PEACEFUL CO-EXISTENCE

An Analysis of Soviet Foreign Policy

FOUNDATION FOR FOREIGN AFFAIRS SERIES

PEACEFUL CO-EXISTENCE

An Analysis of Soviet Foreign Policy

by

Wladyslaw W. Kulski

Published in cooperation with
FOUNDATION FOR FOREIGN AFFAIRS, INC.

HENRY REGNERY COMPANY
Chicago: 1959

FOUNDATION FOR FOREIGN AFFAIRS SERIES, NUMBER 3

The Foundation for Foreign Affairs, 64 East Jackson Boulevard, Chicago 4, Illinois, is a non-profit corporation devoted to the promotion of a wider understanding of international relations— political, economic, and cultural. Books in the Foundation for Foreign Affairs Series are published in the interest of public information and debate. They represent the free expression of their authors and do not necessarily indicate the judgment and opinions of the Foundation.

Also by WLADYSLAW W. KULSKI
The Soviet Regime

Library of Congress Card Catalog Number: 59-13052

To my dearly beloved wife—

with deep gratitude for her

invaluable help in research

CONTENTS

INTRODUCTION

THE SECOND greatest industrial world Power, one of the three nuclear Powers, and the center of a widespread ideological movement, the USSR has pursued a dynamic foreign policy which constantly calls for appropriate readjustments in the foreign policies of other nations. Its exclusive ideology cannot be reconciled with the vast array of opinions held by non-Communists. Nationals of non-Communist countries (and they represent two-thirds of mankind)—Western, Asian, African, Near Eastern, Latin American, West-committed, and uncommitted nations—support a wide range of beliefs, and among them are found political democrats and authoritarians of all possible shades other than the Communist type, socialists, conservatives, religious believers, agnostics, and atheists. All of these people, whatever their nationality and belief, have a common goal: they wish to preserve their ideals and their ways of social life, and they do not intend to surrender them to foreign encroachments. All face the challenge of Communism, both at home, in the person of Communists among their own countrymen, and abroad, in the diplomatic relations of their respective countries with the Soviet-Chinese bloc.

Soviet foreign policy and the Communist ideological drive rest solidly on impressive power potentials. First, there are the economic and, in particular, the industrial potentials, and these, in turn, are the foundations of the military potential. And there is the nuclear potential, in which respect the Soviet Union is on a par with the United States. Finally, there is the psychological potential, which is reflected in the political prestige that surrounds power in international politics, making it possible for the USSR to influence the foreign policies of other countries by taking advantage of their respect for, or the fear of, Soviet military might.

Soviet territory, extending over 22.3 million square kilometers in Europe and Asia, is populated by more than 200 million people. The accretion of more than one million square kilometers, with a population of more than

25 million, in Europe and Asia between 1939 and 1945 grants a measure of dynamic vigor to Soviet policy at a time when Britain, France, and Holland have witnessed a gradual liquidation of their colonial empires.

A few figures will illustrate the Soviet economic potential, to which must obviously be added the potentials of China and eastern Europe, since these two areas are included in the Soviet military bloc. Eastern Europe has a population of more than 95 million, China about 650 million. The economic potential of China is still that of a medium Power, but she has begun to industrialize and will probably become a world Power of the first magnitude in twenty to thirty years. In 1955, the Soviet production of steel was 45 million tons (55 millions in 1958), compared with 106 million tons in the United States and 78.6 million tons in the whole of western Europe (including the United Kingdom). If one includes the steel production of eastern Europe (almost 15 million tons in 1955) and China, one arrives at the figure of 64 million tons for the entire Soviet bloc. Since steel production is a world symbol of industrial output, these figures show that the Soviet bloc has an industrial potential equivalent to one-third that of the Western Powers (slightly less if one adds to the Western potential, as one should, the potentials of Canada and other West-committed countries).

The inferiority of the Soviet position is heightened by all the by-products of speedy industrialization and a highly centralized national economy, e.g., failing to renew worn or inadequate plant equipment in order to build new factories; neglecting transportation; low labor productivity because of poor living conditions, including inadequate housing; bottlenecks in the supply of raw materials; etc. On the other hand, this situation is counterbalanced by a faster rate of industrial expansion in the USSR (the Soviet advantage over the United States is 2.5 to 1) and by Soviet concentration on heavy industries. For instance, between 1955 and 1956, the Soviet output of the means of production increased by 11.4 per cent, compared with an increase of 9.4 per cent in the output of consumer goods. The highest rate of increase in any one sector was in the machine-building industry. Furthermore, the output of the means of production reflected 70.5 per cent of the total industrial output for 1955. This rapid rate of industrial expansion may slacken in the future, but this is mere speculation.

Over-all economic potential is important, even in our nuclear age, because it determines a nation's ability to influence the economies of other countries, especially those which are underdeveloped. But there is another factor, one regarding the means of mass destruction, that is perhaps even more important: the technological potential. An economically inferior country possessing the ability to destroy or mortally wound an economically superior country is the equal of that country because its technological potential makes it a possible nuclear belligerent. Considering Soviet advances in the intercontinental ballistic missiles field (proved implicitly by its launching of heavy earth satellites), one may conclude that the USSR is the peer of the United States in weapons of mass destruction. Russia has the advantage of totalitarianism, which assures speed of decisions, the ability to concentrate on a few selected projects, those deemed the most urgent and most important, and the facility for allocating, without long discussions, the financial resources required for carrying out such projects. But the experience of the last war proves conclusively that a political democracy, once it has fully realized what is at stake, is able to implement a concentrated, rapid, and intense defense effort. Moreover, the history of industrial patents proves that countries which are highly industrialized are apt to make parallel scientific-technological progress.

It is very probable that Soviet-American parity in weapons of mass destruction will be maintained, with sporadic, short-lived advances by one country over the other. If, however, the Soviet Union were to advance more rapidly and establish a long-term superiority in nuclear weapons, it would certainly exploit the resulting psychological advantage to the hilt. During 1956–58, the Soviet Government repeatedly used the potential threat of utter annihilation while trying to dissuade West-committed nations from granting the United States bases for atomic weapons. If this same Government had an obvious technological superiority, it would surely advance the same argument in order to paralyze the will power of the committed nations and persuade them to adopt the policy of non-commitment. Hitler successfully used this technique to split up the European nations, which, terrorized by their fear of a war with Nazi Germany, sought security in a policy of neutrality, only to be overrun, eventually, one after the other.

The non-commitment policy rests, in the last analysis, on the existence of a strong Western bloc as a counterbalance to the Soviet-Chinese bloc. If the USSR were to win the technological race with the West and establish its own superiority for a long period of time, the uncommitted nations would learn, as small European neutral states did from 1939 to 1941, that a great Power thoroughly dissatisfied with the existing *status quo* does not tolerate forever the existence of neutrals. There is no doubt that the USSR is unhappy about the existing *status quo* in the world; it would be very glad to change it. But as long as there is risk of a conflict with the West, the *status quo* survives, including the non-commitment policies.

The Soviet potential in skilled manpower is also increasing. Compulsory junior high school education, with stress on technological and professional training, is gradually expanding in the USSR, and during the next several years, this plan of education will become universal, resulting in a steady supply of youthful, well-trained manpower. The number of students in and graduates from the universities and secondary technical schools is growing steadily; in 1955–56, the enrollment in Soviet universities and equivalent schools totaled 1,867,000. In 1955, students who graduated from universities and similar schools numbered 245,846, of whom 56,466 were qualified to work in industries and building and 9,465 in transportation and communication. The graduates of secondary technical schools trained for work in industries totaled 140,799, and the number trained for work in transportation and communication reached 23,920.[1] This is an impressive record in producing scientific-technological personnel for service in the Soviet Union and for export as technical advisers, not only to China and eastern Europe, but also to economically underdeveloped countries.

The avowed goal of the Soviet Union in rapid industrialization was formulated in 1939 by the 18th Party Congress: "We may and should now practically and fully formulate and carry out the fundamental economic task of the USSR—to overtake and surpass economically the most developed capitalist countries of Europe and the United States." The western European countries have been surpassed. The goal for the coming years, reaffirmed by the 20th Party Congress in 1956, is to do better than the United States in per capita industrial output. The result of this race will be determined by the relative Soviet and Western efforts.

International politics is today dominated by the nuclear stalemate. It seems that all presently existing nuclear Powers have tacitly agreed that an all-out global war would end in suicide for mankind. Marshal G. Zhukov was probably right when he said that any general war involving the nuclear great Powers would become a nuclear war. A Third World War, with everything at stake for the belligerents, including their ways of life, could hardly be pictured as a conventional conflict in which the protagonists master their passions and keep their nuclear swords sheathed, even at the risk of total defeat. As Sir Winston Churchill has said, the existence of nuclear weapons is the precarious (allowing for some risks because of possible political miscalculations) guarantee of peace.

Although the appearance of nuclear weapons has deeply affected international politics, the diplomatic struggle, or "peaceful competition," as Soviet sources call it, continues. All but military weapons are used, and all the known devices of international diplomacy are being practiced. A statesman of the 16th century would not be entirely lost in the welter of our present-day international relations, but our predilection for high-sounding phrases would undoubtedly confuse him.

Let us not forget, however, that the nuclear stalemate does not entirely rule out the use of conventional armaments, tactical atomic weapons, and a violent contest on a limited scale. This line of reasoning leads us directly to one of the most important aspects of the cold war. Would the Soviet or Chinese governments assume the risks of a local war involving a small country, hoping that the Western Powers would be paralyzed by the fear of nuclear retaliation? Would they encourage a Communist revolution or infiltration that would add another member to their camp in anticipation of Western inaction? Or, on the other hand, does the Korean experience warn them that it might be risky to expect Western inaction? If one casts a glance at the predictable and not too distant future, when both the Soviet Union and the United States will be armed with batteries capable of firing intercontinental ballistic missiles with nuclear warheads, and if one assumes that no adequate defense will be invented by that time, the psychological factor acquires crucial importance. The fear of utter destruction could paralyze all the great Powers. The same fear could, however, be just as well manipulated by one of them to frighten the others into accepting local modifications in the *status quo*, modifications achieved by every means short of an all-out conflict. The era of intercontinental missiles might be that of a contest of will power and willingness to assume calculated risks.

In the meantime, the present nuclear stalemate does not guarantee the existing *status quo* in geographical areas where it could be modified without recourse to war. For example, a violent change of government, or even a radical shift in foreign policy, in countries located in the vast zone separating the Soviet bloc from the Western Powers could alter the situation appreciably. This aspect of the nuclear stalemate should not be overlooked, especially since the Soviet Union is unhappy about the political and social *status quo* in the non-Communist world.

Since Soviet foreign policy is a highly important factor in the formulation of policies by other nations, it might be useful to examine it, *in toto*, as it has matured since the 1917 revolution. This, then, is the purpose of this book. There are histories, monographs, and countless articles dealing with particular aspects of Soviet foreign policy. This book is neither a history nor a monograph, but an analysis of the basic patterns, objectives, and means. The astounding fidelity of the Soviet leaders to patterns which were successfully tested makes such a study useful. The author believes that the long-term objectives of Soviet foreign policy have not changed. M. A. Suslov, one of the members of the ruling Party Presidium, said as much at the 20th Party Congress. But tactics do change, and this has, in fact, occurred since Stalin's death. In this respect, the Soviet approach is not different from that of other nations. A nation would be utterly foolish completely to alter its long-term objectives in external relations for such an irrelevant reason as the death of a leader; only a radical modification in the global international situation justifies a basic readjustment of foreign policy.

The experience accumulated during the past forty-one years cannot be forgotten by the present Soviet Government. Only people who learn nothing and forget everything may lightly dismiss this record as the pertinent background of our era of peaceful co-existence—peaceful only in the sense that there are no open hostilities. National life in any country, including the Soviet Union, does not begin anew every morning.

The main enemy of any statesman is his own wishful thinking. Yet statesmen and ordinary people have, for more than forty years, indulged constantly in such thinking about the Soviet Union. Predictions of a forthcoming revolution in the USSR have been mixed with forecasts of a more liberal system to supplant Soviet totalitarianism. One need only to recall the high hopes aroused by Lenin's New Economic Policy or by the Stalinist Constitution of 1936. Between 1941 and 1945, Stalin carefully cultivated the image of "Uncle Joe," a cheerful, wise, and moderate elder statesman, an image later demolished by his own acts and finally buried by Khrushchev in his famous secret speech. Some people now detect in Khrushchev a jovial, good-humored, provincial politician, an evaluation with which Malenkov, Molotov, and Kaganovich would hardly agree.

The hope that the Soviet marshals exert a moderating influence on Soviet foreign policy may or may not be true. A professional soldier can become a peace-loving politician, but, like Cromwell and Napoleon, he can also become fascinated by expansion. The events of 1956 in Hungary did not disclose any intention of retreat on the part of the Soviet marshals; in fact, they probably had much to say about Soviet intervention.

The Hungarian revolt poses a question. If the Hungarians, fighting for their national freedom, were drenched in blood, why should the Soviet Government have a kinder heart for Americans, British, Indians, or others? Perhaps the difference lies not in a greater kindness but in a purely realistic calculation of risks. The use of military force was practical in Hungary, but it would entail a general war if applied against the United States, Great Britain, or India. The actual, world-wide distribution of power, not kind intentions, sets the limits for Soviet foreign policy.

It is the conviction of this author that the Soviet leaders are guided by two motivations: their fidelity to the ideological mission of spreading Communism to the limits of the globe and national devotion to their own country. There is no contradiction between these two motivations. A new Communist regime means an additional Soviet ally or vassal, and it is equally true that a new satellite becomes a Communist state if the USSR has the means to enforce its will. Ideological discussions of whether or not Soviet leaders have remained completely faithful to Marxism-Leninism are rather futile. If one believes the Soviet leaders' own words, they have retained a firm faith in the residue of Marxism-Leninism that has survived the test of experience. They have succumbed, like other people, to the universal law governing the relations between an ideology and an organization created for the purpose of spreading that ideology. Any organization faced with the practical exigencies of its own existence is always compelled to sacrifice many tenets of its original faith for the sake of survival. Actually, if Lenin cared only about his Marxist purity, there would have been no Communist revolution in economically underdeveloped Russia. If Stalin had not been fascinated by the prospect of making his nation a powerful state through the process of rapid industrialization, he would not have fallen victim to the cult of efficiency and would not have produced an un-Marxist social stratification. His successors must, of necessity, take good care of the survival and power of the Soviet state, the mainstay in the expansion of a diluted Marxism. This factor has loomed larger in their practical minds than theological purity. They are not the first—or the last—to subordinate ideology to the needs of the organization. But this does not mean that they are, in a manner of speaking, "atheistic" apostles who do not believe in the essentials of their creed or that they are indifferent to its triumph. Almost all of them were born of Russian parents; they have been influenced by Russian history; they are limited in their actions by Russian geography. They say that they are Russian patriots, and there is ample proof that they mean it. Sixty per cent of the Soviet population is Russian, a people which does not yield to any nation in patriotism. Their love of Russia cannot be disregarded, even by totalitarian leaders, for their nationalistic motivation adds force to the ideological drive.

The argument that all ideological factions of mankind have eventually made peace with their enemies and have come, in the end, to tolerate the existence of their opponents as an inevitable evil is not very convincing if applied to the Soviet Union and Communism. Actually, the analogy turns out to be rather depressing. It took Christians eight Crusades to abandon their armed expeditions to conquer the Holy Land. The Moslems had expanded as Arabs or as Turks for a thousand years before their dynamic energy was exhausted. It took a hundred years of bloody religious wars to convince the Catholics and the Protestants that they had to tolerate each other. The military drive of the French Revolution was short lived only because its ideals conquered the whole of Europe quickly and peacefully. One might hope that these analogies do not apply to Communism.

A British historian has rightly noted that more than once in history has a marriage been concluded between a creed and a territorial or ethnic unit. The Roman Empire identified itself with the Hellenistic civilization, the Byzantine Empire with the Greek Orthodox faith, the medieval Roman Empire with the Western church, the Arabs and, later, the Turks with Islam, the Hapsburgs with Catholicism, and Revolutionary France with equality before law. The USSR has identified itself with Communism.

It would be fruitless to discuss the foreign policy of the Soviet Union without a parallel analysis of current policies in the various Communist parties, all of which look toward Moscow as their ideological center. For a Soviet or other Communist, there is only *one* struggle waged against capitalism, even though it is fought on two fronts: the diplomatic (by the USSR and other Communist states) and the domestic (by each Communist party in a non-Communist country). This, then, is why many pages of this book are devoted to the programs and tactics of these Communist parties and their relations with the Soviet Communist Party. Lenin's teaching concerning the unity of the Communist cause in Russia and every other part of the globe has never been repudiated. Khrushchev reaffirmed the fidelity to the Leninist doctrine in 1955 when he said at Bombay: "We have never abandoned and will never abandon our political line which Lenin formulated for us; we have never abandoned or will abandon our political program. . . . This is why we tell those gentlemen who wait for a change in the

political program of the Soviet Union: 'Wait till the crayfish whistles!' "[2]
It is not Khrushchev's fault that some people eagerly expect the crayfish to
whistle.

Having a faith and a missionary spirit does not preclude the calculation
of risks. Soviet leaders, from Lenin through Stalin to those of the present
day, have proved that they have had the capacity to compute the distribution of power on the international stage and to limit their risks. Their
Marxist training familiarizes them with history, however distorted their
interpretation of it may be. History teaches a great political wisdom: patience and planning, not for one day but for years. The Soviet leaders are
human beings and are therefore fallible. Stalin erred in the postwar years,
as did Khrushchev in his downgrading of Stalin, but they have also shown
that opportunity in international politics often comes from the errors committed by other states.

Are the Soviets impressed by foreign opinion? Yes and no. They never
retreated under the pressure of that opinion. The withdrawal of Soviet
troops from Iran in 1946 was prompted not by public debates in the United
Nations but, as President Truman wrote, by the sharp diplomatic intima-
tion from the United States that they would otherwise face a conflict with
the West. The USSR, exhausted by the Second World War, was not ready
to pick up the challenge. Persuasive speeches and resolutions in the United
Nations did not force Soviet troops to stop their intervention in Hungary
or withdraw later. The violent indignation that followed the Communist
coup in Czechoslovakia in 1948 has not affected the existence of the Communist regime in that hapless country in the least. But the Soviet Government attaches great importance to foreign public opinion in a different
sense, namely that of using it to influence the foreign policies of other countries. The importance of propaganda has certainly not been overlooked in
the Soviet Union.

The research entailed in the writing of this book has convinced the author that, after Stalin's death, the Soviet leaders chose the economically
underdeveloped countries as the principal battlefield in their "peaceful
competition" with the West. The great prize, Europe, has a *status quo*,
frozen for both sides by the nuclear stalemate, but nonmilitary means can
change the situation in underdeveloped areas, as Soviet Near Eastern policy
has proved. The Soviet Union has not created the problems which besiege
the West, in relation to the underdeveloped countries, or the economic

and social difficulties that face those nations, but it does exploit them for its own benefit and does it very skillfully. This is a battle for one billion people.

The present-day Soviet leaders are conscious of the power at their disposal. Khrushchev was asked by a French journalist whether the fear of capitalist encirclement (a true apprehension for Lenin and Stalin) influenced the present Soviet policy. He replied, in a condescending tone:

It is unknown today who encircles whom: the capitalist countries, the socialist states or the opposite. One should not look at the socialist countries as though they were some sort of an island situated amidst a stormy capitalist ocean. One billion out of the two and a half billion world population live in the socialist camp. And how many people share the socialist views in other countries? Therefore, one should not talk about a capitalist encirclement in the former sense of these words.[3]

The practical conclusions which the Soviet leaders draw from this position of strength seem to be as follows: to avoid an all-out nuclear war (we are apt to forget that this fear is shared by the USSR as well); to defend, at any price, the Soviet part of the present international *status quo*; and to change, piecemeal and without an all-out war, preferably by political, economic, and ideological means, the *status quo* in the non-Communist world to the detriment of the West in order to reach, eventually, the ultimate goal which Khrushchev depicted, in his usual picturesque style, as the burial of all capitalist (non-Communist) systems.

Khrushchev clearly stated his intention to use force, as had been done in Hungary, to preserve the Communist share of the present *status quo:*

We declare that, if a new provocation is staged against any socialist country, the provocateurs will have to deal with all the countries of the socialist camp, and the Soviet Union will always be ready to come to the help of its friends and to give the required rebuff to the enemies of socialism, if these enemies attempt to disturb the peaceful labor of peoples of the socialist countries.[4]

These words, spoken in a Hungarian city, had a particularly ominous ring.

Of course, Khrushchev is not to be blamed if wishful thinkers ascribe the present international tension to a regrettable Soviet misinterpretation of the Western intentions, a misunderstanding to be quickly dispelled by a summit conference. Our *status quo* mentally makes difficult the comprehension of the goals of other people who are bent on gradually demolishing the existing international *status quo*. Our pragmatic (case by case, day by day) approach to international events does not help in understanding that the Communists integrate these events within a global framework of their concept of history. Thus while we are inclined to disconnect the sequence of events for lack of a conceptual interpretation of our time, the Communists link all events into a logical chain. We talk the language of the *status quo;* they think in the terms of a long-term revolutionary change.

One must concede that the Communists fully realize that our world is caught in the chaos of three simultaneous revolutions: the Leninist, the awakening of the underdeveloped countries, and the scientific-technological. They want to exploit the other two revolutions for the full promotion of the Leninist. Scientific-technological progress and rapid industrialization are seen as eventually assuring the USSR of a predominant position in the world if they are properly directed. The awakening of the underdeveloped areas is to be diverted into two channels. On the one hand, Soviet policy encourages every trend that promotes a split between these countries and the West; the aim of this policy is to align these countries with the Soviet-Chinese bloc to form a common anti-Western platform. On the other hand, these same countries are considered as a potentially fertile ground for sowing the seeds of Communist revolutions.

Those well-intentioned people who believe that Soviet friendship may be bought with warm handshaking or unilateral concessions can profit from this frank statement which Khrushchev, at that time both Party boss and Soviet Prime Minister, made at the end of March, 1958: "Friendship is true and strong if people share the same views on events, history and life."[5]

WLADYSLAW W. KULSKI

SYRACUSE, NEW YORK
JUNE 19, 1959

PEACEFUL CO-EXISTENCE

An Analysis of
Soviet Foreign Policy

CHAPTER I

REVOLUTION FROM ABOVE AND ITS SOVIET BASTION

1. Soviet Concept of the Revolution

MARXISM-LENINISM is as important a key to the understanding of the Soviet Union and its foreign and domestic policies as Christianity is for the comprehension of medieval Europe or Islam for that of the Arab Caliphate and the Ottoman Empire. The central tenet of Marxism-Leninism, the official creed of the Soviet Union, refers to a complete political, economic, and social change in the existing world set-up. This change is rightly called revolution. The Soviet Government considers its country as the center, sometimes referred to as the bastion, of the vast international movement which plans to bring about this profound change in the existing condition of all mankind.

The *Soviet Great Encyclopedia*, in its 1955 edition, defines the revolution as follows:

The social revolution . . . is a period of radical change and a turning point in the life of a society; a period of violent overthrow of an obsolete social regime and of the establishment of a new, progressive regime; a period of the conquest of the state power by a leading and progressive class which makes use of this power for a further development of society and for its revolutionary transformation.[1]

While it is self-evident that every true revolution, as distinguished from a mere coup, brings about a radical change in the life of a society, there may be some doubts concerning the reality of the seizure of power by a social class, the latter concept being rather hazy in any past or present society. But the important part of the Soviet definition is its reference to the seizure of power, although in the case of a Communist revolution it is the Party, rather than any class, that seizes power in order to proceed with a radical political and economic transformation of society. One may therefore agree with the *Encyclopedia* when it says: "The fundamental question of every revolution consists in the problem of State power, its conquest, retention and strengthening."[2] Stalin laconically formulated this crucial issue of the revolution: "the important thing is to retain power, to consolidate it and make it invincible."[3] Those who doubt that it is legitimate to quote Stalin after the 20th Congress of the Communist Party of the Soviet Union may be reassured on this score by the following evaluation of him in an article printed in *Kommunist* in April, 1957:

... as is known, [Stalin's] book: *Foundations of Leninism,* correctly and masterfully expounded those new elements Lenin had contributed to the treasure-house of Marxism, which had enriched Marxism, and had made certain that it would correspond to the new conditions of the class warfare by the proletariat. ... One must say that Stalin conformed, on the whole, to correct Marxist-Leninist positions, although he formulated some imprecise and at times even erroneous theses in some of his works, mainly in those produced in his last years.[4]

Thus Stalin remains an authority on Marxism-Leninism, except for his latest views—corrected at the 20th Congress.

The factor of power in the definition of the revolution given by the *Soviet Great Encyclopedia* calls for filling in a gap therein, for the definition visualizes only a revolution accomplished against an existing government. But Soviet sources also mention another type of revolution which they call "the revolution from above" and which is carried out by the Communist party in control of a state. This concept of the revolution was invented after the Soviet mass collectivization of agriculture. *Pravda,* commenting in 1949 on a new volume of Stalin's *Works,* had this to say:

The mass collectivization and the liquidation on this basis of the kulaks as a class were the deepest revolutionary upheaval, equal in respect of its consequences to the revolutionary upheaval in October 1917. As is known, the peculiar nature of that upheaval consisted in the fact that it was accomplished from above, on the initiative of the Soviet State, with the widest support from below on the part of the multi-million peasant masses.[5]

Several million peasants were wiped out or forcibly resettled during this revolution from above, whose tragedy consisted in its lack of support from below. The collectivization was decreed by the Party. It was a revolution carried out by the government against the will of the peasant masses, whose resistance had to be broken by the use of state power. It was, therefore, rightly called the revolution from above. We may, for the time being, call a revolution carried out by the Party against a government a revolution from below.

The distinction between the two types of revolution is a matter of semantics. Actually, both concepts are also current in Western terminology. Revolution against a government calls forth images of the storming of the Bastille, of the barricades, and of a civil war. It is the same sense in which the word is exemplified by such historical instances as the English revolt against Charles I, the American Revolution, the French Revolution, the Russian revolutions, and the Chinese Revolution of the late 1940's. We might add the Hungarian Revolution of 1956 to the list, although the Communists conveniently call this a counterrevolution. In all these events, revolution is seen as a struggle against the existing government for a radical political, economic, or social change. This is the first meaning of revolution, and it has been firmly established by long usage.

But we sometimes talk about a revolution accomplished by the government, that is, by legal means and through constitutional procedures, whereby a series of legislative or other measures brings about a considerable change in the policies of a country. Some people say that the United States experienced such a revolution through the New Deal legislation of the 1930's and that Britain also went through a peaceful revolution, thanks to her welfare state and nationalization legislation. However, such legal and peaceful revolutions are still changes from below, if carried out in a democratic country where the government (executive or legislative) is freely elected in an unhampered competition of parties and must follow the aspirations of the electorate. The same type of revolution in a totalitarian state is rightly called a revolution from above.

Soviet sources adduce another example of a revolution from above:

In full conformity with the Leninist plan of a peaceful development of the revolution . . . the passage from the democratic stage of the revolution to the socialist was achieved in the countries of the people's democracy, not by an upheaval and the overthrow of the state power, but peacefully through a revolution from above which took place on the initiative of state authorities with the support of the large masses from below.[6]

The Polish and Hungarian revulsion against this revolution from above disposes of the claim that this type of revolution was carried out with the support of the large masses from below. But it is true that the radical transformation of the regimes in eastern Europe, the passage to a totalitarian regime, took place as a revolution from above, imposed by the Party and supported by Soviet military might, which always remained visible to the masses in the backstage of that revolution.

A short analysis of the elitist nature and philosophy of the Communist Party will justify the contention that Communists know, in fact, only of the revolution from above. There are, however, two types of Communist revolution from above. The first is a revolution carried out against an existing government and therefore requiring the support of a sizable fraction of the masses and the indifference of the remainder. Its long-term objectives are unknown to the masses aroused by the Party short-term slogans. The Party alone fully realizes the ultimate goal of that revolution and casts itself in the role of a leader of the masses, who are unable to comprehend the true meaning of historical events. Thus this type of revolution may also be called a revolution from above because the masses act in ignorance of the true long-term objectives of an upheaval in which they participate. The main and immediate aim of a revolution of this kind is to seize power.

The second type of revolution occurs after the Party has seized power. The Party can then proceed with fundamental changes in the structure of society without support from below. It has the monopoly on the state means of coercion, is able to break down the resistance of the masses, by force if necessary, and certainly does not need to ask the masses for support. The genuine assent of the masses was no longer necessary at the time of the collectivization of agriculture in the USSR and in China, nor was it needed during the profound remodeling of life in eastern Europe.

2. Party, the Elitist Instrument of the Revolution

The entire doctrine of Leninism would fall to pieces if the elitist outlook were removed from it. There is a curious contradiction in Lenin's views between his genuine enthusiasm for the future welfare of the masses and his no less profound belief that those masses were incapable of understanding their true long-term interests; they had to be led, he thought, by a small minority of revolutionary people, the Party. Born in a country of autocracy and skeptical of political democracy, Lenin thought that a small group of people, aware of the true interests of the masses, could do everything for the people but not through the people. The people (masses) could serve as a tool for remodeling society in their ultimate interests, but they were incapable of indicating the direction to their leaders. This is why he was strongly opposed to the spontaneity of the socialist movement, spontaneity that meant following the desires of the proletariat instead of imposing on it the goals determined by the Party.

Stalin correctly interpreted the Leninist concept of a vanguard Party:

> The Party should be, first of all, a vanguard detachment of the working class. . . . The Party cannot be a true party if it limits itself to the registration of what the working class is experiencing and is thinking of, if it trails in the rear of a spontaneous movement, if it does not know how to overcome the inertness and political indifference of the spontaneous movement, if it does not know how to raise itself above the momentary interests of the proletariat. . . . The Party should . . . see further than the working class . . . should lead the proletariat, not trail with the tail of spontaneity. . . . The Party is the political captain of the working class.[7]

A contemporary interpreter of Lenin's thought explains this claim of the Party to be the vanguard by its superior wisdom: "The Party is the vanguard detachment of the working class primarily because it is armed with the knowledge of social life, of the laws of social development and of class struggle, and thus is able to lead the working class and to direct its struggle."[8] This is a far cry from the idealization of the proletariat. Lenin's intellectual contempt for the masses did not interfere with his genuine sympathy for them, the same sympathy that had inspired the Utopian socialists and the founders of the so-called scientific socialism. He did not foresee that his elitist view of the masses would eventually lead his disciples toward the building of an elite, hierarchical society, a society ruled by a group of professional politicians, divided into first-class citizens (the Communists) and second-class citizens (non-Party people) and composed of social classes, with a new socialist bourgeoisie (the higher stratum of the intelligentsia) placed, by its social prestige, its high incomes, and its share in power, at the top of the social pyramid.[9]

The elitist outlook cannot appeal to countries with a solidly rooted democratic tradition which rejects the concept of a single elite; such countries take a hopeful view of the political abilities and discernment of the average citizen. We have, of course, in every democracy several elites, in the sense that they are groups of people who, more than average men, excel in the knowledge of certain problems, but we also accept the fact that an individual may be quite average in certain things and belong to one of the elites in some others. Thus musicians form an elite which guides average people in music; scientists train others in the ways of science; there are professional historians, and so forth. But the musician, or scientist, or historian becomes one of the millions in the average crowd when it comes to matters in which he does not specialize. Above all, we do not think that only certain people are endowed with political sense and that the average man cannot understand what his basic political and social interests are. The peaceful social evolution of the democratic societies in all fields of interest to average men (the masses) during the last several decades supports this optimistic view. The elitist doctrine may, however, find favor in societies unaccustomed to democracy. It is not a sheer accident of history that the Leninist concept of society triumphed in Russia and China, and Walter Z. Laqueur is right when he emphasizes this point in his book on the Middle East.[10] Will this elitist view of the Party and the actual Soviet elitist structure of the society prove repulsive to the frustrated intelligentsia in the underdeveloped countries, especially those where democracy has not become a habit in politics?

It was logical for Lenin to think of the revolution and the ensuing social transformation in terms of processes accomplished by a relatively small group of the "best" people, the Communist elite, who should never defer to the current wishes of the masses. He wrote: "We are bound not to let ourselves fall down to the level of the masses, to that of the backward layers of the class. This is incontrovertible."[11] The masses were unable to think correctly; if they disagreed with the Communists, they fell to the level of backward layers, and some of their sections were not capable of thinking at all: "In each class . . . there are always . . . representatives of the class who *do* not think and are unable to do it."[12] Lenin therefore had to forge an elitist weapon for the transformation of the society in the interest of the masses. A contemporary Soviet writer explains the deep sense of Lenin's fight against the Mensheviks at the 2nd Congress of the Social-Democratic Party in 1903:

Lenin and his [Bolshevik] followers . . . fought for the formation of a party of a new type. They resolutely and consistently defended the Marxist basic tenet that the party should be a vanguard, a conscious and organized detachment of the working class, and should be armed with the knowledge of the laws of development of society and with the experience of the revolutionary movement.[13]

Following Lenin's teaching, every Communist party must be an elitist organization of those who accept the Marxist-Leninist doctrine as their creed, who claim therefore to know where history leads, and who assume the burden of guiding the masses toward the revolution and, later, of transforming society according to their own wisdom. Marxism-Leninism without the Communist Party would be like the bed of a river without water.

The history of the Communist Party of the Soviet Union teaches that the victory of a proletarian revolution and the dictatorship of the proletariat are impossible without a party of a new type which is free of opportunism, uncompromising toward those who are ready to make concessions or to capitulate, and which is revolutionary in relation to its own bourgeoisie and its state power. The usual social-democratic party of the Western-European type, educated in the spirit of opportunism, dreaming only of "social reforms," and afraid of the social revolution, could not become such a party; only the Marxist-Leninist party could, since it was capable of training the proletariat for decisive battles against the bourgeoisie and of organizing the victory of the proletarian revolution.[14]

Lenin said the same: "the unity of the proletariat may be achieved in the epoch of social revolution only by an extremely revolutionary Marxist party and only in a pitiless struggle against all other parties."[15] The Communist Party is, by definition, a party of the minority within both the proletariat and the total population of a country: "The political party may include only a minority of a class, as the truly conscious workers in all capitalist societies represent only a minority among all the workers."[16] Lenin says elsewhere: "the whole or almost the whole working class acts 'under the supervision and leadership' of the Party organizations, but it does not and should not be enlisted as a whole in the party."[17] His contemporary commentator adds: "The Marxist-Leninist party cannot admit all who desire to join it. It grows and becomes stronger through individual admissions to its ranks of only the leading fighters for Communism."[18] This conforms to Lenin's view that a proportionately small party should accomplish the great task of transforming society: "Our party, a small group of people in comparison to the total population of the country, has taken over [this task]. This grain of sand has placed before itself the task of changing everything and it will do it."[19] In 1920, the 2nd Congress of the Comintern adopted this pattern for all Communist parties, and it remains valid to the present day:

The Communist party is part of the working class, the most advanced, most class-conscious, and hence the most revolutionary part. By a process of natural selection the Communist party is formed of the best, most class-conscious, most devoted and farsighted workers. . . . The Communist party is differentiated from the working class as a whole by the fact that it has a clear view of the entire historical path of the working class in its totality and is concerned, at every bend in this road, to defend the interests not of separate groups or occupations, but of the working class in its totality. . . . [If the majority of the working class has sentiments different from the party policy], it must be . . . the task of the proletarian party in such a state of affairs to come out against the sentiments of the majority of the workers and, in defiance of them, to represent the historical interests of the pro-letariat. . . . Political power cannot be seized, organized and operated ex-cept through a political party. . . . The proletariat must resort to armed insurrection. Whoever has grasped that must also understand that an or-ganized political party is essential. . . . A really determined minority of the working class, a minority that is communist, that wants to act, that has a programme, that is out to organize the struggle of the masses—that is pre-cisely what the communist party is. . . . The working class needs the com-munist party not only up to the seizure of power, not only during the seizure of power, but also after the transfer of power to the working class. . . . When the proletariat seizes power its party remains, as before, only a part of the working class. Only if there is such a disciplined organization of the working class elite, is it possible to surmount all the difficulties confronting the workers' dictatorship on the morrow of victory.[20]

Although the Party is the vanguard not only of the proletariat but also of history, it may enter into short-term alliances with other parties, but it must remain the only directing force, both during and after the revolu-tion. Communists like to use "the working class," "the proletariat," "the toiling masses," and "the people" as synonyms for "the Party." They do this not only for propaganda's sake but also because of their conviction that the Party represents the permanent interests of the masses and may, in this sense, identify itself with them. Lenin held the same view, claiming that the will of the Party was also the will of the whole class:

The Party is a conscious and leading layer of the class, its vanguard. The strength of this vanguard is ten, a hundred and more times greater than its numbers. Is it possible? Is it possible that the strength of hundreds were superior to that of thousands? It is possible; it is superior if the hundreds are organized. . . . It [the Party] acquires a single will through organization, and this one single will of the leading thousands, hundreds of thousands, a million, *becomes* the will of the class.[21]

This strange claim becomes easier to understand if one recalls that the Party reflects the permanent interests of the proletariat, which has knowl-edge only of its transient interests; hence the Party expresses the will of the proletariat as it should be, not as it is at any given moment.

For Lenin the masses were a tool which the Party had to operate in order to seize power:

To win with the vanguard only, is impossible. To throw only the vanguard into a decisive battle, while the whole class, the large masses, have not taken the position of either directly supporting the vanguard or, at least, of remaining benevolently neutral toward it and completely refusing to support its adversary, would be not only folly but a crime. . . . The best vanguards express the consciousness, the will, the passion and the imagination of tens of thousands, while the revolution is accomplished by . . . the consciousness, the will, the passion and the imagination of tens of millions.[22]

For him, the masses remained a tool for the post-revolutionary transformation of society: "The dictatorship [of the proletariat] is exercised not by the whole people but only by the revolutionary people [the Party]."[23] *Kommunist* echoes the same thought: "When socialism is now being built not in one but in several countries, it is clearer than ever that there is not and cannot be any dictatorship of the proletariat in any form, including that of a people's democracy, without a Marxist-Leninist Party."[24]

When Lenin talked of the Party as part of the industrial proletariat, he did not mean at all that its membership should be recruited only from among the workers. In his mind, the Party was identified with the proletariat by its objectives; therefore, the social origin or actual occupation of Party members was not an essential matter. Judged by the social composition of the Party during his lifetime or since and by that of all other parties, the higher leadership of the Party is reserved for only the most conscious—to use his words, those who have mastered the difficult intricacies of Marxism—these may be either formally educated people or persons who, despite their former manual profession, have acquired the good equipment of informal education. They become workers in a symbolical sense, that of defending the interests of the proletariat. Lenin, talking about himself and his fellow intellectuals in the Party, said more than once: "We, the . . . conscious proletarians."[25] Practically speaking, this is an important point because the Party, in any country, relies mainly on members of the intelligentsia for its leadership. It expects to induce frustrated, educated persons to become its leading personnel in the underdeveloped countries. A Soviet author justifies this symbolical "proletarianization" of members of the intelligentsia, whatever their social origin, in the following manner:

One should not deduce from what has been said before that the moral outlook of every man must be directly derived from the material conditions of his existence, while ignoring political and ideological influences [on his

outlook] and the possibility of the passage of individuals from the exploiting classes to the side of the proletariat, etc. Such passages do take place in
fact and become more frequent in this century of disintegration of capitalism and of the spreading of Marxist outlook.[26]

The Party itself is founded on the same elitist principle. The best among
the best are its leaders, and the other Party members owe them the strictest
obedience. As early as 1902, Lenin stressed the importance of having a
group of leaders: "the steadfast struggle of any class in the contemporary
society is impossible without a 'score' of talented leaders (and talented are
not born by hundreds), experienced, professionally trained by a lengthy
schooling, men in perfect agreement with each other."[27] After the Revolution he said: "political parties are, as a general rule, directed by a more or
less stable group of the most authoritative, influential and experienced
persons. . . . This is the A.B.C. . . . We need the strictest centralization and
discipline within the political party of the proletariat."[28] It was not a rabid
anti-Communist but Lenin himself who explained, in 1920, the structure
of the Soviet Communist Party and the directing role of the Central Committee and its Political Bureau (now called the Presidium) and concluded:
"this appears to be the most genuine 'oligarchy.' "[29]

In 1920, the Comintern set a pattern for all Communist parties in the
following words:

. . . the communist party must be built on foundations of iron proletarian
centralism . . . without the strictest discipline, without complete centralization, and without the fullest comradely confidence of all party organizations in the party center, the victory of workers is impossible. . . . There
shall be a strong party center whose authority is universally and unques-
tionably recognized for all leading party comrades.[30]

The organizational pattern of the Party was conceived by Lenin as a division of functions between the professional politicians, who were to be the
leaders, and the rank-and-file members, who were to carry out the leaders'
instructions:

Lenin proposed to organize a party composed of two parts: a narrow circle
of professional revolutionaries and a wide network of local party organizations. The professional revolutionaries were to be the leading group within
the party, free of all other occupations except for party work, having a
necessary minimum of theoretical knowledge, political experience, organizational habits, and a capacity to fight with the police.[31]

Pravda, in an article devoted to the purge of Malenkov, Molotov, Kagano-vich, and Shepilov, echoed Lenin's concepts in saying: "The unity of will and actions of the Communist Party is irreconcilable with the existence of factions and groups within it. . . . The Party is not a debating club."[32] These last words are taken from Lenin himself.[33]

Each party passes through two stages: the first is its foundation; the sec-ond is its efforts to conquer power:

[Leninism] teaches that each proletarian party unavoidably passes through two stages in its historical development, after its foundation and before the seizure of power. The first stage consists in the formation of the party itself and the conquest of the vanguard of the proletariat for Communism. The second stage consists in the conquest by the party of the majority of the proletariat and the large masses of the peasantry.[34]

The first stage is usually preceded by the existence of loose Marxist groups, which are merged, at an appropriate time, into a highly disciplined party, ready to begin its operations for the seizure of power.

According to recent Soviet data, the army of this revolutionary elite is rather large:

The ranks of the Communist parties have increased during the last ten years by almost twelve million people; the Communist and Workers' par-ties now number in the whole world about thirty-two million members. The figure includes seventeen millions (including the C.P.S.U.) in Europe, over fourteen millions (including the Communist Party of China) in Asia, and over one million in the countries of Africa, America, and Australia.[35]

Deducting approximately twenty million for the Communist parties ruling in different states of Europe and Asia (the Soviet and the Chinese parties have a membership of about eight and ten million, respectively), there re-mains the rather impressive figure of twelve million revolutionary elite in capitalist countries; these, together with the ruling parties, form one army:

Communists are people of various nationalities, and citizens of countries often very distant from each other; yet they are always ideological brothers and comrades-in-arms. . . . The source of strength of the Communist and Workers' parties lies in the community of their Marxist theoretical out-look, in the singleness of their strategic goal, and in their loyalty to the indispensable ideals of the international workers' movement.[36]

Sheer numbers of Communists are not without importance because "for the Communists the interests of the Party are the highest."[37] However, it would be a disastrous mistake to appraise the strength of various Communist parties by the mere figures of their membership because "V. I. Lenin taught that the Party is strong, first of all, not by the quantity but by the quality of its membership; after all, quality is more important than quantity."[38] The non-Communists may be well advised to heed this reminder: "The Communist Party numbered in its ranks, on the eve of the Great October Socialist Revolution, all told, only 240,000 members."[39] The influence of the Party is measured not only by the quality of its members but also by the army of fellow travelers at their disposal and the degree of successful penetration by its members and sympathizers into crucial positions within a given non-Communist society. A Soviet author lists the vast millions of organized and open sympathizers:

The international democratic unions defend peaceful co-existence: the World Federation of Trade Unions which has over 85 million members, the International Democratic Federation of Women with more than 200 million members, and the World Federation of Democratic Youth with 85 million members.[40]

Another Soviet author assures us confidently: "There is no country in the world where there would be no Marxist-Leninist party. The Communist and Workers' parties have grown into a great army of militants for socialism which, by its influence, embraces the whole globe."[41] Other Soviet sources say that there exist now only Marxist groups in the African countries south of the Sahara, that these groups act through the labor unions, and that there are no full-fledged parties. There is but one strategic objective for all of those parties:

The millions of toilers united under the banner of struggle for peace and democracy, the Communists, the vanguard of the popular masses in every capitalist country, do not forget for a moment their ultimate goal: the inevitability of the struggle for the complete reconstruction of society [the revolution].[42]

Lenin taught (and contemporary Soviet sources confirm this) that the passage to socialism can take place only through a revolution. He said:

This struggle is of such a nature that it may be at any moment transformed and is being transformed, as experience has already proved, from the use of the arm of criticism into the criticism by arms. . . . That which appears before the victory of the proletariat as only a theoretical difference of views concerning the question of "democracy" becomes tomorrow, after the victory, a question to be solved by arms.[43]

A contemporary author says: "Marx and Engels proved that the proletariat could overthrow the capitalist regime only by revolutionary means."[44] *Kommunist* wrote in 1957:

Marxism-Leninism considers that the passage from capitalism to socialism takes place not automatically but as the result of an uncompromising class struggle which leads to the socialist revolution and the establishment of the dictatorship of the proletariat.[45]

The formula of the dictatorship of the proletariat means, in Communist parlance, the Communist Party's monopoly of political power.

3. A Universal Revolution

Lenin himself said in 1918 that the ultimate goal of Communism was revolution in all countries: "We are fighting not only against Russian capitalism. We fight against capitalism in all countries, against universal capitalism, and for the freedom of all workers."[46] He defined the contemporary historical period as that of a universal revolution: "The destruction of capitalism and its works and the laying down of the foundations of a Communist order, make up the contents of this new period of universal history that has now begun."[47] He interpreted the October Revolution as an example for other countries: "we have raised before [the eyes] of the whole world the banner of struggle for a complete overthrow of imperialism."[48]

Turning to contemporary Soviet authors, one finds the same idea of a universal revolution. One of them says:

The Great October Socialist Revolution opened a new era, the era of the proletarian revolutions in the capitalist countries, and thus was the beginning of a world proletarian socialist revolution. . . . The international significance of the October Revolution consists in its being not only a great initiative of one country in the venture of breaking down the system of imperialism but also the first stage of the world revolution, and in its founding a powerful base for the further spreading of the world revolution. . . . The task of the international proletariat, as comrade Stalin pointed out, now consists in the efforts which aim at widening the breach in the imperialist system, at assisting its vanguard that has forged ahead, and in preventing the enemy from encircling it and tearing it from its base.[49]

The author of a recent textbook on the Communist strategy and tactics (destined primarily for the use of foreign Communist parties) writes:

"Leninism teaches that the Communists must use their whole energy and all their revolutionary strength to lead mankind towards a victory of socialism through the most direct and the shortest path."[50] He adds significantly: "The last strategic stage in the liberating struggle will be completed only with the emancipation of the whole of mankind from the chains of imperialism."[51]

The basic difference between Lenin and his contemporary followers on the one hand and the democratic socialists on the other consists in the attitude toward revolution as a violent seizure of power for the purpose of carrying out a social-economic program. The origin of this difference goes back to the pre–October Revolution period and may be understood only if one pays attention to the divergent nature of the national backgrounds of Lenin and his Western socialist contemporaries. The cleavage between socialists of the western European nations and Lenin and his Bolshevik followers was apparent long before the 1917 revolution. The western European socialists were talking about an ultimate proletarian revolution, thus paying a verbal tribute to Karl Marx and Friedrich Engels, but in reality they were acting as legal parties in various states, all of which were law abiding and not seriously impeding socialist activities in parliaments or in labor unions. Formed initially to foster a Marxist revolution, the Western socialist parties were increasingly adopting the habits of democratic processes and revealing a growing interest in a peaceful, step-by-step reform of society by social legislation and, possibly, economic legislation. All of them could reasonably expect growing successes with the electorate, and they had no reason to feel frustrated in their manner of defending the interests of the laboring classes, since such action promised to be effective. For them, the Marxist revolution was becoming a holiday slogan, to be remembered at the time of party meetings but not to be taken too seriously. Lenin was faced with an autocratic regime that hardly gave room for action by any political party, least of all a socialist party, even after the 1905 revolution. If he wanted to pursue his aim of a radical social-economic transformation of society, he had to have recourse to illegal means, including, eventually, a violent revolution. The western European socialists grew up in a multi-party system of government (even though socialist parties could only voice their criticism in parliaments in Germany and Austria-Hungary and had no influence on the actual policies of their governments, independent of those parliaments), and they were acquiring the habits of that system. This opportunity was denied to Lenin, whose mind was formed under the influence of an autocratic Russian environment several centuries old. The schism was not visible to the naked eye because the western European socialists had not yet had the opportunity to participate in their governments, nor had they fully tested their ability to introduce reforms by legal means. Hence Lenin himself had grossly misjudged the "revolutionary" spirit of German socialist leaders and was bitterly disappointed at the outbreak of the First World War when those leaders, with a few exceptions, aligned themselves with their governments and forgot their revolutionary slogans.

Lenin faced another practical problem. His stage of action was Russia, predominantly agricultural but beginning to develop industrially at a rapid pace, although the industrial proletariat was proportionately small. Actually, Russia was in the formative stage of capitalist development. But Lenin was a man of action and could not resign himself to the idea that his political group would have to wait, perhaps several decades, until Russia became a highly industrialized country before it could carry out its plans for reform. Karl Marx predicted a socialist revolution for economically developed countries with a strong proletariat. For him, the revolution would be a natural consequence of the highest development of industrial capitalism. To follow Marx in this respect, Lenin would have had to act as a faithful lieutenant of the Russian bourgeois parties in promoting a purely bourgeois revolution, thus creating a regime more suitable than the autocratic for the beginning of a capitalist-industrial era in Russia. However, he could see that the Tsarist regime was weakening and that there were revolutionary possibilities. Primarily a practical politician, he could not let a revolutionary opportunity go by. Hence he was led to make a profound modification in the Marxist doctrine. He elaborated a theory of a new, so-called imperialist stage of capitalism, a stage, according to him, unknown either to Marx or to Engels; he placed the beginning of that new stage at the turn of the century, after the deaths of both founders of the so-called scientific socialism, which continued to be the foundation of his outlook. Thus his theory of imperialism was for him not heresy but a development of Marxist doctrine. According to Lenin's theory of imperialist capitalism, capital ceased to be merely industrial; it became financial with the growing control by the banks. Various industries were connected by banks and cartels, and capital became a co-ordinated venture on a national scale and acquired international ramifications. Financial capital, in turn, produced great monopolies which economically and politically controlled all the highly industrialized countries. But the quick development of industries required foreign markets and sources of raw materials. The capitalist monopolies therefore had to divide the world of underdeveloped countries, which division usually took place through strife or wars among the imperialist states. Unlike its former self during the lifetime of Marx and Engels, capitalism could no longer be understood within its national scope; it became international, with the whole world as its stage.

The rise of capitalism to a world-wide status had to be accompanied by a world-wide concept of the revolution. There were two fronts facing each other across the globe: the capitalist, in its new imperialist form, and the proletarian. The logical conclusion was that world capitalism could be weakened anywhere; the imperialist chain (in Lenin's metaphor) could be broken, even in an underdeveloped country, so that socialist revolution could secure one link, not the most important, it is true, and thereby sever the chain. While Karl Marx wanted to attack capitalism in its strongholds, the highly developed countries, Lenin said that the attack could be made in either a stronghold or an underdeveloped country. This innovation, un-Marxist as it was, had practical results. The revolution could take place anywhere, in Russia or any other underdeveloped country, if only the revolutionary conditions were propitious.[52] Thus Lenin prepared his Bolshevik party for an active and independent role in the Russian revolution. Unlike his rivals, the Mensheviks, he had no doctrinal scruples; he seized power in a predominantly agricultural country.

Lenin said in 1916, on the eve of the Russian Revolution:

Socialism cannot win simultaneously in all countries. It will win at first in one or several countries, while the remaining countries will remain bourgeois or pre-bourgeois for a certain period of time.[53]

Stalin correctly formulated the important conclusion that Lenin had deduced from this premise:

The Leninist theory of the revolution says: No, not necessarily where industry is most developed, and so forth; it [the imperialist chain] will be broken where the chain of imperialism is weakest, for the proletarian revolution is the result of the breaking of the chain of the imperialist world front at its weakest link. . . . Where in the near future will the chain be broken next? Once more, precisely where it is weakest.[54]

If the amount of attention given by contemporary Soviet commentators to the problem of the revolution and the passage to socialism in the underdeveloped countries is a reliable guide, there is not much doubt that those countries are considered to be just such weak links in the "imperialist" chain.

Lenin was, of course, too sensible to predict a definite time for the revolution in any country. As early as 1902 he said:

. . . the aim of Social Democracy is radically to transform the conditions of life of the whole of humanity, and . . . for that reason it is not permissible for Social-Democrats to be "disturbed" by the question of the duration of their work.[55]

He refused, in 1915, to prophesy the date of the revolution in his own country or the further development of the war:

Will this situation [the war] continue for a long time and to what extent will it become more acute? Will it lead to a revolution? We do not know, nobody can know . . . not one socialist did ever or anywhere guarantee that the revolution would be born out of this and not the following war, or out of the present, not the future revolutionary situation.[56]

Any Leninist of our day would take the same position; nobody knows when the revolutionary opportunity will arise, but it surely will, in a country which is the weakest link. The opportunity may come suddenly and in more than one country, or a long period of time may elapse between one opportunity and the next. Stalin said in 1925: "The revolution does not usually develop along a straight, upwardly aspiring line, in the unceasing process of growth of the [revolutionary] uplift, but along a zigzag path, the path of attack and retreat, the path of flow and ebb."[57]

When does a revolutionary opportunity arise? Lenin gave an answer which seems to be historically correct:

What, generally speaking, are the symptoms of a revolutionary situation? . . . 1. When it is impossible for the ruling class to maintain their rule in an unchanged form; when there is a crisis in one form or another among the "upper classes," a crisis in the policy of the ruling class making for fissures through which the discontent and indignation of the oppressed masses burst forth. Usually for a revolution to break out it is not enough for the "lower classes" to refuse to live in the old way; it is necessary that the "upper classes" should be unable to live in the old way; 2. when the want and sufferings of the oppressed classes have become more acute than usual; 3. when as a consequence of the above causes there is a considerable increase in the activities of the masses, who in peace time quietly allow themselves to be robbed, but who in turbulent times are drawn both by circumstances of the crisis and by the "upper classes" themselves into in-

dependent historical action. . . . Revolution arises only out of such a [revo-
lutionary] situation when, to the above mentioned objective changes, a
subjective change is added, namely, the ability of the revolutionary class
to carry out revolutionary mass actions strong enough to break (or to undermine) the old government which never, not even in a period of crisis, "falls"
if it has not been "dropped."[58]

Richer by the experience of the events of 1917, Lenin reaffirmed, in 1920,
the same view formulated in the above statement, which was made in 1915:

The fundamental law of revolution, confirmed by all revolutions and particularly by all three Russian revolutions in the twentieth century, is as
follows: it is not sufficient for revolution that the exploited and oppressed
masses understand the impossibility of living in the old way and demand
changes; for revolution it is necessary that the exploiters should not be
able to live and rule in the old way. Only when the "lower classes" do not
want the old and when the "upper class" cannot continue in the old way,
then only can the revolution be victorious. This truth may be expressed
in other words: revolution is impossible without a national crisis affecting
both the exploited and the exploiters.[59]

Stripped of its Marxist terminology, the Leninist interpretation of the
history of revolutions may be reduced to the following conditions: 1. a
national crisis (a military disaster, a calamitous economic depression, the
inability of the government to cope with pressing and extremely important
problems of the country, and so forth); 2. the discontent of the population
caused by such a crisis or intensified by it to a point where the population
does not want to tolerate the existing situation any longer; 3. the loss of
faith by the ruling groups in their ability to cope with the situation and,
consequently, in their moral right to govern the country; 4. the existence
of revolutionary leaders who are able and willing to lead the country to
a revolution. The fourth factor is not mentioned in the above quotations
but constitutes the essence of Lenin's teaching concerning the role of a
Communist party.

One may easily check the accuracy of Lenin's analysis, which applies, by
the way, to any regime and any revolution, be they the Communist regime
and a revolution directed against it. France was confronted in 1789 by a
grave financial crisis, Russia in 1917 by a military disaster. In both cases
the population was discontented and wanted some change, a reform of the
royal government in France or the conclusion of peace and the reform of
the regime in Russia. Revolutionary leaders were ready to assume the responsibility for the change—the bourgeois leaders in France, the Bolshe-

viks in Russia. But the important fourth condition was extant; the ruling group lost the ability to rule in the old way, and its supporters, both in France and in Russia, were lacking a strong faith that they themselves could find new ways of governing the country.

If the present-day Communists are correct in thinking that the under-developed countries are the weakest links, they base their analysis on the above-mentioned factors. Actually, such countries are faced with a national crisis, namely, the pressing need of economically transforming the existing conditions to cope with low standards of living and rural overpopulation. The masses are becoming more conscious of their unwillingness to continue with the old ways, and the local Communist parties are bracing themselves for the historical opportunity. The question yet remains: Are the present ruling groups able and willing to find new ways, the old having become obsolete?

Lenin considered that a socialist state in Russia would face an implacable hatred of capitalists in the industrialized states. In the first years after the Bolshevik Revolution, he thought that this revolution was doomed unless the proletariat in the industrialized countries came to the rescue by making their own revolutions. He hoped eagerly for those revolutions, particularly in Germany. They never materialized. One might have described Lenin's mood in the period immediately following the October Revolution as defeatist if he had not been animated by a strong hope for revolutions in the West, revolutions which would come to the rescue of his party. Soviet Russia was feeble and surrounded by hostile capitalist Powers. Her chances of survival seemed to be infinitesimally small. Addressing the 7th Party Congress in March, 1918, he said frankly:

If one looks at the problem from the universal-historical point of view, there is not the slightest doubt that the indispensable victory of our revolution, if this revolution were to remain isolated and if there were no revolutionary movement in other countries, would be a hopeless [expectation]. If we have taken the whole matter into the hands of the single Bolshevik party, we have done it in the conviction that the revolution matures in all countries, and that, by the end of ends, but not at the beginning of the beginning, whatever difficulties we should experience, whatever defeats might be reserved for us, the international socialist revolution would come, is coming, will ripen, because it ripens and will be ripe. Our salvation from all those difficulties, I repeat, lies in the all-European revolution.[60]

Yet the Soviet system survived without a revolution in the West. Lenin quite correctly ascribed the reason for this survival to the conflicts among the capitalist states: the war between Germany and Austria-Hungary on the one hand and the Western coalition on the other and, later, the difference in views among the great Powers participating in the intervention in Russia and between those great Powers and small capitalist states in the immediate neighborhood of Russia. After civil war and foreign intervention, Soviet Russia was still alive.

4. Soviet Union, the Bastion of the World Revolution

Because Lenin, immediately after the October Revolution, hoped for a revolution in a highly industrialized state, he did not think of Soviet Russia as the permanent center of the revolutionary movement. If the revolution in Germany had materialized, Lenin would probably have moved his headquarters from Moscow to Berlin, casting himself in the role of leader of the international revolutionary movement, not as a Russian national leader. He could accept such a transfer of power to an alien city because he was not a Russian nationalist and because he thought in international terms. He said in 1917:

> . . . only the particular historical circumstances have made the proletariat of Russia the pioneer of the revolutionary proletariat of the whole world, but for a definite, perhaps very short period of time. . . . The Russian proletariat cannot successfully complete the socialist revolution by its own effort only. . . . It can [only] ease the situation for the entry into the decisive battle of its principal, most faithful and most hopeful ally, the European and the American socialist proletariat.[61]

Two years later, talking about the role of the Communist International, he repeated this view: "For a time, it is self-understood, only for a short period of time, the hegemony in the revolutionary proletarian International has passed to the Russians."[62]

Even though he expected the center of world revolution to shift to a Western country, Lenin regarded Russia as a pioneer and a provisional base in forthcoming revolutions. He placed the universal cause of the revolution above the Russian national interests; addressing the Party Central Committee on May 14, 1918, he said: "for us the interests of world socialism rank higher than national interests; we are defending the socialist fatherland."[63] This superiority of the cause of world revolution over the national interests of Russia was to become increasingly less pronounced in the minds of his successors when Russia had been identified as the permanent basis of the revolution. One of the first acts of the new Soviet Government, over which he presided, was a decree, adopted on December 26, 1917, which solemnly promised help to foreign revolutionaries:

Taking into consideration that the Soviet Government is based on the principles of the international solidarity of the proletariat and on the brotherhood of the toilers of all countries . . . the Council of People's Commissars considers it necessary to offer assistance, by all possible means, to the left internationalist wing of the labor movement of all countries. . . . For this purpose the Council of People's Commissars decides to allocate two million roubles for the needs of the revolutionary international movement and to put this sum at the disposal of the foreign representatives of the Commissariat of Foreign Affairs.[64]

Later on, the Soviet Government would not so naïvely offer such information to foreign governments threatened by its assistance to subversive groups.

The *status quo* that had emerged, by the end of 1920, with the end of fighting on Soviet borders made it clear that Russia would remain, for the time being, the only Communist state. Her provisional role as center of the revolution looked as though it had to become permanent. Lenin's hopes for a revolution in the industrialized states did not disappear, but their realization had to be postponed for an indefinite time. In the meantime, Russia had to exist amidst the encircling capitalist states, which could one day combine to intervene again. Russia had to become strong in order to survive, but she also had to promote universal revolution for two reasons: the justification of her existence as a Communist state lay in its being the stimulus for further revolutions, and the triumph of the revolution elsewhere, even in an underdeveloped country, would further weaken the imperialist chain and thus give her greater security.

After the external situation of Soviet Russia had been stabilized and after the prospects for an immediate revolution in other countries had receded, Lenin reaffirmed, on November 6, 1920, his conviction that the reason for the existence of a Soviet regime in Russia was to assist in spreading the revolution to other countries: "We have always known, and shall never forget, that our task is an international one, and that our victory is only half a victory, perhaps less, until an upheaval takes place in all the states, including the wealthiest and the most civilized."[65] Yet he announced, as early as 1918, an idea which was to become the source of difficulties for Soviet and foreign Communists:

By preserving the Soviet power we render to the proletariat of all countries . . . the best, the most effective support. There could be no greater
blow to the cause of socialism at this moment than the collapse of the Soviet
power in Russia.[66]

It was as true in his time as it is in ours that the collapse of Soviet power
in Russia would be the greatest calamity for the Communist movement;
logically, then, foreign Communists were driven by this interpretation to
become servants of a strong Russia. Lenin's thought unintentionally contained an identification of the interests of universal revolution with those
of Soviet Russia.

The concept of Russia's becoming the center and the bastion of the universal revolution was thus born. This bastion had to become economically
strong in order to influence the fate of the world and to survive. When
Lenin said that socialism was the Soviets plus electrification, he had in
mind Russia herself. He knew, of course, that the same formula would
have made no sense in an industrialized country. The bastion had to become stronger in order to be ready for two eventualities: a new attack by
the capitalist states or a new opportunity abroad for a further revolution.

Stalin developed the same concept practically. The interwar period offered no real opportunities for the extension of the Communist system; all
the passing hopes of the Soviet leaders were frustrated, one after the other.
But this era was also a period of peace, which gave Soviet Russia the opportunity of building up the potential of the bastion. Stalin did not renounce the ideal of the universal revolution when he advanced the concept
of building socialism, or rather industries, in one country. He only followed Lenin's advice of making the bastion strong by providing it with
industries. Stalin was not mistaken. Thanks to her newly acquired industrial potential, the USSR could benefit by this new opportunity, which
was similar to the one that had saved her during 1917–18. In 1939, a major
war broke out among the capitalist states, and this permitted Russia to
strengthen the bastion of the revolution through a formidable extension of
territory and, later, to export the revolution to eastern Europe on the
bayonets of the Red Army. The defeat of Japan, the weakening of British
power, and the existence of a powerful Soviet Union contributed to the
creation of conditions which were propitious for the Chinese Communists.

Today, the bastion is no longer the insecure and feeble Soviet Russia
of Lenin's time; it is the second industrial Power of the world and is well
provided with nuclear weapons. This reinforces Russia's position as the

center of the international Communist movement. The bastion, in Stalin's time and now, has had its own temporal interests, but this does not mean that its rulers have betrayed Lenin and his dedication to the cause of a universal revolution. Elimination of capitalism remains a goal of Communism; it is the self-acknowledged duty of the USSR to help in this achievement to the fullest possible extent.

Lenin, whom no living Soviet leader has ever repudiated, said in 1917:

There is one and only one kind of internationalism in deed, working wholeheartedly for the development of the revolutionary movement and the revolutionary struggle in one's own country, and supporting (by propaganda, sympathy and material aid) such and only such a struggle and such a line in every country without exception.[67]

In 1918, still thinking of an approaching revolution in the highly developed countries, he said:

History has given us, the Russian toiling and exploited classes, the honorable role of vanguard of the international socialist revolution, and today we see clearly how far the development of the revolution will go. The Russians commenced, the Germans, the French and the English will finish, and socialism will be victorious.[68]

Although he realized that Soviet Russia would be an infinitely greater provocation to the capitalist states if, not content with her own revolution, she promoted the revolution in other countries, he did not hesitate to say, in 1918:

Here lies the greatest difficulty of the Russian revolution, its great historical problem, viz., the necessity of solving international problems, the necessity of calling forth an international revolution, traversing the path from our strictly national revolution to the world revolution.[69]

Stalin remained faithful to the same reasoning. Commenting on Lenin's thought in 1924, he said:

Lenin never regarded the Republic of the Soviets as an end in itself. To him it was always a link needed to strengthen the chain of the revolutionary movement in the countries of the West and the East, a link needed to facilitate the victory of the working people of the whole world over capitalism. Lenin knew that this was the only right conception both from the international standpoint and the standpoint of preserving the Soviet Republic itself.[70]

He reasserted the same view at a time when socialism was gaining a foothold in one country (industrialization was under way). Addressing the Party Central Committee in 1928, he said:

For us there is one of two alternatives: either we continue in the future to wage a revolutionary policy, uniting around the working class of the USSR the proletarians and oppressed of all countries (whereby international capital will impede us in every way in our movement forward), or we renounce our revolutionary policy, make a number of concessions in principle to international capital, and then the international capital, no doubt, will not be averse "to helping us" in the regeneration of our socialist country into a "good" bourgeois republic.[71]

He never failed to follow the first alternative, although his fear that foreign capital might impede the industrial development of the USSR proved to be vain, since American, German, British, and other Western capital was helpful in laying the foundations of the Soviet industrial might during the First Five Year Plan. He remained faithful to the Leninist concept until his death. Not only did he export the Communist system to eastern Europe and start the policy of helping Communist China in her own industrialization drive, but, in the short speech he made to the last Party Congress he attended in 1952, he mainly devoted his attention to the problems facing foreign Communist parties in the capitalist lands, promising them the brotherly support of the USSR:

This trust [on the part of the foreign Communist parties], which means the readiness to support our party in its struggle for the radiant future of the peoples . . . is particularly precious to us. . . . When comrade Thorez or comrade Togliatti declares that their nations would not fight in a war against the peoples of the Soviet Union, this is primarily support given to the workers and peasants of France and Italy who are fighting for peace; while secondly it is support given to the peace-loving efforts of the Soviet Union. . . . It is self-evident that our party cannot remain indebted to the brotherly parties; it must in turn give its support to them as well as to their peoples in their struggle for emancipation and for the preservation of peace. As is known, our party acts in this manner. After the conquest of power by our party in 1917 and after its taking effective measures for the liquidation of the capitalists' and landowners' oppression, the representatives of the fraternal parties, full of admiration for its courage and its successes, called it the Shock Brigade of the world revolutionary workers' movement. . . . It was obviously very difficult to carry out this honorable task as long as the Shock Brigade was the only one and had to carry out this leading task almost in isolation. But this was true in the past. Now the situation is completely different. Now, when new Shock Brigades have appeared in the persons of the peoples of democratic countries from China and Korea to Czechoslovakia and Hungary, it is easier for our party to struggle and the work has become more enjoyable. Those Communist, Democratic, and Workers' and Peasants' parties, which have not yet come to power and which continue to work under the heel of the bourgeois Draconian laws, deserve our particular attention.[72]

After saying that the task of those parties was easier than that of the Russian party before the October Revolution, he proceeded to give the reasons:

First of all, they have before their eyes such examples of struggle and successes as those of the Soviet Union and of the people's democratic countries. Consequently, they may learn from the errors and successes of those countries and thus alleviate their own task. Secondly, the bourgeoisie itself . . . has seriously changed, has become more reactionary, has lost its ties with the people, and thus has weakened itself. . . . Formerly the bourgeoisie was considered the leader of the nation, it defended the rights and independence of nations, placing them "higher" than anything else. Now no trace has remained of the "national principle." Now the bourgeoisie sells the rights and the independence of their nations for dollars. The banner of the national independence and national sovereignty has been thrown overboard. There is no doubt that this banner will have to be raised by you, the representatives of the Communist and Democratic parties; you must carry it forward if you want to be the patriots of your countries and if you want to become the leading force of nations. . . . Obviously all these circumstances should ease the work of the Communist and Democratic parties which have not yet come to power. Consequently, there are reasons for expecting successes and victory of the fraternal parties in the countries where capital is now the master.[73]

The delegates of forty-four parties were listening to Stalin's words. These words, encouraging foreign parties to seize power, were spoken by a man who was not only the head of his own party but also the Prime Minister of a great Power. One can well imagine the indignant charges of illegitimate interference in the domestic affairs of other countries—which the Soviet press would surely raise—were the same words addressed by a "capitalist" Prime Minister to opposition groups of Russia, China, or eastern Europe. Stalin never lost his fierce interest in world revolution. It is interesting to note that he advised his foreign comrades to act as nationalists of their respective countries; his advice has not been forgotten, especially in underdeveloped countries, where the Communist parties brandish the sword of vociferous nationalism, its point leveled at the West.

The concepts of nationalism and world revolution have not been abandoned since Stalin's death. There is no reason to suspect that the ideological faith of Stalin's successors, including Khrushchev, has been broken. Indeed, the world-wide struggle for universal Communism has been vigorously renewed, indicating that the Soviets have not lost sight of their ultimate objective. There is a second reason for their current attitude: it would be politically foolish for them to demolish the ideological foundation for co-operation with the Communist parties which control China and eastern Europe and those in non-Communist nations which constitute a faithful phalanx of supporters of Soviet foreign policy and whose seizure of power would provide the Soviet Union with new allies. The debates of the 20th Party Congress offer ample proof that Soviet ideals remain unchanged. Significantly, one of the major topics of that Congress was the use of various methods for effecting Communist revolution. The new theory of a peaceful transition to Communism (which, it should be noted, is of no practical significance to the USSR, China, or eastern Europe because revolution has already placed the Communists in power in these areas) was elaborated for the benefit of those Communist parties which exist under capitalist regimes.

Khrushchev, like Lenin, has expressed an unshakable faith in the ultimate world victory of Communism:

Our certainty of the victory of communism is based on the fact that the socialist mode of production possesses decisive advantages over the capitalist mode of production. Precisely because of this, the ideas of Marxism-Leninism are more and more capturing the minds of the broad masses of the working people in the capitalist countries, just as they have captured the minds of millions of people in our country and the people's democracies.[74]

He has even quoted Lenin: "As far back as the eve of the Great October Socialist Revolution, V. I. Lenin wrote: 'All nations will arrive at socialism —this is inevitable.' "[75] One may cast aside the highly debatable question of the alleged superiority of the socialist mode of production over the capitalist mode and consider, in another context, the question of whether Communism wins by capturing human minds or by other means (the revolution in Hungary did not prove that Hungarian minds were captured but that Hungarian bodies were crushed by Soviet tanks). The interesting point in Khrushchev's statement is his lively concern with the extension of Communism to other countries. He proceeded to discuss the various ways of effecting revolution without concealing the fact that socialism, in his interpretation, meant revolution: "True, we recognize the need for the revolutionary transformation of capitalist society into socialist society. It is this that distinguishes the revolutionary Marxists from the reformists, the opportunists."[76] Unlike the democratic socialists of Europe and Asia (the reformists and the opportunists), Khrushchev was depicting the road to economic and social advance not as a series of progressive reforms but as a revolution, that is, a sudden and complete change in the existing situation. He pointed out the ways and means of achieving revolution, obviously in the capitalist states, in the pattern of revolution already carried out in all the countries of the Soviet bloc. He added what might seem a revision of the Leninist doctrine, namely the possibility of making the revolution peacefully by parliamentary votes, assuming that Communists and their allies would have a parliamentary majority. The theses adopted by the 2nd Congress of the Communist International in 1920, when Lenin was the acknowledged leader of the organization, took a dim view of the possibility of a parliamentary transition to socialism:

Communism rejects parliamentarianism as the form of the future society; it rejects it as a form of the class dictatorship of the proletariat; it rejects the possibility of the protracted process of winning over parliaments; it pursues the aim of destroying parliaments. Hence one may talk only about making use of the bourgeois state institutions with the objective of destroying them.[77]

Khrushchev accepted, at the 20th Congress, the remote possibility of winning over parliaments by a Communist majority; however, he upheld Lenin's main point: that parliamentarianism could not be the form of government for a Communist state. He could not disagree with Lenin because a parliament can function only with the existence of competing parties, a situation that is incompatible with the Communist monopoly of political power. The Comintern theses rejected the very concept of national will:

Parliamentarianism cannot become a form of the proletarian state administration ... any fiction of the all-national will is harmful to the proletariat at that stage [of the existence of a Communist state]; a Soviet Republic is the form of the proletarian dictatorship of the proletariat.[78]

Khrushchev did not reject violence as the principal means of a successful revolution; he mentioned the parliamentary way as a substitute, to be used, as he and his colleagues clarified it, only in certain specific conditions:

There is no doubt that, in a number of capitalist countries, the violent overthrow of the dictatorship of the bourgeoisie [the bourgeoisie is supposed to be the dictator in all non-Communist countries, even if the form of government is the purest political democracy and if the socialists, or, as Khrushchev called them, the reformists and the opportunists, are in power] and the sharp aggravation of class struggle connected with this are inevitable. . . . Leninism teaches us that the ruling classes will not surrender their power voluntarily. And the greater or lesser degree of intensity which the struggle may assume, the use or the non-use of violence in the transition to socialism, depends not so much on the proletariat but rather on the degree of resistance by the exploiters, and on whether the exploiting class itself resorts to violence. . . . The winning of a stable parliamentary majority, backed by a mass revolutionary movement of the proletariat and of all the toiling people, could create for the working class of many capitalist and former colonial countries, conditions needed to secure fundamental social changes. In the countries where capitalism is still strong and has a huge military and police apparatus at its disposal, the reactionary forces will, of course, inevitably offer serious resistance. There the transition to socialism will be attended by a sharp revolutionary class struggle.[79]

Thus he kindly offered non-Communists two choices: either surrender peacefully to the Communists or resist. If the non-Communists resist, the Communists must have recourse to violence. It follows from Khrushchev's argument that if the "bourgeoisie" is strong enough to capture parliamentary majorities consistently, the Communists will have no choice but to overcome this "resistance" by violence.

Khrushchev's colleague, A. I. Mikoyan, mentioned another factor which was and could again be decisive in assuring a "peaceful" transition to socialism. He said:

And now, when considering the question of the ways of revolution during the contemporary period, we are compelled, as in their time Marx and Lenin were, to proceed from a precise assessment of the balance of class forces both in every individual country and on a world scale. It is clear to everyone that in our time no country can develop by itself without being subject to certain influences from other countries. Lenin foresaw that in a small bourgeois country, with the presence of socialist countries in the neighborhood, the transition to socialism can take place by peaceful means. Lenin made it understood that not only the correlation of class forces in one country should be taken into consideration, but also the presence of victorious socialism in neighboring countries.[80]

Did Mikoyan refer to the contagious example of triumphant Communism in neighboring countries or to something else? He hastened to give the answer by citing the examples of past "peaceful" transitions to socialism in the small countries bordering the USSR:

Because of the favorable postwar situation in Czechoslovakia the socialist revolution was carried out by peaceful means. . . . In their own way, yet also without civil war, the working class of Bulgaria, Rumania, Hungary, Poland, and other people's democracies arrived at the victory of the socialist revolution.[81]

Communist revolution in all of these countries was assured by a simple device: the presence of Soviet troops in or around their territories. Many thousands of victims of Communist violence, members of non-Communist parties, and millions of people in eastern Europe, on whom the Communist system was imposed by the USSR, would take a dim view of the "peacefulness" of this transition to socialism. Another delegate to the Party Congress, I. G. Kebin, cited, as an example of the peaceful transition to Communism, the Baltic countries, which had been "peacefully" occupied by Soviet troops and then annexed to the USSR.[82]

Mikoyan, one of Stalin's sharpest critics at the 20th Congress, did not care to support his interpretation of the peaceful transition by quoting from the writings of his former idol, but Stalin himself predicted, in 1924, such a transition under auspicious international circumstances. He said at that time:

. . . the law concerning the violent revolution by the proletariat, the law concerning the breakdown of the bourgeois state machinery, as a pre-condition of that revolution, is an inescapable law of the revolutionary movement in the imperialist countries of the world. Of course, in a more remote future, if the proletariat wins in the most important capitalist countries and if the present capitalist encirclement is replaced by a socialist encirclement, a "peaceful" road of development will be fully possible for some capitalist countries where capitalists will have recognized the opportunity of serious "voluntary" concessions to the proletariat because of the "unfavorable" international situation.[83]

Stalin applied his theory in the Baltic States and eastern Europe, without waiting for Communist victory in the most important capitalist states, by making use of a propitious international situation.

After all these explanations, one may have doubts about peaceful transition. Polish Communist leader Gomulka cautiously commented, in May, 1957, on the possibility of a peaceful transition:

. . . the 20th Congress of the C.P.S.U. suggested the possibility, but only the possibility (that is to say, it did not yet foresee the existence of an established principle) of the conquest of power by the working class without bloodshed, for instance, by parliamentary means.[84]

But the most interesting comment came from Khrushchev himself:

Whatever the form of transition to socialism, the decisive and indispensable factor is the political leadership of the working class, headed by its vanguard. Without this there can be no transition to socialism.[85]

Peaceful or violent, the transition to socialism must be controlled by the vanguard of the working class (the Communist Party) and therefore must always result in its seizure of power. This interpretation could have been underwritten by both Lenin and Stalin. Mikoyan did not leave any doubt concerning the meaning of the words "transition to socialism"; he said: "any transition from capitalism to socialism, any upheaval in social relations, is revolution, varying in acuteness but nevertheless revolution which all peoples will experience."[86]

The 20th Party Congress, held for the benefit of Communist parties in capitalist countries, had an interesting audience: the delegates of these parties. Mikoyan exhorted the delegates to draw upon the experience of Communist parties already in power, presumably their experience in overthrowing their national governments. He said:

The fraternal Communist parties of the capitalist countries possess an inexhaustible treasure-house of knowledge in the theory of Marxism-Leninism. They possess a rich school in the practical experience and historical lessons of the victories of our country, China, and other people's democracies.[87]

The roster of foreign delegates at the Congress was rather imposing. Excluding the guests representing parties of the so-called people's democracies, there were forty-four delegates from capitalist states. (The following countries were named in Soviet sources: France, Italy, Indonesia, India, Finland, Spain, Britain, Austria, West Germany, Argentina, Syria and Lebanon, Sweden, Mexico, Denmark, Norway, Holland, Belgium, Canada, Iceland, Switzerland, Luxemburg, Israel, Uruguay, Brazil, Japan, Venezuela, Chile, Bolivia, Cuba, Costa Rica, Colombia, and Australia.) Parties which could not send delegates conveyed their greetings to the Congress.

The new line concerning the various modes of transition to socialism and the desirability of temporary co-operation between Communist and non-Communist parties in capitalist countries during the transitory period was formulated for the benefit of the foreign parties. M. E. Saburov told the delegates: "The creative working out by the Central Committee of the most important issues of Marxist-Leninist theory allows our Party and the Communist parties of foreign countries to follow a correct orientation in their practical work."[88]

In September, 1956, Mikoyan, acting as chief guest delegate to the 8th Congress of the Chinese Communist Party, displayed lively interest in the revolutionary changes in non-Communist countries. He reaffirmed the Communist faith in the ultimate world victory:

And here is the place to recall the brilliant foresight of Vladimir Illyich Lenin, who, in his famous article "Better fewer but better" (1923) said: "In the last analysis, the outcome of the struggle will be determined by the fact that Russia, India, China, and so forth, account for the overwhelming majority of the population of the globe. And it is precisely this majority that, during the past few years, has been drawn into the struggle for emancipation with extraordinary rapidity, so that in this respect there cannot be the slightest shadow of doubt as to what the final outcome of the world struggle will be. In this sense the complete victory of Socialism is fully and absolutely assured."[89]

This quotation deserves particular attention for two reasons. First of all, it shows that Lenin, discouraged in 1923 by the frustration of his former hopes for a speedy advent of the revolution in the West, was turning his eyes toward the underdeveloped countries. Secondly, Mikoyan disclosed, in citing this particular quotation, the present hopes of the Soviet Party. The revolution is expected to progress in the countries which are considered the weakest links, its triumph there being deemed a decisive factor in the outcome of the universal Communist struggle. In his speech, Mikoyan indicated the new, post-Stalinist line of thought in distinguishing between the conditions in various capitalist countries and calling, by implication, for different tactics in both the highly industrialized and the underdeveloped countries. He made it clear that the latter countries did not need to go through a Western type of economic development and might pass directly from the pre-industrial stage to that of socialism (Communism). He said:

And it is definitely harmful to lump together, as it is done sometimes, all the countries not belonging to the socialist system, and to include them mechanically in one camp of capitalism. Although actually the capitalist system of production relations dominates or prevails in all these countries, we must not overlook the fact that the capitalist world itself is largely not homogeneous. . . . The supporters of progress [Communists] in those lands [of Asia and Africa] do not want their countries to go through all the tortuous stages of capitalist development. . . . It should be assumed that there is no need for these countries to traverse again the entire tortuous path of capitalism to reach socialism.

Mikoyan made it clear that the Soviet Party considered itself, as before, the center of the Communist movement, a center entitled to indicate to other parties the correct path. Referring to the 20th Congress, he said:

Comrades, together with other important questions of the theory and practice of Marxism-Leninism, well known to your Party, the 20th C.P.S.U. Congress gave serious thought to problems pertaining to the present-day international communist movement and working-class movement as a whole. The conclusions of the 20th Congress on these questions have met with a broad, positive response not only in your Party, not only in all fraternal Communist and Workers' parties, but also among the broad masses of the working people and progressive public in all countries.

He coupled this with an appeal for close co-operation by all Communist parties:

The international essence of our cause demands fraternal friendship and mutual understanding, ties, and contacts between all Marxist-Leninist parties. Contacts and ties between political parties, which base their activities on the principles of Marxism-Leninism, naturally must be closer. What is most valuable is the exchange of experience and the mutual assistance which can be rendered by Workers' parties inspired by one great idea and marching together toward one common goal.

One of the leaders of the Chinese Communist Party, Liu Shao-chi, formulated the same thought—that the Communist movement was not the affair of particular countries where Communists were in power but a world cause: "The Chinese revolution is part of the revolutionary cause of the international proletariat."

The Leninist cause calls for overthrowing all non-Communist political, economic, and social systems and helping the Communists to seize power throughout the world. If the opponents are feeble or can be overwhelmed with the assistance of the existing socialist states, the revolution does not require bloodshed; otherwise, violence must be used. This is the essence of the "new" teaching adopted by the 20th Congress, and it hardly supports the thesis that the USSR is less actively interested in world revolution today than in Lenin's time.

The USSR, the most powerful of the Communist states, continues to play its role as leader. *Kommunist* reported in 1957:

Thanks to the fact that the Soviet Union is the first country of victorious socialism, and is, after the coming into being of the socialist camp, the most powerful country within this camp, a country with the richest experience, and capable of giving the greatest assistance to the peoples in other socialist countries, it has invariably been for forty years the center of the international communist movement.[90]

This statement differs very little from many statements made during the preceding forty years. The central idea is that the USSR, the first and now the most powerful socialist state, is duty bound to support other Communist parties, either in retaining power, as in Hungary, or in conquering power, if these parties still represent opposition groups in capitalist states. The forms of co-operation may change. At one time there existed the Communist International, founded by Lenin in 1919 and dissolved by Stalin in 1943, a universal organization for all the Communist parties of the world. At another time, it was the Communist Information Bureau, which formally included only the Soviet, eastern European, French, and Italian parties; it was an organization founded by Stalin in 1947 and dissolved by his successors in 1956. The contacts are now on a bilateral footing, but their essence remains the same. For Soviet Communists, the USSR remains the center and the base of the universal cause. *Kommunist* said it in 1957, but the same thought has been consistently expressed since Lenin's time. Lenin wrote in his theses on the national and colonial problems which he submitted to the Second Congress of the Comintern (June 5, 1920):

. . . proletarian internationalism requires, firstly, the subordination of the interests of the proletarian struggle in one country to the interests of the same struggle on a world-wide scale; secondly, the ability and the willingness of a nation which has won the victory over the bourgeoisie to accept the greatest national sacrifices for the sake of overthrowing international capital.[91]

The program of the Communist International stated:

. . . the USSR unavoidably is becoming the base of the world movement of all oppressed classes, the center of the international revolution, the greatest factor in universal history. . . . The USSR represents the most important factor not only because it has split up from the world capitalist system, while creating the base for a new socialist economic system, but also because it plays generally an exceptionally great revolutionary role, the role of the international bearer of the proletarian revolution that instigates the proletarians in all countries toward the seizure of power.[92]

The 7th plenary meeting of the Executive Committee of the Comintern declared in 1926:

The Seventh enlarged plenary session of the Executive Committee of the Communist International considers that the Soviet country objectively is the principal organization center of the international revolution.[93]

This frank admission came at a time when the USSR had already undertaken, in international treaties, the obligation not to interfere in the domestic affairs of other countries. The Soviet Party itself has frequently reaffirmed the same thesis. For instance, the 17th Party Conference declared in 1932:

All this [the economic development] makes even more the USSR the center of attraction for the workers of all countries and for the oppressed of the whole world. The revolutionary significance of the USSR is increasing. The USSR, as the base of international socialism, is growing in strength.[94]

This stand differs little from the early pledge adopted by the 7th Party Congress in 1918:

The Congress sees the most hopeful guarantee for the consolidation of the socialist revolution, which has won in Russia, only in its transformation into an international workers' revolution. . . . The Congress declares that the socialist proletariat of Russia shall support, by all its forces and all the means at its disposal, the fraternal revolutionary movement of the proletariat in all countries.[95]

Current comments in Soviet literature uphold the same outlook. For instance, a book published recently by the Soviet Academy of Sciences defined proletarian internationalism as an integral part of Soviet patriotism:

The Party reveals the organic unity between Soviet patriotism and proletarian internationalism, and points out that the toilers, living in a country where the front of imperialism was broken earlier than elsewhere, cannot look on their victory as something self-sufficing and independent of the struggle of the proletarians against capitalism in other countries. On the contrary, the victory of the socialist revolution in one country must be viewed as a buttress, as a means of the victory of toilers in other countries. After the victory of the proletariat in one country, the latter country becomes the base and the buttress for the development of the socialist revolution in other countries. After breaking off one link from the chain of imperialism, the victorious proletarian revolution is shattering the system of imperialism as a whole; it promotes the splitting off of new links, and revolutionizes the proletarians of other countries. The sacred duty and the in-

ternational obligation of the proletarians who won victory in one country
is to assist the toilers of other countries. . . . This assistance takes the form
of a direct support given to the proletarian struggle and the revolutionary
movement in other countries.[96]

A contemporary Soviet political writer says:

The Communist Party of the Soviet Union has always assumed that the
"national" and the international tasks of the proletariat of the USSR merge
into one general task, the liberation of proletarians in all countries from
capitalism, and that the problem of building socialism in our country
merges with that of the revolutionary movement in all countries into one
single problem of victory of the socialist revolution in all countries. The
interests and tasks of the proletariat of the USSR are interwoven and indissolubly tied up with interests and tasks of the revolutionary movement
in all countries, and, vice versa, the tasks of the revolutionary proletarians
of all countries are indissolubly linked with the tasks and successes of the
proletarians of the USSR.[97]

N. V. Tropkin, a Soviet expert on Communist strategy and tactics, wrote
in 1955:

It would be an error to think that the proletarian revolution and the socialist construction in the country of the victorious proletariat could proceed
without a connection with the world revolutionary movement. . . . Only
close cooperation and mutual support among the working people in vari-
out countries may secure the success in the liberating struggle. This is why
the strategy and tactics of any Communist or Workers' party assign the
first place to the interests of the international proletariat, while strictly
reckoning with conditions in its own country. . . . Founded on the solid
basis of proletarian internationalism, the Communist Party of the Soviet
Union considers the victory of the socialist revolution in individual countries not as a self-contained goal but as a means of assuring a bright future
for the toilers of all countries and as a bulwark in the struggle for the free
and happy life of the whole of mankind.[98]

In another contemporary note, *Kommunist* said in 1957:

The essence of the proletarian internationalism consists precisely in the
mutual support given to each other by the national detachments of the
workers' world movement and in their common defense of the socialist
cause everywhere. . . . After October 1917 . . . internationalism was manifest in the support given by the workers' world movement to the Soviet
State and in the support by the toilers of the USSR given to the latter
movement.[99]

All these views might be dismissed as windy propaganda or as a purely
verbal tribute to a dead ideology but for two facts: (1) The Communist

revolution spread from its base in the USSR to China, Korea, Vietnam, and eastern Europe. (2) The Soviet press is constantly commenting on visits to Moscow by representatives from foreign Communist parties. Even after the confusion created by the violent criticism of Stalin at the 20th Party Congress, foreign Communist parties have never failed to rally in support of their elder, the Soviet Communist Party, an example of which was seen on the occasion of Soviet military intervention in Hungary.

Soviet publications in the post-Stalinist era abound in discussion of the future revolution in other countries, notably in the underdeveloped areas. They stress the need to fight for those revolutions and discuss the strategy and tactics of the parties which still face the problem of the seizure of power. Assuming that the Soviet politicians are not mere academicians, one may conclude that they and their collaborators have practical aims in mind. However, this does not mean that they have set a time for a series of revolutions in various countries. Lenin did not do so, and any sensible politician would avoid such a thing. A revolution requires propitious circumstances. Life itself sets the date for a revolution. The task of the Communists is to make use of conditions favorable to their victory, to be ready to seize the opportunity when it offers itself. Both the Russian Bolsheviks and the Chinese Communists have proved that this is not beyond the human capabilities of a well-organized and determined revolutionary organization.

Khrushchev cautiously expressed (he was talking to the representative of a Japanese newspaper, *Asahi-Shimbun*) both the living faith of Soviet Communists in a Communist victory in other countries and the Leninist concept that revolution will come when the conditions were ripe for it:

I believe that Communism will win in Japan. . . . You want the bourgeois system to exist forever. But I want Communism. I sympathize with the Japanese Communists, but we do not allow ourselves any interference in Japanese affairs. . . . Each fruit ripens at an appropriate time and depending on circumstances. The same is true of the revolution. . . . The whole world will come to Communism.[100]

CHAPTER II

RUSSIAN NATIONALISM

1. Lenin, the True Internationalist

THE USSR REMAINS the bulwark of militant Communism simply because it is the most powerful Communist state; it was, moreover, the only Communist state until the postwar emergence of "people's democracies" in eastern Europe and the only base of world revolution for almost three decades. This gives the Soviet Communist Party the role of an elder "brother."

The same background provides the Russian Communists with a feeling of pride in the achievements of both their party and the Russian people, the willing or unwilling mainstay of the ever increasing power of the Soviet base of revolution. The present nationalism among Soviet leaders is thus the result of a long evolution. Lenin was not a nationalist; he thought basically in international terms. His people was not the multi-class, pre-Revolutionary Russian; this was the international proletariat. Tsarist or capitalist Russia was not his fatherland, as he proved in 1914. While most of the European socialists succumbed to the appeal of their respective belligerent countries and wholeheartedly supported the national war effort, Lenin opposed the Russian cause, believing that the war was imperialist on all sides, not excluding the Russian. For him, the defeats of the Tsarist armies were welcome because they could produce that national disaster which he considered a condition of revolution. His fatherland was to come and was to be any socialist country. If the revolution had taken place in Germany, he would have supported Germany against Russia.

Reminding his readers of the refusal of the Bolshevik parliamentary fraction in the Duma to vote for war credits, Lenin wrote in September 1914:

We, the Russian Social-Democrats, have not the slightest doubt that, from the standpoint of the working class and the toiling masses of all the peoples of Russia, the least evil would be the defeat of the Tsarist monarchy, the most reactionary and barbarian government, which oppresses the greatest number of nationalities and the most numerous population of Europe and Asia.[1]

In 1915, addressing a conference of the foreign section of his party, he said again:

The struggle against one's own government, which wages an imperialist war, should not stop in any country before the prospect that the revolutionary propaganda might bring about the defeat of his country. The defeat of the governmental army weakens the government, facilitates the liberation of nationalities which it enslaves, and makes easier the civil war against the ruling classes. . . . A victory of Russia would result in the strengthening of world reaction and of domestic reaction within the country, and would be accompanied by the complete enslavement of the peoples living in the territories already conquered. This is why the defeat of Russia represents in all circumstances the least evil.[2]

The 1917 revolution created a fatherland for Lenin, not because it had taken place in Russia, but because his concept of a socialist regime could be realized there. In 1918, he said that he and his followers had recovered a fatherland, and he showed an amazingly unperturbed attitude toward the fact that his native country was at that time reduced to ethnic Russian territory, the rest having been temporarily lost:

We have been for defense since October 25, 1917; we have won the right to defend the Fatherland . . . we defend the Fatherland against imperialists. . . . We defend, not a Great-Power status; there is nothing left of Russia except for Great-Russia; we do not defend national interests. We declare that the interests of socialism, the interests of world socialism, are superior to national interests and to the interests of States. We defend the socialist Fatherland.[3]

As we have seen, Lenin's mind was set on enlarging this socialist fatherland to include other countries; he hoped that other peoples, especially industrialized peoples, would join in a world Soviet Republic, a fatherland for the whole international proletariat. Addressing the 1st Congress of the Communist International, he said:

The alliance of Communists grows in the whole world. The Soviet authority has won in several countries. We shall soon see the victory of Communism in the whole world, we shall witness the foundation of a World Federated Republic of the Soviets.[4]

For him, Russia was only a stepping stone to the realization of his dreams, and there is no indication that he ever changed his views.

Lenin was, of course, completely familiar with the Russian national culture and mentality. He was not ashamed of his national origin and was, in fact, quite proud of it. While opposing the Russian national war effort, he wrote, in 1915:

> Is the feeling of national pride foreign to us, the Great-Russian conscious proletarians? Of course not! We love our language and our country; we work above all for raising its [Russian] toiling masses (i.e., nine-tenths of its population) to the level of a conscious life of democrats and socialists. It is more painful to us than anything else to see and feel the acts of violence, the oppression and mockeries to which the Tsarist hangmen, gentry and capitalists subject our beautiful country. We are proud that those acts of violence have been answered from our midst, from among the Great-Russian community, that *this* community brought forward Radishchev, the Decembrists, the revolutionaries-*raznochintsev* [the 19th-century revolutionary intellectuals not of noble origin] of the seventies, that the Great-Russian working class created in 1905 a powerful revolutionary party of the masses, that the Great-Russian peasant began at the same time to become a democrat and to overthrow the priest and the landlord. . . . We are filled with a feeling of national pride, because the Great-Russian nation *also* created a revolutionary class, *also* proved that she was capable of providing mankind with the great images of struggle for freedom and socialism.[5]

This was a kind of conditional patriotism, Russia was dear to Lenin only to the extent that she contributed to the march of the revolution. As a matter of fact, it is amazing how able he was in keeping abreast of Russian developments during his long years of exile, so that when he returned to Russia after several years abroad, he moved on the national stage with complete ease and a keen sense for political opportunities. He was able to perform the astonishing feat of combining a thorough familiarity with his national background and a detached international outlook, but he realized that many of his followers might succumb to the appeal of nationalism after the revolution. After all, the socialist fatherland was, at that time, Soviet Russia. The socialists acquired responsibility for the Russian government, but they were in danger of becoming "nationalized," a peril that overshadowed the prospect of socializing the rest of the world. He warned his fellow Party members against the danger of Russian nationalism. For example, he said in 1919:

> There are among us, for instance, at the Commissariat of Education or around it, such Communists who say: "One school, hence do not dare to teach in any other language than the Russian." Such a Communist is, for me, a Great-Russian nationalist. He sits in many of us, and we must fight against him.[6]

Addressing the 8th Party Congress in the same year, he repeated the same warning: "scratch some of the Communists and you will find a Great-Russian chauvinist."[7]

The Party remained alert to this danger for several years, although the problem was becoming increasingly difficult. Russia, conceived at first as an accidental and short-time base of world revolution, was becoming, for lack of other revolutions, a permanent base which would have to be manned by Russians. The national environment was taking its revenge on those internationalists who had denied having any fatherland before 1917; the depth and intensity of national feelings peculiar to modern men were asserting themselves. Much later, the same cause was to account for Soviet troubles in Yugoslavia, Poland, and Hungary. It is possible that nationalism in various Communist countries may eventually become the principal source of the undoing of their political and ideological unity.

However, the Party tried throughout the twenties to control the national feelings of Russian Communists. For instance, in 1923, the 12th Party Congress adopted a resolution as follows:

This pre-revolutionary heritage consists, firstly, in the survivals of Great-Russian chauvinism which is a symptom of the former privileged position of Great-Russians. These survivals live still in the minds of our Soviet officials, central and local; they nest in our economic institutions, central and local. . . . In these conditions the talk about the superiority of Russian culture and the advancement of the thesis concerning the inevitability of victory of the superior Russian culture over the culture of more backward peoples (the Ukrainian, the Azerbaijani, the Uzbek, the Kirghiz, etc.) are nothing but an attempt at consolidating the mastery of Great-Russian nationality.[8]

It is significant that this resolution was adopted at the suggestion of Stalin, who said at the same Congress:

We must consider as one of the most flagrant symptoms of the old heritage the fact that a considerable number of Soviet central and local officials look at the Union of Republics, not as at a union of equal state units destined to secure the free development of national Republics, but as a step toward the liquidation of those Republics, as a beginning of the restoration of the so-called "one and indivisible" [Russia]. . . . The presence of a numerous personnel of old Party officials of Russian descent at the central Party institutions as well as at the offices of the Communist parties of national Republics, who are not familiar with the mores, customs and languages of the toiling masses in those Republics (and who are hence not always sensitive to their [the Republics'] problems) has bred in our Party a tendency to underestimate national peculiarities and national languages in Party activities, a high-handed and contemptuous attitude toward these peculiarities; a deviation toward Great-Russian chauvinism.[9]

Stalin now realized that a new force had been born among the former internationalists, and, still faithful to Lenin in this respect, he sounded an alarm:

. . . a new force is being born in our domestic life—the Great-Russian chauvinism which nests in our institutions, penetrates into not only the Soviet but also the Party institutions, and haunts every corner of our federation. . . . This trust [of the Soviet non-Russian nationalities] which we had then [in 1917] won, we may dissipate completely if we do not arm ourselves against this new, I repeat, Great-Russian chauvinism which crawls without form or physiognomy, yet drop by drop, infiltrates the ears and the eyes.[10]

2. Stalinist Nationalistic Revival and the Current Trend

It is one of the ironies of history that Stalin eventually succumbed to what he had called, in 1923, "the new force in our domestic life." Beginning with the revision of history textbooks in the mid-thirties, which he himself ordered, Stalin gave Russian nationalism the green light.[11] The Second World War intensified it, and it continues to prosper today. The base of world revolution was first identified with the Soviet state and later (largely, but not completely) with the Russian nation. It is an error to interpret Stalin's morale-boosting appeal to the Russian people in 1941 as a tactical move; judged in the light of his postwar policies, it sincerely reflected his feelings. He knew—before, during, and after the war—that in the last analysis, his regime rested on the loyalty and perseverance of the Russian people. In 1941, he was no longer a Georgian; he had become a Great Russian chauvinist, many of whom he had castigated in 1923. Making a political "marriage of convenience" between Lenin and pre-Revolutionary Russian heroes, Stalin exclaimed on November 7, 1941: "Be inspired in this war by the gallant examples of our great ancestors: Alexander Nevskii, Dimitrii Donskoi, Kuz'ma Minin, Dimitrii Pozharskii, Alexander Suvorov, and Mikhail Kutuzov. . . . Forward to victory under the banner of Lenin."[12]

After the war, Stalin referred to the all-Slavic concept: "The age-old struggle of the Slavic nations for their existence and independence has ended with victory over the German invaders and German tyranny."[13]

The opposition of the Slavs to the Germans (not just Nazis) sounded like a proclamation by the Tsarist Government of 1914 and certainly not that of Lenin. Stalin raised his famous toast to the Russian nation on May 24, 1945, at a reception in the Kremlin for the commanders of the victorious Soviet armed forces:

I raise the toast, first of all, to the Russian people because it is the most outstanding nation among all the nations forming together the Soviet Union. I raise this toast to the Russian people because it has gained in this war a general recognition as the leading force of the Soviet Union among all the peoples of our country. I raise this toast to the Russian people not only because it is the leading people but also because it has a clear mind, a reliable character, and the power of resistance.[14]

The pattern was set and has never been abandoned.

It is quite possible that any other Communist leader who might have been in Stalin's place would also have succumbed to Russian nationalism; one can rarely escape one's environment. Attachment to one's country comes naturally and requires a great deal of effort to overcome; few people are able or willing to accomplish it as Lenin did. A current Soviet pamphlet, printed for rank-and-file soldiers and sailors, depicts this native-land attraction rather well:

Fatherland, Motherland, is that country where a man was born and whose citizen he is. When a man pronounces this sacred word: Fatherland, the images of his native country and its landscapes appear in his mind; the word personifies for him his people with their customs and traditions. . . . This love is passed on from generation to generation, from one family to another.[15]

In Stalin's case, there may have been two particular personal reasons for his nationalism, one of which may have been the fact that his mind was formed entirely by Russian cultural environment. Unlike other old Bolsheviks, Stalin never spent much time abroad; Russia was his world. He challenged his colleagues as early as August, 1917, as they looked for salvation toward the West:

It is not impossible that Russia will be precisely the country to pave the road to socialism. . . . We must reject the obsolete notion that only Europe can open this road for us.[16]

The other personal reason may have been the fact that he was born in Georgia. He was not the first example of a foreign-born individual who surpassed his native countrymen in nationalism, as if the better to affirm his assimilation, and the Soviet press certainly hailed him correctly as a Russian on his 70th birthday. For instance, *Sovetskoe Gosudarstvo i Pravo*, the organ of Soviet lawyers, paid Stalin this tribute:

Many people in the Russian past personified in their works and in their moral character the best qualities of the sons of our great Motherland. But not one of them, except the immortal Lenin, can be placed on the same level with I. V. Stalin. Stalin is the mind and the will of our young Soviet Russia. . . . The culture of the Russian people, its heroic past, and the achievements of Russian learning, literature and arts, are close and dear to his heart.[17]

Once Russian nationalism had recovered its birthright in the USSR, it became impossible to distinguish between the various motivations of Soviet leaders, whether in Stalin or in his successors and former collaborators. The expansion of world revolution depended on the strength of its base, while the power and resilience of the base depended, in turn, on the Russians. After the removal of Party barriers against Great Russian chauvinism, the Soviet Communists acknowledged the continuity of the history of their nation. While Lenin had only contempt for the history of Tsarist Russia (as a land of political and social oppression), his disciples found pleasure in tracing their ancestry, discovering in the process that historical events had emotional appeal. Former Russian generations were a source of pride; after all, the greatness of Russia lay not only in the October Revolution and the Soviet regime but also in the earlier achievements of historical significance. The former aspirations and the pre-Revolutionary dreams of Russia became their own.

One may illustrate this Communist pride in past Russian achievements with a few examples. The Russo-Japanese War of 1904–1905 interested Lenin only to the extent that it revealed the rotten timbers in the Tsarist structure and prepared the stage for the Revolution of 1905. For Lenin, that war was just another imperialist war over the spoils of a semi-colonial nation—China. But Stalin espoused the pre-Revolutionary Russian resentment against the Japanese with a thirst for revenge. He said on September 2, 1945, at the time of the Japanese surrender:

The defeat of the Russian troops in 1904, during the Russo-Japanese War, left a bitter memory in the consciousness of our country; it left a black stain on our country. Our people believed in and waited for the day when Japan would be crushed, and the stain removed. We waited forty years, we who belonged to the old generation, for the coming of that day; and behold, the day has come. Japan has today acknowledged her defeat and signed the instrument of unconditional surrender.[18]

Khrushchev must have felt this same revengeful pleasure when he explained to a correspondent of the Japanese newspaper *Asahi-Shimbun* the reasons for the Soviet attack on Japan in 1945, in open violation of the Japanese-Soviet treaty of neutrality concluded in 1941. He mentioned the Japanese participation in foreign intervention and the unfriendly attitude of the Japanese toward the USSR, including the military skirmishes between the troops of the two countries in 1938 and 1939, but he reminded his Japanese guest of 1904 as well: "But remember how Japan attacked Port Arthur in 1904, attacked without a declaration of war and any forewarning."[19] The Soviet press commemorated the 50th anniversary of the same war in 1954 as though there had been no interruption in Russian history between 1904 and 1954. A Soviet admiral of the fleet wrote an article reminding his readers of the glorious feats of the two Russian warships which fought the Japanese:

The glory of the heroes does not wither away, it lives in the memory of the people. . . . The feat accomplished by the *Variag* [a Russian cruiser] personifies the heroism of our whole nation which has never bowed her head before the enemy and has always fought selflessly for the honor and glory of her Fatherland. . . . The Soviet sailors, successors to the fighting glories of the Russian Navy, safeguard and multiply its sacred military traditions. . . . The heroic feat of the sailors of the *Variag* stands before us as a symbol of greatness and military prowess.[20]

The admiral, a high-ranking member of the Communist Party, did not say a word about the fact that the defeat in the Russo-Japanese War was a signal for the Revolution of 1905 and was therefore welcome to Lenin. The survivors of the crew of the *Variag* were given great publicity in *Pravda*, although not one of them had joined the sailors who had revolted against the Tsar in 1905. Their Russian patriotism was the only fact that counted. *Pravda*, printing, in 1954, an article commemorating the death of Admiral S. O. Makarov, Commander-in-Chief of the Tsarist fleet in the Far East, who perished when his battleship was sunk by a Japanese mine, proudly wrote: "Makarov's merits received their full tribute only in Soviet times. The Soviet Armed Forces and the whole Soviet people piously honor the memory of a great Russian patriot who perished at his battle station."[21]

In 1947, Stalin praised Moscow on the occasion of her 800th anniversary in words which acknowleged the continuity of Russian history:

The merits of Moscow consist only only in the fact that she had liberated our Fatherland three times during its existence from foreign oppression: the Mongolian yoke, the Polish-Lithuanian invasion, and the French intrusion [he was referring to events of the 15th, 17th and early 19th centuries]. The merit of Moscow consists, first of all, in the fact that she became the cornerstone of the unification of a divided Russia into one State, with one government and one leadership [this was, of course, the Tsarist leadership]. . . . The historical merit of Moscow consists in the fact that she has been and remains the cornerstone and the initiator of a centralized State in Russia.[22]

To Stalin's successors fell the honor of unveiling in Moscow a monument to Yurii Dolgorukii, the medieval prince who founded the city.[23]

Another occasion for manifesting Communist attachment to Tsarist history was the solemn celebration, in Sebastopol, of the 100th anniversary of the Crimean War. At the celebration, which was held on October 15, 1955, all of the important Soviet leaders heard K. Ye. Voroshilov deliver a fervently patriotic speech in which he said, while bestowing on Sebastopol the Order of the Red Banner ("to commemorate the 100th anniversary of its gallant defense and its great military merits before the Motherland"):

[Founded] by the great military commander of Russia, Alexander Vassilievich Suvorov, and by the celebrated naval commander, Admiral Fedor Fedorovich Ushakov . . . the Black Sea Fleet grew and hardened in battles against the enemies, under the command of Seniavin, Lazarev, Nakhimov and other outstanding naval commanders of Russia [all of them Tsarist officers]. Like Suvorov and Ushakov, they were the best representatives of the Russian armed forces, limitlessly devoted to their Motherland. . . . We may say with pride that the first defense [in 1853–54] of Sebastopol, like the Poltava battle [fought by Peter the Great] and the Borodino battle [in 1812], are piously kept in the memory of our people, as the greatest epics of military prowess, of the courage and valor of the Russian people in the struggle for its independence and its national honor.[24]

This curious blend of Russian nationalism with a solemn duty to world revolution makes it very difficult to distinguish between the two motivations of Soviet foreign policy during the period of imperialist expansion (1939–1945). One may assume that both motivations were happily co-existing in the minds of Stalin and his colleagues and that the annexations reflected pre-Revolutionary ambitions and helped to strengthen the bastion of revolution. A nationalist but non-Communist Russian and a foreign Communist could both approve the annexations, though for different reasons, reasons which did not need to be separated in the minds of Soviet leaders. A Soviet dramatic artist, N. K. Cherkassov, related in his memoirs (published in 1953) an interesting interview he had with Stalin in 1947. Cherkassov played the title role in the well-known Soviet film *Ivan IV*. During the filming of the second part, Stalin asked Cherkassov and the producer (Eisenstein) to visit him and tell him about their progress. Stalin expressed to them his great admiration for Ivan the Terrible, saying, "Ivan IV was a great and wise statesman who protected the country against the infiltration of foreign influence, and strove to unify Russia."[25] Cherkassov writes:

Toward the end of our visit, Jossip Vissarionovich [Stalin] asked how we planned to end the movie. I answered, as intended in the original draft of the scenario, that the movie would end with the march on Livonia and Ivan IV victoriously reaching the coast. Ivan IV, surrounded by his military commanders, standard-bearers and warriors, would stand on the beach facing the oncoming waves. His cherished dream to see "the blue, far-reaching, Russian sea" was being realized. Looking far into the distance, he would end the movie with the words: "We stand on the sea and shall remain here." Comrade I. V. Stalin smiled and gaily cried: "You see, all this took place and in a much better manner."[26]

Lenin did his best to spread the Soviet regime to the Baltic States in the name of the revolution but failed to do so. Ivan IV had tried to conquer the Baltic coast for Russia but had also failed. Stalin, like his predecessors, Peter the Great and Catherine the Great, had been more successful and was proud of it.

In 1940, the publising house of the Soviet armed forces published a pamphlet in the nationalist vein; its author was probably instructed to write it on the eve of the invasion of the Baltic countries, and it therefore expounded the rights of Russia to the Baltic coast:

The Russian Army, led by Peter I, routed the troops of the Swedish King, Charles XII, and the Russian Navy destroyed, in a series of brilliant victories, the naval power of Sweden in the Baltic Sea. From that time the Russian people consolidated their hold on the Baltic coast, and Russia had there, until the Great October Socialist Revolution, immensely long frontiers. . . . As the result of the formation of those new states [Finland, Estonia, Latvia, and Lithuania] the frontiers of our Fatherland on the Baltic extend only to a little more than 300 kilometers. However, the Baltic Sea continues as before to have exceptionally great importance for our country. It is across this sea that our shortest sea lanes lead to Western Europe and the United States of America, and it is there that we carry a significant foreign trade. The importance of the Baltic Sea for the USSR is further increased by the location of Leningrad on its coast. . . . Yet the USSR, through its [present] frontiers, has access in fact not to the Baltic Sea, but only to the most eastern part of the Finnish Gulf. The exit from the Finnish Gulf does not belong to the USSR.[27]

Fourteen years later, a Soviet vice-admiral advanced the same strategic and economic argument: "The struggle of the Russian nation for access to the Baltic Sea was dictated by historical necessity."[28]

These are arguments which could have been propounded by an imperialist of any country, including Tsarist Russia, but both the pamphlet and the article were published in the USSR. The three independent Baltic republics, which had the same right to exist as any Asian state, were annexed in 1940 in the name of Russian vital interests in the Baltic Sea and expansion by the Communist regime.

3. Soviet Patriotism

The concept of Soviet patriotism is very complex, and of its three facets, the first relates to the idea of the bastion of world revolution and the center of the Communist movement. Mindful of this idea, all Communists are expected to pledge their loyalty to the USSR and, if they rule other nations, to give a high priority to Soviet state interests. The second idea centers in the Soviet state as such; in its name, all Soviet citizens, whatever their nationality, owe their allegiance to it. The third factor is the Russian nation, which expects a particular loyalty on the part of Soviet citizens of Russian descent. This last aspect is greatly stressed in contemporary Soviet publications, though not at the expense of the other two.

The first factor, of concern only to non-Soviet Communists, is defined clearly in the following passage:

The ideologists and politicians of the imperialist camp and their "socialist" lackeys slander the Communists and revolutionary workers, claiming that they allegedly betray national and state interests of their respective countries for the sake of state interests of the Soviet Union, and that they defend a "foreign" Fatherland while betraying "their" Fatherland. . . . In fact the defense of the socialist Fatherland, which was born as the result of the October Revolution, is the best way for the working class in all countries to defend the vital interests of the proletariat and the national interests of people in their respective countries. . . . Consequently the support of the

Soviet Union, the principal force of the anti-imperialist front, coincides with the interests of class warfare of the proletariat in the capitalist countries, and with the national interests of peoples in the colonial and dependent countries. . . . It is impossible to defend the national interests of one's own country without mentioning the interests of socialism in the contemporary historical conditions, without taking bearings on the USSR, without fighting together with it and under its leadership against all the forces of international reaction. . . . This is why the leaders of the Communist parties of all countries, expressing the interests and feelings of the working class and of all toilers in all countries, announced their decision that they would not allow the toilers of their countries to be dragged into a war against the Soviet Union. . . . The Communists, who educate the masses in the spirit of the proletarian internationalism, in devotion to the interests of socialism, in the spirit of devotion and love for the USSR, the bulwark of peace in the whole world, in the spirit of hatred for domestic and international reaction, are precisely the true patriots of their country and the most active defenders of the interests of their people. In our time the question may be formulated only in the following manner: either with the Soviet Union against imperialism, reaction and war, or with the USA against peace, democracy and socialism. There is no third road.[29]

The conclusion is obvious: "The attitude toward the USSR is the criterion of proletarian internationalism. A revolutionary and an internationalist is only one who is ready to defend the USSR without reservations, hesitation and conditions, because the USSR is the base of the world revolutionary movement."[30] This conclusion for the benefit of non-Soviet Communists illustrates the usefulness, for Russia at least, of the whole concept of the bastion of world revolution.

Non-Soviet Communists must combat traditional patriotism in their own countries and substitute for it the concept of class warfare:

A revolutionary party of the proletariat unmasks the falsehood of bourgeois propaganda about the "Fatherland" and explains that true patriotism consists in the struggle against the bourgeoisie and this social-political regime of which the bourgeoisie is the bearer. In the process of this struggle grows the class consciousness of the proletariat; here is born the understanding of the community of class interests among the workers of various countries, and here occurs the tendency to unify the efforts of proletarians on an international scale. . . . The workers' movement thus acquires an international character.[31]

Traditional patriotism is a privilege reserved for Russian Communists; Lenin's internationalism, with its Soviet center, is binding on Communists of other nationalities.

The second factor in the concept of Soviet patriotism concern the loyalty of all Soviet citizens, whatever their particular nationality, to the Soviet state and its regime:

The Soviet man considers as his Motherland not only that place where he was born but our whole powerful State of victorious socialism, the Union of Soviet Socialist Republics. . . . Soviet socialist patriotism manifests itself not only in the love of and devotion to the people but also in the love of and devotion to the social and political regime.[32]

. . . Soviet patriotism is not only love for native places, for one's own people, for a native language and culture; it is patriotism of a higher and new order . . . indissolubly tied up with the unconditional devotion to . . . our Communist Party, to the Soviet social regime, to the Soviet State.[33]

The Soviet Communist Party does not tolerate the existence of any deep patriotism among the non-Russian nationalities of the USSR. Since this kind of patriotism is reserved for the Russians, the Party must offer the non-Russians a variety of rather dry and hardly emotional patriotism in the form of allegiance to the Soviet state and its social and political regime.

4. Present Russian Nationalism

The third factor in Soviet patriotism is Russian nationalism. One must concede that Stalin and his present-day disciples have always devoted great attention to the vitality of national feelings. No wonder they have not overlooked, since the mid-thirties, Russian nationalism as a source of vital energy in the USSR! " 'Patriotism,' V. I. Lenin wrote, 'is one of the deepest feelings consolidated by centuries and thousands of years of the [existence] of individual Fatherlands.' This feeling expresses the devotion of man to his Fatherland and his preoccupation with its fate."[34] Unlike certain Western commentators who consider patriotism to be a temporary product of the French Revolution and a passing phenomenon of the 19th and 20th centuries, Soviet writers take it for granted that patriotism is as old as nations themselves:

Devotion to the Motherland and patriotic love for her appeared a very long time ago. This lofty feeling expressed itself in the traditions and folklore of each people. . . . The devotion to one's native country, a passionate love for it, and aspiration to the freedom and independence of the people, speak with immense force in the Russian folklore epics; e.g., "Poem about Igor's Host." This heroic epic, Russian tales, songs, proverbs and sayings narrate the brave struggle of the people for independence. . . .

The Russian soil was often the stage of fierce battles with foreign invaders. The unbending will and the heroic spirit of the Russian people were hardened; their courage, selflessness and love of country manifested in those battles. The Pechenegs and the Polovtsi, the Mongolian conquerors, the German dog-knights, the Swedish and Polish gentry interventionists, Napoleon, and other invaders, frequently tried to conquer the Russian land, and madly attempted to enslave the Russian people. However, all attempts of the enemies broke on the rock of the invincible steadfastness of the Russian people. . . . From the struggle against foreign invaders emerged the outstanding Russian military commanders and statesmen: Alexander Nevskii, Dimitrii Donskoi, Minin and Pozharskii, Suvorov, Kutuzov, and many others, all of them representing the glory and pride of the Russian people. . . . Our people more than once saved, with their own blood, European Civilization from destruction by the barbarians. In the thirteenth to the fifteenth centuries, when Europe enjoyed the era of the Renaissance, the blossoming and development of its culture, the Russian people protected it from the East against the Mongolian hordes. . . . At the beginning of the nineteenth century the Russians saved, by their heroic struggle, the European nations from Napoleon's tyranny. . . . In the realm of military science and art there are no names among the most outstanding military commanders of that time equal to those of Suvorov and Kutuzov. . . . The establishment by the Soviet State in 1942–44 of the orders named after Suvorov, Kutuzov, Alexander Nevskii, Bogdan Khmelnitskii, Ushakov and Nakhimov, had great significance [in patriotic education].[35]

This passage is certainly not an understatement of the pre-Revolutionary glories of the Russian nation. It mentions with pride the names of Tsarist statesmen, princes, generals, and admirals of that period and even goes so far as to place Generals Suvorov and Kutuzov above all their contemporaries, among whom was Napoleon himself. The desire to tie up present-day Russian patriotism with the pre-Revolutionary record is obvious; the intention is frankly stated by another author:

The leading people of Russia were always proud of the contribution which our nation made, during the history of its struggle for the honor and independence of the Fatherland, toward the world revolutionary movement and world culture. The Russian nation gave to the world the greatest philosophers and scientists, writers, artists and composers, military commanders and political leaders. The great names of Plekhanov and Lenin, Belinskii and Chernyshevskii, Pushkin and Tolstoi, Glinka and Tchaikovskii, Gorki and Chekhov, Sechenov and Pavlov, Repin and Surikov, Suvorov and Kutuzov, are a source of Russian national pride.[36]

The list of names the Russian Communist should be proud of, men who allegedly contributed to the revolutionary movement, includes those of eminent composers and painters who did not contribute anything to any revolution, as well as that of General Suvorov, who commanded Russian troops in a punitive expedition against the peasant insurrection in southern Russia and also against the troops of Revolutionary France.

The teaching of national history is considered a means of instilling patriotism in youth: "The most important task of an ideological-political education, during the process of teaching history, consists in instilling in students Soviet patriotism and Soviet national pride."[37] The kind of history used to inculcate Soviet patriotism and proletarian internationalism in Soviet youth can be better understood if one peruses a book written by several prominent Soviet historical authorities. Its opening chapter displays a vigorous pride in the extension of Soviet frontiers from 1939 to 1945, a feat accomplished by the sheer might of Soviet military power:

The state frontiers of the USSR were considerably modified in favor of the Soviet Union in recent years. In the extreme North-West the district of Pechenga [Petsamo] was taken over by the USSR. . . . After the Great Patriotic War Finland restored it to our country by virtue of the treaty concluded with the USSR. . . . Thus the foreign frontier was pushed back away from the ice-free Murmansk port. . . . The frontier on the Karelian Isthmus . . . had bordered the immediate neighborhood of Leningrad, only at a distance of 32 kilometers from that city. It was pushed back in 1940 several tens of kilometers toward the North, beyond the city of Vyborg. . . . Three bourgeois Republics of Latvia, Lithuania and Estonia, allegedly independent but in fact dependent on the Western imperialists, had existed since the Civil War in the Baltic area which had been before a part of Russia. . . . In 1940 . . . Latvia, Lithuania and Estonia became Soviet Socialist Republics joined to the Soviet Union. . . . The territory of the USSR in the Baltic area now reaches the Baltic sea-coast, our historical maritime frontier. . . . The Kaliningrad [Koenigsberg] region of the RSFSR is located on the Southern coast of the Baltic Sea. This land, seized hundreds of years ago by the German conquerors, had been a part of East Prussia and hence of Germany. The German imperialists had established there a bastion for their aggressions against our Fatherland. . . . After the rout of fascist Germany the city of Koenigsberg [now Kaliningrad] and the surrounding region were incorporated into the Soviet Union. . . . In 1921 the toilers of Tuva, which is located on the upper reaches of the Yenisei River, established, with the assistance of the great Russian people, a People's Democratic Republic. In 1944 Tuva was accepted at her own request as a part of the Soviet Union. A Tuva autonomous region was created within the RSFSR . . . the whole length of the Yenisei River is now included within the frontiers of our country. . . . The Southern part of Sakhalin and the Kurile Islands have been Russian lands since time immemorial [sic!], but they remained for a long time in Japanese hands. Those lands separated the Soviet Union from the open Pacific Ocean. . . . Now these territories no longer cut off the USSR from the Pacific but, on the contrary, open to it free access to the Pacific; this fact has great importance for our country.[38]

The author continues, in the same vein, to enumerate all the annexations effected from 1939 to 1945 and "justifies" all of them on grounds of strategic and economic needs or historical "rights" of Russia. The tone is that of Cecil Rhodes, not Lenin. The fact that Soviet annexations were carried out at the expense of small nations like Finland or that they ended the existence of small countries like the Baltic Republics does not make any difference to the apostles of anti-imperialism and anti-colonialism.

A good portion of the same book is devoted to the eulogy of the Russian nation:

In the midst of this great constellation of Soviet Union Republics there is one which the Soviet people call the first among the equal. This is the Russian Soviet Federated Socialist Republic. . . . Our people call the Russian Republic the first among the equal, not only because it is the greatest by its territorial size and its population but, first of all, because its political, state and economic importance is exceptionally great. The main mass of the Russian people live in the Russian Republic. . . . The great Russian people holds the leading position within the family of Soviet peoples. . . . The Russian people is the creator of a great culture. The Russians made a priceless contribution to the world learning, literature and the arts. . . . Vladimir Illyich Lenin, the founder and wise leader of the Communist Party and of the Soviet State, came from among the great Russian people. . . . The Russians distinguished themselves during the Great Patriotic War by their heroic exploits. There were 7,000 Russians among the 11,000 Heroes of the Soviet Union. . . . The Russian people is the most outstanding among all the nations composing the Soviet Union.[39]

George Orwell had in mind the Communists as compared to ordinary Soviet citizens when he wrote: "All the animals are equal, but the pigs are more equal." His quip also applies to the Russians in relation to their non-Russian fellow-citizens. They are the salt of the earth—according to Soviet sources.

While the book devotes entire pages to the description of the glories and superior qualities of the Russians, other nationalities of the USSR receive either a condescending pat on the back in one or two sentences (the Ukrainians, the Georgians, and the Armenians) or no mention at all for the most part. A very revealing part of the book is entitled "The Historical Past of the Soviet People."[40] One would expect a historical survey of the past of all the nationalities of the Soviet Union, since all of them together form "the Soviet people," but this entire portion is devoted only to the history of the Russians. The first chapter bears the title "Our Ancestors, the Slavs"—as if the Slavs were the ancestors of all the nationalities of the USSR. The fact is that only three Soviet nationalities—Russians, Ukrainians, and Byelorussians—are of Slavic descent. The great multitude of other nationalities bear as little relation to the Slavs as they do to the Burmese or the Spanish. It was a standing joke in France in time past that the school primers used in French Africa began with: "Our ancestors, the Gauls. . . ." That was in an "imperialist" colonial country. But the Uzbeks, Tadjiks, Turkmenians, Azerbaijanis, and others in the Soviet Union have to learn about their Slavic "ancestors" as did the French Negroes about their Celtic "forebears."

The whole tone of this part of the book is highly patriotic. The non-Russian nationalities of the USSR are afforded only the current humiliating interpretation of the meaning of Tsarist annexations and conquests of their native lands:

The annexations by Russia of various peoples, whether voluntary or forcible, had for all of them a beneficial and progressive meaning. It helped them to be united with the great Russian people in the struggles against the common enemy, Tsarism, and strengthened the economic and cultural ties among all the peoples of the Russian Empire.[41]

Communists of all nationalities would loudly denounce any such assertion in a British, French, Dutch, Belgian, or Portuguese book, but it becomes a legitimate statement if printed in this and many other Russian Communist books.

Traditional Russian heroes are glorified in the book, whether they were medieval rulers or Tsarist statesmen, generals, and admirals:

Sviatoslav [a medieval Russian prince] was a martial and gallant prince. . . . Sviatoslav's son, Vladimir, continued to enlarge and consolidate the ancient Russian State which achieved during his reign the peak of its power. . . . Prince Alexander [Nevskii, another medieval Russian Prince] was, despite his youth, outstanding by his wisdom, energy, strong character and a warm love for the country. [He was] a talented Russian military commander. . . . Prince Dimitrii Donskoi [another medieval prince] was a gallant and bold warrior and a remarkable Russian military commander. . . . Peter [the Great] was a man of unwavering will. . . . [Thanks to him] Russia became a mighty military and naval Power. . . . Peter's historical merit consists in his finding the ways and means for placing Russia among the leading countries. . . . Peter resolutely brushed aside all obstacles which stood in the path of his reforms. He did not stop at using, as V. I. Lenin said, "barbaric means in the struggle against barbarity." During Peter I's reign Russia was transformed into a powerful Empire endowed with a mighty Army and Navy and a skilled peronnel of officials and diplomats. . . . Peter I was a great man because he correctly understood the tasks which history had placed before our country and energetically fought for their achievement. . . . The future famous military commander, Suvorov, with whose name the development of Russian military art is closely bound up, began his military career during the Seven Years' War. . . . The French [Revolutionary] troops in Northern Italy were defeated thanks to Russian soldiers' heroism and Suvorov's generalship. . . . The remarkable Russian naval commander, Fedor Fedorovich Ushakov, whose name is related to the blossoming of Russian naval art, was Suvorov's contemporary [he also fought against Revolutionary France]. . . . The Soviet Government created during the Great Patriotic War Sovorov and Ushakov Orders to honor those great Russian captains. . . . The outstanding Russian military commander, Mikhail Illarionovich Kutuzov, was widely known for his military successes. [He commanded Russian armies during the war against Napoleon in 1812.] Pavel Stepanovich Nakhimov [an admiral who was the commander of Sebastopol during the Crimean War of 1853–55] continued the best traditions of such naval commanders as Peter I, Ushakov and others. . . . Admiral Makarov, the talented fleet commander in Port Arthur, was getting ready for the decisive naval battle with the Japanese, but perished at the very beginning of the war on his battleship, sunk by a Japanese mine.[42]

Interestingly enough, this imposing gallery (it is much longer in the full text) does not include one single name of a national hero of any Soviet nationality other than Russian. Ironically, none of the listed princes, emperors, generals, and admirals contributed one iota to a revolution or even a social movement.

Soviet Russian patriotism has the naïve freshness of a new development. Look at this example: "The writers of Antiquity describe the Slavs as a gallant, warlike and freedom-loving people."[43] Of course, they had to have those qualities if they were the ancestors of the Russians, although the "writers of Antiquity" knew, in fact, next to nothing about the Slavs, who were at that time barbarians on the fringes of Europe! And Russian troops invariably display outstanding courage:

The Russian troops [in the tenth century] showed valor, absence of fear and steadfastness in their battles against the [Byzantine] Greeks. . . . The courage, heroism, steadfastness and warm love of country which the defenders of Sebastopol demonstrated [in 1854–55] became a part of the Russian tradition. . . . Soldiers and sailors showed, during the Russo-Japanese War, heroism, self-denial and high military qualities characteristic of the Russian Army.[44]

Nationalistic Russian propaganda if also fed to the non-Russian nationalities of the USSR. A recent book written for central Asians in the

USSR contains the following passages about the superiority of their elder brothers:

The great Russian people is the foremost, directing, cementing and leading force within the brotherly family of peoples of the USSR. . . . The peoples of the Soviet Union are now engaged in building a Communist society in indestructible co-operation with, and following the lead of, the great Russian people, the most outstanding nation among all the nations. The Uzbek people, like other peoples of the Soviet Union, looks, with unlimited trust, warmest love and deepest respect, at its elder brother and friend, at the great Russian people which plays the principal and leading role in the construction of the Communist society in our Soviet country. . . . The toilers of the whole world turn their eyes with immense expectation and a feeling of deep gratitude, toward the great Russian people, the hero-people, the warrior-people, the liberator-people, the creator-people, and the faithful friend and powerful defender of all the oppressed and exploited peoples. The peoples of the whole world know that the great Russian people is their loyal defender, the exponent of the most progressive achievements in world culture of all peoples and all civilizations, the herald of the highest ideals of progressive mankind, and the standard-bearer of peace, democracy and Communism in the whole world. . . . The Russian people has made the greatest contribution to world civilization and culture and to the history of the liberating-revolutionary movement. . . . The great Russian people has always been and will remain forever the first among equals within the family of brotherly peoples of the USSR. . . . The Russian annexation brought about the integration of Central Asia within the world economic community and tied up the development [of the central Asian peoples] with the leading Russian culture. . . . The peoples of Central-Asia, the Uzbeks, the Tadjiks, the Kazakhs, the Turkmenians, the Kirghiz and the Karakalpaks, have been and are learning from the great Russian people, the first among the first amidst the peoples of the Soviet Union.[45]

This sounds like a religious litany, not like excerpts from a book which is supposed to be taken seriously. If such words were written by an Algerian Arab about Frenchmen, we would write it off as abject flattery; it is an actual sample of the usual glorification of the Russian nation in the Soviet Union today. Of course when the Soviet authors refer to the Russians as "the great Russian people," they do not use the word "great" in the ethnic sense of "Great Russians" but in its usual meaning in all languages.

Soviet soldiers and sailors are currently indoctrinated in the same creed of Russian superiority: "The great Russian people plays the leading role within the brotherly family of Soviet peoples. The unity of all the peoples living in our country, with the Russian people as its center, is the source of strength and firmness of the Soviet multi-national state."[46]

Language being the usual vehicle of national feelings, Soviet education attaches great importance to teaching Russian to Russian and non-Russian Soviet youth:

Teaching the Russian language has a great significance for the upbringing in Soviet patriotism. Students receive, during the Russian language classes, a distinct idea of the rich vocabulary of that language. . . . [After mentioning various methods of teaching Russian, the authors continue.] All this gives a clear perception of the greatness and power of the Russian language as the language of a great people, and educates the growing generation in the spirit of love for the Russian people.[47]

We shall see later the role that the teaching of Russian plays in the Russianization of other nationalities of the USSR.

Since Stalin's death, there has been greater discretion concerning the fancy claims to Russian priorities in inventions and discoveries, but the list has not been completely forgotten. For instance, a Soviet admiral claimed, in 1954, Russian priority in inventing the telegraph, torpedoes, submarines, and radio, while a marshal of the Soviet air force did the same with the airplane.[48] One member of the Presidium of the Party Central Committee, himself the first secretary of the Uzbek Party, N. A. Mukhitdinov, provided us with the most official version of the same theme in a speech delivered on October 11, 1956, at a conference of the Uzbek intelligentsia:

The Russian people has won, by its great deeds, clear mind, generous heart and brotherly attitude, the universal respect and warm recognition on the part of the peoples of our country and the democratic forces of the world. The Russian people is the force which, under the leadership of the Communist Party, cements the friendship of the Soviet peoples and rallies them together under the banner of proletarian internationalism.[49]

Cosmopolitanism is as opposed to patriotism today as in Stalin's time:

Cosmopolitanism is a reactionary bourgeois ideology which preaches an indifferent attitude toward the Fatherland, claiming that the whole world is the Fatherland of all men. . . . The bourgeois cosmopolitans falsely pretend that patriotism is a harmful survival of the past, deny the necessity of existence of individual independent states, and ask for the creation of a "world state" with one government and one regime, i.e., a bourgeois regime.[50]

Of course, Soviet patriotism also includes much pride in the Communist achievements since the October Revolution:

The Soviet national pride, which includes pride in the great past of our people, is founded, first of all, on the fact that our people, after making the October Revolution, after building up socialism, successfully accomplishes the passage toward Communism, and thus has far surpassed all peoples of the world.[51]

From this premise ensues the natural duty of Soviet citizens toward other nations:

... the international duty of the working class of any country requires from it a selfless assistance toward the toilers of other countries in their struggle for national independence, freedom, democracy and socialism, and an unceasing strengthening of one front of the revolutionary forces and of the camp of peace, democracy and socialism in the whole world.[52]

This side of Soviet patriotism thus takes us back to the concept of the bastion of world revolution.

CHAPTER III

RESIDUE OF
THE COMMUNIST FAITH

1. Objective Truth of Marxism-Leninism

WE MAY at first be surprised by the strange union between Leninist devotion to world revolution and the very un-Leninist Russian nationalism. However, we should remember that human beings are not simply rational animals and that they frequently live rather happily with intellectual contradictions in their minds. The Russian Communists are no exception.

When Soviet Communists speak of world revolution or the triumph of Communism in all countries, what do they have in mind with respect to the practical changes promised in the wake of the revolution? What is the "residue" of Marxism-Leninism to which they remain faithful in practice in Communist lands, particularly in the USSR? The answer to this question is certainly much more important to non-Communists than the reading of copious writings by Marx, Engels, and Lenin. Analysis of the Soviet and other Communist sources allows one to outline the following residue of the Communist faith as reflected in actual practice and policies. The Marxist dialectical-materialist philosophy of the universe and of history must be accepted by every Communist in the same spirit in which Lenin said:

Marx's theory is the objective truth. Following the path of this theory, we will approach the objective truth more and more closely, while if we follow any other path we cannot arrive at anything except confusion and falsehood.[1]

This outlook makes it impossible for religious believers of any denomination, or even agnostics, to belong to the Party. The *Soviet Great Encyclopedia* makes this clear: "The scientific materialistic world outlook is incompatible with belief in God; it arose and developed in an acute and constant struggle with religion."[2] However, Communism offers instead a

58

definite explanation of the universe and of the meaning of history which must be accepted as an objective and final truth:

> ... for its devotees Communism has the *value* of a religion insofar as it is felt to provide a complete explanation of reality and of man as part of reality, and at the same time to give to life, as does religion, a sense of purpose. . . . If reason is to be our *sole* guide, the only intelligible attitude towards the riddle of existence is agnosticism, seeing that all our knowledge is conditioned by the nature and limitations of our human faculties and that there is nothing outside ourselves and the products of our minds by which its final truth can ever be tested. As neither Communism nor religion is content to rest in this position, each is ultimately driven to appeal to certain propositions which have to be accepted by faith, but from which, once accepted, whatever else it is desired to prove, logically follows. Only while religion frankly accepts this, Communism maintains that its fundamental dogmas are guaranteed by science, which they certainly are not, since one and all are very disputable. Nor indeed would the issue be affected if they were so guaranteed, since a belief in the hypotheses upon which science rests requires an act of faith like any other.[3]

The Marxist-Leninist philosophy of the universe and human history proceeds from a quasi-religious claim to an absolute truth founded on the writings of threee mortal men, Marx, Engels, and Lenin, who allegedly escaped the general law of human fallibility. Their view of the universe, for instance, had been formulated before Einstein's theory of relativity became known and modern physics established, the latter theory and physics thus being unrelated to the Marxist concept of nature.

Preaching a quasi-religious and militant creed of their own, Communists must fight all religions in accordance with Lenin's statement: "Marxism is materialism . . . it is . . . relentlessly hostile to religion. . . . We must combat religion—that is the rudiment of *all* materialism, and consequently of Marxism."[4] This does not preclude a reluctant toleration of religious worship, but it does rule out proselytism. Not only religion but any other philosophy of the universe and human history is held false; Einstein's philosophy of relativity, for example, means nothing to the devoted Communist. In other words, Communists offer a rigid world outlook which becomes the official outlook of the state in which they assume power.

2. The Millennium

The quasi-religious Communist outlook is illustrated by its own picture of Paradise. Karl Marx promised his followers a Communist millennium following the post-revolutionary dictatorship of the proletariat. The elimination (by the revolution) of private ownership of the means of production would allegedly eradicate all social evils and transform human nature. People would work for the common good of their own volition, while their productivity would increase by leaps and bounds, thanks to the socialist system of production. Great abundance of goods would result. Eventually, everyone would work according to his abilities and would receive, in turn, consumer goods according to his needs. Coercion becoming unnecessary, the state would gradually wither away. Lenin vividly depicted this remote Paradise:

> Communism is the name we apply to a system under which people become accustomed to the performance of public duties without any specific machinery of compulsion, when unpaid work for the common good becomes the general phenomenon. . . . Only in Communist society, when resistance has been completely broken, when the capitalists have disappeared, when there are no classes . . . only then does "the state . . . cease to exist," and it "becomes possible to speak of freedom." . . . people will gradually become accustomed to observing the elementary rules of social life . . . without the special apparatus for compulsion which is called the state.[5]

> In a higher phase of communist society . . . society inscribes on its banners: from each according to his ability, to each according to his needs.[6]

A Communist has a believer's faith in the advent of the Communist millennium. Its hold on him must be stronger now than it was before 1917 because at that time he could well have imagined that the millennium would follow the revolution. Now, after more than forty years of the USSR, he must be content with a remote and unspecified dawn of the great day. In reality, the Soviet state apparatus continues to follow the policy of totalitarian regimentation and strict compulsion; consumer goods are scarce; labor productivity is notoriously lower than in Western countries; the promised change in human nature has not yet come, as can be seen from constant Soviet complaints about crimes, bribes, and thefts committed by Soviet citizens, despite the complete elimination of the "root" of all evils, the private ownership of means of production. Yet this almost religious belief in ultimate salvation on earth remains part and parcel of the Marxist-Leninist creed.[7]

3. Monopoly of Power

Political monopoly in the hands of the Communist Party is another article of faith. It is called the dictatorship of the proletariat, although the dictatorship is exercised by the Party and not by the workers. Two recent Soviet statements announce this tenet: ". . . Marxist-Leninists believe that there is nothing more important than to defend resolutely the teaching on the dictatorship of the proletariat. . . . The teaching concerning the dictatorship of the proletariat . . . is the principal element of Marxism-Leninism."[8] The joint statement adopted by the Soviet and Hungarian Communist parties in March, 1957, made it clear that the dictatorship of the proletariat meant that of the Party:

The Communist Party of the Soviet Union and the Hungarian Workers' Socialist Party stress that the Hungarian example once again vindicated the views of the great teachers of the proletariat, Marx and Lenin, concerning the decisive role of the Marxist party of the working class as a mobilizing, organizing and directing force of the people. . . . They resolutely take a stand against any attempts to revise such fundamental theses of Marxism-Leninism as the teaching on the dictatorship of the proletariat and the leading role of the Party.[9]

According to the generally accepted view by all Communist parties, a Communist who would share power with another party after the revolution would be a renegade.[10]

Political monopoly inevitably leads to the strict regimentation of not only the whole social life but also all aspects of creative human activity in a nation. A monolithic society is the natural product of total control by a monolithic political party. Lenin accepted this consequence in a speech made at a congress of workers' co-operatives in 1918:

Capitalism deliberately split up various layers of the population. This split should finally and forever disappear, and the whole society should be transformed into one co-operative of toilers. There must be no question of any independent individual groups whatsoever. . . . All the layers of the populations which fight for their freedom must be merged into one strong organization. . . . In order to achieve this, it is necessary that everything be subordinated to Soviet authority and that all illusions about any "independence" either of particular strata or of the workers' co-operatives be forgotten as soon as possible. This hope for an "independence" can exist only where a hope for some kind of return to the past still survives.[11]

4. Socialization of All Means of Production

Faithful to the Marxist teaching that private ownership of the means of production is the root of all social evils, Communists are committed to the total socialization of all the means of production. A Chinese Communist newspaper says categorically: "After the victory of the proletariat under the leadership of the Communist Party . . . industries are nationalized and the collectivization of agriculture is gradually carried out . . . the system of private ownership of means of production being thus liquidated."[12] Communists agree on this goal, although they may pursue it in various countries at different speeds, depending on local circumstances. The Soviet Union has socialized all of its means of production, either through nationalization or collectivization of agriculture. Other Communist states are in different stages of development, but all are guided by this same principle, and in all of them the controlling "heights" of national economy, to use Lenin's expression, such as basic industries, banks, transportation, insurance, wholesale and foreign trade, etc., are in the hands of the state. This socialization of the means of production is not just the result of Communist faithfulness to one of the major tenets of Marxism-Leninism; it represents a practical advantage to the Party, whose leaders concentrate in their hands the monopoly of both political and economic power. Thus the leaders of the Party become both political rulers in the traditional sense and the dispensers of jobs and regulators of wages and incomes; their hands are on the levers of the whole economic life of the country.

A Soviet source lists the following percentages of "socialization" in the industries of eastern Europe in 1954: Poland, 99.4 per cent; Czechoslovakia, 99.7 per cent; Hungary, 97.0 per cent; Rumania, 99.0 per cent; Bulgaria, 99.0 per cent; Albania, 99.0 per cent.[13] The collectivization of agriculture in these areas was proceeding much more slowly; the state and collective farms of various kinds accounted for the following percentages of socialization in total agricultural production in 1954: Poland, 23 per cent; Czechoslovakia, 43.1 per cent; Hungary, 30.5 per cent; Rumania, 24.0 per cent; Bulgaria, 61.0 per cent; Albania, 14.6 per cent. The above percentages for Poland and Hungary have since been considerably reduced because the events of 1956 turned back the clock of collectivization in both countries. Even W. Gomulka, who refused to force Polish peasants to join the so-called producer co-operatives, did not abandon the concept as an ultimate goal. He said in May, 1957: "We know only one form of transformation of small peasant households into socialist economic units, namely the producer co-operative."[14] The Chinese Communist Party beat the Soviet record by collectivizing agriculture in a wholesale manner. Liu Shao-chi said in September, 1956: ". . . 110 million of China's 120 million peasant households, or 91.7 per cent of the total number of peasant households, have joined agricultural producer co-operatives."[15] And this was accomplished at a faster rate than in Russia, i.e., in seven instead of thirteen years after the revolution. Liu Shao-chi also reported that the peasants represented over five-sixths of the total population (approximately 500 million people). The share of national industries in the over-all industrial production of China in 1954 was 47.1 per cent; the remaining industrial production represented the so-called joint state-private corporations (see Chapter X). The state share in China's wholesale trade in 1955 was 95.6 per cent; in retail trade, 82.5 per cent.[16]

While the nationalization of industries proceeds quickly in all Communist states, the pace of collectivizing agriculture is variable, although the ultimate goal remains the same. The reason for this follows.

The necessity for the socialist transformation of agriculture is determined by the basic economic laws of socialism. The socialist system cannot be founded on two antagonistic economic bases: a big socialist industry which develops with great speed and excludes any possibility of a resurgence of capitalist elements, and many millions of small peasant households which are a base for the reappearance of new capitalist elements. Socialism must have only one economic foundation.[17]

This should be borne in mind by those people in the underdeveloped countries who hear the Communists speak only about land reforms and not about the final goal of collectivization. D. T. Shepilov, when he was still talking on behalf of the leadership of the Party, said: "The cornerstone of state regime in all countries of the socialist camp is public ownership of means of production."[18]

5. Centralized and Planned National Economy

Socialization of the means of production requires central economic planning, which, in turn, entails central control over production, wages, and prices and central regulation of the supply of consumer goods. Central planning and administration of national economy are repudiated neither by W. Gomulka, who called it "the fundamental feature of socialism,"[19] nor by any other Communist leader. The Chinese view is reflected thus: "The State, directed by the proletariat and the Communist Party, leads the popular masses in planned development of socialist economy and socialist culture."[20] Soviet sources, of course, subscribe to the same view.[21]

6. Rapid Industrialization

Communist triumphs, with or without the help of the Soviet Army, have been in economically underdeveloped countries, with the exception of the Bohemian part of Czechoslovakia. The new regimes had to face the problem of rural overpopulation. Moreover, they were all interested in the speedy growth of their economic potentials and thereby the military might of the Communist bloc. Industrialization became the order of the day. The pattern of quick industrialization laid out by the USSR has since been followed by all Communist countries, although some of them, like Poland, have had to slow down the pace because of internal difficulties. Industrialization as a long-term objective remains a tenet of the Communist creed:

The construction of socialism and communism involves a transformation and an expansion of all branches of national economy, including agriculture, on the basis of the most modern techniques. There is only one way of solving this problem, namely the expansion of heavy industries in all their aspects. . . . The industrialization of a country begins with the heavy industries and its heart, the machine-tool industry, but never with light industries.[22]

Industrialization therefore means that the building of heavy industries is a top priority:

Great Lenin taught (and the practice of socialist construction in the USSR has fully confirmed this proposition) that heavy industries were the true and only basis for the establishment of a socialist society. . . . The preferential growth of output of the means of production in relation to the production of consumer goods is the law of increasing production, as it is scientifically proved by Marxism-Leninism.[23]

It is obvious that Lenin had industrialization in mind when he said: "Communism is Soviet power plus electrification."[24] The modern version of his thesis would be: Communism is the power of the Party plus industrialization. W. Gomulka, who accepted the slower pace of industrialization for his country, did not change the goal: "the future of Poland consists in socialism, in the unceasing industrialization of the country, in the mechanization of agriculture, in the rural self-governing and collective forms of agriculture."[25] The Director of the Economic Institute of China writes in the same vein:

We stand on the ground of giving top priority to the development of heavy industries. . . . In this connection the decisions of the 8th All-Chinese Congress of the Communist Party of China concerning the Five Year Plan of development of national economy (1958–1962) formulated the task of twice increasing the gross industrial production . . . in comparison with the plan for 1957, and the agricultural production by 35 per cent. The gross production in 1962 should consist approximately of equal halves of output of means of production and of that of consumer goods.[26]

Since Communist countries do not want to rely on long-term loans and foreign investments but wish to achieve industrialization by their own means, the net result is very costly to their people. A large part of their national incomes must be reserved for capital investment, mainly in heavy industries, at the expense of the consumer, the average citizen. Such a rapid pace of industrialization cannot be maintained through consultations with the average man; it can be met only if he is completely regimented by a totalitarian regime.

7. Proletarian Internationalism

Another generally accepted principle of Communism is the so-called proletarian solidarity of the Communist parties, all of them supporting each other in maintaining or seizing power. The Yugoslav Communists do not subscribe to this tenet of faith, which implies the denial of freedom in foreign policies, and the Polish Party also has reservations concerning its interpretation. The Soviet view that a true Communist Party must stand by the unity of the common front of all Communist parties, whether they hold power or represent an opposition group, is reflected in this sentence: "The Communist parties are unanimous in believing that it is necessary to achieve a maximum unity and solidarity among all the Communist and Workers' parties."[27] Such unity has but one major objective in foreign politics, namely "the struggle against imperialist aggression"[28] or, in other words, against the Western Powers.

These, then, are the basic tenets of the Marxist-Leninist creed as currently interpreted by Lenin's disciples. The rejection of any of the tenets would be heresy, but there is latitude for interpretations. Lenin himself said:

We do not look at all at Marx's theory as something completed and intangible; we are convinced, on the contrary, that it has laid down only the cornerstones of that science which socialists must develop further in all directions if they do not want to remain estranged from life.[29]

The practical question is: Who has the right to give an authentic interpretation—Moscow, Peking, or each Communist Party? Tito has claimed such a right since 1948. There is no doubt that Moscow would prefer to hold the monopoly on interpretation, as it did in Stalin's time.

This residual creed does not offer anything tempting to industrialized countries. Its real attraction lies in industrialization and is limited to the underdeveloped countries, if they are prepared to pay the price, in the form of a totalitarian regime, and to accept the other parts of the Communist doctrine.

8. Mystical Faith in Victory

Communism is a pseudo-religious movement led by hard, practical politicians. It has its own mysticism. Its devotees have a deep, though not necessarily rational, faith in the final triumph of their creed, and they have no doubt that it will eliminate other creeds and other social regimes. Lenin is the first example of the fusion, in one mind, of uncanny political perception and a mystical and unshakable faith in the final victory of Communism. But we would probably greatly underestimate both Stalin and his present successors if we considered their faith a choice political morsel for the consumption of rank-and-file devotees. It is risky to assume that generals of opposing armies have no faith in their own cause and in their own victory.

The 8th Congress of the Russian Communist Party, led by Lenin, proclaimed, in 1919, in one of its resolutions: "Whatever might be the difficulties of the Revolution and its possible temporary failures or waves of counter-revolution, the final victory of the proletariat is unavoidable."[30] This was courageously affirmed at a time when few outsiders believed that the shaky Soviet regime would survive for more than a few months in the face of civil war and foreign intervention. Molotov, speaking with authority as Soviet Foreign Minister, said on November 6, 1947:

The Great October Socialist Revolution opened the eyes of nations to the fact that the age of capitalism is coming to its end and that hopeful roads to general peace and great progress of peoples have been discovered. Frantic efforts by imperialists, under whose feet the ground is trembling, will not save capitalism from its approaching doom. We live in a century when all roads lead to Communism.[31]

D. T. Shepilov, not yet accused of being a double-dealer, said, on February 13, 1957, in his capacity as Foreign Minister: "A young social regime, full of vigor and creative forces, comes to relay the old which is decrepit and stricken with incurable ailments."[32] Although he was transferred a few days later to a position as one of the secretaries of the Central Committee, his views were upheld by Khrushchev on February 18 of the same year:

The foreign policy of the Soviet Government is clear and understandable. Our former Minister of Foreign Affairs, comrade Shepilov, talked about this policy at the recently closed session of the Supreme Soviet of the USSR. The new Minister of Foreign Affairs of the Soviet Union, comrade Gromyko, will pursue the same policy which was followed by the former Minister. Our foreign policy is that of the Soviet Government. This is completely comprehensible and does not require particular qualifications.[33]

This was understandable. The foreign policy of any country in its right senses does not change with the appointment of a new foreign minister when the general situation remains the same. The long line of Soviet foreign ministers, from Chicherin to Gromyko, carried not a personal foreign policy but that of the Party leadership. Only wishful thinkers would believe otherwise.

The faithful bard of successive rulers of the Soviet Union, Il'ia Ehrenburg, affirms a similar faith in Communism:

It is time that the Western intelligentsia gave up the over-simplified idea of Soviet society which for decades has been depicted abroad as either hell or paradise. We live on earth. We have many difficulties. But we are happy that we were the first to enter the new path, the path which will be that of all mankind.[34]

Another author says confidently: "the toilers of the Soviet Union firmly know that the future belongs to Communism, that time is working against capitalism, and that the final victory of the new social regime is inevitable."[35]

Time is working for them, the Communists believe. *Kommunist* enumerated in its New Year's, 1957 issue four factors to support this belief: the faster rate of industrial development in the USSR (compared to the West), the industrialization of China and eastern Europe, the activities of Communist parties, and

the national-liberating movement in all its forms and manifestations, which leads to a complete liquidation of the shameful system of colonial enslavement of peoples, has confronted the old world with many preoccupations and invincible difficulties. . . . Lenin's prophecy has been fulfilled—the immense East has awakened. . . . We talk about countries which have approximately a population of 600 million people. The importance of these gigantic reserves is very great for the outcome of world competition. The bosses of the imperialist camp are more alarmed by the growing rapprochement between the two main torrents of the contemporary era, socialism and the national-liberating struggle, than by anything else.[36]

One may take those four factors seriously or shrug one's shoulders, depending on one's judgment, but *Kommunist* was certainly earnest in giving this answer to its own rhetorical question: "For whom does time work?"[37] This mystical faith in ultimate victory, whether supported by rational arguments (more numerous today than in 1919) or not, imbues the Communists with fighting spirit and endurance. It is an asset:

The conviction as to the inevitability of the triumph of Communism inculcates in the fighters for Communism a feeling of optimism which is not and cannot be possessed by the doomed classes. . . . There are no illusions or utopian plans concerning the future in this revolutionary optimism. It is the optimism of fighters who, believing in the inevitable victory of Communism, strive to hasten this victory and hence devote themselves to the struggle with a total revolutionary passion, subjecting to pitiless criticism everything that represents an obstacle to victory. The Communist Party has always striven to strengthen in the working class and the toiling masses this faith in victory, however serious might be the conditions of struggle and whatever the difficulties encountered along the road. The Communist Party has always seen in this faith the most important condition of victory.[38]

The inculcation of this faith in Communist followers is psychologically intelligent because an army that doubts final victory is of no use to its generals. The same burning faith did not prevent Lenin from being a practical politician who calculated all the risks. Shepilov was probably right in claiming the same aptitude for Lenin's successors: "We, the Soviet people, are no Utopians but realistic politicians."[39] His own personal misfortune proves, however, that a practical politician inspired by faith in victory may sometimes make disastrous miscalculations.

CHAPTER IV

COMMUNIST MORALITY, STRATEGY, AND TACTICS

1. Morality

IF TWO basic motivations, the driving urge to convert the world to Communism and the national interests of Russia as the bastion of world revolution, dwell in the minds of the Soviet leaders and inspire their foreign policies, the ultimate goals of the USSR are correspondingly ambitious, for they cannot be reconciled with the existing *status quo*. Revolutionary change in the present social-economic world set-up is itself an almost unlimited goal because the whole earth is its stage. The traditional aspirations of Tsarist Russia have not only affected the neighboring nations in Europe, the Near East, and the Pacific but have been of great concern to the other great Powers. For example, the desire to control the Turkish Straits not only clashed with the right of Turkey to her independence and territorial integrity but also affected the interests of the great Powers which had vital stakes in the Mediterranean area. This was as true in Tsarist times as it was in 1945–46 when Stalin raised the same claim for Soviet control of the Straits. A nationalist Russia, aspiring, in addition, to promote everywhere a basic change in the regime and endowed with the might of a first-class great Power, remains a potential source of international trouble.

The Soviet Union's goals are ambitious. To approach them even step by step, as Stalin did at the appropriate time, requires not only patience but also great flexibility in tactics. M. A. Suslov said at the 20th Party Congress: "The foreign policy of the Soviet State, worked out by our Party, has been carried out with strict adherence to principles and, at the same time, with maximum elasticity."[1] Principles were for him the basic objectives. Tactical flexibility meant the ability to adjust the current policy to the existing circumstances, to what was possible at a given time: "The Communist Party is guided in the realm of foreign policy by the necessity

69

of reckoning most seriously with actual conditions and the perspective of historical development."[2] "Actual conditions" include the relative power of the USSR as compared to that of other powers and other factors extant in international politics; "the perspective of historical development" means being patient while never losing sight of ultimate objectives.

This flexibility, illustrated so vividly by the conclusion (on August 23, 1939) of a neutrality pact with Nazi Germany, is related to Communist moral concepts. One cannot understand Soviet foreign policy or policies pursued by other Communist parties without knowledge of Leninist morality. It is the key which may be disregarded only at his own peril by a non-Communist politician who has to face both the USSR in foreign relations and his domestic Communists at home. He should remember what the late Soviet Foreign Minister A. Ya. Vyshinsky said in 1948: "When interests speak, morality keeps silent."[3] Sentiment must not be allowed to interfere, as was made clear in 1933 by another late Foreign Minister of the Soviet Union, M. Litvinov: "We Marxists are the last who may be reproached with allowing sentiments to prevail in our policy."[4] These men heeded their master, Lenin, who advised his disciples in 1922: "We cannot, in any case, be stopped by sentiments . . . to rely on conviction, devotion and other lofty spiritual qualities, is not a serious attitude in politics at all."[5]

The whole concept of Communist morality differs radically from traditional Western moral ideas. Every traditional morality evaluates the means independently of the aim. The Ten Commandments do not permit murder, theft, adultery, and other reprehensible acts in certain circumstances and in regard to certain people. They do not say: "Kill your enemy but do not murder your friend." Traditional morality does not sanctify the means in the name of any aim.

Of course, neither individuals nor governments have been guiltless of many transgressions against this moral code, which imposes the same standards of behavior on all men. Yet the requirements of this absolute morality, which never justifies the use of foul means, do constitute a restraint to our actions. We may bypass this barrier, but we then have a feeling of guilt. Our conscience, schooled in these precepts, feels uneasy. The very existence of such morality represents a monitor, even in dealing with foreign nations. The 1956 Egyptian crisis brought this consideration to the fore. England was split at the time of the invasion of Egypt, not because Englishmen held different views on the vitality of the Suez Canal for the British economy or because some were pro-Israeli and others pro-Arab, but because a large section of the British public felt a revulsion against military action undertaken in violation of a solemn pledge contained in the United Nations Charter. When President Eisenhower refused, in his speech of November 1, 1956, to apply two measures, one to nations hostile to the United States and another to her friends, Britain and France, he was motivated by traditional morality more than anything else. But when the Communists of the whole world excused the Soviet military intervention in Hungary in the name of the revolution, they evaluated this action from the point of view of its goal; a different morality inspired their judgment.

It is interesting to note that only two parties openly challenged the very foundation of traditional morality: the Nazis and the Communists. Both denied the eternal nature of morality and both placed the ultimate goal of human actions above the morality of the employed means. Both considered that moral precepts had been the temporary fruit of each historical period, the content of morality changing with the change of historical circumstances. For the Nazis, the greatness of the German race was the ultimate criterion of what was moral or immoral. For the Communists, the cause of the revolution is the criterion for judging actions as moral or immoral, depending on their relation to the ultimate goal.

Communists insouciantly indulge in a contradiction. On the one hand they are determinists, deeply convinced that history must unfold itself, according to Marx's analysis, towards its final stage—world revolution and the universal triumph of Communism. On the other hand they are convinced voluntarists, firmly believing that their own actions will hasten the course of history, whose ultimate direction cannot, however, be modified by any human act. The birth of world revolution is certain, and they cast themselves in the role of midwives.

Human behavior, in accordance with an accepted morality or in violation of it, the appraisal by man of his own acts, assume the existence of a relative autonomy in deciding the question how to act in definite situations. If there were no such relative freedom of choice in behavior, there could be no question of any morality. This choice does not exclude at all . . . the dependence of human acts on the definite social-historical conditions, on the class membership, etc. But if human acts were fatally determined by external conditions, and if the possibility of control over human behavior by the society or by man himself were ruled out, there could be no question of a moral appraisal of human acts.[6]

The existence of an eternal morality is rejected:

Having proved the dependence of human moral outlook on the material conditions of life and the class structure of society, Marxism has rejected all attempts at building up an absolute system of morality which would be independent of the social conditions and would be applicable in all times and by all nations. . . . In contradistinction to bourgeois ethics, Marxism does not accept any dogmatic system of morality which would fit all times and all nations, and does not conceal the class origin of its ethics and does not substitute moral views for class struggle.[7]

Moralities, different from each other, succeed themselves throughout the development of the economic history of mankind:

Moral views, like the philosophical, political, artistic and religious, have the nature of a superstructure. The economic regime of a given society is the source of the moral views of men. . . . Morality, being a part of the superstructure of the economic basis of society, changes with the [corresponding] alterations in the basis from which it derived. New moral principles and new rules of behavior are related to the new economic base of society.[8]

Lenin formulated the basic criterion of Communist relativist morality:

We say: morality is what serves to disrupt the old exploiting society and to rally together all the toilers around the proletariat, which is building up a new society of the Communists. . . . At the root of the Communist morality lies the struggle for the strengthening and achievement of Communism.[9]

His contemporary disciple, Shishkin, says the same:

Marxism-Leninism sees the highest criterion of the Communist morality in the struggle for Communism. . . . The struggle for Communism is the only true and scientific criterion of Communist morality because it correctly reflects the historical development of contemporary society.[10]

Another author writes:

History has entrusted to the proletariat the greatest mission of liquidating class society, of destroying the exploitation of man by man and its causes, and of creating a new, classless, communist, social regime. From the proletarian point of view, only such human behavior is, therefore, moral which serves the great cause of the struggle for the liberation of mankind from exploitation.[11]

A third author says it with the same emphasis:

"At the root of the Communist morality," V. I. Lenin teaches, "lies the struggle for strengthening and achieving Communism." This is why from the viewpoint of Communist morality, that is moral which promotes the destruction of the old, exploiting society, and the construction of the new, Communist society. Everything that hinders this [development] is immoral or amoral. . . . To be a moral man, in our understanding, means to devote all his forces and energy to the cause of the struggle for a new Communist society.[12]

We may now better understand why the use of force by Britain and France was termed immoral, while the use of force by the USSR in Hungary, although parallel and simultaneous, was moral. The criterion was the same: Britain and France were capitalist nations and hence their actions were immoral, while the USSR acted as the guardian of the Communist system and her action was therefore moral. This kind of morality may be very helpful in a relentless pursuit of one's goals in foreign policy, but it makes impossible the finding of a common language in politics with people of different moral and political convictions except for contingent political expediency. It is rather difficult to disagree with the Soviet writer when he says: "Morality and politics cannot but remain in close relation to each other."[13]

The Communist concept of justice also becomes a relative value:

Having tied up ethics with the class struggle of the proletariat, Marxism has rejected all appeals to "an eternal justice" so characteristic of the old moral doctrines. . . . "For us," wrote V. I. Lenin, "justice is subordinated to our interest in overthrowing capitalism."[14]

The same author illustrates this flexible morality from the example of patriotism, which also is not an absolute notion:

It [the Marxist morality] does not proclaim every moral rule as being equally fit for all situations. The same moral requirement to love one's country has a totally different content for the conscious workers and toilers in the condition of a bourgeois society and in the condition of a socialist country. . . . For instance, the conscious workers and toilers in a contemporary capitalist society, although they love their country, their language and their democratic culture, cannot consider it their moral duty to respect the interests of the bourgeois state which is subject to and serves the monopolies. On the contrary, in the Soviet regime where power belongs to the people, the strictest respect for the state interests is the unconditional duty of a Soviet citizen and a patriot devoted to his Fatherland. Equally, the application of the same rule cannot but reckon with the various actual situations in which man is called upon to act in a given society. The Communist morality condemns lies and dishonesty in human relations, but this does not entail that a Communist should, for the sake of an abstract "hon-

esty," deliver to his class enemies his organization, his comrades in the same
struggle, etc. . . . A correct solution of one or other practical question of
human behavior, and the appraisal of this behavior may be only *concrete*.
In all actual cases the criterion of Communist morality provides the guiding thread for the solution of practical questions of behavior and protects
our moral judgments and appraisals against dogmatism.[15]

Hence the moral duties of a Communist in any country must be centered
in the cause of Communism and the interests of its base: "The duty of the
fighter for Communism in every country consists in his obligations towards
his own country, his people, the Marxist Party, and the general tasks of the
camp of peace, democracy and socialism headed by the USSR."[16]

Another example of such elasticity of moral judgment is the discussion
of violence:

Violence of the first kind [the bourgeois] serves a reactionary goal and
contradicts the most elementary moral standards; violence of the second
type [Communist] serves the noble goal of freeing society from slavery. The
latter violence promotes the historically rife necessity of replacing the old
society by the new. This is why it meets the requirements of the highest
morality.[17]

While traditional morality does not condone the hatred of other men,

the hatred against the enemies of the Soviet people, the socialist Fatherland and human progress, is an integral part of socialist humanitarianism.
. . . He who shows indifference and a false sense of security regarding the
manoeuvers of the enemy, who does not know how to hate him, does not
love his own people and does not know what is the true love of his own
Fatherland.[18]

A textbook for use in teachers colleges says the same: "Communist morality
is, above all, the devotion to the cause of Communism, the hatred against
the enemies of the people, and the readiness to give up one's life for the
freedom and independence of our great socialist Motherland."[19] In case
of doubt about the morality of an action, there is an adviser and a judge:
"Lenin used to say that the Bolshevist Party was the mind, the honor and
the conscience of our era."[20] The morality of an act is appraised not by
the intentions but by the results, beneficial, of course, to the Communist
cause: "The Marxist-Leninist ethic demands that we judge the moral character of a man, not on the strength of his words, not even his motivations,
but according to his acts and the results of these acts."[21] It is therefore

obvious that such a morality provides Communists with the utmost malleability in their strategic and tactical concepts.

2. Strategy

It is common knowledge that General von Clausewitz's *On War* had a great influence on Lenin's thinking. This was due, among other things, to the fact that both the Prussian General and the Russian Communist saw political life as a perpetual struggle. "War is the continuation of politics by other means" could only imply that peace was a period of struggle waged by non-military means. Lenin, as a Marxist, not only agreed with this view but enlarged it to apply to the whole social life. History was at any time a never ending class warfare which would continue until the great and final victory of the proletariat. The termination of the struggle would usher in the era of peace, the construction of a new society.

Before 1917, the world was, for Lenin, the stage of this perpetual class war, waged by the proletariat against capitalists through domestic battles within each nation. International politics belonged to a different plane of internal struggle among the capitalist monopolies, a sort of civil war within the same capitalist class. The Revolution of 1917, however, changed the picture. The proletariat continued to wage its war on capitalism through its political organizations, but its state, Soviet Russia, had to fight its own parallel battles with the capitalist monopolies, which used their imperialist states as weapons. The unity of the class war was not lost, but the conflict was henceforth fought on the two fronts: that of the Communist parties in each capitalist state and that of Soviet diplomatic relations. Were the USSR to accept the concept of a permanent suspension of hostilities with the capitalist states, it would betray the Marxist-Leninist call for social struggle until the final defeat of capitalism. This is the reason why the Soviet sources prefer the term "peaceful competition" to "peaceful co-existence" and often qualify "peaceful co-existence" by adding the word "lengthy." It is not unfair to Lenin to interpret his Marxist concept of class warfare by reversing Clausewitz's statement: Peace among states with different social regimes is the continuation of class war by other means.

It is not surprising that Lenin adopted military terminology for the description of class warfare, waged either by the Communist parties on each domestic battlefield or by the Communist states on the global interstate battlefield; both he and his followers have always talked about the strategy and tactics of that never ending war. We must remember this concept of the unity of class warfare, whether on the part of a Communist party at home or one controlling the USSR or another Communist state, because otherwise we should miss a vital point in Communist thinking. Whatever Lenin and his later commentators have had to say about Communist strategy and tactics is applicable *mutatis mutandis* to the domestic policies of the various Communist parties and to the international relations of the USSR.

We shall discuss the Communist ideas of strategy and tactics, taking as our guides Lenin, the great acknowledged master of present and past Soviet leaders, and N. V. Tropkin, one of the contemporary Soviet authorities. The latter writer stresses the importance of the Leninist concepts of strategy and tactics and clearly indicates the global unity of the war waged by various Communist "armies," one of them being the Soviet Communist Party itself:

The strategy and tactics of Leninism are one of the most important component parts of the great Marxist-Leninist teaching regarding the transformation of the world according to the new Communist principles. . . . Integrating the experience of the whole world Communist and workers' movement and, first of all, the immense and victorious experience of the Communist Party of the Soviet Union, the strategy and tactics of Leninism determine the direction and the methods of struggle, promote the integration of the various torrents of the liberating movement into one stream, and trace out the roads leading to the overthrow of the dominion of landlords and capitalists, the establishment of the dictatorship of the working class, and the destruction of all forms of exploitation and oppression. The strategy and tactics of Leninism point out to the Communist and Workers' parties the ways and methods of forming the political armies for the liberating struggle, and the direction of the revolutionary activities of these armies. . . . Each truly Marxist party, heading the revolutionary struggle of the proletariat and of all the toiling masses, founds its activities on the strategy and tactics of Leninism. A thorough knowledge of the strategy and tactics of Leninism helps the fraternal Communist and Workers' parties in expertly directing the class struggles and in achieving the strategic objectives at the price of lesser sacrifices and within a shorter historical period.[22]

The class war must be fought to its bitter end: "The Marxist thesis concerning the unavoidable destruction of capitalism . . . represents the indestructible foundation of the strategy and tactics of Leninism."[23]

Stalin supplied a clear definition of the Communist strategy in his *Foundations of Leninism*, which the most recent Soviet sources declare to be a correct interpretation of Leninism:

Strategy consists in the determination of the direction of the main assault of the proletariat within the period of a given stage of the revolution, the working out of a corresponding plan for the unification of the revolutionary forces (the main and the subsidiary reserves), the struggle for the realization of that plan during the whole period of a given stage of the revolution.[24]

Depending on the conditions facing it, a Communist party follows one of three strategic plans: "The experience of the C.P.S.U. and of the whole contemporary liberating movement proves that three strategic stages and three strategic plans of the liberating struggle of the toilers are possible during the imperialist era."[25] The first strategic plan is of concern to such parties as have not yet won power. Its aim is to prepare a "democratic" revolution, whose immediate objectives are to carry out only those reforms that are most attractive to the population of a given country (for instance, land reforms in an underdeveloped country) and to give power to the Communist Party. The true objective of that stage is to prepare the ground for socialist revolution, entailing the socialization of all means of production, which is possible after the Party has consolidated its power:

The first strategic plan is calculated on the victory of the democratic revolution, directed in the imperialist era not only against the feudal and national oppression but also against the establishment of the bourgeois democracy. Hence the principal question of the revolution, that of power, is solved by the democratic revolution not in favor of the bourgeoisie but in favor of the people led by the proletariat. . . . The management of the revolutionary dictatorship by the working class secures a speedy transformation of the people's democratic revolution into a socialist one. . . . Leninism teaches that the bourgeois-democratic revolution is not a goal in itself but only a gigantic step towards the socialist revolution. Leninism places before the revolutionary proletariat the task of doing all that is possible to prevent the revolution remaining in the democratic stage and to transform it into a socialist one.[26]

One may better understand the meaning of these passages if one substitutes the Communist party for the working class and the revolutionary proletariat and if one bears in mind the past experience of the Chinese and eastern European revolutions. The Party prepares the revolution by advancing a temporary and minimum program of immediate reforms which may appeal to large strata of the population, the peasantry in particular, and thus gains allies. After seizing power, the Party carries out these reforms and consolidates its power; then the time comes for its maximum program: the complete socialization of the means of production and the establishment of a totalitarian regime. The Party discards talk about being "agrarian reformers," just as the Chinese did, and the second strategic plan is ushered in:

The second strategic plan is calculated on the victory of the socialist revolution. This plan is determined by the requirements of the maximum program of the Communist party involving the revolutionary transformation of a socialist nature: the overthrow of the bourgeoisie and the establishment of the dictatorship of the proletariat.[27]

At this stage the bourgeois allies, the various democratic and peasant parties, are either eliminated or reduced to impotence; the Communist Party assumes absolute power, as it did in 1948 in Czechoslovakia.

The third strategic plan calls for a nationalized economy, centrally planned and administered, rapid industrialization, and the full control, by the Party, of all social life. This is the stage in which the USSR, China, and eastern Europe have been since the consolidation of Communist power.

The most important mission of the Communist Party, after the October Revolution [in the third strategic stage], has consisted in completing, within the shortest historical period, the liberating struggle in the country by the full liquidation of exploiting classes, by quickly expanding productive forces, and, supported by economic successes, by doing its maximum, within the power of one country, in helping to achieve victory of democracy and socialism in all countries.[28]

Not only the Soviet Union but also China, with her multi-million population, and the European people's democracies find themselves in the third strategic stage, which begins with the seizure of power by the proletariat. ... The strategic goal of the Communist and Workers' parties in all countries of the socialist camp is the same: to consolidate the people's authority in their countries, to develop the victorious socialist and communist construction, to strengthen by all means the socialist camp as a bulwark of struggle by the proletariat and the toiling masses in the capitalist, colonial and dependent countries.[29]

The second and third stages are of little direct interest to countries where the Communists have not seized power. From the point of view of their foreign relations with the USSR and their domestic relations with their own Communist parties, the first strategic plan is of vital interest to them. Non-communist countries are enemy bastions, to be stormed at the propitious time by the joint efforts of their own Communists and the Soviet bloc. Hence they have a stake in understanding Communist tactics applicable to both foreign and domestic relations, for one must not forget that the Soviet sources never separate the former from the latter relations, the "proletarian" war being a single war. Because it is only one war, waged on the two fronts of diplomacy and domestic subversion, "the fraternal Communist and Workers' parties boldly rely on the assistance and support of the powerful socialist camp headed by the Soviet Union in their struggle for peace, democracy and the bright future of their own nations."[30]

3. Tactics

One cannot but agree with this evaluation of Lenin: "Lenin developed Marxism in more than one direction, but broadly speaking, it is true to say that his most important contribution was in the field of Party organization and tactics."[31] He provided his followers in all countries with a political tool of utmost practical importance to them. His teaching of political tactics makes him, as a thinker, an equal of Machiavelli and Clausewitz. Stalin gave the following definition of Leninist tactics:

Tactics is the determination of the line of action of the proletariat within a relatively short period of time of the flow or ebb of the movement, the rise or the decline in the revolution, the struggle for the carrying out of that line through the replacement of the old forms of struggle and organization by the new, of old slogans by new ones, through the combination of these forms [of struggle], etc. If the strategy has for its purpose to win the war, let us say against Tsarism or the bourgeoisie, tactics pursue less substantial aims, because they try to win, not the whole war, but only individual battles and engagements, to conduct successfully individual campaigns, individual actions, in accordance with the concrete circumstances of a given period of the rise or decline of the revolution. Tactics are a part of strategy and are subordinated to it.[32]

The guiding idea is the utmost flexibility of tactics, whether applied to the diplomatic battles waged by the USSR or those fought by various Communist parties on the domestic front:

As the political and economic circumstances of the class struggle are subject to quick changes, it is unavoidable to proceed frequently with alterations of forms and methods of the revolutionary movement. During each strategic stage of revolutionary struggle tactics may be altered many times. The liberating movement cannot develop in the form of one unceasingly growing gigantic wave; it develops through tides and ebbs, offensives and defensives. The tactics of the revolutionary proletariat must reckon with these changes. Their most important task is to determine the ways and means, the forms and methods of struggle which best fit into a given situation and most certainly prepare the strategic success. . . . The Leninist tactics demand from the Communists that they master all forms of struggle, and be ready for a most rapid and unexpected passage from one form to another.[33]

To be elastic, tactics must be adjusted not only to changes in time but also to particular circumstances in each country:

The struggle for democracy and national independence cannot proceed uniformly in all countries. The tactics change depending on the economic development in a given country, the composition of its class forces, the political maturity of the working class and of other toilers, the nature of the political authority, the international situation, and so forth. . . . This is why one of the most important tactical principles of Leninism is that of an obligatory reckoning with what is nationally particular and specific in each country.[34]

The tactics of a Communist party in eastern Europe, protected by the military might of the USSR, cannot be the same as those of a party working in a capitalist country immune to direct Soviet interference. The tactics in a highly industrialized country must be very different from those in an underdeveloped country. The tactics in the USSR's foreign policy could not have been the same before the seizure of power by the Nazis as it was after Hitler proclaimed his anti-Bolshevik crusade. The period of armed conflict among the capitalist great Powers (1939–1945) called for tactics that were entirely different from those of the postwar period, when the Communists could exploit a different type of conflict among capitalist states, namely those which were industrialized and those which were underdeveloped.

Leninist morality is extremely useful in devising tactics. If the goal of the universal revolution justifies all the means, the flexibility of tactics becomes almost infinite. Lenin said this openly: "If you cannot adjust yourself, if you cannot bring yourself to crawl on your belly in the mud, you are not a revolutionary, but a chatterbox."[35] He meant by mud such means as are condemned by traditional morality but not by the Communist variety. He reaffirmed this concept of tactics when explaining what the policy of Communists should be within the labor unions:

One must know how . . . to accept any and every sacrifice, even—in case of necessity—to resort to every kind of trick, cunning, illegal expedient, concealment, suppression of truth, in order to penetrate into the trade-unions, to remain in them, to conduct in them, at whatever cost, communist work.[36]

This teaching opens the way to a skillful manipulation of words, a technique to be considered later.

Tactics depend on a judicious choice of the main battlefield in each strategic stage: "Political events are always very confused and complex. They may be compared to a chain; in order to hold the whole chain, one must grasp the main link."[37] But a chain is only as strong as its weakest link, which thus becomes the main link. It is not surprising, therefore, that the post-Stalinist leadership of the USSR has selected the weakest links in the capitalist chain for their special attention: the underdeveloped countries. Western countries, with their democratic traditions and high standards of living, are the strong links and cannot be broken loose.

Although Communist tactics are always oriented towards final victory, the offensive cannot be pursued at all times. Lenin frequently advised his disciples to be cautious, to avoid open battles where the enemy was much stronger, never to underestimate him, not to indulge in wishful thinking, not to expect miracles, to make concessions to the enemy in order to cover up a retreat or to sow confusion in his ranks, and, above all, to be patient. Marxist training familiarizes Communists with historical perspective, and this gives them a notion of time that is different from the one held by many other politicians, who see only the present moment or, at best, the following day. Communists are able to wait for opportunity while consolidating their forces. Stalin did this in a masterly way by remaining on the defensive during the period of industrialization and by contriving the offensive at the very appropriate moment when war broke out among the other great Powers. The present Soviet leadership is pursuing the same strategy, patiently biding their time, which they measure, as Stalin did, in decades, not in months.

Having selected the weak link in the capitalist chain and having concentrated their attention on the underdeveloped countries, the Soviet Communists have adjusted their tactics in foreign politics accordingly. The problem presented by the underdeveloped countries is twofold: they must be split off from the Western nations, and they must be gradually prepared for an all-out revolution. Tropkin follows in the footsteps of Lenin when he writes that a revolution may take place in a non-industrialized country:

As Lenin teaches, the Marxist thesis concerning the existence of conditions for a socialist revolution only in the countries of a developed capitalism has lost its validity in the era of imperialism. Leninism has concluded that the proletariat wins in the first place in such countries which are the weak links in the chain of imperialism. Such weak links are not necessarily countries with the highest level of industrial development; for these countries may prove, by virtue of the law of unequal development of capitalism, less prepared politically for the socialist revolution. The first victory of socialism, as the Leninist theory teaches, is possible only in a country with no less than an average level of capitalist development, but the following victorious socialist revolutionary transformations are possible, with the support of the country of the victorious socialist revolution, even in the backward countries. . . . The Leninist theory of the socialist revolution has opened wide vistas for the struggle for democracy and socialism in the colonial and dependent countries.[38]

Neither the agricultural nature of the economy nor the absence of a large industrial proletariat is considered an obstacle; not even a relatively small Party membership should be a hindrance. Everything depends on favorable circumstances and the political acumen of the Party:

. . . capitalism will not die of itself. . . . The problem of the Party and its role in carrying out a proletarian revolution occupies the most important place in the Leninist theory of socialist revolution. . . . Lenin stressed the role of the Party as a decisive factor in the process of revolutionary transformation of society. . . . V. I. Lenin pointed out that the proletariat of any country should not miss a favorable opportunity and should seize power regardless of its proportionate numerical size within the total population.[39]

The numerical weakness of the Party should be compensated by grouping together all the temporary allies whom the Party is able to secure:

Having introduced into the theory of socialist revolution the most important thesis of an alliance between the proletariat and the half-proletarian elements in cities and villages, V. I. Lenin proved thereby that it was not necessary for the victory of socialist revolution that the proletariat represent the majority of the population in a given country. . . . The proletariat can counterbalance the inadequate numbers of its own class by its ability to concentrate forces at the decisive moment and the decisive place, by finding allies at each stage of the revolution, and by dividing the enemy forces and destroying them one after another and at different times.[40]

Obviously, the underdeveloped countries are in the first strategic stage, which precedes the Communist seizure of power. In that stage, the Communist Party publicizes only its minimum program, which should be palatable to the non-Communist strata of the population:

The fraternal Communist and Workers' parties in the colonial and semicolonial countries place the first strategic plan at the foundation of their activities. One may understand the strategic direction of the liberating struggle in those countries by examining, for instance, the draft program of the Communist Party of Brazil published in the press. This program represents in substance a minimum program. Drafted with due consideration for the particularities of that country and for the remarkable experience of the victorious, anti-imperialist and anti-feudalist Chinese revolution, it constitutes a very important document of the contemporary communist movement. . . . It does not include the direct tasks of the struggle for socialism; it directs the working class of Brazil towards an agrarian, anti-feudal and anti-imperialist revolution. . . . The existence of significant feudal survivals in these [underdeveloped] countries is combined with the foreign imperialist oppression. The people's democratic revolution is not only anti-feudal but also an anti-imperialist and national-liberating revolution. This circumstance widens the social base of the revolution in the colonial and dependent countries. The proletariat may rely on attracting to the liberating struggle not only the peasants, the petty bourgeoisie and intelligentsia, but also the national bourgeoisie interested in liberating the market and national economy from foreign competitors, and in the destruction of feudal survivals. However, the policy of making use of the revolutionary potential of national bourgeoisie does not eliminate the problem of the struggle of the working class against the national bourgeoisie for the hegemony in the liberating movement.[41]

It follows that the Communist parties in underdeveloped countries should advance a minimum program of change that is acceptable to large sections of the population while keeping silent about the maximum program, which would be frightening to the Party's temporary allies. Such moderate reforms must be combined with an anti-Western stand, an aspect of great importance to the foreign policy of the USSR.

Soviet authors cite the minimum program of the Communist Party of Brazil as a pattern to be followed by other Communist parties, this for the self-evident reason of the skill with which it was drafted. It appeals to every section of the population and successfully camouflages the Brazilian Communists as patriotic and moderate reformers. The Brazilian Party pays due attention to peasants because they, as the Brazilian Communist leader Louis Carlos Prestes writes,

represent the majority of the population; they live oppressed by the big landowners and the majority do not own land. . . . This is why the Party program devotes a great deal of attention to agrarian reform and the peasant question. . . . The Party program . . . asks for the confiscation of land belonging to large landowners and the transfer of this land without any payment to the landless and poor peasants as well as to such other people who want to cultivate it. . . . At the present time it is of importance for the victory of the Brazilian revolution that the peasants should realize, during their own struggle, the need for a revolutionary annihilation of the present regime of big landowners and capitalists. This is why the Party program does not include the nationalization of land and takes into consideration the clearly expressed will of the peasant masses who want in our country, first of all, land to be transferred to their private ownership.[42]

It would, of course, be a tactical error to tell the Brazilian peasants about the future collectivization of agriculture. But Prestes also has something to offer the national bourgeoisie of his country:

The program guarantees freedom of initiative for the industrialists and merchants and the defense of the interests of national industries. It foresees the confiscation of assets and enterprises of only big capitalists who have betrayed national interests and have concluded an alliance with the North-American imperialists.[43]

However, even the minimum program does not beat around the bush about the most vital question, that of power; the "democratic" revolution must transfer power to the Communist Party, which would otherwise be unable to carry out its maximum program: "It [the Brazilian government formed after the revolution] will be a government of a coalition of all anti-feudal and anti-imperialist forces led by the working class and its vanguard, the Communist Party of Brazil."[44]

The Communist Party of Brazil, like other Communist parties in under-developed countries, twists patriotic feelings into a hatred of the United States:

Patriotism of the people is a great force. . . . The slogan of struggle against the yoke of North-American imperialism has become the watchword of vast strata of the Brazilian people. . . . The Party program is directed mainly against North-American imperialism, asking for the confiscation of all assets and enterprises which belong to the North-American monopolies in Brazil, the cancellation of the foreign debts of Brazil whether owed to the government or banks in the U.S.A., and the expulsion from Brazil of all military, cultural, economic and technical missions of the U.S.A.[45]

The program counterbalances this claim for cutting all ties to the United States by insisting on closer relations with the Soviet bloc. Soviet commentators also want to promote a close co-operation between the Latin American countries and the Asian-African nations in order to spread the practice of non-commitment.[46] The slogan of industrialization is part of the minimum program, and it specifies that equipment should be exported by the Soviet bloc in exchange for Latin American livestock, coffee, sugar, cotton, and other agricultural products and such raw materials as copper, rubber, etc.[47] The same minimum program is applicable, with necessary adjustments, to other Latin American countries and, in general, to the economically underdeveloped nations.[48]

According to Communist tactics such a moderate but anti-Western program should be the platform of a national front for the joining together of the Communist Party and all other parties which are ready, for their own reasons, for such a union: "The experience of the contemporary liberating movement proves that the key to the solution of all problems of a democratic, anti-feudal and anti-imperialist revolution is the foundation of one democratic and national front."[49] A parallel concept in the Soviet official policy is the establishment of a common front with the underdeveloped countries, a front directed against the West and founded on an agreement concerning immediate objectives only.

These fronts may be achieved by advancing such slogans as are palatable to non-Communist partners: "It is necessary to issue political slogans and directives which have a familiar ring for and may be understood by the masses."[50] Says Tropkin:

The struggle for the general democratic goals and national independence secures in the best way, in contemporary conditions, to the working class the [acquisition] of the largest reserves and the attraction of all sorts of temporary fellow-travelers to the liberating struggle. The slogans of struggle for democracy and national independence give to the Communist parties an opportunity of intensifying and exploiting to a maximum degree, in the interest of the proletariat, all the contradictions and waverings within the camp of the enemies of socialism, of bringing about misunderstandings and splits within the ranks of the adversaries of the proletariat, and of preventing the unification of the forces of reaction. A clear evidence of this is the growth of contradictions among the enemies of the working class . . . and the increasingly frequent statements made by various bourgeois politicians against the aggressive plans of warmongers.[51]

This is why the USSR and the various Communist parties manipulate so skillfully the slogans of peace, prohibition of nuclear weapons, liberation from Western influence, anti-colonialism, and so forth. Tropkin presents examples of slogans adjusted to particular national audiences:

. . . the Communist Party of the USA appeals to the American people to rally under the slogans of a struggle for peace, for the reduction of the military budget, and for the defense of democratic freedoms. The slogan of the defense of national sovereignty is particularly popular among the

English people because the existence of foreign military bases and forces in England wounds the English high sense of national pride and dignity. This is why the English Communists advance, with a special force, the slogan of the defense of national independence of England and of the autonomy of English foreign policy.[52]

Of course, the eastern European Communists are not encouraged to advance the slogans of national independence, but Communist slogans have only a relative value equal to their usefulness for a particular purpose.

4. Manipulation of Words

It does not take great intellectual effort to discover that each Communist slogan serves a purpose alien to its direct meaning. Peace, for example, means support for the current objectives of Soviet foreign policy; democracy means either the Communist regime or a struggle against the existing order of things, if even democratic in the current sense; national independence means anti-Americanism, and so forth. Words are twisted to give an entirely new meaning; the late Soviet educator A. S. Makarenko provided an example of this procedure when he said: "Discipline is freedom."[53] V. M. Molotov gave another example in a speech delivered to the Supreme Soviet on August 1, 1940, following the invasion of eastern Poland by Soviet troops, after the war with Finland, after an ultimatum had been delivered to Rumania, and after Soviet troops had occupied the Baltic States prior to their annexation. In reference to all of these actions, carried out by the military might of the USSR at the expense of neighboring small countries, Molotov said: "The successes of the foreign policy of the Soviet Union are the more significant in that we have achieved them all by peaceful means."[54] After the reversal of Soviet foreign propaganda and the replacement of anti-Nazi slogans with anti-imperialist slogans directed against Britain and France (a change that followed the conclusion of the neutrality pact with Nazi Germany on August 23, 1939), Molotov advised his listeners to substitute a new meaning for aggression and aggressors:

Some of the old formulas, which we quite recently used and which became a habit for many, have obviously become obsolete and cannot be employed any longer because of those important modifications in the international situation. . . . It is known, for instance, that such notions as "aggression" and "aggressor" have acquired in the last few months a new concrete content and a new meaning. It is not difficult to guess that we cannot now use these notions in the same sense, as, say, three or four months ago.[55]

It is possible that the great Russian scientist I. P. Pavlov had some influence on the Soviet use of words. Pavlov wrote:

The word is for men just as true a conditioned stimulus as all other stimuli which are common for men and animals, but, at the same time, it is such an all-embracing stimulus as no other is, and cannot be in this respect, either quantitatively or qualitatively, equated with the conditioned stimuli of the animals. The word is tied up, thanks to the whole previous life of a grown-up man, with all his internal and external stimuli, which take place in the great lobes [of the brain], transmits all of them, replaces all of them, and hence may cause all the actions and reactions of the organism which are conditioned by these stimuli.[56]

He did not, of course, advocate a perverted use of words to obtain desirable human conditioned reflexes, but he observed: "We know, however, that there is a great multitude of men who want, only by manipulating words without relation to reality, to deduce everything from them and cognize everything through them; they want to order their own and social lives on this basis."[57] A Soviet commentator adds: "On this form [the word], however, has been fixed the reflection of those particular objects or phenomena which it symbolizes."[58]

Communist politicians seem to have comprehended the meaning of Pavlov's teaching that the word is a very powerful stimulus. Perhaps they remembered Pavlov's experiment with dogs, who were trained to associate the sound of a bell with food and whose saliva flowed at that sound although no food was in sight. Could not the word be manipulated in the same way? Could one produce desired human conditioned reflexes by the mere sound of words while having previously detached from them their former meaning? Soviet and Communist propaganda generally seems to follow this procedure, whether under the influence of Pavlov's theory or not. A word is associated with an attractive or repulsive flavor for the conveying of an idea. The original idea is detached, but a favorable or hostile reaction follows the sound of the word. The Communist vocabulary has not been purged of words which have no true meaning for Communists. They desire, for instance, to establish or maintain the rule of one party, yet they talk about democracy; certainly no pacificists, they talk of peace; they control foreign nations yet inveigh against colonialism; they have one-slate elections while speaking of free and democratic elections. The USSR is the only great Power that emerged after the last war with an immensely larger territory and a vast zone of influence, and yet it exploits anti-imperialism. The sad part of it is that Pavlov was right about multitudes of people wanting to guide their own social lives by mere words; the successes of verbal Communist propaganda abundantly prove this point. The hooked bait of words is irresistible, and Soviet deeds are forgotten for the sake of happy-go-lucky wishful thinking. The depreciation of the word may lead to the debasement of the idea it represents. Lenin said: "The most certain way of discrediting a new political (and not only political) idea and to harm it, consists in reducing it to the absurd in the name of defending it."[59]

5. Specific Tactical Devices

Verbal manipulations are but one of many methods used by the Communists to promote their political ideas. Lenin recommended the use of all sorts of tricks:

To wage a war for the overthrow of international bourgeoisie, a war a hundred times more difficult, longer, more complex than the most difficult of the ordinary wars among states, and to renounce manoeuvering, making use of the contradictions of interests, even temporary, among the enemies, and accepting compromises and agreements with possible allies (even if temporary, unsteady, precarious and conditional), is it not infinitely ridiculous? Is it not similar to renouncing to advance in zigzags, to fall back, to abandon the direction selected before, and to try all sorts of directions, while making a difficult ascent of an inaccessible and unexplored mountain?[60]

He never tired of stressing the policy of exploiting any contradictions among enemies:

One may vanquish a more powerful adversary only with the utmost straining of all the forces, and with the indispensable, most careful, thoughtful, cautious, and skillful use of every, even the least, "crack" among the enemies, of every contradiction of interests among the bourgeoisies of various countries, and among the various groups and types of bourgeoisie within particular countries, and of every, even the least, opportunity of acquiring a mass ally, even a temporary, precarious, unsteady, unreliable and conditional one.[61]

Of temporary domestic or international allies, Lenin proposed that they be supported as "the rope supports the hanged man."[62] "It is necessary," he wrote, "to combine the strictest devotion to the ideas of Communism with the ability of making all the necessary compromises, manoeuvers, agreements, zigzags, retreats and similar moves."[63] Suslov expressed the same idea when he said, at the 20th Party Congress, that the Soviet foreign policy was faithful to principles but elastic to the utmost. It is still of interest to the Communist parties in capitalist states that Lenin instructed them to combine "the illegal forms of struggle with *all* the legal forms."[64] Of course, some Communist parties are outlawed and must use only illegal means; others exist legally but cannot be sure that this legal status will not be revoked and must be trained to use illegal means as well. For those people who are tempted to dismiss Lenin's teachings as outmoded for modern Communists, here is a contemporary idea:

Lenin taught that in order to conquer the masses the Communist Party must be active in labor unions, master all methods of struggle, non-parliamentary and parliamentary, illegal and legal, learn from the example of the Bolsheviks how to manoeuver with dexterity and how to make use, in the interest of the proletariat, of the least contradictions among the enemies.[65]

Another author affords this lesson to foreign Communist parties:

Only such a structure, an illegal, underground, and highly centralized party, as Lenin proposed, was capable of securing a high ideological level of leadership under conditions of conspiracy, to safeguard and strengthen the party, to deflect from the leading personnel the blows of counter-revolution, and to promote, from among the workers, new leaders for the revolutionary struggle of the proletariat. This structure, first successfully achieved by our party, lies at the roots of the organization of Communist parties in the capitalist countries. The structure and experience of the Communist Party of the Soviet Union have a tremendous significance for those Communist and Workers' parties which have not yet come to power.[66]

N. V. Tropkin has called for the adjustment of policies pursued by various Communist parties to international circumstances; he means, of course, the foreign policy of the USSR and the Soviet capacity to be helpful to foreign parties: ". . . the tactics of the Communist parties should be devised with strict attention paid to the relation of class forces not only within a given country but also on the international stage."[67] Tropkin thus interprets the Communist role in national fronts:

This is why the Communist Party must have recourse to agreements and compromises with various groups of the workers and petty bourgeoisie, all sorts of petty-bourgeois and sometimes bourgeois parties, without retreating however one step from its ideological revolutionary principles. These tactics help in depriving the adversary of wide public support, in rallying around the proletarian vanguard the toiling masses of the population, and in accumulating strength for the revolutionary assault on capitalism.[68]

The Chinese concept of the national front is given as an example to be imitated:

The Chinese Communist Party demonstrated good patterns of tactical flexibility when it attracted, during the revolution, the national bourgeoisie to the struggle against the forces of feudal-imperialist reaction and successfully followed the line of making use of the pro-American fraction of the comprador bourgeoisie during the anti-Japanese war. Having temporarily abandoned in 1937 the slogan of the confiscation of land of the landlords, it pulled also a fraction of landlords into the struggle against the Japanese interventionists. The tactical flexibility of the Chinese Communist Party allowed the proletariat to create a mighty people's democratic front without which the victory of the Chinese revolution would not have been possible.[69]

The Chinese Communists, who reduced to impotence their former allies, the non-Communist parties, collectivized agriculture after masquerading as "agrarian reformers" in order to gain peasant support, and expropriated both the comprador and the national bourgeoisie, have the right to apply to themselves this description of the Bolshevik treatment of "fellow-travelers": "The Bolshevik Party always safeguarded, while concluding compromises, its own freedom of unmasking its temporary fellow-travelers. . . . This is why it was gaining strength at the expense of those parties with which it had concluded compromises."[70] The same idea inspires the Communist parties in the national fronts and other combinations with non-Communist parties:

The tactical principles of Leninism, in particular the principle of admissibility of compromises concluded in the interest of the working class, determine the contemporary struggle of foreign Communist parties for the rally of all forces of democracy within one powerful people's front of struggle against imperialism and war.[71]

One of the most important tactics in promoting Communism is to infiltrate labor unions and other large organizations and undermine there the influence of "opportunists and reformists" (socialists):

One of the most important tactical forms of struggle is the work of Communists in the labor unions and other mass organizations of the toilers. . . . If the labor unions are led by the reformists (reformists are the agents of the bourgeoisie in the workers' movement) . . . one should not conclude from this at all that Communists should refuse to work in such reformist labor unions. On the contrary, Communists must work with particular energy in such labor unions in order to emancipate the masses from the reformist influence and to win them over to the side of the revolutionary proletariat. . . . V. I. Lenin pointed out that the struggle against the opportunists should necessarily result . . . in the complete putting to shame and expelling all the incorrigible opportunist leaders from the labor unions. . . . Thus the Communist Party of Spain considers the Communist activities in the Franquist labor unions as one of its most important tasks, because the refusal to work in the fascist labor unions would weaken the ties between the Communists and the working class and would deprive the Communist Party of one of the means of inciting the proletariat to the struggle against the Spanish fascism.[72]

This method is of interest to all countries, developed or underdeveloped, and in particular to Africa, where, according to most recent Soviet sources, the Communist influence is penetrating mainly through the labor unions.

Tactics for infiltrating non-Communist organizations are as old as Lenin:

Groups or cells of Communists must be organized without exception in all organizations, unions, associations; first of all the proletarian, and then the non-proletarian of the toiling and exploited masses (political, professional, military, co-operative, educational, sport, and others).[73]

The parliamentary tribune should not be neglected:

The Communists favor the use by the revolutionary proletariat of the parliamentary forms of struggle as well . . . the Communists may successfully exploit the elections to parliaments and the tribune of the bourgeois parliament in order to unmask the exploiting classes and their agents and politically to educate and enlighten the large popular masses.[74]

The parliamentary struggle, however, should not be taken for a form of conquering power by votes (except, as the 20th Congress decreed, where the non-Communist opposition cannot resist the Communist seizure of power, for instance, because of the assistance provided by a neighboring Communist state):

It is characteristic only of the bourgeois agents in the workers' movement [socialists] to consider the parliamentary form of struggle as the principal form and to delude the people with the possibility of conquering power by the proletariat through an electoral competition.[75]

As usual, everyone is invited to join the national fronts:

The most dangerous form of sectarianism [among the Communists] in the contemporary situation is the under-estimation of the task of widening the mass base of movements of peace partisans, of movements for the struggle for democratic freedoms and national sovereignty, of the work in the labor unions and other mass organizations of the toilers, and the equation of rank-and-file members of the Catholic and socialist parties with the reactionary leaders of these parties.[76]

When the Communists "fight" for democratic freedoms in countries which uphold such freedoms, they follow the tactics which Montalembert accused the French Catholics of using: "When I am the weaker, I ask you for liberty because it is your principle; but when I am the stronger, I take it away from you because it is not my principle." R. N. Carew Hunt explains it in the following words:

At the 3rd Comintern Congress of 1921 it was recognized that Communism would make no rapid progress if it was to be fostered only by such organizations as were avowedly Communist, and that they must therefore be reinforced by others which would attract sympathizers and so provide a screen under cover of which the Communists could advance their policy. . . . The most effective arrangement has been to appoint as president a politically colorless but otherwise prominent non-Communist, but to have a Communist or crypto-Communist secretary in the background who exercises control. Such organizations covering every social problem and sphere of activity, proliferate today, and are of the utmost assistance to the Communists in their task of manipulating public opinion. . . . A government has only to suppress a Communist newspaper for sedition, or to arrest a leader for proved treasonable conspiracy, to arouse an outcry, in the name of the freedom of the press or of political liberty, led by persons who are not Communists at all, but whom no amount of experience will convince that the principles for which they stand would count for nothing were the Communists themselves to come into power.[77]

When the fruit is ripe, to use Stalin's and Khrushchev's metaphor, the Party may proceed with the revolution:

One of the most important tasks of the leaders of a Communist party is not to overlook, but to take hold of the moment of a ripening armed insurrection.[78]

But this moment comes only when

a general national political crisis, pervading not only the "low levels" but also "the summits," is a condition without which a socialist revolution is impossible. . . . The crisis of the "summits" manifests itself in that the class groups hostile to the proletariat have fought among themselves and have exhausted themselves by their mutual struggle, while the bourgeois State machinery of oppression and repression is being paralyzed, is no longer serviceable, and has ceased to function normally.[79]

The Chinese example of armed struggle by degrees, starting in the remote rural areas, is recommended for Communists working under similar conditions in underdeveloped countries:

Learning from the experience of the liberating struggle of the toilers of China, comrade Mao Tse Tung, the leader of the Chinese people, has worked out an important strategic thesis concerning the necessity of beginning the people's revolution in the conditions of a semi-colonial country by establishing the authority at the start in separate districts and later on by progressively expanding this authority, in the process of a lengthy struggle, to the whole country . . . the Communist Party of China correctly concluded that it was necessary to wage a lengthy revolutionary war in the Chinese villages and to transfer for a time the center of the Communist activities from the cities to the rural places. It pursued the policy of building up the bases of the revolutionary war in the rural places, to be followed by making use of these bases for the encirclement and liberating of the cities. . . . The path of the Chinese Revolution is also that for the peoples of many colonial and semi-colonial countries.[80]

The Brazilian Communist leader, Louis Carlos Prestes, applies this teaching in his own country, pointing out that the Party devotes much attention to even the distant rural districts because local successes in remote rural areas may lead "to the formation in a number of districts of democratic governments of national liberation."[81] This technique of beginning the revolutionary movement in the rural areas and later transferring it to the cities might be practical in large countries in which control through a national center is not always easy.

6. Violence and Wars

Neither Lenin nor the 20th Congress of the Soviet Communist Party has denied the necessity of using violence to assure the success of the revolution. Communists are neither pacifists nor believers in the virtues of passive resistance. Lenin laconically formulated his philosophy of history in *Two Tactics of Social-Democracy* in 1905:

The great questions of freedom and class struggle are decided, in the last account, only by force, and we must get busy gathering and organizing this force and using it actively not only for defense but also for the offensive.[82]

He rejected individual political terror only because of its inexpediency, but he heartily approved of mass terror:

Of course, we have rejected individual terror only because of its inexpediency; but Plekhanov, when still a Marxist and a revolutionary, already in 1900–1903 laughed and jeered at people who were ready to condemn, as a matter of "principle," the terror of the French Great Revolution, or generally terror applied by a victorious revolutionary party besieged by the bourgeoisie of the whole world.[83]

When Khrushchev condemned Stalin in his secret speech, he did not denounce him for using mass terror but for doing it in an indiscriminate way against innocent Communists. Believing in violent revolution as the means of salvation for mankind, Lenin was simply being logical when he said: "They ask whether the Social-Democrats can be generally opposed to violence. Of course, they cannot be."[84] He expressed the same outlook in a letter:

"Assassination is no murder," wrote our old *Iskra* in relation to attempts [on the lives of Tsarist dignitaries]; we are not against political assassinations at all . . . but individual attempts as a revolutionary tactic are inexpedient and harmful. . . . Individual terroristic acts can and should bring about benefits only if related directly to a mass movement.[85]

Kommunist published in 1957 a previously unknown speech by Lenin in which he had reaffirmed the same thought: "History has proved that it is impossible to win victory without revolutionary violence."[86] He rejected pacifism and welcomed such wars as would bring closer the final victory of the revolution:

We are no pacifists. . . . We have always declared that it would be stupid if the revolutionary proletariat promised not to wage revolutionary wars which might become indispensable in the interest of socialism.[87]

A Soviet book upholds the same view: "To be a patriot does not mean to be a pacifist."[88]

Lenin condoned violence for two purposes: the socialist revolution, which he sometimes called the civil war, and such types of international wars as would promote the cause of the revolution.[89] If war is the continuation of politics, the choice between war and peace is not a moral question but one of political expediency. The main problem is simply whether the policy, peaceful or warlike, of a state is moral or immoral from the point of view of Leninist ethics. Hence the distinction between defensive and offensive wars does not make sense to a Leninist. Lenin, discussing the problem of offensive and defensive wars, said:

It is self-evident that the only possible point of view regarding this question [of war] as the other question of "patriotism" consists not in the defensive or aggressive character of a war but in the interest of the proletarian class struggle or, to say it better, of the international proletarian movement; this is the only possible point of view from which one can examine and solve the problem of the attitude which Social-Democrats should take regarding any event in international relations.[90]

Writing to A. M. Gorki in 1913, Lenin expressed a faint hope for a Russian-Austrian war as an opportunity for the revolution: "A war between Austria and Russia would be a very useful device for the revolution (in the whole of Eastern Europe), but I have little hope that Franz Joseph and Nicolasha would give us such a pleasure."[91] In 1939, Stalin acted according to this precept by precipitating the war among the capitalist states in the hope, which was not in vain, as events proved, of promoting a revolutionary situation.

Applying his own moral concepts, Lenin proposed a theory of wars, just and unjust, which he himself summarized in the following passage:

If the class of exploiters wages a war in order to strengthen its dominion as a class, such a war is criminal . . . if the proletariat, after having vanquished its own bourgeoisie, wages a war in the interest of strengthening and developing socialism, such a war is legitimate and "sacred."[92]

Thus every war waged by a capitalist Power was unjust, but the following wars were considered just: a civil war waged by the revolutionary proletariat (headed by the Communist Party) against its own bourgeoisie,[93] a war waged by a revolted colonial population or by an underdeveloped country against an imperialist Power,[94] or a war waged by a Communist state ("A war on our part would be legitimate and just; it would be a war for socialism, for the liberation of nations from the bourgeoisie.").[95] He thus absolved in advance every Communist state, including the USSR, from guilt in any war waged by it, whether offensive or defensive. We may better understand this classification by looking at a few examples. The Chinese Civil War was a just war because it was conducted by the Communist Party. The guerrilla wars in Indochina or Algeria were just wars because they were fought against a capitalist colonial Power. But the Hungarians, of course, fought an unjust war against Soviet troops, which represented revolution; their action could therefore not be classified as the revolt of an oppressed nationality against a colonial Power. The Soviet offensive war on little Finland in 1939–1940, waged for the sake of territorial acquisitions, was a just war because it was fought by the socialist fatherland against a bourgeois state. Every Communist would agree with these illustrations of the Leninist doctrine of wars.

Let us look at another situation. If two "imperialist" Powers fight each other, it is of no consequence to the Communists except as a possible revolutionary opportunity. Lenin said in 1916:

Bourgeoisie of all the imperialist Great Powers (England, France, Germany, Austria, Russia, Italy, Japan, the United States) has become so reactionary and so permeated with aspiration to world dominion that *every* war on the part of the *bourgeoisie of these* countries can be only reactionary. The proletariat must not only oppose any such war but should desire the defeat of "its" government in such wars and should make use of them for revolutionary insurrection.[96]

Of course, a war waged by the imperialist Powers might become "democratic and progressive" if those Powers happen to be the allies of the USSR, as was the case in 1941–1945. The bourgeois allies are redeemed by the sanctity of every war in which the USSR participates. Molotov could say, on October 31, 1939: "The imperialist nature of this war is obvious to everyone who wants to see the true situation and who does not shut his eyes to facts."[97] But Stalin restored, *ex post facto*, a progressive character to the same war:

The Second World War against the Axis Powers, in contradistinction to the First World War, assumed from the first the character of an anti-fascist and liberating war. . . . The entry of the Soviet Union into the war against the Axis Powers could only strengthen and actually did strengthen the anti-fascist and liberating character of the Second World War.[98]

Words, for the Communists, have only relative value.

If a war is just, then its cost is fairly immaterial: "History frequently knew wars which, regardless of their horrors, bestialities, miseries and sufferings, were beneficial for the evolution of mankind."[99] The attitude to be taken in a war is defined by this classification of wars:

In the wars which the proletariat itself or the proletarian State wages against imperialism, it must defend its Socialist Fatherland. In the national-liberating wars the proletariat takes part in the defense of the country against imperialism. But in the imperialist wars it should stigmatize energetically "the defense of the Fatherland" as the defense of exploitation, and as a betrayal of socialism. . . . If "the defense of the Fatherland" in the imperialist countries is impermissible, it represents a fundamental revolutionary duty in the State of the proletarian dictatorship.[100]

The USSR used military force to expand its territory, and Lenin unintentionally absolved it *a priori* by holding that a progressive war remained such despite the accompanying conquest of foreign territories. He said of the French revolutionary wars:

For instance, there was an element of French plunder and conquest of foreign territories in the revolutionary wars of France, but this does not in the least alter the fundamental, historical significance of those wars which shattered and demolished feudalism and absolutism in the whole of old Europe of serfdom.[101]

The threat of nuclear annihilation hanging over the heads of all men, both Communists and non-Communists, has introduced a new element that was unknown to Lenin. He said:

Pacifism and an abstract apostolate of peace are one of the forms of fooling the working class. Wars are inescapable under capitalism, especially during its imperialist stage. Moreover, the Social-Democrats cannot deny the positive significance of revolutionary wars, i.e., not of imperialist wars but such wars as were waged, for instance, between 1789 and 1871 for the sake of overthrowing a foreign yoke and founding national capitalist states out of feudal splinter states, or those which the victorious proletariat might wage in order to safeguard its achievements in the struggle against the bourgeoisie.[102]

The 20th Congress modified this thesis through its spokesman, Nikita Khrushchev:

There is, of course, a Marxist-Leninist precept that wars are inevitable as long as imperialism exists. . . . In that period [before the Second World War and earlier] this precept was absolutely correct. At the present time, however, the situation has changed radically. Now there is a world camp of socialism which has become a mighty force. . . . Moreover, there is a large group of other countries, with a population running into many hundreds of millions [the uncommitted nations], which are actively working to avert war. . . . As long as capitalism survives in the world, the reactionary forces representing the interests of the capitalist monopolies will continue their drive toward military gambles and aggression and may try to unleash war. But war is not fatalistically inevitable.[103]

This new thesis revises Lenin's teaching about the inevitability of wars in the imperialist period of history, but it does not exclude them as a possibility. What was probably the main reason for adopting this new thesis was stated by Khrushchev in another part of the same speech: "Indeed, there are only two ways: either peaceful co-existence or the most destructive war in history. There is no third way."[104] The May 24, 1958 issue of *Pravda* revealed his apprehension of the risks involved in a nuclear war:

A future war, if the aggressors succeed in unleashing it, threatens to become the most devastating war in the history of mankind, because there is no guarantee that it would not become an atomic war with all its catastrophic consequences. Millions of people would perish, big cities and industrial centers would be swept from the surface of the earth, and many irreplaceable cultural monuments created by mankind throughout centuries would be destroyed; vast territories would be poisoned by the radioactive fallout. ... It is extremely dangerous, for fear of crushing retaliation, to have recourse to nuclear weapons of mass destruction in our time where these weapons have ceased to be the monopoly of one Power.

It would be unwise to exclude the possibility of a nuclear surprise attack at such time when the preponderance of offensive over defensive weapons would remain significant and the large stocks of ballistic missiles and their accuracy would make such a surprise attack a "rational" proposition. The surprise attack would become "rational" in this technical sense if it were almost certain that not only would the enemy country be devastated, but his retaliatory power would also be annihilated, all at one stroke. If this becomes true one day, the meaning of nuclear stalemate would be changed, and it would then be risky to rely on the Soviet assurances regarding the horrors of nuclear war. But for the time being, one can assume the sincerity of Khrushchev's statement because, like any other politician, he must be aware of the horrible risks involved in a general war. The new thesis does not rule out the use of violence by local Communists in a domestic revolution, however, for Khrushchev upheld (in the same speech) violence as a means of bringing about the transition to socialism, his euphemism for revolution.

7. Exploiting Conflicts among Capitalist States

The technique of exploiting conflicts among enemies, dividing them, and then conquering each one separately has been practiced in international relations since the dawn of history. Lenin adopted it as one of the fundamental rules of Communist tactics. The bourgeoisie was rent by internal conflicts, he observed, and the Communists could make good use of this fact in regard to either the bourgeoisie in each country or to all capitalist states whose divergencies of interest might be turned to good account by the Soviet republic.

To understand Lenin's teaching, one should remember that capitalism in all its forms and in all countries is, for the Communists, a single enemy who must be completely destroyed. Therefore, the political form of government or the particular social system that prevails in a capitalist state, in contradistinction to another, does not make any difference to the Communists. Our distinctions between democratic, authoritarian, or fascist states, modern states or states with feudalistic survivals, states guided by the concepts of a welfare nation and favoring partial nationalization of the means of production or highly conservative states—none of these distinctions make any sense to the Communists. For them, every non-Communist state is controlled by capitalists, sometimes hiding behind the backs of "opportunists and reformists," socialists who are nothing but bourgeois agents. Thus *Pravda* did not express an unusual view in its issue of September 21, 1938: "The Soviet Union views with equanimity the question as to which imperialist robber gives orders in one or another colony, in one or another vassal State; for it sees no difference between German and English robbers."[105]

The problem in 1939 was not one of choosing between Nazi Germany and democratic Britain and France; it was a question of selecting the capitalist nation which would offer most to the USSR. This uniform basic hostility to all non-Communist states (hostility that in some instances may be temporarily suspended in order to exploit conflicts among those states, e.g., the period of cordial Nazi-Soviet collaboration in 1939–1940) provides the Soviet Government with great flexibility in dealing with particular capitalist nations because the choice of temporary partners is not hindered by any preference. Lenin illustrated this aspect of Soviet relations with capitalist states in the following example:

When the robbers of German imperialism had led their troops in February 1918 against the disarmed Russia which had demobilized her armies . . . I entered, without any hesitation, into the known "agreement" with the French monarchists. The French captain, Sadoul, who verbally expressed his compassion for the Bolsheviks but who in fact served with his whole soul French imperialism, brought to me the French officer de Lubersac. "I am a monarchist; my only goal is to defeat Germany," de Lubersac told me.

"This goes without saying (*Cela va sans dire*)," I answered. This did not hinder me at all from "agreeing" with de Lubersac concerning the services which the French officers, specialists in laying mines, wanted to offer to us in order to blow up the railroads to hinder the offensive of the Germans. . . . We shook hands with the French monarchist, realizing that one would, with pleasure, hang the other "partner." But our interests temporarily coincided. . . . We made use, in the interest of Russian and international socialist revolutions and against the attacking German robbers, of the equally rapacious counter-interests of other imperialists. . . . We resorted to the legitimate and necessary, in any war, manoeuvers, tacks, and retreats.[106]

Stalin probably looked at Hitler in 1939–1941 and at Churchill in 1941–1945 in the same way that Lenin had regarded de Lubersac in 1918. Substantially, the same feelings probably animate the present Soviet leaders when they warmly shake hands with statesmen from Asian and Near Eastern countries; they bear in mind the chance of making a limited and temporary deal against other "robbers," namely the Western Powers.

Lenin was able to stem the German offensive in 1918 by concluding the Treaty of Brest-Litovsk, thereby forcing the French and their allies to face fresh German reinforcements from the Russian front. He changed his "partners" because they were equally hateful to him. Stalin did the same in 1939; after attempts at a *rapprochement* with the West against the Nazis, he concluded an agreement with Hitler. Today, the Soviet Union is using an anti-Israel card to court the Arabs, although both the Israelis and the Arabs are only pawns in the game against the West.

In 1948, the USSR hoped to play a pro-Israel card. The USSR hastened to recognize the new state of Israel as readily as did the United States. The Soviet Government sent, three days after receipt of the proclamation of an independent state of Israel and the Israeli request for recognition, a warm telegram (which now seems unbelievable) of *de jure* recognition. Foreign Minister V. M. Molotov said in the telegram:

The Soviet Government hopes that the creation by the Jewish people of its own sovereign State will serve the cause of strengthening peace and security in Palestine and the Near East, and expresses its reliance on a favorable development of friendly relations between the USSR and the State of Israel.[107]

Soviet-Israeli diplomatic relations were established in the same month, May, 1948, despite the anti-Semitic domestic policy pursued by the Soviet Government at that time. However, the anti-Western tinge of Arab nationalism, the errors committed in the Near East by the Western Powers, and the refusal of Israel to become a pawn in the Soviet policy have altered the picture. The state of Israel is currently portrayed as a Western puppet and a source of troubles in the Near East; Soviet policy had shifted, in the interim, to favoring other "temporary partners," the Arab states.

Lenin condensed his advice on the matter in this short sentence: "From the political point of view, we must make use of the divergencies of views among our adversaries [the capitalist states]."[108] Discussing the various possibilities of conflict between the great Powers and between those Powers and smaller nations, he defined the task of Soviet foreign policy: "The practical task of the Communist policy consists in exploiting these animosities, inciting them [capitalist Powers] to fight each other."[109] He clearly saw that the best opportunity for doing it was during a war among the capitalist states:

We should have been saved [during the foreign intervention] even better, if the imperialists were mutually involved in a war. If we are compelled to tolerate such rogues as the capitalist thieves, each of whom sharpens a knife against us, it is our obvious duty to deflect these knives against each other. When two thieves fight each other, honest people benefit by it.[110]

He was not foolish in claiming: "We have so far been winning against the world bourgeoisie because it does not know how to unite."[111] The non-Communist states could not at that time (or even now) unite because they had (and still have) a different view of international politics. Their outlook, founded on the concept of various national interests but not on a common ideology, is pluralistic, while the Communist outlook is monistic, with two main adversaries facing each other across the globe: the Communists and the capitalists.

Lenin believed that his strategem, the exploitation of conflicts of interests among capitalist states, was to remain basic in Soviet policy until the final elimination of capitalism:

Fundamental . . . is the rule which we have not only theoretically learned but have practically applied and which shall remain a fundamental rule for a long time, until the final victory of socialism in the whole world; this is the rule that we must exploit the contradictions and divergencies of views between two imperialisms, between two groups of capitalist states, pushing one against the other. . . . If we have not abided by this rule, we all should have hanged a long time ago on the trees to the satisfaction of the capitalists.[112]

Stalin understood this Leninist teaching: "The sense of the existence of the People's Commissariat for Foreign Affairs consists in keeping a record of all those antagonisms [among the capitalist states], in exploiting them and in manoeuvering among them."[113] In 1922, referring to the birth of the Soviet state, he said:

What was the Soviet authority five years ago? A minuscule, hardly notice-able unit which provoked jeers among all its enemies and compassion among its many friends. It was the period of devastation when the Soviet authority relied not so much upon its own forces as on the impotence of its adversaries, when the enemies of the Soviet authority, split up into two coalitions, the Austro-German and the Anglo-French, were busy with the war between themselves.[114]

This highly practical teaching has not been forgotten. Contemporary au-thors repeat it constantly:

Marxism-Leninism teaches the Communist parties to pursue tactics which make possible the exploitation of contradictions among foreign and do-mestic enemies of the proletariat. . . . The Soviet Government has known how to exploit in its foreign policy the contradictions among the various groups of imperialists as an indirect reserve in the struggle against the forces of world reaction. . . . An outstanding example of these tactics was the Soviet-German agreement of non-aggression concluded in 1939. A wise diplomatic step of our Party.[115]

In this connection, it is interesting to note that Khrushchev, in his sharp denunciation of Stalin in the famous secret speech, never criticized Stalin for the agreement with Hitler or for subsequent territorial conquests. A recent Soviet book has this comment: "The Soviet foreign policy has made and is making use of the antagonisms within the imperialist camp."[116]

Lenin did not hesitate in 1917 to use the services of the German general staff, eager to transport him and his anti-war group of followers from Switzerland to Finland with the intention of undermining the fighting spirit of Russia; he accepted a "temporary agreement" with the German army, as he was later ready to do with French officers in the German offen-sive against the new Soviet Government. He saved that Government from an unavoidable disaster by concluding the costly Treaty of Brest-Litovsk, speculating on German-Western hostility. During the civil war and foreign intervention, Soviet Russia was saved by the inability of the Western Pow-ers to make a co-ordinated and full effort, by differing interests of the intervening Powers, and by discrepancies between these Powers and small nations (Poland, Finland, and the Baltic States). The latter were distrustful of the ultimate intentions of the White Russian generals, supported by the great Powers, and they finally made their choice in favor of the then weak Soviet Government, considered a lesser evil than a restored and nationalistic old Russia. Lenin was then able to split off the small nations, one after the other, from the anti-Soviet front by offering them recognition of their independence. Speaking on that situation, he gave two reasons for Soviet survival: the inability of the Western Powers to make a full military effort because of the demobilization of their troops and the disagreements between them and the small neighbors of Russia: "We have won because the Entente had no longer their own troops which they could throw against us; they were compelled to use the forces of small nations, but those small nations . . . did not go, in the final analysis, against us."[117]

The stabilization of the international situation in 1921 opened up new possibilities: "In the new situation that emerged in 1921 the Soviet Government had much more to benefit from these antagonisms peculiar to the imperialist stage of capitalist development."[118] Not only were the interests of the victorious great Powers far from identical, but there existed two fundamental antagonisms: the first was between the defeated nations, particularly Germany, and the victorious Powers; the second was between small nations in the Near and Middle East (as well as China) and the Western great Powers. The Soviet Government moved in with consummate skill. It was completely dissatisfied with the postwar *status quo*. Russia had lost large territories to her neighbors, mainly newly independent states, and she was inimical to the whole social-political *status quo* of the world; she desired to see a universal triumph of Communism. Nor was it very difficult for her to find a common language with Germany, bitter about the Treaty of Versailles. It is true that Germany, a capitalist republic, had nothing against the social *status quo* in the world, but she could become a "temporary" partner in the struggle against that aspect of the *status quo* equally hateful to both countries, namely the Treaty of Versailles. After preliminary contacts, the Treaty of Rapallo was concluded in 1922, to become the foundation of their mutual relations. As long as Germany pursued her diplomatic fight against the treaty, Soviet support was unreserved, although this did not prevent the Soviet Government from encouraging and hoping for a Communist revolution in the land of its political ally.

After the conclusion of the Treaty of Locarno in 1925 Germany pursued a more complex policy of *rapprochement* with the Western Powers but did not abandon her friendship with the USSR (the Berlin treaty with the USSR was concluded in 1926, barely six months after Locarno, to appease Russia and to give her a renewed pledge that the Locarno policy would not mean a cancellation of Rapallo). This pleased the Soviet Government less, especially since its efforts to counterbalance the two-pronged German policy with its own *rapprochement* with the Western Powers did not yield any appreciable results. Even after Locarno the two Powers had common interests: the secret co-operation between the two armies, which helped Germany in evading the military restrictions imposed by the Versailles treaty and assisted Russia in developing her war industries; a mutual dissatisfaction with the territorial *status quo* in eastern Europe; economic co-operation, which was important to the USSR, especially during the period of initial industrialization; and the ability to use each other diplomatically in dealing with the Western Powers, a game in which Germany was more successful.

In the early twenties, Soviet Russia skillfully made use of the antagonisms between Turkey, Persia, Afghanistan, and Kuomintang China on the one hand and the Western Powers, notably Great Britain, on the other by giving support to lesser capitalist states against the great Powers. The normalizing of relations between Turkey, Persia, and Afghanistan and Britain and the conflict between the Kuomintang and Chinese Communists in the late twenties cut the ground from under the feet of Soviet diplomacy, while the general stabilization of the international situation in the later twenties provided fewer opportunities for following Lenin's advice. However, the capitalist states never intended or were able to unite against the USSR, who could pursue in peace her main task of building an industrial potential.

Stalin told the 14th Party Congress in 1925 that the USSR had to seek "a *rapprochement* with the countries defeated in the World War, countries which have been most hurt and robbed and which, consequently, are in opposition to the dominating concert of the Great Powers."[119] Addressing, in 1934, the 17th Party Congress in circumstances radically changed by Hitler's rise to power, he stressed that a *rapprochement* with any capitalist state was always motivated only by Soviet interests and that the political regime of that state did not make any difference:

Of course, we are far from being enthusiastic about the fascist regime in Germany. But the crux of the matter does not lie in fascism if only because fascism, for instance, in Italy, has not hindered the USSR in establishing the best relations with that country. . . . We were not oriented toward Germany, as we are now not oriented toward Poland and France. We were oriented in the past and are oriented now toward the USSR and only the USSR. And if the interests of the USSR demand a rapprochement with these or other states which are not concerned with disturbing peace, we shall do it without hesitating.[120]

The rise of Hitler was fraught with danger for the USSR, but it seemed to offer a new opportunity of exploiting the conflicts among capitalist states. The USSR propagated the concept of an indivisible peace and of a coalition of "peace-loving" nations, especially the Western great Powers and the USSR, against Nazi Germany and possibly Japan. These diplomatic efforts failed because of the Western policy of appeasing both Germany and Japan. Only the year 1939 afforded the great opportunity which would have gladdened Lenin's heart. Hitler needed Soviet neutrality before starting war on the Western Powers. The pact was sealed on August 23; it precipitated the conflict which began seven days later.

At last the imperialists were fighting each other. The neutral USSR could, then, by agreement with Hitler, fortify the bastion of the revolution by expanding its territory. Happy about Soviet neutrality amidst the contending capitalist Powers and knowing the contents of the secret protocol signed with Germany on August 23, 1939, concerning the future division of spoils in eastern Europe, Molotov repeated, on August 31, 1939, the thought expressed by Stalin in 1934:

Is it really difficult for these gentlemen [certain leaders of the socialist parties of Britain and France] to understand the purpose of the Soviet-German non-aggression pact, on the strength of which the USSR is not obliged to involve itself in war either on the side of Britain against Germany or on the side of Germany against Britain? Is it really difficult to comprehend that the USSR is pursuing, and will continue to pursue, its own independent policy, based on the interests of the peoples of the USSR, and only those interests?[121]

The lightning German victories in the West cast a shadow on Soviet-German co-operation. The former opportunity of doing good business, thanks to the imperialist conflict, was gone. It reappeared in 1941–1945, when the USSR was, by the Nazi attack, forced into the Western camp. Speculating on Western hostility to Germany and Japan and on the lack of a complete co-ordination between Great Britain and the United States concerning the policy toward their Soviet ally, the USSR could consolidate her gains of 1939–1940 and acquire additional territory in Europe and the Far East. To be sure, her gains of 1944–45 were due mainly to her own military exertions and the defeat of both Germany and Japan, but she could now extract from her Western allies the diplomatic recognition of most of these territorial gains as a result of the conflict between the capitalist states.

The period of the Grand Alliance provided a tragic example of Soviet ability to exploit dissension among non-Communists. This is the story of the Soviet attitude to the Warsaw uprising, in 1944, against the occupying Nazis.[122] Warsaw, occupied by the Germans, was not only the cultural capital of Poland but also the center of the Polish underground movement against the Nazis. The program of this movement was anti-Nazi and included the restoration of a Poland independent of both Germany and the USSR, with the promise of radical reforms for the postwar period (political democracy, a complete land reform with the distribution of larger estates among the peasants, the nationalization of key industries, and a welfare state).

By the end of July, 1944, advancing Soviet troops were posted close to Warsaw, separated from the main part of the city by the Vistula River. It was natural to expect that the Soviet high command would welcome an uprising in the city, since that would make the crossing of the river much easier. On July 29, Radio Moscow broadcast a call to arms on behalf of the Soviet-sponsored Union of Polish Patriots, which was manipulated by Polish Communists: "Fight the Germans! . . . For Warsaw, which did not yield but fought on, the hour of action has already arrived!" On the following day, Radio Kosciuszko relayed another Moscow appeal: "People of Warsaw, to arms! Attack the Germans!" Since the Soviet troops, under the command of Marshal K. Rokossovsky (who was later to become commander-in-chief of the Polish Army), were only a few miles away, the leaders of the Polish resistance movement ordered an uprising on August 1. It ended sixty-three days later in the smoldering ruins of Warsaw.

The Polish non-Communists fought the Nazis, and the heart of Polish political and cultural life of the time was all but destroyed in the battle. From the Soviet point of view, the "capitalists" (the Nazis and the people of Warsaw, including the industrial workers) were weakening each other in the struggle. The Nazis were assuming the odium for wiping out political forces which could have offered a counterbalance to the Polish Communists, who were ready to follow in the footsteps of the Soviet armies and take power. No wonder the Soviet high command did not move!

Granting the benefit of doubt, one may concede that its strategic plans possibly did not allow for a frontal assault on Warsaw at the time of the uprising; however, this leaves unsolved the problem of the Soviet radio stations' appeals to arms. The Soviet armies could easily have helped in other ways, something which they did not do. Soviet fighters could have intercepted German bombers attacking the Polish insurgents' positions, and Soviet bombers could have bombed German airfields around Warsaw and German gun positions in and around the city. Certainly the Soviets could have dropped supplies to the fighting people of Warsaw. The Soviet air force, which had been bombing military targets in Warsaw before the uprising, remained inactive.

Appeals by Great Britain and the United States to allow British and American supply planes to land on near-by Soviet-held airfields after dropping supplies to the Warsaw people were stubbornly refused by the Soviet Government, although the same procedure was accepted in other cases (e.g., Allied bombing of the Rumanian oil fields, the cities of Königsberg and Gdynia, and other German-held objectives closer to Soviet bases than to Western airfields). As a result, American and British planes had to fly 1,300 miles to and from Italian airfields on missions that were extremely costly, hardly effective, and finally abandoned. Only in the final stage of the uprising, beginning on September 14, did Soviet planes drop supplies, without parachutes, and most of those supplies were damaged in landing. Moreover, this help came at such a late hour, after the forces of Warsaw resistance had been exhausted by the previous seven weeks' fighting, that it could not in any case avert ultimate defeat.

On October 1, Warsaw fell. The city was a shambles. Out of its original population of 1,200,000, more than 240,000 had perished in the fighting, while 630,000 had been deported by the Nazis. The Polish Communist periodical *Nowe Drogi* correctly remarked in August, 1957:

The fate of the uprising depended on whether the Soviet Army undertook on time an offensive that would free Warsaw from the German claws. This is an unquestionable truth which no one probably would dispute.

The Soviet objective was attained—the road was cleared by the Nazis for a Soviet-sponsored government to take over coveted power in Poland.

The postwar period provided the Soviets with the opportunity to advance their cause for only a short time, mainly the period when the Western Powers were still guided in their policies by wartime animosity toward former enemies and before their trust of Soviet intentions had evaporated. The aggressive policies of Stalin cemented the Western bloc, but between 1946 and 1953, he accomplished nothing in the way of gains for the USSR.

After his death, Stalin's successors corrected what they considered his major error, that of relying only on Communists in Asian countries and dismissing newly independent states as vassals of the West. A new opportunity was seized—to exploit the conflicts of interests between the two major groups of non-Communist states, the industrialized and the underdeveloped. The friction between those two groups is considered "a real chance of isolating the imperialist Powers on the world stage."[123] The success of the Soviet policy in exploiting this friction would also bring about the isolation of the underdeveloped countries in the face of the powerful Soviet bloc, but this consequence is, of course, never mentioned in Soviet pronouncements.

When Soviet commentators on international affairs talk about isolating the West by cutting it off from the underdeveloped countries, they mean many things. It is not only the embittering of political relations between industrialized and underdeveloped countries, not only the question of depriving the West of its military allies and bases on foreign territory, but also the economic isolation that they wish to promote. The Western position would be dangerously weakened if the flow of raw materials and oil from underdeveloped areas encountered political obstacles. If the Soviet Union were successful, for instance, in its Near Eastern policy of pitting the Arabs against the West, the use of the Suez Canal would again be endangered and the supply of oil, so vital to Great Britain and western Europe, would either be stopped or greatly hindered. It would hurt the Arab countries to be deprived of national income derived from oil or its transportation through the Suez Canal and the pipelines, but the Soviet gain would be immense. In this, as in other cases, the long-term interests of Western and underdeveloped countries coincide, but then the Soviet Union speculates on short-term conflicts. Its policy could be counterbalanced only by the wisdom of both parties, the West and the underdeveloped countries, in finding compromise solutions for their short-term divergencies of views and in founding their policies on the long-term coincidence of national interests.

This is the lodestar idea of the current Soviet policy, which, however, also looks with hope toward possible antagonisms among the Western states as well. Leaving aside for later treatment the Soviet policy towards the underdeveloped countries, one has difficulty in making a choice from among many current Soviet articles devoted to alleged, true, or potential divergencies of interests among the industrialized states, including Japan. D. T. Shepilov, acting as foreign minister, devoted a large part of an exposé to this problem of detecting rivalries between the United States and Great Britain and France and between Germany and Japan and the other Western Powers.[124] One finds the same thought expressed in the following article:

The sharpest antagonisms among the imperialist Great Powers continue to grow. The antagonism between the USA and England remains as before the principal one. The American monopolies storm the crucial strategic and economic positions of the British Empire. They try to install themselves across the imperial communications, to smash the system of preferential tariffs, and to demolish the sterling zone. This is why a section of the British bourgeoisie promotes the thesis that England should acknowledge the necessity of strengthening the relations with the countries of the socialist camp. . . . The imperialist antagonisms become more acute also because of the resurgence of the Western-German and Japanese competitions on the foreign markets. The reappearance of the German competition is much more dangerous for the other capitalist countries because it proceeds on the basis of a quick growth of Western-German industries and the increase of their share in the total industrial production in the capitalist world. . . . The situation on the capitalist market becomes more difficult. Reckoning with this, some influential circles in Western Germany promote an expansion of trade relations with the countries of the socialist camp.[125]

The author sums up present-day Soviet opportunities in the following words:

An objective factor of peaceful co-existence is the imperialist antagonisms: the antagonisms between the metropolitan countries and the colonies, those between the various bourgeois groups, and those between the imperialist states themselves. Lenin wrote in his *The Slogan of the United States of Europe* and in his other works that all sorts of agreements, blocs and alliances among the imperialist states might have only a temporary character and that the sharpest contradictions among them were unavoidable in the conditions of capitalism.[126]

The interests of the several Western Powers are by no means identical, but these Powers have so far been able to maintain a basic unity. The opportunity seems to be slimmer than Soviet writers hope for. Indeed, the situation is very different from that following World War I. The two defeated nations, Germany and Japan, are, it is true, dissatisfied with the *status quo*, but their dissatisfaction is, for the most part, directed against the USSR because the latter expanded her territories and her zone of influence at their expense.

The Western Powers do not stand in the way of German unification, although they may not all be equally enthusiastic about it, but the Soviet Union bars it quite effectively with military occupation of East Germany. All of the territorial grievances of Germany could be satisfied, but only at the expense of the Soviet bloc. Japan would welcome the return of the Ryukyu and Bonin Islands by the United States, just as she would welcome the return of the Kurile Islands and South Sakhalin by the USSR.

The Soviet-Chinese alliance is expressly directed against Japan; Japanese fishermen encounter constant difficulties in waters close to Soviet territory. And there is little reason to expect that the interwar pattern of German-Soviet co-operation will ever be reproduced again in relation to either Germany or Japan. The USSR has too much to lose by making preliminary political and territorial concessions to either state.

The Western Powers have had their periods of disagreement, but the need of maintaining unity in the face of the might of the Soviet Union has always prevailed. It is possible that the Soviet Government, in this respect, hopes for nothing, taking its wishful thinking for stern facts. This has happened before in the Soviet history. For instance, Lenin predicted in 1920: "A war between England, which has amassed colonies by robbery, and France, which feels frustrated, is inevitable."[127] After having mentioned the "fundamental antagonism" between England and the United States, Stalin forecast in 1928: "With what is this fundamental antagonism pregnant? It probably is pregnant with war."[128]

8. Diplomacy

The USSR has recourse to open diplomacy (speech-making at the United Nations and other public conferences) but uses the method of secret diplomacy when it intends to proceed with serious business. The unlucky experience of Britain and France in 1939 proves that negotiations with the Soviet Union, if accompanied by Soviet indiscretions and public comments, do not augur well for their success. Conversely, the utmost secrecy of the simultaneous German-Soviet conversations betokened the serious intention of the Soviets of coming to terms with Germany. There is merely coincidence in the fact that Lenin and Wilson condemned, at the same time, the very idea of secret diplomacy. Wilson was inspired by idealism when he denounced secret diplomacy as the source of international evils.

Lenin believed for a while that secret diplomacy was a bourgeois method that was useless for a proletarian state, which would do better by appealing to the masses (over the heads of government), thereby breaking down governmental resistance in diplomatic negotiations by means of pressure from the aroused masses. In any event, he hoped that in the period after the Revolution secret and other types of diplomacy would be swiftly abolished by a universal upheaval that would usher in a world socialist republic. The famous Decree on Peace stated: "The [Soviet] Government abolishes on its part secret diplomacy, expressing its firm intention to conduct all negotiations absolutely openly before the entire people."[129]

This was soon forgotten as an impractical proposition. Democratic governments are reluctant to conclude secret agreements because the existence of such agreements makes popular control of governmental transactions too difficult. The Soviet Government has no qualms of conscience in such matters, as was proved by the secret agreements concluded with Nazi Germany in 1939, but it does not like to acknowledge their existence, even belatedly. V. M. Molotov, speaking on August 31, 1939, barely one week after his signing, with von Ribbentrop, of the secret protocol concerning the sharing of spoils in eastern Europe, summarily dismissed Western suspicions by saying: "Finally, there are wiseacres who read into the pact [the public treaty concluded with Germany] more than is written in it."[130] This cavalier statement might fit the home-made image of Soviet politicians: "We, the Soviet people, are not Utopians but realistic politicians."[131] It also reflects Stalin's view of bourgeois diplomats, which the Soviet diplomats might have taken too much to heart:

. . . words should be at variance with deeds; what would a diplomat be if he acted otherwise? Words are one thing; deeds, an entirely different one. Good words are like a mask to cover up nasty actions. A sincere diplomat would be like dry water or wooden iron.[132]

A Soviet professor of international law has evidently tried to imitate a bourgeois diplomat of Stalin's pattern by saying emphatically: "The Soviet Union has rejected [the concept] of secret treaties."[133] He has then proceeded to acknowledge the existence of the Yalta Far Eastern Secret Agreement of 1945 by making a subtle distinction between such agreements and secret treaties:

One must make a distinction between secret treaties and such treaties which are not to be published for a definite time, for instance, because their contents must remain concealed from the states with hostile intentions. Examples of such treaties are provided by the agreements concluded during the Patriotic War by the USSR and its allies against the Axis Powers concerning the time and place of the opening of the second front, the military supplies, the action to be taken by the USSR against Japan, etc., etc.[134]

There is no word in this statement about the secret agreements concluded with Nazi Germany; moreover, every secret treaty is secret only for the reason he mentions, namely to conceal it from unfriendly states.

An experienced former Soviet diplomat, V. P. Potemkin, writing as the editor of a textbook on history of diplomacy, quotes, perhaps not without reason, a dictum attributed to the 17th-century Swedish Chancellor, Axel Oxenstierna, that a diplomat should always have ready for his service "two obedient slaves: simulation and dissimulation; to simulate what does not exist, and to dissimulate what does exist in fact."[135] One chapter in the book is devoted to the "bourgeois" methods of diplomacy and is intended for young Soviet diplomats, presumably as a model:

Those who are preparing themselves to serve the Fatherland in the diplomantic walk of life are bound, of course, to learn in detail this business [of bourgeois diplomacy]. They must remember that Engels' advice applies not only to military business but also to the diplomatic struggle—it is necessary to know as well as possible the methods and subterfuges of the class enemy at the time not only of meeting him on a battlefield but also in diplomatic controversies.[136]

This reduction of diplomacy to the business of methods and subterfuges, combined with the general morality of Communists, might be useful to Soviet diplomats, but Potemkin forgot the main thing, namely that a diplomat is truly useful to his country, not once or twice, but throughout his career, only if trusted by his foreign counterparts. Such confidence is hardly compatible with subterfuge. To be tough and clever is not synonymous with being a good diplomat.

It is interesting to note some of the historical figures who earned Potemkin's praise:

Precisely because Frederick [the Great] was wise and subtle, he never expressed his intimate views for all to hear. He was satisfied with quick notes "for myself" and the confidential "counsels" for his successors, not destining these literary exercises for the immodest eye of a bystander.[137]

Then he quotes from Frederick's *Political Dreams:* "When you like any country and you have the means and power, occupy it with your troops, and when you have occupied it, you will find lawyers and historians who will prove that you have incontrovertible rights to that territory."[138] The Soviet method was slightly different. Soviet troops first occupied eastern Poland and the Baltic States, and then public referenda, conducted under Soviet supervision, proved that the Soviet Union had a right to those territories. In other cases, such as the Kurile Islands, Soviet historians acted exactly as Frederick had advised by discovering historical reasons after the annexation.

"The method of camouflaging aggression by 'self-defense' is more frequently practised than that of concealing aggression under the 'lofty' reasons of allegedly entirely 'disinterested' support given to this or other highest idea of truth, freedom, mankind, etc."[139] Was not the Soviet aggression against Finland justified in 1939 by reasons of self-defense? Was not the Soviet attack on Poland on September 17, 1939, at a time when Germany was invading that country and the USSR was formally neutral, explained by the lofty reason of protecting Ukrainians and White Russians? Was not the Soviet military intervention in Hungary made in the name of defending the freedom of Hungarian toilers?

Did Potemkin think of the ardent Soviet apostolate of a crusade against Nazi Germany in the late thirties when he wrote, with unconcealed admiration for Catherine the Great, the following?

Louder than any other was ringing in Europe the indignant voice of Empress Catherine II who called upon the monarchs and all well-intentioned people to undertake a joint attack on the French revolutionary monsters in the name of everything that was sacred to men. Catherine herself, the wisest and most resourceful diplomat of her time, did not send one soldier to fight against the Frenchmen. She shouted about the necessity of a "crusade" against the revolution mostly in order surely to involve in the war her two rivals in the partition of Polish loot, the Prussian King and the Austrian Emperor. She succeeded brilliantly. At the time of the second and the third partitions of Poland (1793–1795) Austrians and Prussians had their hands tied by their war against revolutionary France. This was what the Russian Empress needed.[140]

He further praised General Kutuzov for his clever outmaneuvering (in 1812) of the Turkish Government. On the eve of the French invasion, Kutuzov was sent by Alexander I to end the war with Turkey and thus allow Russian troops to concentrate against the French armies. He persuaded his Turkish interlocutors that France really did not intend to invade Russia but that she was actually negotiating with Russia for an alliance that would terminate in a partition of Turkey. The Turks fell into the trap. They not only concluded peace but ceded Bessarabia to Russia. Potemkin ends his story with evident pleasure:

Kutuzov secured for Russia Turkish neutrality; not only did he not pay anything for it, but even obtained from the Turks themselves, for no reason, a rich territory into the bargain. Kutuzov's success in Bucarest [the place of negotiations with the Turks] may serve as a classic example of a successful use by the diplomat of the method of subtle threat.[141]

He does not forget threats as a diplomatic method:

The method of threats is . . . widespread and has often been used successfully for a long time in the history of international relations. One must distinguish between two categories in historically known cases of the use of this method: firstly, diplomats very often frightened the adversary without having in fact the slightest intention of carrying out their threats; secondly, they sometimes truly were ready to follow their words with action.[142]

Actually, Soviet diplomats applied both methods. For instance, when an ultimatum was sent to Rumania in June, 1940, its rejection would have been followed by a Soviet military action. More often, threats were meant only to frighten other states, as was the case of the Soviet notes dispatched to Britain and France in the fall of 1956 with a brusque reminder of the horrors of a nuclear war which the USSR most probably never intended to unleash. The Soviet leaders simply wished to be popular with Egypt. This was also the case when a number of notes were sent, in 1957–58, to various countries threatening dire consequences if the United States were allowed to establish atomic-weapons bases within their borders. No recipient of those notes was particularly frightened. Here was a chance to remind the USSR of the following melancholy observation made by Potemkin: ". . . there is a danger for anyone who tries to follow the policy of frightening without serious intention of carrying out his threats. It is fine if the adversary takes fright. But what to do if he disregards the threats?"[143] One can only hope that this excerpt does not apply to current Soviet policy:

The concept of disarmament has been from time immemorial one of the favorite forms of diplomatically camouflaging the true intentions and plans of those governments which become dominated by such a sudden "love of peace." This phenomenon is entirely understandable. Every proposal concerning a reduction of armaments can invariably expect to win a wide popularity and the support of public opinion.[144]

The Soviet Union has violated many non-aggression pacts; one need only mention those concluded with Finland, Poland, and the Baltic States. Writing after those events, Potemkin says:

Pacts of non-aggression, declarations of friendship, etc., become in the hands of diplomacy of the capitalist states "instruments" of the same type as the effusive statements concerning their peace-loving policy made by the imperialist governments. More than often they only serve as a kind of smoke screen behind which it is easier and safer than otherwise to get prepared for war or for a sudden forcible upheaval in the existing international situation.[145]

He says further: "One of the variants of the so-called pacifist tactic has always been the principle of 'the localization of conflicts' proclaimed allegedly in the name of humanitarianism and the limitation of bloodshed."[146] Yet when the USSR had "localized the conflict" in 1939, Foreign Minister Molotov was very proud of it:

The chief importance of the Soviet-German non-aggression pact lies in the fact that the two largest states in Europe have agreed to put an end to enmity between them, to eliminate the menace of war and to live at peace one with the other, making narrower thereby the zone of possible military conflicts in Europe. Even if military conflicts in Europe should prove unavoidable, the scope of hostilities will now be restricted.[147]

Hitler bought this localization of conflict in exactly the same manner described six years later by Potemkin, who was, in 1939, Molotov's chief assistant: "The aggressor proposes to one of his possible adversaries a share in the future loot; he thus calculates to render him harmless for the duration of a planned aggresion against another adversary."[148] The USSR learned this through experience in 1941.

Potemkin's survey of "bourgeois" diplomacy was to serve as a lesson for Soviet diplomats:

The study of documents relating to diplomatic history, as well as the observation and analysis of facts of current international life, allow one to conclude that there are several definite methods which have been and are used, either alternately or in combination, in the incessant diplomatic struggle. This struggle precedes armed conflicts, succeeds them, and does not stop, though it acquires a somewhat slower pace, even at the time of those conflicts.[149]

This gloomy picture, which overlooks the other aspect of international relations, namely co-operation among states, certainly does not encourage Soviet diplomats to be friendly or co-operative. Yet this diplomatic history was written especially for them. Moreover, a Soviet textbook of international law reminds them of the power factor:

> It must be conceded that the economic and political might of a State must be reckoned with in international intercourse because of the uneven economic and political development of various States. . . . The sovereign equality of all the members of the international community should not make one ignore the real strength and importance of Great Powers.[150]

Armed with such advice, Soviet diplomacy faces both camps—the capitalist and the socialist.

CHAPTER V

TWO OR THREE CAMPS

1. Two Camps

F OR LENIN, there were two mutually hostile camps into which the world was divided: the capitalist and the proletarian. The revolution was to wipe out the former and transform the whole world into one socialist camp. This Marxist picture was not essentially altered by the events of October, 1917; said Lenin in 1921: ". . . there are now, I regret to say, *two* worlds in the world: the old one of capitalism, which has got muddled up but will never give up, and the rising new world, which is as yet very weak but which is growing because it is invincible."[1] The only difference, a big one, consisted in the fact that the proletarians had conquered a state for themselves and henceforth could face the bourgeoisie on two fronts: the domestic struggle, waged internally by the Communist parties, and the diplomatic struggle, fought by Soviet Russia as an advanced detachment of the proletarian army. However ("state," in the Leninist interpretation, predicating the tool of power), the emergence of a Communist state was a phenomenon of first importance. While formerly the notion of two camps was concerned only with the horizontal division of each nation into the exploiters and the exploited, after the 1917 revolution, the interstate pattern of relationships was, for the first time in history, cut across by the exploiter-exploited dividing line. A single (as yet) state of the exploited was facing the many states of the exploiters. Stalin expressed the thought of all his political colleagues, including Lenin, when he said, in 1922: "Since the formation of the Soviet Republics the States of the world have been split up into two camps: the camp of capitalism, and the camp of socialism."[2] The Soviet Constitution of 1923 repeated the same words, and the Comintern proclaimed it, too:

A fundamental antagonism between two systems, two worlds, now overshadows the whole world situation. A more or less unstable equilibrium has been, for the time being, maintained between them; on the one hand, there is the world of capitalism headed by America, and, on the other, the world of proletarian revolution headed by the Union of Soviet Socialist Republics.[3]

This basic thought cannot be rejected without abandoning Leninism as a whole. The criterion of this division of the world is twofold; it is both economic and political. A socialist country is one in which all the means of production are nationalized, or at least the economic heights are state owned, while the socialization of the remaining sectors is a foregone conclusion. But this is not enough; the Communist Party must, in addition, be in full control. Any country not fulfilling these two requirements is capitalist, although its government may be controlled by those "opportunists and reformists," the socialists, who, of course, are the intentional or unintentional "agents of the bourgeoisie." A Soviet author, writing before Stalin's death, said:

The world has split up, as comrade Stalin has said, decisively and irrevocably into two camps: the camp of imperialism and the camp of socialism. ... The struggle between these two camps constitutes the axis of the whole contemporary life, fills the whole content of present domestic and foreign policies of statesmen in both worlds, the old and the new.[4]

His colleague, writing in 1956, says the same:

By disrupting the front of world imperialism on a territory equal to one-sixth of the globe, the October Revolution shook the foundations of the world system of capitalism and divided the world into two opposed systems: the capitalist and the socialist.[5]

Kommunist, strongly opposing (in 1957) the Yugoslav thesis that the notion of peaceful co-existence was equally applicable to relations between capitalist and socialist states, as well as to those between socialist states, said:

Some people, who consider themselves Communists, deny, strange as it might be, the fact of the co-existence in the world of two antagonistic camps. We have in view a series of statements in the Yugoslav press. It appears from these statements that the very concept of existence of two antagonistic camps, a socialist and an imperialist, "with clearly defined state frontiers," is declared to be incorrect for the alleged reason that the socialist forces have grown up even there where power does not belong to the working class. ... From the denial of the fact that the world is split up into two antagonistic systems and consequently into the two camps, the conclusion has been deduced that the socialist states allegedly cannot make a distinction in their foreign policy between the socialist and the bourgeois states. This is a point of view alien to proletarian internationalism; it amounts in fact to undermining the unity among the brotherly socialist countries. By glossing over the antagonism between the social and political regimes of socialist and capitalist countries, one pours water for the mill of the reformists who fight Marxism-Leninism and the Communist movement. . . . It is impossible to erase by any arguments the fact that the two antagonistic world social systems and the two camps are a living reality of our day. The two camps, the socialist and the capitalist, do exist and wage a struggle with each other.[6]

The thesis of the existence of two camps cannot be abandoned without throwing overboard the concept of world revolution. In addition, it would be impractical for the USSR to renege on this thesis, since it carries an important implication. As long as the two basically hostile camps face each other, all the socialist states must close their ranks around their powerful elder brother. Their relations with the states in the capitalist camp cannot exceed the bounds of peaceful co-existence, which, as we shall see, is an unceasing political, economic, and ideological struggle. Hence peaceful co-existence is a synonym of peaceful competition. The Yugoslav claim that there should be peaceful co-existence between capitalist and socialist states alike entails a change in the very meaning of peaceful co-existence, which would, if the Yugoslav suggestion were carried out, become a condition of normal, friendly relations with all states, whatever their regime. Furthermore, the degree of friendliness which a socialist state would have towards any other state, capitalist or socialist, would depend not on the regime of the latter state but on its attitude towards the national interests of the socialist state. In other words, the Yugoslav thesis would lead to a return to the pre-1917 international situation, in which national interests, but not ideological considerations, were the only standard of relations between any two states.

The above thesis reflects the foreign policy that Yugoslavia has pursued for the last several years. As we have seen, the Soviet magazine *Kommunist* rejects it, especially since the national interests of the USSR would not be served. Yugoslavia is a small country which wants to be on good terms with both the West and the East, while the USSR is a great Power engaged in fierce competition with other great Powers and having its own constellation of friends and satellites in the form of other socialist states. The concept of the two camps, apart from the doctrinal aspect of the question, namely that this concept is truly Leninist, accurately reflects the national interests of the USSR.

2. Lenin's Subdivision of the Capitalist Camp

The concept of two hostile camps did not prevent Lenin from making a distinction among various capitalist nations. There were highly industrialized, imperialist Powers representing the interests of financial monopolies, and there were nations exploited by these Powers, the colonial and semi-colonial countries. We shall later analyze this distinction, which is all important for our time, but for the time being, let us say that such colonial and semi-colonial (dependent) nations, whose interests collided with those of the imperialist Powers, were considered by Lenin as natural allies of the proletariat. They represented the other sector of the revolutionary front. They would eventually enter the socialist camp through the door of the revolution, but meanwhile, their conflicts with the imperialist Powers could be exploited by the proletariat in its fight against imperialism. Lenin's followers have never lost sight of this differentiation within the general category of capitalist nations, although they have been giving it various practical interpretations. Their views concerned the crucial matter of the attitude to be taken towards the bourgeoisie living in colonial or semi-colonial nations. Could this bourgeoisie lead those nations in the struggle for political independence, or would it unavoidably, sooner or later, betray the national cause by switching to the imperialist side? Could it be trusted always to assert the claim to complete independence of Western imperialism after a colony had achieved formal political autonomy? Practically speaking, could the Communists be sure that conflict between the bourgeoisie of the underdeveloped countries and that of the imperialist Powers would be of long duration? Could it therefore be reckoned with as an important strategic factor, or was it a transient phenomenon that was too risky to rely on? If the latter hypothesis were true, then one could rely only on the local Communists in the colonial and semi-colonial countries. If it were false, one could recruit two sorts of allies: the native bourgeoisie, as a temporary ally against the Western Powers, and the local Communists, both as partners in the anti-Western struggle and as permanent allies in the long-term war for universal revolution.

Lenin was definitely inclined to accept the second hypothesis. Therefore, a temporary alliance with the bourgeois but nationalist elements in the underdeveloped countries seemed to him highly desirable. He was sensitive before the October Revolution to the strategic opportunity offered by the conflict between nationalism of the underdeveloped areas and the policies of the Western Powers. After the Revolution, his policy in this respect was inaugurated by the famous appeal to the Moslems of Russia and the East and was continued by Soviet support given to the Near Eastern nations struggling against the Western Powers, notably Great Britain, although those nations were led by a "bourgeoisie" that was personified by a Mustapha Kemal or a Riza Khan. Stalin faithfully continued Lenin's policy, both in the Near East and in the Far East, where he favored continuation of co-operation between the Chinese Communists and the Kuomintang. He reaped bitter disappointments; the Kuomintang massacred the Communists in 1927, while the Near Eastern countries, including Turkey, began to seek an equilibrium between Soviet Russia and the Western Powers by improving their relations with the latter Powers. Although neither Lenin nor Stalin ever overlooked local Communists as a permanent ally, Stalin seemed to become convinced, after his disenchantments with the Chinese and Near Eastern bourgeoisie, that the latter bourgeoisie was too unreliable an ally to bother about.

3. Stalin's Distrust of the Bourgeoisie in the Underdeveloped Countries

Before World War II, Stalin had little opportunity to display his new convictions, but after the war, the bourgeois (non-Communist) parties came to power in newly liberated former colonies or protectorates, both in the Near East and in Asia. Stalin took the unbending attitude of denying that those bourgeois politicians and parties could be truly inspired by a nationalism that was uncompromising towards the West. He definitely suspected them of betraying the national interests of their countries by serving the general cause of capitalism and by seeking accommodations with the Western "imperialist" bourgeoisie. Thus he believed that Gandhi was merely an agent for Western imperialism. The interpretation of Gandhi's role was crucial for the general attitude of the Soviet Union towards the underdeveloped countries, as we shall see later, because it had a symbolical meaning for the Soviet policies towards these countries. But if one could not conclude even temporary alliances with such bourgeois politicians, then native Communists would be the only reliable allies.

The change, pregnant with all-important modification in Soviet foreign policy, was brought about by new developments. The Chinese Communists proved that it was worth while to enlist the co-operation of their own bourgeoisie in the fight against Kuomintang and the West. They introduced the new theory of national bourgeoisie (that section of native bourgeoisie that was ready, for its own reasons, to co-operate with the Communists). This practical lesson was not lost on Russian Communists, but there was an obstacle in the USSR—Stalin, who was perhaps too old and who had probably lost any previous flexibility of mind. His speech at the 19th Congress indicated his mood. Did he not say—with emphasis—that the bourgeoisie of our time had abandoned the banner of national independence and that the Communists had to pick it up? Surely he had the underdeveloped countries in mind, and it is therefore not surprising that he promoted an uncompromising struggle of local Communists against their own governments in the newly independent states of Asia, together with armed insurrections, or that he neglected to exploit conflicts of interests between those governments and the Western Powers. Thus he confined the USSR to a sterile policy.

4. Current Concept of the Three Camps. Peace Zone

Stalin's successors digested the Chinese experience and revised the appraisal of the role of bourgeois governments in underdeveloped countries. The bourgeoisie, if only anti-Western, could usefully play three roles: (1) they could become a temporary ally of the USSR in its foreign policy and, knowingly or not, help to weaken the Western bloc, in which event Soviet relations with the non-Communist governments in the underdeveloped states should be as friendly as possible (even though the local Communists had to tune down their revolutionary song); (2) they could lead the colonial movements for independence from the Western Powers insofar as such movements had an anti-Western direction (local Communists should help the national bourgeoisie in this particular fight); and (3) were conditions in a given underdeveloped country propitious for a revolution, the local Communists could enlist every possible ally, including, as the Chinese Communists did, their own national bourgeois, which could be expected to co-operate in a revolution carried out under the banners of a minimum program of economic and social changes and of hostility to foreign (Western) influence. This new outlook, reflected not only in Soviet foreign policy and in the new tactics of local Communist parties but also in the doctrinal discussions among Soviet Orientalists, has much practical significance for the Western Powers; they may ignore it only at their own risk and peril.

Although we reserve for a later section of this book the discussion of problems in underdeveloped countries, national movements, and the crucial question of national bourgeoisie, we shall here indicate the present trend. The new Soviet decision of exploiting to the utmost conflicts of interests between the highly industrialized Western (particularly colonial) Powers on the one hand and the underdeveloped countries on the other was clearly formulated in Khrushchev's report, submitted on behalf of the Party Central Committee, to the 20th Congress. He said:

Comrades, between the 19th and the 20th Congresses of the Communist Party of the Soviet Union very important changes have taken place in international relations [Those changes took place not so much in international relations as in the Soviet interpretation of international relations.]. . . . processes have also taken place on the international arena during these years, processes showing that in the world today by no means everything is under the thumb of the monopolist circles [He thereby rejected the former view held by Stalin until his death in 1953.]. . . . The forces of peace have been considerably augmented by the emergence in the world arena of a group of peace-loving European and Asian states which have proclaimed non-participation in blocs as the principle of their foreign policy. . . . As a result, a vast zone of peace, including peace-loving states, both socialist and non-socialist, of Europe and Asia, has emerged in the world. This zone embraces vast areas inhabited by nearly 1,500,000,000 people, i.e., the majority of the population of our planet. . . . More than 1,200,000,000 people, nearly half of the world's population, have been freed from colonial or semi-colonial dependence during the last ten years. The disintegration of the imperialist colonial system now taking place is a post-war development of world historic significance. Peoples who for centuries were kept away by colonialism from the high road of progress followed by human society, are now going through a great process of regeneration. The People's China and the independent Indian Republic have joined the ranks of the Great Powers. We are witnesses of a political and economic upsurge of the peoples of Southeast Asia and the Arab East. The awakening of the peoples of Africa has begun. The national liberation movement has gained strength in Brazil, Chile, and other Latin-American countries. The new period in world history which Lenin predicted has arrived; the peoples of the East are playing an active part in deciding the destinies of the whole world and are becoming a new and mighty factor in international relations. In contrast to the prewar period, most Asian countries now act in the world arena as sovereign states or states which are resolutely upholding their right to an independent foreign policy. International relations have spread beyond the bounds of relations between the countries inhabited chiefly by peoples of the white race and are beginning to acquire the character of genuinely world-wide relations. . . . The friendship and cooperation between the Eastern peoples who have thrown off the colonial yoke and the peoples of the socialist countries are growing and strengthening. . . . The Soviet Union will continue to strive unswervingly for the extension and strengthening of friendship and cooperation with the Eastern countries.[7]

We have here the key to a better understanding of the post-Stalinist foreign policy, with its emphasis on closer relations with the underdeveloped countries, especially those which pursue a policy of non-commitment. They are cast in the role of one of two constituent parts of a "zone of peace," the other part being the Soviet bloc. Together, they should seek a common understanding, which they can find only in opposing the Western policy or some of its aspects. The road has been opened to a very flexible Soviet policy in regard to underdeveloped countries, but it leads to making distinctions among the states of the capitalist camp. The latter concept remains valid, as we have seen and shall see further, because any capitalist state is eventually destined to go through a Communist revolution, and the underdeveloped countries are considered fertile ground for social upheavals. The revolution may take place only under propitious circumstances; one may wait for it for years. In the meantime, the most pressing job is to weaken the Western Powers, competitors of the USSR and the major obstacle for the revolution. The Soviet Government therefore goes back to Lenin's teaching on the alliance between the proletariat and the "exploited" nations of the world, the present preoccupation in Soviet foreign policy; hence the subdivision of the capitalist camp is purely pragmatic. There are the Western nations, where prospects of co-operation with the Soviet bloc or of a Communist revolution are rather dim, and there are the underdeveloped countries, where both prospects are much brighter. There are the uncommitted nations of Asia and the Near East, with whom one may now make some headway, and other underdeveloped states which are committed to the West but which might perhaps be persuaded to take the road of non-commitment. The Soviet foreign policies must consequently be adjusted; this is what Stalin could not see in his old age.

5. National Bourgeoisie as a Temporary Ally

The new Soviet outlook called for a doctrinal re-evaluation of the bourgeoisie in the underdeveloped countries. We shall restrict ourselves here to a brief outline, which will be illustrated by the discussion which the

Soviet Orientalists held in 1956. This discussion pointed out the errors committed in the Stalinist period as the result of his rigidly hopeless view of the bourgeoisie in the underdeveloped countries, and it defined the new outlook:

In his opening words the candidate of sciences, V. V. Balabushevich, discussing the condition of the Soviet Oriental Studies regarding the problem of contemporary East, noticed in particular that Soviet Orientalists had committed many mistakes in the evaluation of economic and political views of national bourgeoisie in the colonial and dependent countries. . . . The acuteness of the antagonisms between imperialism and the bourgeoisie of the colonial and dependent countries was under-estimated. . . . Gandhi's positive role in the national-liberating movement was too often ignored.[8]

These opening remarks contained the substance of the new outlook. The importance of the discussion was such that four reports and thirty speeches were delivered at that meeting of members of the Section of History and Economics of India and Countries of Southeastern Asia (part of the Institute of Oriental Studies of the Academy of Sciences of the USSR). An eminent Soviet Orientalist, Dr. I. M. Reissner, joined in the condemnation of Stalin's error:

The thesis that a political split had taken place since 1925 between the conciliating [towards the West] and the remaining parts of national bourgeoisie, was not confirmed by actual events. It is necessary to revise this thesis of I. V. Stalin and some other dogmas, in particular the untrue definition of Gandhi as an agent and accomplice of imperialism.[9]

A candidate of sciences, G. G. Kotovskii, redeemed the reputation of the Indian National Congress: ". . . the thesis, which usually prevailed in the works by Soviet Indologists that, after each success of the national-liberating movement, a great *rapprochement* was taking place between the National Congress and imperialism, has been disproved by true facts. The intensification of antagonisms and of the struggle of national bourgeoisie against imperialism was taking place."[10] The rehabilitation of the national bourgeoisie in India or elsewhere does not mean that the latter should rule forever in the underdeveloped countries. It remains a bourgeoisie, a class representing a non-Communist system, and it must one day be eliminated. In this long-term sense, then, the division of the world into two camps remains valid. V. V. Balabushevich, who submitted the results of the discussion, said:

The co-existence of two opposite world economic systems, the capitalist and the socialist, and of two world markets, as well as the fact that the world socialist system is getting stronger and proves its superiority over the capitalist system, remain the principal and decisive factors in the international situation.[11]

This fundamental view does not prevent one from being practical and seizing any opportunity that might appear. The occasion for finding common ground between the bourgeois governments in the underdeveloped countries and the USSR must not be overlooked. Hence the national bourgeoisie is rehabilitated, and even called progressive, in opposition to the reactionary Western bourgeoisie. Balabushevich said in his concluding remarks:

The majority of those who have taken part in this discussion have agreed with the opinion that the national bourgeoisie in such countries as India, Burma, and others, is still progressive. . . . But another thought, though unclearly formulated, has broken through some speeches, namely whether the thesis concerning the progressiveness of the bourgeoisie in those countries during the epoch of the general crisis of capitalism and of its decline, is not a deviation from Marxism-Leninism.

V. V. Balabushevich considers such views mistaken. Capitalism as a world system has outlived its age and follows, as a whole, a descending line. But it does not follow from this proposition that individual capitalist countries cannot develop. The bourgeoisie of India, Indonesia, Burma, Egypt, and other countries, which builds up its own national economy, strengthens and develops the State-capitalist sector, fulfills a progressive function. To deny it is equal to ignoring facts and overlooking new phenomena.[12]

The eminently practical desire to seek a *rapprochement* with the underdeveloped countries, in the name of the Leninist tactics of exploiting all possible conflicts among the capitalist states, is reflected in his mentioning by name only uncommitted nations. This new distinction among the members of the capitalist camp and the corresponding differentiation among the various bourgeoisie are important things to remember for a better understanding of the Soviet concept of peaceful co-existence.

CHAPTER VI

PEACEFUL CO-EXISTENCE

1. Lenin's and Stalin's Concepts

WHAT HAS a man to do if he wants to assure the universal victory of Communism and the expansion of the political influence of his own country but refuses to be involved in suicidal adventures? Common sense indicates the answer: you bide your time, wait for an opportunity, and accept peaceful co-existence with your enemies as a regrettable but unavoidable fact. Lenin, who was richly endowed with political acumen, found this simple answer as early as 1918; in his article "Strange and Monstrous," he said that "the leftist Communists" were opposed to any sort of peace with the imperialists. But if there were no peace and no peaceful co-existence, the socialist state could not successfully grow. "The socialist Republic, situated among imperialist Powers," he wrote, "could not, from that point of view, conclude any economic treaties and could not exist unless it were to fly off to the moon."[1]

Any politician in his right mind would have given the same answer at that time; a young Soviet Russia, faced with the alternative of an onslaught by powerful Germany, had either to fly off to the moon or to conclude the Treaty of Brest-Litovsk, the first experiment in peaceful co-existence. After the period of foreign intervention, Lenin faced the same problem, and again his answer was the same: peaceful co-existence with the capitalist states, with whom he was actually eager to enter into economic relations in order to make them help Soviet Russia in her process of rehabilitation.

Stalin could not provide, during the interwar period, a different answer to Lenin's problem. He needed peace, mainly because the USSR was much weaker than the great Powers of that time but also because he wanted to make his country strong by means of intensive industrialization.

At the 15th Party Congress, in December 1927, I. V. Stalin stressed with utmost force that the maintenance of peaceful relations with the capitalist countries was a compelling task for the USSR. "The foundation of our relations with capitalist countries," said I. V. Stalin, "consists in the assumption of co-existence of the two opposite systems."[2]

It was not Stalin's fault that Hitler terminated the era of peaceful co-existence in June, 1941.

After the war, Stalin realized (much better than did the Western governments) the urgent need to heal the deep wounds inflicted on the USSR by Nazi Germany. An extremely heavy loss of human life, numbering in the millions, and the material devastation of all territory west of the Volga made it impossible for Russia even to think about a war against the Western Powers. His boisterous and aggressive policy covered up the military inferiority of the USSR for several years. Foreign Minister V. M. Molotov, speaking in 1945, said clearly that the USSR would need peace for a long time. He could not mention the urgent need for rehabilitation because this would damage the Soviet prestige, a card which Stalin was playing quite skillfully at that time. He justified the need for peace by displaying the grandiose goal of overtaking—economically—the strongest capitalist Power:

You remember that the Party and the Government had proclaimed shortly before the war that the time had come practically to formulate and realize the fundamental task of the USSR. This fundamental task was thus formulated: to overtake and surpass economically the most developed capitalist countries of Europe and the USA and finally to resolve this task within the shortest period of time. This is the task: we must produce in our country per capita of population no less than the industrial output in the most developed capitalist country. . . . It is obvious that we need a lengthy period of peace and security in order finally to resolve this greatest task.[3]

It is very probable that this thought dominated Stalin's mind until his death. Decline in his old age made him engage in adventures, such as the Berlin blockade or the Korean War, which could have put an end to peaceful co-existence, but these adventures were the result of his miscalculations and did not reflect a desire to unleash a general war.

2. Current Views

Stalin's successors did not need to modify his basic proposition of peaceful co-existence; they had only to avoid "adventures" and thereby cut off unnecessary risks. Their first acts were the conclusion of the armistices in Korea and Indochina. G. M. Malenkov, speaking as the first post-Stalinist

Prime Minister, stressed, in his programmatic speech of August 8, 1953, peaceful co-existence and the urgent need of reducing international tension.[4] This leitmotiv was carried further by Foreign Minister Shepilov, who said:

Our great teacher, Lenin, proved in his works the possibility and necessity of peaceful co-existence between the two systems, the socialist and the capitalist. Guided by this teaching of Lenin and the whole experience of historic development during the last decades, the 20th Congress of the Communist Party of the Soviet Union formulated the following theses of great theoretical power and practical importance: 1. concerning peaceful co-existence between the two systems; 2. regarding the possibility of preventing wars in the contemporary period; 3. about the forms of passage of various countries towards socialism.[5]

We should be reminded of the fact that Khrushchev emphatically stated a few days later, after Shepilov's resignation as Foreign Minister, that his speech reflected a considerate policy of the whole Soviet Government. As a matter of fact, Khrushchev himself said at the 20th Congress:

The simultaneous existence of two opposite world economic systems, the capitalist and the socialist, developing according to different laws and in opposite directions, has become an indisputable fact. . . . The Leninist principle of peaceful co-existence of states with different social systems has always been and remains the general line of our country's foreign policy. . . . And this is natural, for there is no other way in present-day conditions. Indeed, there are only two ways: either peaceful co-existence or the most destructive war in history. There is no third way.[6]

3. Nuclear Stalemate

The menace of a nuclear war can only reinforce the desire for peaceful co-existence, since the USSR does not have a monopoly on nuclear weapons. Khrushchev said in 1957: "War will be, under contemporary conditions, an atomic war with all its consequences."[7] He added a homely parable: "The lamb and the wolf live on the same earth; but the wolf devours the lamb by virtue of the right of the stronger."[8] Fortunately, the USSR does not possess the comparative strength of a wolf and the Western Powers are not lambs. Soviet writers deny the possibility of a limited use of tactical nuclear weapons:

Allow us to ask the question: on whom actually is it calculated, this whole "polemic" of the propagandists of "small" atomic wars? Only a very naïve person cannot see that their arch-wisdom is built on sand, and that an atomic war under any conditions may be only a war of mass destruction of the world population. Any attempt to prove that an atomic war might remain a "small" war is a big lie.[9]

The then best-informed man on those matters in the Soviet Union, Marshal G. K. Zhukov, denied the possibility of any major war without the use of atomic weapons:

At the time of my visit to India, Burma and other countries I was asked the question as to whether atomic and hydrogen weapons would be used in future wars. I also heard arguments casting a doubt on the sense of their use, as those weapons if applied were capable of mutually annihilating both parties. They said that it was clear that, in view of these circumstances, atomic weapons would not be used, as chemical weapons had not been used in the last war. I assume that such questions and arguments are incorrect. Firstly, atomic weapons now and particularly in the near future, unless forbidden, will increasingly be adopted in lieu of conventional armaments. In the event of a major military conflict atomic weapons will unavoidably be used as an essential means of combat. Secondly, the chemical weapons were in the past a weapon supplementary to the conventional weapons. The adversaries could reach their objectives by using conventional armaments without recourse to chemical weapons. However, atomic weapons, as I have already said, will be widely used by the troops as their regular weapons.[10]

Marshal Zhukov did not conceal the fact that an atomic war would also affect the Soviet territory:

We believe that the Soviet Armed Forces must be perfectly prepared for the anti-atomic defense of our Fatherland as well as for an effective use of the atomic and hydrogen weapons in the necessity of immediately dealing crushing retaliating blows to an aggressor. In training our troops we must assume that our probable adversaries have a sufficient stockpile of those weapons and the means of delivering them to our territory.[11]

He ended this coldly realistic speech with an appeal to Soviet-Russian patriotism:

Our Army, permeated with the moral strength of the Soviet people and having developed and multiplied everything that was of the best and heroic in the Russian Army, has always been and continues to be noted for the moral steadfastness, valor, and courage of its soldiers.[12]

Even if the Soviet leaders sometimes say for domestic consumption that an atomic war would bring about the destruction of the capitalist system only, they have too much common sense not to realize that nuclear weapons have no political conviction and are equally destructive for both sides. One may dismiss as meaningless, even to himself, this statement made by Khrushchev at the 20th Congress:

Nor is it fortuitous that prominent leaders of bourgeois countries with increasing frequency frankly admit that "there will be no victory in a war in which atomic weapons are used." These leaders still do not venture to state that capitalism will find its grave in another world war, should they unleash it, but they are already compelled openly to admit that the socialist camp is invincible.[13]

Shepilov, then speaking on his and the Soviet Government's behalf, said, however: "The atomic bombs are a threat to the whole of mankind."[14]

4. Peaceful Competition

Peaceful co-existence is the only way out of the Communist-capitalist dilemma. A naïve non-Communist, deceived by the word "peaceful," may imagine that an era of friendship between the two social systems has begun. This is firmly denied by Soviet sources. Let us recall General von Clausewitz's statement (which Lenin liked so much): "War is the continuation of politics by other means." If peace is therefore a struggle, it differs from war not by its objectives but by the means used. In other words, peace is the absence of military hostilities, nothing more. Lenin was for the Brest-Litovsk peace and, later, for peaceful co-existence with the capitalist states, yet he never abandoned his ultimate goal of universal revolution. He said: "A free union of nations in socialism is impossible without a more or less lengthy and stubborn struggle of the socialist Republics against the remaining States."[15] In 1919, he made this gloomy prediction, which expressed his hostility toward "imperialist" states:

We live not only in a State but in *a system of States,* and the existence of the Soviet Republic beside the imperialist states during a lengthy period of time is inconceivable. In the very end either one or the other will win. And before this result, a series of most horrible conflicts between the Soviet Republic and the bourgeois states is unavoidable.[16]

This dire forecast has not yet come to pass, and, ironically, the Soviet Union found, during World War II, some very helpful allies among those "imperialist" states.

The mental outlook of Lenin's present-day followers is no different from his own. Peaceful co-existence is for them a struggle waged by non-military means:

The Soviet Union proceeds from the Leninist thesis that in the situation where there are socialist and capitalist states on our globe their co-existence is historically inescapable. Even in 1921 Lenin had said at the 9th All-Russian Congress of the Soviets: ". . . Is it, however, quite conceivable that the socialist Republics exist amidst the capitalist encirclement? . . . It is already a fact that this is possible in the political and military meaning." However, peaceful co-existence is not a conflictless life. . . . This fact that the co-existing social systems are not only different but opposite (since in the one the toiling social classes are masters, in the other the bourgeoisie) presupposes the existence between them of irreconcilable contradictions, political, economic and ideological. A struggle is and will be waged in these fields. But it is not necessary for that struggle to be fought with armed forces.[17]

The final goal of a universal revolution is not abandoned but postponed until propitious circumstances materialize:

Creatively formulating a new theory of the socialist revolution, V. I. Lenin scientifically proved that states with different social regimes might co-exist for a lengthy period of time. The co-existence of states with different systems was not an accident but a historically legitimate phenomenon. It was caused by the fact that the socialist revolution could not simultaneously win in all countries because of the uneven economic and political development of capitalism in the imperialist era. The revolution was to win initially in a few or even in one country. Consequently, the split of one capitalist world into two worlds and two social systems was inescapable.[18]

But the ideological struggle for the same goal must go on:

One of the perfidious suggestions, which the adversaries of peaceful co-existence make, consists in proposing "to terminate" the ideological struggle. . . . There is not and cannot be anything in common between the question of relations between states with different social systems and that of the ideological struggle. Peaceful co-existence between the bourgeois and the communist ideologies, a compromise or an armistice between them, are impossible.[19]

Khrushchev upheld this same concept:

Messrs. capitalists accuse us of simultaneously proclaiming the policy of peaceful co-existence and talking about the struggle between the communist and the bourgeois ideologies. Yes, this struggle goes on, because it expresses the interests of different classes. This is fully legitimate. Capitalists . . . defend by all means the private ownership of means of production. . . . We Communists . . . are opposed to private ownership of means of production. . . . But the capitalist and the socialist countries are situated on the same planet; they cannot depart anywhere from this planet. This means that we must co-exist. . . . Our ideas will conquer mankind.[20]

When Khrushchev mentioned the social classes, he meant that this ideological struggle was going on not only between the socialist and the capitalist states but also between the Communist parties (in the capitalist states) and their opponents. He again proclaimed his faith in the final victory of Communism as the result of this non-military struggle at the time of his visit to Finland in 1957: "We are confident in the victory of the Marxist-Leninist ideas, just as we are sure that today will be followed by tomorrow. We feel confident that mankind will build up its life on the foundation of these ideas."[21] A Soviet commentator frankly states: "To abandon the ideological struggle would mean to abandon . . . the struggle for socialism in the countries of the bourgeois world."[22]

Recalling that the 20th Party Congress declared that any transition to socialism was a revolution, one may legitimately conclude that peaceful co-existence does not mean either an irrevocable acceptance of different ways of life in non-Communist states or the cessation of struggle for revolution in all those states. Nor does peaceful co-existence entail a suspension of the diplomatic struggle by the USSR. As Shepilov put it:

Peaceful co-existence is not a conflictless life. As long as different social-political systems continue to exist, the antagonisms between them are unavoidable. Peaceful co-existence is a struggle, political, economic and ideological. . . . Co-existence means that one does not fight the other, does not attempt to solve international disputes by arms, but that one competes through peaceful work and economic and cultural activities. But we would cease to be Marxist-Leninists if we forgot the elementary laws of social life, the laws of class struggle.[23]

One may better comprehend the full meaning of peaceful co-existence conceived as struggle by reverting to the parallel concept of the socialist camp. Khrushchev openly stated that friendship and brotherly co-operation were reserved only for the socialist states; explaining to a Japanese newspaper correspondent that the concept of peaceful co-existence was applicable only to states divided by antagonistic contradictions and could not preside, therefore, over the relations among socialist states, he said:

We are guided by the principles of proletarian internationalism, friendship and brotherly co-operation between peoples, in mutual relations between socialist states. . . . When we talk about co-existence, we have in mind socialist and capitalist states. Those forces oppose each other; antagonistic contradictions exist between them.[24]

Please note that he did not mention a different—a third—policy in favor of the uncommitted capitalist states, such as Egypt, Syria, India, or Indonesia.

Khrushchev logically upheld the concept of the two hostile camps against the Yugoslav claims to the contrary:

Some [Yugoslav] politicians express their disagreement with the very notion of a socialist camp and want to substitute for it the word commonwealth or some similar word. I believe that there is not and cannot be any more precise definition than the term socialist camp, which expresses most completely the nature of relations among the socialist countries in a situation where the two systems, the socialist and the capitalist, exist. As long as these two systems representing two poles exist, the two camps opposed to each other must also exist.[25]

A Soviet author develops the same idea:

One of the views alien to Marxism-Leninism, which is being expressed nowadays, consists in saying that proletarian internationalism is a survival of old times and an anachronism. This point of view is, for instance formulated in Yu. Gustinchich's article "Principles for All," published at the end of December, 1956, in the Yugoslav newspaper *Politika*. It is stated there that in "the era when socialism prevails in many countries" the working class, its parties and the toilers of socialist countries, should be guided in their mutual relations not by the principles of proletarian internationalism but by those of co-existence. . . . In fact, Lenin formulated the principle of co-existence in relation to international conditions existing after the Great October Socialist Revolution that had split up the world into the two antagonistic systems, the socialist and the capitalist. It is the principle of a peaceful co-existence between countries which have different, opposite social-economic systems. . . . Communists moreover believe that peaceful co-existence must not include ideology, and they have waged and are waging the struggle against the bourgeois ideology. It is not difficult to understand that it would be deeply mistaken to apply the principle of peaceful co-existence to the relations between single-type socialist countries or to those between Communist parties which have one goal and one ideology. . . . Discussions about the inapplicability of proletarian internationalism to modern conditions and the necessity of replacing it by "co-existence" of Communist parties, are objectively nothing but an appeal for the dissipation of unity in the socialist camp, for the separation of the Communist parties from each other, and for the isolation of the various detachments of the world workers' movement. . . . It follows from this point of view that the proletariat, living in a country where capitalists rule and pursue a policy hostile to the socialist countries, and the working class in the socialist countries, should not give each other international support. . . . [To ignore the existence of the two hostile camps] means to orient oneself to a split-up movement of socialism and communism. But this road hides a great danger. Under the conditions of imperialism the proletariat of any country is unable to consolidate its dictatorship and to secure the construction of socialism without the support of international revolutionary forces. This applies even more to small countries. . . . The socialist regime in any country is the achievement not only of national but also of international significance; the working class bears the responsibility before the international workers' movement and before history for safeguarding its achievements.[26]

This lengthy argument conveys the following principal ideas: the existence of two hostile camps, the necessity of close solidarity within the socialist camp (a call for such solidarity in the capitalist camp would, of course, be called an appeal for capitalist encirclement), and the mutual support given to each other by the socialist states and the Communist parties in the capitalist states. Obviously, this concept of unfriendly but peaceful co-existence with the capitalist states could only do harm to Soviet interests if transferred to relations with the allies and satellites of the USSR.

Variety in foreign policies is welcome, but only as regards capitalist states. Hence the policy of non-commitment practiced by such states is greeted as a buttress of peaceful co-existence: "An increasing number of bourgeois countries favor the policy of neutrality which provides them with the possibility of following an independent foreign course. The partisans of policy of neutrality naturally agree with the principle of peaceful co-existence between states with different social systems."[27] However, when Hungary tried to follow this policy of neutrality and attempted to quit the Warsaw military bloc, she was knocked on the head. The sauce for the capitalist goose is not good for the socialist gander.

Peaceful co-existence does not entail any domestic change within the USSR; Shepilov said this on behalf of all his colleagues, including Khrushchev:

Taking their wishful thinking for reality, they [the strategists of the bourgeois world] have begun to rely on some "evolution" of the Soviet regime and on our rejecting "some aspects" of the dictatorship of the proletariat, on our becoming if not "white" then at least "pinkish" . . . all those conjectures regarding an "evolution" of the Soviet regime towards a bourgeois regime are an empty figment of imagination.[28]

Peaceful co-existence excludes the freedom for the people of a socialist country to choose a different regime: "Helping the Hungarian people, the USSR carried out its international duty towards the toilers of Hungary and of other socialist countries; this action corresponded to the interest of the defense of peace in the whole world."[29] This view simply means that the USSR wants to safeguard all it has throughout the period of peaceful co-existence. The USSR does not intend to make any unilateral concessions out of its dominions:

But "the spirit of Geneva" does not presuppose unilateral concessions. . . . Concessions have their limits; they cannot be made by a socialist state regarding the basic questions on which depends the fate of the achievements by workers and peasants. "We," said Lenin, "go and will go to the merchants to make business, continuing our policy of concessions, but the limits of these concessions are already fixed." (V. I. Lenin, *Sochineniia*, Vol. 33, p. 199.) This advice of V. I. Lenin has an immense present importance and is consistently followed by the Communist Party and the Soviet Government.[30]

To refuse any unilateral concessions requires strength:

V. I. Lenin, while proving the possibility of peaceful co-existence, established several objective conditions which would enable the Soviet State to fight for the consolidation of peace. Among these conditions there is, first of all, the domestic strength, material and moral-political, of the socialist State. The growth of the economic might and defense capacity of the socialist country constitutes a convincing argument for the capitalists in favor of peaceful co-existence.[31]

Further:

The forces of the socialist system have considerably increased. This system now covers more than 25 per cent of the territory of the globe and includes over 35 per cent of the world population; it has approximately a 30 per cent share of world industrial production.[32]

Within the framework of peaceful co-existence, however, there must exist a flexible Soviet foreign policy:

Following the Leninist principle of peaceful co-existence between states with different social systems, the Central Committee of the Communist Party and the Soviet Government pursue an active and flexible policy which takes into consideration actual characteristics of the international situation, the true relationship of forces, and correctly appraises differences and nuances in the policies of particular countries.[33]

Bismarck himself would not disagree with this realistic statement!

The slogans for peaceful co-existence are the famous "Five Principles" (*Pancha Shila*, as the Indians call them):

The five principles: mutual respect for the territorial integrity and sovereignty; non-aggression; non-interference in the domestic affairs of each other; equality and reciprocal benefits; peaceful co-existence and international co-operation . . . were for the first time proclaimed in April 1954 in the preamble to the Chinese-Indian Treaty on Tibet. They were later reaffirmed in the joint declaration by Chou En Lai and Jawaharlal Nehru on June 28, 1954. These five principles are approved and supported by the Soviet Union and all the countries of people's democracy in Europe and Asia. . . . The five principles should become the foundation of peaceful relations among all the states in all parts of the world.[34]

We shall later examine these five principles in the light of the past record of the USSR, but for now, let us say that it is both ironical and ominous that these principles were proclaimed for the first time in a treaty which recognized China's conquest of her colonial protectorate in Tibet.

In summary, one may say that peaceful co-existence means absence of military hostilities but not a truce in the ideological, political, and economic struggle between the socialist and capitalist camps. Any and all non-military means may be used in this struggle for the ultimate termination of the capitalist system, a struggle which is legitimately called, by Soviet sources, a "peaceful competition." In the meantime, the USSR does not intend to allow a change in the *status quo* that would be to its detriment; this it grimly proved in Hungary.

CHAPTER VII

CURRENT OBJECTIVES

1. Five Periods of Soviet Foreign Policy

SETTING ASIDE for the time being the question of revolution, later to be discussed in relation to underdeveloped countries, we should ask ourselves: What are the current objectives of Soviet foreign policy within the framework of peaceful co-existence with the capitalist states? We may better understand these objectives by surveying the past foreign policy of the USSR and by dividing the years since the October Revolution into five periods.

The first period, 1917–1920, covers the era of a militant but weak Soviet state facing the incomparably stronger and unfriendly capitalist states, first Imperial Germany, later (during foreign intervention) the Western Powers and Japan, and the smaller states in its immediate neighborhood. This was also the period of civil war and Lenin's illusions about a fast-approaching revolution in the highly industrialized countries, notably Germany. Soviet Russia, extremely weakened by the First World War and civil war, was struggling against immense foreign and domestic odds. It was touch and go whether she would survive as a Communist state, yet Lenin openly upheld his goal of universal revolution, although he could not effectively support the short-lived Communist regimes in Hungary, Bavaria, the Baltic countries, and Finland. Force was used by and against Soviet Russia. She used it with success in reuniting most of the territories that had been parts of Tsarist Russia. By the end of 1920, she and her adversaries had to call it quits and end the armed struggle. Foreign intervention, civil war, and wars with neighbors, formerly Tsarist-controlled nationalities, were terminated.

The second period of Soviet foreign policy, which stretches from 1921 to 1939, was a defensive policy that avoided military adventures. Stalin correctly sized up the change when he said in 1923: "... since that time [the beginning of 1921] we have felt a slowdown in tempo of the international revolutionary movement; since that time our policy has become defensive instead of offensive."[1] Soviet Russia badly needed a respite to concentrate on building her economic potential. A historian of the Soviet foreign policy in the years 1917–1929 ascribes this defensive nature of Soviet foreign policy to lack of power:

"World revolution" by Russian cannon and sword rather than by foreign working classes may have been implicit in Bolshevism from birth. Perhaps the chief variable between 1917–1930 era and the present is the element of power; Russia is relatively stronger, Europe and Asia relatively weaker.[2]

The policy of reconquest, mainly by force, of the former territories of the Russian Empire in 1917–1920 (including the conquest of Georgia in 1921) and the vain attempt to subdue Finland, the Baltic States, and Poland within the same period of time, supports his view:

. . . it is therefore possible to assume that Soviet imperialism existed from the genesis of the Bolshevik regime but lay dormant from 1921 until Hitler pushed the button that started World War II.[3]

He correctly sums up the initial causes that made both parties accept peaceful co-existence in 1921:

The Western world's condescension to peaceful symbiosis with the Soviet regime arose (1) from that world's failure to destroy the Soviet regime by force, and (2) from the economic necessity of exploiting business opportunities latent in Russia. The Soviet regime's condescension to peaceful co-existence with the Western world arose (1) from that failure of the international revolution to eventuate, and (2) from the miserable economic situation in Soviet Russia.[4]

During that eighteen-year period, the Soviet Government hoped in vain for a war among the "imperialist" Powers to provide it with an opportunity for a less defensive policy. In the meantime, it had to concentrate on building industries in the Soviet Union. All this time, the Soviet Government used force in three cases: in the reconquest of Georgia in 1921; in Manchuria to compel, in 1929, the Chinese authorities to abide by the terms of the Soviet-Chinese contract concerning the Chinese-Eastern Railroad (this was a capitalist-like method of forcing a "semi-colonial" government to respect an economic concession granted on its territory to a foreign Power); and in 1938 and 1939 in the battles, limited in scope but not negligible, with the Japanese troops attempting to encroach on Soviet and Outer Mongolian territories. (In this case the blame must be placed on

Japanese shoulders, since Japan had deliberately provoked these serious incidents).

Louis Fischer is right in saying: "In foreign affairs, too, Russia's orientation can never be wholly Eastern or wholly Western. It must be both. Yet the differences of emphasis are inevitable and result from changing circumstances."[5] This is due to the geographic situation and is just as true with respect to American foreign policy. However, Europe, with its heavy concentration of skilled manpower and industries, remains the main stake for both extra-European great Powers. During the years 1921–1939, as today, the main blow against the USSR could have been struck only from the West. Then, as now, the Soviet foreign policy had to watch first of all the developments in the West rather than in the East. This is why the present Soviet active policy in the underdeveloped countries becomes fully understandable only if viewed as a maneuver to weaken the Western Powers, the main Soviet adversaries.

The years 1921–1939 can obviously be divided into two sub-periods, the dividing line being the events of 1931–33, when Japan began her imperialist adventure by seizing Manchuria and Hitler was appointed Chancellor of the German Reich. Until those fateful events, the USSR could quietly concentrate on her domestic tasks, the "normalcy" obtaining in international relations assuring a propitious atmosphere. The open Nazi hostility toward the Soviet Union radically changed the picture. However, the Soviet Government was reluctant to embark on a countercrusade. After Hitler had ratified, on May 5, 1933, the Protocol of June, 1931 (negotiated by the pre-Nazi German Government) concerning the extension of the Berlin German-Soviet Treaty of Friendship and Neutrality of 1926, *Izvestia* commented:

The people of the Soviet Union will undoubtedly endorse the re-entry into force of the Berlin Treaty . . . in spite of their attitude to Fascism the people of the USSR will to live in peace with Germany . . . and have no desire to make any changes or revisions in Soviet policy with regard to Germany.[6]

Since fascist or other forms of "dictatorship of the bourgeoisie" in any capitalist state made little difference from the Communist point of view, this Soviet attitude towards Nazi Germany was only natural. The main objective was to let the capitalist states fight each other while the USSR concentrated on building her military and economic potential. Foreign Commissar Litvinov said on July 25, 1930: ". . . the larger the scale of our constructive work, the more rapid its tempo, the greater our interest in the preservation of peace."[7] Even after having been forced by Hitler's belligerent speeches to shift to the propaganda of an anti-fascist crusade, Stalin denied in his speech at the 17th Party Congress in 1934 that the USSR pursued an anti-German policy and placed the blame for the deterioration of mutual relations squarely and justly at Hitler's doorstep. Then Chairman of the Council of Commissars Molotov said on January 28, 1935: "As for ourselves, we can say that we had not and do not have any other wish than to continue further good relations with Germany."[8] He repeated this thought on January 11, 1936: "I must say quite frankly that the Soviet Government would have desired the establishment of better relations with Germany than exist at present. . . . But the realization of such a policy depends not only on us but also on the German Government."[9]

The USSR followed the same policy in the Far East, doing its best to avoid being dragged into an open conflict with Japan. The Soviet management of the Chinese-Eastern Railroad becoming increasingly difficult in a Japanese-occupied Manchuria, the USSR hinted on May 11, 1933, that it would be willing to sell it to the Japanese puppet state of Manchukuo. Despite the Chinese protest that such a sale would violate the terms of the Chinese-Soviet agreement of May 31, 1924, concerning the joint administration of the railroad, the USSR sold it to Manchukuo on March 23, 1935, for slightly more than 25 per cent of the original asking price. She wanted to get rid of an object that could involve her in a dangerous dispute with a great Power. This policy contrasted with the use of force in 1929 against a weak China to enforce rights to the same railroad. The sale of the railroad did not prevent the USSR from asking and obtaining in 1945 the "restoration" of her rights to the railroad, a restoration to be imposed again on a weak China.

The main Soviet preoccupation in the years 1931–1939 was to avoid armed conflict with either or both of her powerful neighbors in Europe and the Far East and to remain neutral in the event of a war between either of them and the other great Powers. One may therefore have some doubts concerning the sincerity of the declared Soviet willingness to assist Czechoslovakia in 1938. The Soviet-Czechoslovak Treaty of Mutual Assistance of 1935 was to be applied against Germany, according to the Soviet assurances given at that time to Czechoslovakia, in the following two cases: (1) if France abided by her Czechoslovak alliance; or (2) if the League of Nations branded Germany as an aggressor. It is difficult either to affirm or to deny that the USSR would have taken to arms in either of these two cases because she was never compelled to lay her cards on the table. France refused to abide by her alliance (any recommendation by the League would have been prevented by lack of unanimity), and Czechoslovakia decided to accept the Munich dictate rather than risk a war.[10]

After the Western Powers had recognized the Nazi danger and recovered from the shock that followed the German march on Prague in March, 1939, the USSR regained her freedom of maneuvering. She entered (in March) into negotiations with Britain and France for the conclusion of an alliance against Nazi Germany, but a month later she opened, in utmost secrecy, informal diplomatic conversations for a *rapprochement* with Germany.[11] It is difficult to say with absolute certainty that her real objective was to come to terms with Germany, but this interpretation seems quite probable. If we bear in mind her obvious interest in remaining neutral in order to continue her build-up of economic and military potential and if we remember the Communist teaching about exploiting conflicts among capitalist states, we may conclude that Stalin dragged out the conversations with Britain and France for several months for two reasons: (1) to have reassurance in case of failure of the negotiations with Germany; and (2) to raise his price in Berlin by demonstrating that he had an alternative British-French solution. This interpretation is supported by the utmost secrecy of the Soviet-German negotiations and, in contrast, by several public statements, made by Soviet politicians, to the effect that they doubted the successful outcome of conversations with the Western Powers. For instance, Molotov (at that time both Chairman of the Council of Commissars and Foreign Commissar) said on May 31, 1939, at the meeting of the Supreme Soviet:

As yet it cannot even be said whether these countries [Britain and France] are seriously desirous of abandoning the policy of non-intervention, the policy of non-resistance to the further development of aggression. May it not turn out that the present endeavor of these countries to resist aggression in some regions will not serve as an obstacle to the unleashing of aggression in other regions? We must therefore be vigilant . . . we must remember comrade Stalin's precept to be cautious and not to allow our country to be drawn into conflicts by war-mongers who are accustomed to have others pull the chestnuts out of the fire for them.[12]

He added that the USSR did not intend "to renounce business relations with countries like Germany and Italy." His colleague, Zhdanov, wrote in *Pravda* on June 29, 1939:

It seems to me that the British and French desire not a real treaty accept-able to the USSR but only talks about a treaty in order to speculate before public opinion in their countries on the imaginary unyielding attitude of the USSR, and thus make easier for themselves the road to a deal with the aggressors.[13]

Although Britain and France were themselves guilty of proceeding leisurely with negotiations, the fact remains that this was not the manner to use when speaking in public about would-be allies—if they were seriously meant to become allies. Zhdanov's accusation sounds retrospectively like an attempt at building up an alibi for the USSR. Moreover, the Soviet negotiators, cordial and polite in simultaneous conversations with the Germans, were deliberately rude to the British and French delegations, raising successive difficulties as though to gain time for the completion of the deal with Germany.

The Soviet choice was dictated by the terms offered by the two parties. Britain and France proposed an alliance and therefore war; this would have been very costly to Russia and perhaps mortally perilous to the regime. No one could be sure in 1939 whether Germany would not, in such event, concentrate on the eastern front and try to smash Poland first and Russia afterwards before turning against the West. It was fairly obvious that Britain and France were unable to offer any immediate, effective assistance to the USSR. Had the USSR suffered a major German onslaught in 1939 instead of 1941, while the United States was still neutral and without the benefit of the intervening two years of further effort at building up her potential, would she have emerged victorious, as she did later on? Even if the Allies had won the war in the final account, would they have cared to restore the Soviet regime (which would probably have been engulfed in a military disaster inflicted by Germany)? These retrospective arguments, submitted in full knowledge of the events of 1941, would have been sufficient for Stalin to make his decision. He could see in 1939 the great danger of being involved in a war with Germany, while Japan, visibly hostile and tied to Germany since November 25, 1936, by the Anti-Comintern Pact, could attack the USSR from the rear. But as a good Leninist, he was certainly motivated by the desire to push the capitalist great Powers toward involvement in war, with the USSR remaining neutral and gathering forces for a later harvest at low cost. For those two reasons, he could hardly have wavered between belligerency and neutrality.

Moreover, Britain and France offered nothing as a reward for the Soviet alliance and could offer nothing. In 1939, they raised the flag of defense of small nations; how could they concede to a prospective ally an expansion that would sacrifice the small nations of eastern Europe if they refused such to Germany? Hitler, however, offered to share the spoils with the USSR on the best terms imaginable, namely that these spoils would be secured by the German war effort, while a neutral Russia would have only to pick the ripe fruit at no expense to herself.

The conclusion, on August 23, 1939, of the neutrality treaty and the attached secret protocol concerning the division of eastern Europe between the two great Powers was a logical conclusion surprising only to wishful thinkers in the West.[14] We now see that Stalin made two miscalculations. The first was an overstimation of French power, an error committed by almost everyone in Europe at that time. He believed in 1939 that Germany would have her hands tied to the western front for a long time. His second error was that he could not believe that Germany, with an unfinished war against Britain and with the United States speedily drawing closer to full belligerency, would be foolish enough to attack, without provocation, a neutral great Power. It was not his fault that he considered Hitler to be as shrewd as he was, but had he known in 1939 the sequence of events in 1940–41, he would probably have chosen the pact with Germany as the lesser of two evils and as a means of postponing war until the propitious circumstances when Britain and the United States would be irrevocably committed to a war against Germany to the bitter end. It is not surprising, then, that Khrushchev, in his secret speech, did not criticize Stalin for his decision in 1939 but only for his disbelieving in a German attack in 1941, despite several warnings.

The third period of Soviet foreign relations, 1939–1945, was one of Soviet territorial and political expansion. The secret German-Soviet protocol of August 23, 1939, assigned the following territories: to Germany went all of western Poland up to the Narev, Vistula, and San rivers, plus Lithuania; to the USSR went eastern Poland, Finland, Estonia, Latvia, and the Rumanian province of Bessarabia.[15] After the German conquest of Poland, the German-Soviet Boundary and Friendship Treaty, signed on September 28, 1939, modified the line of partition of Poland in favor of Germany, but an attached secret protocol compensated the USSR by transferring Lithuania to its zone of influence.[16]

Carrying out the terms of the secret agreements with Germany, the USSR occupied eastern Poland in September, 1939. During September and October, she imposed on Lithuania, Latvia, and Estonia treaties of mutual assistance, with the establishment of military and naval bases in their territories. Failing to force Finland to accept major territorial concessions and a Soviet base in Finnish territory, she attacked in November and imposed these conditions in the ensuing peace treaty, which was signed on March 12, 1940. In June, 1940, Soviet troops entered the three Baltic states; "elections" were held under Soviet supervision, and Lithuania, Latvia, and Estonia were annexed to the USSR at the beginning of August. Also in June, Rumania received a Soviet ultimatum to cede Bessarabia and northern Bukovina to the USSR. Soviet territory was thus greatly expanded.

Soviet attempts in September-October, 1939, to conclude pacts of mutual assistance with Turkey and Bulgaria and to include them in a Soviet Black Sea coastal zone of influence failed because of the refusal of those two states to agree to such pacts. Later on, German opposition effectively prevented the USSR from expanding her influence to the Danube and Balkan areas. We now know, from captured German documents, that the Soviet Government informed the German Government of its minimum program of expansion in November, 1940. This program included Finland, Bulgaria, and Turkey, with Soviet control over the Straits, as parts of the Soviet zone of influence, plus an expansion in the general direction of the Persian Gulf, this involving at least Iran and possibly other Near Eastern territories.[17] The German refusal to accept this minimum program (the larger program, also officially known to the Germans, included a few other Danube and Balkan states) was the cause of the breakdown in the Soviet-German negotiations of November, 1940.[18]

The German attack deprived the USSR of all of her recent territorial acquisitions, but by 1941, Stalin had begun to concentrate on receiving Western recognition of Soviet frontiers as gained through his co-operation with Hitler. He had not forgotten his previous plans for a zone of influence in eastern Europe, but in order to achieve it, he had to be first with his troops in the countries he wanted to include within that zone. The distribution of Allied forces in Europe in 1944–45 made it certain that eastern Europe would be occupied, after the common victory, by Soviet troops. The Soviet victories in 1944–45 resulted in the expected political consequences. The whole of eastern Europe, from the northern frontiers of Greece to the Baltic, from the River Elbe to the Black Sea, became a Soviet zone of influence and the stage of new Communist regimes. The Soviet frontiers of June, 1941, were re-established (co-operation with Hitler brought this final result), and in addition, the USSR forced Finland to cede the region of Petsamo, with its nickel mines, and obliged Czechoslovakia to relinquish Subcarpathian Ruthenia. The northeastern part of East Prussia was taken away from Germany.

In the Far East, the Allied victory permitted the USSR to carry out the provisions of the Yalta Far Eastern Agreement concerning the annexation of Southern Sakhalin and the Kurile Islands (lost by Japan), the restoration of Soviet rights to the Chinese-Eastern Railroad and the establishment of a Soviet naval base at Port Arthur and a Soviet commercial port at Dairen. Moreover, China, an ally of both the USSR and the Western Powers, had to pay the cost of the Soviet Union's short-lived participation in the Far Eastern war by recognizing the final loss of Outer Mongolia.

Stalin, looking around him, could feel proud of the services he had rendered the USSR—a territory, except for a part of Poland and all of Finland, larger than that of Imperial Russia in 1914 and a vast zone of influence such as Imperial Russia had never had. As a Communist, he must have been no less happy; almost a hundred million people in eastern Europe had been added to the Communist realm.

For a short time during the years 1939–1945, Stalin was forced by circumstances to submit to a humiliating policy of appeasement; this was in May and June of 1941. Hoping that a German-Soviet war would be averted despite the obvious deterioration in mutual relations by German default, he went to the limit of humiliation permissible for a great Power. On May 9, 1941, he ordered the closing of the Moscow legations of Belgium, Norway, and Yugoslavia, all three of which countries were occupied by German troops.[19] On May 12, he recognized the short-lived pro-German government of Rashid Ali in Iraq.[20] In June, he published a statement to the effect that German-Soviet relations were normal and that

. . . according to information at the disposal of the USSR, Germany is abiding by the provisions of the Soviet-German pact of non-aggression as steadfastly as is the Soviet Union, in view of which, in the opinion of Soviet quarters, rumors about Germany's intentions to disrupt the pact and to undertake an attack upon the USSR are devoid of any foundation.[21]

He thus rashly dismissed both the British and American warnings concerning the impending German attack and the very fact that Germany was concentrating troops on the Soviet Union's western frontiers. Since Stalin did not accelerate Soviet military preparations despite this obvious danger,

Khrushchev was right in criticizing him for this in the secret speech. Stalin probably miscalculated on two points: (1) he could not believe that a man in his senses would attack a neutral great Power without some sort of preliminary negotiation to wrest concessions peacefully, and (2) he did not think it possible that Germany and Japan, two allies, would have an unco-ordinated policy. In April, 1941, Japan had concluded a treaty of neutrality with the USSR; was it not a sign that Germany, visited by the Japanese Foreign Minister a few days before, approved of that step and thus did not intend to attack Russia? Stalin's appeasement policy is worth noting because this is the only one he indulged in during his long political career. Desiring to save Soviet neutrality at any reasonable cost and faced with a great Power ruled by a ruthless man, he appeased Germany up to the last day (Soviet economic supplies were delivered regularly until the German attack) in deference to the power and brutality of his partner. He was never confronted with any such situation thereafter.

It is worth noting that Stalin's anxiety to assure peace on the Soviet Union's western borders made him forget his dislike of the Nazi system in Germany and co-operate wholeheartedly with the Nazi Government, especially from September, 1939, to June, 1940, i.e., when the Nazis needed his co-operation. The foreign Communists were told to concentrate their attacks on "imperialist" Britain and France and not to impede German administration in the Nazi-occupied countries. Soviet economic deliveries to Germany included not only foodstuffs and basic raw materials but such strategic raw materials as rubber, which was bought by the Soviet Union in her status as a neutral Power and then resold to Germany. This economic assistance helped Germany in overcoming the effects of the Allied blockade. The USSR violated her obligations as a neutral Power by extending naval facilities to German warships, particularly submarines, which were allowed to use a naval base near Murmansk as a refueling station.[22]

The last years of Stalin's life comprise the fourth period of Soviet foreign policy. These years contrast with Stalin's previous record as a cautiously calculating politician. Instead of quietly digesting the enormous war gains, concentrating on the rehabilitation and further economic and military development of the USSR, and benefiting from the capital of trust and friendship he had accumulated in the West through Soviet participation in the Grand Alliance, Stalin tried in vain to expand Soviet influence without adequate means. In the late forties, the USSR was in no condition to enforce her claims. She had to live during that period by the prestige of her great war exertions. It was fortunate for the USSR that the Western Powers hastened to demobilize their forces, that their public opinion would not then have tolerated a showdown, and that they did not call the Soviet bluff. The quick Sovietization of eastern Europe, from which the remnants of Western influence had been effectively eliminated, was a challenge that the Western Powers would have accepted, grudgingly, only because they deemed it impossible to do otherwise without facing the possibility of war with their former ally. But Stalin did not stop there. His demands on Turkey, in 1945–46, for the cession of two provinces and for control of the Turkish Straits, his refusal, for several months, to evacuate Northern Iran in violation of treaties, his proposal to grant to the USSR a trusteeship over Tripolitania, the assistance granted by his Balkan satellites to the Communist rebels in Greece—these things clearly indicated that he wanted to make Russia a Mediterranean Power. The inclusion, in 1947, of the French and Italian Communist parties in the Cominform and Stalin's violent opposition to the Marshall Plan indicated that he did not desire any rehabilitation of western Europe and hoped to extend Communist influence to that part of Europe. Having no adequate force to support him in case of a showdown, he reaped only one result—that of alarming the Western nations, thereby precipitating the Brussels Treaty of 1948 and the North Atlantic Treaty of 1949 as the consequences. He could blame only himself for building a united Western bloc.

Stalin mishandled his quarrel with Tito, but in this respect, we should remember that Tito's example could have been contagious in other satellite countries and that Tito's plan for a Balkan federation would have weakened Soviet influence in eastern Europe. In Europe, Stalin not only did not advance a single inch but actually retreated from the Yugoslav Adriatic coast. Moreover, the Berlin blockade, staged perhaps to divert Western attention from the fateful events in China, could have led to incidents of such gravity that the USSR, as yet unprepared for a major and protracted war, might possibly have been involved in a major catastrophe. Stalin allowed the Korean War to drag on with all the risks of a major war between the United States and China. It was not yet the era of nuclear wars. He could have been faced with the alternative of either leaving China alone, despite the treaty of alliance, or engaging in a major war with the United States and, probably, other Western Powers, a war that did not promise to end well for the USSR, however costly for the West.

This record was brightened from the Communist point of view only by the Chinese Revolution, whose causes were mainly beyond Stalin's control, though he helped the Chinese Communists by delivering captured Japanese arms to them and by delaying the arrival of Nationalist troops in Manchuria. But despite all, he left Soviet Russia incomparably more powerful than she ever had been under the Tsars, with vast annexed territories, a ring of satellites, and China as an ally. All this, together with the risky adventure in Korea, became the heritage of his successors.

The fifth period in Soviet foreign policy began in 1953 and is still continuing. Stalin's heirs cut off unnecessary risks and reduced the international tension created by his postwar policies. We may now, after several years of adjusted Soviet foreign policy in the post-Stalinist period, try to reconstruct the current objectives of that policy.

2. *Status quo* in Europe

Assuming that the Soviet Government realizes the dangers involved in a nuclear war and wants to achieve its objectives by non-military means, one may accept as sincere this criticism offered by Khrushchev in his secret speech at the 20th Party Congress: "During Stalin's leadership our peaceful relations with other nations were often threatened."[23] He was probably referring to such events as the Berlin blockade and the Korean War, but he implied also that the new leadership would not assume such incalculable risks. This does not mean that the Soviet Union is particularly happy about the postwar *status quo*. Stalin did much for the extension of the Communist realm, but two-thirds of the world remained non-Communist, while several traditional Russian objectives were never reached (for instance, control over the Turkish Straits, exit to the Mediterranean Sea, or the Danish Straits, exit to the Baltic Sea). The present *status quo* is much better for the USSR than the prewar, but it is not yet completely satisfactory for a great Power inspired by a missionary spirit.

The paradox of the present situation is that the present *status quo* does not make any victorious great Power happy. The Western Powers are certainly not elated by the division of Europe, with its eastern part cut off by the Soviet Union, and the loss of China cannot possibly be a source of satisfaction for them. Thus the victorious great Powers, usually the more or less satisfied beneficiaries of a new *status quo* created by a major war, feel frustrated in this instance, although for opposite reasons. In the final account, the Soviet Union—were she to abandon her aspiration of spreading Communism to the confines of the world—would have the least reasons for feeling unhappy. She is the principal beneficiary of common victory. Great Britain, weakened by the last war, retreated from most of her colonial possessions and did not acquire one square inch of new territory; France lost her former status of world Power; the United States did not extend her territorial realm, except for several sparsely populated islands in the Pacific; the Soviet Union acquired approximately one million square kilometers of territory in Europe and the Far East (with a population of about 25 millions) plus the addition of 95 million people within her zone of influence in eastern Europe. Because of the weakening of other great Powers (Britain, France, Germany, Japan, but not the United States) and her own economic effort, the USSR rose to the rank of second world Power, a rank that she had never before held.

Since the use of her military power in a major war would mean nuclear risks, the USSR must adjust her current objectives to those that can be achieved with non-military expedients. Judged by Soviet statements and articles, the following are the principal Soviet objectives. The maintenance of the postwar *status quo* in Europe, where any change would of necessity require the use of force and would involve the USSR in an all-out war against the West is one of them. Hopes entertained in Moscow for a Communist upheaval in Europe must, therefore, be very faint. There are only two Communist parties in Europe which have the stature of major parties, the French and the Italian, but their influence has remained stationary and is not a decisive factor in the domestic life of these two countries. Only a major economic depression like that of the thirties could conceivably improve Communist chances of success in Europe.

By the same token, the USSR does not intend to retreat from her part of Europe, and could not be forced to do so except by a nuclear war. A Soviet journal specializing in international affairs said very earnestly: "We do not make of it a secret that a crushing answer will be given to any attempt the imperialist would make, to change by arms in their favor the distribution of forces in the world arena."[24] The USSR proved in Hungary that she was determined to defend her zone of influence with arms if necessary. The nuclear stalemate has brought about a freezing of the European *status quo* along present lines of division. This also entails the division of Germany into two separate states; doubtless the German problem, among all the European problems, remains the principal one for the USSR. The

Soviet sources carefully note the economic re-emergence of West Germany as a second Western Power with respect to industrial production. They do not, for instance, overlook the fact that West German steel output in 1956 reached 23 million tons as compared to 21.3 million produced in Britain, nor do the Soviets fail to see the fast-rising role of West Germany in international trade.[25] It would not require much mental effort for Moscow to visualize the power of a unified Germany, which would include the economic potential and almost 20 million people of eastern Germany.

People who are fascinated by historical analogies think with fear of renewed political co-operation between the USSR and Germany. Their fears seem to be unfounded, however, because the present situation is unlike any known previously in either German or Russian history. The former tradition of Russian-German friendship goes back to the 17th century, when expanding Brandenburg sought contacts with Russia. Later on, Prussia and Russia co-operated, doing excellent mutual business through a concerted expansion in eastern Europe. The same tradition was maintained by the unified German Empire until the reign of William II. In each period of mutual relations, both Powers were of comparable strength and were able to found their co-operation on a division of influence in eastern Europe. Political collaboration was further reinforced from the time of Peter the Great by German cultural influence on Russia. The mutual hostility that marked their relations in the decades before the First World War, along with the results of that war, could not but make clear to both countries that it was more profitable to work together than to fight each other. At the beginning of the twenties, Soviet Russia and Germany returned to the age-old pattern of friendly relations. The political, military and economic benefits were mutual, although the differences in social regimes made co-operation less pleasant. Hitler, too, returned to the old pattern in order to free his hands for the war in the West. The two years of Nazi-Soviet co-operation were again mutually profitable, and Hitler had time to conquer most of Europe while Soviet territory was being expanded.

The German-Soviet war changed the traditional picture completely. The cruel Nazi treatment of Soviet prisoners of war and civilian populations in German-occupied territories left a scar of hatred. Stalin, who had never before had any anti-German feelings, did not conceal his resentment at the Allied conferences. Addressing the Soviet people on May 9, 1945, at the time of the German surrender, he said bitterly: "Knowing the wolfish habits of the German bosses, who consider agreements and treaties as empty pieces of paper, we have no reason to trust their word."[26] For the first time in history, the power of the two nations is no longer of comparable magnitude, the Soviet Union having become the second world Power and Germany divided into two separate states. There is no longer any profitable business to transact. On the contrary, the vital interests of the two countries are for the first time deeply at variance. Soviet territory now includes the northern part of East Prussia, along with Königsberg, the city where Prussian kings used to be crowned. Eastern Europe as a whole is included within the Soviet exclusive zone of influence, while Poland, controlled in the last resort by the USSR, has advanced her frontiers, with Soviet encouragement, to the Oder and Neisse rivers. East Germany, of course, is also part of the Soviet zone.

Germany was stripped of vast territories and was divided, although Molotov reminded the Council of Foreign Ministers on April 11, 1947, of the following assurance made by Stalin in 1945: "The Soviet Union celebrates its victory although it does not intend to dismember or to destroy Germany."[27] Not only did the USSR—the only great Power to do so—recognize the Oder-Neisse frontier as final, not only did she repeat frequently that she would uphold that frontier, but she forced the East German Government to accept it, too. This was done in a Polish–East German treaty signed on July 10, 1950. One may be sure that East German Communists did this not out of friendship for the Polish Communists but in order to hew to the line of Soviet policy. They must have realized, though, that this act did not endear them to Germans in either part of the country. Yet they consented to celebrate, on July 10, 1955, the fifth anniversary of the treaty and issued, with the delegation of the Polish Government then in Berlin, a joint communiqué to the effect: "During the conversations [between the two Governments] it was stressed that . . . the attitude towards the frontier on the Oder-Neisse which unites both nations is the criterion for one's devotion to peace and security. They fully agree that the frontier of peace on the Oder-Neisse is the final frontier between Germany and Poland."[28]

The Soviet stand regarding German-Polish frontiers has remained invariably the same since 1945. On November 17, 1956, N. S. Khrushchev told Polish Party representatives on the occasion of their visit to Moscow: "It is known that the German militarists dream of revenge and demand a revision of the Polish frontiers on the Oder and the Neisse. We must take a resolute stand against those avengers and not allow German militarism to unleash again a bloody war against the Polish people, against the peoples of our countries."[29] A joint Polish-Soviet declaration signed at that time contained unequivocal passages referring to the same problem: "The Soviet-Polish alliance, which is of equal interest for Soviet and Polish peoples, constitutes a hopeful guarantee of their security. This alliance is also the most important factor in strengthening the independence of the Polish People's Republic and the intangibility of its frontier on the Oder-Neisse, a frontier of peace."[30] This declaration bore the signatures of Khrushchev and Gomulka, acting as First Secretaries of their respective parties, and of Bulganin and Cyrankiewicz, the two Prime Ministers. A month later, at the signing in Warsaw of a treaty concerning the stationing of Soviet troops in Poland, the Polish Prime Minister claimed, in the presence of the Soviet delegation, that the Soviet Army on the Elbe was a guarantee of security for the whole Soviet bloc: "The presence of Soviet troops on the Elbe is a fundamental guarantee of the security of Poland, as well as of the whole camp of peace in the present situation, where there is neither a peace treaty [with Germany] nor a treaty of collective security, but there exist aggressive ambitions among the revenge circles."[31]

Any outsider can easily analyze the problem of German unification, the preliminary condition of any Soviet-German *rapprochement*, from the point of view of Soviet vital interests. The Soviet assent to unification, following free elections in all Germany and with unified Germany having the right to remain a part of NATO, simply does not make sense to the USSR. Why should she add the economic and human potential of East Germany to an unfriendly coalition? Any number of non-aggression treaties which a unified Germany or the Western Powers could offer as a price would be of small comfort to a country which not only remembers the Nazi attack (despite a treaty of non-aggression) but which itself violated several such treaty pledges. But if a unified Germany had to quit NATO and become a neutral state—like Austria, for example—the new situation would still be unsatisfactory from the Soviet point of view.

Would Germany remain neutral very long if her eastern aspirations were to continue to be frustrated? The USSR could not control the foreign policy of a unified Germany by force because of the risk, or rather certitude, of a general war following a Soviet armed intervention. A unified Germany would either remain frustrated in her eastern aspirations and thus return to the Western fold out of resentment against the USSR, or she would sell her friendly or truly neutral policy to the USSR only at the price of the return of former eastern territories lost after World War II. Thus a retreat from the Elbe would either lead to the hostility of a unified Germany or to a further retreat from the Oder. Nor probably would this be the end of the story, because a powerful Germany, with seventy million people, highly skilled scientific and technical manpower, and an expanding industrial production (in fact, a great Power second in rank only to the United States and the USSR) would sooner or later become interested in eastern Europe, her traditional market. To cement a fruitful co-operation with her, the USSR would have to accept German influence in eastern Europe.

Would Germany forego her claim to the Königsberg area after recovering the territories lost to Poland? Would she abandon the claim to Czech Sudetenland? In making these concessions at the expense of her satellites, Poland and Czechoslovakia, the USSR would lose the only political trump card she has in those countries, namely, her role as their shield against Germany. Poland would have to pay the price of a Soviet-German *rapprochement*, while the events of October, 1956, have already proved that there is not much love to be lost between Russia and herself. Both Poland and Czechoslovakia remember that ten million German expellees from those two countries (approximately three million from the Czech Sudetenland) want to return to their ancestral homes. The other satellite nations, such as Rumania, Hungary, and possibly Bulgaria, having no grudges against Germany, would be tempted to gravitate towards her if she made another appearance in eastern Europe.

For Russia, a unified Germany would mean an eventual disintegration of the empire she has built in eastern Europe. All of these consequences are clear to the Soviet Government, and the Soviets probably prefer to assume the one risk of the present situation: a revolt in East Germany could lead to the implication of West Germany and, eventually, to a general war. The Soviet-East German joint communiqué of January 7, 1957, clearly indicated the Soviet intention to use force in the event of a revolt in East Germany:

Bound mutually by the obligations of alliance resulting from the Warsaw Treaty, the Governments of the Soviet Union and the German Democratic Republic declare that any attempts to use violent methods in settling the German question and to subvert the people's democratic regime of the German Democratic Republic through hostile activities, will be suppressed.[32]

One may assume that the current Soviet objectives in Europe include the petrification of a divided Germanay, for Soviet statements certainly support this view. The Soviets always infer two conditions for a unification: the neutralization of Germany and direct negotiations between the West German Federal Republic and the Democratic Republic of East Germany. Moreover, they add a third condition which makes unification practically impossible, namely that the economic and social achievements of East Germany must not be lost through a merger of the two Germanies. On his way back from the Geneva "summit" conference, Khrushchev stopped in Berlin and formulated, in a speech addressed to a vast crowd of East German Communists, the current Soviet program for the unification, or rather division, of Germany:

How can the German problem be solved? There are two ways. The one proposed by the Western Powers is that of the remilitarization of Germany. But this would lead to the resurgence of German militarism. Obviously this way is pregnant with dangerous consequences for the European nations and in particular for the German people, because a remilitarized Germany might be dragged into new military adventures; she would thus become the battlefield of the most devastating and destructive war, and the cause of grave calamities for all the peoples of Europe, and not of Europe alone. But there is another way, a correct way of settling the German question, a method which the Government of the Soviet Union has been and is supporting; and this is the unification of Germany as one peace-loving and democratic State which would not become a menace to other peoples. . . . We sincerely declared at the Geneva Conference that the settlement of the German problem was a difficult task in the situation where two States with different social-economic systems existed on the territory of Germany, and where Western Germany participated in the North-Atlantic Pact and the Western-European Alliance. . . . The best solution would consist in the settlement of the German question by Germans themselves, who can surely choose the correct road for the development of Germany. . . . Is it not obvious that a mechanical unification of both parts of Germany, which develop in different directions, is an unrealistic task? . . . It is impossible to settle the German question to the detriment of the interests of the German Democratic Republic. . . . Can the German Democratic Republic agree to its inclusion in the North-Atlantic Pact and the Western European Alliance and to carry on its shoulders the burden of an armaments race? Can the toilers of the German Democratic Republic agree to the liquidation of their political and social achievements and of all the democratic transformations? We are convinced that the toilers of the German Democratic Republic will never agree to enter that road.[33]

The last sentences in this quotation dealt with the third Soviet condition, namely that the Communist political and social system of East Germany should not be lost through unification. This third condition simply means that the USSR adjourns the unification *ad calendas greacas*. A joint Soviet-East German communiqué issued on January 7, 1957, reaffirmed this same line of policy. It stressed the need for direct negotiations between the two German Governments as a precondition:

Both Parties consider that the security of Europe and national interests of the German people demand from the Government of the Federal Republic of Germany to abandon the policy of the militarization of Western Germany, and seek the achievement of an agreement between the Governments of the German Democratic Republic and the Federal Republic of Germany concerning problems of an all-German nature, in order to open the road to a final settlement of the German question.[34]

Khrushchev, answering a West German journalist at a press conference in Helsinki on June 13, 1957, said bluntly:

It is not our view that the United States of America and the Soviet Union should settle the German problem. We have no desire to meet anyone whomsoever to discuss the German problem. We have often declared and now declare that the German problem can be solved only by Germans themselves, and that no one else should poke his nose in this business. . . . There are two Germanies. He who has not forgotten how to think realistically cannot make an abstraction of this existing reality. This is why the Germans themselves must agree.[35]

But how can the two German Governments agree on unification? The one represents a political democracy with several parties freely competing, with an all too vivid memory of the evils of Nazi totalitarianism, and with an economic system founded on private ownership of means of production. The other upholds the political monopoly of the Communist Party, is entirely devoted to the USSR and the whole Communist movement, and is bound by its economic program to the nationalization or state control of its whole economic life. Their unification would spell the end of the one or the other of them, and both know it very well. A Soviet writer implicitly stated this insuperable difficulty in the following words:

In fact there are two German states which embody two different social systems within Germany herself. . . . A part of the German nation has achieved political and economic freedom and is rising to the heights of socialism, while the other continues in the chains of capitalism. A mechanical settlement of the German question is impossible under such conditions.[36]

These words reveal the impossibility of settling the reunification problem through direct negotiations between the two German Governments, especially since the USSR has no interest in prodding the East German Government to make concessions in its political and social program.

West German Chancellor Konrad Adenauer's attempt, in September, 1955, to improve Soviet–West German relations can be very instructive in understanding Soviet policy. Whatever hopes the German Chancellor might have entertained at that time, he was unable to effect any concessions. In reality, the Soviet Government received a concession from Adenauer: the establishment of diplomatic relations between Moscow and Bonn. Thus the USSR became the only great Power to have direct diplomatic channels to both German Governments. Soviet negotiators must have had tongue in cheek when they issued the following statement at the close of Adenauer's visit:

. . . the establishment and development of normal relations between the Soviet Union and the German Federal Republic will promote the settlement of unsolved questions relating to Germany as a whole, and should thus help in the settlement of the principal national problem of the German people, namely the restoration of unity of the German democratic State.[37]

To prove that talks with the West German Chancellor did not affect Soviet intentions to rely on the East German Government, an East German delegation was invited to come to Moscow, literally on Adenauer's heels— it came a week later. In contrast to the dry tone of the communiqué issued at the end of Adenauer's visit, the tenor of the communiqué published at the end of the East German delegation's visit was warm and cordial and full of assurances for further close co-operation guaranteed by Soviet garrisons:

The Soviet troops, which are now stationed on the territory of the German Democratic Republic in accordance with existing international agreements, will temporarily remain in the German Democratic Republic by assent of its Government.[38]

Thus the West German Government was again notified of the fact that the USSR did not intend to drop its ally, the German Democratic Republic, and considered it, as before, a partner in all negotiations concerning German unification. One must not forget that the heavy concentration of Soviet troops in East Germany serves two purposes: it is the most advanced outpost from which to watch the West, and it guarantees the loyalty of Poland and Czechoslovakia.

It is true that the Soviet Government has assented to two alterations in the *status quo* in Europe since Stalin's death. The first was the conclusion (by all four great Powers) of a treaty with Austria on May 15, 1955, which freed that country of all foreign troops and made it independent and neutral. This move was motivated not only by the desire to reduce international tension, which had reached a dangerous peak during the last years of Stalin's life, but also by a strategic consideration. The neutralization of Austria created in central Europe a Swiss-Austrian belt that cuts off air and land communications between NATO armed forces stationed in Germany and in Italy.

The second change was the Soviet abandonment of its military base at Porkalla-Udd in Finland, which was finally evacuated in January, 1956. The possession of nuclear weapons makes the conquest of Finland, in the event of general war, a problem incomparably easier than it was in 1939–40. Moreover, the USSR is now a dominating Power in the Baltic and need not fear for the security of access to Leningrad through the Finnish Gulf. Finland pursues a policy of non-commitment. It was clever of the USSR to show that it knows how to reward the uncommitted nations, for the relinquishment of the Porkalla-Udd base was also calculated to please another uncommitted nation—Sweden. Soviet propaganda against American bases in foreign territories obtained a new argument. Those who are rash in deducing conclusions may now point to the Soviet withdrawal from Porkalla-Udd as an example to be followed by the United States. However, this base in southern Finland did not mean a shorter distance between the Soviet Union and possible targets in the West for the Soviet bombers or long-range missiles; bases in the Soviet Union proper are just as convenient.

It is entirely understandable that the Soviet Union, a great Power desiring total change in the existing *status quo*, would not relish the prospect of any consolidation among the non-Communist states. This general reason would be sufficient for Soviet lack of sympathy regarding organizations of any type among the western European nations. Of course an integrated western Europe, with Britain participating in or supporting it in any way, would constitute a world Power of the same magnitude as the United States and the Soviet Union. Long-range Soviet hopes for penetration into western Europe would be effectively quashed, but the Soviet Government might also fear that such a western European union might be tempted to exert strong pressure in the eastward direction in order to fulfill West German aspirations.

Judging by the Soviet official statements and press articles, this apprehension is quite evident in Soviet minds; they visualize West Germany as the most vigorous and economically strongest among the western European nations and fear that she, with so many accounts to settle with the Soviet bloc, might dominate a united western Europe and use it as a tool of pressure on the Soviet Union. An official statement, issued by the Soviet Ministry of Foreign Affairs and published on March 17, 1957, concerning the Common Market and the Euratom reflects these fears and apprehensions. Both projects were denounced as serving only to reinforce NATO, especially Germany:

It is certain that the revenge-seeking Western-German groups will not miss the opportunity to make use of the Euratom to accumulate atomic raw materials in order the more quickly to begin production of their own nuclear weapons. . . . The Euratom will clear for German militarism the road towards the preparation of new military adventures. . . . The establishment of the Euratom . . . will unavoidably result in repealing all limitations on the production of atomic weapons in Western Germany.[39]

Soviet apprehension that a western European Union in one form or another would make West Germany the true and aggressive leader of the whole group was expressed in a statement concerning the Common Market:

The project of a "common market" is particularly convenient for the Western-German monopolies. . . . The creation of the "common market" will result in the subordination of France and other Western-European countries to the economic hegemony of German monopolists, and will disarm those countries in the face of Western-German militarists and avengers.[40]

There is no doubt that the German problem remains, in the Soviet thinking, the crucial one in Europe.

While the Soviet Government opposes any form of integration of western Europe, it has made a great effort in compelling eastern Europe to become militarily, politically, and economically integrated, together with the Soviet Union itself, into one closely knit unit. But as always, the Soviets imply that sauce which is good for the goose is not good for the gander.

3. The Far East (China, Japan)

In all of her Far Eastern history, Russia has never had a situation as favorable as the present one. Her imperial expansion at the expense of China was not viewed with favor by other great Powers—Great Britain, the United States, Germany, and France—and was finally checked by the Japanese victories of 1904. In the interwar period, Soviet Russia was held firmly in check by Japan, and only the events of 1945–1949 changed the picture beyond recognition. Japan was eliminated as a major power in Asia, and China became a Soviet ally. The Soviet-Chinese alliance will undoubtedly remain the main factor in the Far Eastern situation for years to come. One cannot but agree with the general conclusion of the authors of *Moscow-Peking Axis* that all the chances are in favor of the enduring life of that alliance.[41] The USSR did its best to remove from mutual relations the most irritating causes of possible disagreements. She ended the existence of the Soviet-Chinese joint companies in Sinkiang, where they could be a tool of Russian economic infiltration. Soviet troops evacuated the naval base of Port Arthur, the Manchurian railroads were returned to China, and the Chinese, in turn, acknowledged the "independence" of Soviet-protected Mongolia.

Of course a powerful and imperialist China would have quite a few scores to settle with Russia. She could demand the return of the Soviet Far Eastern provinces detached from China in the 19th century, and she could reclaim Outer Mongolia, which was once an integral part of China. But China is not yet strong enough to challenge any world Power successfully. It would be vain to guess what her foreign policy might become in twenty to thirty years, when, probably fully industrialized, she will be a world Power in her own right. In the forties, Japan had a choice—to turn against Russia or to make a southward expansion. She chose the latter. An expansionist China might do the same thing for the same reasons; she would find raw materials, foodstuffs, and also large Chinese settlements in southeastern Asia.

At the present time, close co-operation between the two Communist nations corresponds to their mutual interests, while a community of ideological beliefs cements the coincidence of national interests. Although Peking is an autonomous center of power that is totally unlike the eastern European Communist capitals and although China could follow its own ideological line, the national interests of both China and Russia would demand a toning down of any possible ideological discrepancies. The Soviet and Chinese leaders have a definite ideology; however, they are practical politicians, not theologians, and would not sacrifice vital national interests for the sake of a doctrinal quarrel. Moreover, what appears to be a scholastic dispute over words in the Communist movement is an ideological cover for political divergencies. Political differences result in doctrinal disputations, but not the other way around. The fine splitting of the Leninist hair during the Soviet-Yugoslav (and to a lesser degree the Soviet-Polish) dispute camouflaged a divergence between national interests. Western journalists enjoyed embarrassing Khrushchev by forcing him to acknowledge publicly that the Chinese theory of the possibility of conflicts within a socialist state did not apply to the USSR. Probably neither Moscow nor Peking took seriously to heart the fact that the other country had a different view of the matter. Whether the existence of domestic conflicts is acknowledged or not, the Communist Party in either country has the last word. Mao's theory, much advertised in the West, of "a hundred blossoming flowers" seemed to challenge the Soviet conformist pattern, but Mao did not say that the Party would abandon its monopoly of power. Eventually, the Chinese critics, invited to come into the open by the hundred-flower theory, were brutally forced to recant and to proclaim that the Party knew best. The one hundred flowers were cut. Only one flower can bloom in a one-party garden, the Party flower, and Soviet Communists did not worry about their flower—the Party line—in China. Moreover, it should be remembered that Marxism-Leninism is for modern Communists a residual creed that is not challenged in either Russia or China (see Chapter III).

Although the Soviet Union cannot militarily force China (as it can force the eastern European countries) to follow any policy, she has means of economic pressure, her assistance being of utmost importance to Chinese industrialization. Until China is fully industrialized, Moscow will remain the senior partner, both in international politics and ideology.

China gives the USSR several additional assets. First, she secures the previously vulnerable Soviet Far Eastern flank. Since she is an authentic Asian state, her voice is naturally listened to with greater trust by the Asians than is the Russian, which is, after all, a European voice. China serves as a symbol of Asian revolt against the West. Her industrialization, if it proceeds successfully, will be even more persuasive for those Asians who are tempted to sample the Communist method of industrialization. She started from scratch, while Russia already had a substantial industrial basis to begin with. She may talk with an air of sincerity about Asian unity.

China also has assets in southeastern Asia in the form of the old Chinese settlements from Burma to Vietnam and Indonesia. The Chinese settlers in these areas are now split in their allegiance between Communist China and Taiwan, but the Chinese Communists offer an attraction to the patriotic feelings of foreign Chinese. China, bitterly humiliated by the great Powers, including Imperial and Soviet Russia, has become a truly independent Power; she is again united under one government and is industrializing with a view to acquiring the potential of a great Power. This patriotic compensation for the past plays a vital role among a great many foreign Chinese who are not otherwise Communists. They frequently occupy important economic positions in the countries of their adoption. The fact that they are often disliked in their environment has a dual effect. On the one hand, it makes them look more eagerly towards a compensating symbol of Chinese strength abroad, but on the other hand, it makes the Communist infiltration promoted by Chinese settlers suspect to native eyes. However, the latter role is also assigned to non-Chinese native Communists.

China offers a trade market to Asian countries, notably Japan. It is true that this market, under conditions of complete freedom of exchange, would never be what it was in the past, when Japan was overlord of Manchuria and, later, a large part of China. At that time, Japan could not only impose her own trade conditions on China but could purchase, on advantageous terms, strategic Chinese raw materials, especially coal and iron ore, with her textile products. The Chinese now want capital equipment on their own terms, but Japan and other Asian countries would find a limited market in China. This the USSR knows well and plays her hand accordingly, for instance, in her endeavors to win Japan over to a non-commitment policy.

China's unlimited manpower was very useful in securing a stalemate in Korea and could again be useful. China could provide a geographical springboard for discreetly assisting a Communist uprising in the neighboring countries or even in another local war, which is not entirely impossible in the nuclear age, since the very fear of nuclear implications of a global conflict could force the West to fight within local limits.

The Chinese alliance would become a liability for the USSR only if

China lost her head and wanted to assume undue risks in achieving her immediate national goals: the recovery of Taiwan and the coastal islands and the unification of Korea and Vietnam under Communist regimes. However, if the Chinese Communists are guided by common sense, they will imitate Stalin, who wisely concentrated on quietly building the economic potential of Russia and did not act until the USSR was ready for action.

An important aspect of Soviet-Chinese mutual relations is the present economic dependence of China on the USSR and the Soviet satellites in eastern Europe. An increased trade with non-Communist states would not radically alter the situation, although China will welcome the influx of capital goods from both sources, especially since she is vitally interested in speeding her industrialization. She could not safely rely on Western supplies—or believe that such trade would not be used as pressure on her— if she cut off the stream of Soviet supplies. The Western Powers, unlike the USSR, would probably be wary of granting generous loans to China for the purchase of Western capital equipment. The West's experience with the USSR during her initial industrialization drive has not been very encouraging. During the First Five Year Plan, Western private business provided capital goods and technical assistance (engineers helping to build Soviet plants, dams, and power stations), and the political result of this aid has been all but rewarding for the West. Who would venture to prophesy that a China industrialized with Western and Japanese help would break off her alliance with the USSR and not turn against her former helpers? The answer to this crucial question is a gamble. The present Chinese capacity for exporting raw materials and foodstuffs needed for her own expanding industries and increasing urban population is limited; she is in dire need of commercial credits and loans.

China needs the USSR both economically and politically. Were China to abandon the Soviet alliance, her own status would immediately sink to that which she still actually is—an enormous country with the potential of a medium nation. All of these reasons militate against the optimistic view, sometimes entertained in the West, that the Soviet-Chinese alliance is bound to disintegrate soon or that China has an influence on the course of Soviet policy in eastern Europe. The Chinese, junior allies, may have derived in 1956 some pleasure in contemplating the troubles of their senior partner, a circumstance which seemed to equalize their respective positions. Yet if Russia were seriously menaced by a disruption of her empire in eastern Europe, she would be weakened not only by the loss of the economic resources of that area but also by the loss of 95 million people. China would be weakened by the repercussion. Hence in 1956 the Chinese Communists looked with smiling sympathy at Polish Communists, who asked for greater domestic autonomy though they did not challenge their Soviet alliance, but they condemned the Hungarian revolt, which, if successful, would have disrupted the Soviet bloc in the Danubian region. A Polish Communist would be foolish to expect China to support Poland in an open conflict with the USSR. Common sense indicates that China's own industrialization, conditioned on the regular Soviet supply of capital equipment and on Soviet advisers, is infinitely more important (among other things, in gaining equality with Russia) than are Poland and all of eastern Europe. Moreover, geography has a role to play in this respect. Even a powerful China could never—in those parts—play the role of competitor with Russia, not to mention the fact that the natural room for Chinese expansion, as for the Japanese in the past, is Asia, not Europe. Japan could easily co-operate with Nazi Germany, and this type of relationship holds good for the USSR and China to the extent that Soviet European interests are concerned.

The cost of Soviet-Chinese trade is increased by lengthy lines of transportation. However, both countries have been making great efforts to ease this problem and, at the same time, acquiring new rail links which would be strategically safer than the Manchurian–Trans-Siberian railroads, which are located close to American Pacific air bases. The amount and importance of Soviet-Chinese trade may be measured by the fact that its volume increased almost five times between 1950 and 1955.[42] All routes of transportation have been used, the respective shares being: 81 to 85 per cent for railroads; 10 to 15 per cent for costly maritime transportation between Soviet European ports and Chinese ports; 2 to 3 per cent for trucks; and only 0.1 to 3.5 per cent for fluvial transportation (Amur, Ili, and the Black Irtysh). Thus railroads have played the predominant role. Until January 1, 1956, the rail communications were two: the Chinese Manchurian railroads leading west towards the Soviet Trans-Baikal regions and those leading east towards Vladivostok. However, since the main Soviet centers of supply were located on the western line, the volume of trade for the western link was three times that of the eastern link.[43] The principal use of one railroad for the bulk of Soviet-Chinese trade was a restrictive factor until January, 1956, when a new line was opened from Tszinin, China, through Outer Mongolia (Ulan-Bator) to join the Soviet Trans-Siberian main line. This new railroad is managed in Mongolia by a joint Soviet-Mongolian corporation whose existence is another evidence of the colonial status of Mongolia. The 1956 traffic on railroads linking China with the USSR was distributed approximately as follows: Western-Manchurian Railroad, 40 per cent; the new Trans-Mongolian Railroad, 40 per cent; and the Eastern-Manchurian Railroad (towards Vladivostok), 20 per cent.[44]

Further industrial development of Siberia, Kazakhstan, and the Soviet Far East, carried out under the current Seven Year Plan, will ease mutual trade, since the centers of supply will, in time, be located closer to the Chinese borders. Furthermore, the planned oil pipelines in Siberia will facilitate the export of Soviet petroleum products to China.

The Soviet-Chinese agreement of April 7, 1956, provides for the construction of a fourth railroad link, the Lanchzhou-Urumchi-Alma Ata line, which is scheduled for completion in 1960. "This railroad, which is being built, will link the richest regions of Northwestern China with the Central-Asian Republics and will become the shortest commercial route between the central regions of China and the European industrial regions of the Soviet Union."[45] This intense building of railroads—commercially and militarily vital to both states—does not indicate that they consider their alliance an ephemeral one.

The Chinese dependence on trade with the USSR and eastern Europe may also be measured by the figures for 1954. Eighty-one per cent of all Chinese foreign trade was with the other "socialist" countries, while 97 per cent of China's imports of capital goods came from the USSR. The USSR provided from 50 to 70 per cent of the capital equipment for 156 large, newly built Chinese industrial plants. In 1950, Soviet credits amounted to 1,200 million roubles, and in 1954 another 500 million roubles were added. All of these loans aimed at financing Soviet imports of capital goods.[46]

On February 7, 1959, the USSR and China signed a new agreement whereby the Soviet Union pledged herself to supply the heavy-industry equipment for seventy-eight large enterprises—to be built from 1959 through 1967—in China. The total value of this equipment, five billion roubles, was to be repaid by Chinese imports. Soviet experts will help to build these enterprises and put them into operation.

The two economies might not be naturally complementary. China could probably buy capital goods at a lower price in the West, while Russia could go elsewhere for most of the foodstuffs and raw materials now imported from China. Moreover, she could do this without exporting capital goods that are so important for her own potential. Yet political considerations are paramount for both countries. Alexander Eckstein considers that the Soviet exports of capital goods to China do not represent an undue strain on Soviet production, since they amount to only 1.5 to 2.5 per cent of the total Soviet output and up to 2 per cent of the total annual domestic investment in the USSR.[47] But these exports, which are bound to increase with the augmenting Chinese capacity of absorption, limit the Soviet ability to play a decisive role in the industrialization of underdeveloped countries taken as a whole.

Turning to the other important Soviet neighbor, Japan, one might expect less mutual coolness than exists at present if Japan desired more scope for maneuvering with the United States (by seeking an improvement in her relations with the USSR). Japan, former and potentially future enemy and the only industrialized Asian state, and China, the major Soviet Asian ally, now in the process of industrialization, are equally important problems from the point of view of Soviet security. But while the political, economic, and ideological common bonds between the USSR and China seem to be solid and durable, there is much to divide Japan from Russia. There is not only the record of long rivalry and hostility during the past several decades but also current frictions regarding such matters as fisheries along the Soviet coasts, the existence of an anti-Japanese Sino-Soviet alliance, and, above all, the divergence of views concerning Soviet territorial acquisitions in the Far East at Japan's expense. No quarrel affects relations between two independent states more adversely than a territorial one. However, the USSR annexed, without waiting for the conclusion of a peace treaty with Japan, not only Southern Sakhalin, which was conquered by Japan in 1905, but also the Kurile Islands.

There exists in the Japanese mind an analogy between the loss of the Kurile Islands to Russia and the Ryukyu and Bonin Islands to the United States. Japan established her firm sovereignty over all of these archipelagos in the 1870's, long before the beginning of her imperialist drive. Her sovereignty was not contested by any Power until 1945. However, the United States has never annexed the Ryukyu and Bonin Islands; they have merely been placed under an exclusive American administration for strategic reasons. Looking into the future, one may visualize a return of those two archipelagos to Japan. The situation is notably different in the case of the Kurile Islands, formally annexed by the USSR, who makes no secret of her intention to keep them forever.

At the time when the USSR and Japan signed their Joint Declaration of October 19, 1956, concerning the formal re-establishment of peace and normal diplomatic relations, the Soviet stand concerning the territorial question was clearly defined. The progressively reduced Japanese pleas for the return of Southern Sakhalin and the Kuriles, of the Kuriles only, and eventually only of the southern Kurile islands of Iturup and Kunashir were firmly rejected. Asked in June, 1957, by a Japanese journalist whether the USSR could envisage the return of Iturup and Kunashir, Khrushchev refused to consider the matter because, as he said, "they have an important strategic significance."[48]

However, mindful of an American concession made to Japan in 1953 in the form of returning to her the northernmost of the Ryukyu Islands, the Amami Oshima Islands, the Soviet Government promised in the Joint Declaration of October 19, 1956: "The USSR . . . agrees to return to Japan the islands of Habomai and Shikotan but under the condition that the actual return of these islands will take place after the conclusion of a Peace Treaty between the Soviet Union and Japan."[49] The Amami Islands are already Japanese, while the USSR made only a promise of returning the islands of Habomai and Shikotan after the conclusion of a formal peace treaty in which Japan would have to grant her formal recognition of the annexation of other much more important Kurile Islands and Southern Sakhalin. This Japan refused to do; these two islands remain in Soviet hands.

Khrushchev reaffirmed this position in June, 1957, but seized the opportunity of an interview with a Japanese newspaper to make one of his heavy jokes at the expense of Japanese susceptibility: ". . . if the Americans return Okinawa to you tomorrow, I shall place before our Government the proposal to return to Japan the Habomai and Shikotan Islands before the conclusion of the Peace Treaty."[50] His joke reflected perhaps his "law of the jungle": "This is the true law of the jungle—I am strong, you are weak, hence you must obey me."[51] He surely demonstrated to the Japanese the Communist relativity of values. It was impossible to give them back the islands of Iturup and Kunashir because of their strategic value to the USSR; he suggested that the United States should evacuate the all-important military base on Okinawa before the USSR's giving up of the militarily insignificant islands of Habomai and Shikotan, conveniently forgetting that America had already made an equivalent concession to Japan by the return of the Amami Islands. All this can hardly encourage Japan to become pro-Soviet, despite Japanese interest in trade with China and Russia. Trade does not necessarily mean trust or friendship.

4. Undermining NATO. Western and Soviet Bases and Troops on Foreign Territories

One of the ABC's of politics is to weaken, if not disintegrate, the enemy coalition. Therefore, the Soviet Government and press never tire of their violent denunciations of the NATO, Baghdad, and SEATO agreements. It is less understandable that the uncommitted nations join in these criticisms. Were they to look at the global problem of the balance of power, the question would take on a different hue. A disintegration of Western alliances would remove the main prop from under their non-commitment policy. Could they therefore defend, by themselves, their neutrality policy in the face of the dynamic Soviet-Chinese bloc without being able to rely implicitly on the stabilizing counterbalance provided by the West's unified front?

Former Prime Minister Malenkov, in his programmatic speech of August 8, 1953 (which remains important despite his downfall), hinted at the pious Soviet wish when he said:

The aggressive [Western] circles also believe that, if the North-Atlantic Bloc is being now, in a tense international situation, rent by internal struggle and contradictions, the situation might deteriorate, with the reduction of that tension, as far as the disintegration of the Bloc.[52]

Malenkov and his colleagues relied on the rule of international politics, often tested in practice, that a coalition ends with the elimination of a common foe and weakens in proportion to the fading visibility of the common danger. This is why Malenkov's era was—and the present era continues in this—one of Soviet efforts to reduce tension while refusing to make any major concessions. The conclusion of the armistices in Korea and Indochina not only helped to cut off unnecessary risks but also aided in creating a feeling of security in the non-Communist world. When Malenkov declared that "the Soviet Union has no territorial claims against any State whatsoever, including the neighboring States," he meant to reassure not only Turkey—over which had hung, since 1945–46, the Soviet claim to the provinces of Kars and Ardahan—but all the nations of the world. He further declared that the USSR was prepared to negotiate on all outstanding problems and mentioned the first steps towards a normalization of international relations: a formal note to Turkey abandoning former claims, the re-establishment of diplomatic relations with Israel, and an exchange of Ambassadors with Yugoslavia and Greece. Characteristically for the new Soviet policy, he did not spare friendly words for India; no less characteristically he said: "Our people did not shed the blood of millions of its sons and daughters during the war against militarist Germany in order to re-create this most dangerous war center in Europe."

The USSR closely watches relations among the NATO and other committed nations in order to seize any opportunity to undermine their unity through a conflict of interests.

Even an armchair strategist would realize that a Russia strong enough to participate in great Power competition and desirous of modifying the *status quo* in her favor would not be very happy about American bases, which greatly reduce the distance to Soviet targets for American bombers and long-range missiles. This will remain a first-class problem for the USSR until she acquires a sufficient stockpile of intercontinental ballistic missiles and is able to counterbalance this strategic disadvantage with equal power of retaliation against the continental United States, the arsenal of the West.

For the time being, one should not be surprised at the Soviets' indignant vituperations. But when the USSR appeals to mankind in the name of peace in her campaign against the Western military alliances and American bases abroad, she stands on weak legs. She herself provided the example of establishing bases in foreign territory, but with a rather important difference—her bases were created without the free assent of the nations concerned. She also led in building up a network of alliances directed against the Western Powers. Her moral arguments therefore do not have a persuasive ring, especially since the long record of her expansion (1939–1945), her support of civil war in Greece, her pressure on Turkey in the postwar period, her reluctance to withdraw troops from Iran, her forcible sovietization of eastern Europe, and her adventure in Korea cannot be dismissed because of the recent reassuring words of post-Stalinist leadership.

Soviet opposition to Western alliances and American bases abroad is usually expressed in the form of moralistic arguments. The West menaces the peace of the world and pursues aggressive aims, while, of course, Soviet alliances and bases abroad serve peace and have only a defensive purpose. Two quotations will illustrate this type of propaganda, which infects un-committed nations (who are seldom reminded of the Soviet military blocs and bases). An article in *Pravda* said in 1956:

The establishment of the American military bases on foreign territories does not pursue any other objectives but the preparation of an aggressive war and the imperialist expansion of the USA. . . . The American bases represent a serious threat to the peoples on whose territories they are located. . . . Millions of simple people in all countries, acting in the interest of peace and security, demand the evacuation of American armed forces from foreign lands.[53]

The declaration by the signatories of the Warsaw Pact—themselves par-ticipants in a military bloc—of January 28, 1956, detected the mote in the Western eye:

. . . the policy of building up aggressive military blocs, directed against peace-loving States, of the type of the North-Atlantic bloc, the Baghdad bloc, and the military bloc in Southeastern Asia (SEATO), not only cannot promote the settlement of divergencies of views between States but, on the contrary, intensifies those divergencies and leads to a greater irritation in relations between various countries.[54]

The Soviet picture in this, as in other cases, is all white-and-black; on the one side there are only evil, aggressive intentions, but on the other are pious and peace-loving wishes. The implications in Pavlov's teaching have certainly not been wasted on Soviet propagandists.

In 1946, Molotov said at a committee meeting of the United Nations General Assembly:

The war has ended, but the allied troops continue in certain cases to re-main on the territories of other United Nations [he had in mind principally the presence of British troops in Greece]. It is completely clear that the former reasons and causes of this [situation] have disappeared because of the passage from war to peace. If the troops of the United Nations remain, after the termination of war and more than a year after the rout of the enemy, on the territories of friendly states, this cannot be explained in the former manner. Obviously, there are other reasons. . . . It is impossible to deny that the stationing of foreign troops on the territory of a State con-stitutes an inadmissible means of pressure in the domestic affairs of that State. In some cases this presence of foreign troops pursues not only the aim of the foreign pressure in the domestic affairs of a country but is also used as a means of threatening its neighbors from outside. It is necessary to put an end to this situation.[55]

He unintentionally set a standard for evaluating Soviet policy in the same speech:

It is not permissible to act in such a manner as to apply one yardstick in certain cases and another in other cases. One must use one and the same yardstick in all cases and in relation to all states.[56]

Let us inquire whether the Soviet Government has taken its own counsel regarding foreign troops and foreign bases on the territory of other states and with regard to the question of military blocs. One need not even glance at Western sources; Soviet ones are preponderant enough to prove that the Soviet Union has never fostered (for her own use) any doctrine against military alliances, or the stationing of troops, and the possession of bases on foreign territories. Stalin indicated the two-yardstick policy of his government in an interview granted to Mr. Hugh Bailey, President of the United Press, on October 29, 1946:

Question: "How does the USSR look at the presence of British troops in Greece? . . .
Answer: "As unnecessary."
Question: "What is the size of the Russian military contingents in Poland, Hungary, Bulgaria, Yugoslavia and Austria, and how long do you believe they should remain there in the interest of securing peace?"
Answer: "In the West, that is to say, in Germany, Austria, Hungary, Bulgaria, Rumania and Poland, the USSR has at present altogether 60 divisions (infantry and armored together). . . . There are no Soviet troops in Yugoslavia. . . . In two months . . . 40 Soviet divisions will remain in those countries."[57]

With sixty divisions in eastern and central Europe and the promise of keeping forty later—without any date for withdrawal—Stalin was raising a storm about the small British contingent in Greece!

In 1921, the USSR, following in the footsteps of her predecessor, Imperial Russia, absorbed the province of Outer Mongolia, which had been part of China from time immemorial. On March 12, 1936, the Soviet Government entered into a treaty of mutual assistance (this is the term used in modern times in lieu of "alliance") with the puppet state of the People's Republic of Mongolia. This Treaty acknowledged in its Preamble that the People's Republic of Mongolia owed its existence to Soviet military intervention since 1921: "The Governments of the USSR and the Mongolian People's Republic, proceeding from the unchanging friendship that has existed between their countries since the liberation in 1921 of the territory of the Mongolian People's Republic thanks to the support of the Red Army. . . ."[58] A recent Soviet source openly concedes Soviet military intervention in Outer Mongolia at the time this province was detached from China: "The People's Government of Mongolia asked on July 12, 1921, the Council of People's Commissars of the RSFSR not to withdraw the detachments of the Soviet Army from Mongolia for as long as the external danger was not eliminated; the Soviet Government acceded to this request."[59]

Article 1 of the 1936 treaty formulated the *casus foederis* against any outside Power: "The Governments of the USSR and the Mongolian People's Republic are obliged, in case of a military attack against either party, to help one another with all means, including military assistance."[60] This alliance was at that time directed against China, the former sovereign in Outer Mongolia and a "semi-colonial nation," as a Communist would say, and Japan, then overlord of Manchuria, Inner Mongolia, and northern China.

The Treaty of 1936 was replaced on February 27, 1946, by another agreement. Article 2 of the 1946 treaty stated: "The Governments of the USSR and the Mongolian People's Republic shall be bound, in case of a military attack against either of the High Contracting Parties, to provide each other every assistance, including military."[61] Article 3 is very interesting because of the Soviet "reluctance" to keep her troops on foreign territory:

The Governments of the USSR and the Mongolian People's Republic consider it self-evident that the troops of one of the Parties, which remain by mutual agreement on the territory of the other Party in consequence of carrying out the obligations resulting from Articles 1 or 2 [of the present Treaty], shall be withdrawn without delay after the disappearance of the cause [of their presence].[62]

There is a strong suspicion that the cause of the presence of Soviet troops in Mongolia has not yet disappeared. This treaty remains in force (it was originally concluded for ten years but had to remain valid until 1966 if not denounced before; it has not yet been denounced). While the Treaty concluded in 1936 was directed against Japan and "semi-colonial" Nationalist China, its replacement of 1946 had in view only China (Japan being defeated in 1945). At present, its point is directed against another ally of the USSR, Communist China, as a healthy reminder that the Soviet Union maintains her interest in Outer Mongolia.

Before the last war, the USSR had also concluded (in 1935) treaties of mutual assistance with France and Czechoslovakia, but these lost meaning when the Munich agreement was signed. Soviet co-operation with Nazi Germany brought treaties of mutual assistance with the Baltic States, which dared not reject this Soviet suggestion after having seen Soviet troops deployed in eastern Poland. These treaties are worth recalling because of the later history of Soviet-Baltic relations. The first treaty to be signed was that with Estonia. Its Preamble stated: ". . . In order to re-enforce their friendly relations, initiated by the Peace Treaty of February 2, 1920, and founded on the recognition of their independent statehood and on the non-interference in the domestic affairs of each other." Article 5 supported this statement: "The enforcement of the present pact must not infringe in any way upon the sovereign rights of the Contracting Parties, in particular upon their economic system and constitutional regime."[63]

The Soviet-Latvian treaty of mutual assistance, signed on October 5, 1939, repeated the same assurances, both in the Preamble, and in Article 5, which was even more precise, mentioning, in addition, the intangibility of the social (not just the constitutional and economic) systems of the contracting parties.[64] The Latvians received an additional assurance, in the form of a joint communiqué, on October 6, 1939, which predicted safe and peaceful co-existence between the two states:

Having placed the Pact of mutual assistance on the foundation of firm provisions of their Peace Treaty and Non-Aggression Treaty, both Parties have again reaffirmed their unconditional recognition of the sovereign rights of either State, and of the principle of non-interference in domestic affairs of the other Party. Having been convinced by many years of experience that the differences in the constitutional regimes of the two countries have been no obstacle for a fruitful co-operation between them, each Party declares that it shall, in the new conditions created by the Pact of mutual assistance, always be guided by respect for the constitutional, social and economic structure of the other Party.[65]

The Soviet-Lithuanian treaty of mutual assistance, which was signed on October 10, 1939, contained identical provisions in its Preamble and Article 7.[66] Barely seven months later, this peaceful co-existence, founded on non-interference in domestic affairs and respect for national independence, was suddenly ended with the wholesale annexation of all three Baltic States. Finland was asked in October, 1939, to sign a similar pact, refused to do so, and the USSR did not insist, demanding only territorial cessions and the establishment of a Soviet base on the Finnish territory. As we have said, Turkey and Bulgaria declined (in September-October, 1939) the Soviet invitation to accept similar treaties of mutual assistance.

We may omit a discussion of the Soviet Union's World War II treaties of mutual assistance with Britain and France, which were denounced in May, 1955, in response to the British-French assent to West German rearmament and which became politically obsolete anyway. In 1943, the USSR began building her own network of treaty alliances in eastern Europe, which she treated as a future zone of influence. The first such treaty was signed with Czechoslovakia on December 12, 1943, although a third ally, Great Britain, notified both parties that she would prefer an adjournment of the signature until after the armistice with Germany.[67] This first treaty, concluded for the wartime and the postwar periods, was soon followed by several others, and together they covered the entire eastern European zone of Soviet influence. Article 4 is worth quoting in view of the events of 1948, which reduced Czechoslovakia to the status of a Communist satellite:

The High Contracting Parties, taking into consideration the interests of security of both of them, agree to maintain a close and friendly co-operation in the period following the restoration of peace and to act in accordance with the principles of mutual respect for their independence and sovereignty, and of non-interference in the domestic affairs of the other State.[68]

On April 21, 1945, before the USSR, the United States, and Britain had time to carry out the agreement concluded at Yalta in February of the same year (concerning the establishment of a Polish Government to be recognized by all three of them), the Soviet Government created a *fait accompli* by signing a treaty of mutual assistance with the Communist-controlled Polish Provisional Government in Soviet-occupied Warsaw. It was concluded for twenty years, with an automatic proviso for renewal every five years thereafter. Article 2 sounded rather ironical, even in the conditions of 1945: "The High Contracting Parties . . . shall strengthen the friendly co-operation between both countries in accordance with the principle of mutual respect for their independence and sovereignty and of non-interference in the domestic affairs of the other State."[69]

On April 11, 1945, Yugoslavia signed a similar treaty of mutual assistance.[70] Strangely enough, it was the only treaty concluded in eastern Europe which did not contain a provision concerning non-interference in domestic affairs. However, Soviet interference was one of the reasons for the rift between the two countries in 1948. Practically identical treaties were signed with other satellites—Bulgaria, Rumania, and Hungary. Article 2 of the Rumanian-Soviet Treaty (signed on February 4, 1948) made it even more clear that these treaties were directed not only against a renewal of German aggression but also against other states, presumably the Western Powers:

In a case where either of the High Contracting Parties is involved in hostilities with Germany, attempting to renew her aggressive policy, or with any other State which directly or in any other form would combine with Germany in an aggressive policy, the other High Contracting Party immediately shall provide to the High Contracting Party involved in hostilities, military and other assistance with all the means at its disposal.[71]

Article 2 of the Soviet-Hungarian Treaty of February 18, 1948, and Article 2 of the Soviet-Bulgarian Treaty of March 18, 1948,[72] reproduced, almost literally, the same provision, mentioning other states besides Germany.

Which German policy (not necessarily an armed action) would be aggressive and thus call for Soviet military action? When could a third state, say the United States or Britain, be accused of espousing such a policy? It would probably be the right of the stronger ally to provide the answer to these crucial questions. The treaties do not say that the alliance would be applied in case of an armed attack by Germany or a third state, but they do use the all-embracing formula of one of the parties being involved in hostilities. A state may be involved in hostilities after having attacked another state, as was Germany in 1939. At any rate, Molotov was inexact when he told American Ambassador Walter Bedell Smith on May 9, 1948: ". . . all the mutual assistance treaties concluded by the Soviet Union with Eastern-European countries as well as with England and France aim at preventing a new German aggression and are not directed against any allied State whatsoever."[73] He hardly reassured Smith when he proclaimed, in the same conversation, a sort of Soviet Monroe Doctrine for Europe:

As is known, the United States of America follows the policy of strengthening its relations with neighboring States, for example, Canada and Mexico, and also with other American countries. This is fully understandable. It is equally understandable that the Soviet Union also pursues a policy of

strengthening its relations with neighboring and other European countries.[74]

Whatever Molotov had in mind, his mentioning "other" European countries sounded rather ominous in 1948.

A Soviet memorandum to the United States, the United Kingdom,
France, Belgium, Holland, Luxemburg, and Canada at the conclusion of
the North Atlantic Treaty in 1949 stated:

All the treaties of friendship and mutual assistance between the USSR and
the countries of people's democracy have a bilateral character and are directed only against a repetition of German aggression. . . . Moreover, any
interpretation that those treaties are directed to any extent against the
last-war allies of the USSR, the United States, Great Britain, or France, is
entirely excluded.[75]

The mention of third states other than Germany was not erased by protestations.

Stalin was not satisfied in tying all the satellites to the militant Russian
chariot. On February 22, 1948, he asked the President of Finland to conclude a treaty of mutual assistance with the USSR.[76] Finland had to agree
but was able to obtain a very different treaty which obliged her only to
defend her own territory in case of aggression against the USSR by a third
state and only if that state should try to use Finnish territory.[77] By granting
this treaty, unusual in Soviet practice, Stalin had assented implicitly to
the Finnish policy of non-commitment a long time before the USSR began
to favor that policy for all non-Communist states. He may have feared that
the armed language he used in talking to the Finns in 1939 would this time
involve him in a war with the West; he also wanted to reassure another
uncommitted state—Sweden. The Soviet-Finnish Treaty was signed on
February 4, 1948, and was extended in 1955 for another twenty years.

Treaties with satellite countries were concluded for twenty years, with
automatic and indefinite renewals for five-year periods thereafter.[78] When
the Soviet-Hungarian Treaty was signed, Molotov could say with satisfaction: "With the conclusion of this Treaty the Soviet Union will have pacts
of friendship and mutual assistance with all the States on its Western
frontier, from the Black Sea to the Baltic Sea."[79] Could he be legitimately
surprised that the western European Powers answered by concluding, in
1948, the Brussels Treaty of Mutual Assistance or that the United States,
Canada, and several European Powers concluded, in 1949, the North Atlantic Treaty?

Turning from the Black and Baltic seas to the Pacific area, one discovers that the USSR followed the same policy of establishing treaties of mutual assistance or, in Soviet parlance, building up military blocs. One may overlook the Soviet-Chinese Nationalist Treaty of August, 1945 (a mutual assistance treaty), because it was directed against a common enemy, Japan, and had but a very short life. After the victory of the Chinese Communists, however, the USSR hastened to sign a treaty of alliance with the People's Republic of China. It was concluded on February 14, 1950, several months before Communist aggression in Korea and several years before the United States signed the SEATO Pact. The initiative in building military blocs continued to be dominated by the Soviets in both Europe and Asia.

The Soviet-Chinese Communist Treaty stated in Article 1 that it was directed against Japan and any other third state: ". . . in a case where either of the High Contracting Parties becomes the object of an attack by Japan or by a State allied to Japan, and is thus placed in a state of war, the other Contracting Party immediately shall provide military and other assistance by all the means at its disposal."[80] This agreement was concluded for thirty years and was to be renewed for five-year periods thereafter if not denounced.

The European treaties were crowned, rather than replaced, by the Warsaw Treaty. It is well to remember this fact because the Soviet Government has frequently offered to barter the Warsaw Treaty for the North Atlantic Treaty and to replace both by an all-European security agreement, but never did the Soviets mention that they would cancel the bilateral treaties concluded between 1943 and 1948.

The Warsaw Treaty of May 14, 1955, formally added two more partners to the Soviet European network of alliances: East Germany and Albania. Communist China was represented at the Warsaw conference and promised its support. This Treaty combined the forces of the USSR, Albania, Bulgaria, Hungary, East Germany, Poland, Rumania, and Czechoslovakia into one military bloc. While the Western blocs were denounced as a threat to the peace and an imperialist venture, the Warsaw Treaty signatories expressed the belief that "the success of the present conference will promote a further rallying of peace-loving countries and peoples, and will significantly help in strengthening world peace and security in Europe and in the whole world."[81]

The very first Article of the Warsaw Treaty evokes mixed feelings in view of Soviet intervention in Hungary against a government that refused to obey Moscow: "The Contracting Parties undertake the obligation, in accordance with the United Nations Charter, to refrain in their international relations from the threat or use of force."[82] Article 4 defined the *casus foederis* as an armed attack in Europe against one of the parties by a third state; the other parties would then be obliged to give immediate assistance. Article 5 placed the armed forces of the signatories under a unified High Command; this Article actually ratified, *ex post facto*, an existing fact. Soviet Marshal I. Konev was appointed Commander in Chief of the combined forces. Article 5 probably served as a basis for later secret agreements concerning the stationing of Soviet troops on territories of other signatories: "They will take other measures agreed upon which will be indispensable for strengthening their defense capacity."[83] Article 6 created a joint Political Consultative Committee in which all of the signatories were represented. The Treaty is formally open for the adhesion of other states, but, like the North Atlantic Treaty, it makes such adhesion conditional on the assent of the signatories. It is thus a closed bloc. Its period of validity is twenty years, but it will be extended for an additional ten years if not denounced. Such denunciation cannot take place, in fact, without Soviet agreement, as was pertinently proved by the tragic consequences of the Hungarian denunciation of November, 1956.

The declaration of the Chinese delegate at the Warsaw Conference and the comments by the Chinese press that followed the signature of the Warsaw Treaty made it clear that one should regard the Warsaw bloc, connected with China through the Soviet-Chinese alliance, as a single military camp extending from the Elbe to the Pacific coasts of both the USSR and China.

Peace is indivisible, *Dagunbao* stresses, and the interests of the Chinese people cannot be separated from those of the European peoples. The same newspaper points out the declaration by Piu De Khuaia at the Warsaw Conference that, if European peace is violated and the imperialist aggressors unleash a war, then "our Government and our 600-million-strong, heroic people will, jointly with the Governments and peoples of our fraternal countries, wage a struggle against aggression until the final victory"; this declaration expresses the will and decision of the Chinese people.[84]

Thus the Soviet Union, before the Western Powers had time to provide a similar answer, had built up her own military bloc from the frontiers of Greece to the Baltic Sea and from the River Elbe to her Pacific coast. Those listening to the Soviet diatribes against military blocs could well have reminded the Soviet propagandists of this historical fact.

The USSR was reluctant neither to station her troops on foreign territories nor to establish her military bases there. She actually set an example
for the United States as far as the Eastern Hemisphere was concerned. The
nations which offered their territories for American bases have not yet lost
their independence, nor have they been forced to adopt a democratic form
of government if they had some other kind. The Soviet story, however, is a
different one.

In the early Leninist period of Soviet history, a "semi-colonial" country,
Iran, was compelled to accept a treaty with Russia which gave the latter
the right to station her troops on Iranian territory if she felt threatened
by a third power. There might be a cause-and-effect relation between the
signing of that treaty and the presence of Soviet troops in the Persian
Caspian Sea province of Ghilan. Those troops entered Iranian territory in
hot pursuit of White Russian detachments during the civil war but remained there until the treaty was signed. It was concluded on February 26,
1921, and is still in force. (The Iranian Government denounced Article 6
of the Treaty on March 2, 1959. However, this Article remains in force as
far as the USSR is concerned.) Article 4 says: "Recognizing the right of
each people freely to settle its political fate, both High Contracting Parties
renounce . . . interference in the internal affairs of each other."[85] This
solemn pledge neither prevented the USSR from promoting the activities
of the subversive Tudeh Party in the Soviet-occupied part of Iran nor did
it prevent the USSR from encouraging the separatist movements of the
Persian Azerbaijanis and Kurds during the later part of the last war.

The crux of the Soviet-Iranian Treaty is Article 6:

Both High Contracting Parties agree that, if any third country were to try,
through an armed intervention, to pursue an annexionist policy on the
territory of Persia, or to use this territory as a base for military action
against Russia, if this menaced the frontiers of the RSFSR or of Powers allied to the RSFSR, and if the Persian government, after a warning from
the Russian government, were unable to eliminate such a threat, the Russian Soviet government shall have the right to introduce its troops into the
territory of Persia in order to take necessary measures of self-defense. The
Russian Soviet government shall immediately withdraw its troops from
the territory of Persia after the elimination of danger.[86]

This article has been hanging over Iranian heads ever since the Treaty
became effective. The crucial question of just what action by a third power
would menace the USSR and justify the entry of the Soviet troops will
always depend on the convenience and strength of the USSR as compared

with that of other great Powers. Weak Iran had nothing to say on the matter in 1941 when the USSR invoked this article to occupy the country jointly with Britain. In spite of the infiltration of German influence into Iran, the fact remains that both great Powers put an end—by force—to the neutrality of a small nation and thus opened mutual communications across the territory of a "semi-colonial" country. Britain at least kept her promise and withdrew her troops soon after the war; the USSR at first refused to do so, tried to use the delay for the promotion of separatist movements in Northern Iran, and eventually recalled her troops at the price of an oil concession. After the conclusion by Iran and the United States of an agreement on military assistance in 1947, *Tass* published an official communiqué on April 4, 1948, in which the Iranian Government was accused of following a policy contrary to the Soviet-Iranian treaty of February 26, 1921.[87] When Iran adhered to the Baghdad Pact, Soviet protests mentioned only the Soviet-Iranian friendship treaty of 1927, but that treaty had expressly reaffirmed the Treaty of 1921. Thus the Soviet right to move troops into Iran has been used in attempts to frighten Iran; it is an obvious Soviet mortgage on Iranian sovereignty.

As recently as 1957, a Soviet journal specializing in Eastern affairs reminded Iran of her ominous mortgage:

The Soviet-Iranian negotiations were concluded on February 26, 1921, by the signature of the Treaty. The Iranian Government took the obligation not to allow the stationing on its territory of the armed forces of States hostile to Soviet Russia, and Russia received the right to introduce in future her armed forces into Iran in order to liquidate the threat of intervention in case Iran were unable by her own forces to protect her independence.[88]

If the Iranian Government has been free to follow an independent policy this has been due to Soviet fear of a conflict with the Western Powers.

The year 1939 allowed the Soviet Government fully to display its own convictions concerning bases on foreign territory. The Soviet-Estonian mutual assistance treaty of September 28, 1939, contained the following in Article 3:

The Estonian Republic grants to the Soviet Union the right to possess naval bases and military airfields on the Estonian Islands of Saavemaa (Ezel) and Hiyumaa (Dago), and in the city of Paldiski (Baltic Port). . . . The USSR has the right to keep in the areas, reserved for bases and airfields, at its own expense, strictly limited numbers of Soviet land and air armed forces in order to protect those naval bases and military airfields.[89]

The Soviet-Latvian Treaty of October 5, 1939, stated in Article 3:

In order to assure the security of the USSR and to strengthen its own independence, the Latvian Republic grants to the Soviet Union the right to possess naval bases and several military airfields in the cities of Liepaia (Libava) and Ventspils (Vindava). . . . To protect the Irben Bay the Soviet Union is granted the right . . . to build up a coastal artillery base on the coast between Ventspils and Pitragas. In order to protect its naval bases, airfields and coastal artillery base, the Soviet Union has the right to keep, at its own expense, strictly limited numbers of Soviet land and air armed forces in the areas reserved for those bases and airfields.[90]

Finally, the Soviet-Lithuanian Treaty of October 10, 1939, stated in Article 4:

The Soviet Union and the Lithuanian Republic undertake the obligation jointly to defend the state frontiers of Lithuania. Hence the Soviet Union is granted the right to keep within the Lithuanian Republic, at places mutually agreed upon, strictly limited numbers of Soviet land and air armed forces.[91]

This defense of the frontiers and the independence of the Baltic States ended in their incorporation within the territory of the protecting Power.

One of the causes of the 1939–40 Soviet-Finnish War was the Finnish refusal to grant to the Soviet Union a naval base on the peninsula of Hangö. The Soviet Union imposed this concession on Finland in the ensuing peace treaty of March, 1940. The peace treaty with Finland concluded in 1947 replaced this base with another, at Porkalla-Udd, which was to be leased for fifty years. Finland was also compelled to grant to the Soviet Union the unhampered use of Finnish territory for the maintenance of transportation and communication lines between the USSR and the Soviet base. The USSR withdrew from that base in January, 1956.

The end of hostilities found Soviet troops in eastern Europe. Molotov conceded, in a speech made on March 10, 1950, that these troops were a factor in imposing a Communist regime on several nations in this area:

Look towards the West, beyond the frontiers of the USSR. There arose and were consolidated the states of people's democracy—in Poland, Czechoslovakia, Hungary, Rumania, Bulgaria and Albania. They arose in the wake of the military rout of Fascism in Europe and thanks to the assistance provided by the Soviet Army to the peoples of those countries in their task of national and social liberation.[92]

For a time, these troops remained for two official reasons: to assure the security of Soviet military communications with East Germany and as occupying forces in former enemy states. The first reason is still invoked against Poland, but the 1947 peace treaties with Rumania, Hungary, and Bulgaria provided for the evacuation of Soviet troops within three months after the treaties became effective (Article 21 of the Treaty with Rumania, Article 22 of the Treaty with Hungary, and Article 20 of the Treaty with Bulgaria). While the Bulgarian Treaty provided for unconditional withdrawal, the Rumanian and the Hungarian treaties delayed this evacuation for a period needed by the USSR to secure its communications with Soviet troops in occupied Austria. The treaty with Austria in 1955 removed this particular reason, yet Soviet troops remained in both Hungary and Rumania.

At the present time, Soviet troops are stationed in East Germany, Poland, Rumania, and Hungary. Marshal G. K. Zhukov acknowledged this in 1957: "The presence of Soviet troops on the territories of the Rumanian People's Republic as well as of the German Democratic Republic, Hungary and Poland, is founded on the Warsaw Treaty and is caused by the need of guaranteeing the security of the whole socialist camp."[93] Only at the insistence of the Polish Government did the USSR negotiate, in December, 1956, its first formal agreement concerning the stationing of its troops and their legal status. This treaty was followed by others that were practically identical. There arises the question of the legal basis for the presence of Soviet troops on territories of those several states before December, 1956, when the Polish-Soviet treaty was signed. The public text of the Warsaw Treaty does not mention this particular problem anywhere.

Were secret agreements concluded to this effect? The Soviet Government's Declaration of October 31, 1956, conceded the existence of such unpublished agreements in the case of Hungary and Rumania: "It is known that Soviet troops are stationed in the Hungarian and Rumanian Republics in accordance with the Warsaw Treaty and the governmental agreements."[94] Those agreements, probably also concluded with Poland, must have been highly unsatisfactory if the Polish Government gave, after the October days, the highest priority to the question of concluding a more precise agreement. That such Soviet troops did not refrain from interfering in the domestic affairs of the countries concerned is borne out by more than the Hungarian events. The Polish Communist periodical *Nowe Drogi*, reporting on the debates of the 8th Plenum of the Party Central Committee held during the fateful October days (when a delegation of Soviet leaders suddenly descended on Warsaw to impose on Polish Communists the retention of Soviet Marshal K. Rokossovsky in their Political Bureau) related such an exchange:

Comrade Starewicz: . . . today, at the time of difficult and extremely serious conversations with the delegation of the Communist Party of the Soviet Union, movements of troops towards Warsaw have been taking place in our country. . . . A few columns of tanks have been advancing on Warsaw; there have been some maneuvers of certain Soviet detachments on our Western frontier, and inside the country in the area of Wroclaw. Hence I would like to ask comrade Marshal Rokossovsky [then still the commander-in-chief of the Polish and Soviet troops in Poland] what has been the purpose of these movements of troops? Secondly, on the basis of whose decisions have these movements taken place?[95]

Three other members of the Central Committee pressed the same questions. Eventually, Marshal Rokossovsky replied:

The Soviet troops have been advancing indeed. . . . These troops have been advancing in the direction of Bydgoszcz and Lodz. At the instruction of the Political Bureau [of the Polish Party] I have requested Marshal Konev [the commander-in-chief of all the Warsaw Bloc troops], who has directed those maneuvers, to stop the advance eastward of the troops of the Northern group and to order their return to the garrisons of their permanent location. This is all I know.[96]

He, as well as his impatient audience, knew something else: namely that a further advance on Warsaw would have resulted in a full-scale resistance by the workers of Warsaw and probably the Polish troops as well. The Soviet delegation in Warsaw decided not to assume this risk.

The Polish-Soviet Treaty of December 17, 1956, is interesting, not only in what it says, but also in what it leaves undefined. Article 2 left for future agreements such important matters as the numerical strength of Soviet troops in Poland and their exact location. Articles 15 and 16 did the same in regard to questions of troop transportation routes and dates, the amount of payments due to Poland for the transportation of Soviet troops and equipment, the rates of customs duties due, and the definition of the right to import or export currencies by Soviet military personnel and their families. Article 9 conceded to Polish courts the jurisdiction over the military and civilians who were members of the Soviet military personnel in Poland, but with one important reservation, namely, that crimes committed while on duty would belong to the jurisdiction of Soviet courts-martial. Article 10 equated crimes committed by Polish citizens against Soviet troops or their members with crimes committed against Polish troops or their members but left such crimes to Polish jurisdiction. Article 18 defined the meaning of the Soviet troops' "places of garrisons" as the territory reserved for their use, including training fields, shooting ranges, etc. The Treaty was concluded for the duration of the stationing of Soviet troops in Poland—thus for an indefinite time—and cannot be terminated except by mutual agreement (Article 21).[97]

The treaty concluded with East Germany on March 13, 1957, follows closely the Polish pattern except for Article 18, which clearly allows Soviet troops to quell any disturbances:

In case of a threat to the security of Soviet troops stationed on the territory of the German Democratic Republic, the High Command of Soviet troops in the German Democratic Republic may take measures to eliminate such a threat, while simultaneously consulting the Government of the German Democratic Republic, and taking into consideration the actual situation and steps taken by the authorities of the German Democratic Republic.[98]

This Article is drafted in such a way that it allows for immediate Soviet military intervention without preliminary German Communist assent. Nevertheless, the East German Government gave this its unreserved blessing in the Preamble, which says: ". . . stationing of Soviet troops on the territory of the German Democratic Republic is indispensable."[99] One of the signatories of the Treaty, Marshal Zhukov, thus explained the reasons for the Soviet military presence:

Insofar as the Soviet people and the Soviet Armed Forces are concerned, we very well remember the lessons of the past war and will never forget the sacrifices we suffered in the struggle against imperialists and fascists. The stationing of Soviet troops on German territory is at the present time dictated by the need of guaranteeing the security of our whole socialist camp.[100]

Having personally signed this agreement and that with Poland, Zhukov, then chief military expert of the Soviet bloc, denounced bases on foreign territory and military blocs: "The toilers of all countries need . . . neither foreign military bases on their native soil nor military blocs."[101]

Treaties drafted in terms practically identical with those of the Soviet-Polish Treaty were signed on April 15, 1957, with Rumania,[102] and on

May 27, 1957, with Hungary.[103] The Soviet-Hungarian Treaty, signed by Foreign Minister A. Gromyko and Marshal G. Zhukov, contained a curious Article 1, which made strange reading after the 1956 intervention:

The temporary presence of Soviet troops on the territory of the Hungarian People's Republic does not in any way infringe on the sovereignty of the Hungarian State. The Soviet troops do not interfere in domestic matters of the Hungarian People's Republic.[104]

The Soviet Government announced on May 24, 1958, on the occasion of a meeting of the Warsaw Treaty Political Consultative Committee, that it intended to withdraw its troops from Rumania in the near future. Assuming that the troops would be completely withdrawn (there are practically no means for outsiders to check on movements of troops in eastern Europe), this move does not mean at all that the USSR would henceforth rely less on its army to enforce obedience in its colonial protectorates. A glance at the map would show that Soviet troops in the Soviet Union and Hungary encircle Rumania and could quickly move in at the first sign of anti-Communist or anti-Russian disorders. The geographical situation will now make it even more imperative for the Soviet troops to remain in Hungary in order to keep a close watch on Czechoslovakia and Rumania.

Bold in the assent given by the United States and Britain in the Yalta Far Eastern Agreement, the USSR imposed on Nationalist China in 1945 the lease of a naval base at Port Arthur, a lease held before the Japanese War of 1904 by the Imperial Government of Russia. After the Chinese Civil War, Stalin extorted from his new allies a confirmation of this lease in an agreement on February 14, 1950. He was, however, clever enough to be ready to make a delayed concession to a China allied to Russia. The agreement provided for the evacuation of Port Arthur, either after the conclusion of a peace treaty with Japan or no later than the end of 1952, but the naval base could again be used by Soviet armed forces in a war by Japan or a third power against China or the USSR. The promised evacuation was delayed, by mutual agreement in 1952, until the conclusion of the peace treaty with Japan. Probably both parties then considered that the Korean War made the presence of Soviet forces in Port Arthur desirable. After the conclusion of the Korean armistice, the two governments agreed, in 1954, on Soviet evacuation of Port Arthur, which actually took place in 1955, ten years after their taking over this Chinese harbor. The foregoing record makes one a little doubtful about the Soviet moralistic vituperations against American bases.

5. Underdeveloped Countries—the Main Battlefield

The prospects of a Communist revolution in Europe being dim and hopes for the disintegration of NATO being faint, Soviet foreign policy must concentrate on extra-European countries in the attempt to weaken the capitalist camp as a whole and the Western Powers in particular. The Soviets exploit conflicts of interests among non-Communist nations and devote the utmost attention to underdeveloped areas as the weak links in the imperialist chain. This is, at present, their most vital objective. The author of an article on peaceful co-existence states some of the conditions which he deems propitious for the Soviet policy as follows:

The development of antagonisms between metropolitan territories and the colonies has acquired a new character in contemporary conditions; it consists in the disintegration of the colonial system of imperialism. . . . The question of the complete liquidation of the shameful system of colonialism has been placed on the current agenda as one of the most acute and fateful problems. The peoples of the East, which had played an important role in the development of human civilization but which later fell under the yoke of imperialism, are in the process of regeneration. These peoples take an increasingly more active part in decisions concerning the fate of the whole world. . . . The disintegration of the colonial system of imperialism means the loss by the monopolies of an important source of profits. This leads not only to a weakening of the general position of capitalism and of the aggressive forces that it generates, but imperialism loses the opportunity of manoeuvering and overcoming difficulties at the expense of colonial countries. It looses markets, spheres of investment, and millions of colonial slaves on whose sufferings and bones the wealth of multi-millionaires was built up. Imperialism loses the opportunity to receive cheaply military-strategic raw materials.[105]

This quotation is interesting, but not because of its diagnosis, which can be easily turned upside down. Actually, the political emancipation of former colonial possessions may become a firm foundation for other and much better relations between them and the Western Powers once colonialism, the source of their former national antagonism, has been removed. Their economic development may, for one thing, greatly increase the size of the international market. One hardly follows the Soviet author in his opinion that independent states would suddenly cease to sell raw materials or would refuse foreign investments or assistance in various modern forms (grants, governmental and private loans, or private investments) which they sorely need. Taking the long view, one may just as well come to the opposite conclusion, viz., that future relations between the former colonial nations and the West would develop on a much healthier, a much more friendly basis than that which characterized the colonial period.

The important points in the above quotation, reflecting current Soviet views, are of a divergent nature. First, hostility against Western nations is openly stated, and this gives a peculiar flavor to the slogan of peaceful co-existence with the same nations. Second, the significance of the "revolution" going on in the underdeveloped areas is fully understood by watchful Soviet authorities, their clear intention being to exploit it to the utmost in order to divide the capitalist camp.

One must precede the discussion of Soviet and general Communist policies towards the underdeveloped areas by an analysis of the Communist concepts regarding nationality, the colonial and semi-colonial countries, the principle of self-determination, and kindred subjects. The Communist doctrine on these lines is well developed. Lenin fathered this secular gospel, which is just as flexibly relativist as Communist morality and has great practical potentiality.

CHAPTER VIII

COMMUNIST NATIONALITY DOCTRINE

1. Definitions

L ENIN'S WRITINGS on politics are, on the whole, clear and logical, but the same cannot be said of his views on nationalism. Having been born in a multi-national Russian state, itself a colonial great Power, he observed the animosities dividing Russians from Russian-controlled nationalities. The phenomenon of nationalism was as familiar to Lenin as to any other eastern European, yet the problem bothered him, for he believed sincerely in the empty words of the *Communist Manifesto*—that the proletarians had no fatherland, lived in chains beside their exploiting capitalist countrymen, and should follow, in their own vital interest, not their national preferences and dislikes but the *Manifesto:* "Proletarians of all countries, unite!"

The universal revolution was the only thing that really interested Lenin; the problem of nationalism, although real, was a nuisance that diverted the proletarians from the main task of overthrowing the bourgeoisie. Something had to be done about it in order to assure proletarian international solidarity. He was torn between contradictory emotions—between his abhorrence of Russian nationalism, together with his shame of Tsarist Russian oppression of other nationalities, and his definite preference for large economic units, a preference that would leave Russian territory intact, even after the Bolshevik Revolution. He was also torn between his aversion to the exploitation of one nationality by another (with consequent recognition of the right of all nationalities to self-determination, including secession) and his suspicion of nationalism of the oppressed nationalities subversive of proletarian internationalism; between his fanatical concentration on one social problem (that of universal revolution against capitalism) and, for him, the subordinate problem of national self-determination; between his recognition that large economic units should not be disrupted and his practical urge to exploit, for the benefit of revolution, conflicts between nationalities of the colonial and semi-colonial countries on the one hand and nationalities controlling colonial empires on the other.

Lenin's doctrine of nationalities was therefore not exempt from contradictions, which were finally resolved by deft application of his moral yardstick. Granted that the cause of revolution was the supreme standard of moral judgment, Lenin was entitled to deduce highly relativist conclusions concerning the nationality problem. A national struggle directed against a capitalist state was to be supported by the Communists because it tended to weaken the imperialist chain. A similar movement against the socialist state, however, was to be looked upon as a crime against the revolution. This relativist theory, fully developed by Stalin and very convenient for the Russians after the October Revolution, has remained firmly entrenched in the minds of successive Soviet leaders.

It is appropriate here to recall Khrushchev's words of February 18, 1957 (a year after his devastating attack on Stalin):

Our Party has criticized Stalin for those mistakes and shortcomings against which V. I. Lenin had already come out and which manifested themselves especially in the last years of Stalin's life. But Stalin, with whom we worked, was an outstanding revolutionary. . . . [After referring to the rout of Party enemies, the building of a mighty socialist State, and the victory in the last war, Khrushchev continued.] This great victory was achieved under the leadership of our Party and its Central Committee headed by comrade Stalin. Stalin devotedly served the interests of the working class and the cause of Marxism-Leninism; we shall not surrender Stalin to our enemies.[1]

Stalin's views are important because he was the Party's expert on nationalism; he was appointed Commissar for Nationalities after the 1917 revolution. It was he, not Lenin, who provided the basic definitions for Party use. He defined "nation" in his early dissertation *Marxism and the National Problem*, which was written in 1912–1913, as follows:

A nation is, first of all, a community, a definite community of people. This community is neither racial nor tribal. How does the national community differ from the state community? Among other things, because a national community is inconceivable without a common language, while a common language is not indispensable for the state community. . . . Thus *community of language* is one of the characteristics of a nation . . . There is no nation which would use simultaneously different languages, but this does not entail that there cannot be two nations speaking the same language. . . . Nations arise only in consequence of long and regular mutual relations [among their members], and a lengthy common life is impossible without a common territory. . . . Thus, *community of territory* is another characteristic feature of a nation. . . . Community of territory does not by itself make a nation. This requires moreover mutual economic ties which unite particular parts of a nation into a whole. . . . Thus, *community of economic ties, the economic community*, is another characteristic particularity of a nation. . . . Nations differ from each other not only by the conditions of their life but also by their spiritual outlook which is expressed in the peculiarities of national culture. . . . Thus, *community of the psychological complex*, which manifests itself in the community of culture, is another characteristic feature of a nation. . . . A nation is a stable human community, arising through a historical process and on the basis of community of language, territory, economic ties, and mentality expressed in a common culture. . . . It is necessary to underline that not one of the above mentioned characteristics, taken separately, is sufficient for the definition of a nation. Moreover, the absence of one of them is enough to make a nation cease to be a nation.[2]

A specialist on nationality could easily quarrel with this definition; for instance the Swiss certainly constitute not only one state but only one nationality, yet they speak four languages. Nevertheless, it is amazing that Stalin (who was no scholar) was able to disengage the principal features of a nation—common language, common territory, and common mentality and culture—although he added, as a Marxist, still another one: the economic community. He was wrong in requiring the simultaneous presence of all of these characteristics in a nation according to his definition, but no one has, as yet, found a truly satisfying and all-embracing definition of this real but elusive phenomenon. Stalin's definition expressly excluded the Jews as a nationality.[3] Lenin held the same view. This opinion allowed both Stalin and his successors to refuse Soviet Jews facilities for the free cultivation of their culture; such refusal was a step toward a policy that was, in effect if not in intention, anti-Semitic.

Stalin, as ruler of a multi-national state, had good reason to believe that nations were not an ephemeral phenomenon: "It is known that nations and national languages have a remarkable stability and a colossal power of resistance to a policy of assimilation."[4] The Marxist-Leninist dream that nations will disappear as separate entities sometime after the world revolution continues to be mentioned, but probably without conviction:

Marxism-Leninism teaches that nations are not eternal categories. In the future, when the socialist revolution vanquishes the whole world, not only will national isolation be destroyed but nations will merge into one nation. This merger may take place only in definite historical circumstances, namely in conditions of highly-developed Communist society triumphant on a world scale. But a period of existence and development of peoples within the framework of independent, sovereign, national or multi-national, socialist states, with the conditions of life, culture and language peculiar to the people of each nationality, lies on the road of mankind towards the merger of nations.[5]

This implicit recognition that the nationality problem will remain vital for quite some time has a practical significance; it prompts the Soviet Government to be on guard against nationalism within the USSR and to exploit it abroad at the expense of other countries.

Soviet writers see very clearly the simultaneous existence in our time of two contradictory tendencies: the trend towards large economic units, which offer the advantage of a large domestic market and are thus able to develop more quickly, and the irresistible tendency of various nationalities to form their own states, usually through the process of splitting off from large economic units, the multi-national states or colonial empires. These writers must, of course, deny the existence of such a contradiction within the multi-national Soviet state and limit the problem to capitalist states, but they know only too well that the aspiration to independent statehood could become a disruptive factor for the USSR. They say:

The development of capitalism has disclosed two tendencies which are irreconcilable in capitalistic conditions. The first is the trend towards the internationalization of the means of production and exchange, the destruction of national self-sufficiency, the economic *rapprochement* of nations, and the progressive unification of immense territories into a compact whole. . . . [This process] has been and remains progressive, because it prepares the material pre-conditions of a future socialist world economy. . . . The economic unification of territories under capitalism has been and is taking place through a forcible subjection of some nations to others. . . . All this violence and oppression have evoked in the popular masses a second trend towards "the destruction of forcible forms of this unification." Hence the struggle for the liberation of oppressed colonies and dependent nationalities from the imperialist oppression has been growing in strength. Insofar as this second trend means the rebellion of oppressed masses against the imperialist forms of unification, insofar as it demands the unification of nations on the basis of co-operation and free union, it has been and remains a progressive trend.[6]

Of course, as we shall see, the same trend towards national self-assertion is reactionary if it affects the Russian dominions.

2. Division of Nations into Exploiting and Exploited

Lenin's most significant contribution to the problem of nationalities was his division of mankind into oppressing and oppressed nations, un-Marxist but politically all important for the current Soviet policy. Karl Marx, who was interested in revolutions in the highly developed industrial countries, divided every nation into two mutually hostile domestic camps, capitalist and proletarian, while Lenin superimposed his division of whole nations into two groups. Writing in 1907, he said: "Imperialism is an epoch of the increasing oppression of nations of the whole world by a handful of 'Great' Powers; thus the struggle for the socialist international revolution against imperialism is impossible without the recognition of the right of nations to self-determination."[7] He repeated this idea in his famous *Imperialism, the Last Stage of Capitalism*, which was written ten years later:

As has been proved in this booklet, capitalism singled out a small group (less than one-tenth of the world population, and by the most "generous" and exaggerated account, less than one-fifth) of the wealthiest and most powerful states which rob the whole world simply by clipping coupons. . . . The world has been divided into a small group of States-usurers and the gigantic majority of States-debtors. . . . Hilferding correctly points out the connection between imperialism and the aggravation of national oppression: "Concerning the newly-discovered countries," he writes, "the imported capital intensifies antagonisms and provokes steadily-growing resistance against the newcomers on the part of peoples who are awakening to national consciousness; this resistance may easily grow into dangerous actions directed against foreign capital. . . . The capital itself slowly gives the ways and means of emancipation to the conquered. And they advance towards the same goal which the European nations once considered as supreme—the formation of a national state as a tool of economic and cultural freedom."[8]

Lenin did not forget this division after the October Revolution. He said in a speech in 1920:

I told the 3rd Congress of the Communist International that the whole world was divided into oppressed and ruling nations. The oppressed nations represent no less than 70 per cent of the whole world population. . . . We act now indeed as the representatives not only of proletarians of all countries but also of the oppressed peoples. The journal of the Communist International recently appeared with the headline: "Peoples of the East." The Communist International has issued the following slogan for the peoples of the East: "Proletarians of all countries and the oppressed peoples, unite!" One of the comrades asked: "Since when has the Communist International had the power to change slogans?" I cannot truly remember it. Of course, from the point of view of the Communist Manifesto this [slogan] is incorrect, but the Communist Manifesto was written under completely different circumstances; from the point of view of the present policy this slogan is correct. The conditions have changed . . . all of Asia is boiling up.[9]

The same year, addressing the Comintern Congress and commenting on the theses adopted by that Congress with respect to national and colonial problems, he said:

First of all, what is the most important and fundamental idea in our theses? The distinction between the oppressed and the oppressing peoples. . . . This idea of making a distinction between, and of dividing peoples into oppressing and oppressed, permeates all the theses.[10]

Lenin, who had good reasons to feel a little disappointed in the lack of vigorous revolutionary enthusiasm among the Western workers, went so far in his division of mankind into the oppressing and oppressed nations that he even included part of the Western proletariat in his concept of exploiting nations. Writing in 1907, he said:

The extensive colonial policy has resulted in a situation where the European proletariat *partly* finds itself in a condition where the whole [European] society is subsisting *not* on its labor but on the labor of almost enslaved colonial natives. For instance, the English bourgeoisie derives more income from the tens and hundreds of millions of the population of India and other colonies than from the English workers. A material and economic base is being formed, under those conditions, in certain countries for contaminating the proletariat with colonial chauvinism.[11]

Stalin faithfully interpreted this Leninist concept when he envisaged one front of struggle against the imperialist West, a front composed of the Communist parties (the proletarians) and the national movements in the colonial and semi-colonial countries:

Leninism is founded on the following theses concerning the settlement of national question: a. the world is divided into two camps: the camp of a small group of civilized nations which possess financial capital and which exploit the immense majority of the world population, and the camp of the oppressed and exploited peoples in the colonies and dependent countries which represent this majority; b. the colonies and dependent countries, which are exploited and oppressed by financial capital, represent an immense reserve and a serious source of strength for imperialism; c. the revolutionary struggle of oppressed peoples in the dependent and colonial countries against imperialism is the only way for their liberation from oppression and exploitation; d. the more important colonial and dependent countries have already entered this road of a national-liberating movement which cannot but result in a crisis of universal capitalism; e. the interests of the proletarian movement in the developed countries and of the national-liberating movement in the colonies require a unification of these two aspects of revolutionary movement into one front opposing the common foe, imperialism; f. the victory of the working class in the developed countries and the liberation of the oppressed peoples from the imperialist yoke are impossible without the establishment and consolidation of a common revolutionary front.[12]

Both Lenin and Stalin thought of this common front as a line of attack against industrialized Western countries. Of course the emancipation of most of the colonies during and after the last war was not a welcome event, since it reduced the prospects of a common-front struggle. However, it would be risky to dismiss this Leninist-Stalinist concept as obsolete, for it has acquired new meaning for the Communists in its division of the independent nations into those that are wealthy and those that are underprivileged. The latter nations are considered a vast reserve for the anti-Western front built up by the Soviet-Chinese bloc. The importance of glaring difference in the distribution of wealth between the two types of nations is not overlooked in modern Soviet sources: "The division of nations into oppressing and oppressed is most important and fundamental from the point of view of international relations in the era of imperialism. . . . During that era the national-colonial question becomes a part of the general question of proletarian revolution."[13]

To support the colonial movements directed against the Western Powers or to espouse all possible grievances of the underdeveloped countries is simple and easy. It does not cost a penny and is an investment in the struggle against the West. But both Lenin and his successors have had to face a much more difficult question of national movements which were or could be directed against a Communist state. To proclaim, without reservations, the principle of national self-determination could possibly result in the disintegration of a multi-national socialist state and in a weakening of the revolutionary front. Lenin was rescued here by his relativist morality. If the cause of the revolution was the supreme standard, it was logical to make a distinction.

An eminently practical politician, Lenin demonstrated a peculiar blind-

ness in believing that the mere fact of a Communist revolution would automatically solve national problems and eliminate all possible sources of
national friction. If the cause of all social evils, private ownership of the
means of production, were uprooted, why should any national animosities
survive? This simplicist Marxist view led Lenin to endorse, after the Bolshevik Revolution, a largely forcible reunification of the former Tsarist
empire into a single Soviet state. For him, this state was not the successor
of Imperial Russia but the predecessor of a world Soviet Republic in which
all nationalities would be free and equal. For his successors, it became the
tool of Russian oppression in the name of welfare and might of the socialist
state. When Lenin invited the Social Democrats (future Communists)
representing various nationalities of the Tsarist empire to combat the
separatist trends (while he and his Russian colleagues fought against Russian chauvinism), he did not realize that he unconsciously promoted the
idea of an indivisible Russia.

3. Relativist Theory of National Self-determination

Lenin's relativist concept of national self-determination was formed
very early in his career. Writing in 1903, he said:

We have included in the Party draft program the demand for a Republic
with a democratic constitution which would guarantee, among other things,
"the recognition of the right to self-determination for all nations which
are component parts of the State." . . . But this unconditional acceptance
of the struggle for a free self-determination does not compel us by any
means to support every demand for national self-determination. . . . We
must *subordinate* the demands for national self-determination to the interest of [class struggle of the proletariat]. . . . Russian Social-Democracy
does not tie up its hands at all. It reckons with all possibilities, even with
all theoretical conjectures, when it includes in its program the recognition
of the right of nations to self-determination.[14]

Later he said:

We demand the freedom of self-determination, i.e., independence, i.e., the
freedom of secession, for the oppressed nations not because we dream of an
economic parcelling out [of big States] or of an ideal of small States, but
on the contrary because we want big States, and a *rapprochement*, even a
merger of nations on a truly democratic and internationalist basis which
is inconceivable without the freedom of secession.[15]

He believed, rather naïvely, that the proletarians of various nationalities
emancipated by the socialist revolution could be safely granted the right

of national self-determination, since they would be inspired by a mutual brotherly love: "The more a democratic regime of a State nears the full freedom of secession, less frequent and weaker will be in practice the trend towards secession, because the advantages of big States from the standpoint of economic progress and of the interests of the masses are beyond any doubt."[16]

In this respect, Lenin relied on the enlightening propaganda of the Social Democratic parties representing the oppressed nationalities: ". . . the socialists of the oppressed nations should in particular defend and realize a full and unconditional unity, including the organizational, of the workers of oppressed nations together with those of oppressing nationalities."[17]

Thus Lenin was led to make a subtle distinction between the theoretical right of secession and its practical application, which should be refused by the conscious proletarians of oppressed nationalities. Little wonder, then, that the Polish moderate socialists, who wanted full independence for their country, suspected him of Russian hypocrisy and rejected his idea: "The conscious workers do not preach secession; they know the advantages of big States and of the unification of large masses of workers."[18] His relativist creed, which was to become so expedient for his Russian disciples, was summed up in 1913:

The question of the right of nations to self-determination (i.e., to a completely free and democratic procedure of resolving the problem of secession, to be guaranteed by the state constitution) should not be confused with the problem of expediency of secession by a particular nation. The latter problem must be decided by the Social-Democratic Party in each particular case (completely independently of other cases) from the point of view of the whole social development and of the class struggle of the proletariat for socialism.[19]

This pragmatic viewpoint, combined with his identification of Communists with the proletariat and the toiling masses, led Lenin, after the October Revolution, to use the Red Army to dissuade the various nationalities of the former Russian Empire from seceding from the new Soviet state. He said bluntly on January 20, 1918: "But no Marxist, without flying in the face of the principles of Marxism and of Socialism generally, can deny that the interests of Socialism are higher than the interests of the right of nations to self-determination."[20]

In 1919, Lenin deduced a practical conclusion for Soviet Russia from his own teaching, namely that all the nationalities of the former Russian

Empire should stand fast in the hope that other nations of the world would join them later, eventually forming the world Soviet Republic: "We strive for a close unity and a full merger of the workers and peasants of all nations of the world into one World Soviet Republic."[21] It is no wonder, then, that he disclosed an open hostility towards those Communists who wanted to avail themselves of the right of national self-determination and who would thereby weaken the Russian foundation of the future World Republic:

If a Ukrainian Communist insists on an unconditional State independence of Ukraine, he may be suspected of defending such a policy not from the point of view of temporary interests of the Ukrainian workers and peasants in their struggle against the capitalist yoke, but because of his petty-bourgeois and petty-peasant national superstitions. The experience has proved a hundred times to us that the petty-bourgeois socialists of various countries, that mixture of Polish, Latvian, Lithuanian, and Georgian pseudo-socialist Mensheviks, Social-Revolutionaries and their kind, have disguised themselves as defenders of the proletariat with the sole aim fraudulently to smuggle in a policy of co-operation with "their" bourgeoisie against the revolutionary workers.[22]

This language, employed by the head of a government which could use the Red Army to enforce its views, was hardly encouraging for the self-determination and secession of various nationalities of the former Empire.

Lenin thought that his early policy of recognizing the independence of border nationalities would convince these nationalities of the new Russian rulers' sincerity in desiring to treat them all as equals of the Russians; he trusted they would understand this and refuse the offer of secession. He said in 1919:

It is precisely through recognition of the independence of the Polish, Lithuanian, Estonian, and Finnish states that we slowly but surely win the trust of the most backward toiling masses in the minuscule states who are mostly misled by their capitalists. In this manner we sever these masses more effectively from the influence of "their" national capitalists, and lead them more truly towards a full trust [in us] and towards the future single international Soviet Republic.[23]

Frustrated in these hopes, he later used other more convincing arguments to lead the recalcitrant nationalities back to the common fold. He viewed the Communists of various nationalities as a cementing force of the Soviet multi-national state and therefore flatly refused to consider the existence of several distinct national parties and organizations:

The interests of the working class demand the merger of workers of all nationalities of Russia into unified proletarian organizations, political, professional, co-operative, educational, etc. Only such a merger into the unified organizations of workers of various nationalities provides the proletariat with an opportunity of waging a victorious struggle against international capital and bourgeois nationalism.[24]

However, this single party, with monopoly of political power, was to make the federal structure of the USSR a mere illusion.

Lenin's definite preference for big states and his hopes for a universal Soviet Republic made him follow a policy of salvaging the integrity of the former Russian territory, a policy which he did not think of as resembling the colonial policy, which he detested and denounced. That which was still lacking—later to be supplied by Stalin—was Russian nationalistic motivation. However, the Leninist concept could excuse anything, and it provided a pretext for Stalin and his successors in suppressing national aspirations of the non-Russian nationalities of the USSR. Leninist theory could excuse the annexation of any satellite country of eastern Europe, just as it condoned the annexation of the Baltic nations. The Chinese Communists did not betray Lenin when they forcibly annexed Tibet. Actually, the Leninist theory could, against the intentions of its founder, serve as a cloak for any imperialist expansion of a Communist great Power if one large socialist state were deemed better than a multitude of small ones.

Stalin followed Lenin's relativist doctrine of self-determination, but he put it in a slightly cruder form:

The question of the *right* of nations to free secession has been impermissibly confused with that of the *necessity* of secession by a nation at a given time. The latter question must be decided by the Party of the proletariat completely independently in each particular case and only in the light of actual circumstances. Conceding the right of the oppressed nationalities to secession, the right to decide their own fate, we do not solve thereby the other question as to whether this or another nation *should* secede at a given moment from the Russian State. . . . We remain, therefore, free to agitate for or against secession depending on the interests of the proletariat and of the proletarian revolution.[25]

These words were pronounced on April 29, 1917, at a time when Stalin and other Bolsheviks decided to seize power in Russia and when he could foresee the problem that would face the Party in a multi-national Soviet state. After the Revolution, he repeated (in 1918):

The nationality problem is not a self-contained question with [its component elements] given once forever. Being only a part of the general question of transformation of the existing order, the nationality problem is entirely determined by the conditions of a given social situation, by the nature of the government in any given country, and, generally, by the whole process of social development.[26]

He gave an even more pragmatical turn to this concept when he said in 1921:

. . . central Russia is in no position to maintain her military and economic power without fuel, raw materials and agricultural assistance of the border territories.[27]

Therefore, the border nationalities had to be persuaded, by the Red Army if necessary, not to invoke their right to self-determination or, as Stalin said in 1920:

Of course, the border territories of Russia and the nations and tribes on those territories, like all other nations, have an inalienable right to secede from Russia. . . . But the interest of the popular masses tells us that the demand of secession in the border territories is deeply counter-revolutionary at the present stage of the revolution.[28]

In 1922, he justified the Soviet military offensive undertaken in 1920 in a vain attempt to make Poland a Soviet republic by appealing to the relativist theory:

. . . the right of self-determination cannot and should not hinder the realization of the right of the working class to its own dictatorship. The former must make room for the latter. Such was, for instance, the situation in 1920 when we were compelled to march on Warsaw in the interest of the defense of power of the working class.[29]

He formulated another aspect of the question just as clearly: "We must support every [national] movement directed against imperialism."[30]

A contemporary historian of the early Soviet period justifies the Bolshevik refusal to accept the claim to secession of the border areas in the same Stalinist terms:

Central Russia, center of world revolution, would have been unable to survive without the assistance of the border territories abundant in raw materials, fuel resources, and foodstuffs. The working class of Russia could not have consolidated the dictatorship of the proletariat in its own country without the assistance of the toiling masses of national border territories.[31]

The *Soviet Great Encyclopedia* has enshrined the same relativist theory:

This postulate [the right of national self-determination, including seces-
sion] must not be confused with the question of expediency of secession of
one or another nation. The Party looks in each particular case at the question of a nation's secession from the point of view of promoting the revolutionary struggle of the proletariat.[32]

And a contemporary Soviet writer upholds the same point of view:

It is necessary to reckon with the actual historical conditions at the time
of application of the slogan of national self-determination. . . . One must
examine the practical question of realization of the right of nations to
free secession from the point of view of interests of the working class and
of the proletarian revolution. The construction of socialism in the Soviet
Union required, not the secession but the unification of various peoples
in one multi-national State.[33]

The disruptive weapon of national self-determination should therefore
be used only against the capitalist states; when and how it should be used
is a question of practical politics. Thus the Indian Communists did not
hesitate to benefit by the support they gave to the aspirations of various
linguistic groups in India, and they hold this weapon in reserve lest the
foreign policy of the Congress Party become less friendly to the USSR.
Bulganin and Khrushchev, in speeches during their visit to India in November-December, 1955, were careful to leave the hands of Indian Communists free in this respect. They alternately referred to the Indian people
as if they recognized only one Indian nationality and to the Indian multi-
national state as if each linguistic group were a separate nationality.[34]
R. P. Dutt, a British Communist, wrote in *India Today* at a time when
the Soviet-Indian relations left much to be desired:

Unity of the Indian people in their struggle for freedom against imperialism does not mean that the Indian people must, therefore, be regarded as
a single homogeneous whole. On the contrary, there are strong grounds for
recognizing the multi-national character of the Indian people. . . . The
free [he meant Communist] India of tomorrow might take the form of a
federation or union of autonomous States of the various nationalities such
as the Pathans, Punjabis, Sindhis, Hindustanis, Rajasthanis, Gujeratis,
Bengalis, Assames, Biharis, Oriyas, Andhras, Tamils, Kamadigas, Maharas-
trians, etc. . . . Every section of the Indian people which has a contiguous
territory, has its common historical tradition, common language, culture,
psychological makeup and common economic life, would be recognized as
having a just claim to play its part within a free India as a distinct na-

tionality, with the right to exist as an autonomous State if it so wishes within the free Indian Union or Federation, including the right to secede.[35]

The Third Indian Communist Party Congress pledged its support (in December of 1953 and January of 1954) to the constitution of linguistic provinces, which, in their understanding, were to be nationality provinces.

The relativist view leads the USSR towards the worst type of political opportunism at the expense of the principle of national self-determination, not only in its nationality policy at home, but also in relation to the under-developed countries. In 1945, Stalin had no qualms of conscience in asking for a Soviet trusteeship over Tripolitania, although this would have placed the USSR in a position dangerously close to that of a colonial Power. His urge for making the USSR a Mediterranean Power proved to be stronger than the anti-colonialist slogans. V. M. Molotov publicly conceded on September 19, 1945, at a press conference in London that his government had asked for that trusteeship: *"Question:* 'Would you care to tell us your opinion concerning the news in the *New York Herald Tribune* about the request by the Soviet Union relating to Tripolitania?' *Answer:* 'There is a grain of truth in this news.' "[36] Later, after the Western refusal to consider a Soviet trusteeship in North Africa, Molotov melancholically concluded the whole affair on May 28, 1946: "We have not insisted any longer that Tripolitania be placed for several years under a trusteeship to be exercised by the Soviet Union alone or jointly with Italy, although this would have had great importance for the Soviet merchant ships traveling in the Mediterranean Sea."[37]

Molotov mentioned the alternate proposal made after the failure to get trusteeship for the Soviet Union alone. The Soviet Government then became generous towards the Italian Government, in which the Communists still participated at the time, and offered to it a joint trusteeship. When this proposal failed, the subsequent suggestion was to leave all Italian colonies in Africa to Italy, probably because she was the weakest among the Western Powers. This diplomatic move ignored completely not only national self-determination but the fact that the Italians were not particularly liked, especially in Libya. The existence of this suggestion is conceded in an official Soviet publication which says that V. A. Zorin, then Deputy Minister for Foreign Affairs, informed, on February 14, 1948, the Italian Ambassador to Moscow of the proposal (made by the Soviet Government in May, 1946, at the meeting of the Council of Foreign Ministers) to place all former Italian colonies in Africa (Libya, Eritrea, and Italian Somaliland) under an Italian trusteeship and told him that this proposal remained standing in 1948.[38] Despite this Soviet plan, Libya became independent, Eritrea was federated with another underdeveloped country, Abyssinia; only Italian Somaliland was temporarily placed under an Italian trusteeship.

Another illustration of the relativism of views regarding the underdeveloped countries is provided by a comparison of two opinions expressed by Soviet sources concerning the nature of the presence of British troops in Egypt. An official Soviet publication, referring to events of the last war, said in 1948:

Did the English Government act correctly in stationing during the war its troops in Egypt, disregarding Egyptian protests and even the resistance of some elements in Egypt? Absolutely yes. This was the most important means in stopping the march of Hitlerite aggression in the direction of the Suez Canal. . . . Only enemies of democracy or crazy people may claim that those acts of the English Government represented an aggression.[39]

But a recent Soviet booklet on Egypt published in 1956 takes a different view: "Lawlessness of the English colonial troops in Egypt, their cruel terror and provocations, intensified the hatred of the Egyptian people against the colonizers."[40] For the Egyptians the presence of British troops was equally obnoxious before, during, and after the last war. From the Soviet Union's point of view, one fact made the whole difference—the USSR was allied to Britain during the last war but not before or after.

CHAPTER IX

COMMUNIST DOCTRINE OF UNDERDEVELOPED COUNTRIES

1. Communist View of the Awakening of the Under-developed Countries

AN ANALYSIS of Soviet policy towards the economically underdeveloped countries requires, first of all, a clarification of terminology. Soviet sources seldom refer to these countries as economically underdeveloped, although their economic and social problems are fully understood. Until recently, they preferred (and sometimes prefer at present) to call them the colonial and semi-colonial, or the colonial and dependent, countries; they now refer to them frequently by their individual names or by the collective name of a geographical area (the Near East, Southeast Asia, Latin America, etc., or the East, a term which embraces not only Asia, including the Near East, but also Africa). To the Soviets, a colonial country is, as for us, a country governed by a foreign Power. A semi-colonial or dependent country is a country that is politically independent but economically dependent on Western assistance, loans, investments, and trade. Practically all economically underdeveloped countries with non-Communist regimes are, in this sense, classed as dependent countries. Of course, the proletariat, the toiling masses, and the progressive people are terms that are used, generally speaking, not in their direct sense but as synonyms for Communists and their ardent sympathizers.

One must also remember that Leninists think in terms of class relations. For them, therefore, international relations are part of a bigger picture of class relations on a world scale. There is a permanent fund of Soviet thought on the underdeveloped areas that goes back to Lenin, but there is also a temporary ideational fund of only passing value for a given historical situation. With alterations in the Soviet view of the outside world, these terms acquire accommodating meanings.

One must pay tribute to the political genius of Lenin for his early understanding of the emergent changes in the economically backward countries. What is now a commonplace for all of us was not a commonplace for Lenin's generation. His contemporaries were fully aware of national movements in Europe but paid scarcely any attention to the same problem— already growing—in non-European countries. Lenin detected this new trend well before 1914 and foresaw that it would bring about a revolutionary change in the relations between the industrialized West and the non-industrialized majority of mankind. He was therefore naturally led to speculate on how the revolutionary socialist cause might benefit from this new international phenomenon. Was a conflict of interests to divide the West from the rest of humankind? If so, could not the revolutionary proletarians, like himself, promote the revolution by exploiting those conflicts and making common cause with the national emancipation movements in the underdeveloped countries? Was it possible to build one anti-Western front from two disparate materials—the Communists and the non-Communist nationalists of the underdeveloped countries? Of course Lenin was confronted with an international situation that was largely different from that of the present. There were, it is true, independent states that were economically underdeveloped—as they are today—and they had their quarrels with the Western Powers, but the main problem was that of colonial peoples ruled by one or another Western Power.

Writing in 1916, before the October Revolution, Lenin noted the link between the problem of revolution in Europe and the question of recruiting allies in the colonial areas of the time:

We shall make every possible effort to come closer to and unite with Mongols, Persians, Indians, and Egyptians; we believe that it is our duty and also *our interest* to do so, because socialism in Europe would not otherwise become solidly rooted.[1]

In his famous speech made in 1919 at the Second All-Russian Congress of the Communist organizations of Eastern peoples he said:

We know that the popular masses of the East will rise as autonomous participants in and creators of a new life, because hundreds of millions of those populations belong to nations which are dependent, deprived of equality of rights, have been until now the object of international politics, and have existed only as fertilizers for capitalist culture and civilization.... This majority [of the world population], who had remained until now completely outside the historical progress because they could not act as an independent revolutionary force, ceased, as we know, to play a passive role at the beginning of the 20th century. . . . During the contemporary revolution, the period of the awakening of the East will be followed by a period of participation by all peoples of the East in the settlement of the fate of the whole world. . . . The peoples of the East are awakening in order to act practically and to make every nation decide the problem of the fate of all mankind.[2]

The Manifesto of the Second Comintern Congress of August 8, 1920, reflected Lenin's ideas:

The working people of the colonial and semi-colonial countries have awakened . . . all this is transforming the growing army of the colonial insurrection into a great historical force, into a mighty reserve for the world proletariat. The pariahs are rising.[3]

The Fourth Comintern Congress (also held in Lenin's lifetime) issued, in November, 1922, theses on the Eastern question with a correct diagnosis of the then colonial aspirations: "The chief task which is common to all national-revolutionary movements is to bring out national unity and achieve political independence."[4] In his draft of theses on national and colonial problems, which he submitted in 1920 to the Second Comintern Congress, Lenin sized up the depth and susceptibility of colonial nationalism born out of foreign rule and disclosed his own contemptuous condescension for those feelings in this way:

The age-old oppression of colonial and weak nationalities by the imperialist powers has left behind among the toiling masses of the oppressed countries not only bitterness but also a distrust towards the oppressing nations in general and towards the proletariat of the latter nations in particular . . . the more a country is backward, the stronger are the petty-agricultural modes of production, patriarchy and remoteness, which unavoidably result in great strength and stubbornness of superstitions, deepest among the petty-bourgeoisie, superstitions of national egoism and national narrow-mindedness. . . . Hence the conscious communist proletariat of all countries must take a particularly cautious understanding attitude towards the survivals of national feelings among the most oppressed countries and nationalities, and make concessions in order quicker to eliminate this distrust and superstition.[5]

This lesson, which is certainly useful for anyone dealing with former colonial nationalities, has not been lost on Lenin's disciples. One need only read Soviet speeches made on the occasion of visits to such countries or watch the red-carpet receptions reserved for their representatives to realize that the USSR is making a great effort to show the utmost respect for the touchy national feelings of countries that have known foreign rule. Unfortunately, the Soviets do not display the same respect for similar feelings in eastern Europeans. Khrushchev demonstrated in his speech in Burma in 1955 how one should talk to former colonial populations that are highly sensitive to a foreign superiority complex: "Are not the Burmese as gifted as are the Russians or the Englishmen? Nations are not divided into gifted and incapable. If one provides them with equal opportunity, all of them will be successful in their development."[6]

N. A. Mukhitdinov, then an alternate member of the ruling Presidium of the Soviet Party Central Committee, a man who seems to devote much attention to the Asian problems, perhaps because of his Uzbek descent, almost used Lenin's very words in describing the processes going on in Asia: "Peoples of the foreign East and of the whole of Asia live through a stormy period of their history. A mighty national-liberating movement has been taking place in the whole colonial world. One after the other, countries have liberated themselves from colonial dependence and achieved their national independence and sovereignty."[7] The Soviet press devotes much of its space to what is called "the disintegration of the colonial system." One of the prominent Soviet Orientalists, E. Zhukov, writes, for instance:

The process of the disintegration of the colonial system has taken on at present gigantic dimensions. The population of the colonies and dependent countries numbered in 1939, on the eve of the Second World War, about one and a half billion people, i.e., approximately 66 per cent of the whole world population. 1,200 million people overthrew during the last decade the yoke of colonial oppression. The world of colonial slavery has radically shrunk. About 200 to 250 million people, i.e., 9 per cent of the world population still remain colonial slaves of imperialism. This simple juxtaposition of the two figures, 1.5 billion and 250 millions, discloses the scale of the crumbling of the colonial system.[8]

He explains in another article the global figure of 1,200 million people who have become independent by including in it the 600 million Chinese because of their revolution.[9]

Such articles show that the Soviet Union is fully aware of the deep change taking place on the international stage. Naturally, Soviet authors never mention the fact that the withdrawal of the colonial Powers has been taking place not only because of the awakening of colonial peoples but also because of free recognition of this fact by the colonial Powers, nor do they mention that this withdrawal has proceeded, with but few exceptions, by peaceful understanding between the colonial people and the colonial Power.

The fact remains that Lenin's forecast is coming true in our generation. It is of paramount interest to the Western countries, forced to fight the main battle against the Soviet-Chinese bloc in the underdeveloped countries, to understand with sympathy the deep processes of transformation taking place there. Except for Communist phraseology, the following picture is close to truth:

The 19th century passed under the sign of mastery of industrial countries of Europe and the United States of America. . . . The present 20th century has all the reasons for becoming the century of the rise of Asian and African countries, of the progressive liquidation of their economic backwardness, of their liberation from foreign domination, of their industrialization, and of the blossoming of their national culture.[10]

One can foresee the time when the relative power of the present industrialized countries, Western and USSR, will decrease because of the growth of the economic potential in several underdeveloped countries, to mention only China and India, while the voice of these countries in international affairs is bound to be much weightier in a few decades than it is now. The USSR endeavors to swim ahead of the historic wave.

2. Common Front against the West

A colonial population is separated from the colonial Power by natural antagonism. A former colonial country may continue to nourish anti-colonial resentments; an independent but economically underdeveloped country may still have some outstanding accounts to settle with the former colonial Power, or it may simply feel, rather strongly, its economic inferiority and be disappointed in the Western response to its urgent problems. Here is fertile ground to exploit for the benefit of Communism, and Lenin saw this very clearly. Where there are two forces antagonistic to the West—the Communists and the national movements in the colonial and semi-colonial countries—they should combine against the common foe. Accordingly, Lenin's government addressed, on December 3, 1917, a passionate appeal to the Moslems of Russia and the East (actually, it was addressed to the non-Moslem colonial and dependent populations as well).

It ended by saying: "Moslems of the East, Persians, Turks, Arabs, and Hindus. . . . We inscribe the liberation of the oppressed peoples of the world on our banners."[11] Stalin aptly summed up Leninist thought on this matter in 1921:

If Europe and America may be called the front-line, the stage of principal battles between socialism and imperialism, the semi-independent nations and colonies, with their raw materials, agricultural products and immense manpower, should be acknowledged as a hinterland, the reserves of imperialism. In order to win a war, it is necessary not only to win victories on the front, but also to revolutionize the hinterland and the reserves of the enemy. This is why the victory of the world proletarian revolution may be assured only where the proletariat knows how to combine its own revolutionary struggle with the liberating movement of the toiling masses in the semi-independent nations and the colonies, against imperialists and for the dictatorship of the proletariat.[12]

In his celebrated lectures on the foundations of Leninism (delivered in 1924), Stalin listed among the various antagonisms rending the capitalist world that between "a handful of ruling 'civilized' nations and the hundreds of millions of the colonial and dependent countries of the world."[13] He continued:

. . . all this . . . has split up the world population into two camps, the handful of "leading" capitalist countries which exploit and oppress vast colonial and dependent countries, and the immense majority of colonial and dependent countries which are compelled to wage a struggle for emancipation from imperialist oppression. . . . A coalition of the proletarian revolution in Europe with the colonial revolution in the East within one world front of the revolution against the world front of imperialism is unavoidable. . . . The question is as follows: are the revolutionary possibilities existing in the womb of the revolutionary-liberating movement of the oppressed countries exhausted or not? If not exhausted, are there hope and reason for making use of these possibilities for the benefit of the proletarian revolution, for transforming the dependent and colonial countries from a reserve of the imperialist bourgeoisie into a reserve, an ally of the revolutionary proletariat? Leninism answers affirmatively those questions.[14]

Does this sound much different from what *Kommunist* had to say in 1957? While listing the factors which make time work for the final victory of Communism, it said: "Lenin's prophecy has been fulfilled—the immense East has [awakened]. . . . The importance of these gigantic reserves is very great for the outcome of world competition."[15] The very word "reserves" conveys the meaning of the role assigned to the underdeveloped areas; their conflicts with the Western nations should hasten the final Communist victory. Their problems are not viewed in themselves but only as issues placed within the framework of a gigantic struggle against the West.

Since Lenin's time the elements of the question have changed greatly. Not only has the Communist army grown immensely in strength, but the nature of the "colonial reserves" has been profoundly modified. Lenin thought in categories of colonial armed insurrections; his modern disciples face the same problem, but as a minor aspect of the large question of underdeveloped countries. The main aspect consists of Soviet relations with newly independent countries. It is interesting, therefore, to see the modern classification of the underdeveloped countries, since each category requires a different approach and handling:

At the present time one can find the following types of countries in Asia and Africa (looking at them from the point of view of the particularities of their internal development and the task which confronts them): 1. Eastern countries which belong to the socialist camp; 2. Eastern countries which have won their independence, pursue their own independent policy, are free of enslaving economic agreements, and do not participate in aggressive blocs; 3. countries which are politically independent but which are entangled in the net of enslaving economic and military-political agreements that have been imposed on them; 4. countries which still remain colonies of the imperialist powers.[16]

In the third category, which embraces the countries committed to the West, the object of Soviet endeavors is and will remain to win these countries over to a non-commitment policy. A. A. Guber says this in so many words: "It is entirely self-evident that the inclusion of this or that country within one of the types characteristic for the period of disintegration of the colonial system is not immutable and given for all time."[17]

Lenin, as we have said, thought mainly in terms of colonial uprisings. In 1916 he wrote: "The Socialists should not only demand an unconditional, gratuitous and immediate liberation of the colonies. . . . The Socialists should also . . . assist in their revolts and in their revolutionary wars *against* the imperialist powers which oppress those countries. . . . The national wars of colonies and semi-colonies are not only probable but unavoidable in the period of imperialism."[18] When one recalls the armed insurrections and guerrilla wars that took place before or after the last war, one cannot deny that he was partly right in his forecast, although he grossly erred in thinking that the emancipation of colonies could be brought only by revolution or in dismissing as fraud the independence which the "imperialist" Powers could grant. In theses submitted to the Second Comintern Congress in June, 1920, he expressed those views:

> . . . the national-liberating movements of the colonies and oppressed nationalities . . . learn from bitter experience that they cannot expect any salvation except from the victory of Soviet authority over world imperialism. . . . It is necessary resolutely to explain and unmask . . . this fraud, systematically performed by the imperialist Powers, of founding States, fully dependent on them economically, financially and militarily, under the pretext of creating politically independent states. In the contemporary situation there is no salvation for the dependent and weak nations except in the Union of Soviet Republics.[19]

This skepticism concerning the peaceful parting of ways between the colonies and colonial Powers, and consequently concerning the true independence of former colonial countries, was to lead Stalin into a blind alley in the postwar years, when he stubbornly refused to acknowledge the reality of truly independent India, Burma, Indonesia, and other countries. As a result, he remained inactive in those countries, which he blindly treated as crypto-colonies.

Stalin's successors promptly corrected this error, which was originally committed by Lenin. A typical modern commentator sounds a little un-Leninist in this respect but reflects the new, much more flexible view of his government:

> The peculiar nature of the post-war situation consists . . . in the fact that a constellation of independent states have replaced the former colonies or semi-colonies (India, Indonesia, Egypt, Burma, Tunisia, Morocco, Sudan, etc.). Although the social regime is, in those countries, founded on private ownership of means of production, one should not mechanically include them within the imperialist camp hostile to socialism. . . . Is it possible to include those countries, those young independent States, which recently freed themselves from colonial oppression, which do not want to be subject to the dictates of the big imperialist States, and which desire to strengthen their political independence and at the same time achieve their economic independence? Of course not.[20]

As we see, at least a country which is not committed to the West now deserves to be called independent despite its capitalist system. However, the main problem posed by Lenin remains intact: how to use those nations against the West. Lenin formulated this question without much respect for these countries:

The dialectic of history is such that small nations, although they are powerless as an independent factor in the struggle against imperialism, play the role of one of the ferments, one of the bacilli, which help the coming onto the stage of the true force against imperialism, namely the socialist proletariat. . . . We would be very poor revolutionaries if we did not know how to make use, in the great liberating war of the proletariat for socialism, of any national movement and of any particular misfortune of imperialism, in the interest of deepening and widening the crisis.[21]

Any national movement which may be identified as having an anti-Western tinge is welcome and should be supported, whether represented by a colonial group claiming the autonomy or independence or by an independent government distrustful of the West or in process of settling accounts with a Western Power. It is a simple and eternal rule of politics that one combines, or seeks contacts, with those who happen to have some quarrel with one's principal enemy. The Comintern resolutions on the matter are not obsolete, despite the changed circumstances. Lenin advised the Second Congress of the Comintern in 1920: ". . . it is necessary to follow a policy of closest alliance between all national and colonial-liberating movements and Soviet Russia."[22] The platform of the Comintern adopted on March 4, 1919, followed the same line: "International proletarian communism will support the exploited colonial peoples in their struggle against imperialism, in order to promote the final downfall of the imperialist world system."[23] The Fourth Congress, in 1922, was very broadminded in promising support for every movement, whatever its social complexion might be:

Taking full cognizance of the fact that those who represent the national will to State independence may, because of the variety of historical circumstances, be themselves of the most varied kind, the Communist International supports every national revolutionary movement against imperialism.[24]

3. National Bourgeoisie. Fluctuations in the Appraisal of Its Role

Modern adjustment of this traditional doctrine of support for any country or movement engaged in a conflict with the West consists in two alterations, the first of which concerns terminology. The term "one front of revolutionary struggle" could arouse some suspicion in the minds of governments not wanting to be treated as pawns by the USSR. The 20th Congress very cleverly substituted a much better sounding term, a zone of peace, which, according to Khrushchev's report, was composed of the Soviet-Chinese bloc and all uncommitted nations in the East. They should be aligned for the noble purpose of defending the peace against the machinations of Western imperialists. Actually, the old wine is poured into new bottles, peace being, in the adroit Soviet terminology, merely another synonym for Soviet foreign policy objectives. The other alteration consists in a very important revision of views concerning the bourgeois (non-Communist) governments in the underdeveloped countries. Since every new approach in Soviet foreign policy must be explained in terms of classes and their mutual relations, this one cannot be fully understood without an analysis of the Soviet concept of national bourgeoisie as opposed to the comprador bourgeoisie.

Lenin knew before and after the Bolshevik Revolution that only in Europe did the socialist movement truly exist as a sizable political force. He had no choice but to look towards the bourgeoisie as a possible ally in the underdeveloped countries. He wrote in 1916: ". . . the socialists should most resolutely support the most revolutionary elements in the bourgeois-democratic national-liberating movements in these countries [colonies] . . . against the imperialist powers which oppress these countries."[25] He did not change this point of view after the Revolution. He stressed again in 1920 "the necessity for all the Communist parties to help the bourgeois-democratic liberating movements in those [colonial and semi-colonial] countries."[26] In reality, Lenin's government supported Turkey, Persia, and Afghanistan against Britain, although the governments in those countries were "bourgeois." This did not prevent him from including the underdeveloped areas within his scheme of universal revolution. He told the Second Comintern Congress in 1920: "The imperialist war [of 1914–1918] dragged the dependent peoples into universal history. Hence one of the most important of our present tasks is to think how to lay down the cornerstone of an organized Soviet movement in the non-capitalist countries."[27] He repeated this theme shortly afterwards:

We must not only form independent cadres of fighters, the party organizations, in all colonial and backward countries, not only immediately proceed there with propaganda for the organization of peasants' soviets and strive to adjust them to the precapitalist conditions, but the Communist International must adopt and theoretically justify the proposition that . . . the backward countries may pass to the Soviet regime . . . avoiding the capitalist stage of development.[28]

His teaching of making friends with the local bourgeoisie against the imperialist West and at the same time preparing the ground, through Communist organizations, for a revolution is the key to present Soviet policies, which pursue both aims.

For several years, Stalin acted according to the same pattern, founded, as he said, on ". . . the unavoidability of a coalition between the proletarian revolution in Europe and the colonial revolution in the East within one world front of the revolution against the world front of imperialism."[29] Explaining the friendly Soviet attitude towards the bourgeois governments and movements, he said:

The revolutionary character of national movement in the condition of imperialist oppression does not presume at all the necessary existence of proletarian elements in this movement, of a revolutionary republican program, or of a democratic foundation. The struggle of the Emir of Afghanistan for the independence of Afghanistan objectively is a revolutionary struggle regardless of his and his followers' monarchical views, because it weakens, disintegrates and subverts imperialism. . . . The struggle of Egyptian merchants and bourgeois intelligentsia for the independence of Egypt is for the same reasons an objectively revolutionary struggle regardless of the bourgeois descent and position of leaders of the Egyptian national movement, and irrespective of their hostility to socialism. . . . Lenin is right in saying that the national movement of the oppressed countries must be viewed not from the point of view of a formal democracy but from that of actual results within the total balance-sheet of struggle against imperialism, that is to say, "not in isolation but within a world framework."[30]

Speaking in 1927, after bitter disappointment with the Chinese Kuomintang, Stalin upheld this same thesis:

Were we right in helping Canton in China and, let us say, Angora in Turkey, as long as Canton and Angora were waging a struggle against imperialism? Yes, we were right. We were right, and we followed in Lenin's footsteps, because the struggle of Canton and Angora was dissipating the imperialist forces, was weakening and debunking those forces, and thus was making easier the task of developing the USSR, the center of the revolution.[31]

Stalin originated the present Communist division of the bourgeoisie into a section that sought to co-operate with the imperialists and a second group, the nationally minded. Speaking in 1925, he said: "With the growth of the revolutionary movement the national bourgeoisie of those [colonial and semi-colonial] countries splits into two parts: the revolutionary (petty bourgeoisie) and the opportunist (big bourgeoisie). The former continues the revolutionary struggle while the latter joins the imperialist bloc."[32] Two years later, he took a more generous view of the whole bourgeoisie in the same countries:

There where the oppression by imperialism of other countries becomes one of the factors of the revolution, this oppression must also be of concern to the national bourgeoisie; this national bourgeoisie may, at a given stage and for a given period of time, support in its country the revolutionary movement against imperialism. The national factor is there a revolutionary factor insofar as it is a factor in the struggle for liberation.[33]

In 1928, the Sixth Congress of the Comintern sounded almost like Soviet contemporary sources in dividing the bourgeoisie into the comprador and the truly national:

The national bourgeoisie in those colonial countries does not take the same position towards imperialism. A part of this bourgeoisie, in the first place the commercial bourgeoisie, directly serves the interests of the imperialist capital (the so-called *comprador* bourgeoisie). . . . The remaining part of the native bourgeoisie, in particular this part which has an interest in native industries, stands on the ground of national movement. . . . The independence of the country from imperialism corresponds to the interests of the whole colonial people and also to the interests of national bourgeoisie.[34]

So far the Soviet doctrine allowed for all sorts of accommodations with the anti-Western bourgeois politicians in the underdeveloped countries. However, the same Comintern Congress prepared the ground for a radical change in doctrine by expressing its suspicion regarding the political reliability of national bourgeoisie. Gandhi served then, and later, as a symbol. In 1928, the 6th Congress of the Comintern adopted a resolution stating that:

Trends such as Gandhism in India, thoroughly permeated with religious concepts, idealize the most backward and economically reactionary forms of existence, seeking the solution not in proletarian socialism but in a return to the most backward forms; propagandize passivity and reject class struggle. Such trends are being transformed, in the process of development of the revolution, into an openly reactionary force. Gandhism increasingly becomes an ideology directed against the revolution of popular masses. It should be the object of a resolute struggle on the part of Communists.[35]

Two Soviet Orientalists place this change of doctrine at a very early date:

The incorrect appraisal of the role of national bourgeoisie in the liberating struggle originated in the description of national bourgeoisie that I. V. Stalin had given in 1925 in his speech at the Communist University of Toilers of the East. Stalin talked in his speech about the alleged split of the Indian bourgeoisie into two groups: the conciliatory and the revolutionary. He included the most influential bourgeois layers in the conciliatory group which allegedly had already entered into a bloc with imperialism and had stood with both feet in the camp of counter-revolution. Stalin's concept was developed in the theses and resolutions adopted by the Sixth Congress of the Comintern concerning the national-colonial question. These resolutions stressed the lack of consistency of the bourgeoisie in the struggle for national independence, its tendency to ally itself with imperialists against the growing colonial revolution, and the impossibility of victory of national-colonial revolution without the hegemony of the proletariat. Precisely the Indian bourgeoisie and Gandhi, as its leading representative, received the most negative evaluations in those resolutions. ... As Kuusinen said at the 20th Congress of the C.P.S.U., these evaluations were incorrect even at the time of the adoption of the resolutions, i.e., in 1928.[36]

To be fair to Stalin, one must say that his speech of 1925 did not at all preclude his friendly attitude towards the Chinese, Turkish, Iranian, and other bourgeoisie as long as they were involved in quarrels with the West. By the time of the 6th Comintern Congress in 1928, Stalin had definitely changed his mind—after the bitter disappointment with Kuomintang. His new views were not very harmful to Soviet foreign policy until the end of the last war, there being no great opportunities for anti-Western co-operation with the native bourgeoisie. However, the appearance of newly independent states in the Near East and in Asia placed the matter on the agenda. Stalin stubbornly stuck to his guns, and the Soviet Orientalists were forced to follow his line of thought and to ignore obvious facts. Moreover, the tempo of serious Oriental studies slackened, with the result that only during the last few years has the USSR started to repair the damage and to intensify its scholarly interest in Asia and Africa.

It is possible that Stalin had some doubts in 1952 about his own approach. Two texts printed in 1952 and 1954 respectively reflect the new line and the old. The pertinent volume of the *Soviet Great Encyclopedia* said in 1954:

The peoples of the colonies and dependent countries have been convinced by their own experience that only Marxism-Leninism points out the right road towards freedom and independence, and that they can achieve the liquidation of social and national oppression and a correct solution for the national-colonial question only under the leadership of the Communist and Workers' parties.[37]

This view simply ignored the native national bourgeoisie. But a book published in 1952 could express, despite strict Stalinist censorship, an opinion diametrically opposed:

In the epoch of imperialism the national bourgeoisie can play, under certain conditions, a relatively progressive role in colonial and dependent countries, insofar as it participates in the national-liberating struggle against foreign oppression and feudal survivals. This applies in our days to the national bourgeoisie of India and some other colonial and dependent countries which fight for their national independence and state autonomy.[38]

However, this view remained isolated until Stalin's death.

Why was the criticism of Gandhi, and opinions for which it stood, harmful to Soviet interests? "The attacks on Gandhi, in which the Soviet press indulged, were in fact helpful to the imperialists who were extremely interested in making more difficult the relations between India and the USSR and in promoting mutual distrust and alienation from each other."[39] The practical reasons for the new line are stated very frankly:

Whatever may be the difference in the social and economic structure of those countries and the countries of socialist system, their struggle for peace and economic independence objectively deepens the general crisis of capitalism, leads to further disintegration of the imperialist colonial system, strengthens the positions of peace, democracy and socialism in the whole world. There lies the positive international meaning of the struggle of people in Asia and Africa which were only recently the hinterland of imperialism and which march now on the road of independent development.[40]

4. Contemporary Theory of National Bourgeoisie

The 20th Congress, with its concept of a vast zone of peace embracing the Soviet-Chinese bloc and the uncommitted nations of Asia and the Near East, spurred a fundamental revision in the appraisal of native bourgeoisie. The Soviet journal devoted to Oriental studies reserved, throughout 1956, much of its space for the castigation of mistakes committed in the Stalinist period and outlined the new Party policy. The list of past errors helps one to understand better the new approach. Both the errors and the new policy are usually illustrated by the case of India for the simple reason perhaps that she is the most important uncommitted country. Former mistakes are listed as follows: (1) the interpretation of the proclamation of Indian independence in 1947, glossed as though India became only a semicolony instead of a colony (the true source of power remained in London); (2) the thesis that the Indian bourgeoisie, represented by the Congress Party, led by Gandhi, made a deal with British imperialism and camouflaged this continued status of dependency on Britain by sham talk of independence; (3) the fact that the same interpretation was automatically extended to other newly independent nations, such as Indonesia, Burma, Ceylon, Egypt, and others; (4) the Soviet sole reliance on local Communist organizations while exaggerating their domestic influence and strength and expecting true independence from the West only after a Communist revolution (as Soviet authors put it, "We took our wishes for reality");[41] (5) the denial of the obvious fact that leadership in the struggle for independence was held in the hands of native bourgeoisie and its parties, such as the Congress Party of India, and that even the majority of industrial workers actually followed that lead but not the Communist; (6) the thesis, essentially correct, of the merger between the two revolutions (a bourgeois-democratic for ending foreign rule, and the Communist social revolution) was mistakenly extended to countries where Communist parties were too weak to assume leadership in the purely national revolution and thus were unable to transform it immediately into a Communist one; (7) the lack of effort in making more subtle distinctions among the various layers of native bourgeoisie and the writing off of all of them as hopeless in the struggle against Western influence (one of the critical articles went so far in the opposite direction that it partially rehabilitated the comprador bourgeoisie, i.e., the bourgeoisie making business with foreign firms, and claimed that the comprador bourgeois might become patriotic under the impact of the formation of a national market protected against foreign imports); (8) the thesis that co-operation with the bourgeoisie was impossible because of its philosophy (e.g., that of Gandhi), which was unacceptable theoretically to Communists; (9) the view that a country politically independent but economically dependent could not afford an autonomous foreign policy (the examples of Indonesia and Saudi Arabia were adduced to prove the falsehood of this particular view); and (10) the thesis that countries ruled by native bourgeoisie could not dream of economic development because no capitalist country might develop in the general period of the decline of capitalism.[42]

The meaning of these mistakes, couched in Marxist-Leninist terminology, becomes clearer when expressed in the language of practical politics. These past errors prevented Soviet politicians and scholars from seeing the true domestic distribution of forces in the Asian and Near Eastern countries, led them into wishful thinking and a fruitless denial of the possibility of finding temporary partners among native bourgeois parties, and precluded any active Soviet foreign policy towards the underdeveloped countries. Moreover, this essentially negative attitude towards the native bourgeoisie resulted in forbidding local Communists to form national fronts with that bourgeoisie for the purpose of opposing Western influence and thus assisting the USSR in its foreign policy. These practical reasons, dictated by the Soviet principal objective to cut the West off from the underdeveloped countries, would have been sufficient in themselves for a thorough revision of the previous doctrine. However, the Chinese experience, whereby parts of the Chinese bourgeoisie were enlisted as allies in the civil war against the Kuomintang, also had its influence, as we shall see in another context, on Soviet ideas concerning the native bourgeoisie.

The new picture of the underdeveloped world, emergent after the revision of the doctrine, is depicted in the following words:

The decomposition of the colonial system is a complex and many-sided process. The liberation from the colonial oppression proceeds in various countries in different ways. In some cases people immediately achieve full independence, both political and economic, and embark on the venture of accomplishing not only democratic but also socialist transformations. In such cases the new sovereign States adopt the form of people's democracy [the author mentions China, North Korea, North Vietnam, and Mongolia, as such fully independent states]. . . . The active role of the working class in the anti-imperialist movement and of its militant vanguard, the Communist parties, grows everywhere, and one must, of course, expect that the working class will win everywhere in the future the position of a leader in the struggle. But this is a long and complex process.[43]

The preference and the long-term hope are clearly formulated: the full economic and political independence may be achieved only in a Communist people's democracy; the Communists will win power everywhere, but it will take time. Meanwhile, one must reckon with the existing distribution of forces in each country:

The workers are not the only force waging the struggle for national liberation and against imperialism. Peasants, craftsmen, merchants, industrialists, the intelligentsia, including students, lower-rank officials and military officers, actively participate in that struggle in the colonial and dependent countries. Even some feudal elements (khans and princes) are dragged into the general torrent of the national-liberating movement.... This happens in particular when the imperialists engage in a colonial war for the complete enslavement of a nation, or take away some land belonging to certain tribes or nationalities.... Frequently at the helm of the movement are found such leaders or such political parties which represent the interests of propertied classes.... The peasantry in colonies and semi-colonies is a great revolutionary force, but the peasant struggle against local and foreign oppressors bears as a rule an elemental character ... the peasants, although they form the immense majority of the population, are completely dispersed, internally lack cohesion and fail to make up one compact mass. It is largely for this reason that the representatives of national bourgeoisie find themselves more than often at the helm of the movement in those countries of Asia and Africa where the working class has not yet achieved the position of a generally acknowledged leader.... This is not accidental. National bourgeoisie is an organized force which has the most numerous trained personnel and which puts forward an independent political program.... At present the leading position in many former colonial and dependent countries, which have achieved independence, belongs to national bourgeoisie and its parties. Such is the situation in India, Egypt, Indonesia, and many other countries.... These are not socialist countries. The constitutional regime in these countries is not that of a people's democracy but all sorts of forms of a bourgeois state, from a parliamentary republic (India) to a limited monarchy (Morocco). It would be, however, the greatest mistake to minimize the world-historical significance of the process of decomposition of the colonial system only because this decomposition has brought in its wake non-socialist sovereign states.... Whatever the form of national liberation of colonies and semi-colonies might be ... this liberation is a blow to imperialism and, in consequence, necessarily does not strengthen but weakens the world capitalist system.[44]

If the native bourgeoisie holds power because of insufficient strength of local Communists, the practical conclusion must be for the USSR to acknowledge this regrettable fact and make the best of it:

The question of establishing correct mutual relations [between local Communists and the bourgeois parties] within a single anti-imperialist front, and in particular the question of the attitude of the working class and its party towards national bourgeoisie, acquire great importance under such conditions.... Of course, nationalism and communism are two different ideologies. The bourgeois nationalism is deeply alien to the working class. ... But as national bourgeoisie plays the role of an active participant (and sometimes leader) in the all-national anti-imperialist struggle, its nationalist ideology must not become an impassable barrier between the bourgeoisie and the toiling masses in their co-operation and alliance against imperialism.... Of course, there is a possibility of co-operation between Communists and the bourgeois nationalists.[45]

This is a sound political conclusion from the Soviet viewpoint, although an orthodox pre-1914 Marxist would have wept on hearing the proposition for political co-operation between Marxists and their proclaimed major enemy, the bourgeoisie. But Lenin was already un-Marxist in this respect; his hatred, concentrated on the Western (imperialist) bourgeoisie, made him accept the concept of temporary co-operation with the native bourgeoisie, so easy to eliminate after the final rout of the Western bourgeoisie. His disciples follow in his footsteps. Their major enemy is the West; its defeat would undoubtedly bring about the universal triumph of Communism. Why not co-operate with anyone, including the native bourgeoisie, if he pursues aims unfriendly to the West? Thus the USSR recovers full freedom of maneuvering within the capitalist camp by helping one of its sections in fighting the other. Local Communist parties must, on their part, seek a common anti-Western platform with non-Communist parties.

This line is pursued with rigorous consistency. Whenever a conflict divides a Western Power from an underdeveloped country, one may be sure the USSR will stand by that country. The policy of *rapprochement* with individual members of NATO, followed in the hope of weakening this Western coalition, is sacrificed in such a case for the other major objective of widening the gulf between the West and the underdeveloped countries. The swift Soviet support of Egypt after the nationalization of the Suez Canal, despite the earnest efforts in the first half of 1956 to establish better relations with France and Britain, provides a pertinent illustration. This aspect of the question is sometimes overlooked in the West, which for the Soviet policy is the main enemy but not the major objective of current policy.

E. Zhukov provides the Soviet people with a lesson that is useful for anyone who has to deal with countries that are newly independent:

It is necessary to remember Lenin's most important observation that one must treat, with the deepest understanding and caution, the sensitive national feelings of peoples which recently acquired their independence and whose bodies still bear fresh scars left by the chains of colonial enslavement. ... It is incorrect, for instance, to call some small states in the United Nations satellites of the USA only because their official representatives are sometimes compelled, under the pressure of American diplomacy, to vote against their convictions. Global inclusion of several economically backward and hence weak countries within the category of satellites of one or another imperialist State produces a primitive and simplified image of international relations. . . . Imperialism is not as powerful as it is erroneously depicted by those who are ready to classify every insufficiently strong state . . . as a mute American or British "vassal."[46]

The tone and language here are worth attention because they have a realistic ring that was impossible to attain in the last years of Stalin's rule. The Soviet Government, helped by advisers free to deduce conclusions from actual facts they observe, is now enabled to pursue a much more flexible and efficacious policy. The rest depends on the orientation of a given foreign government or party.

The USSR welcomes the non-commitment policy, especially if it leans towards the Soviet-Chinese bloc:

National bourgeoisie does not see now just one prospect, namely the need for dealing with the imperialist world and the strong imperialist countries. The objective possibility of another orientation has now appeared, namely to have contacts with another world, the system of socialist States, not because socialism as a socio-political system pleases national bourgeoisie, but because countries of the socialist camp are active champions of national freedom and state sovereignty of all peoples.[47]

In other words, a policy dictated by resentment against the West will always find Soviet support.

It would be a naïve error to think that the revision of the doctrine concerning national bourgeoisie was the cause of a new Soviet foreign policy. The reverse is true. The scholarly debates of 1956 only followed Khrushchev's and Bulganin's resounding journey to India, Burma, and Afghanistan. But a government and a party that uphold a creed need *ex post facto* doctrinal justification for the new active policy towards the bourgeois governments in the underdeveloped countries. The new theory does not pay any attention to Marx; it is highly practical and elastic—to suit current political exigencies. It is impossible to disengage a clear definition of national bourgeoisie from a multitude of scholarly articles and discussions. In the past, there was a theoretical difference between the comprador and the national bourgeoisie; the former, making business with foreign capital, was given up as a possible ally. Now even a comprador bourgeois may become patriotic after his country has won independence and his interests are predominantly tied up with domestic profits. National bourgeoisie should not be confused with petty or middle bourgeoisie. A very rich native capitalist may be a national bourgeois only if his economic interests make him hostile to foreign competition. Actually, any capitalist or pseudo-capi-

talist is welcomed if he has reason to be anti-Western; even landlords may
now be patriotic (anti-Western). At this stage in the game, when the opportunities for a revolution in a given underdeveloped country are not
immediate, class distinctions have practically lost their meaning for pragmatic "Marxists." A Soviet author, typical in this respect, writes:

The growth of capitalist productive relations gave birth to national bourgeoisie in the colonies and dependent States. At present there are in those
countries various layers of national bourgeoisie: petty, middle, and big
industrial or commercial bourgeoisie. In some countries a thin stratum of
monopolistic bourgeoisie of national origin has also made its appearance
. . . national bourgeoisie aspires to create such conditions where it could
exploit the working class and toilers of its country entirely by itself and
independently [of foreign capital]. It not only does not want to share profits
with foreign imperialists but wants itself to get the highest profits. These
basic antagonisms between the interests of national bourgeoisie in each
colonial and dependent country and those of imperialism are objective
facts bearing a fundamental character, and cannot be ignored. These antagonisms have a deep political significance because they determine . . . its
participation in one national anti-imperialist front. . . . The interests of
the petty, middle, and part of the big bourgeoisie, as well as of the planters
and landlords who are busy with the production of raw materials destined
for export, are harmed by the imperialist monopolies. This is the reason
that important strata of the bourgeoisie in the colonies and semi-colonies
. . . join the struggling popular masses [against the Western Powers].[48]

The great debate of Soviet Orientalists, specialists in the Near East,
Asia, and Africa, held in 1956, did not help to clarify the issues from a
Marxist point of view. But this was not its purpose; it was not expected
to culminate in (to use Communist words) sectarian, scholastic, and dogmatic definitions. Its aim was to notify all Soviet Orientalists of their new
freedom to deduce conclusions from observable facts and thus help the
Soviet Government in its new policy. The main conclusions of that debate
were that not the whole comprador bourgeoisie served always and only
imperialist capital; that national bourgeoisie was not a matter of wealth
but of being tied up with the development of domestic economy independently of foreign influence; that an economic definition was insufficient and
must be supplemented by a political definition, namely, an anti-imperialist
attitude of that bourgeoisie; that the native national bourgeoisie did not
like Communism but might have other reasons for co-operation with the
Soviet-Chinese bloc; and that this co-operation did not eradicate domestic
class antagonisms between that bourgeoisie and other classes.[49]

5. Revival of Soviet Oriental Studies

The Stalinist period of a rigid policy towards the underdeveloped countries, or rather the lack of any active policy, and of reliance only on local Communists had a very harmful effect on Soviet studies of Asia and Africa. This is a practical matter. The Soviet diplomatic corps is not inferior in talents to any other, although its rigid manners and restriction of movements by iron and detailed instructions reduce its efficiency. It is true that the USSR now has a great number of scientific-technical personnel, which allows for sending skilled missions to the underdeveloped countries. It is no less true that the principal Soviet universities offer good opportunities to students from those countries for a training in natural sciences and technology, where, unlike social sciences, Marxism-Leninism does not interfere with studies. It is even more true that the USSR has one notable advantage over Western Powers in that its message is carried to a foreign public not only by an embassy or other official institutions but also by members of that public, the local Communists. They know how to speak to their countrymen and how to sell them Soviet stuff better than a foreign diplomat, and they enjoy, as natives, greater initial trust, confidence a foreigner may win only after long effort.

But all this leaves other questions unsolved. Who will advise the Soviet Government and its diplomats? Who will give background training to a Soviet citizen sent abroad? Will this citizen be able to establish, right away, confident relations with natives in their own language, and will he understand their mentality? Who will tell the Soviet university personnel and students about how to handle foreign students? These various responsibilities must be managed, directly or indirectly, by competent scholars who follow up, without wishful thinking, on foreign developments and by teachers of foreign languages.

The new turn of Soviet foreign policy towards the various underdeveloped countries, notably in Asia and Africa, created new problems. Soviet scholars were caught largely unprepared for their new task, for the Stalinist policy was sterile in this respect. It will probably take several years to repair the damage. This does not mean that Soviet Orientalists are small fry and that their knowledge is contemptible. It means only that they could not produce, for a long time, truly scientific works on current affairs. One may take as an example Leningrad University, one of the four universities with an Oriental Studies Department (the other three are those in Central Asia, Baku, and Tbilissi) having chairs of history of the Far East, history of the Near East, history of the Ancient East, and nine philological chairs (Chinese, Korean, Japanese, Mongolian, Hindi, Iranian, Arabic, Turkish, and African). Students of this department may learn the languages, literature, and history of almost all Asian countries and the principal African languages. In 1955, the teaching of the Tibetan language was introduced. This same department published, in 1951–53, the Russian-Hindi and Russian–Urdu dictionaries.[50]

Even such distinguished effort would be inadequate for the large demand created by the new foreign policy. N. A. Mukhitdinov expressed the apprehension and wishes of his colleagues when he said:

Our Orientalists do not pay enough attention to a study of the contemporary situation in the East. . . . It is necessary to improve radically the all-embracing research in the fields of economics, culture, history, and contemporary conditions of the foreign Eastern countries. It is indispensable to improve substantially the training of our Orientalist personnel. When we wanted to publish in Hindi the periodical *The Soviet Union,* we discovered a lack of specialists who had mastered that language which, as you know, is the official language of the Indian Republic. The question of teaching languages and histories of the bigger Eastern countries in our high schools has been rife for a long time . . . languages of Eastern peoples are not taught in all such schools.[51]

He did not hide one of the reasons for this sudden interest in Oriental languages: "We face the great and responsible task of publicizing abroad the achievements of the Soviet Union."[52] He returned to the same subject in June, 1957:

We must restore and intensify scholarly work in many sectors of Eastern philology, in particular regarding teaching languages and literatures of Southeastern-Asian and African countries. . . . There is not enough scientific research particularly regarding countries of the immense African continent. Our Orientalists have poorly worked on problems of countries of Southeastern Asia. . . . Training the personnel of Orientalists occupies the most important place in the further development of Oriental Studies; it is its foundation. . . . It is necessary to supply the Oriental Studies' schools and other universities with qualified teachers, inviting them in case of necessity to come from the Eastern countries concerned. . . . It is very good that our [high] school students learn Western languages, but one should not, at the same time, underestimate the importance of learning Oriental languages which are spoken by a large part of the world population. . . . A good beginning was the introduction of teaching the Chinese,

Arabic, and Hindi languages in several schools in Uzbekistan. This should be encouraged and extended further. One should think about an improvement in teaching history in the middle schools. The present school curriculum reserves an inadequate place for the East. We must send our scientific workers and students to the Eastern countries, to make them better understand and watch on the spot the life of those peoples under conditions of actual reality. It is also indispensable to encourage by all means students from Eastern countries to travel to the USSR.[53]

He disclosed in the same article some new developments: the reorganization of the Oriental Institute and the opening of a Chinese Institute at the Soviet Academy of Sciences and the opening of an Oriental Languages Institute at Moscow University and an Oriental Institute in Tashkent. The interesting point to note is the present concentration on learning Oriental languages in the Uzbek middle schools; Uzbeks, who are a Turkic people with distinctly Asian features, will play the role of "brothers" of other Asians better than the Russians. That this teaching of Chinese, Hindi, and Arabic, is not treated lightly, even on the high-school level, is proved by the curriculum; it requires five hours weekly in the second, third, and fourth grades, seven hours in the fifth, sixth, and seventh grades, with supplementary teaching of language by way of literature in the eighth, ninth, and tenth grades.[54]

The Geographical Society of the USSR established, at the end of 1955, an Eastern Commission, with the seat in Leningrad; its program of Asian-African studies is not limited to geography but extends to ethnography, history, and linguistics.[55]

A considerable number of people fluent in foreign languages is important for many reasons, one of them being the export of translated Soviet books, pamphlets, and other publications; circulation abroad is greatly helped by the low price of Soviet publications. "The Soviet Union exports annually tens of millions of books. . . . A considerable number of Soviet books are translated and published in foreign languages: English, French, German, Italian, Spanish, Swedish, Chinese, Korean, Persian, Arabic and Japanese."[56] The enumeration of languages in which books are translated is certainly not exhaustive, but it is noteworthy that only a few Oriental languages are listed. The same source mentions the success abroad of Soviet publications for children and high-school students.[57]

What were the principal lacunae in the Soviet Oriental publications? "There is not a single important monograph devoted to the African colonies in the Soviet literature."[58] "There are many 'white' pages in the Soviet

scientific literature devoted to Africa. The economic problems of many
African countries are poorly studied or not studied at all. Many problems
relating to postwar development of the African continent have not been
investigated."[59] "There is very little literature on Africa as a whole or on
particular African countries."[60] This new interest in Africa south of the
Sahara not only follows recent developments in that part of the world but
presages an increased Soviet activity there. A Soviet author stressed in
1957 the growing importance of the "Black Continent":

Africa has become in fact the last colonial reserve of imperialism and at
the same time the front line of the national-liberating struggle of oppressed nations. Its contemporary role is determined, first of all, by these
circumstances. . . . It is known that the Belgian Congo is the most important
source of supplies of uranium ore in the capitalist world. The extraction
of uranium from the waste of gold-mining has considerably increased during the last several years in the South African Union. . . . The rapid growth
of the mass anti-imperialist movement in Africa is one of the most significant events of the middle of the 20th century.[61]

The editors of the Soviet Orientalist journal, which had begun to appear only in April, 1955, deplore the fact that

. . . the collaborators of the [Oriental] Institute have not yet published
one book on the Chinese People's Republic or the Democratic Republic
of Vietnam. There is no publication on Indonesia or Burma. There are
no recent studies on the contemporary situation in Egypt and other Arab
countries, in Turkey, Iran, Afghanistan, and Pakistan. Very few scientific-
popularizing pamphlets have been printed on particular Eastern countries, pamphlets destined for the wide-reading public interested in the
East. The Institute has not yet truly begun to investigate African problems
although these problems should be a part of its learned activities. . . . The
study of India, Pakistan, Indonesia and all the countries of Southeastern
Asia taken together, occupies the same number of senior scientific collaborators as the study of Iran and Turkey or of the Mongolian People's
Republic.[62]

The same article makes it clear that all Soviet scholars and institutions
dealing with Asia and Africa will henceforth work under the co-ordinating
supervision of the Oriental Institute of the Academy of Sciences.

One may detect other lacunae by examining the program of current
studies of political significance. This program includes such topics as (1)
the infiltration of Western capital in the underdeveloped countries, the
co-operation or competition between various foreign corporations, their

links with domestic capital; (2) a detailed study of Black Africa; and (3) the agrarian problem, including the nature of landholding and land tenancy, and the agrarian policies of the newly independent states. This particular study is important because, as we shall see later, Communists hope that the dissatisfied peasants may serve as tools of the revolution.

Finding out who holds land in each Eastern country, what is the trend in the process of re-distribution of land and in allocating land to the main peasant masses, investigating the various forms of land tenancy and of mutual relations between various categories of landowners and tenants, either landless or with small plots of land, allow for depicting a correct picture of the class structure in the villages and disclosing the basic antagonisms.[63]

A detailed program of Eastern studies was published in 1957 by the Soviet Orientalist journal. The Oriental Institute of the Soviet Academy of Sciences became the center of all Eastern studies. The staff of the Institute was enlarged to include experts on rarely studied problems and to promote the training of young scholars. Soviet senior and junior experts will be sent to Asian and African countries for further studies, while specialists from Eastern countries will be invited to co-operate with the Institute. Two new journals began publication: *Vostochnaia Literatura* and *Sovremennyi Vostok*. The Institute was subdivided into six sections: African, Near and Middle Eastern, Indian-Pakistani, Southeastern Asian, Far Eastern, and International Problems section. The Institute approved a Five Year Plan of studies for the years 1957–1960 which included history, economics, linguistics, literature and culture, publication of treatises, monographs and collective works, etc. Other Soviet institutions, such as the Institute of World Economics and International Relations, the Institute of Eastern Languages of Moscow University, the Eastern Department of Leningrad University, the Institute of International Relations, and Orientalists from China and the European people's democracies will closely co-operate with the Institute. Special attention is paid to such matters as the role of the working class (Communists) in the Asian-African countries, the native national bourgeoisie, and the competition among Western Powers in Asia and Africa. Monographic studies will be published on particular countries —India, Vietnam, Sudan, Tunisia, Malaya, Iran, Indonesia, Thailand, Burma, Iraq, Morocco, Ceylon, Turkey, Syria, Afghanistan, etc. One item is of special interest: "the working class as the leading force in the revolution."[64] A special group will study Africa with particular attention to the significance of African raw materials for the West. Another topic to be studied is that of the prevailing ideology, including religion, in all Eastern countries. Several dictionaries and grammars are to be published: the Pushtu (this is of interest to Pakistan, which has a conflict with Afghanistan over the Pushtu area, with the Soviet Union supporting Afghanistan, of course), Vietnamese, Hindi (second edition of the dictionary), Japanese, Arabic, Bengali, Kurdish (the Soviet Union is now the only great Power inclined to foster the Kurdish national aspirations against Iran, Turkey, and Iraq, this problem being of lesser importance in Syria), Mongolian languages, Telugu, Tamil, and other Indian languages. The inclusion of the various Indian languages points to Soviet alertness to one of the most serious domestic problems of India.[65]

These and other studies are to be made by using both Soviet and foreign sources:

... it is necessary to widen the volume of literature and sources particularly concerning Eastern countries, to organize systematically scientific expeditions of Orientalists for work at the libraries and archives of foreign countries, and to take serious steps in improving the study of Eastern languages, especially those which have never been learned by us or whose learning has been interrupted.[66]

Rich factual material concerning colonial questions and colonial policy is to be found in numerous monographs published by the bourgeois specialists, principally in those written after the Second World War. A critical use of those works, frequently based on sources which are inaccessible to a Soviet student, is indispensable in examining those problems.[67]

As a matter of fact, Soviet publishing houses have started publishing translations of foreign books, especially those on Black Africa. All this indicates that the new approach to underdeveloped countries is not going to be amateurish.

CHAPTER X

SOVIET CURRENT POLICY TOWARDS THE UNDERDEVELOPED COUNTRIES

1. Basic Patterns

A NEW Soviet approach towards the underdeveloped countries was outlined in many speeches which Bulganin and, especially, Khrushchev made during their long visit to India, Burma, and Afghanistan in November-December, 1955.[1] The aims of the pattern are as follows: (1) to show utmost deference and friendliness to former colonial or semi-colonial countries, taking good care of their national pride and susceptibility; (2) to exploit the resentment accumulated in the previous period of their relations with the West in order to estrange them from it; (3) to make the most not only of their anti-colonialism but also of anti-racialism; (4) to promote the trend towards political neutrality; (5) to espouse each quarrel they might have with a Western nation; (6) to encourage their ambition to develop their own economies through industrialization, to some extent by granting Soviet loans and increasing mutual trade; (7) to evoke suspicion against foreign capital or assistance as alleged means of endangering their independence; and (8) to place before their eyes the quick industrialization of the USSR as a model to copy, with a hopeful implication that local people will understand that only Communists could realize such achievements within a short period of time.

This pattern is another application of the Leninist advice to exploit antagonisms between capitalist states, which is nothing but the ancient Roman formula, *divide et impera*. The Soviet Government pays lively attention to all underdeveloped areas but seems to expect results sooner in Asia, the Near East, and Africa than in Latin America. Most of the current literature is devoted to those three large regions of the world. Antagonism between the West and the underdeveloped countries is seen in the following way: "The imperialist contradictions are becoming more acute between the 'great' imperialist powers, on the one hand, and small bourgeois countries, on the other."[2] Therefore, the Soviet bloc must be active in their relations with the "small bourgeois" countries: "The mutual relations between the socialist States and former colonies and semi-colonies exert a deep influence on contemporary international relations."[3] These relations should take the shape of the peace zone proclaimed by Khrushchev from the 20th Congress tribune:

A vast "zone of peace," which includes the socialist and non-socialist peace-loving states of Europe and Asia, has made its appearance on the international stage. This zone comprehends an enormous surface of the earth where almost one and a half billion people, i.e., the majority of the world population, live. Thus, the cause of peace is now defended not only by the countries united under the socialist banner but also by a group of other states which only recently for the most part were freed from foreign domination.[4]

Shepilov, while Foreign Minister, made no secret of the fact that the animosity against the West, or, as he called it, the colonial system, should be the cement of that peace zone: "The Soviet people regard with sympathy and compassion the selfless struggle of Eastern nations against dying colonial imperialist system."[5] However, he also made it clear to Frenchmen that the Soviet Union was not uncompromising in her anti-colonialism and could make concessions to the Western "imperialists," presumably if this would weaken their own coalition. Probably mindful of a possible Soviet-French anti-German platform, he said: "We think that every people has an inalienable right to its national freedom, independence, and self-determination. This applies entirely to the Algerian people. But one must not deny at the same time the existence of known historical ties between France and Algeria."[6]

The new love for the Arabs did not prevent a Soviet international lawyer from writing in 1955:

The Jewish State of Israel was proclaimed on May 14, 1948, at a meeting of the "Jewish National Council." The League of Arab States, incited by the American and English imperialists, declared on May 15, 1948, that the Arab States were in a state of war with Palestine. The Egyptian Government issued an order to its armed forces to enter the Palestinian territory. . . . Pursuing her aggressive plans, Great Britain strove to oppose to the State of Israel, not only Egypt but also Iraq and other Arab States.[7]

Individual underdeveloped countries are expendable in various forms of "peaceful war" against the West.

The Asian-African Bandung Conference was very warmly greeted by the Soviet Union for several reasons. It is true that the representatives of the Western-committed nations did not hide their distrust of the Soviet-Chinese bloc, but the uncommitted nations gave tone to the conference, which included the *Pancha Shila* in its final declaration. The Chinese delegation made a good impression, and its country was received into the Asian-African family. The most important point for the USSR was, however, of a different nature.

The concept of an African-Asian unity is void of meaning in many respects; culturally, taking this word in its non-political sense, one may talk of a European cultural unity extending from the Pacific coasts of the Western Hemisphere to the Pacific coasts of the USSR. Asia and Africa are the home of several, often unrelated, civilizations. The long-term interests of those countries are not only far from identical, but they sometimes clash with each other (one thinks immediately of problems that divide India from Pakistan, India from Ceylon, the Chinese from the Malayans, the Arabs among themselves, etc.). Is there anything in common between a Vietnamese and an inhabitant of Ghana or between an Egyptian and a Thai? Their feeling of vague unity is not altogether untrue. They harbor the same resentment against the West about the former colonial period, a resentment which has no present objective and which time alone will heal. They experienced, in the past, humiliating treatment by many Europeans who were proud of their "racial" superiority. Most important of all, they face the same fundamental problem of economically developing their countries at a speedy rate. This kind of unity easily acquires an anti-Western undertone. The Western Powers were the colonizers and are highly industrialized. In the latter respect, they belong to another world. It is this intentional or unintentional anti-Western tinge of Asian-African unity that really interests the Soviet Union.

Pravda acclaimed the Bandung Conference immediately after its close in terms which were cordial but also unequivocal concerning the true Soviet interest.

Although the social-economic systems of the Asian-African countries are different, all those countries are united in their common aspiration to a full emancipation from the miseries of the colonial policy of imperialism, to peace, freedom, and national independence. . . . For the first time in history the representatives of 29 countries on the Asian and African continents, where more than half of mankind live, gathered together to examine problems common to all of them. The fact alone of the convocation of the Conference was eloquent evidence of a deep historical change that had taken place. Asia and Africa of today are not Asia and Africa of yesterday when the imperialist powers wholly dominated. . . . The Conference succeeded precisely because it acted independently of the United States. . . . The most essential feature of the decisions of the Conference, one that had an important international significance, was their general hostility to the colonial system of imperialism and the exploitation and oppression of Asian and African peoples. . . . The conference participants condemned the policy and practice of racial segregation and discrimination. . . . The Bandung conference contributed greatly to the strengthening of national consciousness among the Asian and African peoples.[8]

A year later, another Soviet article stressed the same factor of Asian-African unity, underlined by anti-Western animosity:

The Bandung Conference rallied together the Asian and African peoples in their struggle against colonialism and for its complete liquidation. . . . For the first time in history the representatives of African States, which had achieved their political independence to a greater or smaller extent, met with the representatives of the Asian continent. The Conference proved that Africa, following the footsteps of Asia, had entered the wide arena of international life and of the struggle against colonialism.[9]

2. Uncommitted Countries

One may rest assured that the USSR intends to be active in relation to all underdeveloped countries. However, opportunities are not the same everywhere. One may try hard to win a committed country to the concept of non-commitment, but one cannot achieve impressive results as long as that country wants to remain committed and entertain cordial relations with the West. Similarly, Britain, which had recognized Communist China at the beginning of 1950, has not yet reaped spectacular results. The United States has granted loans to Poland for the sake of her nuisance value, but this cannot be expected to change the basic pattern of Soviet-Polish relations. Meanwhile, the Soviet Union works away. The long list of distinguished foreign visitors who have come in the last few years to the USSR includes not only representatives of uncommitted nations but those of the West-committed, e.g., the Shah of Iran. The warm shower of grandiose and cordial receptions is, however, mainly reserved for guests from the uncommitted nations, such as the Prime Ministers of India, Burma, Cambodia, Yemen, or the Presidents of Indonesia and the United Arab Republic. Soviet leaders have thus far limited their visits to the uncommitted nations of Asia: India, Burma, Afghanistan, and Indonesia. They hope that the zone of peace will in this way become a political reality:

The countries of socialism, the Indian Republic, Indonesia, the Burmese Union, Egypt, and other Eastern countries actively follow the principle of peaceful co-existence. . . . Thus the "zone of peace," which embraces the countries of the socialist camp and several non-socialist Asian and African countries, is being widened.[10]

Khrushchev, while enumerating at the 20th Congress the cardinal points of the Soviet foreign policy, mentioned as one of them: "To support countries which refuse to be involved in military blocs."[11]

The uncommitted Asian nations, which found their own foreign policy on the existence of two counterbalancing blocs, would have to abandon the true non-commitment policy in order to form a "peace zone" with one of the two blocs. However, it is the avowed Soviet objective to make them lean increasingly more heavily towards the Soviet bloc. There lies one of the contradictions of interest between those countries and the Soviet Union. The Soviet interpretation of the non-commitment policy follows an old pattern which Communists apply to domestic relations in the capitalist countries. Various intermediate classes (for instance, peasants and petty bourgeoisie) are placed between the two main protagonists, the proletariat and the capitalists. The intermediate classes should be at least neutralized and if possible won over to the proletarian side. Similarly, the present world is conceived as being composed of three main groups: the Soviet-Chinese bloc, engaged in the struggle against its main adversary, the Western coalition, and the intermediate group of underdeveloped countries to be neutralized in this struggle and, if possible, joined to the Soviet side as temporary political allies.

Relations with non-committed nations are placed under the aegis of the *Pancha Shila,* the five principles of peaceful co-existence with capitalist countries. These five principles, introduced into international intercourse by China, are as follows:

The best formula for mutual relations between states with different social regimes is, under present circumstances, the known five principles of international relations: 1. mutual respect for the territorial integrity and sovereignty; 2. non-aggression; 3. non-interference in the domestic affairs of each other; 4. development of international relations on the foundation of equality and mutual benefits; 5. peaceful co-existence and economic co-operation. These principles could serve as a foundation for solidly peaceful relations between states of the whole globe.[12]

We shall later analyze these five principles against the realistic background of the actual Soviet record. For the time being, however, let us note that these principles were not suddenly invented; they could be found in any international-law textbook published in the 19th century as the basic duties of independent states. They are a part of customary international law and do not gain vitality by being repeated in formal treaties. Moreover, the record of this century, to which the USSR greatly contributed, is such that one may view with some skepticism solemn pledges embodied in international treaties unless they are grounded firmly on coincidence of national interests. The cheapest concession, if it is a concession at all, is to sign a high-sounding agreement incorporating lofty principles which should in any event be respected; as ever, the taste of the pudding is in the eating. People are, however, seldom cured, even by bitter experience, of the modern disease of pactomania.

Soviet attention is mainly concentrated on the uncommitted nations, on India, Indonesia, and the United Arab Republic in particular, and the reasons are not the same in each case. India is the most important uncommitted nation; she has great prestige in both Asia and Africa, and her policy cannot simply be dismissed by other nations as an insignificant factor; she has the potential of a future great Power. The attention paid to India may be measured by the following facts: a month spent there by Bulganin and Khrushchev while both men were among the busiest people in the world; the enthusiastic reception reserved in the USSR for Prime Minister Nehru; the loans granted to India; the Soviets' calling India a great world Power in anticipation of the future; and their bestowing on the Indian nation the unusual honor of being called great, an adjective usually reserved only for Russians and Chinese. Indonesia is another great Asian country, but she suffers from chronic instability and has a very large Communist Party. A Soviet journal notes:

The Communist party of Indonesia has considerably grown in recent times and has become a political party of over a million people. It received in the last parliamentary elections towards the end of 1955 over six million ballots and gained 39 seats in parliament.[13]

The Indonesian Party ranks, therefore, together with the French and the Italian, as the largest outside the Communist-controlled areas. The United Arab Republic might well become the key to the Near East should Soviet policy succeed there, a matter of vital importance to any Russian government.

This is how the Soviet press sees the Indian role:

The Indian Republic plays an outstanding role on the international stage. ... The Government, the public and the politicians of India stand for universal peace and against the policy of building military blocs ... the intensification of economic relations with the Soviet Union, the People's Republic of China and other socialist countries, demonstrates the creative resoluteness and will of the Indian people in their struggle for independent development.[14]

Probably the most important element in this picture is Indian opposition to the Baghdad Pact and to SEATO.

The Soviet Union enjoys a clear advantage over the United States in having no political friends among the colonial Powers, all of them being members of NATO. It may espouse any quarrel between an Asian or African country and a colonial Power at no cost to itself. Thus Khrushchev, in November, 1955, threw his support behind the Indian claim to Portuguese Goa and just as readily supported the present partition of Kashmir against West-committed Pakistan.[15] Marshal K. E. Voroshilov, while on a long official visit in Indonesia, did not miss the opportunity of saying: "The Soviet Union has unalterably supported and is supporting the legitimate claim of Indonesia to union with Western Irian."[16] There was no reason for him to do otherwise—Indonesia is uncommitted, but the Netherlands is a member of NATO; if their positions were reversed, he would just as gladly have supported Holland against Indonesia.

Egypt is considered by Soviet sources to be the key point in the Near East: "Egypt has become the key point in the anti-imperialist movement in the Near East after the victory of the national revolution in July 1952."[17] Another Soviet author says: "Egypt, supported by all Arab countries [sic!], marches at present in the vanguard of the Arab national movement directed against all forms of colonialism."[18] A Soviet pamphlet devoted exclusively to Egypt states some of the reasons why Egypt is considered a key country in the Near East:

She rejected the Baghdad Pact and is waging a resolute struggle against it. ... Friendly relations have been established in recent years between the Soviet Union and Egypt. ... Egypt has become the center of opposition of Arab peoples to colonialism. ... Present-day Egypt plays in the Near East an important and progressive role, winning for herself at the same time a merited international prestige by her independent foreign policy.[19]

In its unqualified enthusiasm for Soviet-Egyptian friendship, the pamphlet discovered one of the foundations for this cordiality in archeological excavations:

> This friendship has a solid foundation and sound tradition rooted in time immemorial. The excavations in the Trans-Caucasus, Crimea, and even in the Urals and Altai area, have enabled Soviet archeologists to discover many bronze and other figurines representing Egyptian gods. This proves that commercial and cultural relations had existed a long time ago between the peoples of the Soviet Union and Egypt.[20]

In their excitement, the authors overlooked the fact that the Soviet Union did not peacefully co-exist with ancient Egypt and that the areas indicated had not been a part of the Russian state in that historical period for the sufficient reason that no such state then existed.

Anti-Semitic inclinations of Soviet leaders and their political expediency, of course, make it easy for them to exploit to the hilt the Israeli-Arab dispute, using Israel as a scapegoat:

> The situation in this area is aggravated by the fact that the aggressive circles of those [Western] Powers make use of the State of Israel as a tool for the realization of their military plans. With this goal in mind, they intensively arm Israel thus promoting the armament race in the Near and Middle East.[21]

Another author frankly indicts Israel:

> The ruling clique in Israel has chosen a policy oriented towards Israeli-Arab enmity, the conquest of territories of the Arab countries, and the squeezing out and extermination of the Arab population. This is due to the fact that power in Israel has been taken over by the Zionists. . . . The Zionists have been successively the instrument first of the Germans, later of the English, and finally of American imperialism. . . . Arab hostility towards Zionists has been caused by the expansionist policy of the Zionist organizations which enjoy the support of the Western imperialist circles.[22]

However, when the USSR had a different view of the Near Eastern situation, she was one of the first to grant recognition to Israel.

This analysis of the Soviet attitude towards non-commitment policy does not imply criticism of the latter policy. First of all, there are as many variations in that policy as there are states which practice it. The only common factor is the non-participation in any Western or Soviet political and military arrangement. But this common factor allows for three basic attitudes: remaining truly aloof of both blocs, or leaning towards either of them in actual words or deeds. The reasons for that policy also vary widely from one state to another. It may be the question of traditional neutrality, sanctified by treaties or not, as in the case of Switzerland and Sweden; it may be the price to be paid for independence, as in the case of Austria; it may be the result of having quarreled with one bloc and having an ideological aversion for the other (Yugoslavia); it may be determined by anti-colonialist resentment, prevailing disputes with the Western Powers, and local rivalries with states of the same area, as with the United Arab Republic; it may arise from firm conviction that a long period of peace is absolutely necessary for solving grave and pressing domestic problems and that participation in a Western bloc would cause only irritation to Communist neighbors, one of the Indian motivations. With all new states, the policy of non-commitment is, moreover, largely dictated by the desire to be independent of any foreign influence and entanglement.

Furthermore, non-commitment is an elastic word used to cover up various policies. There is obviously a wide difference between the strict political neutrality of Switzerland and the anti-Western tone of the United Arab Republic's policies, determined by factors unknown to the Swiss, such as present quarrels or the memory of past disputes with Western Powers, the anti-Israeli stand, and inter-Arab rivalries. Again, some of the uncommitted governments seem to take a different view of Western and Communist patience; they think, not without good reasons, that it is a safe venture to cite only the Western alliances as examples of harmful military blocs and to denounce only Western bases on foreign territories, while a similar and parallel condemnation of the Soviet military bloc and Soviet bases abroad would certainly involve them in a deterioration of relations with the Soviet bloc.

Another root of certain non-commitment policies lies in an approach, different from the Western, to the central problem of the distribution of international forces. The Western great Powers, like the USSR and China, are forced by their global interests to pay most of their attention to world distribution. They see a Soviet-Chinese bloc growing in power and watch its dynamic policy; they have to build up a co-ordinated universal dam to protect themselves and, in fact, all other non-Communist states. They experience bitter disappointments in any other policy towards the USSR. Such bitter experience is unknown to the Asian–Near Eastern uncommitted nations. Moreover, the latter nations know that they are sheltered against the immediate dangers from the East by the existence of the Western bloc. Their national interests, limited within a geographical area, make them more sensitive to the problem of the local balance of power than to world distribution of forces. Thus the increase in the military capacity of Pakistan through her participation in the Baghdad and SEATO arrangements looms more important on the Indian horizon than Western-Soviet competition, although the latter is vital to all states of the world. The United Arab Republic pays more attention to its rivalry with other Arab states and its hostility to Israel than to the global picture.

Then there are some practical attractions in the non-commitment policy. If one is on good terms with both blocs, one may hope to receive financial and economic assistance from both sides, as exemplified by the Indian and other experiences. If one has an open dispute with a Western Power, it is tempting to counterbalance this with Soviet support, which will certainly be forthcoming. Egypt thus acted on a large scale, and Indonesia has welcomed Soviet support in her anti-Dutch claim to Western Irian.

Since the Soviet-Chinese bloc has not yet had any direct disputes with the Asian-African countries, at least since the suspension of claims against Turkey and the inauguration of a more peaceful policy towards Iran, it may support, at no cost to itself, not only any such country in its conflict with a Western Power but also back up the Asian-African bloc in the United Nations on certain general issues, notably anti-colonialism. The USSR does not risk embroilment in a quarrel with an ally by voting with that bloc on all colonial issues; she gains only by making anti-Western propaganda.

3. Africa and Latin America

After Asia and the Near East, current Soviet attention is directed towards that part of Africa south of the Sahara. Since for the time being this is still the last colonial area of importance, the Soviets think of it in the old Leninist terms—the struggle of a colonial people against a colonial Power. (In the case of independent African countries, like Ghana or Ethiopia, the problem obviously belongs to the realm of foreign policy.) The plan is to win over both the native national bourgeoisie and the working class, whose professional struggle is viewed as an anti-colonial one but not as a conflict of interests with the native bourgeoisie. The main preoccupation is to align all native social classes against the colonial Power:

The characteristic feature of economic battles of the African working class consists in the fact that the working class is opposed not by the local national bourgeoisie but mainly by the foreign, imperialist bourgeoisie, because the main enterprises where hired labor is employed are owned by foreign monopolistic corporations. This is why the economic struggle naturally merges with the political against foreign monopolies and colonial authorities which serve those monopolies. The struggle of the working class for its professional interests naturally becomes an integral part of the all-national anti-imperialist movement in countries with an underdeveloped national bourgeoisie and a preponderance of foreign monopolies.[23]

The same author concedes readily: "National bourgeoisie stands, for the time being, at the helm of the liberating movement in the African colonies."[24] He complains of the lack of Communist parties in Black Africa, probably meaning the absence of tightly organized and highly disciplined parties:

Legal and illegal Communist parties exist only in the countries of the Maghreb [Tunisia, Algeria, and Morocco] and in Egypt. The Communist party of the South-African Union, the oldest on the African continent (founded in 1921), was dissolved in 1950. . . . There were and are no Communist parties in the other African countries; only Marxist circles exist here and there. In those conditions the labor unions are called upon to unite the large toiling masses around the working class.[25]

If we substitute "Communists" for the "working class" in the last sentence, we realize that the plan is to infiltrate these countries through labor unions. This is implicitly conceded: "A struggle for influence over tens of millions of African working class is going on between various international labor-union confederations."[26]

Although Latin America is given less space in the Soviet press, it is far from forgotten:

The struggle of the peoples of Latin America against the domination by American monopolies, against the implication of their countries in the military blocs, and against the interference in their domestic affairs, is constantly growing in vigor. . . . The struggle of the Chilean people, which formed a National Front uniting all democratic forces in the country, has attained significant scope. The anti-imperialist struggle of the Brazilian and other Latin-American peoples is developing. . . . The single National Front is organized in many countries. It represents a wide coalition of patriotic forces—workers, peasants, the intelligentsia, craftsmen, urban petty-bourgeoisie, and other strata of national bourgeoisie. All the patriotic forces of the country unite, independently of their political opinions and convictions, in the struggle against colonialism, the oppression by foreign monopolies, against the participation of the colonies and semi-colonies in closed military blocs, and for the liquidation of economic and cultural backwardness.[27]

This indicates that the concept of National Front, which is by no means limited to Latin America, is the key to the Soviet plans for that part of the world. It must, as we shall see, fulfill two tasks: to multiply the Communist force by an alliance with the non-Communist parties and organizations, primarily to carry out an anti-American policy, and to split up local non-Communists in order to break the ground for the ultimate revolution. All Latin American Communists have supported, since 1955, the concept of an association of Latin American states, which, unlike the existing Organization of American States, would not be open to the United States. This concept was launched in July, 1955, at a Communist-sponsored conference of Latin American parliamentary deputies and other politicians held in Chile.[28]

4. Communist Revolution

It is so easy and comfortable to forget the ultimate Communist aim. However, they do their best to remind us, particularly in the underdeveloped countries, of their final goal:

Ideas know no frontiers and no obstacles. There is no force which could hinder the infiltration of Marxist-Leninist ideas to the consciousness of peoples. The oppressed peoples of the world find in Marxism-Leninism the answer to the burning questions of their life, to the main question of how to achieve a human existence and how to free oneself from poverty. Is there anything surprising in the fact that they increasingly follow that teaching which corresponds to their vital interests?[29]

"Poverty?" Would not a Westerner shrug his shoulders? There is poverty in the Soviet Union. In June, 1957, Khrushchev gave a clever answer:

They say that capitalism assures high living standards for the population. But one must not judge the living standards in the capitalist countries by England, France and other Western capitalist countries. . . . One should appraise what capitalism gives to people according to the living standards of the populations in the dependent countries of Asia, Africa and Latin America. Only then will it become clearer which system is better and which gives more benefits to the whole people.[30]

There are degrees in poverty, and poverty in the underdeveloped countries is incomparably greater than that of the Soviet people. However, non-Communists in those countries, radical as they might be, should read the conclusion which Khrushchev deduced; he indicated that the Communist system was better and immediately deployed before the eyes of the underdeveloped countries the following example:

> The pre-revolutionary Russia was a backward agrarian country. . . . During the past forty years the volume of industrial production has increased more than thirty times. The Soviet Union has overtaken in regard to the volume of industrial production, all capitalist States except the United States, and has occupied the second place in the world.[31]

Addressing professors and students on the Rangoon University campus, he harped on the same theme of the Soviet Union having shown the quickest road to industrialization:

> During a short period of time, thirty-eight years, of the Soviet regime, our country has been transformed from a backward Russia into the land of mass literacy. The higher learning institutions of the Soviet Union graduate each year a much greater number of engineers, agronomers and other specialists than the United States. This conveys the meaning of the workers' and peasants' power. . . . We have proved that our Soviet regime is the most progressive. Socialism, built in the Soviet Union, is the best society and the greatest achievement mankind has ever known. . . . The days of the capitalist regime are numbered.[32]

He drove this home in another speech in Mandalay, where he frankly said that economic progress in the underdeveloped countries was a matter of "correct" leadership (only Communist leadership could be "correct" for Khrushchev): "Your country is wealthy in natural resources. You want to work intensely for the well-being of the people, using your resources. You have manpower. You can achieve, under correct leadership, a rapid development of the country."[33] He thus pointed to a tangible goal of the revolution—industrialization!

One may treat lightly this question of the revolution as a remote possibility, but Lenin did not use a timetable. He left the matter to historical opportunity, certainly more probable in poor countries which do not want to remain poor than in the prosperous West. We would do well to remember Stalin's prophecy on China and not look with indifference at the economic-social problems of other countries which could become Chinas of tomorrow. Does it not now appear that what he told the 14th Party Congress in 1925 is true?

The forces of the revolutionary movement in China are immeasurable. They have not yet fully revealed themselves; they will reveal themselves in the future. The rulers of the West and the East, who do not see these forces and who do not sufficiently reckon with them, will pay for it. We, as a State, cannot but reckon with these forces. . . . He who does not pay attention to such, will certainly lose the battle.[34]

Why are the underdeveloped countries more vulnerable to Communism than the industrialized West? Communism thrives on two weeds: frustration and ignorance. Thorough knowledge of actual Communist practice, as opposed to its alluring propaganda, would cure most of the people attracted by Communist slogans. The actual practice is better known to the Western countries, where a multitude of books and articles have been devoted to the subject. This is not true in the underdeveloped countries, where an average educated man usually has a rather hazy idea of the actual Communist regime, whether as a sympathizer or an enemy of the movement. This ignorance helps the Communist in his propaganda. His second assistant is the frustration of his audience. It may be personal frustration of an individual who feels insufficiently rewarded by his environment or lost in the maelstrom of modern life, who yearns for a rock of faith for his convictions and actions. Agnostics are few among thinking men; usually, a man needs a fundamental hypothesis on which to build his outlook on life. Science cannot provide this, being itself built on hypotheses. Religion performs such a function, but a man who has lost his religious faith and feels unhappy as an agnostic looks about for another basic hypothesis which is also acceptable as an article of faith. So Communism, with its claim of scientific certitude, comes to him as a new religion, brought down to earth and yet founded on the faithful acceptance of its fundamental premises. These premises, once accepted (the infallibility of Marx, Engels, and Lenin, their philosophy of the universe and of human history, and the deterministic expectation of the victory of Communism), the rest flows therefrom as logically as a geometric theorem. The converted man becomes intellectually and morally happier. Where the same man feels that his environment needs a radical change to right his personal wrongs, he becomes a devoted Communist.

Frustration may also be of a social nature. The seeking person may feel that his society is based on injustice, with no change in sight. Communism seems to offer such change, the most radical he could desire. He then has a powerful social reason for militant devotion to his new church.

All of these factors that are true for a Western society must be multiplied in the case of an economically underdeveloped society. Often, traditional religion has lost its grip on educated people, whose recruitment for the Party is much more important than that of manual laborers. The native intelligentsia provides the leaders and the cadres, the toiling masses being only the tools. Anti-colonialism gives to nationalism an anti-Western complexion. If the rulers of an underdeveloped country sometimes divert the attention of the poor from the domestic problems towards the Western "devils," a prospective convert to Communism may easily be incited in such atmosphere frankly to give his nationalism not only an anti-Western but also a pro-Soviet twist.

The intelligentsia of the underdeveloped countries often has an unusually high proportion of people who have graduated in social sciences and law and for whom there are not enough jobs. University students know that their prospects are dim. Hence unemployment is produced, together with frustration, which may be channeled not only against the West but also against the present native regime. Personal frustration is then married to social indignation.

Democracy, which requires a long tradition and the formation of political habits in the whole population, is usually novel in the underdeveloped countries and at first has weak roots. But in many cases, Communists compete not with democratic but with authoritarian regimes and often military dictatorships. The question might then be oversimplified and largely reduced to the problem of which undemocratic regime, the present or the Communist, would be more efficient.

Native politicians are sometimes inexperienced or have only hazy or short-term objectives. Their competitors, the Communists, are schooled in the Leninist theory of politics, which is far from impractical and has definite goals. The long-term program of the Party may not be repulsive to the frustrated section of the native intelligentsia. First of all, it offers political power to the elect. Secondly, neither the nationalization of industries, usually foreign owned, nor collectivization of agriculture need be of great concern to an urban intelligentsia. The patriarchal pattern of tutelage over the toiling masses is deeply rooted in tradition; Communists do not upset it except for a change in the personnel who exercise the tutelage. The Communist revolution, which is always a revolution from above, being engineered by a minority, also fits into the traditional pattern of reforms decreed by higher authority.

Milovan Djilas' brilliant explanation of the sense of the Communist revolution may cure many a Western daydreamer, but it will have scant influence on frustrated educated persons in the underdeveloped areas.[35] He said that property was nothing but control and profit and that both control and profit were shifted by the Communist revolution to a new social class, the Communist upper stratum of the intelligentsia. After the nationalization of all means of production, they control the distribution of the total national income and reserve for themselves a copious serving. This is the modern form of the exploitation of man by man. But need it repulse an unemployed member of the native intelligentsia? His reward will be both power and high income. Yet he would be well advised to familiarize himself with the actual post-revolutionary Communist practice and the unhappy lot of the so-called "temporary allies" before embarking, with closed eyes, on a venture of co-operation with Communists. He might be referred, among others, to the ruthless Chinese treatment of "temporary allies" (see Section 6 of this chapter) and to the bitter complaints of the Left Wing Polish Communists (see Chapter XIII). Everyone may safely profit before the Communist revolution from the unfortunate experience of other people, but one's own unhappy experience *after* that revolution is no longer of any practical use.

There is the last attraction: Soviet power. Unfortunately, power has a magnetic spell for many people in both the West and the East. The success of Communism in eastern Europe, in China, and above all, in the second world Power, is a telling argument.

The main change that Communists promise and carry out is industrialization, the ambition of all underdeveloped countries as a panacea for their social ills. It must solve the problem of rural overpopulation, provide jobs, raise the cultural level of the masses, and terminate misery. Poverty is not a source of revolution in itself, but when a man realizes he is poor by comparing his lot to that of other people, he has an urge to do something about it. People in underdeveloped countries have awakened or are awakening to the realization of their poverty by comparing their status with that of Western nations.

Such countries have entered a period of flux. They are truly the weak links in the non-Communist chain. Stalin formulated briefly in 1924 the whole problem of this revolutionary opportunity:

Where will the revolution take place, where can the front of Capital be breached in the first place, in which country? The usual answer was in former times: "Where industries are more developed, where the proletariat represents the majority, where there is more culture and democracy." No, objects the Leninist theory, not necessarily where industries are more developed, etc. The capitalist front will be broken where the imperialist chain is weaker, because the proletarian revolution is the result of the break of the weakest sector in the world imperialist front. It might happen that the country that has begun the revolution and breached the capitalist front is less developed in the capitalist sense than other countries which are more developed, but which remain, however, in the capitalist condition. In 1917 the chain of the imperialist world front proved to be weaker in Russia than in other countries; therefore, it broke there. . . . Where will the chain break in the immediate future? Again, where it is weakest. It is not excluded that this chain may break, let us say, in India.[36]

If we substitute China for India, he was far from wrong. Lenin cited the economic backwardness of Russia as one of the reasons of her October Revolution:

It has become our lot to take over the whole burden and, in our estimation, the great honor of acting as pioneers in the world struggle against imperialism, because of several circumstances (among others, the backwardness of Russia, her immeasurable territory, and her being the frontier-land between Europe and Asia, between the West and the East).[37]

He foresaw the future attraction of a Russia, formerly backward and later industrialized: ". . . if Russia is covered with a thick network of power stations and powerful technical equipment, then our Communist economic construction will become a model for the forthcoming socialist Europe and Asia."[38]

It happened that the Communist revolution had taken place so far only in the economically underdeveloped countries. W. Gomulka said in May, 1957: "History has taken such a turn that socialism as a social order has come on the historical stage in the economically backward or underdeveloped countries."[39] This is neither a historical accident nor does it contradict the Leninist theory. Communism, as it has proved in actual practice, delivers neither freedom nor abundance of consumer goods, but it does deliver speedy industrialization at the cost of consumption and freedom, a cost that must be borne by several generations. Viewed from this point of view, it offers nothing to the West, but it might have an attraction for the economically backward countries if the West is slow in providing them with the alternative of an economic transformation by foreign assistance and if local governments fail to see the ominous writing on the wall. Contemporary Soviet commentators draw these conclusions:

The immortal success of the Russian workers and peasants has convinced the progressive elements in Eastern countries that the October ideas are invincible, that those ideas are international in their nature, and that the great Marxist-Leninist teaching can be creatively used in Eastern conditions. The example of the Russian workers and peasants, who have achieved with their own hands the emancipation from oppression by capitalists and landlords, has become the inspiration for other peoples of the world, including those of the colonial and dependent East.[40]

This does not make for pleasant reading, even for the governments of such uncommitted nations as look for Soviet support against the West. But Lenin's prophecy, quoted in the same article, is no more pleasant for the West:

Socialism has become a real prospect of world development. "The outcome of the struggle depends, in the inescapable analysis," V. I. Lenin wrote, "on the fact that Russia, India, China, etc., form the gigantic majority of the population. This majority is being dragged, as a matter of fact, with unusual speed in recent years, into the struggle for their liberation. There cannot be, in this sense, a shadow of doubt as to what the final solution of the world-struggle will be. The final victory of socialism is in this sense fully and unconditionally secured." (Lenin, *Sochineniia*, XXXIII, 458).[41]

As we remember, Lenin considered before and immediately after the October Revolution that the Western revolutions would decide the issue and that the colonial and semi-colonial movements would play a subsidiary role. Disappointed in his hopes, he increasingly relied on revolutions in the underdeveloped countries. This is also the hope of his modern disciples. Their current slogan sounds like this: "The October Revolution opened the new epoch of colonial revolutions led by the proletariat and its vanguard, the Communist parties."[42]

Lenin believed that his type of revolution could be carried out only by a determined and disciplined group of native disciples. Addressing a group of such disciples who had come from Asia and the Near East, he said in 1919:

It is now the lot of our Soviet Republic to group around itself the awakening peoples of the East in order to wage together the struggle against international imperialism. You face there a task which has never before confronted world Communists. Relying on the all-Communist theory and practice, you must know, adjusting yourselves to those special conditions which do not exist in European countries, how to use this theory and practice in the situations where the peasants form the bulk of the masses and where it is necessary to find solutions for questions involving struggle not against capitalism but against medieval survivals. This is a difficult struggle but it is a gratifying one, because those masses, which have not yet participated in the struggle, are being drawn into it. . . . Thanks to Communist organizations in the East which you represent here, you have contacts and the opportunity for making a further effort in spreading Communist propaganda in every country, using a language accessible to its people. . . . Your task consists in awakening revolutionary activity, self-reliance and organization of the toiling masses independently of the level they have attained, and to translate the true Communist teaching, destined for the Communists of more advanced countries, into the languages of all peoples . . . and to join in the common struggle of proletarians who wage it in other countries. . . . You will have to lean on the bourgeois nationalism awaking those peoples, which cannot but awake them, and which has historical justification. But at the same time, you must trace the road for the toiling and exploited masses of each country and tell them in accessible language that the only hope of liberation lies in international revolution, and that the international proletariat is the only ally of all the toiling and exploited masses of those hundreds of millions of Eastern peoples.[43]

This was the gospel that inspired Mao Tse-tung, Ho Chi-minh, the Korean and other Communists of the underdeveloped countries; not one iota need be changed.

The very word "socialism" is extremely fashionable in Asian countries. This is due not only to the Soviet-Chinese experience but also to the popularity of socialism in large sections of western European countries and to the nature of Asian capitalism. The latter capitalism is still in the stage Western capitalism was in during the 19th century. An Asian capitalist desires to make profits quickly, and the easy way is to keep wages low and prices high. The revolution that transformed American capitalism in the twenties has not affected Asia. To an American capitalist, the worker is not only a producer but also a consumer who assures wide demand for goods. His high wages entail a big market, while profits are expected not so much from a wide margin between the cost of production and the price as from large sales. This philosophy, which makes possible high standards of living, has not affected Asian economy. There, capitalism means low wages, misery to the workers, and huge profits quickly amassed by the few. Marx's picture of England in the middle of the 19th century still holds true for Asia and other underdeveloped countries. The western European postwar trend towards partial nationalization of industries has also exerted its influence. The concept of a planned economy, founded on the nationalization or building of the key industries by the state, is appealing to countries which want to give clear direction to domestic economic development.

All of this makes the word "socialism" popular. However, socialism has in our time acquired a confusing meaning. The British Labor Party, which is as much attached to political democracy as the Conservatives, is socialist, but Communists claim to be socialists as well. To the Asians socialism usually means some sort of mixed economy, composed of state-owned and private enterprises, but not a Communist political and social system. However, Communists have not overlooked the trend; they intend to capitalize on the popularity of the word:

The popularity of socialist ideas among the broadest popular masses in all Eastern countries is so great that even the national bourgeoisie in several non-socialist countries (India, Burma, and others) officially advances the slogan of building socialism and forming an economy of socialist type, etc.[44]

Another Soviet writer says the same thing:

It is not an accident that the leading statesmen of such large countries as India, Indonesia, and Egypt, who do not themselves represent socialist parties, often favorably mention socialist ideas. Although their concept of socialism is not identical and does not coincide with Marxism, it is obvious that they more and more frequently turn their attention towards socialism. This is a sign of the times. It is also characteristic that, while the workers' and socialist parties had before acted in the main only in the highly-developed capitalist countries, the position of socialist parties is now being strengthened in the underdeveloped countries. For instance, the 3rd Conference of the socialist parties of Asia and Africa, held in Bombay in November 1956, was attended by the following heads of governments: U Ba Sve (the chairman of the conference), Prime Minister of Burma, Bandaranaike (Ceylon), Kwame Nkrumah (Gold Coast), Abdullah Khalil (Sudan), Nnamdi Azikiwe (Nigeria), and by other outstanding statesmen of several Asian and African countries.[45]

Another Soviet specialist on Asia says:

The leaders of the Burmese Government declare that they intend to build "the society according to the socialist pattern." Although the meaning of socialism is different for the Burmese leaders from that which the Marxists follow, it is impossible not to see in these statements the evidence of that immense influence which the great ideas of socialism and democracy exert in our time not only on workers and peasants but also on the leading representatives of other classes.[46]

Khrushchev was very careful to avoid possible confusion in the minds of his Asian sympathizers. He made it clear that the socialism of the national bourgeois Nehru was not *his* socialism, and that Prime Minister of Burma, Mr. U Nu, who had greeted him and Bulganin as "comrades," was not really a socialist comrade.[47]

When the historical opportunity had materialized and when the Communists in an underdeveloped country were able to control events, then they would perform two revolutions almost at the same time, the bourgeois-democratic against feudal survivals and the socialist, introducing a Soviet-like or Chinese-like regime. This is a basic Leninist teaching already applied in Russia and China; the absence of developed capitalism is not an obstacle to a socialist revolution that is possible after a few preliminary reforms effected by Communists themselves. A recent Soviet handbook on Communist strategy and tactics, written mainly for use by foreign Communists, thus explains the Leninist theory:

> The theory of the transformation of the bourgeois-democratic revolution into a socialist revolution, which V. I. Lenin formulated in the first years of the Russian Revolution is, equally with the concept of the hegemony of the proletariat, one of the cornerstones of the strategy and tactics of Leninism. . . . V. I. Lenin proved that the necessity for a long interval between the victorious bourgeois-democratic revolution and the coming socialist revolution was excluded in the period of imperialism. . . . The bourgeois-democratic and the socialist revolutions become two links of one chain, two strategic stages in one revolutionary-liberating movement and in one process of powerful popular revolution, vanquishing one after the other, all exploiters; it establishes at first a revolutionary-democratic dictatorship of the proletariat and peasantry, to be followed by the dictatorship of the proletariat. The short interval between the democratic and socialist revolutions is, at the same time, filled not with the dictatorship of the bourgeoisie, but with the transformation of the people's democratic revolution into a socialist one; during which period the proletariat, in alliance with the peasantry and other democratic strata of the population, exercises the revolutionary-democratic people's dictatorship.[48]

Stripped of its esoteric language, this means that the Communists (the proletariat) take power, hold it during both revolutions, and proceed, with the initial, so-called democratic reforms, to sweep the ground for the Soviet-like regime. The same author points out that both revolutions may be carried out by local Communists with the assistance of other Communist states, probably according to the eastern European pattern:

> Lenin said . . . that the national-liberating struggle was part of the revolutionary struggle of the proletariat for socialism, and that the oppressed peoples, after throwing off the yoke of colonizers and feudal lords may take,

with the assistance of countries where the proletariat has already won, the road of socialist transformation while by-passing the capitalist stage.[49]

North Korea, Mongolia, and North Vietnam are vivid illustrations, besides eastern Europe, of Lenin's meaning.

Current Soviet articles support this view. For instance a Mongolian writes:

Now, when the age of capitalism is nearing its end, when the colonial system of world imperialism is in the process of disintegration, when all roads lead to socialism, the existence of the mighty camp of democracy and socialism makes the non-capitalist way of developing the underdeveloped countries towards socialism not only possible but historically necessary and fully legitimate. . . . He [Lenin] proved that the material-technical and cultural premises required for the passage to socialism might be created not only within capitalism but also after the overthrow of the power of exploiting classes, and that the working class holding political power was capable of dealing successfully with the gigantic difficulties of the passage from pre-capitalist conditions to socialism. Lenin pointed out that the revolutionary overthrow of the dominion of landlords and capitalists and the establishment of the dictatorship of the proletariat were the main premises for the transition of economically underdeveloped countries to socialism.[50]

A Mongolian knows from experience that a Communist revolution, especially if assisted by the Red Army, may take place even in a country populated by nomads. Such a queer interpretation of Marxism recalls Lenin's forecast: ". . . the movement of the majority of world population . . . will play a much greater revolutionary role than we expect (Lenin, *Sochineniia*, XXXII, 458)."[51]

The present intense interest in revolution in the underdeveloped countries is also due to Chinese events. While the Russia of 1917 was already on the road to industrialization, China in 1949 was still an agricultural country. Her example is more convincing than the Russian. Moreover, the revolutionary strategy followed by the Chinese Communists is surrounded by a halo of success. The Chinese Revolution, coming as it did at such an early stage, must have taken even Stalin by surprise. Molotov, speaking soon after the Chinese victory, admitted this: "It became clear only recently [*sic!*] that the triumph of the national-liberating movement in China was the most important result of the allied victory over German fascism and Japanese imperialism."[52] If the rapid Chinese success came as a surprise, the impression it produced in Moscow must have been proportionately deeper. Since that time, Chinese strategy and tactics have been recommended to Communists in all the underdeveloped countries.

5. Temporary Allies before the Revolution

A survey of Chinese experience points to its giving a new turn to the theory of two revolutions carried out by the Communists and to an adroit use of all social classes in the process of conquering power:

It [the Communist Party of China] demonstrated that the most important historical particularity of the Chinese Revolution consisted in its having two stages: first, the democratic revolution, and second, the socialist revolution. . . . The Communist Party explained to the masses that the edge of the democratic revolution was not directed against capitalism and capitalist property in general, but that its main enemies were the class of feudal landlords and foreign imperialists, together with the Chinese comprador bourgeoisie serving those imperialists. Only a united Chinese people could achieve this upheaval, the proletariat, the peasantry, petty-bourgeoisie and the representatives of other classes, all of them capable of fighting imperialism, feudalism and bureaucratic capitalism. . . . But, while forging this single anti-imperialist and anti-feudal front, the Chinese proletariat fought for its own hegemony within this front, for the Communist Party being the center of the National Front, and for the revolutionary-democratic alliance of the proletariat with the peasantry as the foundation of the Front. . . . Striving for a widening of the front of revolutionary forces, the proletariat also recruited for the revolutionary movement various layers of the bourgeoisie, following the policy of "alliance and struggle." When the bourgeoisie acted in alliance with the proletariat against imperialism and feudalism, the proletariat made use of its revolutionary potentialities, but fought at the same time for the elimination of the bourgeoisie from the leadership of the revolution and for its own hegemony. This struggle had an outstanding significance; if the antagonism between imperialism and the Chinese people, as well as that between feudalism and the popular masses, were the principal contradictions in semi-colonial and semi-feudal Chinese society, the struggle between the bourgeoisie and the proletariat for revolutionary leadership of the popular masses was the determining form of class struggle within the National Front itself.[53]

This may be reduced in ordinary words to its essence: the Chinese Communist Party deployed the flag of Chinese anti-foreign nationalism and agrarian reform and recruited followers not only from the proportionately small proletariat but also from among the peasants, for whom the Communists masqueraded as innocent agrarian reformers, and from all other social classes, including the bourgeoisie, if they were interested in the vision of a powerful industrialized China, if they were tired of the Kuomintang, and if they wanted to modernize Chinese society. Nothing else needed to be said at that stage of the game; the principal goal was to control the movement and to win political power.

The Chinese victory was followed, in 1949–1952, by the so-called new-democratic revolution:

Speaking of the economic contents of the new-democratic revolution, Mao Tse Tung said: "This revolution economically consists in the transfer to State administration of large capitals and large enterprises, belonging to the imperialists and to the national reactionary traitors, in the distribution of the landlords' land and its transfer to peasants' private ownership, but it also presupposes the survival of private capitalist enterprises in general and does not involve at all the liquidation of the kulak homesteads." (Mao Tse Tung, *Selected Works*, III, 174). The carrying out of these economic measures was one of the main tasks of the democratic people's dictatorship in 1949–1952. The confiscation and nationalization of bureaucratic capital and also of foreign capital uprooted imperialism and liquidated the big comprador bourgeoisie closely connected with it. All banks, railroads, means of communication and air transport, the main sectors of the automobile and fluvial transport, with industrial enterprises, such as plants, factories, mines, owned by the comprador clique, were transferred to national ownership. All branches of economy were transformed into one state economic sector. The share of the State industrial output represented as early as 1949 37 per cent of the total national industrial production.[54]

The new-democratic revolution, which lays down the foundations for the next stage, consists in the nationalization of what Lenin called the controlling economic heights. The Party founds its political power on its ability to direct the whole national economy. But it needs to consolidate its power by keeping, for a time, the peasants and the bourgeoisie fairly contented; it therefore proceeds to distribute land to the peasants, though it is well aware that it will take this back in the next stage—collectivization. It does not nationalize the property of the national bourgeoisie, unopposed to the revolution, though it will do so in the near future. The country is left to settle down before the opening of the socialist revolution. This clever tactic misled not only millions of Chinese but also a number of Western observers.

Chinese strategy and tactics have left their imprint on the current Communist concepts concerning the method of handling various social classes in the underdeveloped countries. After all, the Communist parties have small memberships and want to be so; they must be sure of the passive neutrality or benevolence of the masses in all cases where Soviet or Chinese military assistance is not readily available. China is cited as an encouraging example for the underdeveloped countries: "People's China is the inspiring example for people in the underdeveloped countries."[55] Of course, it is not expected that the revolution will take care of itself; the Communists must carry it out:

However much the correctness of teachings of scientific socialism is proved in actual life, they cannot by themselves spontaneously master the con-sciousness of the masses and provide toilers with a clear revolutionary vision and a faith in the victorious outcome of their struggle. The Marxist-Lenin-ist parties play a decisive role in that struggle.[56]

Communists isolated from the rest of the population would remain an insignificant and sour group. The theorist of Communist strategy therefore says:

Lenin frequently taught that the working class could not vanquish the ex-ploiters merely by its own force: the victory requires a close alliance be-tween the proletariat and the broadest non-proletarian strata of the toilers. The formation of such an alliance is the most important component ele-ment of the general question of recruitment of a mass political revolution-ary army and of the conquest and use by the working class of its main reserves in the liberating struggle. The peasant democratic movement for the seizure of land owned by the landlords . . . is such an essential reserve. The peasant question . . . is that of essential allies of the proletariat.[57]

This is an obvious tactic to be followed in any agrarian country where the industrial workers represent a small class. The peasants should carry the Communists to victory on their shoulders. Lenin saw this perfectly before the October Revolution. His three slogans—peace, bread, and land—were understandable to everyone; long dissertations on Marxism would have evoked no response from his audience of soldiers, workers, and peasants. Peace meant the end of a war which had brought only ghastly human hecatombs to Russia; bread was an alluring offer to a country with dis-rupted food supplies; land attracted peasant support for the Bolsheviks, who did not waste time on legal niceties but told the peasants to grab land belonging to powerful landowners and to the Church. His peasant policy was a crucial factor in the October Revolution and in the subsequent civil war. It is no wonder, then, that he advised the Second Congress of the Com-intern in 1920 to stress "the necessity of supporting especially the peasant movement in the backward countries against the landlords, the large es-

tates, and against all manifestations or survivals of feudalism, and of trying
to give the most revolutionary character to this movement."[58] It is quite
true that "the October Revolution demonstrated that it was possible and
realistic to combine the 'peasant war' with the proletarian revolution."[59]
The 4th Comintern Congress upheld the same thesis:

Only an agrarian revolution, whose object is to expropriate large estates,
can set in motion the enormous peasant masses; it is destined to exercise
decisive influence on the struggle against imperialism. . . . The revolutionary movement in the backward countries of the East cannot be successful
unless it relies on the action of the broad peasant masses. Therefore the
revolutionary parties of all Oriental countries must formulate a clear agrarian programme, putting forward the demand for complete abolition of the
feudal system and its survivals in the form of large landownership and tenant farming.[60]

A contemporary Soviet writer remains faithful to this line of thought when
he says:

The peasants represent the most numerous class in the Asian countries,
about 70 to 80 per cent of the populations of India, Indonesia, Burma,
Pakistan, Iran and other States. . . . This is why the revolutionary movement of the masses against imperialism is usually interwoven with the struggle of the peasants against the landlords.[61]

The battle for the peasants requires the defeat of the main competitor,
the peasant or other "bourgeois" parties, which also favor an agrarian
reform. This is why the peasant parties were the butt of a pitiless Communist campaign in eastern Europe in the forties. A Soviet expert puts it this
way:

. . . the struggle against the bourgeoisie and its agents for the peasant reserves and for influence among the broadest strata of the peasantry is one
of the most important strategic and tactical tasks of the revolutionary proletariat in all countries of the capitalist world.[62]

The Chinese Communists did not invent this concept, but they did apply
it brilliantly:

Following the Leninist tactical principles concerning the peasant question,
Mao Tse Tung considered the peasant question as the central one within
the problem of the hegemony of the proletariat. "Poor and middle peasants," Mao Tse Tung said, "may achieve their liberation only under the
leadership of the proletariat, and the proletariat in its turn may lead the

revolution to a victory only in close alliance with the poor and middle peasants. Victory is otherwise impossible." (Mao Tse Tung, *On the Dictatorship of People's Democracy*, Gospolitizdat, 1949, 14) It is precisely because of the hegemony of the proletariat and the alliance between the working class and the peasantry that the Chinese new-democratic revolution won a final victory and made possible the transformation of that revolution into a socialist one.[63]

Having promised a radical agrarian reform, the Chinese Communists, cut off from the eastern seaboard, with its urban workers, were able to establish the center of their movement and recruit their armies in purely rural areas. The same Chinese author writes:

After 1927 the Communist Party of China transferred the center of its activities to the villages and created there, with the help of the armed revolutionary people, revolutionary bases, gathered its forces and then, acting from this center, started encircling the cities and finally conquered them. Comrade Mao Tse Tung says that: "... a protracted revolutionary struggle waged in the villages, this bulwark of the revolution, is essentially a peasant partisan war directed by the Communist Party of China." (Mao Tse Tung, *Selected Works*, III, 156) One of the peculiarities of the Chinese revolution consists in this protracted armed struggle, beginning with the establishment of revolutionary bases in the villages and ending with the victory of the revolution in the whole country.[64]

This is a peculiarly Chinese lesson, and it is not yet lost to sight.

After the victory, the Chinese Communists could not disappoint the peasants by proceeding immediately with the collectivization of land. They needed time for settling down. They therefore carried out the agrarian reform during the civil war to attract peasants to their banners and continued it after that war. A territory inhabited by 120 million people witnessed the agrarian reform accomplishment before the proclamation of the People's Republic in 1949; after the victory, the reform was carried out in the remaining territory. A law on agrarian reform was formally adopted on June 28, 1950. The procedure was rough, with the express intention of inciting the peasants against the landlords; Communists organized people's tribunals to terrorize the landlords and richer peasants, as well as peasant unions (two-thirds composed of poor peasants and one-third middle peasants), for the division of land. As a result, 47 million hectares, confiscated from larger landowners, were transferred to poor and middle peasants as their short-term reward.[65]

The other element to be drawn into the situation is that urban population which eludes classification as the industrial proletariat, in other words, the various strata of the bourgeoisie, from the petty to the big. Here is an important matter because this urban bourgeoisie includes the educated class, a decisive factor in social movements and also indispensable after the revolution for running the state machinery in the transitory period until the Communists are able to install their own intelligentsia. Of course a penniless member of the intelligentsia remains a bourgeois as long as he is not transformed into a proletarian by his admission to the Party. Chinese Communists did not scare their so-called bourgeoisie by advertising their ultimate intentions to regiment all thought and to nationalize, in the last analysis, all means of production. Did not Mao Tse-tung say that the "democratic" revolution "presupposes the general survival of private capitalist enterprises"? Were not the various small Chinese parties invited to join with the Communists in getting rid of the Kuomintang?

These Chinese techniques, a great improvement on the Bolshevik ones in 1917, are now cited as a pattern to be followed by the Communist parties in all underdeveloped countries. The minimum program especially commended is that of the Brazilian Party; it mentions only such points as are palatable to various sections of the population (see Chapter IV). Actually, the Chinese Communists and their present-day imitators in other underdeveloped countries have recourse to a technique known to other politicians. It is so easy to promise Paradise to the constituents before elections; thereafter it is just as easy to forget your promises. Only a political democracy places certain practical restrictions on this type of pre-electoral demagogy; there are other parties, one's term of office is limited, and if you fool the electorate, you will not be re-elected. There is no such sanction for the Communists. They may promise anything before their "elections," the revolution, but no one may call them to account after the revolution for the sufficient reason that political competition has already been eliminated. Their demagogy may thus be unlimited; it goes unchecked.

6. Fate of Temporary Allies after the Revolution

The social classes to which Communists appeal may ask the vital question concerning the fate of the same classes in other countries which have already had their revolution. The politicians who think that they can outsmart the Communists in the venture of mutual co-operation (this is no easy job, for Communists have gone through the excellent political school of Lenin's teaching on tactics) and who believe that they may lean on Communist support in order more easily to reach their immediate objectives (of defeating a domestic enemy or fighting a foreign Power) may also cautiously ask the question concerning the fate which befell other non-Communist politicians in lands now ruled by Communists. Industrial workers would then learn that labor unions become, in a Communist state, the right arm of the general employer, the state, that strikes are forbidden, that equality of incomes is repudiated in favor of hard work for the workers and high incomes for the state and Party dignitaries and industrial executives. Peasants would discover that the plots granted them by Communist agrarian reform are taken back some years later in the collectivization drive. The intelligentsia, whose main social function is to think, will discover that their brethren in Communist lands must toe the Party line in every sphere of thought. The bourgeoisie will learn that their enterprises will soon be nationalized despite promises to the contrary. As for non-Communist politicians, they might contemplate the sad fate of non-Communist parties and their leaders in China and eastern Europe. Politicians who showed courage to the bitter end, e.g., the Bulgarian peasant leader Petkov, were physically exterminated. Their parties were split up, one fraction being retained after Communist infiltration to serve as a channel of propaganda to those sections of the population easier to be reached in that way. The National Front, organized before the revolution as a co-operative venture of various parties and organizations, simply becomes a smoke screen for the only party which, in fact, remains and holds all of the power. These practical lessons are patently available; wise politics includes, first and last, the ability to learn from the experience of other people.

The Chinese experiment may serve as but one illustration. The maximum Communist program began to be carried out only a few years after the revolution; the new-democratic revolution made room for the socialist one: "In contradistinction to the democratic revolution, directed against imperialism, feudalism and bureaucratic capital, the edge of the socialist revolution is turned against capitalism and capitalist property in general."[66] What is the general line of the socialist revolution to which the democratic is only a preamble?

In 1952, after the rehabilitation of national economy had neared its completion, the Central Committee of the Communist Party of China . . . formulated the general Party line for the period of transition from a new-democratic society to a socialist one. This general line consists in a gradual carrying out of socialist industrialization of the country, in the socialist transformation of agriculture and craftsmen's trades, capitalist industries and commerce, and in building up in this way a Chinese socialist society.[67]

The peasant masses were forced to accept collective farming at a speed that put the USSR to shame; over 500 million peasants were driven into collective farms within a few years. The collectivization drive began in the years after the end of the civil war but was a small-scale movement until 1955:

It [collectivization] has accomplished capital successes only in recent times, especially after Mao Tse Tung's report on agricultural co-operatives submitted on July 31, 1955, and the decisions of the Plenum of the Central Committee of the C.P.C. adopted in October of the same year on the basis of that report. . . . The movement for co-operatives soon began irresistibly to develop. By the end of 1955 the number of co-operatives was more than 1,900,000 with 70 million peasant homesteads having been integrated [there were only 100,000 such collective farms in 1954]. By the middle of 1956 the co-operatives had integrated 90 per cent of all peasant homesteads.[68]

These figures and the short period of time they cover implicitly provoke one comment, namely that those untold millions of Chinese peasants were not asked to express their opinions but were forced to abandon private husbandry for the sake of collective farming, which no peasant, be he European or Asian, likes.

This rapid mass collectivization did not satisfy the Chinese Communists. Outbidding their Soviet comrades, they suddenly decided in 1958 to inaugurate a policy for which there was no example in the Soviet Union. They decreed to organize the so-called "communes," each of them covering large rural areas of the size of a county. The whole manpower of each commune was organized as a quasi-military unit. The Party assumed the power to direct each section of that manpower to any work: industry, public works, or agriculture. Family life, traditionally essential for the Chinese society, was disrupted, the father being assigned to one work brigade, the wife to another, while the aged and the children were to be taken care of by communal institutions. Communal feeding was substituted for family meals. The sacred ancestral family burial plots were plowed over to increase the size of agricultural areas. The most zealous local Party organizations even cast a doubt on the right of members of communes to own any personal property. This policy had two purposes: to assure full mobility of manpower, each individual remaining at the Party's call, available for any kind of work that was assigned to him; and to replace the highest Chinese loyalty to the family with undivided allegiance to the Party and the state.

This system, barbarian in its harshness, left even the Soviet leaders somewhat perplexed. It caused such discontent that the Party had to moderate it several months later by making it clear that private property in goods of personal use should be respected and that family life could be tolerated insofar as work assignments of the parents would leave any free time for it.

This Chinese policy of communes appears so ruthless even by comparison to the Soviet record that eastern Europeans, themselves subject to Communist regimes, joke that they are lucky to be separated from China by a "big buffer State." However, the peasants and non-peasants in the underdeveloped countries could usefully digest the post-revolutionary policy of China as a warning to themselves.

The fate of the "national" bourgeoisie was no better. The procedure adopted by the Chinese Party was subtle and effective; they did not hang all the capitalists on lamp posts, as a naïve anti-Communist would have expected them to do, for these capitalists represented precious human material for an underdeveloped country intending to become industrialized. Their skills had to be used, but their capital was to be taken away, and this was done by degrees. Immediately after the revolution, the state went to work in two directions: (1) to build up new state-owned industries, not only in order to proceed with industrialization, but also to control the general economic life of the country, an objective made much easier by the immediate confiscation of important large enterprises, either foreign owned or under the pretext that they had been owned by the comprador bourgeoisie; and (2) to install controls over enterprises owned by the national bourgeoisie through purchases of their output.

Beginning in 1950, a second step was taken: the state monopolized the purchase of output from, and the supplies of raw materials to, privately owned enterprises while leaving to their owners the heavy responsibility for the quantity and quality of production. This system allowed the state to cut down profits by fixing prices for raw materials and finished goods.

The third step taken in the current period consists in forcing owners to accept the state as a partner and to form mixed state-private enterprises in which the role of the owner is limited to that of a manager under state supervision.[69] The result is that "they [those enterprises] become State-private and are placed under direct State administration."[70] The control of property is thus transferred to state bureaucracy. What of the profit?

This is detached from its previous relationship to actual production and reduced to a fixed commission proportionate to the value of the enterprise as appraised, of course, by the Communist state. The net result is not too pleasant for national bourgeoisie:

It is quite obvious that the annual income of former owners of smaller industrial and commercial enterprises, under the system of a fixed 5 per cent annual commission, is significantly lower than the average wages of skilled workers. Such smaller enterprises constitute the majority. . . . At present almost all former owners of commercial and industrial enterprises have already become the employees at mixed or state enterprises.[71]

The next step will be to abolish the small commission and to transform mixed enterprises, already, in fact, state owned, into openly nationalized ones. The national bourgeois, like the industrial worker or peasant, will become a state employee. Soviet sources admit that a great number of these former enterprise owners have already become ordinary workers. But those who represent a pool of administrative-managerial skills are "re-educated" for the service of the state:

The use of former owners of private industrial and commercial enterprises as technical specialists and administrative employees is dictated, of course, by production interest. The transformation of small capitalist industrial enterprises employing small numbers of workers (those enterprises represent the majority) will not result in a reduction of production and an increase in unemployment where former owners are used as organizers of production under strict control of workers and the State. This applies even more to private trade. Former owners who have technological and organizing habits may also become very useful in big enterprises.[72]

The results of this process of socialization are summed up thus:

Approximately 92 per cent of peasants and 90 per cent of craftsmen were already in the middle of 1956 united in all sorts of producer co-operatives. The capitalist production to the extent of 99 per cent of its value and 98 of its total number of employees, has already been transformed into a higher type of mixed State-private industry where the administration is completely concentrated in the hands of the State. By the end of June 1956, 68 per cent of private commercial and private catering enterprises were already converted into mixed State-private enterprises, co-operative stores or co-operative groups. The conversion of capitalist industries and trade into mixed State-private enterprises, transformation of capitalists into people receiving a fixed commission, and the passage of management of private enterprises into the hands of the State, have prepared the ground for full nationalization of those means of production which belong to capitalists.[73]

The "peaceful" Chinese method of nationalizing the property of national bourgeoisie not only aims at gradually accustoming the owners to their unavoidable loss and psychologically training them for their new managerial or other functions as state officials but also prevents economic disorganization as a consequence of violent and rapid confiscation. A Chinese author thus justified to his Soviet comrades this "sweet" way of despoiling the national bourgeoisie:

As the Chinese experience has proved, the gradual "purchase" of means of production, although it implies the payment of a certain compensation, allows for escaping various losses unavoidable in the procedure of a sudden transfer of means of production from one owner to another. . . . A temporary lowering of the level of social productive force is an almost unavoidable consequence of a forcible change in any form. There lies the greatest advantage of methods of peaceful transfer.[74]

He used a second argument that was decisive for Soviet Communists: he reminded them of Lenin's temporary concessions to the bourgeoisie in the period of the NEP for somewhat similar economic reasons:

The general line and the fundamental tasks in the transitory period in China do not differ in essence and in principle from the new economic policy promoted by Lenin in the period following the Civil War. We tread the Leninist path in carrying out our policy, except for using forms, stratagems, and methods different from those applied in the transitory period in the Soviet Union.[75]

The fate of the non-Communist parties in China which still survive is best illustrated by the one which is supposed to represent national bourgeoisie. A bystander would have expected it to raise a storm at this process of expropriation of its constituents. Let us turn to a Soviet source for an answer:

A very important particular feature of the policy of ideological re-education by the Communist Party of the bourgeois elements consists in the educational and political activity conducted with the assistance of the United National-Democratic Front in which the national bourgeoisie also participates. . . . The All-Chinese Association of the Democratic National Construction is the main political party of national bourgeoisie. This bourgeois party was organized in December 1945, but it became a numerous organization only after the liberation, and particularly during the period of intensification of the socialist transformation of capitalist industries and trade. . . . The Association has become the main national-bourgeois party which actively supports the general line of the Communist Party in the transitory period. . . . The first Congress of the Association was held in the beginning of April 1955. . . . The Congress resolution pointed out that the general line of the Association in the transitory period should follow the general line of the Communist Party of China. . . . The Association Charter thus defines its tasks: "The Association, reckoning with the main State tasks in the transitory period, unites and educates, under the leadership of the Communist Party, the national bourgeoisie for active realization of socialist transformation, for a resolute struggle against foreign and domestic enemies, and for the construction of a socialist society."[76]

Thus a party nominally national bourgeois, therefore non-Communist, openly avows being only an arm of the Communist Party and persuades its constituents that their best choice is to co-operate in their elimination as a class. The economic organization of the same bourgeoisie is the All-Chinese Commercial-Industrial Association, whose national congress decided in 1953:

The Congress unanimously supports the general line of the [Communist] Party [and unanimously acknowledges that] the gradual socialist transformation of private industries and commerce through State capitalism is "the best way" and method of transformation, convenient to the State and the people and also to private industrialists and merchants.[77]

Eastern European experience is basically the same. The surviving "peasant" or "democratic" parties have the same "independence" in relation to the Communist Party as the hapless Chinese Association. The nationalization of industries was completed without the subtle Chinese stages, while collectivization of agriculture has thus far been carried out at a speed and with total results that are more modest than the Chinese. Of course there are no non-Communist parties, even by name, in the USSR, and the socialization of economy was totally accomplished a long time ago, but then the USSR has existed for forty years. Soviet Communists make no secret of their view that non-Communist parties, even though they co-operated with Communists before the revolution, must gradually disappear after the revolution. A monolithic society cannot be reconciled with the survival of more than one party:

The question of a multi-party system must be examined concretely and historically, because the liquidation of exploiting classes and the building up of moral-political unity of the society result in the decline and finally the complete elimination of the multi-party system.[78]

7. National Fronts

As we have seen, the concept of temporary alliances with "unstable and unreliable" allies is an integral part of Lenin's theory of tactics. A national, popular, united, or whatever labeled front is one of the familiar applications of that concept. The universal formula is as follows:

Taking their cue from the strategic and tactical principles of Leninism and from the experience of Communist Parties of the Soviet Union and of China, Communist parties in the colonial and semi-colonial countries follow the course oriented towards the victory of an agrarian, anti-feudal and anti-imperialist revolution. The proletariat [this word is used here as a synonym for Party] of the oppressed countries recruits its political army from among all layers of the peasantry, urban, petty and national bourgeoisie, all the patriotic elements, and strives to build up a powerful alliance of all progressive forces in one democratic national front. The foundation of the democratic national front, based on the alliance of the working class with the peasantry, but with the proletariat as leader in this alliance, represents a firm condition for the success of an anti-feudal and anti-imperialist revolution in those countries.[79]

To combine forces with non-Communist parties and other organizations serves several purposes: (1) it splits the non-Communists and makes possible their defeat, one after the other; (2) it makes victory easier in the battle against the enemy of today by means of the assistance of enemies of tomorrow, for instance, against a political party in power, or against the industrialized West by means of the help of opposition parties or the underdeveloped countries; (3) it gives the Communists an aspect of respectability, since the average man might be inclined to dismiss as rubbish any reflections about their ultimate aims in view of the fact that politicians whom he trusts consent to co-operate with them; and (4) it allows for the gradual infiltration of the rank-and-file partisans of co-operating parties.

Whatever the slogans of the National Front, the Communists, as a rule, readily agree to authenticate the type that sparks the immediate sympathetic response of the public. Such watchwords must refer to current issues, not to the Communist maximum program, which might only frighten the public. When it comes to transforming these slogans into political action, one may be sure the Communists will display greater enthusiasm and less fear of risks than collaborators who have only limited aims. They are thus able to capitalize on the sympathy of the public, which begins to see them as the only true and uncompromising fighters. They have nothing to lose.

Other parties must calculate the risks; they do not desire the country to be plunged into chaos which might deliver it to the Communists alone.

However, the Communist Party never surrenders to its allies. It must preserve its own ideological and organizational identity, make clear to members and sympathizers that it is affianced only temporarily to the "bourgeois or petty-bourgeois" parties and that it may denounce the alliance at any time. The Chinese theory of alliance with, and struggle against, national bourgeoisie is as old as the Communist movement because any non-Communist organization may become an ally for a limited time only and will be a future enemy. The Party should do its best to give the front a political direction suiting its own aims. All of this applies to the "peace zone" with uncommitted nations as well as to the domestic fronts.

Lenin said in 1920:

... the Communist International should support the bourgeois-democratic national movements in the colonial and backward countries only on condition that the elements of future proletarians, Communist parties not only by name, be grouped together in all backward countries, and educated in the consciousness of their particular task of fighting the bourgeois-democratic movements within their own countries.[80]

This sentence, apparently self-contradictory, becomes clear if one understands the main point: to support national-bourgeois movements against the imperialists (the West) and to fight against these movements in order to prepare the ground for domestic revolution. Stalin was just as straightforward in 1927:

The United Front [in dependent and colonial countries] may have revolutionary significance only on condition that it does not hinder the Communist Party in conducting its own independent political and organizational work, in arousing the peasants against the landlords, in openly organizing the revolution by workers and peasants, and in preparing in this way the ground for the hegemony of the proletariat.[81]

These two quotations throw light on the Communist concept of national fronts in the underdeveloped countries, a concept sponsored in 1922 by the 4th Comintern Congress: ". . . in the colonial East the slogan that must be emphasized at the present time is that of the anti-imperialist united front."[82] This concept has never been abandoned, but it could not serve a useful purpose in the last period of Stalin's life because of his negative attitude towards national bourgeoisie. It has since been revived. The 20th

Congress stressed the need for such fronts as one of the means eventually leading to "socialism." Khrushchev said:

> ... the present situation offers to the working class in a number of capitalist countries a real opportunity to unite the overwhelming majority of people under its leadership and to secure the transfer of basic means of production in the hands of the people. ... The working class, by rallying around itself the toiling peasantry, the intelligentsia, all patriotic forces, and resolutely repulsing the opportunist elements incapable of giving up the policy of compromise with the capitalists and landlords, is in a position to defeat the reactionary forces opposed to popular interest, to capture a stable majority in parliament and transform the latter from an organ of bourgeois democracy into a genuine instrument of popular will. ... The winning of a stable parliamentary majority, backed by a mass revolutionary movement of the proletariat and of all toiling people, could create for the working class in a number of capitalist, former colonial countries, conditions needed to secure fundamental social changes.[83]

Of course a united front of all "patriotic" forces need not use parliamentary procedures, especially in countries where parliaments play insignificant roles.

People who believe that the Communist movement has become policentric, with each party having an independent line defined by its own leadership, should sometimes check on the simultaneous pronouncements made by various Communist parties on a topic of general interest. They would be surprised by the identity of concepts, and even terminology, in all such declarations, as though all of them followed the same pattern, fixed by a group of people working at one center. The idea of national fronts would provide useful material for such a check. This idea recently became very fashionable in Moscow. The leading foreign Communists responded from all corners of the world, copying Soviet patterns of thought and Soviet slogans. Some of them, e.g., the Indonesian and Syrian Communists, have been very lucky in going farther than mere propaganda for a national front and in forging such fronts in their countries. The others are still busy advertising the idea.

Khalid Bagdash, the secretary-general of the Communist Party of Syria and Lebanon, could report to *Pravda* in March, 1956, on his success. He applied in Syria the Soviet concept of a very broad national front extending to every willing party, organization, or person, including the national bourgeoisie, about which he wrote in rather sympathetic words. Though an atheist, he welcomed the co-operation of the Islamic clergy as well. His con-

cept of the Syrian National Front consisted in uniting all anti-Western
forces under the slogan of the struggle against the Baghdad Pact. His trump
card was his unreserved anti-Israeli stand. Towards the end of his report, he
made clear the true objective of his national-front policy: "They [the Arab
peoples] find, in their glorious and noble struggle, as usual the assistance
and support of the world socialist camp and of its vanguard, the Soviet
Union and People's China."[84] Dolores Ibarruri, the first secretary of the
Communist Party of Spain, hurried from the other end of the Mediterranean to report, in the same month, her wholehearted support for identical
concepts. She said: "We cannot discount those workers and peasants or the
intelligentsia who are under the influence of socialist parties in the capitalist countries."[85] She gave very practical reasons for a united front with
the socialists, for whom she had not demonstrated particular love during
the Spanish Civil War:

The Social-Democratic parties number, according to 1953 data, ten million
members united in 36 Socialist and Labor parties; 24 of them are European,
5 are Asiatic, 6 are American, and one exists in New Zealand. . . . The International Confederation of Free Trade Unions . . . has 54,525,000 members.
. . . A joint action by Socialists and Communists would have serious influence on the electoral results in France.[86]

If the socialists, with their labor unions, represent a solid force, why not
enlist them as temporary allies, as the 20th Congress recommended a month
earlier? Strong in her Soviet orthodoxy, she denounced those Communists
who felt an aversion to even a temporary co-operation with the "opportunists and reformists":

There are still some Communists who assume that a Communist Party cannot conclude any agreements with non-Communist parties which could become in certain situations our allies. Lenin sharply denounced such views
but unfortunately they recur like measles.[87]

A year later she again reported to Moscow on her own endeavors to form
a broad national front for the purpose of overthrowing General Franco:

The plenary session of the Central Committee of the Communist Party of
Spain held recently, adopted important decisions. . . . The plenary session
reaffirmed the unwavering loyalty of Spanish Communists to Marxist-
Leninist teachings and its trust in the Communist Party of the Soviet
Union. . . . The Frankist anti-national policy has resulted in objective con-
ditions where the broadest strata of Spanish society begin to come together

in their views on some current problems. Those strata, from the working class to the non-monopolistic bourgeoisie, including even some groups from the big bourgeoisie, are all interested, for various reasons, in a deep change in the political and economic orientation of Spain. . . . From this soil of opposition to Frankism have grown up objective conditions favorable to a policy of a broad National Front which could include the leftists and the rightists forces interested in the political change. . . . The Communist Party . . . has called upon all groups and social-political forces desiring political changes in Spain to end the division into "reds" and "blues" which arose during the Civil War, and to establish concord among the Spaniards. . . . The question of the future regime, be it Monarchy or Republic, must not be an obstacle to mutual understanding among various forces of civilian and military opposition.[88]

One may measure the utter opportunism of Communist national-front tactics by this willingness of Dolores Ibarruri, who had won during the Spanish Civil War the reputation of a fiery Amazon of the revolution, eventually to co-operate with the Monarchists for the sake of the revolution.

There are several current instances of national-front policies. For instance, Soviet sources cite the example of the Syrian National Front:

The victory of the Syrian people in the struggle for independence would have been impossible were not all patriotic forces in the country united in a wide national-liberating front. The universal hatred of colonialism, the common aspiration to secure and maintain national independence, and the desire to raise the economic and cultural standards of Syria, are the foundations of this front.[89]

The slogans of the Syrian front did not mention the long-range Communist program but insisted on objectives which were currently popular—anti-Westernism (anti-colonialism) and the legitimate aspirations of an underdeveloped country to raise its economic and cultural standards. The authors cite the elections in 1954 as an example of fruitful results of national-front tactics:

During the [1954] electoral campaign the progressive forces organized the "National Union" which included Communists as well. . . . A Communist deputy, the secretary-general of the Communist Party of Syria, Khalid Bagdash, was for the first time in Syrian history elected to parliament. He held second place among the elected candidates in the Damascus constituency, judging by the number of ballots cast in his favor. The socialist party of Arab Regeneration, which electioneered under the anti-imperialist and democratic slogans, won 16 seats. Many other patriots and democrats were elected to parliament.[90]

Another example was the by-election in the city-of-Homs constituency held in 1955:

> ... the patriotic forces founded a National Progressive Front. The socialist party of Arab Regeneration, a leftist group headed by Khani as-Sabai, the Communist party, and other progressive groups were its members. Thus a wide rally of national forces was for the first time organized in Syria. The National Progressive Front was also supported by the influential National Party whose leader is the President of Syria, Kuwatly. This joint effort bore its fruits. The candidate of the National-Progressive Front, Ahmed-al-Madj Yunis, received four thousand ballots more than his opponents. . . . In March 1956 all the important political parties and organizations of Syria reached an agreement on a joint program called the National Charter. The National Charter stresses in the field of foreign policy the struggle against Israeli aggression and against foreign military alliances, the policy of an "active neutrality" between the two camps, and declares its full support for the Bandung Conference decisions. It foresees a strengthening of the bilateral alliance with Egypt through the conclusion of economic, political and cultural agreements, such agreements being destined to become the foundation of an "all-including Arab unity." . . . The close co-operation between the socialist party of Arab Regeneration and the Communist Party successfully frustrated the attempts by the reactionary elements to give an anti-Communist twist to the Charter. . . . The Syrian people wages an increasingly active struggle against oppression by foreign monopolies, in particular against the English Iraqi Petroleum Company and the American Trans-Arabian Pipe-Line.[91]

The National Front tactics had proved to be so propitious for the Communist infiltration that the non-Communist Syrian politicians became frightened by the prospect of losing power to their "allies." They thought that salvation lay in a merger with Egypt. After the two countries had formed the United Arab Republic, President Nasser hastened to dissolve all parties. The Syrian Communists went underground and have since tried to capitalize on the Syrian discontent with the new arrangements which had resulted in the Egyptian political and economic ascendency in Syria.

Another example concerns an underdeveloped European country, Greece. The 7th Plenum of the Central Committee of the Greek Communist Party, held at the beginning of 1957, adopted the same pattern, with adjustments to different national conditions. The Party declared itself in favor of a national front that would include all patriotic forces, priests (the Church is traditionally influential in Greece), army officers (the Greek army has played, at times, an active political role), and the national bourgeoisie and its parties. The objectives of such a front were spelled out: freeing Greece of foreign imperialist chains; liquidation of foreign bases on

Greek territory; expulsion of foreign military and economic missions; denouncing Greek membership in NATO; and full support for the self-determination of Cypriots. The place of Israel as the whipping boy of Arab nationalism was taken by Britain because of the Greek claim to self-determination for Cyprus. This is immaterial as long as the whipping boy stands for the Western Powers. The point of the sword is there, as elsewhere, directed mostly against the United States, the most powerful enemy. This and other programs suit the current Soviet policy perfectly. By way of contrast, the social-economic program offered to expected co-partners in the united front is amazingly moderate. "The Communist Party of Greece is ready to accept co-operation [with other parties] on the basis of an even more moderate program in order to make easier the consolidation of all patriotic forces."[92] The Greek Communist Party, legally outlawed but active under an assumed name of an ordinary Leftist party, has won, numerically, the second place in parliament.

The same is true in other countries, including those in Latin America. An article written by Salvador Allende, vice-president of the senate of Chile and president of the Chilean National Front, printed by *Pravda* in 1954, brought interesting information on both the composition and program of the front. After stating that 40 per cent of the Chilean population earned a living in agriculture, that 87 per cent of the arable land was owned by less than 2,000 people, and that foreign corporations exploited natural resources like copper and nitrate, Allende said that the National Front had been formed to obtain radical political, economic, and social changes in the present setup. He continued:

Its program is . . . anti-imperialist and anti-feudal. . . . The Popular Front is a broad patriotic movement struggling for political and economic liberation of our country. It includes the Socialist, Communist and Democratic parties. . . . The Front program is sufficiently broad to allow for union within it of peasants and progressive landowners, women and young people, officials and craftsmen, teachers and intelligentsia, university professors, merchants and industrialists, everyone who cherishes national interests; the working class is its backbone. The National Front wages a struggle for a structural change in our economy that would secure the full exploitation of our national resources and wide industrialization, as well as an agrarian reform . . . and for the re-establishment of normal relations between Chile and the USSR, the Chinese People's Republic, and all countries of people's democracy. It is also necessary that our country be freed of its international obligations which tie us up militarily and politically, and limit our independence and sovereignty. . . . The National Front . . . fights for the repeal of that reactionary statute which is called "the law for the defense of democracy," because its provisions hinder political liberty, the freedom of labor union activities, and have placed the Communist Party of Chile and its members beyond the pale of civil rights. The National Front demands the granting to the Communist Party and its members the same rights other parties enjoy. . . . Asia and Africa are awakening. Latin America will do the same in order to achieve its economic emancipation.[93]

Pravda carried an article on the Brazilian National Front written by another Latin American, Egidio Skeff. After a scathing attack on the United States and American corporations, such as the United States Steel Corporation, Bethlehem Steel Corporation, Standard Oil, and others, he continued:

The anti-imperialist movement had become so deep and broad . . . that a patriotic inter-party organization emerged. . . . The League of National Liberation was founded in April of this year [1954] in Rio de Janeiro. . . . The [founding] conference was convoked under the slogans of defense of natural resources and sovereignty of Brazil against the threat of American monopolies, and of a struggle against the danger of war towards which Yankee monopolies are leading Brazil. . . . Members of Congress representing various political parties, generals and officers, representatives of workers' and peasants' organizations, teachers, industrialists, merchants, doctors, judges, lawyers, intellectuals, and State officials, participated in the conference. . . . The League of National Liberation was thus born. . . . The League committees in the States and principal cities of the country, and local cells at plants and factories, universities, plantations, etc., have started work on recruitment of new members and on enlightenment of the popular masses. In several rural districts (peasants constitute 70 per cent of the Brazilian population) League cells are being organized. . . . Labor unions, students' associations, peasants' leagues, workers' unions, and various national organizations have come out from all over the country with declarations of support for the League. It is enough to declare one's support for the League program to become its member. . . . As the result of the national movement for the restoration of relations with the USSR, an Association of Brazilian-Soviet Friendship was founded in Rio de Janeiro. The program of the League of National Liberation, calling to a struggle against imperialism, demands at the same time the restoration of relations with the Soviet Union, China and countries of people's democracy.[94]

Despite the exaggerations in this report, it is worth pausing to compare the program of the Brazilian League with those of other national fronts promoted by Communists the world over. The main pattern consists of the same features; without a mention of the true long-term Communist program, they concentrate public attention on moderate local reforms, nationalistic slogans against the West (the United States in particular), as well as against foreign capital, attacks on the commitment policy, an appeal to all social classes, including the bourgeoisie, against whom Marx had raised his banner of revolution, and propaganda for closer relations with the Soviet bloc. This similarity of front programs cannot be mere coincidence. As long as the initial front program is clearly anti-Western and helps to weaken non-Communist solidarity and to divide non-Communists, its contents are fairly immaterial, and the Communists are told to go as far as possible in their concessions in order to assure the formation of the front.

A narrower version of a united front is that of socialist-Communist cooperation in the name of proletarian solidarity. This is not an easy enterprise because socialists are the competitors among the working class, and Communists have never tired of denouncing them as reformists and opportunists. The 20th Congress did the same. The western European socialists, who remember the sad experience of the popular front with Communists in the thirties, are probably the last to respond to this appeal. Soviet publications hardly encourage them by saying:

The international workers' movement went, during and after the Second World War, through an unheard of experience of united action by the Communist and Social-Democratic parties. This experience proves that the interests of Social-Democrats do not suffer in the least from such unity. This is best seen in the countries of Southeastern and Central Europe where the enemies of the working class failed in their attempts to divert Social-Democrats into the disastrous path of refusing to act together with Communists, and where the idea of unity triumphed . . . in the European countries of people's democracy mighty United Workers' parties were established.[95]

Unfortunately for the Communists, the western European socialists have a good memory and know recent history. Wartime anti-Nazi co-operation with Communists lasting for a few years after the war brought them "fine" results in France and Italy. The French Socialist Party lost the first place it had held in the prewar workers' movement to the Communist Party, while its former control over the General Federation of Labor Unions also passed to Communists. The Italian Party was split, the democratic socialists remaining in a minority. Eastern European socialist parties were shorn of their leaders, some of whom were shot or imprisoned, while the terrorized remnants everywhere were compelled in 1948 to merge with the Communist parties, thereby losing their former identity. This is hardly encouraging, though this bitter experience is less familiar to socialist parties in non-European countries. The narrower concept of a united front is actually destined for them:

The Social-Democratic parties in colonial and dependent countries have become since the Second World War considerably more active. . . . The movement of the popular masses in Asia, Africa and Latin America, has not only an anti-colonial but also in essence an anti-imperialist character. All this cannot but influence the leaders of Social-Democratic parties in those countries. . . . The appraisal of the situation and of the tasks that stand before the national liberating movement in the colonies and dependent countries points to the most favorable conditions for unity of action not only among the Socialist parties but also between them and the Communist parties and all other leading organizations of workers. . . . The Communists will be able to unite all national-democratic elements in those countries only on condition that, while remaining a party of the working class, they express in their proposals on unity of action with other parties the national aspirations and interests of the broadest toiling masses in their countries.[96]

The Soviet adviser counsels the utmost flexibility and adjustment to the conditions of each country:

It is only natural that contacts and unity of action between the Communist and Social-Democratic parties in various countries will be achieved in different ways depending on the historical, social, and political particularities and actual situation in each country. An uncritical imitation and a mechanical transfer of forms and methods of the joint action between Communist and Social-Democratic parties from one to another country may only hinder the establishment, broadening and strengthening of such unity. Demands relating to improvement in material conditions of toilers and to the defense of freedom and peace, can become fundamental points in the unity program in all countries. But the economic demands, realizable within the framework of a given regime, and the nature of the struggle against warmongers [Western sympathizers] and the forces which directly or indirectly assist those warmongers, will assume different complexions in each country. . . . Communists . . . should not try to by-pass these necessary stages of mass movement during which workers gradually lose their illusions through their actual experience, and eventually pass over to Communism.[97]

However broad or narrow the national front, Communists should never lose their identity and should cut the ground from under the co-operating socialists' feet:

The Communists may not of course and should not renounce even for a minute their own independent action relating to Communist enlightenment, organization and mobilization of the masses. . . . Communists will continue as before to defend Marxist-Leninist positions, and explain to the masses that the Marxist-Leninist theory provides the correct orientation regarding all domestic and external problems and the correct ideological foundation for the defense of the cause of the working class.[98]

Strong emotional reaction to the colonial past, fed on current quarrels with one or another Western Power, offers fertile ground for domestic national fronts and for a foreign policy sympathetic to the USSR in countries never reached by the Soviet expansionist policy. An article written for *Pravda* by Dr. Sukarno, president of the Indonesian Republic, throws light on emotions and attitudes in former colonial countries which follow the policy of non-commitment. It begins with a sharp denunciation of past Western colonial policy, whereby the Western Powers subjugated Asia and then acted as a pump, draining the riches of that continent towards the metropolitan countries. Asia not only lost its independence but was also reduced to poverty. He further says that the Indonesian Republic is founded on five principles: "1. One Almighty God; 2. One Indonesian Republic; 3. Humanitarianism; 4. Government by the people; 5. Social justice."[99] He continues:

The experience of the Soviet Union undoubtedly will be useful for the Asian countries after a careful analysis of and adjustment to, the actual conditions of each Asian country determined by national-historical development and the character of each nation. . . . It is very encouraging that the peoples of the Soviet Union look with sympathy and understanding at the struggle of Asian peoples, which has not yet ended. . . . Let us go forward together, let us strengthen our friendship.[100]

Did the President of Indonesia ask himself the question of whether the five principles he mentioned were practiced in Communist countries? Was he concerned to reconcile "One Almighty God" with militant Communist atheism? Or humanitarianism with purges, for which Khrushchev had provided so many details in his secret speech (made several months before the appearance of Dr. Sukarno's article)? Or with correctional labor camps or simply with Leninist morality? How did he square government by the people with the elitist concept of all Communist parties? Or, finally, social justice with Soviet repudiation of so-called egalitarianism and the privileges of the Soviet new upper bourgeoisie? This article illustrates a Western difficulty that is advantageous to the Soviet Union. The West is known to Asian countries, and everything known is never perfect. The Soviet Union is practically unknown as far as its actual practice is concerned; an official visit hardly provides a good opportunity for careful observation. It is only too easy to succumb to the idealization of the USSR, especially if one feels legitimately bitter about a remembered colonial past.

An Indian writing for another Soviet periodical has been more reserved but has joined Dr. Sukarno in the virulent denunciation of Western colonialism. It is useful for people who want to establish confident relations with former colonial countries not to underestimate the depth of these feelings, even though they represent nowadays only emotional reaction to the historical past, unfortunately recent, of nations now free and independent. Let us listen to the Indian accusation:

Thinking about the period of industrial development [of Europe in the 19th century], the inhabitants of Asia remember the dominion of ancient Egyptian Pharaohs and the Athenian democratic State where a small group of elect, leading a leisurely life, enjoyed the benefits of civilization at the expense of the labor of immense popular masses deprived of all rights and privileges whatsoever except for the right to work for their masters. . . . One has the impression that Englishmen, Frenchmen, and Dutchmen realized a similar order of things on a world scale transforming the whole population of Asian and African continents into a labor force and compelling them to work for the sake of the economic prosperity of European countries, prosperity which became in turn the foundation of contemporary Western Civilization.[101]

Although there is a grain of truth in this historical picture, Western civilization had certainly existed and flourished centuries before the conquest of Asia. A quick perusal of Marx's *Das Kapital*, which is rather well known in Asia, would also prove that the 19th-century economic development of Europe was due not only to profits coming from colonial possessions but also to the sweat and labor of European workers. When the same author ascribes all of the ills of contemporary India to British rule, he also exaggerates; to cite one or two examples, the caste system had existed for millennia before the appearance of the first Britisher in India, and the national unity of modern India was forged in the mold of British colonial administration; this indeed had made one whole of disparate regions the British found in the 18th century. But the point is not the exaggeration, but the existence of resentments which make Soviet foreign policy so much more plausible at first than any Western persuasions. The Indian author was at least not blind to another colonialism, which, unlike the Western, is not receding and is very much alive. Speaking with the courtesy due his hosts, he wrote:

We shall not examine this phenomenon in Europe, although we understand by colonialism not only the exploitation but also interference in the free life of peoples in other States, whatever the motivation of such an interference might be. The Indian people, who remember recent foreign rule, condemn every enslavement, whatever its place, either in contemporary Europe or in any other area of the globe.[102]

8. Industrialization Slogan

The underdeveloped countries yearn for the economic transformation that would bring them gradual solution of their pressing social problems. They often visualize it as a process of gaining economic independence, which would strengthen their political independence. The same Indian author says:

Many Indians believe that the battle for freedom either in India or in other countries has been won only by half, only in the political sense. The struggle in the realm of economics is more important. The Indians think that, if this second battle is lost, political freedom will again be threatened.[103]

Dr. Sukarno correlated independence with economic development in the same way:

Opening the [Bandung] Conference [in April, 1955] President Sukarno of Indonesia said: "They often tell us colonialism is dead. We must neither be deluded nor rejoice. I tell you that colonialism has not yet died. How is it possible to say that it is dead, if vast areas of Asia and Africa remain unfree. And I beg you not to imagine colonialism only in its classical form which we in Indonesia and our brothers in various parts of Asia and Africa knew. Colonialism appears also in modern clothes—in the form of economic control, spiritual control, and direct physical control exercised by a small group of foreigners from within the country."[104]

It is true that a country is more independent in foreign relations if it has a strong economy, but this begs the question of how to achieve the desired economic development. Common sense would indicate that this could be done at a less costly and speedier pace if foreign help were forthcoming in the various modern forms of loans, grants, and investments. After all, this is the secret of the quick American industrialization in the 19th century, which was spurred by large foreign investments. Yet the United States remained independent.

Economic transformation is usually equated with industrialization, which would bring a solution to overpopulated countries with no prospects for mass emigration. This is fully understood in the Soviet Union, which constantly plays up to such sentiments in the underdeveloped countries. However, an industrialization with Western assistance is not welcomed, for rather obvious reasons. The underdeveloped countries are asked to look towards the Soviet bloc for assistance, though Soviet capacity in this respect is very limited. For instance, a Soviet author writes:

The immense gulf separating the [attainment] of economic independence by colonial and dependent countries from the rapid formation of their national consciousness is an indisputable fact. . . . The conquest by peoples of several former colonies and semi-colonies of their political freedom is complicated and hindered by the economic imperialist overlordship in the whole colonial world, but the same overlordship intensifies the trend . . . towards economic independence. . . . The liberated Asian countries take the road of establishing their own industries and training their own technological intelligentsia . . . they may make use of the achievements of the world socialist system. . . . These countries cannot now be compelled to turn to their former oppressors for modern equipment. They may acquire this equipment in socialist countries.[105]

Other authors see in the trend towards industrialization a source of new antagonisms between the West and the underdeveloped countries:

The beginning industrialization of those countries helps in strengthening national independence and deepens the economic antagonisms between those countries and imperialism, including the antagonisms between the national bourgeoisie on the one hand and foreign monopolies and local feudal reaction on the other.[106]

When Soviet writers address their own scholarly audiences, however, they concede that there is plenty of room for Western economic co-operation with the underdeveloped countries or that the very economic development of such lands will stimulate international trade with all nations. A well-known Soviet Orientalist says, for instance:

It is obvious that the underdeveloped countries in Asia and Africa need foreign economic and technical assistance. The United States, as a country with great financial and technological possibilities, could play no small role in hastening the process of industrial and cultural development in Asian and African countries.[107]

A Soviet economist presents, in turn, a very sensible picture of the future economic relations between present underdeveloped countries and states already industrialized:

It is self-evident that the industrial development of such big countries as India, Indonesia, and others, will require for a long time to come an immense quantity of all sorts of equipment, machinery, workshops, half-finished products, transportation equipment, and other means. The economically underdeveloped countries are able, in the process of a speedy industrial development, to absorb an incomparably greater quantity of all sorts of goods produced in the industrial States than in the condition where they are principally a market for consumer goods, a condition in which they were until recently. Experience has proved that the more a country is industrially developed, the more it needs goods, including those which are imported from abroad; its foreign trade acquires broader and more diversified character. Hence, it is obvious that the greater the industrialization of India and other Asian countries, greater also will be the opportunity for other States for mutually beneficial trade and economic co-operation.[108]

This is true. Actually, the economic development of presently underdeveloped countries will assure the West of a large market for both capital and consumer goods. The long-term interests of both sides coincide in this respect.

The Soviet approach to the problem of industrialization of underdeveloped countries is rather complex. First of all, there is a contradiction between the long-term objective of converting the whole world to Communism and the short-term goal of making friends with underdeveloped countries. Their successful economic transformation and the eventual solution of the problem of rural overpopulation and of low standards of living would make the prospects of Communist revolution more remote than ever. Popular discontent bred by unsatisfactory economic conditions constitutes the great hope. On the other hand, aspiration for speedy economic development cannot be ignored in the Soviet-Western competition for the friendship of underdeveloped countries.

The West, especially the United States, has already made a great effort in assisting such countries, both economically and technically. The USSR recognized a few years ago that it could not remain inactive; it had to offer at least some proofs of good will. The new Soviet policy of closer trade relations with underdeveloped countries, technical assistance, and occasional loans is meant to prove that good will. It is probably undertaken on the calculation that it may encourage the non-commitment policy by providing another and stronger argument in its favor. A non-committed state is able to benefit from assistance coming from both sources, Western and Soviet, for the Western Powers would be foolish to cut off their aid to countries which have commercial relations with the Soviet bloc and which accept its loans for the sole purpose of hastening their economic processes. Soviet economic policy promotes friendliness towards the USSR and helps the local Communists in clamoring for avoidance of economic ties with the West and for expelling foreign capital from underdeveloped countries under the pretext that there is an alternative in the form of Soviet assistance. It increases the bargaining power of underdeveloped countries in their relations with the West, a clear benefit for the USSR. On the other hand, Moscow might be comforted by the thought that joint Western and Soviet assistance could not rapidly change the basic economic and social conditions in underdeveloped countries and that the initial process of change, unable to produce quick visible results in greatly improved living conditions, may only stir and awake the populations to a more troublesome discontent. Thus the local Communists would, for a long time to come, have fertile ground for their activities.

The unceasing reminder, by Soviet politicians and writers as well as by local Communists, of Soviet experience in industrialization is an investment in the distant future. The enormous Soviet success, especially if supported by similar future successes in China and eastern Europe, will loom large on the horizon of the economically underdeveloped countries should the latter countries fail to achieve economic transformation within a reasonable period and were Western assistance insufficient to hasten the process. Addressing the population of a country in the throes of chronic political instability, Marshal Voroshilov was probably thinking of the one-million-member-strong Indonesian Communist Party when he recalled the Soviet way of industrialization in a speech made in Jakarta:

Thanks to the selflessness, heroism and patriotic devotion of our people, unbelievable difficulties were overcome, and we have been able to transform the Soviet Union from a backward country into one of the most powerful and developed World Powers.[109]

It is quite probable that many people in Indonesia asked themselves the question of whether the same formula could not work in their country; the native Communists are awaiting an opportunity to explain what Marshal Voroshilov had in mind.

The incessant talk about industrialization, increasingly fashionable in underdeveloped countries, creates a dream that lights the eyes of not only the intelligentsia but also the poor masses. Industrialization spells for them greater international power, less dependence on foreign great Powers, diversified production, and the end of economies relying on foreign purchases of a few staple export products. It multiplies jobs for the overpopulated villages (whence emigration to the new industrial centers could begin), yields a more self-contained market that is less dependent on foreign imports and exports, and, in due time, promotes higher living standards. With the closure of mass-immigration countries, this dream becomes more and more attractive. For all of this, the successful industrialization of the West and the USSR acts as a spur. To dismiss this dream as unrealistic would be very dangerous, there being no substitute for the transformation of national economies of underdeveloped countries and no other solution for their social ills. But economic transformation does not necessarily mean only the building up of heavy industries.

Leaders of underdeveloped countries would be well advised to analyze the lesson deducible from the postwar Polish experience in industrialization. They need only read numerous articles written in 1956 by Polish Left Wing Communists to realize the depth of the bitter disappointment that Poland faced after several years of experimenting with the swift building of heavy industries (see Chapter XIII). The net result was a top-heavy economy equipped with several heavy-industry plants, notable increase in production of steel (but also a corresponding neglect of agriculture, light industries, and housing), and generally low standards of living, which were demoralizing to the workers, who could see no point in hard work for meager compensation. Basic investments in transportation vital for industrialized society were also lost to sight. This imbalanced economy broke down, and the new Party leadership had to shift to a new economic policy designed to restore economic harmony by due attention to light industries producing consumer goods, agriculture, transportation, housing, and living conditions of the population. The ambitious program of developing heavy industries was to be reduced and adjusted to the actual capabilities of the country. Moreover, Poland was no Russia; she had no abundance of raw materials. Her industrialization program should have been adjusted to the means of importing foreign raw materials, a limited capacity; the overlooking of this aspect of industrialization cost Poland heavily in breakdowns of output; the new heavy-industry plants frequently had to stop production for lack of raw materials.

If this lesson is digested by underdeveloped countries, they may save themselves the troubles and disappointments which beset Poland in 1956. Economic transformation, a "must" for underdeveloped countries, does not mean concentrating on heavy industries but developing harmoniously the whole national economy, including agriculture and light industries; industrialization must be proportionate to available domestic raw materials and the capacity of the country to import them from abroad. A country which does not have the exceptionally rich natural resources of a United States or a Russia must trim its program to what is possible. The Poles learned this the hard way; others may learn from Polish experience without repeating the same ambitious and costly blunders. In addition, basic investments in transportation, irrigation, public health, training of technological intelligentsia instead of an overproduction of lawyers and social scientists, and raising literacy standards might do more for the basic advancement of national economies than building, from vainglory, another steel plant. Industrialization is only part of the global picture. It would be more reasonable to substitute for the misleading and incomplete industrialization slogan that of economic transformation, the better to reflect the true needs of underdeveloped countries with rural overpopulation and low standards of living. The dream would then become a realistic program.

This economic transformation may be gradually carried out in two ways: either in the Western manner of converting national economy with foreign help, as was done in several European countries and the United States (such help taking the form in our time of governmental and private loans, grants, private investments, and technical assistance), or in the Communist way of keeping down national consumption and feverishly investing a large part of the national income in industries while neglecting agriculture, transportation, and other branches of the economy. The former way is much less painful to living generations, since the burden of the economic transformation is borne by several generations, who slowly repay foreign loans where loans play an important role in the process. It makes for less pressure on the living generation, spared the compulsion of making enormous sacrifices out of its current needs in consumption, and it allows the existence of a non-totalitarian regime. In such soil, democracy may then take root. The other way is inaccessible to a non-totalitarian government because the citizen must be strictly regimented, forced to live on a very low level of subsistence, and obliged to work intensively whether he likes it or not. His right to protest must, as a first measure, be totally eliminated. This can be done effectively only by a Communist party having an uncontested monopoly of power.

Here is the actual single alternative, and the Cmmunists know it only too well. When they cater to popular yearning for industrialization, they hope the West will fail in giving adequate assistance and that local governments will fall down in carrying out the economic transformation, which also requires social reforms for adjustment to modern conditions (land reform, e.g., in the interest of peasants). If such hopes come true in any underdeveloped country, the Communist turn will come.

Soviet propaganda in favor of the Communist formula for industrialization does not necessarily fall on deaf ears. For instance, an Indian major-general, Sahib Singh Sokhey, made a speech on July 14, 1954, on the occasion of receiving the Stalin Peace Prize, in which he said:

The poverty and backwardness of Asia, Africa, and Latin America are the most serious world problem. The Soviet Union has demonstrated how to achieve miracles of production and how to create quickly a cultural existence by giving to science its legitimate place in the social organism and by using the scientific achievements systematically and on a planned scale. The Soviet Union is a leading country . . . we must familiarize our nation with those facts.[110]

In an article published on the same day, he wrote:

These peoples [the economically underdeveloped] want to have the opportunity of developing their own resources and to build for themselves decent conditions of existence. The Soviet people has traced the road and has accumulated a rich experience which is at the disposal of all nations. Peoples understand that they can achieve similar progress and that this cannot be denied.[111]

When one looks at Soviet and Western relations with underdeveloped countries, one may perceive two vistas. A short-range picture does not exclude the usefulness, in several cases, of friendly relations with the USSR. A nation separated from one or another Western Power by a definite quarrel is naturally tempted to counterbalance Western influence with Soviet influence. The non-commitment policy is sheltered behind correct relations with both camps. Soviet economic assistance coming on top of Western aid is very welcome. The long-range picture is different. The Western Powers have been realizing the importance of the battle for the underdeveloped countries. It is not a military battle, and the final objective for both sides is either the extension of the Communist realm or economic and social stabilization. Basic long-term interests of the West and the underdeveloped countries coincide in this respect. Non-Communist politicians in the underdeveloped countries do not relish the idea of being hanged on lamp posts in the event of a Communist revolution; they visualize, instead, the political future of their countries along non-Communist lines corresponding with their own plans and aspirations. The Western Powers have a vital interest in preventing such countries from following the exit of China. A peaceful economic and social transformation is in the interest of both parties. If a Soviet loan or a livelier trade with the Soviet bloc helps to speed this process, no Western vital interests are harmed, except where the USSR monopolizes economic relations with a given underdeveloped country, thus reducing it to the status of economic dependence (the United Arab Republic, for example). Moreover, the very process of economic development requires, for some time, the influx of foreign capital in various forms and the use of foreign know-how. Western capacity is in both respects incomparably greater than the Soviet, a fact not to be overlooked by any sensible statesman in the underdeveloped areas. One should have no illusions that this basic, long-range coincidence of interests will ever eliminate friction, but the USSR also has its share of economic difficulties, of a different type, in dealing with the countries of its own bloc.

Were the Soviet Union guided by sincere interest in the well-being of underdeveloped countries, its press should have welcomed assistance coming from any source, including the West, but this is not the case. One Soviet author says:

The young sovereign states of Asia and Africa take several measures to overcome their economic backwardness and to achieve full independence. This is impossible without a consistent squeezing out of foreign capital.[112]

Another writer echoes the same theme:

The other very important way [besides building state industries] of strengthening the political and economic independence of those countries is the struggle against oppression by foreign monopolies.[113]

Yet the same Soviet sources that talk of squeezing out foreign capital admit that this capital is quite useful in the process of industrialization. For instance, here is the Soviet-adduced example of Burma:

Burma concluded in 1954 an agreement with Japan according to which Japanese firms received the right to invest their capital to the extent of the global sum of 50 million dollars in the joint companies formed together with either Burmese firms or the Burmese Government; the Burmese will have 60 per cent of the stock, and the period for investment of Japanese capital was fixed at ten years. The Burmese Government concluded also agreements with several Western-German, Japanese, Swedish, English and American firms concerning the construction of industrial plants. For instance, a steel mill in Burma is being built by the Western-German firm

Damag; a Japanese firm builds a textile mill, etc. Burma recently . . . received a long-term loan from the International Bank of Reconstruction and Development of 20 million dollars destined to finance the reconstruction of the Rangoon port and the rehabilitation of railroads. The Burmese Government has decided to accept an American loan of 25 million dollars for a period of forty years.[114]

Another Soviet source adduces the no less convincing example of India:

It is expected that the steel mill built in Rourkela by the Indian Iron and Steel Company with the originally planned capacity of 500,000 tons of steel will have its capacity of production doubled; *Krupp-Demag* supplies the equipment, and the International Bank of Reconstruction and Development partly finances its construction. . . . Another steel mill will be built in Durgapure by agreement with the English consortium of metallurgical companies; its capacity will be one million tons of steel annually. . . . The concern Tata concluded in November 1955 an agreement with the American firm of Henry Kaiser and Company concerning the technical supervision over the realization of the project of expanding the capacity of the steel mill in Dzhamshedpure from the present 1.3 million tons to 2 millions. The concern Tata signed in June 1956 an agreement with the International Bank of Reconstruction and Development for a loan of 75 million dollars.[115]

The steel mill constructed by the Soviet Union in Bkhilai with a projected capacity of one million tons of steel remains useful for India but does not seem to be the only foreign project. Co-operation with the West continues to be fruitful.

9. Soviet Trade, Loans, and Technical Assistance

The Soviet bloc economic offensive, which began in 1955, has been concentrated on the underdeveloped countries. Its motivations are probably twofold, though the political drive of making friends with these countries is the most important. There is also a subsidiary economic motivation; the exchange of capital goods for raw materials and agricultural products imported from these countries is profitable for the Soviet bloc countries, suffering as they do from deficiencies of agricultural production and, as Soviet satellites in Eastern Europe are concerned, from shortages of raw materials. Thus this exchange becomes mutually useful. One may expect growth in this trade, but one can hardly expect that it will reach, in the near future, such a volume that it will radically affect the trade trends of all of the underdeveloped countries. The underdeveloped countries want to import principally capital goods from the Soviet bloc; the Soviet bloc countries, whose industrialization is tied up with the underdevelopment of light industries and ensuing shortages of consumer goods, cannot even afford to export appreciable quantities of consumer goods.

The Soviet capacity and willingness to export capital goods is strictly limited by several considerations. The equipment of a plant that remains in the Soviet Union is a safe investment in the total Soviet economic and, indirectly, military potential. The same equipment is almost as safe an investment if it goes to an eastern European country controlled by the USSR. If it is exported to China, there is a small risk that the alliance between the two countries might end someday, but the intensive economic assistance to China is also the best guarantee of the solidity of that alliance, since it makes China temporarily economically dependent on the USSR. The Soviet Union has little choice in the matter. It must give high priority to requests submitted by its Chinese ally, whose capacity of absorption is enormous. It is in Soviet interest to help to the utmost in building up the economic potential of its own bloc. The task is gigantic; China only begins to emerge from an almost exclusively agricultural condition, while eastern Europe is still basically in the stage of a mixed industrial-agricultural economy. Moreover, the Soviet Union takes part in the self-imposed race to outdistance the United States as the first industrial great Power. All of these considerations severely limit the Soviet capacity of exporting impressive amounts of capital goods, especially machinery, to the underdeveloped countries. We may expect a steady increase of Soviet bloc participation in the trade of these countries, but we should not expect this bloc one day to occupy a controlling or decisive position in that trade.[116]

This is not equivalent to saying that trade and loans cannot be used as trump cards in the Soviet policy towards particular underdeveloped countries. Soviet capacity need not be strained by concentrating on a few small countries in a strategically vital area, as the USSR has been doing in Egypt, Syria, and Iraq. Other underdeveloped countries may welcome even proportionately small trade with the Soviet bloc for the sake of selling agricultural or raw material surpluses for which there is no other ready market (as with Burma) and buying additional capital equipment for their economic development.

Soviet economic relations with underdeveloped countries never take the form of sizable grants. Relatively small gifts are sometimes offered as tokens of friendship, and these are usually immediately repaid with gifts of similar value. A discussion of the usual forms of such relations thus far follows.

Bilateral trade in the form of barter of Soviet goods, usually capital goods, for raw materials or foodstuffs is the usual form. The number of such trade agreements concluded by the Soviet bloc with non-Communist states increased from 113 in force at the close of 1953 to 203 by the end of 1956. More than half of them were concluded in 1956 with the underdeveloped countries, yet the total of the Soviet bloc share in the world trade was only 3 per cent.

The Soviet Union showed great skillfulness in exploiting particular situations. When Burma was burdened with a rice surplus and falling world prices, the USSR bartered its goods for Burmese rice. When Afghanistan was blocked by Pakistan from its commercial outlet to the Arabian Sea because of their dispute over Pushtoonistan, the USSR offered its trade routes and barter. When Egypt could not readily find arms in the Western countries and had a surplus of cotton, the Soviet bloc supplied arms and took cotton.

This does not mean that barter trade with the Soviet bloc is always profitable. Often the goods they offer are of inferior quality by Western standards, though some may be less complex and therefore more suitable to an underdeveloped country. The Soviet bloc states are not hampered by profit calculation, as a private Western corporation would be, and can offer goods at prices lower than the world prices, especially in small transactions. Usually, the Soviet bloc negotiators are business-like and are not ready to sell cheaply unless prompted by major political considerations.

According to the figures computed by the State Department (*New York Times*, March 22, 1959), the grand total of credits granted by the Soviet bloc to the eighteen underdeveloped countries reached, by the end of 1958, the sum of $2,373,000,000. Of this total, $1,591,000,000 was for economic aid and $782,000,000 for military aid. Of the nearly $2,400,000,000, the Soviet Union offered $1,600,000,000, the eastern European countries $650,000,000, and China $120,000,000.

The political motivation is evident from the fact that the main recipients were uncommitted nations: Afghanistan, the United Arab Republic, India, Indonesia, and Iraq. Iraq was duly encouraged, after the revolutionary change of regime, by a military aid of $120,000,000 and an economic assistance credit of $137,000,000. The lively Soviet interest in Latin America was evidenced by a sizable credit of $102,000,000 extended to Argentina in 1958. The same political motivation in the Soviet economic relations with the underdeveloped countries was demonstrated by the sudden Soviet breach of promise in the form of cancellation of their credits to Yugoslavia when a new rupture took place in the spring of 1958. Yugoslavia had been promised initially, at the time of mutual reconciliation, $465,000,000 in credits. She actually received only $163,000,000, the remaining $302,000,-000 having been canceled later.

The balance sheet of the Soviet bloc economic credits (excluding the military) as it stood by the end of 1958 was, in millions of dollars, as follows: Afghanistan 116, Argentina 102, Brazil 2, Burma 34, Cambodia 34, Ceylon 58, United Arab Republic (Egypt and Syria) 506, Ethiopia 2, Iceland 5, India 304, Indonesia 194, Iran 3, Nepal 13, Turkey 13, Yemen 42, Yugoslavia (credits actually used before the rift with the USSR) 163. This makes a grand total of $1,591,000,000, to which $137,000,000 granted to Iraq in March, 1959, should be added. Except for Argentina, the countries committed to the West by one or another treaty received only relatively small credits. The size of credits granted to uncommitted nations acquires a more persuasive eloquence if measured by the dimensions of their economies. For instance, the assistance to the United Arab Republic and Iraq was, proportionately, incomparably higher than the relatively small sum of $304,000,000 for India. The USSR visibly had neither the intention or the capacity to underwrite the second Indian Five Year Plan, whose implementation was facing tremendous difficulties. The investment in the United Arab Republic or Iraq was considered to be more profitable, and the amount of credits was of such a nature that it would seriously affect the relatively small economies of these countries. The same is true of the Soviet credits to other small countries strategically located, such as Yemen, Afghanistan, Cambodia, etc.

It is interesting to note that China, herself in need of assistance from the Soviet bloc, distributed grants to the tune of $55,000,000 to Ceylon, Cambodia, Nepal, and Egypt, thus creating good will for the Asian "big brother." It is significant that, except for Egypt, those grants went to countries located on the peripheries of India; Nepal is, in fact, an Indian protectorate. Were they the first harbingers announcing the future Chinese-Indian competition for the leadership in Asia?

The generous credits extended to Egypt and Syria, and later to the United Arab Republic and to Iraq, hardly need a comment. The United Arab Republic is located on both sides of the Suez Canal and close to the most important Near Eastern oil fields, while Iraq is one of the largest oil producers. The policy of friendship towards these Arab countries and Yemen resulted in making the Soviet Union a Mediterranean and Near Eastern Power. She was rewarded by the vociferous anti-Western propaganda poured from the United Arab Republic and Iraq. It is worth while to note that the Egyptian Government consented to holding the Asian-African Solidarity Conference in its capital and to the establishment on its soil of the permanent headquarters of the organization founded by the Conference; this points to the obvious implication that Egypt is being used as a channel for Soviet anti-Western propaganda directed at Asia and Africa. Whatever might be the intentions of the Syrian and Egyptian governments, the effects of their recent policies have transferred these two countries (now forming the United Arab Republic) from the group of genuinely uncommitted nations to a new group of non-Communist states committed in the foreign realm in many ways to the Soviet bloc. This is worth more than several hundred million dollars to the Soviet Union.

The Soviet Union demonstrated once more her political interest in the United Arab Republic by granting, on October 23, 1958, a $100,000,000 loan to help in financing the first stage of the construction of the Aswan Dam. This loan, more than the previous, is a long-term investment. The construction of the dam is planned to last at least eighteen years; although native labor and local materials will be supplied, the United Arab Republic will need further Soviet loans to carry on this tremendous enterprise, which is of potentially great importance for the whole Egyptian economy. Thus the dependence of the United Arab Republic on the Soviet good will is deepened by its need of the present and future loans; this makes a substantial shift in its foreign policy even more difficult.

The policy of credits to the underdeveloped countries may be stepped up. The two and four-tenths billions contributed so far have not affected the Soviet–eastern European economies. Their gross national product in 1957 was 235 billions, and the value of their industrial production was 100 billions. The Soviet bloc is thus able to offer new credits; it seems probable that Indonesia, another key country, will receive a much more generous share than she has been getting thus far.

The appealing factors in these loans are as follows: low rates of interest (2 to 2.5 per cent), long periods of repayment extending from ten to thirty years, and the mode of repayment either in specified goods produced in the recipient country or in its currency, which will eventually be used to buy available goods in that country. Such credits are usually granted to finance the import of capital goods. However, well over one-third of the credits are used to finance the Soviet bloc supplies of military equipment.

A notable proportion of Soviet exports is represented by war material shipped as far as Egypt, Syria, Yemen, Iraq and Afghanistan. This form of exports is profitable because armaments quickly become obsolete in our age of speedy technical improvements. Arms exported by the Soviet Union are seldom of the latest model, but if they are, the USSR, itself having a great production of armaments, can afford it. Of course such exports do not affect the Soviet capacity of production, as they do in capital goods; armaments are, in a sense, consumer goods. Political benefit is obvious in all instances of countries involved in quarrels with the West, such as Egypt and Syria, or with Western-committed Pakistan (Afghanistan). The need to rely on Soviet experts for training armed forces in the use of Soviet-im‧ported arms and on spare parts creates dependence on further Soviet good will, which is not forthcoming without tangible political compensation.

Technical Soviet assistance takes two forms: (1) sending Soviet technicians to train foreign specialists, to offer advice, or to help install Soviet-imported equipment; or (2) training foreign technicians and students in the Soviet Union. This technical assistance program usually goes hand in hand with barter agreements, supplements them, and is founded on a paying basis. Approximately 2,800 civilian technicians sent by the Soviet bloc operated, in 1958, in several underdeveloped countries. Eighty per cent of them were concentrated in the United Arab Republic, India, and Afghanistan; most of the others worked in Burma, Cambodia, Indonesia, and Yemen. Moreover, 1,200 military experts, allocated mainly to the United Arab Republic, served in 1958 in the underdeveloped countries. About 2,000 specialists and students from these countries were studying in the Soviet Union in 1957. This program of exchange enhances the Soviet prestige in the underdeveloped areas and allows Soviet technicians to establish personal contacts. Foreign students coming from underdeveloped countries are also an investment. They may be impressed by the economic-technological results achieved in the USSR and come to the conclusion that the Communist regime could produce the same desirable results in their own countries. At least they will return home grateful for the education they have received and will remain friends of the Soviet Union.

One may be sure that the Soviet Union has the capacity for a much larger program of technical assistance. Khrushchev declared at the 21st Party Congress on January 27, 1959, that the total pool of specialists (professionally trained people with higher or secondary-technical education) amounted approximately to seven and a half million persons.

The USSR likes to concentrate on spectacular projects which attract public attention in an underdeveloped country, such as building a steel mill in India, an aluminum plant in Yugoslavia, a petroleum refinery in Syria, paving streets of the Afghan capital, Kabul, etc. It defers readily to local wishes, avoiding such mutual irritation as often results from offering advice to a foreign government. The Burmese wanted, for instance, large quantities of Soviet cement in exchange for their rice; the USSR agreed, with the result that Burma did not know what to do with the cement, since prior plans had not been made to use it. This policy would hardly be followed by a country genuinely interested in the economic development of the recipient, but the USSR pursues the political goal of becoming popular by attaching no strings to its assistance. Judging by its credit policy, however, there is indeed a string attached, namely, the recipient must be an uncommitted or at least a strategically located nation.

One might expect that the Soviet Union would be ready to make generous offers to committed nations as well if there were a reasonable hope of loosening their ties with the West. The Communist monopoly of foreign trade allows for the heavy concentration on well-selected targets. Already more than 20 per cent of the trade of Afghanistan, Egypt, and Burma is carried on with the Soviet bloc. But two firmly West-committed nations, Turkey and Iran, also had to accept an increasing rate of trade with the Soviet bloc, the figures being 17 per cent of total trade for Turkey and 12 per cent for Iran.

Keeping a watchful eye on the public response in the underdeveloped countries, the Soviet bloc finances projects of industrial nature and, to a lesser extent, projects in transportation, communication, power, and mineral development. This emphasis surrounds the bloc with the halo of helpers in the industrialization drive that is so popular in all underdeveloped countries. There would be nothing wrong with it except that the bloc pays scant attention to the improvement of agriculture, thereby revealing its short-term objectives. The underdeveloped countries cannot expect to find the main resources for their economic transformation anywhere except in increased agricultural production.

The export of capital goods (means of production) ranges from equipment and machinery for a steel mill in India with future capacity of production of one million tons annually to equipment for nuclear research laboratories, an experimental atomic reactor, cement plants, oil refineries, power stations, bakeries, and shoe and porcelain factories exported to Egypt.[117] Therefore, "capital goods" means, in Soviet trade, equipment not only for heavy but also for light industries. Export of the latter equipment does not affect the basic Soviet economic potential, heavy industries, but nevertheless reduces its potential for the domestic production of manufactured consumer goods; this is also true of other exporting countries of the Soviet-Chinese bloc. This is no small matter, there being a shortage of consumer goods in both these countries and in the USSR. Thus a sacrifice is made in exporting the machinery for light industries, a sacrifice at the expense of the average consumer within the Soviet bloc.

The generous supply of armaments, equipment for both heavy and light industries, and other products, such as cement (despite a notorious shortage of housing in all Soviet bloc countries), is also a political investment. The success of Soviet policy in Egypt and Syria proves that this commercial policy has been worth while. To avoid any future quarrels with the importing country, the Soviet bloc never asks for a share in the capital, or participation in the management, of plants they help to build with their equipment and technicians. Of course a country which relies heavily on trade with the Soviet bloc gradually becomes dependent on it both economically and politically. It is not without significance that the share of the Soviet bloc countries in Egyptian exports (mainly cotton) in 1955 had already reached 27.8 per cent of the total and in imports 7.5 per cent of the total.[118] The Soviet bloc's becoming an important buyer of surpluses ties to it the economy of a country relying on exports of one or two staple products. This is true of Egyptian cotton and, to some extent, of Burmese rice. The USSR consented by commercial agreement on July 1, 1955, to buy annually 200,000 tons of Burmese rice for three years. The subsequent agreement of April 1, 1956, raised this contingent to 400,000 tons, to be exported during the following four years.[119] As in the case of Egypt, the other countries of the bloc, China, Poland, Czechoslovakia, Rumania, Hungary, and East Germany, followed suit in concluding with Burma agreements concerning the purchases of rice. Soviet commentators say that Burma thus stabilized the market for its rice; this is true, and it is no less true that the Soviet bloc acquired a means of economic pressure in case they wished to link political matters with continuation of the arrangements for purchasing rice surpluses.

The patterns of Soviet bloc trade and technical assistance with the underdeveloped countries may be illustrated by a few examples. For instance, India is given special attention, not only because of its size and role in Asia, but also because: " 'We,' declared comrade N. S. Khrushchev in a speech he made at the fourth session of the Supreme Soviet of the USSR, 'fully understand and support the policy of the Indian leaders who said that India occupied a neutral place between us and other States.' "[120] The Soviet economic policy aims at encouraging the non-commitment policy in India as an example to other countries.

So India received a contract for the construction of a steel mill, was granted the import of one million tons of Soviet rolled steel, to be supplied in 1956–1958, plus machinery and other equipment; the USSR has proceeded to organize a regular steamship line to India; Soviet specialists supervise the construction of the steel mill and help in geological search for oil; the Soviet Union will equip a polytechnical institute in Bombay to be supplied with a Soviet teaching staff; loans were granted at an interest rate of 2.5 per cent. Czechoslovakia has followed suit. She supplies India with equipment for sugar refineries, an aluminum plant, and a power station. She will import 2,050 railroad trucks. She also supplies tractors, equipment for shoe factories, etc. Hungary exported equipment for two cable plants, Diesel locomotives, etc., and East Germany supplied electrical equipment, precision instruments, equipment for chemical factories, etc.[121]

Respective shares of the various socialist countries in trade with India during the Indian fiscal year April, 1955, to April, 1956, were: the USSR, 35 per cent; China, 40 per cent; Czechoslovakia, 16 per cent; and others, 9 per cent. Despite the considerable growth in the Soviet bloc trade, "the total share of the socialist countries in the foreign trade of India is, for the time being, small and represents just over 2 per cent."[122] This proves that it is not possible for the Soviet bloc to occupy a crucial position in the economic life of a big country.

Egypt is an instructive example of a small uncommitted country in which the Soviet bloc can easily afford to play an important role. The share of the Soviet bloc in Egyptian foreign trade in 1955 was already considerable and the highest by comparison to all non-Communist states taken individually. This share was 15.3 per cent, while the British was 9.8; the American, 9.7; the French, 8.7; the West German, 8.4; the Italian, 6.9; the Dutch, 2.8; and the Indian, 6.2.[123] The crucial problem of cotton is reflected in these words:

The export of cotton to the countries of people's democracy has increased in 1955–56, by comparison with the previous year, by 70 per cent. . . . The purchases of cotton by countries of the socialist camp have for Egypt a particular importance in view of the fall in sales to the capitalist coun-tries.[124]

Other uncommitted nations get their share of Soviet attention. Burma received a very rare Soviet gift in the form of a technological institute in Rangoon, to be built and equipped by the USSR. Afghanistan got a loan in 1955 of 100 million dollars, a considerable sum for a small and totally underdeveloped country. The USSR not only agreed in 1956 to buy 400,000 tons of Burmese rice in each of the following four years, but China prom-ised in 1955 to buy 200,000 tons every year, and Poland, 50,000 to 60,000 tons. Czechoslovakia, Hungary, and Poland agreed in 1955 to buy 30,000 tons of rice from Egypt. The good sense shown in buying surplus goods from underdeveloped countries, such as Burma or Egypt, is clearly stated:

The example of Burma has immense importance for the other economically underdeveloped countries. It proves that if those countries show good will, the problem of sale of their goods can be successfully solved on the demo-cratic world market.[125]

If they show good will! They can show good will by following a non-com-mitment policy, which now suits the "democratic" market.

Burma decided in 1957 to reduce her rice exports to the Soviet bloc to well below the volume stipulated in the earlier agreements. She was moti-vated by the fear that she might lose her former non-Soviet customers and by the rise in prices on the international rice market. She was also dis-satisfied with the quality and price of imported Soviet goods, but she might have felt apprehensive of the expectation that she should "show good will to the democratic market."

The agreement concluded in March, 1956, by the USSR and Yemen il-lustrates the variety of Soviet trade with underdeveloped countries. The Soviet Union will supply industrial equipment (probably mostly of mili-tary nature), agricultural machinery, building materials, oil products, flour, rice (perhaps the Burmese and Egyptian rice will be resold to Yemen), sugar, etc., for Yemeni coffee, dried fruit, leather, etc.[126]

The role of China in trade with underdeveloped countries of Asia and the Near East has been steadily growing. Commercial agreements were signed in 1955–56 with Indonesia, Ceylon, Burma, Egypt, Syria, and, as Soviet sources call them, the business circles in Japan. China took part in the fairs in Delhi, Karachi, Damascus, Tokyo and Osaka. Her trade increased considerably with India, Burma, Indonesia, Egypt, Japan, Pakistan, Malaya, and Singapore. However, it remains a small fraction of the total trade of those countries. China buys rubber, rice, cotton, and other agricultural products, as well as industrial goods and metals, such as chrome, manganese, zinc, lead, wolfram, and tin. Of course Japan is lured to a greater trade with China by such calculations:

According to data for the first half of 1955, the average price of an iron ore ton was, if imported from China to Japan, 9 dollars, if imported from the USA, 15 dollars, if imported from the Philippines, 12 dollars. The average price of coking coal was: from China—12 dollars, from the USA—20 dollars per ton.[127]

Trade with West-committed nations is carried on for economic reasons, but also in the hope that considerable exports to and imports from the Soviet bloc will create a propitious atmosphere for weakening the ties between a committed underdeveloped country and the Western Powers. Bulganin was not too secretive about this when he gave an interview to the telegraphic agency of the United Press of Pakistan. He offered to take Pakistani goods for Soviet machinery, but he also indicated his dislike of the Pakistani foreign policy:

We are hostile to the military-political aggressive blocs like the SEATO and the Baghdad Pact in which Pakistan participates. Friendly relations between the USSR and Pakistan could be built up on the foundation of the known five principles of peaceful co-existence which have been accepted as the basis of relations between the USSR, India, People's Republic of China, Burma, and other countries.[128]

It happens that the five principles govern the relations between the Soviet-Chinese bloc and the uncommitted nations.

Probably because the approach to Latin American countries should be more cautious, Bulganin did not mention mutual political relations in a similar interview granted to the newspaper *Visão*. He limited himself to offering various types of Soviet machinery, automobiles, and technical assistance in exchange for Latin American agricultural products and raw materials.[129]

In October, 1958, Khrushchev made an important statement on economic assistance to the underdeveloped countries (*Pravda*, October 22, 1958). Referring to frequent Western private suggestions of combining the Western and Soviet aid in some sort of an International Development Fund, Khrushchev categorically refused to contemplate any such scheme and insisted on bilateral deals concluded with each recipient country separately.

Somehow, this statement passed unnoticed, but it merits a very serious consideration. It is well known that the governments of underdeveloped countries have been for years practically united in their desire of having a United Nations or other international fund. Their preference for the international rather than bilateral form of economic aid relates to their conviction that this form would protect them against any political implications which could be involved in the bilateral agreements. If Khrushchev believes that the Western bilateral economic aid subverts the independence of recipient countries but that the Soviet is free of any political strings or considerations, why did he refuse even to contemplate a non-political international scheme?

It seems that the Soviet bloc will play a proportionately increasing role in the trade of underdeveloped countries, with probable concentration on nations considered as having key strategic importance for its foreign interests. This policy will probably never become a decisive factor in the global picture, but it may play a crucial role in a few countries or areas, as is already true in the United Arab Republic and Iraq. However, political policy and propaganda are cheaper; they bring satisfactory results by exploiting all possible conflicts between the West-committed countries and the uncommitted or between the Western Powers and one or another underdeveloped country; by harping on anti-racialist and anti-colonialist themes; by warning against economic dependence on "foreign monopolies"; etc.

10. Asian-African Solidarity Conference

The Asian-African Solidarity Conference held in Cairo from December 26, 1957, to January 1, 1958, should have been an eye-opener for all those people who had failed before to notice the main direction of Soviet policy as inaugurated in 1953, namely the choice of underdeveloped countries as the battlefield for the political, economic, and ideological struggle against the West. The Conference was, unlike the Bandung Conference, a meeting of non-governmental delegates who came from forty-two countries. It was impossible to estimate whom these delegates represented, as they had no formal mandates from anyone. The delegates from the Communist countries—the Soviet Union, China, North Korea, North Vietnam, and Mongolia—like any Communist delegation at an international conference, spoke with the full approval of their governments.

The Soviet delegation was carefully selected and was composed almost exclusively of loyal central Asians, Uzbeks, Turkmenians, Tadjiks, and Kazakhs. It was headed by Sh. R. Rashidov, one of the vice-chairmen of the Federal Presidium of the Supreme Soviet and the chairman of a similar presidium in his native Uzbekistan. He knew how to impress his audience favorably. He said: "We resolutely favor the termination of the colonial war in Algeria and a just solution of such questions as those of Western Irian and Goa and of all other problems of national independence for Asian and African countries."[130] He, a renegade Uzbek speaking there on behalf of his Russian colonial masters, did not blush when he thus wound up his closing speech: "The fresh breeze of freedom and independence sweeps away the dark clouds of colonial slavery! Sun of liberty and independence lights up the road of nations!"[131] There was no one in the crowded hall to remind him of the dark Soviet cloud casting its shadow over his native central Asia and the recent eclipse of the sun of liberty in Hungary, one of the Soviet colonial protectorates.

Rashidov's Armenian colleague, A. A. Arzumanian, advised the Conference of a simple means of promoting industrialization by confiscation of foreign assets; he mentioned the "encouraging," as he said, examples of Egypt and Indonesia. At the same time, he offered Soviet assistance in the form of capital goods.[132] Was there a delegate in his audience sufficiently immune to emotions to proceed with a computation of the Soviet capacity to provide *all* the countries represented in Cairo with capital goods in the face of the domestic Soviet commitments and obligations to China and eastern Europe? The actual Soviet capacity, not to mention willingness, was recently tested. When India was faced with the dire need of foreign credits to uphold her second Five Year Plan, the Soviet Union did not display any desire to underwrite the Plan.

Those delegates who came from countries other than the Soviet-Chinese bloc were a mixture of crypto-Communists and non-Communists who had been blinded by their anti-Western hatred to the extent of fraternizing with the representatives of the Soviet Union, the biggest colonial Power of our time, which keeps under her heel two hundred million people belonging to diverse European and Asian nationalities. Those non-Communist delegates were brought to Cairo by the resentful recollection of their recent colonial past, by their present quarrels with one or another Western Power (for instance, the Indonesians and the Arabs), or by their search for allies against a colonial Power still controlling their native land, as was true of the Algerians and Africans from other colonies. Whenever their grievances were legitimate, their ignorance of the Soviet colonial record made them forget that they were exorcizing the Devil with Beelzebub. Whomever they represented, these non-Communist delegates certainly left Cairo determined to act in co-operation with the Soviet-Chinese bloc and their Communist countrymen in the struggle against everything Western. The Soviet Union thus found non-Communist channels for feeding its anti-Western propaganda to the two continents. Her spokesmen will be not Russians but authentic Asians and Africans.

Whatever the intentions of the Egyptian Government were, it made possible the holding of this anti-Western assembly on non-Communist territory. It thus rendered an inestimable service to the USSR. Although the Conference was non-governmental, members of the Egyptian Government attended the opening meeting, while President Nasser was the only non-Communist head of state to send a telegram of welcome along with Mao Tse-tung and Marshal Voroshilov. He offered a reception to the delegates at the close of the Conference. The Egyptian National Assembly sent another telegraphed greeting. All this could hardly be squared with the following statement made by the main Egyptian delegate, Anvar Sadat: "Neutrality in which we believe means that we intend to remain aloof from international blocs and at the same time do our best to promote a rapprochement between these blocs."[133] His colleague, Khalid Muhi ad-Din, interpreted in a peculiar way this aloofness and neutrality when he violently assailed even the Western economic assistance: "Imperialism tries to offer to several countries economic assistance which is in fact nothing but a new form of colonialism. Imperialism attempts through this assistance to seize control over national economies [of underdeveloped countries]."[134]

The goal pursued by the Soviet Union was spelled out in *Pravda* on the eve of the Conference: "History teaches that the guarantee of a speedy emancipation of mankind from colonial dependence and exploitation lies in the co-operation between the national-liberating movements against imperialism and the mighty forces of socialism. It is manifest to all today that the development of socialism and of the national-liberating movement has radically accelerated and will continue to accelerate the process of disintegration of imperialism."[135] *Pravda* commented thus after the close of the Conference: "The ruling circles of Western Powers cannot fail to notice that their isolation grows."[136] The disintegration of imperialism (the West) through its isolation from the underdeveloped countries is to be brought about, thanks to the co-operation of these countries with the Soviet-Chinese bloc. The Cairo Conference was another step towards this co-operation.

One cannot help admiring Soviet skill in selecting such slogans for Asian-African consumption as are sure to evoke a favorable response. These slogans, as we have seen from the preceding pages, were invented long before the Cairo Conference, but they celebrated their triumph in Cairo. All of them were summed up in a single and all-embracing formula of struggle against imperialism, a vague word to which each delegate could append his own interpretation, except that it stood as a symbol for all anti-Western resentments. Imperialism played in Cairo the role of the medieval Devil; it was the incarnation of all evils, whether they could or could not be traced back to colonialism. The fact that the Cairo delegates expressed views corresponding to the Soviet slogans for Asia and Africa does not prove that all of their views were mistaken but, rather, that the Soviet Union had selected its catchwords with a discerning eye on the needs, grievances, and emotions of Asia and Africa. The topics most frequently mentioned in the speeches were as follows:

(1) The denunciation of racial discrimination. The Sudanese delegate, Mohammed Ahmed Mahgoub, who could not divest himself of his official responsibility as foreign minister of his country, violently singled out two countries for particular blame: the Union of South Africa and the United States.[137]

(2) Upholding the *Pancha Shila* as the foundation of peaceful co-existence.

(3) Anti-colonialism that was expressed in the demands for the transfer of Taiwan to Communist China, of Goa to India, of Western Irian to Indonesia, for self-determination for Cyprus (while the Hungarians were never mentioned, the Cypriots were the only European nationality for which the Conference took up the cudgels), and for independence for Algeria and all other African colonies.

(4) Denunciation not only of the Baghdad and SEATO Pacts and of the Eisenhower Doctrine but also of NATO, the Colombo Plan, though supported by such uncommitted Asian countries as India and Ceylon, and of purely western European arrangements, such as the Coal and Steel Community, the Common Market, and the Euratom. While western Europeans were denied the right to found common organizations, the Conference fa-

vored, by contrast, exclusively Asian-African economic and other associations. The Indian delegate, Anup Singh, reflected the general feeling of the Conference when he said that there should be no foreign troops or bases in Asia and Africa.

(5) The support for Communist China to be seated in the United Nations.

(6) Korea and Vietnam to be unified.

(7) The unconditional and immediate suspension of all nuclear tests. The Japanese delegate, Kaoru Yasui, who was the most eloquent speaker on the matter, called for co-ordinated action to stop the American and British tests carried out in the Pacific area, somehow forgetting that the Soviet tests were also taking place in Asia and that Japan had had her share of fallout after each Soviet test. He proposed to commemorate the anniversary of Hiroshima and Nagasaki by holding, in August, 1958, an international conference of protest against the nuclear tests.[138]

The resolutions adopted by the Conference reflected the debates.[139] All of them were adopted unanimously, a rare achievement for an international gathering supposedly representing forty-two countries. The highlights of these resolutions were as follows:

(1) Economic transformation of Asia and Africa through industrialization and planned economic development.

(2) "The Conference does not oppose foreign investments and foreign loans [without any strings]," but the Conference hardly encouraged further private investment in Asia and Africa by declaring that "nationalization is a legal act and a right belonging to each State in virtue of its national sovereignty."[140]

(3) Higher international market prices for exported Asian-African raw materials.

(4) Development of trade with all countries independently of their social regime (in other words, no restrictions on trade with the Communist states).

(5) Denunciation of the blocking of accounts of one country by another, a point of practical importance to Egypt, the host country.

(6) The necessity to proceed with immediate agrarian reforms in Asia and Africa.

(7) Freedom for the labor-union and co-operative movements, encouragement of an all-Asian-African unity of both movements, and development of producer co-operatives.

(8) A state-guaranteed minimum of wages and a social insurance system for industrial workers. (Points 6, 7, and 8 are of no direct concern to the West, but they make clear that the Asian-African Solidarity organization which emerged from the Cairo Conference will become a tool of pressure, not only in international but also in domestic matters. Its domestic activities will not be free of demagogy; the Conference demanded minimum wages for all categories of workers, but the Soviet Union, the so-called socialist state, introduced minimum wages for unskilled workers only as late as 1956, when she was already a fully developed industrial country. To ask for minimum wages in the underdeveloped countries was so unrealistic that it could be interpreted only as a desire to embarrass the Asian-African governments. One may predict that the Asian-African Solidarity organization will become a headache, not only to the West, but also to those governments.)

(9) Denunciation of Western military pacts, the Eisenhower Doctrine, and the western European Common Market as the various instruments of imperialism.

(10) Call for assistance to the Palestinian refugees, who should be allowed to return to their former homes in Israel, to have their properties restored, and to be compensated for losses suffered. Israel was stigmatized as a tool of imperialism.

(11) Support for the transfer of Taiwan to Communist China, of Goa to India, of West Irian to Indonesia, for the self-determination of Cyprus, for the complete independence of Algeria and all African colonies. March 1, 1958, was proclaimed the Day of Algeria, to be celebrated in Asia and Africa.

(12) Condemnation of racial discrimination, with South Africa the only state mentioned by name in the resolution.

(13) Unconditional and immediate termination of nuclear tests.

This program is to be enforced by Asian-African conferences of all sorts and by the permanent organization of Asian-African Solidarity, with its headquarters in Cairo. An Egyptian was to become the secretary-general and was to be assisted by ten secretaries from the following countries: the Soviet Union, China, Japan, India, Indonesia, Sudan, Syria, Ghana, Iraq, and the Cameroons. Thus the Soviet-Chinese bloc will be represented by two secretaries, the uncommitted nations by five, the African colonies by one, and the West-committed countries by one opponent of commitment. The importance the Soviet Union attaches to the Near East as a gate to

Africa and a key area for both Europe and Asia, as well as the active role played by the Arabs at the Conference, are well reflected in the assignment to Arabs of four out of eleven secretarial posts. While the permanent secretariat will be in a good position to pull the strings, another body created by the Conference is the Council of Asian-African Solidarity, which is scheduled to meet only once a year and is composed of one delegate from each Asian and African country. These delegates will be appointed by national committees of Asian-African Solidarity; the Cairo Conference appealed for the formation of such committees in each country. This vast organization will probably co-operate with the Communist-sponsored World Peace Council, whose president, the late Professor Joliot-Curie, did not fail to send a telegram of welcome to Cairo.

The Asian-African Solidarity organization planned to promote other forms of co-operation, such as the formation of the Federation of Asian-African Women, the League of Asian-African Youth, the League of Asian-African Scholars, Writers, Artists, and Educators, and the foundation of an Asian-African University, probably to raise there the young elite for the enforcement of the Cairo program. Various conferences were announced in Cairo: there was to be a conference of Asian-African labor unions and co-operatives; a youth conference was to be held in 1958; youth festivals were scheduled; a conference of Asian-African writers, scholars, educators, and artists was to be held in 1958 in Tashkent (the USSR), in addition to mutual visits of people representing these professions.

This whole organizational scheme promotes the concept of a political and cultural bloc composed of Russia, a basically European country, China, Communist Vietnam, Korea, and Mongolia, and all Asian-African nations, a bloc closed to Europeans, other than Russians, and to Americans. This kind of exclusive club, perhaps politically not too healthy for the Asian-African non-Communists, admirably reflects the Soviet ideal of a vast "peace zone" opposed to the West.

CHAPTER XI

PANCHA SHILA
AND THE SOVIET RECORD

1. *Pancha Shila* of Peaceful Co-existence

THE *Pancha Shila* preside over relations between China and the USSR on the one hand and the uncommitted Asian nations on the other. They promise mutually: (1) respect for territorial integrity and sovereignty; (2) non-aggression; (3) non-interference in domestic affairs for whatever reason—economic, political, or ideological; (4) equality and mutual benefits; and (5) peaceful co-existence. The observance of these five principles should be taken for granted between members of the international community; it is rather sad that they must be solemnly reaffirmed in relations with Communist countries. It is, however, encouraging that the Asian countries concluding *Pancha Shila* agreements with China and the USSR did not feel a need to make similar agreements with the Western Powers, believing, perhaps, that such Powers will observe the principles without special treaties. The previous record of the USSR made it more urgent to restate these principles as a basis of mutual relations. This must have been the view of a popular Indian newspaper: "The Indian newspaper *Blitz* wrote: 'Now, with the signing of the agreement on Pancha Shila, former distrust regarding socialist countries has disappeared.' "[1] It is naïve of anyone who has lived through the last few decades to believe that trust in any government should be founded, not on its record of deeds, but on paper declarations, yet this seems an inalienable human feature derived from literacy and respect for the written or printed word. Pavlov was not so wrong when he said that the sound of familiar words evoked conditioned reflexes in human beings. Hitler was a past master in precipitating such reflexes among statesmen and peoples by solemn promises and treaties so soon to be broken. As we shall see, the Soviet Government followed similar policies at suitable times.

The *Pancha Shila* saw daylight in the Chinese-Indian joint declaration

of April 29, 1954. The occasion for their first public proclamation was in-
auspicious, namely the Indian recognition of the Chinese military conquest
of Tibet and of its being turned into a Chinese colony. The agreements of
that day settled the problem of commercial and transportation relations
between India and the "Tibetan district of China," and liquidated the
former Indian outposts in Tibet (evacuation of an Indian military contingent stationed in southern Tibet and the transfer to China of all Indian
buildings and postal, telegraph, and telephone installations on the Tibetan
territory). Although the *Pancha Shila* are self-evident, they were reaffirmed
for the second time on June 28, 1954, in a joint declaration signed by Prime
Minister Nehru and Prime Minister Chou En-lai on the occasion of the
latter's visit to New Delhi. This apparently useless repetition seemed to
indicate that distrust in relation to the Communist countries was not so
easy to dispel. The *Tass* contemporary dispatch from India made an interesting observation: "The acceptance of the above-mentioned principles
will also promote the creation of a peace zone."[2] This seems to reveal that
the concept of a peace zone, combining the Soviet-Chinese bloc with the
uncommitted nations, was not invented by the 20th Soviet Party Congress
but had emerged in Soviet thinking soon after Stalin's death. That the five
principles were first put into international circulation by China pointed to
another important fact, namely that the USSR acquired in China not only
a military but also a very skillful diplomatic ally who would be extremely
useful in dealing with Asian nations inclined to look with more sympathy
on an Asian Communist country than a European one. *Pravda* noted with
pleasure: "The Indian interest in learning the Chinese language has grown;
it is taught at Allabahad, Calcutta and Shantikinetan. The Chinese youth
learn the Hindi and Urdi languages at Peking University."[3]

Chou En-lai signed another five-principle declaration, this time with
Burma, on June 30, 1954; Indonesia followed suit. Then the Soviet Union
stepped in to sign similar declarations with uncommitted countries in Asia.
The five principles thus became the foundation of relations between the
Soviet-Chinese bloc and the Asian uncommitted nations.

The principles of peaceful co-existence are only five in number, yet the
fourth and fifth are entirely superfluous. There is no point in listing peaceful co-existence as a separate fifth principle because all the other principles
are couched to express the basic ideas of such co-existence. The fourth principle contains empty phraseology which has never done any good to weaker
states. The proclamation of equality neither makes the military and eco-

nomic potential of India or Indonesia equal to that of the USSR nor makes Burma or other small states the equals of Russia and China. If equality means equal respect for mutual independence, external and domestic sovereignty, and territorial integrity, this is stated clearly in the first principle. The equality in any other sense has been repudiated in the practice of the "socialist" camp. Its members are never listed alphabetically, but the first place is always assigned to the USSR, the second to China, while the people's democracies follow in various orders, most of the times according to the size of their respective populations. This and the invariable Soviet insistence on the leading international role of great Powers point out to a hierarchical rather than equal concept of international relations. Mutual benefits of the fourth principle are another empty phrase; if they refer to economic mutual benefits, such wording does not add to or detract a thought from the commercial treaties which the Soviet bloc countries have signed or are going to conclude. Actually, only the first three principles have definite meaning; they repeat the obligations which all members of the United Nations have undertaken in the Charter. Do international obligations acquire greater vitality by repetition? India, Burma, Indonesia, and others have succumbed to the modern disease, which had previously affected the Western states, of finding pleasure in multiplying solemn treaties and reaffirming lofty principles. It would be an innocent game except that it creates a false sense of security among the bona fide contracting parties.

2. Soviet Respect for Treaties

The prime insistent question concerns the Soviet record in the observation of political treaties. This record is long, and it suffices for the time being to adduce the most glaring examples; they are far from encouraging. Molotov, who as Soviet Foreign Minister had been instrumental in 1939–40 and, later, in disregarding the most solemn pledges of non-aggression and respect for national independence and territorial integrity of other states, was apparently at peace with his conscience because he stated at a press conference in London on October 3, 1945: "Everyone knows that the Soviet Union has always been faithful to its word."[4] His predecessor, Chicherin, was much more forthright in 1922 when he thus formulated the Soviet philosophy of international treaties: "Every treaty is merely an expression of forces operative in the realm of facts."[5]

On May 7, 1920, a peace treaty was signed by the RSFSR and the Democratic Republic of Georgia, which had proclaimed her secession from the former Russian Empire and was ruled by a moderate socialist government certainly as progressive as the present-day Indian Congress Party. The Soviet Russian Government promised in that treaty to recognize unconditionally Georgian independence (Article 1), and ". . . Russia renounces intervention of any kind whatsoever in the domestic affairs of Georgia" (Article 2).[6] But "forces operative in the realm of facts" changed a year later; the Soviet Government had its hands untied by the end of the civil war and foreign intervention. The Red Army conquered Georgia in February, 1921, and the country was annexed as a Soviet Republic.

The treaty of alliance concluded by the RSFSR, this time with the Soviet Republic of Bukhara, on March 4, 1921, stated: ". . . the RSFSR unconditionally recognizes the complete autonomy and independence of the Soviet Republic of Bukhara . . . and renounces forever all rights which Tsarist Russia imposed on Bukhara."[7] Similar pledge was given to the neighboring Soviet Republic of Khoresm (Khiva). Four years later, both republics were incorporated into the Soviet Union, Foreign Commissar Chicherin simply advising, on June 10, 1925, all foreign diplomatic missions in Moscow that the territories of Bukhara and Khoresm had been included within the newly formed Turkmenian and Uzbek Soviet Republics, parts of the Soviet Union. Two Asian countries witnessed the Soviet solemn pledges being wantonly broken.

On April 13, 1941, at the time of serious deterioriation in Soviet-German relations, the USSR was very glad to secure her flank in the Far East and to sign with Japan a treaty of neutrality, whose Article 2 read: "In a case where either of the Contracting Parties is the object of hostilities on the part of one or several third Powers, the other Contracting Power shall observe neutrality for the duration of the conflict."[8] Article 3 added: "The present Pact . . . shall remain in force for five years."[9] The treaty should have remained in force until April 13, 1946, but "forces operating in the realm of facts" wanted it otherwise. Those forces were not a sudden revulsion at Japanese imperialist expansion, since Japan had time to conquer Manchuria and most of China before the signing of the treaty. The treaty was not denounced earlier, although Japan had occupied, between 1941 and 1945, the Philippines, Indochina, Indonesia, Burma, and other territories. During that period, the same forces operating in the realm of facts told the Soviet Government that it had to concentrate on its war with Germany and to stay neutral in the Far Eastern war in view of the strong Japanese Kwantung Army concentrated in Manchuria close to the Soviet frontiers. The forces active in 1945 were of a different type—Germany had already unconditionally surrendered in May, 1945; Japan had been decisively defeated on the seas by the United States and had no chance to withstand for long a blockade of the home islands; there were small risks, if any, in entering the war against Japan for the price promised by the United States and Britain in the Yalta Far Eastern Agreement. Japan had confessed her defeat to still neutral Russia in the middle of July, 1945. Molotov told a press conference on August 8, 1945, that the Japanese Government had asked the USSR in the middle of July to offer its good offices for the termination of hostilities; he added that this information had been passed to the United States and Great Britain during the Potsdam Conference (July 17–August 2, 1945).[10] On August 3, 1945, the Soviet Government notified Japan of its denunciation of the treaty of neutrality, to take effect at the end of the treaty's initial five-year duration.[11] Japan could interpret this as meaning that the treaty would not be extended after April 13, 1946. The treaty did not include any provision for a denunciation with immediate effects before the lapse of five years. On August 8, 1945, the USSR declared war on Japan and began operations in Manchuria at the time Japan was in the process of surrendering. But the Soviet Union thus preserved its rights to territorial and political acquisitions at the expense of both China and Japan, as stipulated in the Yalta Far Eastern Agreement.

Turning to Europe, we find a record even less encouraging. Poland, Finland, Lithuania, Latvia, Estonia, and Rumania, all neighbors of the USSR, seemed to be well protected against any risks, if protection consisted in the accumulation of pledges and solemn assurances. The Finnish independence of Russia was recognized by the Soviet Government on December 31, 1917. On October 14, 1920, both governments concluded a peace treaty that contained mutual recognition of their common frontier. On January 21, 1932, they signed a treaty of non-aggression. Both were members of the League of Nations; the League Covenant contained Article 10, whose tone sounded like an improved version of one of the *Pancha Shila:* "The Members of the League undertake to respect and preserve against external aggression the territorial integrity and existing political independence of all Members of the League." The meaning of aggression was clarified for the USSR and her European neighbors, including Finland, in a regional convention on the definition of aggression concluded on July 3, 1933. The text of this convention followed closely the original Soviet draft, and the convention was concluded by Soviet initiative. Its contracting parties were the USSR, Afghanistan, Estonia, Latvia, Iran, Poland, Rumania, Turkey, Finland and a few other states. Aggression was defined in Article 2 as the commission of any of the following acts:

... 1. Declaration of war upon another State; 2. Invasion by armed forces, with or without a declaration of war, of the territory of another State; 3. Attack by land, naval or air forces, with or without a declaration of war, on the territory, vessels, or aircraft of another State; 4. Naval blockade of the coasts or ports of another State; 5. Provision of support to armed bands formed on the territory [of one State] which have invaded the territory of another State, or refusal, notwithstanding the request of the invaded State, to take, on [the aggressor's] territory, all the measures in its power to deprive those bands of all assistance or protection.

Article 3 reinforced this definition by stating that:

No political, military, economic or other considerations may serve as an excuse or justification for the aggression. . . .

An annex to Article 3 stipulated precisely that the following reasons could not justify aggression:

A. The internal condition of a State: for instance, its political, economic or social structure; alleged defects in its administration; disturbances due to strikes, revolutions, counter-revolutions, or civil war.

B. The international conduct of a State: for instance, the violation or threatened violation of the material or moral rights or interests of a foreign State or its nationals; the rupture of diplomatic or economic relations; economic or financial boycotts; disputes relating to economic, financial or other obligations towards foreign States; frontier incidents not forming any of the cases of aggression specified in Article 2.

It was to be one of the ironies of history that these precise definitions of aggression, originally drafted by the Soviet Government and accepted by its neighbors at its insistence, were to be systematically violated five and more years later during the last war and again in 1956 in Hungary. Here the Communists claim that a counter-revolution had taken place; but counter-revolution was expressly mentioned in the convention (on the definition of aggression) as one of the excuses which could not be adduced to justify an armed intervention in another state.

Finland, like all other Soviet neighbors and the USSR itself, was a party to the Briand-Kellogg Pact for outlawing war signed in Paris on August 31, 1928. This Pact said in Article 1:

The High Contracting Parties solemnly declare in the name of their respective peoples that they condemn recourse to war for the solution of international controversies, and renounce it as an instrument of national policy in their relations with one another.

The Soviet Union was so eager in 1928 to display its peace-loving intentions that it proposed to all neighbors to make the Briand-Kellogg Pact immediately valid in their mutual relations, without waiting for its general entry into force. This was done by a regional protocol signed on February 9, 1929.

On April 7, 1934, the Soviet-Finnish treaty of non-aggression was extended for an additional ten years, until 1945. *Pancha Shila* make meager reading against the imposing background of Soviet pledges of non-aggression and respect for independence and territorial integrity of Finland contained in both bilateral and multilateral agreements. Yet Finland was suddenly confronted in October–November, 1939, with Soviet demands for territorial cessions and the lease of a military base on her territory. After Finland had accepted some of these demands and had rejected the others, the USSR attacked her on November 30, 1939, and imposed its demands in the peace treaty concluded on March 11, 1940.

Poland seemed no less well protected. The peace treaty signed by both countries on March 18, 1921, defined their frontiers by mutual agreement. Both were parties to the Covenant of the League of Nations, the Briand-Kellogg Pact, and the London regional convention on the definition of aggression. They signed, on July 25, 1932, a treaty of non-aggression. At the time when it was a public secret that Poland and Germany had quarreled over the fate of Danzig and the Polish-German frontiers, the USSR gave Poland, on November 26, 1938, solemn assurance that it would respect the treaty of non-aggression. Yet barely a year later, while Polish troops were battling against overwhelmingly superior German armies, the neutral USSR sent its troops across the border, stabbed Poland in the back, and met the new Nazi friends on a demarcation line in the middle of the country, which was thus strangled by both mighty neighbors. Polish territory was then divided between them by the Treaty of September 28, 1939.

The three Baltic countries had similar guarantees. Their independence of Russia and the integrity of their territories were recognized by the Soviet Government in peace treaties concluded with Lithuania on April 12, 1920, with Latvia on August 11, 1920, and with Estonia on February 2, 1920. All three were members of the League and parties to the Briand-Kellogg Pact and the convention on the definition of aggression. All three were protected by pacts of non-aggression: Lithuania by the Treaty of September 28, 1926, Latvia by the Treaty of February 5, 1932, and Estonia by that of May 4, 1932. On April 4, 1934, all three non-aggression treaties were extended for ten years and should have expired in 1944. But the Soviet troops invaded those small countries in June, 1940, and the Supreme Soviet of the USSR passed on August 3, 5, and 6, 1940, respectively, laws on the incorporation of Lithuania, Latvia, and Estonia.[12]

Rumania was less well protected legally. She had no formal peace treaty with the USSR, which had never recognized the Rumanian seizure in 1918 of the Russian province of Bessarabia. However, she seemed to have guarantees against the use of force in settling this controversial territorial question. The USSR accepted, on July 4, 1933, her signature to the regional convention on the definition of aggression. Both countries were bound by Article 2 of the Briand-Kellogg Pact to the effect that "the High Contracting Parties agree that the settlement or solution of all disputes or conflicts of whatever nature or of whatever origin they may be, which may arise among them, shall never be sought except by pacific means." The USSR, however, sent on June 26, 1940, a 24-hour ultimatum to Rumania asking for the surrender not only of Bessarabia but also of northern Bukovina, which had never been Russian. The Rumanians had to accept; the alternative was the wholesale invasion by Soviet troops.

In the postwar years, after the 1948 rift between Yugoslavia and the USSR, the Soviet Government sent, on September 28, 1949, a note to Yugoslavia with the following passages:

... Facts discovered during the trial [of Rajk and associates in Budapest] proved further that the Yugoslav government was totally subjected to foreign imperialist circles and became a tool of their aggressive policy. This had to result and actually has resulted in the liquidation of the autonomy and independence of the Yugoslav Republic. ... In view of the preceding the Soviet Government declares that the Soviet Union considers itself free as of today of all obligations resulting from that Treaty [the Treaty of friendship, mutual assistance and post-war co-operation, concluded on April 11, 1945].[13]

This treaty did not provide for a unilateral denunciation before its expiration. The pretext for its denunciation has now been repudiated by the

USSR after the reconciliation with Yugoslavia in 1955 and the rehabilitation of Rajk in 1956. But in the meantime, Tito might have learned that it
was not too wise to trust in treaties signed with the USSR. Actually, other
treaties concluded with Yugoslavia by either the USSR or her eastern European satellites were also unilaterally denounced in 1949. This and other
unilateral denunciations of treaties, about which we shall speak later, deserve this comment, which was made unwittingly in 1955 by a Soviet international lawyer: "A unilateral denunciation of an international treaty, i.e.,
against the will of the other party, is a violation of international obligations."[14] The violations of international treaties in the cases of Georgia,
Poland, Finland, the Baltic States, and other countries do not require any
stronger condemnation than his writing:

Every international treaty should be fulfilled by its contracting parties. . . .
A State which violates an international treaty should reckon with the fact
that its action subverts the trust which other subjects of international relations have in it.[15]

But he adds, tongue in cheek:

The Soviet Union has, since the first days of the Great October Socialist
Revolution, strictly carried out the international treaties which it has concluded.[16]

Of course when a pact of non-aggression was violated to the prejudice of
Soviet interests, the Soviet Government did not like it at all. Molotov said
in a radio speech on June 22, 1941:

This unheard-of attack on our country constitutes a breach of faith unprecedented in the history of civilized nations. Our country has been attacked regardless of the Soviet-German treaty of non-aggression and the
conscientious execution of the provisions of this treaty by the Soviet Government.[17]

No one would deny that the Nazi attack on Russia was treacherous, but
how shall we categorize the Soviet aggressions against Poland, Finland, and
the Baltic States, also committed in violation of treaties? Actually, those
aggressions could have served Germany as precedents, had not the Nazis
their own equally disreputable precedents.

The last sample of Soviet respect for international treaties is of current
interest. The peace treaties of 1947 stipulated that Soviet troops would

evacuate Rumania and Hungary after the conclusion of a state treaty with
Austria. The latter treaty was signed by the Four Powers in 1955, and thus
the need to protect the lines of transportation across Rumania and Hun-
gary between the USSR and its troops in eastern Austria disappeared.
However, Soviet troops remained, and still remain, in both Hungary and
Rumania.

The *Pancha Shila* are divided into five principles, but the actual Soviet
record has entangled them. This renders impossible the separate analysis
of each of them, and pertinent references to the Soviet record, without in-
curring a constant repetition of the same facts. We shall therefore follow
the Soviet record in chronological order, in each case referring to one or a
few *Pancha Shila* involved in the Soviet action. Although the postwar history of satellite eastern Europe provides a rich illustration, we shall reserve
this important matter for a separate treatment (see Chapter XIII). The
Soviet reconquest of various nationalities of the former Russian Empire
during the period of 1917–1921 also requires a separate treatment (see
Chapter XII) because the subject matter is closely related to current Soviet
nationality policy. Thus we shall limit ourselves to cases which affected
relations between Soviet Russia and states which were at the time or are
still independent.

One may easily distinguish two periods in Soviet policy when it challenged principles now embodied in the *Pancha Shila*. The first lasted from
1917 until 1921, the second from 1939 until 1946 at the least. The first is
associated with Lenin, who remains the great teacher for all Soviet and non-
Soviet Communists, the other with Stalin. Anyone inclined to dismiss the
second period as inconsequential because of the downgrading of Stalin at
the 20th Congress should read carefully, page after page, Khrushchev's
secret speech, in which Stalin was mostly criticized for exterminating, without good reasons, Soviet and foreign Communists. This long and emotional
speech did not contain one word of condemnation for Stalin's exploits,
which we shall factually relate. Khrushchev could not make any detrimental
allusion to those facts for the simple reason that the USSR is enjoying the
fruits of Stalin's policy. It is easy to rehabilitate a dead Communist, but it
is not tempting to disgorge territories conquered by Stalin.

The international career of the Bolshevik Government began in a very
promising way. One of the first steps of that Government was to proclaim
on November 15, 1917, "the right of the nationalities of Russia to free
self-determination including secession and to the establishment of their

own independent States."[18] Thus every non-Russian nationality of the former Russian Empire received the right to abandon association with the Russians and to start an independent life. It needed, apparently, only to proclaim its independence and form a state to receive the recognition of the Soviet Government of Russia. After that first step, it was to be protected against new Russian encroachments by another generous Bolshevik declaration relating to annexations. On November 8, 1917, the Soviet Government issued its famous Decree on Peace, in which it said:

The Workers' and Peasants' Government . . . proposes to all belligerent peoples and their Governments the immediate opening of negotiations for a just and democratic peace. . . . By such a peace the Government understands an immediate peace without annexations (i.e., without seizure of foreign territory, without the forcible incorporation of foreign nationalities, and without indemnities). . . . By annexation or seizure of foreign territory the Government understands . . . the incorporation into a large or powerful State of a small or weak nationality, without the definitely, clearly, and voluntarily expressed consent and desire of this nationality, regardless of when this forcible incorporation took place, regardless also of the degree of development or backwardness of the nation forcibly annexed or forcibly retained within the frontiers of the given State, and finally, regardless of whether this nation is located in Europe or in distant lands beyond the seas.[19]

Never before nor after has any government proclaimed such a forthright statement on annexations and forcible control of alien nationalities. Never before and never since has imperialism been denounced in clearer terms or the principle of national self-determination proclaimed in more unequivocal words. Ostensibly, Bolshevik Russia was going to open to the gates of what Lenin had called the prison of nationalities; every nationality, forced before to live together with the Russians within one state, was apparently free to do as it liked. Here was the veritable revolution.

Yet Soviet practice was soon to contradict these generous statements. We remember Lenin's relativist nationality doctrine and his definite preference for large states. The maintenance of the territorial integrity of the former Empire was equivalent to saving the existence of a large economic unit and a potentially powerful base of the universal revolution. Lenin was caught in the web of his own equivocal nationality doctrine, and he solved the problem in a way that would not have displeased the Tsars. The revolution had to expand territorially, and national self-determination was not to become an obstacle. Meanwhile, however, several border

nationalities seized the opportunity provided by the revolutionary upheaval and proclaimed their independence of Russia. The Soviet Government answered, whenever possible by arms, the usual argument of the
stronger. The action of the Red Army basically restored the territorial integrity of the former Empire, but it failed in a few cases. It was Stalin who
repaired that damage caused in 1917–1920 by self-determination and annexed or included within the Russian zone of influence those nationalities
that had escaped this fate in the Leninist period.

3. Finland

This small country had been for over a hundred years a part of the
Russian Empire as an autonomous grand duchy. On December 6, 1917,
the Finnish Diet proclaimed Finnish independence and thus terminated
former association with Russia; on December 31 of the same year, the Soviet Government duly recognized Finnish independence.[20] But on January
27, 1918, a Communist uprising, supported by Red Army detachments still
stationed in Finland, took place in Helsinki; a Soviet Finnish Republic
was proclaimed, and a civil war started. The Soviet Russian Government
immediately hastened to conclude an alliance with the Finnish Soviet
Government, a treaty to that effect having been signed on March 1, 1918.[21]
This marked the first Soviet intervention in Finland. Lenin, speaking on
March 7, 1918, said: ". . . and meanwhile we shall help the Finnish revolution. . . . We are sending arms to the Finns, but no troops, which would be
useless."[22] However, Russian detachments that had been in Finland before
the Communist coup remained there until a request by the Imperial German Government for their withdrawal. The Finnish Communists were
eventually defeated in April–May of 1918, and a non-Communist regime
was fully restored in the whole national territory. The Soviet Government,
busy with the defense of its own existence against the domestic enemies
and intervening foreign Powers, could not but accept the defeat of the revolution in Finland. On October 14, 1920, it renewed its recognition of the
Finnish independence by concluding a peace treaty with a non-Communist
government. Thereafter, mutual relations between the two neighbors remained correct until 1939. The treaty of non-aggression of January 21,
1932, the Finnish accession on January 31, 1934, to the London convention
on the definition of aggression, the adhesion in 1928 of both states to the
Briand-Kellogg Pact, the extension on April 7, 1934, of the validity of

the non-aggression pact until 1945, and their simultaneous membership in the League of Nations (the USSR joined the League in 1934) accumulated so many Soviet pledges concerning non-aggression, respect for the independence and territorial integrity, and non-interference that Finland could feel completely secure. To doubt the sincerity of the Soviet Government would have been an insult to a neighboring great Power whose Foreign Commissar, Litvinov, emphatically said, on the occasion of the visit of the Finnish Foreign Minister to Moscow on February 8, 1937:

Since that time [the recognition of the Finnish independence in 1917] the Soviet Government has striven unwaveringly for the most friendly relations with neighboring Finland, founded on a complete respect for her independence, culture, inviolability of her frontiers, and an undisturbed peace. This trend found its expression in the Peace Treaty of 1920, the non-aggression pact of 1932 and its extension in 1934 for a further ten years, the London convention on the definition of aggression, and in all those other instruments that bear the signatures of the Soviet and Finnish Governments.[23]

The Foreign Commissar reassured all Soviet neighbors on November 24, 1933, in a speech delivered in New York:

This principle [of peace] has enabled us to conclude with all our neighbors, including those who withdrew from the former Tsarist Empire, peace treaties fully satisfying their national aspirations and also representing, by the way, the only consistent and intelligent embodiment of the idea of self-determination of peoples set forth in the message of President Wilson.[24]

Yet Litvinov made, on December 29, 1933, in a speech at the session of the Soviet Central Executive Committee, the enigmatic observation: "We understand very well the difference between doctrine and policy."[25] Did he mean that there could be a difference between Soviet international doctrine as formulated in treaties and its actual policy? However, he again reassured all of the USSR's neighbors in the same speech: "We have no desire to expand to the West or to the East, or in any other direction."[26]

The year 1939 brought the first opportunity for clarification of Litvinov's allusion to doctrine and practice. Nazi Germany offered to pay a generous price for Soviet neutrality in the forthcoming war. On August 23, 1939, two diplomatic instruments were signed. The one made public gave Germany a free hand to attack whomever she desired by pledging unconditional Soviet neutrality. In all previously concluded pacts of non-aggression, the USSR carefully limited its promise of neutrality to a war in which the other contracting party was attacked without provocation by a third state. Such a non-aggression pact would have been useless to Hitler; he intended to attack Poland immediately after securing his rear through a neutrality agreement with the Soviet Union. The Soviet Government knew this very well and conceded to Nazi Germany a new formulation of the non-aggression obligation, namely: "Should one of the High Contracting Parties become the object of belligerent action by a third power, the other High Contracting Party shall in no manner lend its support to this third power."[27] The full meaning of the new formula can easily be gauged by comparison with the pre-1939 Soviet neutrality obligations. For instance, the German-Soviet treaty of friendship and neutrality concluded on April 24, 1926, stated in Article 2: "In a case where either of the Contracting Parties were to become the victim of an aggression by a third power or several third powers, regardless of its peace-loving policy, the other Contracting Party shall observe neutrality for the duration of the conflict."[28] The new formula, used in the treaty concluded with Nazi Germany, mentioned neither the peace-loving policy nor aggression by a third state; it simply promised Soviet neutrality in case Germany were involved in hostilities. Of course, a state may also be involved in hostilities because of its own attack on another country. Japan was granted, in 1941, the same freedom of attacking third states, the USSR remaining neutral; Article 2 of the Soviet-Japanese treaty of neutrality copied the formula used in 1939 in relation to Nazi Germany: "In case one of the Contracting Parties is the object of hostilities on the part of one or several third Powers, the other Contracting Party shall observe neutrality during the whole conflict."[29] Again there was no reference to the crucial question of who would be first to start hostilities, Japan or a third power. The Soviet Union thus gave Japan a carte blanche to expand by aggression in a southern direction at the expense of other states.

The Nazis recompensed the USSR in the secret protocol attached to the public treaty of August 23, 1939. This Protocol included within the Soviet zone of influence the eastern half of Poland (to be attacked by Germany), Estonia, Latvia and Finland (see Chapter VII). Thus the fate of Finland and other neighbors was sealed at the price of Soviet unconditional neutrality in a German war against Poland, Britain, and France. This type of neutrality was unwittingly condemned by Foreign Commissar Litvinov in a speech he made on March 17, 1936, at a meeting of the Council of the League of Nations:

The Soviet Union has itself signed pacts of non-aggression with all its neighbors (except Japan which rejects such a pact to this day). But the Soviet Union has always attached great importance to the point that these pacts should not facilitate aggression against third parties. We therefore always included in these pacts a special clause, freeing either of the contracting parties from any obligation under the pact if the other party commits an act of aggression against a third State. Such a clause, however, will be absent from the pacts proposed by Mr. Hitler, according to the model which he has indicated. . . . Every State which has signed such a pact with Germany is immobilized by her in the event of Germany attacking a third State. This proposal of Mr. Hitler gives me the impression that we are faced with an attempt to divide Europe into two or more parts, with the object of guaranteeing non-aggression for one part of Europe in order to acquire a free hand for dealing with other parts.[30]

This analysis of pacts of unconditional neutrality was to fit exactly the pattern of Soviet agreements with Nazi Germany in 1939 and with Japan in 1941.

The pact with Germany pushed the button. Hitler was free to attack Poland and to face the risk of a war with Britain and France, feeling sure that the USSR would remain neutral. His military action also untied the Soviets' hands. Now their Government had found the long hoped-for opportunity for an armed conflict among capitalist states and could brush aside former promises given to its neighbors. The pre-1939 *Pancha Shila* were forgotten. The turn of Finland came after Poland and the Baltic States. On October 14, 1939, Finland was suddenly confronted with the following Soviet demands:

1. the conclusion of a treaty of mutual assistance on the Baltic model (this demand was quickly dropped in the face of stubborn Finnish refusal);

2. the lease of the Hangö peninsula with its port for a Soviet military and naval base and a Soviet garrison;

3. the cession of various islands in the Gulf of Finland and of the larger part of the Karelian Isthmus;

4. the demolition of Finnish fortifications on the same isthmus, which protected access to southern Finland and the capital of Helsinki.

In exchange the USSR offered the cession of a large piece (militarily unimportant and economically poor) of the territory of the Soviet Autonomous Karelian Republic.[31]

The Finnish-Soviet negotiations dragged on throughout October and November, the Finns offering the cession of some of their islands in the

Gulf of Finland and a rectification of the frontier in the Karelian Isthmus. Speaking at a meeting of the Supreme Soviet on October 31, 1939, Molotov, then Chairman of the Council of People's Commissars and Foreign Commissar, justified these demands on security reasons: a better protection of Leningrad through Soviet control over access to the Finnish Gulf by having naval and military bases located on the territories of the Baltic States and Finland and by pushing the Finnish frontier on the Karelian Isthmus dozens of kilometers northward; and a greater safety for Murmansk by taking pieces of Finnish territory in the North (parts of the Rybachii and Srednii peninsulas). He conveniently forgot that the same territorial modifications and the demolition of fortifications would have reduced the security of small Finland facing a great Power across her borders. This Soviet concept, born in 1939, of annexing, in the name of security, territories and establishing zones of influence, recalled similar concepts of other imperialist great Powers, not excluding Nazi Germany. Did not Hitler claim in 1938–39 that German control over Czechoslovakia was indispensable for German security? This concept could be extended indefinitely; one annexes a territory for the protection of one's state; one must later annex another territory for the greater safety of the territory previously taken, and so on. Small countries disappear from the surface of the earth, immolated on the altar of the greater security of great Powers. Molotov himself acknowledged this on May 28, 1946: "They sometimes say that it is difficult to fix a boundary line between the aspiration for security and expansion. Indeed, it is sometimes difficult to do it."[32]

The Finnish-Soviet negotiations ended in a deadlock. The sequence of events followed the pattern used by Hitler in his aggression against Poland. The Soviet-Finnish frontier, peaceful for nineteen years, suddenly flared up. On November 26, 1939, the Soviet Government complained in a note that its troops on the Karelian Isthmus had been fired on by Finnish troops, as though small Finland had an interest in provoking a war with the USSR while Germany observed a neutrality, benevolent for Russia, and Britain and France were tied up by their war with Germany. The Soviet note demanded the immediate withdrawal of Finnish troops by twenty to twenty-five kilometers, a move that involved the evacuation of Finnish fortifications on the Karelian Isthmus. The Finnish Government replied on November 27 by denying that the Finnish artillery had fired across the border at the Soviet troops and pointing out that the Finns had observed artillery fire within the Soviet territory. It proposed a mutual withdrawal of troops from both sides of the frontier and an investigation of the alleged incident in accordance with the Soviet-Finnish convention of September 24, 1928, on the procedure of settlement of frontier incidents.[33]

This provocative answer by the Finnish Government was qualified by the Soviet Government as an act "calculated extremely to aggravate the crisis in the relations between the two countries." The Soviet Government further said in its note of November 28, 1939, that in view of the excessively hostile and provocative position taken by the Finnish Government which had violated by its action the pact of non-aggression of 1932, the Soviet Government "considers itself free from the obligations undertaken in this pact of non-aggression." The Soviet Government was compelled on November 29 to break off its diplomatic relations with Finland and to call back its representatives.[34]

On the following day the Soviet troops began their operations on all the Finnish frontiers.

No better comment can be made on this unprovoked war against a small country for the purpose of imposing on it at least territorial cessions and at best of annexing it as another Soviet Republic than this one: ". . . an unjust, conquering war has for its objective the conquest and enslavement of foreign countries and peoples."[35]

The Soviet Government expected that a war by a great Power against a small country with a population of four million would be an easy and short affair. It therefore decided to subjugate the whole country by importing there a Communist government on Soviet bayonets. The pattern was familiar enough. Lenin used the same device of importing people's governments in the wake of the advancing Red Army; it served him well in the reconquest of various border nationalities of the former Russian Empire (see Chapter XII), but it failed him in 1920 in Poland. The same pattern was followed in 1956 in Hungary (see Chapter XIII). But this time the People's Government of Finland was formed on the morrow of the outbreak of hostilities, Soviet troops hardly having advanced into the Finnish territory, and while the whole Finnish population rallied around their government, which throughout the war never ceased to function in Helsinki. The USSR chose as the head of the People's Government Otto V. Kuusinen, a Soviet citizen of Finnish extraction, a veteran of the Comintern, and now a member of the ruling Party Presidium of the Central Committee. He proclaimed the formation of this government in the Soviet-occupied border town of Terijoki.

Mr. Kuusinen, Chairman of the People's Government and Minister of Foreign Affairs of Finland, gave out on December 1 of the current year [1939] to the Presidium of the Supreme Soviet of the USSR an official statement concerning the formation of the People's Government of Finland and proposed to establish diplomatic relations between the Finnish Democratic Republic and the Soviet Union. The Presidium of the Supreme Soviet of the USSR resolved to grant recognition to the People's Government of Finland and establish diplomatic relations between the USSR and the Finnish Democratic Republic.[36]

On December 2, 1939, Kuusinen and Molotov concluded a treaty of mutual assistance and friendship with the following preamble:

. . . Convinced that now, when the Finnish people by its heroic struggle and the Red Army of the USSR by its efforts are liquidating the most dangerous hotbed of war created on the frontiers of the Soviet Union by the former plutocratic authority in Finland to accommodate the imperialist powers, and when the Finnish people has formed its Democratic Republic which rests on the active support by the people, the time has come to establish steadfast and friendly relations between our countries and to assure jointly the security and inviolability of our States; . . . in order to strengthen the spirit and the fundamental provisions of the Peace Treaty of October 23, 1920, which was based on the mutual recognition of State independence and non-interference in the domestic affairs of the other party.[37]

After this eloquent preamble, which equated war on Finland (and the attempt to impose on her a government headed by a Soviet citizen) with respect for her independence and non-interference in her domestic affairs, the treaty itself reflected Soviet "respect" for territorial integrity by granting to the USSR all the territorial cessions that had been originally demanded, and the lease of the base on the Hangö Peninsula.[38] All this was done despite assurances given to the Finns by Molotov right after the denunciation of the non-aggression pact, the rupture of diplomatic relations, and on the eve of hostilities. Molotov said on November 29, 1939, in a broadcast:

There are some people who say that the steps we have taken are directed against the independence of Finland or constitute an interference in her internal and external affairs. This is also a malicious slander. . . . It is our steadfast wish that the Finnish people should settle their own internal and external questions as they think fit.[39]

Two days later, he and Kuusinen settled those problems for the Finns.

Having formed the People's Government, the USSR denied the existence of any other Finnish government and therefore of any war between it and Finland. Two Soviet documents evidence this policy which would have been clever but for the fact that Soviet troops displayed less efficiency on the Finnish front than Otto Kuusinen in Moscow and were bogged down for months on the same front, far away from Helsinki. Molotov explained on December 4, 1939, to the Swedish Minister in Moscow, who pleaded on behalf of the mutual neighbor, that

... the Soviet Government did not recognize the so-called "Finnish Government" which had already quit the city of Helsinki [that was notoriously untrue] and gone in an unknown direction; this is why there could be no question now concerning any negotiations with that "government." The Soviet Government recognizes only the People's Government of the Finnish Democratic Republic.[40]

The Finnish Government addressed, on December 3, 1939, a complaint to the League of Nations, of which both countries were still members, and said:

The USSR, with whom Finland maintained good-neighborly relations since the signature of the Peace Treaty of Tartu of 1920, and signed a pact of non-aggression expiring only in 1945, suddenly attacked on the morning of November 30th not only the frontier positions but also open Finnish cities, sowing death and desolation among the civilian population especially by air raids.[41]

The Soviet answer of December 4, addressed to the League Secretary-General, bore the imprint of undisturbed equanimity:

The Soviet Union is not at war with Finland. . . . The Soviet Union maintains peaceful relations with the Democratic Finnish Republic with whose Government it concluded on December 2nd a Treaty of Mutual Assistance and Friendship. . . . The Government of the Democratic Finnish Republic appealed, in its declaration of December 1st, to the Government of the USSR for providing the Finnish Democratic Republic with assistance by armed forces in order to liquidate, by joint effort, as quickly as possible the most dangerous hotbed of war created in Finland by her former government.[42]

As late as March 4, 1940, when the Soviet Government was already contemplating the opening of peace negotiations with the legitimate Finnish Government, the general staff of the Leningrad Military Region still referred in its public communiqué to "the so-called Finnish government."[43]

The Council of the League of Nations expelled the USSR from the

League for its aggression against Finland. This was why the USSR was so glad to replace the League by another international organization whose name, the United Nations, did not recall the existence of its predecessor. While Soviet military operations were dragging on for months in the face of stubborn and successful Finnish resistance, Britain and France toyed with the idea, unwise from their own point of view, of coming to Finnish assistance by opening two fronts against the Soviet Union—one in Finland and the other in the Near East. We may imagine retrospectively the possible results of such a move; the actual war with Germany was not yet fought; to force the USSR to abandon her formal neutrality and to join Nazi Germany would have proved disastrous to the Western Powers in 1940 after the Nazis had commenced their operations in the West. The two Western Powers had an excuse in their impatience with Soviet poltical and economic co-operation with Nazi Germany. The effects of the Allied blockade of Germany were partly nullified by Soviet supplies of raw materials and foodstuffs either regularly exported to Germany from the Soviet territory or re-exported from Asia, where the USSR was buying, for instance, rubber to cover her own and German requirements. British-French security was also threatened by the Soviet Union's granting to German submarines naval facilities close to Murmansk. However, the starting of a war on the USSR would have been folly. The USSR herself did not intend to be dragged into a major conflict with either belligerent camp. Rumors of pending British-French intervention brought to a halt the Soviet operations in Finland, though they were at last scoring successes. On March 7, 1940, the USSR began negotiations with the "so-called Finnish Government," and a peace treaty was signed on March 12. The Finns saved their independence but, exhausted by the unequal struggle, had to grant to the USSR all the demands as formulated in 1939: territorial cessions, which included the important city of Vyborg, and a thirty-year lease of the Hangö Peninsula. The Petsamo area, dividing the USSR from Norway, had not been claimed in 1939 and was left to Finland in 1940 despite its nickel mines. This Soviet omission was repaired by the peace treaty of 1947. Molotov had rather unkind words to say on March 29, 1940, at a meeting of the Supreme Soviet, regarding the People's Government: "The results of the agreement to terminate hostilities and establish peace are contained in the Peace Treaty signed on March 12. In this connection the question arose of the People's Government dissolving itself, which it did."[44] This is the usual unceremonious manner of getting rid of expendable people's governments if Soviet troops fail to install them in the countries for which those governments are destined. They were quickly liquidated in 1920 in Poland and in 1946 in the Iranian Azerbaijan and Kurdistan.

The present version of the Finnish war, supported at each point by the official Soviet collection of documents, may, however, leave doubt in the minds of people who think this era of Soviet foreign policy was closed with Stalin's death. In 1955, a Soviet international lawyer told his readers of these events with no apparent pangs of conscience:

In connection with the provocative acts committed on the Soviet frontier by the Finnish White Guards who worked for the benefit of the fascist states [the Soviet Union but not Finland co-operated closely at that time with fascist Germany], and also in order to protect the security of Leningrad, the Soviet State undertook in November 1939 an action which bore a defensive character. The Soviet Union warned Finland that its action was not directed against her independence. After the rout of the White Finns the Soviet Union concluded on March 12, 1940, a peace treaty with Finland. This peace treaty, which did not infringe on Finnish sovereignty, solved the question of correcting the Soviet-Finnish frontier.[45]

The peace treaty of 1940 did not satisfy the USSR. Captured German documents reveal that the Soviet Union wanted to prevail itself of the secret protocol of August 23, 1939, to reopen the Finnish question with German assent. Hitler was no longer amenable to such suggestions; he thought he did not need the USSR any longer after his western victories and on July 31, 1940, had actually made his fateful decision to attack Russia in the spring of 1941. The conversations he and von Ribbentrop held with Molotov in November, 1940, ended in a deadlock, the Germans refusing to concede to the Soviet Union a zone of influence which, as Molotov claimed, would include at least Finland, Bulgaria, Turkey, and the Turkish Straits. They were willing to offer Russia only the skin of a still living British lion in the form of an expansion in the direction of the Persian Gulf.[46]

The Soviet Government tried to intimidate the Finns. For instance, Molotov told the Finnish minister in Moscow on December 6, 1940:

We do not want to interfere in the matter, or to make any hints with reference to the nomination for a new presidential candidate in Finland, but we are watching closely the preparations for the election. We shall know whether Finland desires peace with the USSR, on the basis of who is chosen as President. It is clear that if some such persons as Tanner, Kivimäki, Mannerheim, or Svinhufvud is elected President, we shall draw the conclusion that Finland does not wish to observe the Peace Treaty she has concluded with the USSR.[47]

Remembrance of the Soviet invasion in 1939 and this constant threat hanging over their heads pushed the Finns into an unwise step. They consented to the arrival of German troops and eventually joined Germany in the attack on the Soviet Union in 1941. Defeated, they had to sign an armistice (on September 19, 1944) which re-established the frontier of 1941, took away from Finland the Petsamo area (thus providing the USSR with a frontier on Norway), replaced the former base on the Hangö Peninsula by a new one at Porkkala-Udd, and demilitarized the Finnish Aaland Islands.[48] This was not the end of the inflicted penalty. The peace treaty signed with Finland on February 10, 1947, not only confirmed the provisions of the armistice, including a fifty-year lease of the Porkkala-Udd base, but imposed reparations of 300 million dollars, to be repaid in goods during eight years.

In addition, the Soviet Union acquired the so-called German assets in Finland (independently of whether those assets had been German before 1941 or gained later by Nazi pressure) for a general sum of 6 billion Finnish marks. These assets were used, according to a Soviet-Finnish agreement concluded ten days before the signing of the peace treaty, for the "purchase" of Finnish goods (3.02 billion marks); for the acquisition of 176 square kilometers of Finnish territory close to Petsamo, with the power station handy for the exploitation of Petsamo nickel mines (1.375 billion marks); for the purchase of the Finnish coastal naval vessels (265 million marks); in payment for repairs to and servicing of Soviet vessels in Finnish naval yards (400 million marks); for the acquisition of British currency from the Bank of Finland (465 million marks); for the transfer to the USSR of Finnish real property in Leningrad and Tallin (60 million marks); for the reconstruction of the Soviet Embassy in Helsinki (75 million marks); payment of the Soviet share in a Soviet-Finnish joint company producing artificial fiber (this corporation, which had been before purely Finnish, came under joint Finnish-Soviet administration) (200 million marks); for building a new factory for the same corporation (125 million marks); finally, the remaining 15 millions were earmarked as payment for Finnish supplies to the Soviet base at Porkkala-Udd.[49]

It was fortunate for Finland that the Soviet bill ended there. Stalin decided to leave her a neutral country, free in her domestic affairs. The treaty of mutual assistance concluded with the USSR in 1948 obliged her only to defend her own territory in an attack on the USSR across that territory.

The Finnish chapter may be closed on this curious recent observation in the Soviet journal devoted to international affairs:

Although mutual relations between the Soviet Union and Finland do not necessarily represent in their entirety an example applicable to other countries, one can, however, find in them certain features and details which deserve studying and even copying in other cases.[50]

4. Poland

Poland, partitioned by Russia, Prussia and Austria in the last decades of the 18th century, recovered its independence after the defeat of Germany in 1918, the disappearance of the Austrian-Hungarian Empire in the same year, and the crippling effect of the war and the revolution on the third partitioning Power. The Soviet Government recognized Polish independence in 1918. However, mutual relations left much to be desired, both governments being to blame for this state of affairs. Poland, fascinated by her pre-partition frontiers of 1772, planned to form a federation of nationalities in which Ukrainians, Byelorussians, Lithuanians, Latvians, Estonians, and others would participate and where the Poles would have the upper hand. The Soviet Government saw a non-Communist Poland as an obstacle on the road to revolution in Europe and especially as a barrier between the Russian and German "proletariats." Lenin had agreed before World War I with the Polish Social Democrats (future Communists) that Poland should remain a part of revolutionary Russia. His action in 1920 did not come as a surprise, although he certainly was not guided by a Russian quest for glory but by his ardent desire to extend the revolution to Germany.

The Poles refused to conclude an armistice with Soviet Russia and in the spring of 1920 engaged in a foolish offensive in the Ukraine that led them to Kiev. This offensive collapsed because of overextended supply lines. Now it was the Soviet Government's turn. Pursuing the defeated Polish troops, the Soviet armies reached the immediate neighborhood of Warsaw, and it seemed that nothing could save Poland from becoming another Soviet Republic. The Western Powers tried to salvage her independence by offering an armistice to Russia on a line which was named after the British statesman Lord Curzon, who signed the pertinent dispatch to the Soviet Government. This line of demarcation would probably have become the final Polish-Soviet frontier—it corresponded roughly to the present boundary line—but Lenin was not interested in frontier problems. He was sure that a Soviet government would be installed in Warsaw within a few weeks. He had no doubt that Polish workers and peasants would rise up at the approach of "liberating" Soviet troops and render them every assistance. For him, those Soviet troops were not Russians, they were soldiers of the universal revolution. He told the Red soldiers going to the Polish front: ". . . you, soldiers of the Republic of workers and peasants, are going to meet them [the Poles] not as oppressors but as liberators."[51] He was sanguine in his hopes: "We expect the Polish proletariat, together with the proletariat of Latvia and Byelorussia, to take care of expelling the Polish bourgeoisie and landlords."[52] The All-Russian Central Executive Committee was less sincere in its proclamation, addressed, in 1920, to the Polish people: "Our and your enemies deceive you when they say that the Russian Soviet Government intends to plant Communism in Polish soil with the bayonets of the Russian Red Army soldiers."[53] This was precisely the aim of Red troops advancing on Warsaw.

However, the Polish workers and peasants could see in these Soviet soldiers only another Russian army coming to subjugate the country which had got rid of foreign domination only two years before. The Red soldiers were for them not brother-liberators but national enemies. Lenin understood his misapprehension only after the defeat of Soviet armies in August, 1920. Talking to the German Communist, Clara Zetkin, a year later, he said:

Yes, what happened in Poland had to happen . . . our unbelievably brave, victorious advance guard could receive no reinforcements from the infantry, could receive no munitions, not even stale bread and other prime necessities from the Polish peasantry and petty-bourgeoisie. These . . . saw in the Red Army soldiers not brother-liberators but foes. . . . The Polish revolution on which we reckoned, failed. The peasants and workers . . . defended their class enemies, permitted our brave Red Army soldiers to die of starvation, and ambushed and killed them.[54]

It was beyond his imagination that anyone could look on his Soviet soldiers as he himself had viewed the Tsar's:

We remain slaves to the extent that we are sent to reduce other tribes into slavery. We continue to tolerate in our country a government which not only crushes every aspiration to freedom in Russia with a hangman's cruelty, but uses moreover Russian soldiers for forcible attacks on foreign freedom. [Written in 1901][55]

The stake in Poland was not only another Soviet Republic, it was the bringing of the revolutionary torch to Germany and western Europe; Lenin said as much shortly after the events: "If Poland had become a Soviet State . . . the Peace of Versailles and the entire international system . . . would have been shattered."[56] Karl Radek, the late Soviet expert on central Europe, defined the issue in very similar terms:

Soviet Poland would have become an advanced fort of Soviet Russia. The dominion of the working class on the Vistula not only would have deprived the Versailles Peace of one of its props in the person of Poland but would have hastened the victory of the German proletariat.[57]

However, the Soviet Government was too feeble to challenge openly the western Powers urging it to conclude an armistice with Poland. It had to assent to the reception of a Polish delegation for armistice negotiations while at the same time pressing with the military offensive in the hope that there would soon be no bourgeois government in Warsaw with which to negotiate. On July 12, 1920, Lenin sent a telegram to Stalin, then political commissar at the Polish southwestern front, which disclosed his innermost desires: "Hasten issuing the instructions regarding a mad intensification of the attack."[58] Happy about a delay in the arrival of the Polish armistice delegation, he sent another dispatch to Stalin on August 11, 1920: "The Poles drag on and have not arrived at the appointed time. This is extremely convenient to us."[59]

Why was it convenient? Another telegram from Lenin to Stalin dated August 2, 1920, brings an explanation: "Dzerzhinsky together with his Polish friends have founded a Polish revolutionary committee and issued a manifesto."[60] *Pravda* reported the next day:

A Provisional Revolutionary Committee of Poland was organized on July 31 on Polish soil. Its members are: Julian Marchlewski (chairman), Feliks Dzerzhinsky, Feliks Kon, Edward Prochnik and Josef Unschlicht. The Provisional Revolutionary Committee addressed a manifesto to the toiling population of Poland calling it to revolt against Pilsudski's government of bourgeoisie and landlords: ". . . The Red Army is coming with the slogan: 'For our liberty and yours.' . . . The Soviet of deputies of city and village toilers will proclaim a Polish Socialist Soviet Republic."[61]

The editorial comment ran as follows:

. . . a Revolutionary Committee of Poland has already been organized on Polish territory. . . . It talks in warm words about a solid peace between

socialist Poland and socialist Russia. It welcomes the Red Army as a libera-
tor. . . . Old and experienced revolutionaries stand at the helm of this new
Government. . . . The establishment of the Revolutionary Committee of
Poland is the first step towards the foundation of a Soviet Poland; this is a
new victory for World Proletarian Revolution.[62]

The choice of members of this new Polish government was very careful. Its
chairman, Julian Marchlewski, had acted in 1919 as the Russian pleni-
potentiary delegate to the armistice and peace negotiations with Poland.
Louis Fischer reproduced in his book a photostatic copy of the original
Soviet full powers issued to Marchlewski on October 4, 1919, under the
signature of Russian Foreign Commissar Chicherin.[63] Feliks Dzerzhinsky
was at that time the head of the Russian *Cheka*, the ancestor of the Soviet
M.V.D. Josef Unschlicht was later to become the Soviet Assistant War Commissar. All of them were old hands of the prewar Polish Social Democratic
Party, which had rejected the idea of Polish independence and which
wanted Poland to remain part of revolutionary Russia. For them, as for
Lenin, the cause of the revolution was infinitely more important than their
native country; Lenin was luckier in belonging to the ruling Russian na-
tionality. The Provisional Revolutionary Committee was proclaimed in
Bialystok, a Russian-occupied Polish city. The pattern to be applied by
Stalin in 1939 to Finland and by Khrushchev and his colleagues in 1956 to
Hungary was set up.

It is little wonder that the Polish armistice delegation was confronted on
August 17, 1920, with such conditions that no independent Government
could accept. They contained the following points, in addition to proposing the Curzon line as the final frontier:

. . . 4. The Polish Republic shall limit all its armed forces, without exception, to a number not exceeding 50,000 men. . . . These armed forces shall
be supplemented by a citizens' militia recruited from among the workers
and destined to preserve public order and security of the population; 5.
The government of the Polish Republic shall, immediately after the conclusion of the armistice and a preliminary peace treaty, proceed with de-
mobilization, and shall terminate it within a period of one month. . . .
6. The Polish Republic shall keep only such armaments and military equipment which are necessary for the armed forces indicated in Article 4. The
remaining armaments and military equipment . . . shall be placed, within
one month after the signature of the preliminary peace treaty, at the full
discretion of the Control Commission of the RSFSR and the Ukrainian
SSR. . . . The RSFSR and the Ukrainian SSR shall distribute such armaments and equipment as are deemed necessary to the militia mentioned
in Article 4. 7. The Polish Republic shall terminate the production of

weapons and military equipment and shall proceed with the demobiliza-tion of its military industry. . . . 8. The Polish Republic shall neither allow on its territory nor accept from foreign States, organizations or groups, any assistance in men and horses, weapons and military equipment. . . . 10. In due relation to the demobilization of the Army of the Polish Republic and the transfer of articles of military equipment to the RSFSR and the Ukrainian SSR, the troops of the RSFSR and the Ukrainian SSR shall proceed with withdrawal. At the time of the actual completion of de-mobilization of the Polish Army and the transfer of equipment, an army not stronger than 200,000 men shall remain in the territory adjacent to the neutral zone. . . . 13. The Polish Republic grants to the RSFSR and the Ukrainian SSR the right to unconditionally free transit for persons and all merchandise across its territory. The railroad line Volkovysk-Bialystok-Graievo, insofar as it passes through the territory of the Polish Republic, shall remain in full possession and management of the RSFSR.[64]

In other words, the Polish Government had to accept the reduction of its armed forces to a small size, with the prospect that this army would be faced across a narrow neutral zone by Soviet forces four times stronger. Deprived of any reserve in weapons and equipment, forbidden to produce or import them from abroad, that army would be of no use. It would be counter-balanced at home by a militia armed at will by the Soviet Government. It is not difficult to guess that Lenin had in mind a militia controlled by Polish Communists. The provision concerning the railroad is interesting for two reasons. It is the first example of a Soviet capitalist-like "concession" on a foreign territory, a concept that Stalin was to apply after the last war on a large scale in Europe and Asia; but it was also meant to provide a link between the Soviet armies and East Prussia, then German territory. The revolution in Germany was not forgotten in those armistice conditions. If they were enforced, Poland would have soon become another Soviet Re-public. The unexpected Polish victory in the second half of August ruined Lenin's plans.

Stalin had to repair the damage by two steps. In 1939, he could only share Poland with Nazi Germany. In 1945, he had her all to himself. The annexation of almost half of Polish prewar territory was an easy affair, since German troops took upon themselves the military conquest of the country. The secret German-Soviet protocol specified on August 23, 1939, that the rivers Bug-Vistula-San would become the demarcation line be-tween Germany and the USSR. German military operations began on September 1; the Soviet Union concentrated its armies on the Polish fron-tier. The Germans wanted the USSR to intervene almost immediately in the hope that such intervention would bring forth British and French declarations of war on Russia. Stalin wisely waited. Only after he was convinced, by the development of the German campaign, of speedy German victory in Poland and, by the peacefulness of the Western front, of the Western inability to assist Poland did he decide to act and to take his share. The Poles did not expect that a neutral Russia would attack them from the rear. Had they not a peace treaty concluded in Riga on March 18, 1921, a pact of non-aggression signed on July 25, 1932, and renewed on May 5, 1934, to last until 1945, and a convention on the definition of aggression of July 3, 1933? Were they not members, together with the USSR, of the League of Nations, and did they not accept the Briand-Kellogg Pact in 1928? Did not *Tass* publish on November 27, 1938, at a time when the German-Polish relations were speedily deteriorating, a communiqué to this effect?

It was established during a series of conversations, which the People's Commissar for Foreign Affairs, Comrade Litvinov, and the Polish Ambassador, M. Grzybowski, have recently held, that: 1. Relations between the Polish Republic and the USSR shall continue to be founded in their entirety on all existing treaties, including the non-aggression treaty signed in 1932; and that this treaty, concluded for five years and extended until 1945, provides a sufficiently broad guarantee of the inviolability of peaceful relations between the two States.[65]

Poland had a full share of *Pancha Shila.*

Only a rabid anti-Communist would have paid much attention to what Lev Mekhlis, then editor of *Pravda,* said in March, 1939, at the 18th Party Congress: "[in case of war] . . . military operations must be transferred to enemy territory; we must fulfill our international obligations and increase the number of Soviet Republics."[66] Or he would have pondered over this warning given by Zhdanov on November 29, 1936, at a meeting of the Congress of the Soviets:

Round us are small countries which dream of great adventures or allow great adventurers to manipulate their territory. We are not afraid of these little countries; but if they do not mind their own business, we shall be compelled to open our borders, and it will be too bad if we are compelled to use the Red Army on them.[67]

Surely such a skeptic would have been then, as now, denounced as a foolish man who mistook his nightmares for daytime reality. After all, the Chairman of the Soviet Council of People's Commissars, Molotov, had enough official authority to be believed when he said on January 28, 1935, at a meeting of the Congress of the Soviets:

The Soviet Government, as a government of workers and peasants, bases itself on another [non-imperialistic] policy which precludes annexationist plans. . . . Who can deny the fact that the gigantic Soviet Union has never held out the threat of annexations to a single state, large or small?[68]

Soviet troops crossed the Polish frontier on September 17, 1939, while assurances of neutrality were conveyed to Polish allies, Britain and France. Polish detachments, taken by surprise and engaged in heavy fighting against the German armies, could pose no effective resistance. This was a mere promenade for Soviet soldiers along the road paved by German victories, just as it was no more difficult six years later to rout the Mukden Army of a Japan already defeated by the United States. Molotov, speaking on October 31, 1939, at a meeting of the Supreme Soviet, conceded that the Red Army had to fight Polish troops. He gloated over its glorious feats:

During the military advance of the Red Army through these districts [of eastern Poland] our military detachments fought at some places serious battles with the Polish detachments; hence there were losses . . . the total figures for the casualties sustained by the Red Army on the territories of Western Byelorussia and Western Ukraine were: 737 killed, 1,862 wounded, that is to say, altogether 2,599 men.[69]

The heavy losses were the lot of the German and Polish armies.

The Red Army did not come to Poland this time to establish a Soviet Republic as it did in 1920 and 1945; its purpose was more limited, namely, to extinguish, by agreement with Nazi Germany, the existence of an independent Polish state and to seize a large part of its territory. The Soviet Government did not even try to conceal its co-operation with Hitler in this enterprise. Molotov said:

. . . it was enough of a swift blow against Poland, firstly by the German Army and then by the Red Army, and nothing remained of this monstrous offspring of the Versailles Treaty. . . . Recent events have fully confirmed the fact that new Soviet-German relations have been built up on a solid basis of mutual interests.[70]

Mutual interests were well taken care of:

The territory which passed to the USSR is equal in size to that of a big European State. . . . The territories of the Western Ukraine and Western

Byelorussia acquired by us represent together 196,000 square kilometers with a population numbering approximately 13 millions.[71]

Molotov no longer had use for former anti-aggression slogans and defended the Nazis against Britain and France:

After this judge for yourselves: has the sense of such notions as "aggression" and "aggressor" changed recently or not? It is not difficult to see that the use of these words in the old sense, that is, before the recent decisive turn in political relations between the Soviet Union and Germany, and before the outbreak of the great imperialist war in Europe, can only sow confusion in people's minds and lead to erroneous conclusions. In order to avoid this we must not allow for an uncritical attitude towards these old notions which are inapplicable to the new international situation. . . . It appears that the English and the French warmongers have declared against Germany some sort of an "ideological war" which reminds us of the old religious wars. . . . But those wars took place in the Middle Ages [sic!]. Do the ruling circles in England and France want to drag us back to the Middle Ages, to the time of religious wars, superstitions and cultural savagery? . . . A war of this type cannot be justified in any manner. . . . The efforts of the British and French Governments to justify their new position on the ground of their undertakings to Poland are, of course, obviously unsound. Everybody realizes that there can be no question of restoring old Poland. It is, therefore, absurd to continue the present war under the flag of restoration of the former Polish State.[72]

The same war was to be retrospectively proclaimed by Stalin as a liberating war in 1945, while his former friends, Hitler and von Ribbentrop, against whom Britain and France had been waging a "religious war" that could not be justified, became "faithless men and monsters."[73]

The Soviet Government displayed remarkable diplomatic ability throughout this difficult operation of remaining neutral regarding Britain and France and co-operating militarily with Germany against their ally, Poland. It could not disavow its agreement with Germany for fear of arousing suspicions in Berlin; it therefore agreed, on the one hand, to publish on September 18, 1939, a joint communiqué with Germany:

To counteract all sorts of unfounded rumors concerning the tasks of the Soviet and German troops operating in Poland, the Governments of the USSR and Germany declare that the operations by these troops do not pursue any objectives which conflict with the interests of Germany or of the Soviet Union or contradict the spirit and letter of the pact of non-aggression concluded between Germany and the USSR.[74]

Molotov reassured Britain and France, on the other hand, in his October 31, 1939, speech, in which he said: "We have consistently pursued this course [of neutrality] which was in no wise contradicted by the entry of our troops into the territory of former Poland."[75]

What, exactly, happened to the Polish *Pancha Shila* during those eventful days? Molotov had given an answer in a radio speech on September 17, 1939:

The Polish State and its Government have *de facto* ceased to exist. In consequence of this situation treaties concluded between the Soviet Union and Poland have become null and void.... Our Red Army, having been strongly re-enforced by the recent call-up of reservists, must carry out with honor the lofty mission placed before it. The Government expresses its deep conviction that our Workers' and Peasants' Red Army will demonstrate also this time its military might, consciousness, and discipline.[76]

The actual sequence of events was somehow different—first, the German and Soviet armies destroyed the Polish state, and second, they partitioned the country while former treaties obviously lapsed for lack of the contracting party. The two partners fixed their new common frontier in a treaty signed on September 28, 1939. This treaty formally noted the extinction of the Polish state and acknowledged the new frontier as "final."[77]

Only then, after having received the German blessing for the new frontier, could the USSR think of the propaganda aspect of this beneficial operation. Lenin had said in 1916: "You may wiggle as you like but you cannot escape the conclusion: annexation is an infringement on national self-determination and a fixing of State frontiers against the will of the population."[78] The Soviet Government did not wiggle but proceeded with popular referenda on the conquered territories. This handy device was to be used again in the Baltic States. It is difficult to say retrospectively whether the majority of the population of eastern Poland would have expressed in a free plebiscite their preference for living under Soviet rather than Polish sovereignty. Out of the thirteen million population, there were three million Poles whose answer to this question cannot be doubted; the others, mostly Ukrainians and Byelorussians, might have preferred or not to pass under a Communist regime for the sake of being united (under the control of one foreign government rather than of two) with their brothers in the Soviet Ukraine and Byelorussia. But no one could express freely his opinion because the referenda were organized in a territory already occupied by Soviet troops, placed under the Soviet administration, and controlled by both the Party and the Soviet fear-inspiring Commissariat of the Interior. No wonder that the familiar pattern, known already from Soviet domestic "elections," was faithfully reproduced in these referenda carried out by open ballot and with the results of voting tabulated by Communist electoral commissions. Of course no rival lists of candidates were allowed.

The results of "voting" were as follows:

The elections took place on October 22, 1939. 4,443,397 voters participated. 4,032,154 persons or 90.93 percent of all voters cast their ballots for the candidates to the National Assembly of Western Ukraine. . . . The National Assembly of the Western Ukraine met on October 26–28 in the ancient Ukrainian city of Lvov. . . . It unanimously proclaimed the establishment of Soviet authority on the whole Western Ukrainian territory, and decided to request the Supreme Soviet of the USSR to accept Western Ukraine as part of the Soviet Union, and to incorporate it within the Ukrainian SSR.[79]

With respect to the other territory, the so-called western Byelorussia, the procedure was identical:

On that day 2,672,280 electors out of the total of 2,763,191 registered voters cast their ballots. 96.7 per cent of all registered electors took part in voting. 90.6 per cent cast their ballots for the people's candidates.[80]

The published figures did not attain the 99 per cent of the Soviet elections, indicating, probably in advance, natural Polish reluctance to come under foreign rule. However, half of the Poles would have had to join in the general desire to be placed under Russian sovereignty should the 90 per cent of the tabulated results be vindicated. This is not surprising because a year later the Estonians, Latvians, and Lithuanians "voted" with the same enthusiastic quasi-unanimity for the annexation of their countries. What could the Supreme Soviet of the USSR do in the face of such a unanimous popular request but bow its head to the people's will?

On that day [November 2, 1939] the Extraordinary Sixth Session of the Supreme Soviet of the USSR adopted the statutes which incorporated Western Ukraine and Western Byelorussia within the USSR, while unifying them with Soviet Ukraine and Soviet Byelorussia respectively.[81]

Thus the first chapter in the new expansionist policy was closed.

This story of events that took place in Poland in the fall of 1939 calls only for a comment given by Stalin in December, 1931, at the time of the Soviet-Polish negotiations for a pact of non-aggression. Talking to German writer Emil Ludwig, he said:

We are, if you want, politicians of a peculiar kind. There are politicians who promise or declare one thing today and tomorrow either forget it or deny what they had stated; they do not even blush at that. We cannot act in this way. . . . If we said one thing and did something else, we would lose our prestige with the popular masses. . . . We and the Poles must declare in the pact that we shall not use force or commit aggression in order to modify the frontiers of Poland or of the USSR or mutually to infringe on our independence. . . . There is no point in talking about a pact without it.[82]

Stalin overlooked only the fact that human memory was short; Soviet prestige does not seem to have been lost, though he had promised one thing, performed something else, and certainly did not blush.

During the period of the Grand Alliance, the USSR could not refer Britain and the United States to the German-Soviet treaty of September 28, 1939, which had fixed its western boundary line in Poland. It founded its right to territories acquired in September, 1939, on those "free" referenda. *Tass*, for instance, published on January 11, 1944, the following statement:

. . . as is known, the Soviet Constitution determined the Soviet-Polish frontier in accordance with the will of the populations of Western Ukraine and Western Byelorussia, which had been expressed in plebiscites carried out in 1939 on the basis of deeply democratic principles.[83]

The two Western allies, in dire need of Soviet co-operation in the war against Germany and in hope of its support in the Far Eastern war, accepted this frontier with some modifications in favor of Poland by returning to the 1920 Curzon Line. This was done informally at the Teheran Conference and formally at the Yalta Conference. Actually, the Western Powers could only acknowledge the results of a strategic situation; Soviet armies had already passed the Soviet frontiers of September, 1939, by the time of the Yalta Conference.

5. Eastern-German Territories

Stalin, whom Hitler had taught to distrust and fear Germany, skillfully, and step by step, obtained American-British assent to detaching eastern territories from Germany and transferring them to Poland and Russia (the northeastern part of East Prussia). He accomplished this at the three Allied conferences at Teheran, Yalta, and Potsdam. The Teheran Conference served him for selling this idea to the Western Allies; the Yalta Conference resulted in British-American assent to support the Soviet claim to north-eastern part of East Prussia at the peace conference and to large but still undefined Polish annexations in eastern Germany. The Potsdam Conference transferred to the Polish administration all eastern German territories east of the Oder and Western Neisse Rivers, pending the final decision of the peace conference. However, British-American assent to the mass expulsion of Germans from the Polish-administered territories could not, at that time, be interpreted other than as final assent to the new eastern German frontier, pending formal approval by the peace conference.

Millions of people are not expelled to be returned to their homes a few years later; in 1945, it was generally expected that the peace conference for the German problem would soon take place. Made strong by these diplomatic victories and by the more important fact of having his troops on the Elbe, Stalin formally annexed the Königsberg area to the USSR, and he advised the Polish Government to do the same regarding the territories east of the Oder-Neisse line. Having a Communist-controlled Government in Warsaw, he was sure that he had built up three Soviet frontiers, the first on the Elbe, Soviet troops being posted in eastern Germany, the second on the Oder, with Poland reduced to the position of a satellite, and the third along the Curzon Line, officially recognized by Britain and the United States at Yalta as the Soviet-Polish frontier. It was easy to obtain approval for the latter frontier from the Polish Government, which signed on August 16, 1945, a treaty with the Soviet Union formally acknowledging the annexations carried out initially in September, 1939. However, the then Polish Prime Minister could turn to his countrymen and point to the western annexations by Poland:

This Treaty on frontiers has for us a particularly and exceptionally important meaning. It is closely and organically bound to our Western frontiers which we have fully restored to their historical extent on the Neisse, the Oder, and the Baltic Sea. . . . The help and efforts of Generalissimo Stalin, Commissar Molotov, and the Government of the USSR regarding the restoration to Poland of her former lands in the West will make disappear once and for all the emotional reactions which the loss of the Eastern lands evoked among the Poles.[84]

Stalin's policy was clear: to write off Germany as a future partner and to weaken her as much as possible by occupation zones and territorial amputations; to tie the Poles to the Soviet chariot by giving them territories which they could keep only with Soviet support; and to create a gulf between Poland and Germany while bridging the gulf between Poland and Russia. It is possible that his flexible mind did not lose sight of another opportunity that could arise for his successors, namely, to make, if needed, a deal with Germany at the expense of Poland by returning the Polish-annexed territories. He knew that among the great Powers only the USSR could offer this royal gift to Germany without general war. He must also have been aware of the fact that Soviet diplomacy could indefinitely play with this hope, dangled before German eyes, even though the Soviet Union did not intend to retreat, either from the Elbe or from the Oder.

We may leave to the reader the solution of the riddle involved in the following contemporary views of a Soviet international lawyer:

Military intervention consists in the entry of armed forces of one State into the territory of another. . . . The position of the Soviet Union concerning the inadmissibility of intervention has been several times declared and has always been followed in practice. . . . Annexation is the seizure of foreign territory without a clearly and freely expressed assent of the population. It violates the right of nations to self-determination and represents a form of national oppression. The Soviet Union and the countries of people's democracy reject annexations. Aggression and seizure of foreign territory are alien to the Soviet Union. . . . The Soviet Union favorably regards the plebiscite if carried out in conditions of a free popular vote without pressure, coercion and force. . . . The plebiscite may express the will of the people if . . . troops are withdrawn for its duration. . . . The expression of their will by the populations of Western Ukraine and Western Byelorussia concerning the union with the Soviet Union (1939) was a true demonstration of the opinion of popular masses. . . . The state boundaries of the Soviet Union have been determined in full conformity with the Leninist-Stalinist principle of the right of nations to self-determination.[85]

These interesting views were written in 1955 after the annexations of northern East Prussia, Southern Sakhalin, and the Kurile Islands, where the USSR had not even taken the trouble of proceeding, as it did in eastern Poland, with the "people's referenda." These views may serve as fit introduction to the story of the Baltic States.

6. Baltic Republics

The Baltic States' story begins like that of Finland, but the end is less happy. The three countries were conquered by Russia in the 18th century. The Bolshevik Revolution and the presence of German troops on their ter-

ritories provided them with the opportunity to proclaim their independence. Lithuania did so on December 11, 1917, Estonia on February 24,
1918, and Latvia on November 18, 1918. The Soviet Government was in
no hurry to grant the recognition. The Allied Powers ordered, on December 23, 1918, the withdrawal of German troops from the Baltic territories,
and the main barrier to the Soviet advance was thus removed. In the same
month, the Soviet Republics of Estonia, Latvia, and Lithuania were proclaimed; Lenin was reassembling the territories of the former Empire.
The Soviet Russian Government immediately granted formal recognition
to all three Soviet Republics, and Soviet troops marched into the Baltic territories in January, 1919, to help local Communists in making those Soviet
Republics a living reality. The Soviet decree of December 8, 1918, on the
recognition of the Estonian Soviet Republic was eloquent:

The Russian Soviet Government instructs all military and civilian authorities of the Russian Soviet Republic which come into contact with Estonia to
provide every assistance to the Estonian Soviet government in its struggle
for the liberation of Estonia from the bourgeois yoke.[86]

The decree of December 22, 1918, on the recognition of the Latvian Soviet
Republic contained an identical passage.[87] The third decree, December 22,
1918, on the recognition of the Lithuanian Soviet Republic did not fail
to include the same provision.[88] Soon after, on December 23, 1918, the All-
Russian Central Executive Committee issued a decree which approved the
three former decrees enacted by the Council of People's Commissars and
gave a specious interpretation of national self-determination conceded by
Soviet Russia to all nationalities of the former Empire:

The Central Executive Committee reaffirms that the fact of these countries
[Estonia, Latvia, and Lithuania] having formerly been part of the old
Tsarist Empire does not impose on them any obligations, but the Central
Executive Committee expresses at the same time its firm conviction that
only now, on the basis of the recognition of complete freedom of self-determination and of the transfer of power to the working class, will be formed
a free, voluntary and indestructible union of toilers of all nations populating the territory of the former Russian Empire.[89]

This was a practical application of Lenin's nationality theory—to concede to all nationalities of the Empire the right of self-determination,
including secession, and then to persuade the proletarians not to avail
themselves of this right. Thus the former Empire could be saved from

disintegration, while the doctrine remained safe. The Central Executive Committee explained in its decree how the toilers should be "persuaded" to stay within the frontiers of the former Tsarist Empire:

The Central Executive Committee testifies to the readiness of the RSFSR to provide any necessary support to the toiling masses of Estonia, Latvia, Lithuania, and Ukraine in their struggle against a regime of exploitation and oppression, and in defense of their freedom and independence from attempts at foreign conquest.[90]

The following month, Soviet Russian troops were to take care of the enforcement of these decrees and of conquering the Baltic countries for fear that someone else might conquer them or that they might remain free. However, the Baltic countries fought for their independence, supported by German volunteer troops under General von der Goltz and also by the Allied naval forces. The Soviet attempt at conquest failed in 1919. The formation on June 1, 1919, of a close (military, economic, financial, transportation, and manpower administration) union between the Russian Soviet Republic and the Soviet regimes in the Baltic countries did not help.[91] The Estonian Minister of Foreign Affairs was fully entitled to point out, in his telegram sent on September 4, 1919, to the Soviet Foreign Commissar Chicherin, Soviet responsibility for hostilities in which the two countries had been engaged since January:

I have the honor to inform you that, as the military operations between Estonia and the RSFSR were caused by the invasion of Estonia by the armed forces of the Russian Republic . . . and if the RSFSR is now ready to put an end to a war started without any reason, the Government of the Republic will see no difficulties in beginning negotiations on this subject and also on future relations between both Republics.[92]

Lenin was not ready for such negotiations in 1918 when he issued, on November 29, the following instructions to the Soviet High Command:

I request you to instruct the commanding personnel of the armed detachments concerned that our troops should support by all means the provisional Soviet governments of Latvia, Estonia, Ukraine and Lithuania, but of course, only Soviet governments.[93]

But he was ready in the second half of 1919, his regime having been exhausted by civil war and foreign intervention. Armistices were concluded with all three Baltic States at the end of 1919 and the beginning of 1920.

The year 1920 ushered in a new area in Soviet-Baltic relations, an era of peace and correct intercourse. Russia soon turned her main attention to the rehabilitation of her national economy. The time of "socialist" conquests had passed. The peace treaties were concluded on February 2, 1920, with Estonia, on July 12, 1920, with Lithuania, and on August 11, 1920, with Latvia. They contained the first Soviet pledges of respecting the national independence of the Baltic States. Article 2 of the Estonian treaty said:

The RSFSR having proclaimed the right of all peoples to a free self-determination, including complete secession from the State whose part they might have been, Russia unconditionally recognizes the independence and autonomy of the Estonian State and renounces, freely and for all time to come, any and all sovereign rights regarding the Estonian people and land which belonged to Russia by virtue of the formerly existing legal order and international treaties, the latter treaties becoming null and void insofar as they conflict with the present Article.[94]

Soviet renunciation of all former Russian rights for "all time to come" was to last exactly twenty years. Article 1 of the Lithuanian treaty and Article 2 of the Latvian treaty also unconditionally recognized the independence of these two states.[95] Their solemn wording was almost identical with that of the Estonian treaty.

These pledges were later multiplied in the non-aggression treaties (concluded with Lithuania on September 28, 1926, with Latvia on February 5, 1932, and with Estonia on May 4, 1932), the Covenant of the League of Nations, the Briand-Kellogg Pact, and the London convention on the definition of aggression. The meaning of the promises stands out clearly from Article 2 of the Soviet-Lithuanian pact of non-aggression: "The USSR and the Lithuanian Republic mutually take the obligation to respect, under all circumstances, the sovereignty, territorial integrity and inviolability of each other."[96] Alas, the circumstances were to change in 1939, and the USSR was no longer able to abide by this or Article 3 of the same treaty: "The USSR and the Lithuanian Republic mutually take the obligation to refrain from any aggressive actions against the other party."[97] The Soviet-Estonian treaty of non-aggression of May 4, 1932, was no less explicit. Its Article 1 said:

Both High Contracting Parties guarantee the inviolability of their common frontier as laid down in the Treaty of Peace signed on February 2, 1920, and solemnly undertake to avoid any act of aggression against one another or any act of force liable to affect the integrity of the territory of the other Contracting Party or its political independence, regardless of whether such aggression or action is undertaken alone or conjointly with other States, with or without a declaration of war.[98]

Article 1 of the Soviet-Latvian non-aggression treaty of February 5, 1932, was no less unequivocal:

Both High Contracting Parties undertake to refrain from any act of aggression directed against the other Party and from any act of violence directed against the territorial integrity and inviolability or political independence of the other Contracting Party, regardless of whether such aggression or such act is committed separately or jointly with other Powers, with or without a declaration of war.[99]

Commissar for Foreign Affairs M. Litvinov reassured all three Baltic States as late as April 4, 1934, on the occasion of the extension of mutual pacts of non-aggression. Addressing the Baltic foreign ministers, he said:

The pacts which bind our States are being extended henceforth for a period of more than ten years, a period never surpassed by obligations of this kind. We have thought of proposing pacts of an indefinite duration, but the absence of any termination date is a sort of abstraction and a philosophical concept. We have feared that such a proposal would produce the impression of an empty declaration, while we have in mind a meaningful act. Anyhow it should be clear to the whole world that our proposal is not of a temporary nature and is not caused by accidental and opportunistic reasons but expresses our permanent peace policy for which there is no termination date. The existence of independent young States which you represent is an essential element of this policy. . . . The Soviet Government . . . has never asked and does not intend to ask for any revision of the existing treaties. The Soviet State . . . does not visualize its national task as conquests, expansion, or acquisition of territories.[100]

However, the secret protocol signed five years later by Litvinov's successor, Molotov, and von Ribbentrop unceremoniously allocated Estonia and Latvia to the Soviet zone of influence and Lithuania to the German; the secret agreement of September 28 of the same year transferred Lithuania to the Soviet zone as well. Their fate was thus sealed. The USSR, perhaps still fearful of possible repercussions of its new policy in Britain and France, took, in September and October of the same year, only the first rather timid step. We must remember that the Baltic governments were asked to sign mutual assistance treaties and to provide the USSR with bases and sites for Soviet garrisons in their territories. The treaties, however, again pledged the USSR to respect the sovereignty of the Baltic States and not to interfere in their domestic affairs (see Chapter VII).

Of course the wholesale destruction of the Polish state undermined Baltic trust in the Soviet pledges, but Molotov reassured the Balts in his speech of October 31, 1939, delivered at the meeting of the Supreme Soviet:

> You know that the Soviet Union has concluded such pacts of mutual assistance with Estonia, Latvia and Lithuania. . . . In view of the particular geographical location of these countries, which represent a sort of approach to the USSR especially from the Baltic Sea, these pacts grant to the Soviet Union such facilities as naval bases and airfields at determined sites in Estonia and Latvia and, regarding Lithuania, provide for a joint defense with the Soviet Union of the Lithuanian frontiers. The establishment of these Soviet naval bases and airfields on the territories of Estonia, Latvia, and Lithuania, and the introduction of a certain number of Red Army detachments for the protection of these bases and airfields, secure a hopeful foundation for the defense not only of the Soviet Union but also of the Baltic States themselves. . . . The particular nature of the above-mentioned pacts of mutual assistance does not involve at all any interference whatsoever on the part of the Soviet Union in the affairs of Estonia, Latvia and Lithuania, as some organs of the foreign press try to insinuate. On the contrary, all these pacts of mutual assistance firmly reserve the intangibility of sovereignty of the signatory States and the principle of non-interference in the affairs of the other State. These pacts are founded on mutual respect for the constitutional, social and economic structure of the other party, and should strengthen the peaceful and good-neighborly co-operation between our peoples. . . . We declare that the idle chat about the sovietization of the Baltic States is convenient only for our common enemies and all sorts of anti-Soviet provocateurs.[101]

It is true that the Soviet Government did not interfere in domestic affairs of the Baltic States until June, 1940. On the whole, the Soviet garrisons behaved properly, but the lightning victories of the German armies changed the picture. France was knocked out, Britain isolated. Neither could afford even to protest against any Soviet action in eastern Europe. Germany, the only great Power of consequence left on the Continent, had given a carte blanche to the USSR in 1939. The Soviet Union was thus freed of all apprehensions. Moreover, it could no longer trust Nazi Germany from the previous certitude that Soviet neutrality was indispensable. It concluded that the time had come for a complete integration of its zone of influence. Baltic states incorporated into the USSR were a safer bet than bases and garrisons, and the Soviet Government proceeded with vertiginous speed.

On June 14, 1940, Molotov handed the Lithuanian Minister of Foreign

Affairs, summoned for that purpose to Moscow, a note, excerpts from which follow:

The Soviet Government considers it absolutely necessary and most urgent:

1. That the Minister of the Interior, Mr. Skuchas, and the head of the political police department, Mr. Povelaitis, be immediately committed for trial as directly responsible for provocative acts against the Soviet garrison in Lithuania.

2. That a government immediately be formed in Lithuania able to assure an honest application of the Soviet-Lithuanian Treaty of Mutual Assistance, and resolutely to restrain the enemies of this Treaty.

3. That a free entry into Lithuanian territory be immediately granted to Soviet troops for their garrisoning at the most important centers of Lithuania; their numbers must be sufficient to assure the application of the Soviet-Lithuanian Treaty of Mutual Assistance and to prevent any provocative acts directed against the Soviet garrison in Lithuania.

The Soviet Government expects an answer from the Lithuanian Government before 10 o'clock on June 15.[102]

This note requires no long comment. Suffice it to say that the alleged incident between Lithuanian citizens and Soviet soldiers happened just at the time when Lithuania would have been most foolish to provoke the USSR; no incidents had occurred between October, 1939, and June, 1940. The time limit of the Soviet ultimatum was only twenty-four hours. The Lithuanian Government, representing a country of less than three million people and facing the demands made by a mighty great Power, had no choice; it accepted the ultimatum on June 15 at 9 A.M.

Although no incidents were alleged to have occurred in Latvia and Estonia, Molotov handed identical notes to the Estonian and Latvian ministers in Moscow on June 16. The USSR demanded:

1. That a government be formed immediately in Latvia [Estonia] that would be able and willing to assure an honest application of the Soviet-Latvian [Estonian] Pact of Mutual Assistance.

2. That free entry into Latvian [Estonian] territory be immediately granted Soviet troops for the purpose of their garrisoning at the most important centers of Latvia [Estonia]; their numbers should be sufficient to assure the application of the Soviet-Latvian [Estonian] Pact of Mutual Assistance and to prevent possible provocative acts against the Soviet garrison in Latvia [Estonia].[103]

Both governments accepted these demands on the same day. Soviet troops poured into the hapless Baltic States. "The representatives of the people came to power in the Baltic countries."[104] These Communist-controlled governments were formed with the helpful assistance of three wise men dispatched from Moscow in the wake of arriving Soviet reinforcements: Dekanozov went to Lithuania, Vyshinsky to Latvia, and Zhdanov to Estonia. The Baltic States having been provided with people's governments, the only thing that remained to be done was to proceed with people's elections under the watchful eye of the Soviet troops and the N.K.V.D. This was the only important task assigned to the people's governments. The electoral mechanism was typically Soviet—one candidate for each seat in parliament, open ballot, and stamping passports of the electors at the polling stations to assure their full participation. The Communist-sponsored electoral blocs did not allow for opposing candidates but were cautious enough not to include in their platform the demand for incorporation into the Soviet Union; their electoral appeals spoke only about close friendship with the eastern neighbor.

For the rest of the story, we may turn to Soviet sources.

These were the first truly democratic elections in the history of Latvia. . . . An enormous number of electors, unprecedented in Latvian conditions, took part in the elections. 94.7 per cent of [registered] electors took part in the vote, and 97.6 per cent of ballots were cast for the candidates of the "Union of the Toiling People of Latvia."[105]

Latvia had an excellent reputation for actual participation in the elections, the percentage of registered electors actually voting varying during her short independent history between 74.8 per cent and 84.8 per cent, but the Communists did much better. No party had previously scored 97.6 per cent of ballots cast for the simple reasons that formerly other parties had competed.

The elections . . . to the People's Seym took place on July 14 and 15, 1940. . . . 95.51 per cent of all [registered] electors took part in the elections. . . . 99.19 per cent of those who participated in the elections cast their ballots for the candidates of the Union of the Toiling People of Lithuania. . . . Mikhail Ivanovich Kalinin [the late Chairman of the Presidium of the Supreme Soviet] wrote in his article: "The Lithuanian people on a new road": "The Lithuanian people could, for the first time in its whole history, freely express its will in the 1940 elections."[106]

591,030 electors participated in the elections to the State Duma on July 14 and 15, 1940. All the 80 candidates sponsored by the "Union of the Toiling People of Estonia" were elected to the State Duma by an immense majority; . . . 548,631 persons or 92.8 per cent of the total number of voters cast their ballots for the candidates of the Union of the Toiling People of Estonia. . . . The Estonian people expressed freely, for the first time in its history, its will in the elections of July 14 and 15, 1940.[107]

The next step was to be taken by the parliaments winning those elections, the "first truly free" elections in the independent history of the Baltic countries. "On July 21 the State Duma unanimously proclaimed the Estonian SSR, and requested the USSR to admit [Estonia] to the Soviet Union."[108] The Seym decided on July 21 to proclaim the Lithuanian Soviet Republic and request the USSR to incorporate Lithuania into the Soviet Union.[109] "The Latvian Seym unanimously adopted on July 21, 1940, the decision to proclaim the Soviet authority on territory of the Latvian Republic and request admission of the Latvian SSR to the Soviet Union."[110]

These decisions contrasted with the national composition of all three countries, where Russian-speaking people were at that time small minorities. For instance, "the population of Latvia is composed [in 1940], as to their nationality, approximately as follows: Latvians—60 per cent, 16.5 per cent Letgalians, 11.5 per cent Russians, and 12 per cent other nationalities."[111] These are the figures conceded by a Soviet author, though in 1940 he invented a new nationality, the Letgalians, who were simply southern Latvians speaking the same language and having a distinct consciousness of being nothing but Latvian. Yet despite this 76.5 per cent Latvian majority and similar proportions in the two other republics, the unanimously elected parliaments unanimously renounced their national independence. The most appropriate comment was provided by M. M. Litvinov in his note of March 18, 1939, sent to the German Ambassador in Moscow in reply to the German notification of the establishment of a German protectorate with the "assent" of the Czech people. He said: "It is difficult to assume that any nation would voluntarily assent to the destruction of her independence and her incorporation within another State."[112]

The Soviet predilection for establishing one central pattern and then applying it in various particular instances, a phenomenon apparent throughout this book, was also demonstrated regarding the Baltic States. All three received practically identical ultimata on June 14 and 16. Soviet motorized detachments crossed their borders on June 16 and 17. The three wise men were dispatched on the same day from Moscow to pick up suitable members for the people's governments. New governments were formed within the short span of June 17 through 20. Elections were held in each country on July 14 and 15. Parliaments asked on July 21 for the incorporation of their

countries into the Soviet Union, and Soviet laws incorporating the three
countries were passed by the Supreme Soviet on August 3, 5, and 6. The
Soviet mechanism of annexation worked with the precision of a clock. V. M.
Molotov summed up the results of the annexation in a speech before the
Supreme Soviet on August 1, 1940:

... the Soviet Government presented the demands of which you are aware
concerning changes in the composition of the Lithuanian, Latvian and Estonian Governments, and dispatched additional Red Army units to those
countries. You know the results of these steps taken by our Government. ...
We can note with satisfaction that the peoples of Estonia, Latvia and Lithuania had solidly voted for their representatives, who unanimously decided
to introduce the Soviet regime and to incorporate Lithuania, Latvia and
Estonia in the Union of Soviet Socialist Republics. ... As a result of the
affiliation of the Baltic countries with the USSR, the population of the Soviet Union will be increased by 2,800,000 people of Lithuania, 1,950,000
of Latvia, and 1,200,000 of Estonia. ... The fact that the frontier of the
Soviet Union will now be shifted to the Baltic coast is of first importance
for our country. We shall now have ice-free ports on the Baltic of which we
stand so much in need.[113]

Ice-free ports as a reason for annexing independent small states—this was
an argument Hitler could well understand.

The period of the Grand Alliance required different arguments to justify
the past and to prepare Western public opinion for the reannexation of
eastern Poland and the Baltic States. The concept of an eastern front was
forged; actually, the USSR expected a Nazi attack and had to extend her
frontiers westward to gain greater depth for her defense. This retrospective
argument continues to be advanced:

The defense arrangements taken by the Soviet Union on its Western frontiers (the voluntary union in 1940 of Lithuania, Latvia, and Estonia with
the USSR, the peaceful settlement with Rumania of the question of Bessarabia and Northern Bukovina, and the conclusion of the peace treaty with
Finland) created the conditions propitious for the establishment of a defensive front ("the Eastern Front") from the Baltic to the Black Seas.[114]

Another author adds the annexation of eastern Poland as another element
in building up the eastern front:

... the first task of the Soviet Government [in 1939–40] consisted of building up an "Eastern Front" against Hitlerite aggression ... and in organizing
in this way a barrier against any unopposed advance of German troops towards the East. ... The reunion of Western Byelorussia and Western

Ukraine with Soviet Byelorussia and Soviet Ukraine ... laid the foundation for the "Eastern Front."[115]

The very name "Eastern Front," which the Soviet sources mention in quotation marks, proves that this argument was invented for Western consumption; geographically, this front was to become for the Soviet Union its western front. Although there is no doubt that adding large slices of foreign territory provided the Soviet Union with a better defense in depth, those arguments about the ice-free ports and fronts had nothing in common with national self-determination (favorite present-day slogan for consumption by the Asian and African nations) and could have been used by any imperialist in the past centuries.

The concept of the eastern front, if it existed in 1939 (it could just as well have emerged in 1940 after the German victories in the west), aimed in 1939–1940 at most in providing a better bulwark for the preservation of Soviet neutrality but not for its participation in a war against Nazi Germany. The last thing Stalin wanted to do was to provoke Hitler. Did the Soviet Union indeed benefit by these enormous territorial acquisitions? Was it better prepared for a Nazi attack? Khrushchev gave a disappointing answer in his secret speech of February 25, 1956:

Documents which have now been published show that by April 3, 1941, Churchill, through his ambassador to the USSR, Cripps, personally warned Stalin that the Germans had begun re-grouping their armed units with the intent of attacking the Soviet Union.... Churchill stressed this repeatedly in his dispatches of April 18 and in the following days. However, Stalin took no heed of these warnings; what is more, Stalin ordered that no credence be given to information of this sort, in order not to provoke initiation of military operations. We must assert that information of this sort concerning the threat of German armed invasion of Soviet territory was coming also from our own military and diplomatic sources.... Despite these particularly grave warnings, the necessary steps were not taken to prepare the country properly for defense and to prevent it from being caught unaware.... The result was that already in the first hours and days the enemy had destroyed in our border regions a large part of our air force, artillery and other military equipment; he annihilated large numbers of our military cadres and disorganized our military leadership; consequently we could not prevent the enemy from marching deep into the country.[116]

Stalin simply could not believe that Hitler would attack a neutral great Power without provocation and despite the unfinished war in the west. The border areas, annexed in 1939–1940, were quickly overrun, and German armies penetrated deeply in 1941 the territory that had been Soviet before 1939.

To terminate the Baltic story, one may quote a current Soviet document, which makes no mention of the eastern front:

The incorporation of the Baltic countries by Russia [sic!] had a great bene-ficial meaning for Russia as well as for the Baltic countries themselves. The peoples of the Baltic area were secured a more peaceful and quiet existence and more propitious conditions for their economic development; com-munion with Russian culture, leading Russian social thought and the Russian revolutionary movement promoted their cultural and political growth.[117]

Probably Asians and Africans remember similar arguments advanced by colonial Powers to justify their rule. But this last is the voice of an "anti-colonialist" Power.

The Soviet Government assures and has always assured that Communism is not for export but can win only in consequence of genuine domestic de-velopment. In 1920, Foreign Commissar Chicherin told the American Sec-retary of State that "the Soviet Government clearly understands that the revolutionary movement of the working masses in every country is their own affair. It holds to the principle that Communism cannot be imposed by force "[118] This was said in the very year Soviet Russia tried to impose Communism on Poland by force and after similar attempts in 1918–1919 in Finland and the Baltic States.

The unceremonious annexation of the three Baltic countries reflected Soviet contempt for small nations, a contempt so well expressed by Molotov on October 29, 1946:

To equate the voice of Honduras with that of the United States of America, or the voice of Haiti with that of the Soviet Union which represents a union of sixteen republics, is allegedly the best democracy that deserves to be gen-erally approved. It seems clear that it is not worth while to waste words on discussing this sort of "democracy."[119]

After Soviet disappointment over co-operation with the great Powers, Molo-tov swiftly changed the sights of his batteries and on November 6, 1947, courted the small countries:

The policy of the Soviet Union is founded on the principle of respect for the sovereignty of great and small States and on that of non-interference in the internal affairs of other States.[120]

When was he to be believed? When could other Soviet statesmen be trusted?

7. Rumania

The problem of Bessarabia is more complex because the history of this province is very checkered. Turkey had ceded this country to Russia in 1812, and Russia held it until 1918. Rumanian troops, seizing the opportunity of the Russian Revolution, occupied it in 1918. It remained in Rumanian possession until 1940, although the USSR never accepted its loss in any international treaty. The province is inhabited by Rumanians, Ukrainians, and Jews. What is interesting in this case is not its merit but the manner in which the USSR provided the solution.

Rumania was protected by the London convention on the definition of aggression and by the Briand-Kellogg Pact against a forceful solution of her controversy with the USSR, both countries having been parties to these diplomatic instruments. The League Covenant no longer applied, since the USSR had been expelled from the League of Nations in 1939. The problem of Bessarabia was potentially solved in the German-Soviet secret protocol of August 23, 1939, which assigned Bessarabia to the Soviet zone. Of course, the Rumanians were unaware of the protocol's contents. The then Rumanian Minister of Foreign Affairs tells the story:

Mr. Molotov invited on June 26, 1940, at 11 P.M. Mr. Davidesco, the Rumanian Minister, to come to the Kremlin and handed him an ultimatum where the USSR called on Rumania to cede Bessarabia and Bukovina in accordance with a map attached to the Soviet note. The Rumanian Government had to give an answer within twenty-four hours.... Mr. Davidesco did not fail to observe that the transmission of the note, given him that night, to Bucarest would take a good part of the period of time granted [to Rumania] and that it would be impossible for him to send within that period of time the map attached to the ultimatum. But all this was to no avail. Mr. Molotov had decided to strike hard, without courtesy or delay.... He remained therefore firm and uncompromising. It was the attitude: take it or leave it, the two provinces or war.... The Rumanian Government was to discover later, after Mr. Molotov's map had been delivered in Bucarest, that the new demarcation line, traced by the head of the Soviet government with a red pencil, separated from Rumania not only the two provinces expressly named in the note but also the township of Hertza and the Northern corner of old [pre-1914] Rumania.[121]

Although Molotov had made an error with his red pencil, the Soviet Government stuck to his line, and Rumania had to deliver strips of territory that had never before belonged to Russia. The Rumanians had little choice. France had been defeated, Britain was fighting for her survival, and Germany counseled acceptance of the ultimatum for fear Soviet troops might otherwise occupy the whole of Rumania to the prejudice of the German plans. Rumanians accepted the ultimatum, but their answer seemed to Moscow to be unclear, so a second note was dispatched on June 27 with the following harsh instructions:

1. The Rumanian troops shall evacuate the territory of Bessarabia and the Northern part of Bukovina within a period of four days, beginning with 2 A.M. Moscow time on June 28.

2. The Soviet troops shall, during the same period of time, occupy the territory of Bessarabia and Northern part of Bukovina. . . . The Soviet Government insists that the Royal Government of Rumania answer the above proposals not later than 12 noon of June 28.[122]

The Rumanian Government accepted these conditions on June 28, although the Rumanian troops and authorities were thus compelled to withdraw in complete disorder, with Soviet troops marching on their heels. This humiliating experience, together with German pressure, resulted a year later in Rumania's joining Germany in war against the USSR.

The German Government, which had been advised before the Rumanians of the contents of the ultimatum, was surprised that the USSR should ask for the surrender not only of Bessarabia, as had been agreed, but also of Bukovina, a province that had never been Russian. The Soviet Government explained that this was in the nature of compensation for moral damages suffered by Russia during the twenty-two years of Rumanian occupation of Bessarabia. After some wrangling with Berlin, it agreed to demand only northern Bukovina.[123]

The manner in which the controversy with Rumania was settled contrasts with the following statement, made in 1955 by two Soviet experts on international relations: ". . . since the very beginning of its existence the Soviet government has rejected the method of ultimata and dictates, and has always proposed peaceful negotiations as a means of settling disputes and divergencies of views."[124] Molotov, at least, felt no pangs of conscience over the 1939–1940 annexations; he proudly boasted in his speech of August 1, 1940:

Thus the territory of the Soviet Union has been enlarged by the addition of Bessarabia, which has an area of 44,500 square kilometers and a population of 3,200,000, and of Northern Bukovina, which has an area of 6,000 square kilometers and a population of over 500,000. As a result the frontiers of the Soviet Union have shifted to the West and have reached the Danube, which, next to the Volga, is the biggest river in Europe and one of the most important commercial routes for a number of European countries. . . . [After referring to the annexation of the Baltic countries, he continued.] Thus, with the population of Bessarabia and Northern Bukovina, the population of the Soviet Union will be increased by approximately 10,000,000. If to this we add over 13,000,000 population of Western Ukraine and Western Byelorussia, the increase of the population of the Soviet Union in the past year will exceed 23,000,000. It should be noted that nineteen-twentieths of this population previously formed part of the USSR.[125]

It is true that these territories, except for eastern Galicia and northern Bukovina, had belonged not to the USSR, which did not exist at that time, but to the Tsarist Empire. But did not the Soviet Government, in 1917, offer the right of free secession to all nationalities of that Empire? However, Molotov could have felt proud; history does not record many cases of annexing twenty-three million people without firing (except for small casualties in Poland) a single shot. This was a diplomatic masterpiece; it was accomplished at the expense of the principles repeatedly advertised by the Soviet Union.

The annexation of Bessarabia again made Russia a Danubian Power, with control of the Danube's mouth shared with Rumania. After the last war, the USSR seized monopolistic control over almost the whole navigable section of that important river, the satellite Danubian countries having little to say on the subject. The Western Powers, the United States, Britain and France, were kicked out at the Danubian Conference in 1948, where the USSR demonstrated what it could do if it controlled the majority of votes. She aligned Rumania, Czechoslovakia, Hungary, Bulgaria, and Yugoslavia against the three Western Powers. The chairman of the Conference, Mr. A. Ya. Vyshinsky, allowed discussion only on the basis of the Soviet draft, discarding the Western drafts and amendments. Thus the present convention on the navigation on the Danube was born. After a British statement referring to the former 1921 Danubian convention and reserving the rights of its signatories, A. Ya. Vyshinsky, who had so often complained of being left in a minority at the United Nations, showed how a minority should be treated: "We shall say in advance . . . that they [such statements] will have for us no significance, we shall pass them by, we shall say: 'This door serves for entry and for exit.' This is how the political situation looks. . . . There is no Benelux here . . . and the language should fit the occasion."[126] Talking to the Western delegations, he unwittingly characterized his own language at the Conference: "Thus may argue only those who feel themselves masters."[127] He felt master of the Conference and behaved so.

The Rumanian armistice concluded on September 12, 1944, re-established the Soviet-Rumanian frontier as it had been after the ultimatum of 1940. The armistice was concluded after such public assurance as that given on August 25, 1944, by the Soviet Government: ". . . The Soviet Union does not have the intention to acquire any part of Rumanian territory or to change the existing social regime in Rumania or to limit in any way the independence of Rumania."[128] Yet Rumania was soon after changed into a satellite Communist state. The Rumanian peace treaty of February 10, 1947, confirmed the cession of Bessarabia and Northern Bukovina and, in addition, contained the Rumanian acknowledgment of Soviet annexation of Czechoslovak Subcarpathian Ukraine.

8. Czechoslovakia

Subcarpathian Ruthenia, or Ukraine, a poor territory lost amidst the eastern Carpathian mountains and populated by Ukrainian-speaking people, was transferred after the First World War from Hungary to Czechoslovakia. The Soviet Government coveted this territory for rather important political and strategic reasons. An extension of Soviet sovereignty over this land, which never before had been Russian, was to provide the USSR with a common frontier with Hungary, earmarked, like the rest of eastern Europe, to become a Communist satellite. (As a matter of fact, the USSR has now a direct access for its troops to Poland, Rumania, Hungary, and Czechoslovakia.)

The problem of annexation of Subcarpathian Ukraine might have been somewhat complicated for people more sentimental than Soviet leaders were or are. The Poles, the Finns, or the Rumanians have never had particular predilection for the Russians, past historical quarrels having cast a shadow on their mutual feelings. But the Czechs, who had no common frontier with Russia until 1945 and who retained the worst remembrance of past experience with the Germans, whom they feared, looked on Russia as the big Slavic brother whose might would protect the Slavs against German expansion; they cultivated for a long time a tradition of friendship for Russia. After the Revolution, the Czechs, except for the Communists, frankly disliked the Soviet regime, so foreign to their democratic ideals, yet

they continued to see the Soviet Government first of all as a Slavic government. A friend of President Beneš says:

In spite of the ideological differences which opposed democratic Czechoslovakia to the Tsarist regime, and later, to the Soviet regime, the whole
nation realized that for geographical as well as ethnical reasons, Russia
ought to be one of its natural defenders against German expansionism.[129]

Czechoslovakia was the first eastern European country to conclude a treaty
of mutual assistance with the USSR, the first time in 1935 and the second
in 1943. Both times it was made by non-Communist governments, although
Czechoslovak Communists participated in the government which signed
the treaty of 1943.

The Czechoslovak Government attached very great importance to the
restoration of their country's territorial integrity as it had existed before
Munich. They were therefore reluctant to make any territorial concessions
to Russia until after full restoration of their pre-Munich frontiers with
other neighbors. As the same member of the then Czechoslovak Government says:

. . . we were prepared to cede to Russia, in case she should become our
immediate neighbor, Subcarpathian Russia. . . . But we were anxious that
this question should not be settled finally until after the war, after our
frontiers with Germany had been fixed and our parliament was in a position to ratify such a cession. However, as soon as Subcarpathian Russia
was occupied by the Red Army, it was sovietized, contrary to the Soviet-
Czechoslovak agreement on the administration of liberated territories.[130]

The Soviet Government was in a great hurry to annex every piece of territory it coveted; it had no time for legalistic niceties or the desires of its
Czechoslovak friends. Soon after the military occupation of Subcarpathian
Ruthenia, people's elections were hurriedly held, and a Congress of people's committees of Trans-Carpathian Ukraine was convoked. "This Congress unanimously adopted a manifesto expressing the wish of the people
of Trans-Carpathian Ukraine to join Soviet Ukraine."[131] The matter was
settled as far as the USSR was concerned. "The treaty on the incorporation
of Subcarpathian Russia into the Soviet Ukraine, concluded on June 29,
1945 [with Czechoslovakia] . . . simply confirmed a *fait accompli*."[132] On
this occasion, Molotov, with his dry sense of humor, said: "The present
treaty is a manifest demonstration of genuine friendship among the Slavic
nations and of fraternal co-operation between the Soviet Union and
Czechoslovakia."[133]

The Second World War brought the USSR enormous European territories and sizable slices of land in the Far East. These gains were achieved mainly at the expense of small nations and defeated Germany and Japan. The great conquering Tsars would have been proud of such successors; neither they nor the Soviet leaders worried very much about national self-determination. Malenkov, speaking then on behalf of Stalin and all his colleagues, proudly boasted in a speech made on the occasion of the 32nd anniversary of the October Revolution (the same revolution which had proclaimed the right of nations to self-determination, including secession):

Never had our Fatherland, throughout its entire history, so just and so well-traced frontiers as now. Look at the map. In the West—Ukraine has brought together into one family the entire Ukrainian people. Historical injustice regarding the frontiers of Byelorussia and Moldavia has been repaired. East Prussia in the West does not exist any longer. . . . Towards the North new frontiers were solidly established in order to strengthen the defense of Leningrad. In the Far East the Kurile Islands were erected into a bulwark of security of our Fatherland, while Sakhalin, entirely restored to us, plays a greater defensive role in the interest of the Soviet Union than formerly half of it did. Never before during its whole history was our Fatherland encircled by neighborly countries so friendly to our State. [He then enumerated Poland, Czechoslovakia, Hungary, Rumania, Bulgaria, Mongolia, and China.][134]

Ironically, he added: "The socialist State does not need external expansion or colonial conquests."[135]

A recent article comments in the same innocent vein:

The Soviet Union has never thought of or planned to destroy capitalist States. . . . There has never been a case in history where the Soviet Union would make use of its power to the prejudice of other countries or peoples. . . . It suffices to point to the latest examples of events in Hungary and Egypt.[136]

This was written after the destruction of the Baltic States, after Communist regimes and Russian control had been imposed on eastern European nations, and after force had been used on Poland, Finland, and Rumania to acquire their territories for the USSR. If the 1956 case of Hungary is cited as the latest example of the Soviet Union never using its power to the prejudice of other nations, then black is white and up is down. There continually arises the question of what weight, if any, to attach to Soviet words which palpably have a meaning that is altogether different from ordinary language.

9. Turkey

The Russian-Turkish relations have never been too happy since the beginning of the 18th century, when the Russian expansionist drive took a southward direction and met the resistance of the Ottoman Empire. Throughout the 18th and 19th centuries, the Turks retreated gradually, losing territories to advancing Russia. Wars alternated with periods of uneasy peace. The main Russian goal was to seize control of the Turkish Straits, along with Istanbul, the capital of the Ottoman Empire. This was the precondition of Russia's becoming a Mediterranean Power. The problem of the Straits had for the Russian Empire, as it has for the USSR, two aspects. The Straits could be regarded as an entrance to the Black Sea and as a gate for the invasion of the shores of the Ukraine and Caucasus. The French-British landing, with Turkish co-operation, in Crimea in 1853 and the use of the Straits for sending Allied armies and supplies to help Bolshevik enemies in the civil war of 1918–1920 proved the importance of the Straits for the defense of Russia. However, it is not easy to distinguish between the defensive and offensive needs of a great Power. The control of the Straits would have allowed the Russian navy to appear in force in the Mediterranean. Then a second chapter would have been opened, since Russia would necessarily get interested in opening an exit to the ocean, probably through the Suez Canal rather than the Strait of Gibraltar. No Russian Government, whether thinking of defense or expansion, could remain indifferent to the matter.

For Turkey, it is a different problem. The Straits are bordered by the Turkish coasts, and Istanbul is the most important Turkish city. Russian control over the Straits would cut off the European part of Turkey from the Asian and sooner or later would have reduced her to the condition of a Russian satellite. What is a strategic problem for Russia becomes for Turkey a matter of independent survival.

Only once did the Western Powers interested in the Mediterranean assent to Russian seizure of Istanbul and the Straits. This was in 1915 in a secret agreement concluded between Britain, France, and Imperial Russia for dismemberment of Turkey, then allied to Germany and Austria-Hungary. The treaty became null and void after the Bolshevik Revolution and the conclusion of a separate peace at Brest-Litovsk in March 1918. Moreover, the Soviet Government itself renounced in 1917 all Russian rights resulting from the London treaty. Isolated, at odds with the great Powers, the Bolsheviks followed Lenin's concept of seeking allies among the small nations who were opposed, for one reason or another, to the European great Powers. On December 7, 1917, the Soviet Government issued its famous manifesto to the Moslems of Russia and the East, calling the latter to revolt in the name of their national independence. This manifesto contained precise assurances for the Turks:

We declare that secret agreements concluded by the overthrown Tsar concerning the seizure of Constantinople, agreements which were reaffirmed by overthrown Kerensky, are now torn up and destroyed. The Russian Republic and its government, the Council of People's Commissars, are opposed to the seizure of foreign territories; Constantinople must remain in Moslem hands. . . . We declare that the agreement concerning the partition of Turkey and of taking Armenia away from her [Armenia was reserved for Russia as a spoil of victory] is torn up and destroyed. As soon as the hostilities are ended, the Armenians will be granted the right freely to determine their political fate.[137]

The Turks could breathe again, although the mention of Turkish Armenia was equivocal; it threatened to reopen the problem after the war.

The peace imposed on Soviet Russia at Brest-Litovsk by the superior force of Germany solved the controversial Russian-Turkish territorial problem in favor of Turkey as a German ally. Russia lost to Turkey the three provinces of Batum, Kars, and Ardahan, all of which she had conquered from Turkey in the war of 1877–1878. The loss of Batum on the Black Sea coast was particularly painful because the port served as an outlet for Baku oil. Black days soon came for Turkey; she and her allies were defeated in the fall of 1918. The Western Powers, in particular Britain, were bent on partitioning her practically out of existence. The movement of national regeneration led by Mustapha Kemal Pasha, future Kemal Atatürk, had to face Western hostility and a Greek invasion of Asiatic Turkey inspired and supported by Britain. It was an irony of history that the secular enemy, Russia, was at this time prepared to help Turkey in the Russian interest. The West was the common enemy, and a Soviet-Turkish friendship was thus born. Russian assistance was precious in that hour of Turkish dire need and isolation. While the Turks were still battling the British-supported Greeks, they settled their territorial controversy with Soviet Russia by means of a compromise. The Soviet-Turkish treaty of friendship and brotherhood signed on March 16, 1921, returned Batum to Russia and left

Kars and Ardahan to Turkey. Mutual friendship between Communist Russia and anti-Communist Turkey was cemented four years later by a treaty of friendship and neutrality signed in Paris on December 17, 1925. The problem of the Straits did not mar these friendly relations. Russia was weak, she had no immediate ambitions, and her navy was almost no navy at all. Article 5 of the treaty of March 16, 1921, stated:

In order to secure the opening of the Straits and freedom of passage through the Straits for commerce of both nations, both Contracting Parties agree to entrust the final elaboration of an international statute for the Black Sea and the Straits to a special conference of delegates of the littoral countries on condition that any decision they arrive at shall not involve any derogation of Turkey's complete sovereignty or of the security of Turkey and its capital, Constantinople.[138]

The Russian attitude is explained by the circumstances of the time; the Straits and Constantinople were in British hands; anything was better than that. Turkey was friendly, and the best solution was to settle the status of the Straits by leaving them to her control.

At the time of the Lausanne Conference, convoked for the purpose of elaborating an international status for the Straits, Russia consistently battled for Turkish sovereignty and against any international control. Chicherin, the Foreign Commissar, said there on December 4, 1922:

... The Russian Government and its allies, basing their argument on the fact that the Dardanelles and the Bosphorus belong to Turkey, and respecting as they do the sovereignty of each people, insist on the re-establishment and full maintenance of the rights of the Turkish people over Turkish territory and waters.[139]

The Soviet Government expressed its deep dissatisfaction with the Lausanne Convention, among other reasons because it demilitarized the Straits and entrusted the control over navigation to an international commission. Fresh in their memory was Western intervention in the civil war, which was carried out partly via the British-controlled Straits.

Voroshilov, paying an official visit to Turkey on the tenth anniversary of her independence, said on October 27, 1933: "We have no desire to conquer foreign lands."[140] This assurance was given at a time when mutual friendship continued to exist, though it had cooled somewhat by reason of the normalization of Turkish-Western relations. When three years later the Turkish Government asked the signatories of the Lausanne Convention to assent to a revision which would restore the Turkish right to remilitarize the Straits and would transfer control over the execution of a new convention from the international commission to Turkey, the Soviet Government replied as follows:

... The Soviet Government has in the past frequently given clear expression to its views on the question of the regime of the Straits. It has always been of the opinion that Turkish sovereignty should be fully maintained in this zone, as the essential condition for the maintenance of peace and order in the Straits.[141]

Foreign Commissar Litvinov, while addressing the Montreux conference on the revision of the regime of the Straits, said on June 23, 1936:

I do not intend to discuss the question of the remilitarization of the Straits. I do not think that this requires much discussion since we all recognize Turkey's right to complete liberty to defend its coasts, its territory, and its Republic.[142]

He was also very reassuring when he told the Conference, which granted to Turkey the right both to remilitarize the Straits and to enforce the new regime herself, on the closing day of July 20, 1936:

The Conference has had to realize that instead of old imperialist Russia, which tried to use the Black Sea as a base from which to take part in the imperialist struggle of the Great Powers and to carry out new territorial conquests, there is today a new Soviet and socialist State, occupying the greater part of the Black Sea, one of the first of whose acts was to renounce completely all imperialist designs.[143]

The Soviet-Turkish honeymoon ended in the fall of 1939. Soviet Russia again had imperialist designs, to use the words of her former Foreign Commissar. Turkey was subjected to heavy pressure to persuade her to sign a treaty of mutual assistance with Russia. Turkey needed only to study closely the treaties of mutual assistance concluded by Russia with the Baltic States to distrust this proposal. She did not want to be included, either, in the Soviet or in the German-Italian zone of influence. She answered Soviet pressure by concluding a pact of mutual assistance with Britain and France, but she carefully excluded its application against the USSR. A few months later, she refused to co-operate in British-French plans to help Finland by opening a Near Eastern front against the USSR, but the USSR drew different conclusions from the cautious Turkish policy of neutrality. Molotov, speaking on October 31, 1939, no longer used the sweet language to which the Turks had been accustomed between the Revolution and 1939. He said:

They write abroad all sorts of nonsense on the subject of these conversations [with Turkey]. . . . In fact the talks concerned the conclusion of a bilateral pact of mutual assistance limited to the area of the Black Sea and the Straits. The USSR considered that the conclusion of such a pact should not compel any action that would drag it into an armed conflict with Germany; again the USSR must have a guarantee that Turkey would not allow warships of the non-Black Sea Powers, in view of the peril of war, to pass through the Bosphorus towards the Black Sea. Turkey rejected both reservations made by the USSR and thus made impossible the conclusion of the pact. . . . As is known, the Turkish Government preferred to tie up its fate with a definite group of European Powers participating in the war. It concluded a pact of mutual assistance with England and France. . . . We shall not attempt to guess whether Turkey will not regret it.[144]

Molotov ended with a veiled threat, and captured German documents reveal that the Soviet Government intended to carry out its threat. During his visit to Berlin in November, 1940, Molotov asked for certain German concessions before the USSR would accede to a pact of four powers: Germany, Japan, Italy, and the USSR. According to the German proposal, this pact would cement political co-operation between the three fascist states and Communist Russia and would be accompanied by a secret protocol dividing the Eastern Hemisphere into four zones of influence. The Soviet Government, always vociferous regarding colonialism, accepted the proposal but asked a price that Hitler was not prepared to pay. The price was fully stated in a note handed by Molotov on November 26, 1940, to the German Ambassador in Moscow:

The Soviet Government is prepared to accept the draft of the Four Power Pact which the Reich Foreign Minister outlined in the conversation of November 13, regarding political collaboration and reciprocal economic support subject to the following conditions:

1. Provided that the German troops are immediately withdrawn from Finland, which, under the compact of 1939, belongs to the Soviet Union's sphere of influence. . . .

2. Provided that within the next few months the security of the Soviet Union in the Straits is assured by the conclusion of a mutual assistance pact between the Soviet Union and Bulgaria, which geographically is situated inside the security zone of the Black Sea boundaries of the Soviet Union, and by the establishment of a base for land and naval forces of the USSR

within the range of the Bosphorus and the Dardanelles by means of a long-term lease.

3. Provided that the area south of Batum and Baku in the general direction of the Persian Gulf is recognized as the center of the aspirations of the Soviet Union. . . .

. . . in case Turkey refuses to join the Four Powers, Germany, Italy, and the Soviet Union agree to work out and to carry through the required military and diplomatic measures.[145]

Germany had her own designs on Bulgaria and Turkey and could not agree to the Soviet proposal. The collapse of the German-Soviet conversations was followed by the Nazi attack that imperiled the very existence of the USSR. This was no time for planning expansion, but one for re-assuring all neutral states that could join the enemy. On June 27, 1941, *Tass* published the following official statement:

Regardless of the fact that the People's Commissar for Foreign Affairs, comrade Molotov, had denied on June 22 the concocted, ante-dated, false and provocative statements contained in Hitler's declaration concerning the alleged claims of the USSR to the Bosphorus and the Dardanelles and the alleged intention of the USSR to occupy Bulgaria, some Turkish newspapers have taken up and are spreading this slander of Hitler against the USSR. *Tass* is authorized to declare that the responsible Soviet circles decisively deny this vile slander against the Soviet Union concerning its position regarding Turkey and the Straits and also Bulgaria.[146]

But for once, Hitler spoke the truth. The Soviet Government had so uneasy a conscience or feared so much that the Germans might reveal to the Turks the official Soviet note on the Black Sea zone of influence and the Turkish Straits addressed in November, 1940, to Berlin that the Soviet Ambassador in Ankara made another reassuring declaration on August 10, 1941:

The Soviet Government reaffirms its fidelity to the Montreux Convention and assures the Turkish Government that it has no aggressive intentions or claims whatsoever regarding the Straits. The Soviet Government, like the British, is ready scrupulously to respect the territorial inviolability of the Turkish Republic.[147]

Turkey could also find comfort in the more general assurances given by the USSR during the first period of the German-Soviet war. The Soviet Ambassador in London, Maisky, declared on behalf of his Government at an inter-Allied conference on September 24, 1942:

... The Soviet Government stands for the right of every nation to her State independence and territorial inviolability, and the right to establish such a social order and to choose such a form of government as she considers the most useful and necessary for securing her economic and cultural well-being.[148]

In the same statement, he also accepted the Atlantic Charter:

... The Soviet Government expresses its assent to the fundamental principles of the Declaration made by the President of the United States of America, Mr. Roosevelt, and the Prime Minister of Great Britain, Mr. Churchill.[149]

The Allied Powers promised in the Atlantic Charter to seek no territorial or other aggrandizement for themselves and to respect the right of every nation to choose her own form of government. Foreign Commissar Molotov himself declared on November 6, 1941:

We cannot have and do not have any such war aims as conquest of foreign territories or enslavement of foreign nations whether those nations and territories are located in Europe or in Asia, including Iran.[150]

Article 5 of the Soviet-British treaty of mutual assistance signed on May 26, 1942, was no less clear: "They ... shall also act in accordance with these two principles: to seek no territorial aggrandizement for themselves, and not to interfere in the domestic affairs of other States."[151] How easy to proliferate such promises when one was fighting an enemy with the back to the wall, and with no means of following a different policy. However, the Soviet Government made it clear to the British that its renunciation of territorial gains did not include those annexations which had been carried out in co-operation with Nazi Germany.

The Soviet victories against Germany radically changed the picture. Forces operating in the realm of fact, again to use Chicherin's phrase, changed their course. The USSR decided in 1945 to apply pressure on Turkey in order to wrest from her the provinces of Kars and Ardahan and control over the Straits. Molotov notified the Turkish Ambassador in Moscow in March, 1945, that the Soviet Government did not intend to extend the validity of the Soviet-Turkish treaty of friendship, non-aggression, and neutrality of December 17, 1925, which had been extended thus far without difficulty, and that it would terminate it at its expiration.[152] Turkey was informed on April 4, 1945, that the USSR was ready to negotiate another treaty.[153] This was the beginning of a campaign of intimidation which aimed at "softening up" Turkey.

Stalin, a man with a keen eye for the true opportunity and sensitive to the distribution of international forces, a man who had proved his political ability at home and in foreign affairs, began to make gross miscalculations. Did he expect Turkey to remain isolated or the Western Powers to accept passively his attempt at making Russia a Mediterranean Power? Did he disregard the relative weakness of Russia, caused by enormous human and material losses in the war just ended? And did he entertain the possibility that Turkey might not be intimidated and might be supported by the West while he was powerless to pass from words to deeds?

On August 7, 1946, the Soviet Government addressed to Turkey a note concerning the Straits:

1. The Straits should remain open for transit to all merchant vessels of all countries.

2. The Straits should always remain open to warships of the Black Sea Powers.

3. The transit of warships of the non–Black Sea Powers through the Straits is forbidden, except for cases especially stated.

4. The determination of the regime of the Straits, the only seaway leading to and from the Black Sea, should fall within the jurisdiction of Turkey and the other Black Sea Powers.

5. Turkey and the Soviet Union, the Powers most interested in and capable of guaranteeing the freedom of merchant navigation and security in the Straits, shall jointly organize the defense of the Straits to prevent their use for purposes hostile to the Black Sea Powers.[154]

The first point of the note was uncontroversial and consonant with established practice. Points 2 and 3 would close the Straits to all maritime Powers except Turkey, the USSR, and satellite Rumania and Bulgaria as far as warships were concerned. Turkey would have been left facing alone in the Black Sea the quickly growing Soviet naval power. Point 4 proposed to discard the Montreux Convention of 1936 without asking the other signatories for their opinion and to replace it by a new regime of transit through the Straits to be formulated by the USSR and Turkey alone, or, taking into consideration their unequal power, rather by the USSR only (it is not difficult to guess that the USSR would then control the navigation in the Straits). This was asked at a time when the United States, Britain, and Turkey had officially declared their readiness to revise the Montreux Convention by agreement to take better care of the interests of the USSR. The fifth point would place military control of the Straits in Soviet hands, for that was the only practical meaning of the proposed joint arrangement. Turkey would lose sovereignty over the Straits and would have entered a stage in relations with Russia familiar to the Baltic States in 1939–1940 before their annexation. No wonder that the Turks, who were not hopelessly isolated as were the Balts in 1939–40, declined to negotiate on such a basis. They cared about their independence, the crux of the *Pancha Shila*.

The Soviet Ministry of Foreign Affairs issued on September 28, 1946, a communiqué which is now intensely interesting because of Soviet support of Egyptian control over the Suez Canal. The USSR has claimed, in 1956 and since, that a waterway situated on the territory of any state should be entirely controlled by that state. But the Suez Canal case was in the nature of a Western-Egyptian controversy. In 1945–46, the USSR argued that a waterway of interest to it and a littoral state should be placed under a joint control, with no attention paid to the sovereignty of that littoral state. But the USSR went further; it claimed in 1946 that the Suez Canal should be controlled by all interested Powers, presumably including the USSR. The communiqué of September 28, 1946, said:

The significance of the Black Sea Straits, which lead to the closed Black Sea, is altogether different from that of such waterways as, for example, the Gibraltar Strait or the Suez Canal. . . . In relation to such world waterways it is indeed indispensable to establish an international control with the participation of the most interested Powers.[155]

This communiqué gave indiscreet warning to Western Powers that the USSR, after seizing control of the Straits, would open next the question of its participation in the international control over both exits from the Mediterranean, a natural consequence of its becoming a Mediterranean Power. Egypt should remember that communiqué; for were the USSR to overcome Western resistance, it would not fail, in obvious self-interest, to raise the question of Soviet participation in control over the Suez Canal.

The USSR did not limit itself to demands pertaining to the Straits; the territorial problem of the provinces of Kars and Ardahan was raised as well. Stalin wanted to settle all questions with Turkey. On December 20, 1945, *Pravda* reproduced an article originally printed on December 14 in the Soviet-Georgian newspaper *Kommunisti*, asking for modification of the So-

viet-Turkish frontier, this in justice to the alleged Georgian claims to
territories once Georgian, but Turkish since time immemorial. The article,
written by two members of the Georgian Academy of Sciences, had an
ominous ring if one remembered Stalin's Georgian descent. The crucial
sentence was as follows:

The Georgian nation should receive back her lands which she has never
renounced and may not renounce. We have in view the districts of Ardahan,
Artvin, Olta, Tortum, Isgir, Baiburt, Giumiushane (Tiumiushane) and
Eastern Lazistan, including the districts of Trabzon and Giresun, i.e., only
[*sic!*] part of the territories taken away from Georgia.[156]

Soviet Armenians raised their own territorial claims against Turkey, asking
for the cession of Kars. This was a tactical error, to burden the question
of the Straits with territorial claims, for the reason that it would only make
Turkey the more reluctant to negotiate.

   The firm attitude of the United States and Great Britain in support of
Turkey and the 1947 Truman Doctrine, which promised American help
and assistance to Greece and Turkey, nullified the effects of Soviet pressure.
Stalin, however, never abandoned his 1945–46 position. A Soviet-Georgian
pamphlet said as late as 1948:

The Georgian people has never recognized the forcible seizure of, and has
never renounced, its southern and southwestern lands. . . . It is therefore
comprehensible that Georgian public opinion insists on demanding the
return to Georgia of territories torn from our Fatherland.[157]

These Georgian claims looked spurious and ordered from Moscow; after
all, Georgia herself had in 1921 been deprived of her independence.

   After Stalin's death, his successors quickly adjusted the situation to their
new policy, which could not be reconciled with demands for foreign territories. In 1953, the Soviet Government sent a note to Turkey informing
her of Soviet abandonment of previous claims anent both the Straits and
the Turkish provinces. This note of May 30, 1953, summarized, at the same
time, former territorial claims:

As is known, in connection with expiration of the period of the Soviet-
Turkish Treaty of 1925, the question of regulating Soviet-Turkish relations
was touched upon in official talks of representatives of both States some
years ago. In these talks there figured certain territorial claims of the Armenian Republic and the Georgian Republic on Turkey, and also considerations of the Soviet Government relative to removal of the possible

threat to the security of the USSR from the side of the Black Sea Straits. This was accepted badly by the Government and public circles of Turkey which could not but in certain degree be reflected in Soviet-Turkish relations. In the name of preserving good-neighborly relations and strengthening peace and security, the Governments of Armenia and Georgia have found it possible to renounce their territorial claim on Turkey. . . . Thus the Soviet Government declares that the Soviet Union has not any kind of territorial claims on Turkey.[158]

Since that time, the USSR has made a great effort to court Turkey by increased trade. However, can one be surprised that Turkey joined NATO and later the Baghdad Pact? She had known the bitter experience of finding, in the forties, the same old imperialist Russia in the person of the new USSR.

It is remarkable how the USSR manipulated, in the 1939–1946 period of actual or attempted expansion, the nationality principle for propaganda purposes. This principle could not be and was not invoked against Finland or for annexations of the Baltic States, the Königsberg area, Southern Sakhalin, and the Kurile Islands, where other arguments had to do: strategic security and historical and economic considerations. But it was used against Poland and Czechoslovakia in the name of uniting all the Ukrainians and Byelorussians within one state and against Turkey in the name of uniting all Georgians and Armenians and lumping together what allegedly or truly had been their historical lands, whether any Armenians or Georgians could now be found there or not.

Conceivably, such opportunity of outright expansion will never again offer itself to the Soviet Union. But its neighbors know that the nationality argument could be used against them under propitious circumstances to make inroads on their territorial integrity. The USSR can no longer present in Europe any claims in the name of this principle, all Ukrainians and Byelorussians having already been united under its aegis. But the same is not true concerning Soviet Near and Middle Eastern neighbors. Azerbaijanis live not only in the Soviet Republic bearing their name but also in northern Iran, close to the Soviet Union. Their autonomous movement was in 1945–46 supported by occupying Soviet troops. Several hundred thousand Armenians are to be found in Iran, Turkey, Syria, Lebanon, and other countries of the Near East. Over 500,000 Turkish citizens are claimed as Georgians by the *Soviet Great Encyclopedia*, which says that they have inhabited "Georgian territories from time immemorial."[159] Kazakhs, Kirghizs, and Uzbeks are to be found in the Mongolian People's Republic and in Chinese Sinkiang; however, their "claims" for unification could not be raised in the present condition where the USSR and China are bound by an alliance; the outright annexation of Mongolia would be deeply resented by China as disturbing a delicate balance on mutual frontiers. Kirghiz, however, also live in small numbers in Afghanistan and northern Pakistan; there are about 2,000,000 Tadjiks, according to Soviet sources, in Afghanistan and Iran;[160] approximately 380,000 Turkmenians are claimed to live in Afghanistan.[161] Uzbeks are also to be found in Afghanistan.[162]

Soviet Near Eastern neighbors know only too well that the USSR has been deeply interested in the national movement of a turbulent nationality, the Kurds. In 1945, Soviet troops proclaimed a short-lived Kurdish autonomous republic in northern Iran. According to the previously mentioned Soviet source, there are about 7,000,000 Kurds outside the Soviet frontiers, while over 45,000 of them live in Soviet Transcaucasus.[163] The exact number of Kurds has not been scientifically established; various sources claim widely different figures, but it is interesting that the *Soviet Great Encyclopedia* mentions the highest figure, which is also that of Kurdish nationalists. It distributes them as follows: 2.5 to 3 million in Turkey, 2 to 2.5 million in Iran, 1.2 in Iraq, 300,000 in Syria, and about 200,000 in Afghanistan and Pakistan.[164] Before the October Revolution, Imperial Russia and Britain encouraged, at various times, Kurdish national aspirations as a means of undermining the territorial integrity of the Ottoman Empire. In our time, only the USSR may use this weapon, since Turkey, Iran, and Pakistan are all members of the Baghdad Pact. Nationalist Kurds have no choice either, and several of their political leaders have been trained from among Soviet citizens and refugees of Kurdish descent. Open Soviet support of the Kurdish claim to create their own state would threaten to undermine Turkey, Iraq, Iran, and Syria, but such a state, if its territorial composition were to correspond to Kurdish ambitions, would not only include large parts of those four states but would also give the Soviet Union direct access to the Mediterranean and the Persian Gulf, assuming that the Kurdish state became a Soviet protectorate or a component republic of the Soviet Union.

10. Iran

Iran has the same recollection as Turkey of the Russian expansionist drive towards the south. She was faced by imperialist Russia from the 18th century; she lived in the 19th century and the first of the 20th through the dangerous experience of being caught between the advancing imperialisms of Britain and Russia. For Russia, Iran meant access to the Persian Gulf and the ocean while bypassing the Turkish Straits and the Suez Canal; it also meant an advanced outpost for outflanking British India. For Britain, it was a question of protecting her dominion in India, her imperial communications in the Red Sea, and in this century, the access to the Near Eastern oil resources. The interests of both Powers continuously clashed until 1907. The German danger made them forget for a time their divergent views in the Near and Middle East and come to an agreement concerning their respective zones of influence. Iran had to pay the price of the 1907 agreement, which divided Iran into three zones, the southern being assigned to Britain, the northern to Russia, and a neutral zone where the Iranians could continue to exist in quasi-independence.

This unhappy situation lasted until the Bolshevik Revolution. The Soviet appeal to the Moslems of the East of December 7, 1917, seemed to bring promise of the elimination of one of two threats to Iranian independence. It said emphatically:

We declare that the treaty concerning the partition of Persia is torn up and destroyed. As soon as hostilities are terminated, troops will be withdrawn from Persia, and Persians will be assured the right of free determination of their fate.[165]

Soviet-controlled Russian troops disappeared from Iran, and Britain moved in and established a sort of protectorate, *de facto*, over the whole of Iran. Russia was eliminated as a threat to Iran for about two and one-half years; she was torn by civil war and assailed by foreign Powers. However, in May, 1920, Soviet troops reappeared on Iranian soil; pursuing the remnants of defeated Denikin's forces across the border, they encamped in the Iranian Caspian Sea port of Enzeli. Soon they occupied the whole province of Ghilan. The local Persian radicals co-operated and proclaimed a Soviet Republic of Ghilan. Ja'afar Pishevari, who became known to foreign public opinion only in 1945–46, had been Commissar of the Interior of that improvised republic protected by Soviet bayonets.

The Ghilan Soviet Republic lasted as long as the Soviet troops were in occupation; it collapsed in the fall of 1921 after the Soviet withdrawal. But the Soviet Government used the trump card of having troops in northern Iran to persuade the Iranian Government into signing on February 26,

1921, a treaty that gave Russia the right to reintroduce her troops if she thought it necessary for her own protection against a threat by a third Power trying to make use of Iranian territory for such a purpose (see Chapter VII). Even so, it was several months after the signing of that treaty before Soviet Russia finally withdrew her troops from Ghilan. There may have been two reasons for the eventual Soviet withdrawal and abandoning the people's government of Ghilan, the first of which was fear that Britain might use Soviet presence on Iranian soil as an argument for consolidating her hold on Iran. The second reason was probably the wish to allay suspicion among those small countries which could serve the purpose of combating, together with Soviet Russia, the Western Powers. The latter policy caused the Soviet Government to reassure Iran on the actual meaning of the treaty of February 26, 1921. Already after Soviet withdrawal from Ghilan, the Soviet note limited the scope of that treaty by saying: ". . . Articles 5 and 6 [of the 1921 treaty] are intended to apply only to cases in which preparations have been made for a considerable armed attack upon Russia."[166] It is of course a matter of interpretation as to the exact meaning of preparations for a "considerable" attack.

At the time of negotiating with Iran the treaty of non-aggression signed on October 1, 1927, the USSR took great care to preserve its right to introduce troops. Article 1 of the non-aggression treaty said: "The mutual relations between Persia and the USSR shall continue to be governed by the Treaty of February 26, 1921, of which all the articles and provisions shall remain in force."[167] During the Soviet-Iranian diplomatic controversy over the Iranian accession to the Baghdad Pact, the Soviet Government availed itself only of the treaty of 1927, but, since this treaty expressly mentions the treaty of 1921, the allusion had a dual meaning. The USSR could not afford a nuclear conflict with the West over Iranian participation in the Baghdad Pact and invoke the treaty of 1921. Iran remained free in her foreign policy, thanks to the nuclear balance between East and West.

Article 2 of the non-aggression treaty makes interesting reading in view of the events of 1941:

Should either of the Contracting Parties become the victim of aggression on the part of one or more third Powers, the other Contracting Party agrees to observe neutrality throughout the duration of the conflict, while the Party which is the victim of aggression shall not violate that neutrality, notwithstanding any strategical, tactical or political considerations or any advantages it might thereby gain.[168]

This did not prevent the USSR from occupying neutral Iran by joint action with Britain. The Nazi machinations in Iran, with the connivance of the Iranian authorities, which had little love for either Britain or Russia, did not represent the danger of a "considerable attack" on Russia across the Iranian territory. The strategic reason was different, namely the need to open direct (safe from German attack) lines of transportation across Iranian territory. The Iranian Government was informed on August 25, 1941:

The Soviet Government itself assumed . . . the defense of interests of the USSR in Iran in case of danger foreseen in the Treaty of 1921. . . . In consequence the Soviet Government has been compelled to take necessary measures, and immediately to avail itself of the right belonging to the Soviet Union by virtue of Article 6 of the 1921 Treaty, namely to introduce its troops into the territory of Iran for a period of time in order to assure its self-defense. . . . The Soviet Government has not the slightest intention [to infringe] upon the territorial integrity or the State independence of Iran. . . . As soon as this threat [of German hostile activities in Iran] to the interests of Iran and the USSR is eliminated, the Soviet Government, in accordance with its obligations assumed in the 1921 Soviet-Iranian Treaty, will immediately withdraw the Soviet troops from Iran.[169]

Britain introduced her troops on the same day. Thus Iran was confronted with a situation recalling that of 1907, but this time its territory was neatly divided into two zones of occupation. Despite protestations of non-interference in the domestic affairs of Iran, the Shah was compelled to abdicate his throne and was deported by Britain. Iran passed into foreign control.

The Allied Powers, including the USSR, multiplied their assurances of restoring the Iranians' full independence after the end of the war. Article 1 of the British-Soviet-Iranian treaty of alliance, concluded on January 29, 1942, said:

The Presidium of the Supreme Soviet of the USSR and His Majesty the King of Great Britain, Ireland and the British Dominions overseas, Emperor of India (named below the Allied Powers), jointly and separately take the obligation to respect the territorial integrity, sovereignty and political independence of Iran.[170]

Article 4 was even more precise:

The Allied Powers may keep on the Iranian territory land, naval and air forces in numbers which they consider necessary. . . . It is understood that the presence of these troops on Iranian territory does not constitute military occupation and shall as little as possible interfere with the usual work of the Iranian administrative and security authorities, the economic life of the country, the usual circulation of the population, and the application of Iranian laws and decrees.[171]

Iran was also reassured on another score in Article 5:

The troops of the Allied Powers should be withdrawn from the Iranian territory not later than six months after the termination of all hostilities between the Allied Powers, on the one hand, and Germany and her accomplices, on the other, through the conclusion of an armistice or armistices, or immediately after the conclusion of peace between them.[172]

The Teheran Declaration by the United States, Britain, and the USSR (December 1, 1943) added another guarantee:

... the Governments of the United States, the USSR, and the United Kingdom join with the Government of Iran in the desire to safeguard the full independence, sovereignty and territorial inviolability of Iran.[173]

As far as political treaty obligations were concerned, Iran was wonderfully protected against any undue interference of the Allied Powers in her domestic affairs or undue delay in the postwar withdrawal of Allied troops. But things did not look so well at the time when the Allied victory was drawing close. The Soviet Assistant Commissar for Foreign Affairs, S. I. Kavtaradze, arrived at Teheran in October, 1944, with the mission to extort from the Iranian government an oil concession that would cover the territory of the five northern provinces bordering on the USSR. The Iranian Government refused, on October 16, 1944, to grant the concession and forestalled the pressure of the USSR and other Powers by stating that all oil concessions would have to wait until after the war, i.e., until after Iran was free of foreign occupation. Kavtaradze responded on October 24 by calling a press conference in Teheran at which he made a threatening statement:

The Soviet Government is interested in additional oil resources. . . . [It] . . . had every reason to expect that its proposal would be accepted. . . . However, the Government of Iran, as it is known, has decided that the consideration of granting the concession to the Soviet Union should be postponed until after the end of war; this is equivalent to a refusal. . . . The Soviet public opinion believes that Saed's government . . . wants to cause deterioration in relations between our countries.[174]

The events in northern Iran showed a year later that the Soviet Government meant business when its representative talked about deterioration in mutual relations. It is a matter of interpretation whether the Soviet policy intended to detach the northern provinces from Iran or only meant to apply pressure to secure the oil concession. The Second World War ended in September, 1945, with the surrender of Japan. By that time Soviet troops should have been making preparations, as the British did, to evacuate the country, at the latest in March, 1946. But the Soviet Government started in December, 1945, to be very active in using its familiar device of people's governments. On December 12, a national assembly of Iranian Azerbaijan, elected under the Soviet military occupation, proclaimed an autonomous Republic of Azerbaijan. It appointed a government headed by Ja'afar Pishevari, who had in 1920–21 been Minister of Interior of the Soviet Republic of Ghilan, had returned to Russia, been active in the Comintern, and had then come back to Iran. The other members of the autonomous government had also been closely connected with the USSR in their previous activities. The commander-in-chief of the Azerbaijani army, General Danishiyan, spoke broken Turkic, did not know Persian, and was fluent only in Russian.

Three days later, on December 15, 1945, the leaders of the Kurds, encouraged by Soviet occupation authorities, proclaimed the Kurdish People's Republic in western Iranian Azerbaijan. The two people's republics concluded a military alliance, and the whole province was thus separated from Iran. When the Iranian Government tried to assert its authority by sending troops, they were compelled by Soviet troops to retreat. The Iranian appeal to the United Nations, and Western support of that appeal, inclined the Soviet Government to negotiate in February–March, 1946. The first proposals were harsh: (1) Soviet troops would remain indefinitely in some parts of Northern Iran; (2) the Iranian Government would accept the autonomy of Azerbaijan with appropriate guarantees for the latter's government; and (3) the USSR and Iran would set up a joint corporation for the exploitation of northern Iranian oil, 51 per cent of the stock being Russian and 49 per cent Iranian. The Iranian Government refused.

In the meantime British troops were evacuated at the appointed time, March 2, 1946. Western pressure and the embarrassing debate at the United Nations made the USSR retreat, but the Iranian Government had to pay for the Soviet military withdrawal. On April 4, 1946, both governments signed an agreement which fixed the date of the Soviet evacuation at one

and one-half months after March 24. A joint Soviet-Iranian corporation for
the exploitation of oil was to be established after the ratification of the
agreement by the Iranian Majlis. In exchange, the USSR abandoned the
people's governments of Azerbaijan and Kurdistan, just as it had done in
1940 in Finland. Those who believe that only oil companies of the West
are able to take care of their interests will be interested in the fact that the
proposed joint oil company was to exist for fifty years. The stock was to be
divided for twenty-five years into a 51 per cent Soviet share and 49 per cent
Iranian share, and for the following twenty-five years into equal 50 per
cent shares. The Soviet troops were eventually completely evacuated on
May 9, 1946, at this "capitalist" price. Once Iranian authority had been
restored, the two people's governments collapsed. But the USSR was for
once cheated, the Iranian Majlis refusing on October 22, 1947, to approve
the oil concession.[175]

The Treaty of 1921 was again invoked in 1950 when the Soviet government learned about the Iranian intention to grant an oil concession, possibly in northern Iran, to a foreign corporation. One of the protesting
notes sent on June 20, 1950, to Teheran said that the search for oil in the
districts close to the USSR

> . . . might create a danger to the [security of] frontiers of the USSR, and
> such activities in those districts would pursue objectives which cannot be
> reconciled with good-neighborly relations between the USSR and Iran, as
> foreseen in the provisions of the Soviet-Iranian Treaty of February 26,
> 1921.[176]

Marshal Voroshilov said in Budapest in April, 1950: "Many people do not
believe, said comrade Stalin, that relations based on equal rights could
exist between a great and small nation. But we Soviet people believe that
such relations may and should exist."[177] The Treaty of 1921 did not provide
for equal rights and actually comes under the typical Soviet definition of
unequal treaties:

> If an international treaty contains the obligations of one party only, it is
> unequal. If an international treaty does not provide for rights and duties
> of each contracting party, or if those rights place formally or in fact one
> of the contracting parties in an unequal, dependent position in relation
> to the other contracting party, such an international treaty is also un-
> equal.[178]

Soviet appetite for expansion had an astonishing capacity of absorption.
Even Norway, the new neighbor of the USSR, was not left in peace in

1944–46. According to an official Soviet statement released in 1947, the Soviet Government approached the Norwegian Government in 1944–45 concerning the future of the Spitzbergen Archipelago. It claimed Soviet sovereignty over one of the islands (*Medvezhii* in Russian) and Soviet strategic and economic interest in the whole archipelago and suggested a joint defense system for the islands. The same matter was raised again in November, 1946.[179] The Norwegians had no reason to submit, while the USSR could not risk a conflict with Norway and the Western Powers. It is small wonder, then, that this unpleasant experience had its part in the later Norwegian decision to join NATO.

11. China

The Soviet image of China was, until the Chinese Communist Revolution, that of a semi-colonial country victimized by imperialist great Powers. This image was, to a large extent, true, just as it was true that Imperial Russia was one of the European Powers seeking to profit from the Chinese weakness by detaching territories and extorting economic concessions. If there is now a difference between the sad Russian and European records in China, it consists in the fact that only Russia has retained some of her former loot to the present day. Russian Far Eastern territories were seized from helpless China in the middle of the past century. The Russian-Chinese treaty signed in Aigun in 1858 detached the Chinese territories on the left bank of the Amur River, and the Treaty of Peking, signed in 1860, transferred to Russia the territories east of the River Ussuri where the Soviet Far Eastern capital, Vladivostok, is located.

Russia had been swiftly expanding at the expense of China until she met a competitor, Japan, and was defeated in 1904. She had established her preponderant influence in Manchuria, where she had had, since 1896, a railroad concession leading eastward to Vladivostok and southward to the Russian-controlled (since 1898) ports of Port Arthur and Dairen (Dalnyi). She was implanting her control in northern China and Korea when Japan sent her reeling back. But the Portsmouth Peace Treaty of 1905 left her with control over the northern trunk of the Chinese-Eastern Railroad (completed in 1903), while that over the southern trunk passed to Japan. Halted by Japan in her steady process of imperialist expansion in the northeast, she found, in 1911, some comfort in encouraging the autonomist movement in Chinese Outer Mongolia. China was forced on May 25, 1915, to sign with Russia and her own province, Mongolia, a tripartite agreement whereby she had to withdraw her troops and grant autonomy to Mongolia. In fact, the power passed to the Russian Minister Resident in Urga (later known as Ulan Bator). The Russians also displayed lively interest in the adjoining territory of Tannu-Tuva, and in 1864 they penetrated into Sinkiang.

The Bolshevik Revolution posed the crucial question of whether Lenin, author of a booklet loudly denouncing imperialism and a man who had never hesitated to condemn Tsarist imperialism, together with his colleagues and disciples, would renounce Tsarist loot in China. On July 25, 1919, Karakhan, the Soviet Acting Foreign Commissar, issued an appeal to China in which he said:

We herewith address the Chinese people with the object of making them thoroughly understand that the Soviet Government gives up all conquests made by the Government of the Tsar, which took away from China Manchuria and other territories. . . . The Soviet Government returns to the Chinese people, without demanding any kind of compensation, the Chinese Eastern Railway.[180]

Reference to conquered territories could only mean Outer Mongolia and the Russian Far East on the left bank of the Amur and east of the Ussuri. This appeal cost little, since all of eastern Siberia was at that time controlled by Japan, a participant in foreign intervention. Although Russia did not recover her Far Eastern province until 1922, when the Japanese evacuated it under American pressure, the second appeal, also issued by Karakhan, took a more cautious attitude towards the problem of the Chinese-Eastern Railroad. The Soviet Government felt by that time that it would survive, since the civil war was drawing to a close. The second appeal, September 27, 1920, said:

The Soviet Government declares null and void all treaties concluded by the former Government of Russia, renounces all seizures of Chinese territory and all Russian concessions in China, and restores to China, without any compensation and forever, all that had been seized from her by the Tsar's Government and the Russian bourgeoisie. . . . The Russian and the Chinese Governments [should] sign a special treaty on the working of the Chinese Eastern Railway with due regard to the needs of Russia.[181]

The Chinese were soon able to test the sincerity of these appeals. In 1921, Soviet troops re-entered Outer Mongolia; on November 5, 1921, the Soviet Government signed together with the People's Government of Mongolia a formal alliance in which it recognized "the People's Government as the only legal government of Mongolia."[182] (Article 1) In 1922, Joffe, and in 1923, Karakhan, the very signatory of the former generous appeals to China, visited China; both made it plain that those appeals should not be interpreted as promises of restoring any Russian territory to China, of withdrawing troops from Mongolia, or of abandoning Russian interest in the Chinese-Eastern Railroad.

The Soviet-Chinese agreements, concluded in 1924 by Karakhan, contained the renunciation by Russia of her former rights in the so-called treaty ports, extraterritoriality, and consular jurisdiction. But the Chinese-Eastern Railroad was to remain Russian property, although China obtained the right to purchase it at a fair price. Chinese sovereignty over Outer Mongolia was recognized as a diplomatic courtesy, copying in this regard the Tsarist-Chinese agreement of 1915. However, both in 1915 and 1924, Russian troops remained in Mongolia to protect an administration that refused to acknowledge Chinese interference. It probably did not make much difference to the Chinese that those troops displayed different national flags in 1915 and 1924.

At the same time, the Soviet Government was building an anti-Western co-operation with the Kuomintang movement. Dr. Sun Yat Sen and Joffe signed on January 26, 1923, a joint declaration which seemed very promising for China:

1. Dr. Sun Yat Sen holds that the Communist order, or even the Soviet system, cannot actually be introduced into China, because there do not exist here the conditions for the successful establishment of either Communism or Sovietism. This view is entirely shared by Mr. Joffe. . . .

2. Mr. Joffe has categorically declared to Dr. Sun Yat Sen (who has fully satisfied himself as to this) that it is not and has never been the intention or purpose of the present Russian Government to pursue an imperialistic policy in Outer Mongolia or to cause it to secede from China.[183]

Dr. Sun Yat Sen indulged in some wishful thinking; he knew the text of the Soviet-Mongolian treaty of November 5, 1921, which had recognized the People's Government as the sole legitimate authority in Mongolia and had established Soviet diplomatic and consular relations with it.[184]

The Soviet-Chinese relations were henceforth founded on the agreements signed on May 31, 1924. The main treaty, signed on that day, guaranteed Soviet rights in the Chinese-Eastern Railroad at the price of recognizing nominal Chinese sovereignty over Outer Mongolia. Article 5 said: "The

Government of the USSR recognizes that Outer Mongolia is an integral part of the Chinese Republic and respects the Chinese sovereignty there."[185] This nominal sovereignty was to be formally liquidated in 1945 and 1950. Article 9 promised the sale of the Chinese-Eastern Railroad to China at some indefinite date: "The Government of the USSR agrees to the purchase by the Government of the Chinese Republic with Chinese capital of the Chinese-Eastern Railroad."[186] But Article 9 gave something more tangible to Russia:

Until such time as various questions relating to the Chinese-Eastern Railroad are settled . . . the rights of both Governments, resulting from the contract of August 27 (September 8) 1896 concerning the construction and administration of the Chinese-Eastern Railroad . . . shall remain in force.[187]

An agreement signed on the same day settled the question of the joint administration in an entirely "capitalist" manner. An administrative board composed of five Soviet and five Chinese citizens was formed. Every decision of the board had to be taken by the majority of six; all documents required, for their validity, the signatures of the chairman and the vice-chairman, one being a Soviet citizen and the other a Chinese. The actual administration was entrusted to the manager, a Soviet citizen, assisted by two assistant managers, one of them a Soviet citizen. All other managerial posts were to be filled in the same manner: a Soviet manager and two assistant managers, one of them, again, a Soviet citizen. All other employees were to be recruited in the same fashion of fifty-fifty participation of both nationalities.[188] Karakhan was very satisfied with this arrangement; he commented on October 5, 1924:

In addition to the political, economic and other advantages, the Soviet Union has recuperated . . . a property which according to the most conservative estimate is worth over half a billion gold roubles. The Soviet Union can consider the restitution of its title to the Chinese-Eastern Railway as one of the most remarkable instances of the return of Soviet property seized by its enemies.[189]

On July 10, 1929, the Soviet Union itself was confronted with a Chinese anti-colonialist move. The Chinese removed on that day the Soviet manager-in-chief of the Chinese-Eastern Railroad and all other Soviet employees. They were deported to the USSR. The situation was somewhat analogous to the Egyptian move in 1956 in nationalizing the assets of the

Universal Company of the Suez Canal and taking over the Canal's administration. The Chinese also tried to nationalize a means of transportation situated on their own territory; if there was a difference, it consisted in the fact that the Suez Canal is of vital interest to many nations of the world, while the Chinese-Eastern Railroad made easier communication only with the Soviet Far Eastern province. What was the answer of the anti-colonialist Power?

On July 17, 1929, the USSR broke off diplomatic, consular, commercial, and railroad relations with China. The People's Commissar of Transportation, T. Rudzutak, on July 19, 1929, told foreign press correspondents in Moscow that the Soviet Government had decided not to use force, not an easy decision in view "of the indignation of the broad popular masses . . . which demanded that we defend our infringed right with armed force. . . . [This decision] constitutes a proof, anyhow superfluous, that our signature of the Kellogg Pact was not an empty sound."[190]

Although it is true that the local Chinese authorities rather foolishly assumed a generally hostile attitude towards the USSR, the Kellogg Pact and the anti-colonialist slogans were soon forgotten. By the order of People's Commissar for Military and Naval Affairs Voroshilov on August 6, 1929, all Soviet armed forces in the Far East were grouped together in a special Far Eastern army.[191] On September 4, 1929, Soviet troops attacked the Chinese frontier garrisons with tanks and artillery. Soviet aviation participated in these border engagements, and the Chinese replied with raids on Soviet territory. It all ended in the decisive Soviet operation across the Chinese border. The USSR was luckier than Britain and France in 1956. Rykov, then Chairman of the People's Commissars, could say on November 29, 1929, at the session of the Central Executive Committee of the USSR:

You know from newspapers that we were compelled recently to undertake some military operations on the Chinese territory. . . . [After referring to Chinese overtures which followed the Soviet military action] I cannot but notice the fact that the direct acquaintance of the Chinese militarists with the might of our Army did not remain without influence on the stubborn attitude of the Chinese Government.[192]

Foreign Commissar Litvinov, who earned his peace-loving reputation in the West, thanks to his tirades against the Nazis in the thirties, was not such a pacifist in his speech of December 4, 1929, at the session of the Central Executive Committee:

Tchang Sun-liang, the commander-in-chief and governor of the province, only in the last days, after the Far-Eastern Army had [struck] a particularly painful blow . . . officially communicated his acceptance of our conditions. . . . In case of further advance our Special Far-Eastern Army would have hardly met any serious obstacles. . . . The counter-measures taken by the Special Far-Eastern Army cannot be considered at all as a violation of the Kellogg Pact.[193]

The conflict was finally settled on December 22, 1929, by the Khabarovsk Protocol, which was signed by both countries; it restored Soviet rights in the Chinese-Eastern Railroad. Soviet troops withdrew from Chinese territory after successfully fulfilling their mission.[194] Litvinov justified this action on May 11, 1933, in an interview with *Tass* in terms that smacked of capitalist concepts of sacred foreign property:

The Tsarist Government pursued without doubt imperialist goals in building the railroads in Manchuria, on a foreign territory. . . . The railroad was, however, constructed with money earned with the toil of the peoples populating the Soviet Union. This is why the Soviet Government considered and still considers its duty to safeguard the property rights in this railroad.[195]

Such was the story of the Soviet Port Said expedition.

After Japanese seizure of Manchuria and the formation there of the puppet state of Manchukuo, the USSR could no longer pursue the same forcible policy of defending property built with Russian money. She was facing a strong imperialist Power instead of a weak, semi-colonial China. Her freedom of movement was, in addition, restricted by the threatening Nazi policy. The Manchurian authorities, in fact the Japanese, made no secret of their intention to kick Russia out of the Chinese-Eastern Railroad. The Soviet Government concluded promptly that the best way out would be to sell the railroad to Manchukuo at any price the Japanese would consent to pay. Litvinov conceded this on May 11, 1933, and took the opportunity to brush aside with contempt the protest of the Chinese Government. The sale of the railroad to Manchukuo was a double blow to China. The deal was with a puppet state unrecognized either by China or by most other countries; it involved an informal recognition by the USSR of Japanese control over Manchuria and conflicted with the Chinese treaty right to purchase the railroad. Litvinov, however, said on May 11, 1933:

It is true that we discussed during our interview with Ambassador Ota [Ambassador of Japan] on May 2 the serious situation on the Chinese-

Eastern Railroad recently created by acts of the Manchurian authorities; this situation threatens to complicate our relations with both Manchuria and Japan. . . . I mentioned the purchase of the Chinese-Eastern Railroad by Manchukuo as one of the radical solutions. . . . It is also true that the Nanking Government conferred with the Soviet Government in relation to this matter, questioning its right to sell the Chinese-Eastern Railroad to anyone but the Nanking Government. . . . It is much more pertinent that the Nanking Government and the authorities subordinated to it ceased in fact over eighteen months ago to be partners of the USSR on the Chinese-Eastern Railroad. . . . The non-fulfillment by the Nanking Government of the obligations imposed on it by the Peking and Mukden agreements [of 1924], during a period of eighteen months deprives this Government of any formal or moral right to invoke these agreements. . . . I am convinced that only such people may protest against the proposal who are interested for some reasons in straining Soviet-Japanese and Soviet-Manchurian relations.[196]

The Chinese Government, referred to rather contemptuously as the Nanking Government, could indeed not fulfill its obligations concerning the railroad because it was expelled by Japan *manu militari* from Manchuria. After hard bargaining with Japan, the railroad was sold, on March 23, 1935, to Manchukuo.

It seemed that only China had the moral right to recover it after the defeat of Japan in 1945, but the Soviet Government was of a different opinion. The Manchurian railroads were now more tempting than ever, since the Japanese had in the meantime invested much capital and energy in the development of both the Chinese-Eastern and the South-Manchurian railroads (they had held the latter railroad since 1905), which they administered as one concern. In the meantime, the USSR further consolidated its hold on Outer Mongolia against both Japan and China; on March 12, 1936, it concluded an alliance with the People's Republic of Mongolia. The Chinese protest was rejected on April 8, 1936, in this peremptory answer:

This note contends that the signature on March 12 last of the protocol between the Governments of the USSR and the Mongolian People's Republic constitutes a violation of Chinese sovereignty and is in contradiction to the Soviet-Chinese agreement of May 31, 1924. . . . The Soviet Government must reject the Chinese Government's protest as groundless.[197]

The United States, believing at the time that it badly needed Soviet participation in the Far Eastern war, was gradually led through diplomatic negotiations to the Yalta Far Eastern Agreement of February 11, 1945. This agreement conceded to the USSR not only Southern Sakhalin and the

Kurile Islands but also other things at the expense of Allied China: the restoration of Soviet rights not only to the Chinese-Eastern Railroad (sold in 1935) but to all Manchurian railroads, including those which had been lost in the Treaty of Portsmouth of 1905, Chinese formal recognition of the loss of Outer Mongolia, and the restoration of the *status quo ante* as it existed before 1905 in Port Arthur and Dairen. Stalin was busy recuperating the possessions and rights lost by Tsar Nicholas II.

The USSR did not take the trouble to seek Western or Chinese approval for an annexation performed in 1944. The territory of Tannu-Tuva, which China had claimed as part of Outer Mongolia and China herself and which had come under the Soviet control in 1921, was formally annexed in 1944 and changed into the Tuvinian Autonomous Region of the RSFSR.

The triumphal Soviet march into Manchuria was followed by a thorough looting of industrial equipment. On August 14, 1945, the Nationalist Government of China had to sign a series of agreements with the USSR in order to carry out the Yalta Far Eastern Agreement, to which it had not been a party. Cut off by that agreement from Western support and hoping to buy at that price Soviet assistance in the extension of its authority over the whole national territory partly occupied by the Chinese Communists, it had little choice in the matter. A thirty-year alliance directed against Japan was signed. It contained the usual Soviet promise in Article 5:

The High Contracting Parties . . . agree to work, after the restoration of peace, in the spirit of close and friendly co-operation and to act in accordance with the principles of mutual respect for their sovereignty and territorial integrity and of non-interference in the domestic affairs of the other High Contracting Party.[198]

This promise was further reinforced by a Soviet note of the same date, which said, among other things:

. . . The Soviet Government agrees to give China its moral support and its assistance in the form of military supplies and other material resources; such support and assistance shall be entirely given to the National Government as the central Government of China.[199]

This pledge did not prevent the USSR from handing over large stocks of seized Japanese arms to the Communist armies or to make all sorts of difficulties in admitting the Nationalist forces to Manchuria. It did not hinder the USSR, in the last stage of the Chinese Civil War, from concluding (in

July, 1949) a commercial agreement with "the Manchurian people's demo-cratic authorities"[200] or from granting recognition to the People's Republic of China on October 1, 1949, at a time when the civil war was not yet ended and a Nationalist administration still functioned in Canton.[201] A British historian writes:

The assistance received from the Russians, whether in the securing of arms from the Japanese dumps or the holding up of the Nationalist forces so as to give the Communists an opportunity of establishing themselves at key points, was so unobtrusive as to make it difficult to challenge the Russians with any overt breach of their agreements.[202]

The Soviet-Chinese agreement of August 14, 1945, restored the Russian *status quo ante* on all the Manchurian railroads as though the Russian-Japanese War of 1904–1905 had never taken place and the USSR had never sold Japan (in 1935) its rights to the Chinese-Eastern Railroad. Molotov said a few months later, on November 6, 1945: "One must also mention the restoration of the rights of our State to the railroads in Manchuria and in the districts of Port Arthur and Dalnyi."[203] He talked about the "restoration" of rights wrested by the Tsarist Government from a semi-colonial China, an Allied country in 1945. The agreement of August 14, 1945, treated all Manchurian railroads as one concern called the Chinese Chanchung Railroad. Those railroads, leading across Manchuria either to the Soviet Far Eastern maritime province or to Port Arthur and Dairen, became the joint property of China and the USSR. A Soviet-Chinese joint company was formed for the purpose of exploiting these railroads. Although the board of administration was to be composed of an equal number of Soviet and Chinese citizens, the manager-general was to be a Soviet official. The whole managerial personnel was to be composed of Soviet or Chinese employees, assisted in each case by an employee of the other nationality. Profits were to be distributed equally between the two countries. The agreement was to expire after thirty years, and the railroads would then revert to China.[204] It is worth while to note that the 1924 Soviet-Chinese agreement concerning the Chinese-Eastern Railroad would have expired in 1961; the new agreement concluded in 1945 was to last until 1975. The joint railroad management also extended to forests, coal mines, power stations, industrial plants, and other enterprises which had been operated before 1935 by the Chinese-Eastern Railroad or before 1905 by the Russian-administered South-Manchurian Railroad, despite the fact that all those concerns had in the meantime been expanded by the Japanese.

Another agreement of the same date provided for Soviet use of Port Arthur as a naval base. The agreement specified that the USSR could keep there any armed forces it deemed necessary. The civil administration was to remain Chinese, but the Soviet military commander could veto the Chinese appointments. The policy of local Chinese civilian administration had to follow the security requirements as laid down by the same Soviet commander. The agreement was concluded for thirty years.[205]

Still another agreement declared Dairen a free port, but a special zone in its harbor was reserved for the USSR. The city administration was to remain Chinese, but the harbor manager was to be a Soviet citizen. The USSR also acquired the right to export and import goods through Dairen and the Manchurian railroads free of any Chinese customs duties; this agreement was also to last for thirty years. The early Soviet renunciation of concessions in China was somehow forgotten.

China had to make another concession, namely to recognize the loss of Outer Mongolia. There was one condition attached to it—"if the people of Outer Mongolia reaffirm this aspiration [to independence] in a plebiscite."[206] The USSR, an experienced expert on people's referenda, organized the plebiscite on October 20, 1945. The disarmingly naïve official Mongolian protocol on the results is worth quoting:

The plebiscite took the form of an open vote; every voter expressed his opinion . . . by apposing his signature in one of the two columns: "For" or "Against." . . . 98.4 per cent of all citizens entitled to participate in the plebiscite [took part]. . . . 100 per cent of all citizens participating in the plebiscite voted in favor of State independence of the Mongolian People's Republic. Not a single vote was cast in the opposite sense.[207]

What is more fascinating than a unanimous open vote is the fact that largely illiterate Mongolians were able on that day to appose their signatures. They presumably used the Russian alphabet, which had been introduced in that "independent" country.

The Communist victory in China changed the picture entirely, even for Stalin, who never relished releasing anything he had. Russia was confronted with an ally. Therefore, new agreements were negotiated in 1950. A numerous Chinese delegation, headed by Mao Tse-tung himself, came to Moscow by the end of 1949. Stalin took part in the negotiations, which must have been hard bargaining on both sides, for they lasted from December 16, 1949, until February 14, 1950, the date of the signature of agreements. The first of them was the Soviet-Chinese alliance directed against Japan and other Powers, concluded for thirty years.[208] The second agreement settled the matter of Soviet rights on Chinese soil: (1) the Soviet rights in the Manchurian railroads were to be retroceded to China either after the conclusion of a peace treaty with Japan or not later than the end of 1952; (2) the Soviet naval base at Port Arthur was to be evacuated by the Russians either after the conclusion of the Japanese Peace Treaty or not later than the end of 1952; and (3) the question of the Soviet rights in Dairen was to be discussed after the conclusion of the Japanese Peace Treaty.[209] These were real concessions made by the USSR to the new ally, but the Chinese Communists had to pay a price. The two governments agreed on March 27, 1950, to form three joint corporations: (1) one for the joint prospecting and extraction of oil in Sinkiang, where the USSR had always maintained a lively political and economic interest; (2) another for prospecting and mining non-ferrous metals in the same province of China; and (3) for the exploitation of the airlines Peking-Chita, Peking-Irkutsk, and Peking–Alma Ata. All three corporations were to function according to the usual Soviet fifty-fifty pattern. The first two corporations were to last for thirty years and the third for ten years.[210] A fourth joint company was established in 1951 for repairing and building ships in the Dairen shipyards. While the USSR made a genuine contribution to the companies created in 1950 in the form of supplied equipment, its share in Dairen was represented by Soviet-confiscated Japanese assets and holdings.

The agreements of February 14, 1950, included another Chinese concession, namely the formal recognition of the "independence" of the People's Republic of Mongolia. However, Stalin granted China large credits which aimed at the rehabilitation of the Chinese economy and the beginning of industrialization. A pattern was established for future Soviet-Chinese economic relations, the USSR supplying basic equipment and machinery and China repaying with raw materials and foodstuffs.

The Korean War cemented the mutual alliance. In the fall of 1952, new Soviet-Chinese agreements of September 15 confirmed Soviet willingness to transfer all Soviet rights to the Manchurian railroads to China, while both countries agreed to postpone the promised evacuation of Port Arthur until after the conclusion of the Japanese peace treaty.[211] By the end of 1952, the Chinese took over from the Russians the property and management of the Manchurian railroads. This long colonialist chapter in the Soviet history was closed.

Another set of agreements was concluded in October, 1954. The USSR, which could no longer invoke the emergency created by the Korean War, agreed to evacuate Port Arthur in the spring of 1955. The joint Soviet-Chinese companies were entirely transferred to Chinese ownership and management, China having to repay by installments the value of the Soviet stock. In 1955, these agreements were implemented, and China was at last freed of the Russian mortgage on her soil.[212]

Only Afghanistan, of all Soviet, European, and Asian geographical neighbors, was not involved in a territorial dispute with the USSR. Otherwise, each of them may point to serious Soviet encroachments on, or claims endangering, their sovereignty and territorial integrity. Three of them were annexed, several others reduced to vassal status, still others either lost territories or were in immediate danger of losing them. Several were compelled to grant either military bases or economic concessions to the USSR; two barely escaped this peril.

One could multiply examples of Soviet policies shedding a strange light on the Soviet attitude towards the principles enshrined in the *Pancha Shila*. However, this book is not a history of Soviet foreign policy. We shall not mention the Soviet role in the Greek Civil War in the late forties, where the USSR, acting by proxy and using Greek Communist guerrillas and the satellite Balkan territories, provided a steady flow of supplies and a haven of refuge to the Communist insurgents.[213] Neither shall we recall the story of the Korean adventure, in which the North Koreans, obviously encouraged by the earlier evacuation of American troops from South Korea and by advice coming from Moscow and Peking, suddenly attacked South Koreans, and in which the USSR and China steadily assisted the North Koreans in the fight against South Korea and the United Nations forces in defiance of the United Nations resolutions. This story is fresh in human minds and is told in many easily accessible sources, including the United Nations documents.[214] We prefer to end this review of the Soviet respect for the *Pancha Shila* by glancing at the Yugoslav experience.

12. Yugoslavia

The whole story of the Soviet-Yugoslav dispute revolves around the *Pancha Shila*, the Soviet lack of respect for the sovereignty and independence of Yugoslavia, interference in the Yugoslav domestic matters, and the unequal treatment of that small Communist country, all the benefits of mutual intercourse being reserved for the Communist great Power. We shall limit ourselves to a few episodes of that dispute.

The Yugoslavs felt that the Soviet Government had broken its former promises and had withdrawn its support for the Yugoslav territorial claims to Trieste and slices of southern Austria. They were bitter and could in nowise understand that the USSR, fatherland of the toilers, should act simply as a great Power in sacrificing the interests and aspirations of its small satellite for the sake of its own general interests and a global settlement with other great Powers. Mutual Soviet-Yugoslav recriminations in 1949 threw a revealing light on the Soviet attitude towards the value of words, in particular "territorial integrity," which occupies a crucial position in the *Pancha Shila*.

Stalin promised, in May, 1945, then Chancellor of Austria K. Renner to respect Austrian independence and integrity; he said in a personal letter addressed to Chancellor Renner: "You may rest assured that your preoccupation with the independence, integrity and well-being of Austria is also my own."[215] The Yugoslavs reminded the USSR in 1949 of that letter and accused Stalin of duplicity—bound by his pledge to Chancellor Renner, he was never sincere in promising the Yugoslavs support of their territorial claims against Austria. Ordinary common sense would indicate that the Yugoslavs were right. The 1945 pledge to Chancellor Renner to respect the integrity of Austria could have referred only to the integrity within the frontiers before the 1938 *Anschluss*, which had provisionally terminated the independent existence of that country. Either the Austrians or the Yugoslavs had to be cheated in order to fulfill such contradictory promises. However, this was not the opinion of the Soviet Government as expressed in its reply to Belgrade on August 29, 1949:

The question of the integrity of this or that State and the question "of not revising its frontiers" are two altogether different problems. Only people who have dissipated the last remnants of Marxism can confuse and equate these two problems. The Soviet Government had declared itself against the partitions of Poland and in favor of the unification of all Polish territories in one integral State. Did this mean that it declared itself thereby in favor of the intangibility of Polish frontiers and that it did not consider it possible to modify these frontiers in one or another direction? Obviously it did not.[216]

One could reinforce the Soviet argument by other examples. Did not the USSR promise to respect the territorial integrity of Finland and the Baltic

States, and did it not proceed with either the forcible revision of Finnish frontiers or the integral incorporation of the Baltic countries? However, the word integrity (in Russian, *tselostnost'*) implies one thing to the Soviet Government and something opposite to other people.

The tone of Soviet notes to Belgrade at that time is interesting for the treatment a small country may get from Moscow. Here are a few samples:

The mendacity and double-dealing of the Yugoslav government. . . . The Yugoslav government acted in this case not as a friend but as an adversary of the Soviet Union and as an agent of foreign imperialist circles. . . . Everyone knows that the Yugoslav government has deserted the camp of socialism and democracy for that of imperialism and fascism. One must observe that the Soviet people and society do not respect deserters. More than that, they cannot feel anything like sympathy towards the deserters. More than that, everyone knows that the Soviet people and society have contempt for deserters. . . . There are such people who desert not only to save their skins but also to harm the camp from which they have fled. Sad as it may be, one must say that the Soviet people and society consider the Yugoslav government not as ordinary deserters but as malicious ones . . . there are malicious deserters who make a profitable venture out of their own shame, loudly display their desertion as some kind of heroism, bring the whole matter onto the stage in order to bark at the camp which they have abandoned, shamelessly brag that they can always afford to bark at that camp, and that they are not, therefore, common deserters but heroes. This absolutely exemplifies Krylov's fable: "Hark, this mongrel must be strong to bark at an elephant." . . . We hope that the Yugoslav government will understand that it cannot expect from the Soviet Government either courtesy or, even less, respect.[217]

The official Soviet collection of diplomatic documents, published in 1953 and containing the Soviet notes sent in 1949 to Yugoslavia, faithfully reproduces the spelling of the original texts; it is noteworthy that the Soviet Government is always spelled with a capital "G," while the Yugoslav Government with a small "g." The Yugoslav Government protested on May 29, 1949, against the Soviet attempt at domestic interference by promoting subversive activities of those Yugoslav Communist *émigrés* in Moscow who had fled to the USSR and had published their own newspaper, which was hostile to Tito and his regime. Since all printing houses were nationalized in the USSR, the Yugoslavs had a strong case; the newspaper could be published only with Soviet connivance. The Soviet Government sent a reply on May 31, 1949:

The Yugoslav government has deprived itself of the right to expect a friendly policy from the Soviet Government. . . . The Soviet Government

has decided to give hospitality and to grant asylum to those Yugoslav patriotic *émigrés* who are persecuted by the Yugoslav anti-democratic regime
for their democratic and socialist convictions. . . . The Soviet Government
does not prevent citizens of the USSR from supporting the activities of
Yugoslav revolutionary *émigrés*. . . . The Yugoslav government "demands"
(literally: demands) in its note that: "the Government of the USSR forbid
. . . further printing by the Yugoslav revolutionary *émigrés* of the newspaper." In other words, it "demands" that the USSR itself establish an
anti-Communist and anti-democratic, terroristic regime of the type that
now exists in Yugoslavia. . . . Does not the Yugoslav government find that
this laughable "demand" amounts to "the most crude interference" in the
domestic affairs of the USSR? Does not the Yugoslav government believe
that it places itself in a ridiculous position by submitting this absurd "demand"? The Yugoslav note qualifies the Yugoslav revolutionary *émigrés*
in the USSR as "traitors to their country." . . . The Soviet Government
considers that the Yugoslav revolutionary *émigrés* are true socialists and
democrats, faithful sons of Yugoslavia, staunch defenders of her independence, and builders of friendship between Yugoslavia and the Soviet
Union. If one has to look for traitors to Yugoslavia, he must seek them not
among the Yugoslav revolutionary *émigrés* but among those gentlemen
who try to undermine the friendship between the Soviet Union and Yugoslavia.[218]

In another note of August 18, 1949, concerning the Yugoslav complaint
about the subversive activities of Soviet citizens in Yugoslavia, the Soviet
Government quoted with approval the following Cominform resolution
relating to Yugoslavia:

The Information Bureau does not doubt that there are enough sound elements, faithful to Marxism-Leninism, the internationalistic traditions of
the Yugoslav Communist Party, and the unified socialist front, within the
Communist Party of Yugoslavia. The task of these sound elements within
the Communist Party of Yugoslavia consists in compelling the present leaders openly and honestly to confess their errors and to correct them, to break
off with nationalism, to return to internationalism, and to strengthen in
every way the united socialist front against imperialism, or, if the present
leaders of the C.P.Y. prove to be incapable of doing it, in replacing them
by a new internationalist leadership of the C.P.Y. The Information Bureau
does not doubt that the Communist Party of Yugoslavia will know how to
fulfill this honorable task.[219]

The very fact that the Soviet Government felt itself authorized to quote in
an official note the resolution of the Cominform and to comment on it implicitly conceded that this "international organization" was nothing but a
Soviet agency.

The "honorable task" assigned to Moscow agents within the Yugoslav

Communist Party consisted in overthrowing their Party leadership and their own government. However, the Soviet note ended with typical Soviet double talk:

As has been seen, the resolution does not contain one word concerning the overthrow, and even less a forcible overthrow, of the State regime in Yugoslavia. The resolution only says that the Communists of Yugoslavia should compel the existing leadership of the C.P.Y. to change the course of their policy or, if this does not succeed, to renew the leadership of the C.P.Y. by electing a new one. Is it a Party-constitutional and fully legal way? Absolutely yes.[220]

The note qualified Tito's regime as a "fascist-Gestapo regime."[221] However, the Soviet Government knew very well that Tito had the solid support of his own Party and that his leadership could be ended only by a violent coup.

An economic blockade was applied to Yugoslavia. On December 27, 1948, her government was compelled to sign with the USSR a protocol that reduced the volume of their mutual trade to one-eighth of that in 1948. The official Soviet communiqué published on that occasion frankly connected this decision with "the unfriendly policy of the Yugoslav government towards the Soviet Union which has made impossible the continuation of the broad economic co-operation between the USSR and Yugoslavia."[222] On February 1, 1949, the Yugoslav Government complained to the Soviet Embassy in Belgrade that Yugoslavia had not been asked to attend, in January of the same year, a Moscow economic conference convoked by the USSR and to which the eastern European satellites had been invited or to join the Council of Mutual Economic Assistance formed at the same Conference. The Soviet Government gave a frank answer:

. . . the Yugoslav government, having assumed a hostile attitude towards the USSR and the countries of people's democracy, has excluded itself from the participation in the Moscow conference. . . . The Soviet Government considers participation of Yugoslavia in the Council of Economic Mutual Assistance desirable. But this participation would become possible only if the Yugoslav government abandoned its hostile policy towards the USSR and the countries of people's democracy and returned to its former policy of friendship.[223]

The "hostile attitude towards the USSR" consisted in the defense of Yugoslav independence against Soviet interference in domestic matters. As the two staunch Communists J. B. Tito and E. Kardelj said in their letter of

April 13, 1948, to Stalin and Molotov: "No matter how much each of us loves the land of Socialism, the USSR, he can, in no case, love his country less, which is also developing socialism."[224]

The Soviet record, established here almost exclusively on the basis of official Soviet documents, is not very encouraging for high expectations regarding the *Pancha Shila*, which the USSR and China proclaimed in their joint communiqué of October 12, 1954, as the foundation of their relations with "the Asian and Pacific Ocean countries, and with other States."[225] However, it is impossible, as Lenin said, for Communist and non-Communist states to fly off to the moon and thus avoid co-existence on earth. They must live together. Unavoidably, non-Communist states are obliged to have day-to-day policies towards the USSR. The practical conclusion from the Soviet record, however, is of a different nature. These policies cannot rely on the affirmation and reaffirmation of lofty principles. Only a masochist would desire to provide the future with yet one more Soviet breach of solemn pledges. There is not much point in weeping over spilled milk. A practical policy towards the USSR should avoid high-sounding declarations conducive only to a feeling of false security; it should be strictly founded on the basis of upstanding give-and-take, a basis which the Soviet Government has always understood, with its business-like attitude towards its own national interests.

Such a business-like approach on both sides precludes neither negotiations nor agreements on specific matters, as was evidenced by the Four Power treaty on Austria, for instance. When people think, however, of negotiations and agreements with the Soviet Union, they should remember that there is a fundamental difference between negotiations conducted by the Soviet Union only for the sake of propaganda and those which it wants to lead to a business-like conclusion, between agreements based on mutual and equivalent concessions and agreements made of unilateral concessions. The latter agreements belong to the realm of appeasement policy, which never benefited the yielding party but always strengthened its opponent. As long as the Soviet Government persists in pursuing its long-term objectives, which consist ultimately in the complete elimination of different political-social regimes (there is no sign as yet that they have changed their views on this score), it is a vain hope to reach a global settlement founded on the mutual acceptance of the present *status quo* in the world and mutual tolerance of the existence of opposite ideologies. Unfortunately, a cautious foreign policy of non-Communist governments cannot overstep these bounds, imposed by the Soviet policy of "peaceful competition."

Neither could the alertness to Soviet long-term objectives and its past record be dispelled nor the trust in Soviet words be increased by the following statement, which N. S. Khrushchev made on May 24, 1958, in defiance of Soviet-published documents:

But could any of these [Western] statesmen cite at least one fact which would bear testimony to an action by the USSR that has threatened the security of any State whatsoever? No one has cited or could cite such facts because they have never taken place. (*Pravda*, May 27, 1958)

CHAPTER XII

SOVIET COLONIAL POSSESSIONS

1. Imperialism, Colonialism, and National Self-determination

W E MAY NOW ask two fundamental questions. What is imperialism? What is colonialism? The very words are of Western derivation; they were born during the process of Western colonial expansion and the building of empires in the non-European parts of the world. Naturally, they remain associated with the West in the minds of people living in former colonial areas.

Let us look at them from the point of view of national self-determination, which is a moral principle of international relations. If one invokes this principle, he cannot say that only a nationality favored by a coincidence of propitious circumstances should be independent. A principle differs from political expediency by virtue of its universal applicability. It ceases to be a principle if applied in certain cases and bypassed in others where its mention would be too embarrassing. Short of being a racialist, one must concede that it is equally applicable to all people, whatever their racial descent, pigment, or language. Viewed from this universal point of view, national self-determination means the moral right of every distinct nationality (an ethnic group fully conscious of forming one entity because of the same historical past and the same culture) to decide its fate freely, with the corresponding moral obligation of other nationalities concerned to respect this decision. A nationality may prefer to stay with another nationality within the same state, as Scotsmen do. It may want only home rule, as Irishmen desired in the 19th century or the Czechs until 1914. It may wish to secede from the state of the controlling nationality or to preserve some links with it. Such were the various choices made by the newly independent nationalities after the last war. Syria, Lebanon, Burma, and Indonesia severed all ties with France, Britain, and Holland, respectively. India, Pakistan, Ceylon, and Ghana preferred, for their own reasons, to stay within the Commonwealth as independent members. But the choice must be made by the nationality itself. It may be expressed only under conditions where the former ruling nationality in no way interferes.

What is imperialism in the light of this principle of self-determination? It is the expansion of political or other control of one nationality by imposing it on unwilling other nationalities. The word is derived from the word "empire," but such an expansion may be pursued by a small nation at the expense of another nationality; Holland, for example, is numerically a small nationality, yet it built up a vast empire. The same is true of Portugal. Spain is not a great Power, yet she controls a few alien nationalities, such as the Catalans or the Basques. Imperialism does not need, within the terms of our reference to the modern self-determination concept, to result in a huge empire populated by many nationalities, as the British, the French, or the former Tsarist Russian. As long as one nationality expands its rule by subjecting another nationality, this is imperialism.

What is colonialism? It is rule over alien and unwilling nationalities. However, both terms, imperialism and colonialism, were forged in western Europe and were traditionally associated with western European overseas expansion. It is high time to give a modern content to these symbols. It is, first of all, untrue that imperialism and colonialism are and were sins committed only by Europeans. The ancient Chinese Empire had its imperialist drives and its colonial protectorates in Korea and Southeast Asia. Communist China has a sizable number of alien nationalities, approximately forty million people, and recently conquered, *manu militari*, formerly independent Tibet. India has had some troubles with the border tribes, who do not feel that they are Indians; she has her own protectorates of Nepal, Bhutan, and Sikkim. Ethiopia controls the Eritreans, who may or may not feel happy about it. The Arabs conquered many peoples of other races, languages, religions, and cultures at the time of their Moslem expansion in the Near East, North Africa, and the Iberian Peninsula. It would be erroneous to think that Asians and Africans were always virtuous, though this does not justify western Europeans.

A second popular misconception is that only Asians and Africans have been the victims of imperialism and colonialism. Actually, it was originally an Asian nationality, the Turks, who had ruled for centuries, not only over the Arabs, but over several European nationalities, such as the Greeks, the

Serbs, the Bulgarians, the Albanians and the Rumanians. Moreover, European nationalities fell victims to the imperialism of other Europeans. The Poles were ruled for 150 years by the Russians, the Germans, and the Austrians. The Austrians and the Hungarians controlled, until 1918, the national life of Czechs, Slovaks, Poles, Ukrainians, Rumanians, Serbs, Croats, Slovenes, and Italians. Irishmen were for centuries oppressed by Englishmen. The evil was not a purely European vice, nor were its victims only Asians and Africans.

A third mistake consists in interpreting the terms "imperialism" and "colonialism" in the traditional geographical sense. A colony is for most Asians and Africans a foreign-controlled overseas territory. But what has geography to do with a political concept? A ruling nationality may live side by side with the ruled, no stretch of ocean dividing one from the other. Blue water does not make the life of an oppressed nationality either lighter or more difficult, nor does it alter the prime fact of unwanted foreign control. The Russians, the Germans, the Austrians, or the Turks did not need to navigate the seas to conquer other nationalities; they had only to march on land with their conquering armies. As a matter of fact, this kind of conquest is technically easier, and the overland control is more effectively enforced. Asians and Africans have seldom paid any attention to the ease with which most of their countries parted company with the colonial Powers—a contrast with the difficulty of applying the principle of self-determination to such areas as Algeria or British East Africa, where sizable alien settlements have been implanted amidst the native populations. Yet this is the serious problem which usually confronts a nationality conquered overland by another nationality. The facilities and cheapness of land communications invite the settlers of the conquering nationality. They begin to form islands of their own language and culture that increase in size. Eventually, the controlling nationality is tempted to round up its national-cultural territory by proceeding with a more or less forcible denationalization of the conquered nationality. It may do it easily because it controls the state and its powerful means of education and coercion. A foreign-controlled nationality is faced with the danger of losing its own identity through the slow erosion of its members' allegiance. Asians and Africans may bless Providence for living in distant areas; distance and climate made European mass immigration both costly and unattractive. Asians and Africans were thus able to preserve their national identity intact throughout the colonial period, but this is not true of nationalities conquered overland.

2. Multi-national Soviet Empire

The Soviet Union of today is heir to the Tsarist Empire, that vast agglomeration of nationalities conquered throughout centuries of Russian overland expansion. Starting with the small Grand Duchy of Moscow, the realm was expanded in all four directions of the compass. European and Asian nationalities alike fell victims to that steady and relentless expansion. Russian settlers followed the Russian flag; their islands were established amidst each conquered nationality; their power and, in the case of less-developed nationalities, their superior culture expanded the numerical size of the Russian nation by constant assimilation. By 1914 it was a vast colonial empire, ruled by the Russians but populated by many nationalities living from the Vistula and the Danube to the Pacific coast and from the northern ocean to the Black and Caspian seas.

The Bolsheviks inherited that empire. At the time of their coming to power, it was falling to pieces, most of its component nationalities desiring to throw off the secular yoke. The controlling Russian center was weak. A vast movement of colonial disintegration was taking place thirty years before the beginning of the present era of gradual but steady liquidation of western European colonialism. But while this latter process continues, while the colonial Powers retreat by strides, while new independent nations emerge, the process of disintegration of Russian colonialism was effectively stopped by the Bolsheviks, who had proclaimed the right of all nationalities to self-determination, including secession. This colonial empire is not only very much alive, but, as we have seen, was greatly expanded in 1939–45 and was enriched by colonial protectorates established in eastern Europe. If the principle of national self-determination is understood by Asians and Africans as a moral principle but not as a weapon of political expediency, why are they usually silent about Soviet Russian imperialism and colonialism? Are they blinded by an inverse racial prejudice, and do they remain indifferent in this case only because most of the Soviet-controlled nationalities are of European stock? Moreover, there are twenty-five million Asians among these Russian-controlled nationalities. Are the other Asians afraid of irritating the Russians, who, unlike the Westerners, have very limited patience with foreign criticism? It does not cost much to shout about Western imperialism and colonialism, which are in any event in full retreat, or about Western military blocs and bases, but it would be more risky to weigh the Russians on the same scale, which could quickly spoil mutual relations. However, national self-determination loses its prestige as a moral principle and acquires the unpleasant taste of political expediency when it is invoked in certain cases but not in others.

There are excellent monographs on the nationality problem in the USSR.[1] Moreover, we are primarily concerned with foreign policies of the USSR. We shall therefore limit ourselves to mentioning briefly several aspects of Soviet nationality policy insofar as they provide strange background for the Soviet anti-colonialist apostolate in the underdeveloped countries. We shall endeavor, as usual, to rely almost exclusively on Soviet sources to dispel doubts in the reader's mind. The large question is, has the apostle himself clean hands? Is he guiltless of any imperialist and colonialist sins?

Soviet sources never deny that the USSR is a multi-national state. The last population census having been taken in 1939, before the large annexations in Europe and the Far East, there exist today no official Soviet statistics on the national composition of the Soviet population. Soviet sources manipulate the figures of 1939, which are obviously obsolete because of the addition of new populations in 1939–45, natural increase, and the migration movements within the USSR. A recent pamphlet sums up the situation as follows:

The Union of the SSR is the model of a multi-national State. Several scores of nations, nationalities, and national groups populate it; Russians represent 60 per cent, Ukrainians—20 per cent, and Byelorussians, Uzbeks, Kazakhs, Georgians, Armenians, Azerbaijanis, Tadjiks, Kirghizs, Turkmenians, Lithuanians, Latvians, Estonians, Moldavians, Karelians and other peoples—20 per cent.[2]

The Russians constitute the prevailing majority, 80 per cent, only within the Russian Republic, one of the fifteen.[3]

The remaining fourteen major nationalities usually form the majority on the territory of the republics which bear their names. The Ukrainians represent 75 per cent of the forty-two million population of their republic.[4] There are also an unspecified number of millions of Ukrainians on the territories of other republics, including the Russian. These figures indicate that the Ukrainian problem is the most serious among the nationality questions in the USSR. They live on a compact territory adjacent to Poland, Rumania, Hungary, and Czechoslovakia and have broad access to the Black Sea. The agricultural and industrial importance of this territory remains vital to Russia, despite the economic development in the last decades of other Soviet territories. A separatist movement there would be the most serious threat to Russia as a great Power. In the absence of free elections, the non-existence of any party except the all-Soviet Communist, and the suppression of all facilities for free expression of national feelings, it is impossible to state the feelings of those millions of Ukrainians. Do they want to be independent or to have autonomy within a state shared with the Russians? Assuming that they are human beings not inferior to Tunisians, Moroccans, or the peoples of Ghana, Nigeria, and Malaya, one may expect that they probably aspire to be masters at home in one form or another. The 1939 annexation of eastern Galicia (western Ukraine), which had never been part of the Russian Empire and had lived under alien rule (the Polish, the Austrian, and the Polish, in that order), might well stimulate this aspiration among the other Ukrainians who had been ruled by Russians since the 17th and 18th centuries. The Ukrainians of eastern Galicia, cut off from the Russians and belonging to a different, Greek Catholic Church, developed a clear national consciousness pervading all social classes. They had their own intelligentsia aspiring to build an independent Ukrainian state. The absorption of eastern Galicia may work as a leaven among the other Ukrainians. Anyhow, this is potentially the most serious national problem of Russia.

The third Slavic-speaking nationality consists of the Byelorussians, who constitute over 80 per cent of the population of their republic.[5] These three nationalities together represent about 85 per cent of the total population; the remainder are peoples speaking other languages, most of them of non-European extraction. The Baltic group (Lithuanians, Latvians, and Estonians) number approximately six million.[6] The so-called Moldavian Republic counts 70 per cent of Rumanian-speaking people out of its 2.7 million population.[7]

Another important group of nationalities live in the Transcaucasus (in the Republics of Georgia, Armenia, and Azerbaijan). Each of these three nationalities forms a majority on the territory of the republic bearing its name, and each has, both culturally and linguistically, nothing in common with the Russians.

The last important group is represented by former Moslem (it is impossible to assess to what extent the Communist atheistic propaganda and the oppression of Moslem religious life have wiped out native attachment to Islam, before the Revolution the backbone of their national culture) populations of central Asia: the Uzbeks, the Kazakhs, the Kirghizs, the Turkmenians, and the Tadjiks. The first four peoples belong to the Turkic-speaking family and the fifth to the Iranian-speaking. The Azerbaijanis, and some of the nationalities of the Russian Republic, such as the Karakalpaks, the Bashkirs, and the Tartars, also speak Turkic languages. The 1939 population census gave these figures for the Asian peoples of the USSR: Uzbeks, 4,840,000; Kazakhs, 3,098,000; Tadjiks, 1,230,000; Kirghizs, 884,000; Turkmenians, 811,000. Among the other Turkic-speaking peoples, the Tartars numbered 4,300,000 and the Azerbaijanis 2,275,000.[8] The Christian Georgians and Armenians, whose history stretches back to antiquity, numbered, in 1939, 2,248,000 and 2,152,000, respectively. The Jews, dispersed over the whole Soviet territory but living mainly within the Russian, Ukrainian, and Byelorussian Republics, numbered just over three million.[9] Those various nationalities (except the Jews) were annexed by the Russians during centuries of expansion, but some of the conquests took place only in the 19th century. For instance, the western European partition of central Africa was accompanied by a parallel Russian expansion in the Far East and central Asia (the conquest was completed between 1864 and 1895).[10] This fairly recent military conquest is the reason why "seventeen million people happily live and work on the territories of the present Soviet Republics of Central Asia and the Kazakhstan."[11]

Lenin inherited this mosaic of peoples in 1917. We already know his relativist approach to the nationality problem and his distinct preference for large economic units. He wanted Russian Communists to concede to other nationalities of the Empire the right of self-determination, while the Communists belonging to those nationalities had to reject the exercise of that right and proudly declare that their respective nations preferred to live together with revolutionary Russians in one Soviet family. Although not a nationalist, he was singularly blind to the fact that his countrymen would then remain, as before, the controlling nationality within the Soviet state by virtue of their numbers and the predominant position they had acquired under the Tsars. He was not a gravedigger of the Russian Empire when he said on May 12, 1917:

Why should we, the Great-Russians, who oppress a greater number of nations than any other people, refuse to recognize the right of secession to Poland, Ukraine and Finland? ... To fortify internationalism it is necessary to insist in Russia on the freedom of secession of the oppressed nations, and in Poland to stress the freedom of union. The freedom of union assumes the freedom of secession.[12]

He must have been bitterly disappointed to see the various nationalities of the former Empire take to the letter the early generous appeals of the Soviet Government. Did not the latter proclaim on November 3, 1917, the right of all the peoples of Russia to a free self-determination, including secession and formation of their own independent states? Did it not say in its famous appeal to Russian and foreign Moslems:

Moslems of Russia, Tartars of the Volga and the Crimea, Kirghiz and Sarts of Siberia and Turkestan, Turks and Tartars of Transcaucasia, Chechens and mountain Cossacks! All of you, whose mosques and shrines have been destroyed, whose faith and customs have been violated by the Tsars and oppressors of Russia! Henceforth your beliefs and customs, your national and cultural institutions, are declared free and inviolable. Build your national life freely and without hindrance![13]

Only an inveterate skeptic could have doubted the sincerity of this promise to respect Moslem mosques and shrines given by a government composed entirely of atheists.

3. Reconquest of the Tsarist Empire (1918–1921)

The tumultuous response of many nationalities started a process of disintegration of the former Empire. Independent or autonomous republics were proclaimed. There was a clear danger that the bastion of the revolution would be despoiled of its economically important territories and would shrink down to ethnic Russia. Yet Lenin was committed to the universal revolution, incomparably more important than the trivialities of national self-determination. For him the Communists represented the elite of each nationality; if they wanted to remain within the Empire, they would reflect the true and permanent interests of their respective nationalities. Their will should be enforced on the "ignorant" majorities. Thus the process of reconquest of the territories of the former Empire began. Since the local Communists were not strong enough, the Red Army had to help. This venture failed, as we have seen, in Finland, the Baltic countries, and Poland, but it succeeded elsewhere. The basic territorial integrity of the Empire was saved. As we said before, quoting Soviet sources, the reconquest of border areas was also motivated by economic considerations. These areas usually supplied central Russia with foodstuffs and raw materials, in addition to coal and industrial products from the Ukraine. Stalin, at that time Commissar for Nationalities, said frankly in 1918: "The October Revolution, having won in the center of Russia and having conquered a number of border territories, could not limit itself to the framework of Russia."[14] It could limit itself even less to central Russia.

However, Lenin had to make one concession out of his preference for one centralized state. The national feelings of non-Russian nationalities were so strong that he had to shift in 1918 to the concept of a federal state, centralized by the existence of one monopolistic Communist Party for all component nationalities. A Soviet historian thus traces this evolution:

It is known that the Bolsheviks rejected until the October Revolution the federal structure of the state and stood by the single centralized Republic, guided in these views by Marx's and Engels' theses. . . . The Communist Party, during the first period of the October Revolution, the process of state-building and struggle against the national-bourgeois "governments" in the border territories, came to the conclusion that the federation, as one of the transitory forms leading towards a socialist unitary state, could be used for the organization of a Soviet multi-national State. . . . The strength of the national movement proved in the process of unification of nations to be much more serious and complex than it had seemed before the World War and the October Revolution. This caused the change in the views of the Communist Party on the problem of federation. . . . The Soviet federation, wrote Lenin, would be the surest step towards the steady unification of the various nationalities of Russia within one, democratic, centralized, Soviet State.[15]

But this formal federation had to be, at the same time, a highly centralized state, thanks to the existence of one Communist Party instead of several for each component nationality. Thus the pre-Revolutionary Bolshevik concept was saved, despite the outward concession made after the Revolution to the non-Russian national feelings. The Party was to be the actual ruling force. The 8th Congress of the Communist Party adopted the following resolution in March, 1919:

At the present time Ukraine, Latvia, Lithuania, and Byelorussia exist as separate Soviet Republics. . . . But this does not mean that the Russian Communist Party should in turn be organized as a federation of independent Communist parties. . . . It is necessary to maintain the existence of *one* centralized Communist Party with one Central Committee which directs all Party activities in all parts of the RSFSR. All the decisions of the Russian Communist Party and of its leading institutions are unconditionally binding on all sections of the Party independently of their national composition. The Central Committees of the Ukrainian, Latvian and Lithuanian Communists enjoy the rights of the Party regional committees and are entirely subordinated to the Central Committee of the Russian Communist Party.[16]

This important aspect of Soviet life should never be overlooked by anyone who wants to understand the true mechanism of the Soviet "federal" state. As a Soviet author says:

Whatever is the Republic where Communists find themselves, they have acted and act under one single direction of the Party Central Committee which carries out the will of the whole Party.[17]

One may only add that this Party and its directing bodies have always been and remain predominantly Russian in composition.

The story of the reconquest may be fully traced through Soviet sources either of the time or of today. A Soviet historian said in 1954:

The Red Army detachments, the revolutionary soldiers and sailors, sent from the center of Russia, and the toilers of the border territories who rose up in the struggle against the bourgeois-nationalist "governments," crushed the counter-revolutionary centers on those territories by their joint efforts. ... The immense political, economic, military, and cultural assistance given by the Russian people to all the border peoples was the decisive factor in the creation and consolidation of the sovereign Soviet republics on the border territories and in the union of the border peoples around the Russian Federation.[18]

In 1956, we saw in Hungary that the Communist terms, counter-revolutionary centers, meant national movements which were neither pro-Russian nor pro-Communist, while the toilers were a synonym for local Communists. Otherwise, the statement is historically correct, the Russians playing the decisive role in the Soviet reconquest of border territories.

The Ukrainians formed their autonomous government in 1917; its name was the *Rada*. It was poorly organized and was unable to put up an effective resistance against the Russian and its own Communists. However, the Soviet Government did not proceed to a free plebiscite among the Ukrainians in order to know whether they wanted to share a common life with the Russians and, in particular, whether they intended to adopt the Soviet regime. On December 4, 1917, it addressed a 48-hour ultimatum to the Ukrainian *Rada* in Kiev, asking it to co-operate with Russia in the war, still being waged, against the central empires and against anti-Soviet Russian military detachments, as well as not to disarm Communist armed detachments on the Ukrainian territory. The alternative was a declaration of war on the Ukrainian *Rada*.[19] The Ukrainian Congress of the Soviets rejected this ultimatum on the next day in the following resolution:

Considering the ultimatum of the Council of People's Commissars as an attack on the Ukrainian People's Republic, and declaring that the demands voiced in it violate the right of the Ukrainian people to self-determination and to a free creation of forms of political life, the All-Ukrainian Congress of Soviets of Peasants, Workers, and Soldiers' Deputies resolves that the centralistic plan of the present government of Moscow (Great-Russia), by leading to war between Muscovy and the Ukraine, threatens to break completely the federal relations which Ukrainian democracy strives to establish.[20]

The Soviet Government replied by building a rival pro-Soviet government in the other Ukrainian large city of Kharkov. Let the rest of the story be clearly told by a Soviet historian:

The Communists of the Ukraine, supported by the Red Guards and revolutionary sailors sent there by the Soviet Government from Moscow and Petrograd, began a struggle for the formation of the Soviet authority in the whole Ukraine and for the liquidation of the *Rada*. . . . The Central Committee of the Party headed by V. I. Lenin directly ordered this struggle. . . . It [a rival Ukrainian Congress of the Soviets hastily improvised in Kharkov which had proclaimed on December 25, 1917, a Ukrainian Soviet Republic] spoke in favor of close federal ties between the Ukrainian Soviet and the Russian Soviet Republics. The Congress pointed out in its decisions that it considered the Ukrainian Republic a federated part of the Russian Republic. The Central Executive Committee elected by the Congress was instructed to extend the decrees of the Workers' and Peasants' Government of the Russian Federation to the Ukrainian territory. . . . The Russian Council of People's Commissars recognized the Soviet Government as the only legitimate government of the Ukraine and decided to provide it immediately with armed assistance in the fight against the *Rada*. . . . On January 5 [1918] the troops, which had arrived from Soviet Russia, and the Red Guard detachments of the Ukrainian Soviet Government began the offensive. . . . On January 26 Kiev was occupied by the Soviet troops.[21]

The German-Austrian occupation soon put an end to Soviet rule in the Ukraine. After the defeat of Germany and the evacuation of the German-Austrian troops in the late fall of 1918, the Ukrainians re-established, in December, their national government in Kiev, the Directory. However, the Central Committee of the Soviet Communist Party, which was the supreme Party body for both the Russian and the Ukrainian Communists, appointed in November, 1918, a new Communist Ukrainian government with its first seat in the Russian city of Kursk. Characteristically enough, its first head (until January 1919) was a Russian, Piatakov, who was succeeded by a Russified Bulgarian, Rakovsky. The Soviet troops reconquered, after various vicissitudes, the whole of the Ukraine in 1919–1920.

The Byelorussian story is given by the same Soviet historian, who readily concedes that the initiative in the process of Sovietization and unification was Russian from the start:

The Central Committee of the Communist Party convened in Moscow a conference of the Byelorussian Communists. This conference adopted a resolution . . . expressing the desire to organize a Byelorussian Soviet So-cialist Republic. [After the Soviet military occupation of Eastern parts of Byelorussia] the First Congress of the Soviets of Byelorussia, opened in February 1919 in Minsk, proclaimed an independent Byelorussian Soviet Socialist Republic. . . . The First Congress of the Soviets of Byelorussia decided to open negotiations with the Russian Soviet Republic concerning the establishment of close economic and political ties between the Byelo-russian people and its elder brother, the Russian people.[22]

It is interesting that the same author mentions a Russian Communist, Ya. M. Sverdlov, as the initiator of all the Byelorussian decisions.[23] The procla-mation of the Soviet Byelorussian Republic was immediately followed by the Soviet Russian recognition and a promise of assistance.[24] After the end of the war with Poland, a major part of Byelorussia remained an integral part of Soviet Russia. Thus the western frontiers of Russia were fixed to last until 1939.

The independent Republics of Armenia, Azerbaijan, and Georgia were proclaimed in May, 1918. Each had a non-Communist government of its own choice. Their fate was sealed, however, in 1920–21. The first step was taken in Baku, a cosmopolitan city with a high percentage of Russians; local Russian and other Communists proclaimed there on April 28, 1920, the Soviet Azerbaijani Republic. They immediately declared that the Azer-baijani Government, supported by the local nationalist party, Mussavat, was to be overthrown; they formed the Provisional Military-Revolutionary Committee of the Azerbaijani Republic, which hastened to send Lenin a telegram asking for military assistance:

. . . Being unable to withstand, by its own means, the pressure of the united bands of the internal and external counter-revolution, the Military-Revo-lutionary Committee proposes to the Government of the Russian Soviet Republic to enter into a brotherly alliance. . . . We beg you to give us immediately real help by dispatching the detachments of the Red Army.[25]

Soviet Russian troops soon conquered the entire Azerbaijani territory. They had advanced into Armenia and Georgia but had to be withdrawn in view of the Polish offensive in the Ukraine. Lenin followed the advice of his favorite author, General von Clausewitz, in turning first against the main enemy while appeasing the lesser ones. Although the Soviet Government had refused, in December, 1918, to recognize the independence of Georgia,[26] it concluded now, on May 7, 1920, a peace treaty with this small country and thereby recognized its independence while renouncing all intentions of intervention in its domestic affairs and promising not to tolerate on its territory any group that would plot against the Georgian government.[27]

The Azerbaijani pattern was copied in November, 1920, in Armenia. A Revolutionary Committee of Armenia was formed and immediately appealed for Soviet-Russian assistance:

The peace concluded with Poland and the rout . . . inflicted on the last Tsarist General Wrangel have freed the Red Army; Soviet Russia has now the opportunity to give us her brotherly assistance.[28]

Russian troops entered the territory and swiftly conquered it. The alliance concluded on December 2, 1920, between the RSFSR and Soviet Armenia in conquered Erivan, capital of the country, conceded in Article 8 that the Armenian Communist Committee, which had appealed for Russian help, was not even located on Armenian soil:

The government of the Republic of Armenia shall be deprived of power after the signature of the present treaty. Power shall be transferred, for the time being and until the arrival of the Revolutionary Committee, to the [Soviet] military High Command.[29]

Georgian independence was suppressed in the same manner in February, 1921. Stalin wrote in *Pravda* in November, 1920, soon after the conclusion of the Polish armistice: ". . . Georgia completes now the last days of her life."[30] Military operations against Georgia were preceded by the formation of a Georgian Revolutionary Committee in the village of Shulaveri. It was formed on February 16, and the march of the Soviet troops began on February 16–17. On February 25, Tiflis, the capital, was taken, and on March 18, the Georgians, attacked from the rear in the area of Batum by Turkish troops, capitulated to the Russians. It is worth while to quote, from the Soviet collection of early diplomatic documents, this appeal addressed by the Georgian Communist Revolutionary Committee on February 16, 1921 (the very day of its formation) from the obscure village of Shulaveri:

We hope and are convinced that the country not only of the great proletarian revolution but also endowed with great material resources will not leave us alone in this unequal struggle and will come to the assistance of the newly-born SSR of Georgia. Long live Soviet Russia! Long live her great leader! Long live the Red Army![31]

This text leaves little doubt that Georgian Communists did not expect to conquer unaided in "the unequal struggle" against their countrymen, who were defending national independence. The story of the conquest of Georgia was aptly summarized by a Soviet author:

An armed insurrection in Georgia was being prepared according to instructions issued by the Caucasian Office of the Russian Communist Party (Bolsheviks) headed by Sergo Ordjonikidze. It began in the middle of February 1921. . . . A Revolutionary Committee was formed. It proclaimed the Soviet Socialist Republic of Georgia and appealed for help to Soviet Russia. The Red Army immediately came to the rescue of the Georgian people in accordance with the decision of the Central Committee of the Russian Communist Party (Bolsheviks) and on direct instructions from Lenin and Stalin. On February 25, 1921, detachments of the 11th Army entered the capital of Georgia. . . . Sergo Ordjonikidze conveyed the joyful news to Lenin and Stalin: "The Red flag of the Soviet authority flies over Tiflis."[32]

A Soviet historian freely concedes that Soviet intervention was the decisive factor in establishing Soviet Republics in the Transcaucasus:

The Trans-Caucasian peoples overthrew their bourgeois-nationalist "governments" with the assistance of the Red Army. . . . S. K. Ordjonikidze stressed at the First Trans-Caucasian Congress of the Soviets that the Azerbaijani, Armenian, and Georgian workers and peasants achieved their liberation in alliance with the Russian workers and peasants. ". . . were there no Soviet Russia," Ordjonikidze said, "there would have been no Soviet Azerbaijan, Georgia, or Armenia."[33]

The same pattern was reproduced in central Asia whenever the native Moslems tried to achieve their independence; recently conquered Moslems of Turkestan strove hard to throw off the foreign yoke. According to a Soviet source:

In November 1917 the counter-revolutionaries proclaimed in the city of Kokanda an "autonomous government" of Turkestan. . . . In February 1918 the Red Army . . . administered a crushing blow to the bands of "autonomists" and routed them. . . . [In 1918] the decrees of the council of people's commissars of the Turkestan territory dissolved the municipal councils in Tashkent, Ashkhabad, Andidjan and other cities because [their composition] did not correspond to the interests of toilers; ... the nationalist periodical *Izakh* was closed. . . . The Tashkent bourgeois-nationalist organization *Ulema* was dissolved.[34]

The Soviet Government, however, lost control of Turkestan between July, 1918, and October, 1919. During the subsequent period of the restoration of Soviet authority in 1919–1920, the affairs of central Asia were concentrated in the hands of the so-called Turkestan Bureau, later renamed the Central Asian Bureau of the Central Committee of the Russian Communist Party. No native Communist was included in the Bureau, which was composed of three Russians—M. V. Frunze, V. V. Kuibyshev and L. M. Kaganovich.[35] The Soviet source concedes the decisive role of Soviet troops in defeating local nationalist detachments, the so-called *Basmachi:* "The offensive operations of the Red Army, undertaken at the beginning of 1920 under the direct command of M. V. Frunze, destroyed *Basmachi* gangs active in the Ferghana region."[36] Referring to later *Basmachi* guerrilla warfare, the same author writes:

The transition to rehabilitation was hindered by an exceptionally tense political situation which existed in the territory because of the intensification of the *Basmachi* movement. . . . *Basmachi* bands were decisively defeated thanks to the tremendous help given by the Government of the RSFSR and the great Russian people.[37]

The help given by "the great Russian people" in subjugating Central Asia and reconquering it for the Soviet Government took two forms: military operations by Soviet Russian troops and the support they could find among the Russian settlers. The debt owed by Soviet Russia to Russian settlers in central Asia is now duly acknowledged:

The Russian workers headed by the railroad employees played the crucial, leading and organizational role in the victory of the proletarian revolution and the establishment and consolidation of Soviet authority in Turkestan. They were the main channels in spreading Leninist ideas among the broad masses of the native population.[38]

Present Soviet central Asia is composed of former Turkestan and two former Russian vassal states: Bukhara and Khiva (Khoresm). These two Khanates became Russian protectorates in 1868 (Bukhara) and 1873 (Khiva). They were left a large measure of internal autonomy. A Soviet attempt at reconquering the Khanate of Bukhara in February 1918 had failed but was successfully renewed in 1920. In February of that year, Khiva was conquered, and in September, the same fate overtook Bukhara. Both were proclaimed people's republics. A Soviet author concedes the active role of Soviet troops in these transformations of the two Khanates into people's protectorates of Soviet Russia:

Armed detachments of Soviet Turkestan, which included many Russian Communists in their ranks, together with the Khivan revolutionary detachments, crossed the river in order to support the people's insurrection in Khiva. . . . Comrade M. V. Frunze, the commander of the Turkestani front, said in his order to the troops of the Red Army dated August 20, 1920: ". . . Regiments of the Bukhara Red Army, which are being formed, are marching to help their people. The Red regiments of workers' and peasants' Russia must march with them."[39]

Another writer confirms it:

The assistance given by the Red Army had a decisive significance for the outcome of the struggle of toiling masses against their masters. The peoples of Khiva and Bukhara would not have been able, without this assistance, to win victory.[40]

After the Soviet conquest and the proclamation of the two people's republics, the RSFSR concluded alliances with both of them. The letter of these treaties promised that the two republics should exist without fear of being eventually incorporated into the Soviet territory. Article 1 of the Khoresm-Russian treaty of September 13, 1920, said: ". . . Russia unconditionally recognizes the full autonomy and independence of the Khoresm People's Socialist Republic . . . and renounces forever all those rights which were imposed on the Khoresm Republic by the former Russian Government."[41] The preamble to the Russian-Bukhara alliance, signed on March 4, 1921, contained an analogous pledge:

. . . The RSFSR unconditionally recognizes the full independence and autonomy of the Soviet Republic of Bukhara with all the consequences resulting from such recognition, and forever renounces all rights and privileges which were claimed by Russian Tsardom over Bukhara.[42]

However, even native Communists of Bukhara and Khoresm were not as servile as Moscow expected.

The Communist parties of Bukhara and Khoresm were badly infected by alien elements. This stratum of Russian workers, who represented the proletarian core and the essential leading force within the Communist Party of Turkestan, did not exist in these Republics.[43]

The first step was taken in 1922: "The Central Committee of the Russian Communist Party (Bolsheviks) decided in 1922 to incorporate the Communist parties of Bukhara and Khoresm into the Russian Party."[44] The next step was to incorporate, in 1924–25, the two people's republics into the Soviet Union. The process initiated by the Tsars was completed.

The outright annexation of Bukhara and Khoresm disregarded not only the solemn pledges given to these two people's republics but also a promise to their neighbor, Afghanistan. A Soviet-Afghanistani treaty signed on February 28, 1921, stated in Article 8: "... the High Contracting Parties agree upon the actual independence and freedom of Bukhara and Khiva, whatever form of government may be in existence there, in accordance with the will of their peoples."[45]

These fragments of the history of the Soviet reconquest of the former Empire bear witness to the fact that it was not a spontaneous movement of native populations towards a union with Russia but a struggle decided in the final account by the Soviet Russian sword.

4. Foundation of the USSR

The following stage of a formal unification in one state of the various Soviet Republics established in this manner was not completely painless. The native "bourgeois-nationalists" wiped out in the process of reconquest could no longer oppose this reconstitution of the former Empire in the Soviet form. In many instances, their place was taken over by native Communists who wanted to preserve some remnants of autonomy. Moscow favored a strict conformity:

The first constitutions of the fraternal Soviet Republics of Ukraine, Byelorussia, Azerbaijan, Armenia and Georgia, founded on the principles of the Constitution of the RSFSR of 1918, took it as their model, borrowing from it many essential provisions. All the Soviet Socialist Republics enforced on their territories the codes of laws of the RSFSR.[46]

This structural uniformity was from the start intertwined with Moscow control over the affairs of the republics.[47] The process of unification took two years—until the formal signing on December 30, 1922, by all Soviet republics of a treaty establishing one federal state known since as the USSR.

Those two years saw also the emergence of a local Communist opposition to the merger of the republics into one state; it was to be highly centralized except in name. A Soviet historian frankly acknowledges this, notwithstanding the epithets he uses to designate native opposition:

The Ukrainian and Byelorussian bourgeois-nationalists and Trotskyites opposed the federation and favored a confederate State, i.e., such a State where the decisions of the highest authorities of the Union would be subject to approval by the governments of the Republics ... the bourgeois-nationalists and Trotskyites of the Ukraine and Byelorussia ... wanted to deflect the historical evolution of the Soviet multi-national State from the road of socialist federation and a close unification of peoples towards the road of separatism. The Georgian nationalist-deviationists and the Bashkir and Tartar bourgeois-nationalists, supported by the Trotskyites and Bukharinites, demanded the liquidation of the Transcaucasian and Russian federations and the direct participation of each Republic in the Union. . . . The national deviationists exaggerated the importance of national peculiarities of various peoples and underestimated the class interests of the proletariat.[48]

The same historian cites an example of the manner in which Moscow imposed conformity:

The national-deviationist leadership was dismissed on October 22 [1922] by the plenary meeting of the Central Committee of the C.P. (B) of Georgia, and a new Bureau of the Central Committee was elected; this Bureau headed the campaign for the establishment of the USSR.[49]

He reports also "fierce" nationalist opposition to the formation of one state within the Central Committees of the Ukrainian and Byelorussian parties.[50] He correctly attributes the reason for this local opposition to:

The heritage of the past consisted ... in the survivals of bourgeois nationalism amidst those peoples who had experienced the heavy yoke of national oppression. . . . The survivals of local nationalism expressed themselves in a kind of defense against the Great-Russian chauvinism.[51]

Thus the Russian Communists met on Soviet soil the very nationalism which they now try to exploit abroad for their own purposes.

The so-called national deviationists among the non-Russian Communists wanted to preserve some autonomy for their nationalities, as may be seen from the following description of their aims:

Insignificant groups of Georgian, Ukrainian and Byelorussian national-deviationists . . . opposed the establishment of one federal State. They favored the concept of a confederate system for the USSR. . . . They smuggled into the Ukrainian and Byelorussian draft constitutions, provisions directed against a common plan for the development of national economy, against a single federal budget, against federal citizenship, and the establishment of united people's commissariats for foreign affairs and external trade.[52]

Even this unfriendly contemporary report on their aspirations shows that the USSR, as a federal state, came into being in December, 1922, against the opposition of fractions of non-Russian Communists. But the will of Moscow was stronger. The former Empire was reconstructed in a different form, though with the same predominance of the Russian center. The socialist republics of Khoresm and Bukhara formally remained outside the Union until the reorganization of the Soviet central Asia that took place in 1924–25; at that time, Soviet Turkestan and the two republics were together regrouped into four present republics: the Uzbek, the Turkmenian, the Tadjik, and the Kirkhiz. Bukhara and Khoresm disappeared from the political map; they became parts of the Uzbek and Turkmenian Republics, which were both integral parts of the USSR.

We have related the events of the reconstitution of the Empire using only Soviet sources, yet even those sources do not vindicate this optimistic statement, which appeared in a Soviet history textbook:

The multi-national capitalist States are usually founded through conquest, enslavement and forcible annexation of peoples. . . . The Soviet Union was created in a completely different manner. It was founded as a free union of peoples within one federal State.[53]

5. Reappraisal of Tsarist Annexations

The manner in which the USSR had been built up led in the later Stalinist period to a re-evaluation of Tsarist annexations. They could not remain condemned in the Leninist manner because this could cause the non-Russian nationalities to wonder whether the Soviet way of reassembling the territories of the former Empire was quite legitimate and also to ask the indiscreet question of why they were initially brought into political association with the Russians. The first official theory was that of the lesser evil; it was better to be annexed by Tsarist Russia than by one of the Western imperialist Powers or by a small underdeveloped country like Turkey or Iran because Tsarist annexations eventually brought in their wake, for the non-Russian nationalities, the blessings of the October Revolution and the Soviet regime, enjoyable by them only because of the political association with the Russians. This theory has never completely disappeared but was largely superseded by another, which pointed to the benefits, economic and cultural, that had followed Tsarist annexations and also to the political advantages accruing from the post-October regime. Stalin's death has not affected this thesis; it is currently repeated for the benefit of non-Russian nationalities. They are actually expected to be grateful for being deprived of their former independence. This thesis does not deny the national oppression policy pursued by the Tsarist government but considers it a minor evil in comparison to the blessings that followed the annexations. It implies that to live together with Russians is an unmixed blessing and reflects the modern current of Soviet Russian nationalism.

The concept of the beneficial effects of Russian expansion was again restated on January 12, 1954, in theses adopted by the Party Central Committee on the occasion of the 300th anniversary of the union of Ukraine with Russia. The Ukrainian Cossacks, who appealed to the Moscow Tsar against Poland to defend their freedoms and their Greek Orthodox Church, did not expect that the Tsars would later gradually suppress those freedoms or that the Tsarist Government would eventually deny the very existence of a separate Ukrainian nationality. But the Central Committee declared in its 1954 theses:

The union of Ukraine with Russia, regardless of the fact that the Tsar and landlords stood then at the helm of Russia, had an immense progressive meaning for the further political, economic, and cultural development of the Ukrainian and Russian peoples.[54]

This thesis

... provided a deep, Marxist-Leninist evaluation of the leading role of the Russian people in the lives not only of the Ukrainian but also of all other peoples of our socialist Fatherland. The annexation by Russia had a decisive and progressive meaning also for the peoples of Azerbaijan, Georgia, Armenia, Northern Caucasus, Kazakhstan, the Baltic lands, Siberia, the Far East, and others.[55]

The Uzbek member of the highest Party body, the Presidium of the Central Committee, N. A. Mukhitdinov, added his authoritative voice:

The annexation of Central Asia by Russia in the second half of the 19th century was a turning point in the history and fate of the Uzbek and other

Central Asian peoples, and was deeply progressive. The union of the peoples of Central Asia with the Russian working class is, together with other factors of an economic and cultural nature, the most important phenomenon which determines the progressive character of the Russian annexation of Central Asia.[56]

All three state and Party supreme bodies, the Presidium of the Supreme Soviet, the Council of Ministers, and the Party Central Committee, upheld the same thesis on June 13, 1957, in their greetings addressed to the Bashkir Autonomous Republic on the occasion of the 400th anniversary of Russian annexation: "The incorporation of Bashkiria within the Russian State had a deeply progressive meaning for the economic and cultural development of the Bashkir people."[57]

Except for one peculiarly Soviet argument concerning the happiness of non-Russian nationalities through participation in the Soviet regime, all other arguments could have been used by any old-fashioned 19th-century imperialist: Russia brought to the conquered peoples a superior culture, contacts with progressive social-political thought, and an acceleration of economic development. The same arguments, whether true or not, could justify the existence of any colonial Empire, but surely they have a peculiar ring in the mouths of professed anti-colonialists. Let us look at a few samples of such arguments. A geographical textbook says:

The Russian annexation of Central Asia had objectively a progressive meaning, because Russia, regardless of her backwardness, was economically more developed and culturally superior. The annexation liquidated the feudal parcelling out of the country and the incessant feudal wars, accelerated the process of the development of capitalism, and promoted the emergence of a working class. It secured the development of cotton production.[58]

Another author writes:

The building of railroads linked Central Asia with Russian and world markets. . . . Local industries began to develop. There were already in 1913 only in Turkestan (excluding Khiva and Bukhara) 705 industrial establishments, chiefly . . . small enterprises engaged in the initial processing of cotton and cotton seeds. . . . The number of cities and the urban population were constantly growing. . . . Cotton production was increasing at an exceptionally quick pace. . . . Thanks to the annexation by Russia conditions were created for the penetration into Central Asia of Russian culture and Russian leading social ideas. . . . Without the Russian annexation and without the fraternal help on the part of the great Russian people, the peoples of Central Asia would have remained aloof from the all-Russian revolutionary movement.[59]

Another Uzbek author embroiders the same theme; he mentions the "civilizing role of Russia regarding the peoples of Central Asia" but also points to the advantages which accrued to Russia herself:

The Russian annexation of Central Asia had a tremendous significance for Russia herself. In consequence of this annexation Russia acquired a large market and an immense source of raw materials. . . . The annexation of Central Asia enlarged the territory and strengthened the Eastern frontier of the Russian State.[60]

He fortifies his positive thesis by the older theory of the lesser evil:

If Central Asia were not annexed on time by Russia, it would have been undoubtedly enslaved by that aggressive colonial State, England. Further developments would have led, under the yoke of English imperialism, only to one result, namely that the historical fate of peoples of Central Asia would have been no different from that of the peoples of Malaya, Ceylon, Algeria, Morocco, and other colonies of the Anglo-American-French imperialism.[61]

The book was printed in 1955, when Ceylon had already become independent. One cannot understand why it would have been a calamity for the central Asian nationalities to attain independence such as Ceylon's, Morocco's, or Malaya's. The author says in the same breath:

Those [Central-Asian] peoples had no rights whatsoever. . . . [However] Russia objectively played a progressive role by including the annexed non-capitalist countries, as those of Central Asia, into the world economy.[62]

Then one has to suffer the self-humiliating confession of Uzbek inferiority:

After the Russian annexation of Central Asia, the leading culture of Russian people, the culture of the great Russian nation, which stood incomparably higher than the cultures of Central Asian peoples, began to penetrate there.[63]

Whatever the nationality, the same thesis and similar arguments are advanced. A few other samples will illustrate this: "Despite the colonizing policy of Tsardom the union of Azerbaijan with Russia had historically a progressive meaning."[64] "The annexation by Russia of Eastern Armenia in 1828 was for the Armenian people a fact of great progressive meaning; a new period of its history began at that time."[65] "The incorporation of the Baltic region into Russia had great positive significance for Russia and the Baltic region itself. . . . The annexation by Russia of the Trans-Caucasus had objectively a progressive meaning."[66]

6. Evaluation of the Anti-Tsarist Native Uprisings

The Russian Empire was built in the two ways familiar to other empires. Whenever Russian expansion met densely populated territories and nationalities with clear national consciousness, the only way to go ahead was to use the sword. But large tracts of the Empire were acquired by the peaceful settlement of Russian and Ukrainian peasants in northeastern Europe and Siberia, areas sparsely populated by culturally much inferior tribes. The colonial policy of the Tsars was neither milder nor worse than that of other colonial Empires. Culturally inferior or economically backward nationalities benefited, as in the case of other empires, by contact with a superior culture, administrative experience, and a large economic market, at the inevitable price, of course, of losing their political self-government. The losers who were culturally and economically the equals of the Russians found themselves without any compensating advantages. However, even in the case of culturally backward nationalities, Russian colonial rule was not an unmixed blessing. Taking as an example the then nomad Kirkhizs, one may reconstruct the Russian colonial record, following a contemporary Soviet writer as guide. This record has a peculiar analogy to other colonial instances where white settlers took away the best lands from the natives. If the Russian record is not particularly worse, this should not lead Soviet anti-colonialists into extolling the Tsarist annexations as being providential for the conquered.

Kirghizia was conquered by Russian troops between 1855 and 1876. The conquest was followed by waves of immigration by Russian and Ukrainian peasants. The Russian Government reserved the best lands for these settlements, while the protests of native nomads deprived of their pastures were severely repressed by local authorities. A decree of 1892 declared all lands used by Kirghiz nomads state property; this land reserve was then used for granting plots to immigrants from European Russia. The Kirghiz paid the price; their numbers were reduced by 7 to 10 per cent between 1903 and 1913. It is little wonder, then, that they took to arms on several occasions. During the First World War, the government changed its previous policy of freeing the central Asian natives from military service and started conscripting them for auxiliary service behind the front. This caused an uprising in August, 1916; it was drastically repressed. Many Kirghizs tried to escape to China, men and cattle dying on the way. The Kirghiz population was again reduced by the effects of the unsuccessful uprising. Yet the very author who describes those tribulations of the Kirghizs ends his sad story with: ". . . the annexation by Russia of Kirghizia had a progressive meaning."[67]

This current evaluation of Tsarist annexations has had a repercussion on Soviet appraisal of the pre-Revolutionary past of non-Russian nationalities, a past frequently interwoven with struggle against Russian domination. The leaders of wars against Russia or of uprisings against Tsarist colonial rule became native national heroes. To allow each Soviet nationality to cultivate freely its historical tradition and to worship at the shrines of its heroes, as the Soviet Russians are currently allowed and even encouraged to do, would entangle the Party in complex difficulties. If historical memories, with their frequent anti-Russian undertone, were constantly kept alive, would it not stimulate aspiration towards greater national freedom? Would not anti-Russian resentment be inflamed? Would not the whole question of political association with Russia be thrown open to question?

During the Leninist and earlier Stalinist periods, it was legitimate favorably to mention national uprisings against the Tsarist colonial rule because the Russians themselves, after all, rose against the Tsar in 1917. However, the Russian nationalist trend in the later Stalinist period, with its glorification of the pre-Revolutionary past, brought on a radical revision. Armed opposition to Tsarist annexations and subsequent uprisings against Russian rule became a reactionary phenomenon to be mentioned only in terms of utter opprobrium. This view prevailed until very recently, surviving Stalin himself. A certain change took place only in 1956, cautiously showing a more lenient view of anti-Russian wars, uprisings, and national heroes. The present thesis seems to be that it was all right to defend oneself against conquering Russian armies and to take to arms against Russian colonialist oppression but that incorporation into the Empire was, nevertheless, politically, economically, and culturally a beneficial achievement. Of course this interpretation must be sparingly employed; one must no describe past wars and insurrections as directed against the Russians but only against the Tsars and their officials; no anti-Russian note may be injected. The new interpretation may be due to three causes: a general trend towards pruning the more absurd exaggerations of Stalinist policies, a desire to reduce the extent to which non-Russian nationalities were humiliated in their pride during the last period of his rule, and possibly the wish slightly to adjust the domestic policy to the external policy of courting foreign colonial and former colonial peoples.

Part and parcel of the Stalinist policy was to forbid publication of ancient epics of non-Russian nationalities (similar Russian epics were, of course, reprinted with care and love), even to frown on their mention, and to qualify them as feudal folklore products to be forgotten as monuments of a hateful past. These epics had two defects: they referred to the independent past of various nationalities and, not infrequently, contained anti-Russian allusions. Thus two yardsticks were applied, the one to Russian epics and pre-Revolutionary literature, the other to the non-Russian. The resulting situation is best described, not without bitter humor, in an article concerning central Asia which appeared in 1956:

Ancient Russian tales often mention "a good Tsar" or "a glorious ruler," and tell how a peasant son became a Tsar or a simple girl a Tsarina. Folklore epics picture Russian heroes vanquishing in "an honest battle" and killing "a Moslem monster." Numerous Russian poets, not the folklore poets but literary writers of world fame, expressed opinions on social problems which were characteristic of their time but which were erroneous by our standards; they often paid homage to religious dogmas. No one, however, withdrew them from circulation and branded those tales, folklore epics, and poems with horrible labels. But a different situation unfortunately existed in some Republics, especially the Central Asian. Were Lermontov a Kirghiz bard and have said in his poems that "the desert worships god," there would have been in that [Stalinist] time people who would have stigmatized the poet as a reactionary, even a Pan-Islamist, as they denounced local bards only for following the customs and laws of their own society and their own time in beginning the poems with the verse: "For the greater glory of Great Allah." Such [an Asian] a Lermontov would have taken a beating for "the evil Chechen," as would have such a Pushkin for his words: "now the savage Tunguz and Kalmyk, friends of the desert," as the popular bards of Kazakhstan and Kirghizia got a beating for the slightest disrespectful mention of the Russians. This is particularly noteworthy because those vulgarizers did not want to remember that these peoples, for instance, of Central Asia, had been subject not only to the influence of the leading Russian culture but, first of all, to the colonial oppression of Russian imperialism. . . . Those nihilist-vulgarizers did not meet with any protest and denounced epic after epic, bard after bard, proclaiming them without reason as anti-people, reactionary, bourgeois-nationalistic, and ideologically mistaken. Thus the wonderful Uzbek epic "Alpamysh" was suddenly qualified as anti-people, thus the Azerbaijani epic "Kitab Dede Korkud," the Turkmenian "Korkut Ata," the Buriat-Mongolian "Ghesser," and others were condemned without appeal.[68]

These folklore epics are now to be published, but the difficulty remains of finding a "correct" expurgated version that will not smack of anti-Russianism too much.

A new interpretation of past native insurrections was submitted by N. A. Mukhitdinov:

The religious outer shell of national-liberating movements does not prejudge by itself their reactionary nature. The historians who try to deny the national-liberating character of events of the second half of the 19th century and the beginning of the 20th century, should not forget that the whole history of Central-Asian peoples was permeated with the struggle for freedom and independence. It is more than strange to claim that the Central-Asian toilers remained inactive for some reason during the period of feudal and colonial oppression, despite the rapid growth of a powerful revolutionary movement in Russia and in the presence of such an ally and leader as the Russian working class headed by the Communists.[69]

Thus the central Asian uprisings are rehabilitated in a very cautious manner. They were part of the Russian revolutionary movement and were directed not against the Russians as such but only against the common oppressor, the Tsar. To avoid any possible misunderstanding, Mukhitdinov added:

The Uzbek people considers it its sacred duty to safeguard, as the apple of its eye, and further to strengthen by all means its eternal, indestructible and brotherly friendship with the Russian and other Soviet peoples.[70]

He ended on a warning to those Uzbeks and others who might be tempted to go too far in their interpretation of the new Party line:

Nationalism expresses itself in history in the glorification and idealization of the feudal past, with the deeds of Khans and Beys being described, instead of telling the story of the popular masses.[71]

Only a year before Mukhitdinov's speech, an Uzbek Communist wrote in the old vein:

The insurrection led by Kenessar Kassymov and directed against Russia and the Russians, which took place in the forties of the 19th century in Kazakhstan, was a reactionary, religious-nationalist movement. Kenessar's movement dragged back the Kazakh people . . . towards the detachment of Kazakhstan from Russia and of the Kazakh people from the great Russian people. The Andijan insurrection in 1898 led by Muhammed-Ali . . . was

also anti-people and nationalistic. . . . Pulat Khan's insurrection in Kokanda [1873] was another such nationalistic rebellion.[72]

Another illustration of the new Party line is the present reappraisal of the
insurrection by Moslem mountaineers of northern Caucasus, led by Shamil,
against Russia. Their war lasted for several years in the 1850's and was
quelled with great difficulty and ruthlessness. The evaluation of those
events traced a full circle; first it was a national-liberating and anti-colonialist movement. Stalin changed his views in 1950, and thus it became a reactionary and feudal movement inspired and abetted by English and
Turkish imperialists (the insurrection happened to coincide in time with
the Crimean War). Now the movement and its leader are again rehabilitated. Those changes were, of course, not the result of new historical discoveries; each time they were imposed by the Party on Russian and other
Soviet historians. For the last change, the decision was made in 1957 by
the Bureau of the Daghestan (the area where the movement had taken
place) Party regional committee. This decision admitted as mistaken the
former view that the national movement of the Daghestan mountaineers
and the Chechens had been "reactionary and inspired by foreign agents"
and characterized it as "an anti-colonial and just struggle against the Tsarist colonizers."[73] The same order, however, circumscribed this reappraisal
by an injunction to Soviet historians to devote their studies as well to "the
objectively progressive meaning of the incorporation of Daghestan into
Russia and the beneficial influence of the Russian material and spiritual
culture on the cultural development of Daghestan."[74]

The central period in the current historical studies relating to the past
of non-Russian nationalities remains the post-Revolutionary. For instance,
the secretary of the Communist Party of Tadjikstan said on November 22,
1956, addressing a conference of Tadjik intelligentsia: "Study of the history
and culture of the Tadjik people during the Soviet period should be the
central object of attention for our scholars."[75]

The new line must be followed cautiously. Two months after the afore-
said Party decision concerning Shamil's movement, a Soviet historian took
a beating at the hands of the editorial staff of the principal Party journal
for justifying the contacts of Shamil with England and Turkey during the
Crimean War as seeking support wherever it was possible to find it, for
overlooking the "feudal and clerical" nature of the movement, and, the
worst offense, for not even mentioning the progressive nature of Russian
annexation of northern Caucasus.[76]

7. Russians—the Elder Brothers

The current formula, established in the Stalinist period but enforced today, for the description of relations between the Russians and the other Soviet nationalities is as follows. The Russians are the elder brother and the leader in the fraternal union of equal nationalities, the non-Russians owing an eternal debt to the Russians for the beneficial effects of past annexations, for the October Revolution and the Soviet regime, for their economic development in the post-revolutionary period, and for the blessings of political and cultural intercourse with the great Russian nation. The Russians are definitely more equal and should be unreservedly loved and cherished. Never before has a controlling nationality formulated such a preposterous claim. The formula is reproduced faithfully in a history textbook:

The great Russian people plays a leading role in consolidating friendship among the peoples of the USSR. Its working class has the most leading revolutionary traditions. The selfless help of the Russian people given to the Ukrainian, Byelorussian, and other peoples of the USSR in overthrowing the power of landlords and capitalists and in the development of economies and cultures of their Republics, has intensified the feeling of gratitude, trust and love of the peoples of the USSR for the brotherly Russian people, the most eminent nation among all the nations of the Soviet Union.[77]

An Uzbek writes:

The Uzbek people, like other peoples of Central Asia, considers the alliance and friendship with the great Russian nation as the source of its national pride. "To have friendship with the great Russian people," N. S. Khrushchev said, "means to march in the foremost ranks of the most progressive people's movement for the destruction of capitalist slavery. Friendship with the great Russian people leads this victorious movement forward on the path of progress, on the path of Communism."[78]

Khrushchev happens to be a Russian and did not display a particular national modesty.

Another member of the Party Presidium, the Ukrainian A. Kirichenko, wrote in 1957: "The Ukrainian culture creatively absorbs the best achievements of brotherly cultures and preeminently of the rich culture of the Russian people."[79] His colleague, N. A. Mukhitdinov, responded from

Uzbekistan: "Who has helped the Uzbek people to achieve a cultural revolution, to make the population literate, to bring up a national intelligentsia? Above all, the Russian people and its representatives working in our Republic hand in hand with the Uzbek people."[80] The secretary of the Party Central Committee of Tadjikistan, T. Yu. Ul'djabaev, admonished the Tadjik intelligentsia in the same vein: "The Tadjik people considers it a sacred duty to strengthen and develop brotherly friendship with the great Russian people and all other peoples."[81] He said in another speech:

The Tadjik people knows very well that it owes, like all the other brotherly peoples of the Soviet Union, all its political, economic and cultural achievements, and the happiness of its life, to the wise leadership of the Communist Party, to its Leninist Central Committee, to the Soviet Government, and to the fraternal and disinterested assistance of the great Russian people.[82]

A Kazakh newspaper wrote in 1957:

The Kazakh people, like all the peoples of our great multi-national Fatherland, feel a limitless love and a brotherly attachment to the Russian people. . . . The Kazakh people is sincerely grateful for everything to its elder brother. It protects this indestructible friendship with the great Russian people . . . as the apple of its eye.[83]

8. Culture: National in Form but Socialist in Content

Common sense indicates that a one-party regime does not leave any room for independent political thought or action among Soviet citizens. Moreover, Stalin defined the scope of local cultures for his and the present times in very narrow terms:

What is national culture under the dictatorship of the proletariat? It is a culture socialist in its content and national in its form; its object is to educate the masses in the spirit of internationalism and to strengthen the dictatorship of the proletariat.[84]

Thus the contents of each culture of the various Soviet nationalities must be identical and follow the current Party interpretation of Marxism-Leninism. Literature, arts and music must be streamlined according to the concept of socialist realism and convey no ideas which are not Party approved. What is the national culture? The *Soviet Great Encyclopedia* gives a clear answer:

The national language is the principal instrument with which a nation develops her culture. Besides, the form of national culture finds its expression in the particularities of music, dance, its own type of painting, dress, architectural style, etc. The socialist nations have in fact a socialist culture, one in its contents but expressed in various national forms. . . . Marxism-Leninism is the foundation of that culture.[85]

This means in practice an ideological uniformity, but expressed in as many languages as exist in the Soviet Union. It means even less, however, from the growing impact of the Russian language, the enforced influence of Russian culture, and the constant warnings against bourgeois nationalism, which is nothing but a genuine local patriotism without genuflexions before the great Russian nation. An influential Uzbek Communist scholar writes:

An exceptional role belongs to the great Russian people in the development of the socialist culture of the Uzbek and other peoples of the Soviet Union. The Russian people has created throughout its history the richest culture which greatly enriched the storehouse of world culture. . . . It is remarkable how the socialist culture of the Uzbek people is organically tied with the cultures of all peoples of the Soviet Union, but preeminently with that of the great Russian people. . . . The construction of socialist culture in our country is planned and directed by the Communist Party and the Soviet State, who perform a colossal work in educating Soviet people in the spirit of socialist ideology. One of the principal places in this work is occupied by the struggle against old customs and habits, traditions and superstitions, which have been inherited from the old society. . . . The building of Uzbek socialist culture has taken place in an incessant struggle against bourgeois nationalism.[86]

Needless to say, old customs and habits, traditions and superstitions, refer to the pre-Revolutionary, many-centuries-old Moslem culture of the Uzbeks. This is being uprooted to make place for a new uniform socialist culture with a distinct Russian flavor.

9. Bourgeois Nationalism

The ever recurring Soviet admonitions against bourgeois nationalists testify, as much as the national awakening of Asia and Africa and the national revolts in 1956 in Poland and Hungary, to the indomitable force represented by patriotic attachment to one's country, its culture, and its history. This powerful yet natural feeling, just as natural as family love, proved more than anything else during the two world wars to be the source of a firm solidarity. During both wars, people otherwise belonging to the same denominations, professing the same social beliefs, members of the same social class, fought each other in the name of their respective countries. This irresistible attraction of one's own country is a source of both strength and weakness to the USSR. For the Russians, the Soviet Government is their only existing government; they will probably rally around it in every international crisis, as they did in the Second World War. But for other Soviet nationalities it is hardly their own government; their patriotism, so carefully suppressed, might again flare up as it did in 1917 and the following years of the Russian Civil War. This peril that menaces all multi-national empires is not ignored by the Party.

It was still the day of Lenin when the 10th Party Congress passed a resolution directed against local bourgeois nationalism in 1921:

. . . Communists who stem from local native populations which lived through the grave period of national oppression, and have not yet freed themselves from the habits of that period, often exaggerate the importance of national particularities in their Party and Soviet work; they leave in the shadow the class interests of toilers, or simply confuse the interests of toilers of a given nation with so-called "general-national" interests; unable to distinguish between them, they found their Party work on the latter interests. This attitude leads in turn to a deviation from Communism towards a bourgeois-democratic nationalism which assumes sometimes the form of Pan-Islamism or Pan-Turkism (in the East).[87]

However, when Lenin was alive, such a resolution was always counterbalanced by a castigation of Russian "Great-Power" chauvinism. Under Stalin, as now, the attack has been waged unilaterally against non-Russian "bourgeois" nationalism.

Stalin's successors have reaped the harvest of his ruthless purges in this and other respects. The purges left the legacy of fear. It will take a long time for the Russians and non-Russians of the Soviet Union to forget the time when hundreds of thousands of mostly guiltless people perished and millions were sent to forced labor camps. Can they be sure that such purges will never be repeated? This fear is one of the psychological instruments in the hands of the Party. The purges of the thirties created a hecatomb among the non-Russian Communists as well.

The non-Russian nationalities have twice lost their political elite, the first time immediately following the Revolution when their non-Communist intelligentsia was decimated, together with the Russian one. They lost their elite a second time during the purges of nationally inclined Communist leaders. To mention only the most eminent among Communist leaders of the non-Russian nationalities who perished in the thirties, let us merely count the victims among the chairmen of the Central Executive Committees and chairmen of the Councils of People's Commissars of the various Republics. The list includes the chairmen of the Central Executive Committees of Ukraine, Byelorussia, Turkmenistan, Tadjikstan (two of them were shot in succession), and Karelia and similar high authorities in three Autonomous Republics—Adjar, Daghestan, and Volga-German, as well as several chairmen of the Councils of Commissars of Union Republics—Ukraine (two of them executed), Transcaucasia (existent for a time, later to be split into the Union Republics of Georgia, Armenia, and Azerbaijan), Uzbekistan, Georgia, and Tadjikstan. The first secretaries of the Uzbek and Buriat-Mongolian sections of the Party were also executed. A few other "nationalist" Communist leaders escaped execution by taking their own lives, for instance the Ukrainians Skrypnik and Lubchenko. Skrypnik's successors as Party bosses in the Ukraine, Postyshev and Kosior, also met violent deaths. The execution of Kosior made room for Khrushchev, who came as his successor. This gives a peculiar flavor to Khrushchev's posthumous rehabilitation of Kosior at the 20th Party Congress in 1956.

Local nationalism has not been extirpated. Judging by contemporary warnings and complaints, it survives and appears at first opportunity in any mild form. N. A. Mukhitdinov conceded on October 11, 1956, that the great purges had taken a toll of innocent people in Uzbekistan:

The Bureau of the Central Committee of the Communist Party of Uzbekistan has examined the cases of several outstanding officials of the Republic repressed in 1937–39 after having been accused of nationalism and treason to the Fatherland. It has become clear that, while a great work had been done to unmask nationalists and traitors of the Fatherland, some leaders of the Communist Party at the same time had innocently suffered.[88]

He immediately dispelled any possible illusions that local patriotism would now be tolerated: "It is necessary to wage a most uncompromising struggle against all sorts of survivals of nationalism."[89] The secretary of the Party Central Committee of Tadjikstan, T. Yu. Ul'djabaev, sounded the same warning a month later:

Chauvinism and nationalism are alien by their very nature to socialist nations. But this does not mean that some backward people among us do not assume unsound and politically harmful attitudes, including the nationalistic one against which we must wage a resolute struggle.[90]

Their Lithuanian colleague, A. Snechkus, was even more explicit, perhaps because of the moral effects of the Hungarian revolt on his recently annexed country:

We cannot be passive observers when some people, grossly distorting the reality, idealize the bourgeois time and implant thereby incorrect views especially among youth which did not know the bourgeois regime. . . . The bourgeois nationalists . . . now try to pose as defenders of the interests of Lithuanian people. . . . We cannot but react against the fact that some of our scientific and cultural workers express in particular cases unsound and alien moods and mistaken opinions. . . . Some people alien to our Soviet student body have found the way to our higher-learning institutions. Some of them . . . disturb the studious atmosphere among the students. We consider that such elements have no place in the Soviet higher-learning institutions.[91]

Perhaps the Arabs, the Indians, or the Indonesians are better placed than other people to understand the reasons why Lithuanian intellectuals and students hark back to the "bourgeois" time; it was simply the period of their national independence, and that period is not even remote, since Lithuania was annexed for the first time in 1940 and for the second in 1944.

In December, 1956, the Ukrainian Union of Writers heard similar admonitions and warnings against bourgeois nationalism, which had reappeared among some of its members.[92] A few months later, A. Kirichenko wrote for the benefit of his Ukrainian countrymen: ". . . the national form of culture if deprived of its socialist content may be used to camouflage bourgeois nationalism."[93] Mukhitdinov, who appears to be one of the top Party specialists on nationality problems, wrote in June, 1957:

We shall always remain irreconcilable towards survivals of nationalism in whatever form they would manifest themselves . . . nationalistic survivals may appear in acts of individual persons in the most various forms; for instance, as the idealization of the feudal past, as an inconsiderate, disrespectful and haughty attitude towards the traditions, culture and language of other peoples . . . in the underestimation of the international debt owed by their own nation, in the inclination to minimize the great help which other peoples have given to the Uzbek people.[94]

"Bourgeois" nationalism will pester the Party as long as the various nationalities live because this is one feeling that nobody has ever yet been able to uproot in any living nation.

10. Deportations

Both Stalin and Hitler used forcible mass deportations as a means of solving embarrassing national problems. In 1935, the Finnish population was removed from the border areas of the Karelian Republic in connection with the building of Soviet fortifications. The whole Korean population in the Soviet Far East was removed to central Asia in 1938 as a measure of security in the period of tension in relations with Japan. During the last war, other mass deportations took place. After the Nazi attack, the Soviet Government removed the Volga Germans from their ancestral settlements and dispersed them over the whole Soviet territory. Then came the turn of small Moslem nationalities, also deported from their homelands and dispersed, the Karachays and the Kalmyks by the end of 1943, the Chechens, Ingushes, and Balkars in the spring of 1944.[95] The Crimean Tartars were overtaken by the same fate in 1944. In each case, from tens to hundreds of thousands of people were involved—men, women, and children. One of Stalin's lieutenants at that time, N. S. Khrushchev, passed this retrospective judgment in 1956:

Not only a Marxist-Leninist but also no man of sense can grasp how it is possible to make whole nations responsible for inimical activity, including women, children, old people, Communists and Komsomols, to use mass repression against them, and to expose them to misery and suffering for hostile acts of individual persons and groups of persons.[96]

Yet Stalin, at that time faithfully served by Khrushchev, exacted a horrible price from entire nationalities for acts of collaboration with the Nazis committed by some of their members. The names of their autonomous republics were simply erased from the official roster of Soviet republics. This pattern could not be applied to forty million Ukrainians. Khrushchev, while mentioning in his secret speech in 1956 the mass deportations of small nationalities, said with grim humor: "The Ukrainians avoided this fate only because there were too many of them and there was no place to which to deport them. Otherwise he [Stalin] would have deported them also."[97]

The present Soviet leaders took four years before they decided to repair this injustice. On January 9, 1957, the Presidium of the Supreme Soviet passed an edict which restored the Chechen-Ingush Autonomous Republic, transformed the Kabardin Autonomous Republic into the Kabardin-Balkar, organized again a Kalmyk autonomous region, and restored the Cherkess autonomous region to its previous status of the Karachay-Cherkess region. The edict was approved by the Supreme Soviet on February 11, 1957.[98] These legislative acts carried the implication that Chechens, Ingushes, Balkars, Kalmyks, and Karachays be allowed at the same time to return to their ancestral homes.

The damage was not fully repaired. Neither Khrushchev's secret speech nor the edict of the Presidium ever mentioned the Volga Germans or the Crimean Tartars. The postwar Russian hatred of the Germans may account for the first omission. The Crimean Tartars could not be returned to their native land because post-Stalinist leadership had made it a present to the Ukrainian Republic in 1954. Crimea, the Tartar homeland for several centuries, was annexed by Russia in 1783. The constant Russian and Ukrainian immigration and the Tartar exodus to Turkey, which had followed the annexation as it did each Russian-Turkish war, radically changed the ethnic composition of Crimea; the Tartars eventually became a minority.[99] On February 19, 1954, the whole of Crimea, already cleared by Stalin of all Tartar traces, was incorporated into the Ukrainian Republic. The Crimean Tartars had no place to go, and their autonomous republic was not restored in 1957.

The mass deportations of whole nationalities must have taken a heavy toll of human lives. This may be deduced from the fact that it was not worth while to restore to the Kalmyks their previous autonomous republic, which was replaced by a lower administrative unit, an autonomous region. Thousands of Buddhist Kalmyks escaped from the USSR during the last war, and some of them eventually found a new home in the United States. Lenin had told them on July 2, 1919:

Brother Kalmyks, the entire past of your people is an uninterrupted chain of suffering. . . . The autocratic Tsarist Government, which extended its power by bloody conquests over many foreign tribes, has likewise fastened the chains of slavery on the freedom-loving Kalmyk people.[100]

Lenin's followers added the most tragic link to that chain of sufferings of a small Asian nationality.

The reader will recall the earlier-mentioned mass expulsions of millions of Germans from the Soviet or Polish-annexed eastern German territories, from Czechoslovakia (the Sudetenland), and Hungary. This mass operation, carried out at an unusual speed and involving much hardship for the expelled millions, had the Soviets' wholehearted blessing, as may be seen from this excerpt from a recent international law textbook:

The transfer differs from option or the exchange of populations in that the factor of free will is excluded. For instance, the transfer of the German population from Poland, Czechoslovakia, and Hungary to Germany was decided at the Berlin Conference in 1945. The transfer of the German population from the Kaliningrad [Königsberg] region also took place. The Soviet State looks with favor on the transfer as one of the possible solutions of the national problem in the interest of a democratic peace.[101]

It is a strangely peculiar "democratic" peace that requires the forceful expulsion of millions of people. This method of assuring peace palpably differs from an option which leaves to each individual free choice of remaining on the annexed territory (acquiring new nationality) or transferring his home to the country of his former allegiance; it differs also from an exchange of populations where the two governments concerned freely agree mutually to transfer their respective national minorities.

11. A Centralized Russian State

The unceremonious attitude of Soviet Communists towards the constitutional structure of their multi-national state may be gathered from other facts. In 1924–25, the Turkestan, Bukhara, and Khoresm territories were reorganized by a fiat of the central government; four republics were established: Uzbek, Turkmenian, Kirghiz, and Tadjik. This redrawing of the political map of central Asia was due to the desire to break down Moslem solidarity of the area and to isolate one nationality from another. As late as July 17, 1956, the Supreme Soviet incorporated one of the sixteen major Union republics (states of the Union) into the Russian Republic as an autonomous republic. Thus the status of the Karelo-Finnish Republic was suddenly downgraded and the territory of the Russian Republic greatly increased. There is no trace in Soviet documents of a referendum held among the Finns and their linguistic brothers, the Karelians, concerning their own wishes in the matter.

The USSR, as we may see from these facts, is a peculiar federal state. Although each nationality is formally granted in proportion to its size a union or autonomous republic, an autonomous region or national area, they have nothing to say about it or about the administration of their affairs. How could it be otherwise in view of the fact that the Soviet state is highly centralized despite its formally federal structure? Its planned and nationalized economy and the monopoly of power vested in the Communist Party do not allow for local self-government. It is much easier to pursue a nationality policy that disregards local aspirations if one rules the country with an iron rod held by a Party that is predominantly Russian in its entire membership, in the composition of its supreme agencies, the Central Committee and its Presidium, and which has Russian secretaries attached to its national sections (where one always finds a Russian together with a native as the main Party agents). After the purge of Malenkov, Molotov, Kaganovich, and Shepilov, the new Presidium was enlarged to include fifteen members. Eleven of them are Russians; four are of non-Russian origin. Even those four—the Armenian Mikoyan, the Finn Kuusinen, the Ukrainian Kirichenko, and the Uzbek Mukhitdinov, have never given any proof of taking care of the interests of their nationalities. Kirichenko is known for his diatribes against the Ukrainian "bourgeois" nationalism. In 1939–40, Kuusinen acquired the sad fame of traitor to his native country when he accepted the Russian appointment to head a Finnish people's government (seated behind the Soviet front) and whose only known act in that capacity was to surrender to Russia, on the very day of the proclamation of his "government," large slices of Finnish territory. The oft-quoted statements by Mukhitdinov, who took Marshal Zhukov's place on the Presidium, do not warrant the expectation that he will defend the interests of the Soviet-Asian nationalities. Although several non-Russians, e.g., the Ukrainian Korotchenko, the Latvian Kalnberzin, the Georgian Mzhavanadze, were in 1957 given positions of alternate members of the Party Presidium, this was the reward for their proven loyalty not to their countrymen but to the Russian "elder brothers." One does not find a non-Russian name among the army marshals; the heads of federal ministries and other departments are nearly all Russians. Membership in the Party Moscow (city and region) organization is almost as large as the total membership in the Ukraine although the population ratio is quite the opposite—about nine million people living in the Moscow region versus over forty million in the Ukrainian Republic. There can be no doubt that Russians are the bosses of the Party and the Soviet state, yet Lenin wanted to have one highly centralized Party for all Soviet nationalities.

Stalin reflected Lenin's thought when he said on April 29, 1917: "All the proletarians of all nations within one State should be organized in one indivisible, proletarian collective."[102] Hence: "The Bolshevik Party considers it harmful to the interests of the proletariat to organize national parties inside the [Soviet] territory, and a federative union of such parties."[103] The existence of one party is certainly harmful for the various Russian nationalities, which have no way of expressing their own desires through the channel of Communist parties composed of their own countrymen.

This system has resulted in many adverse consequences for non-Russians. *Sovetskaia Latvia* (in each Republic there is one principal newspaper in the local language and one in Russian) reported in December, 1952, on the national composition of delegates to the Latvian Party Congress: "Delegates belonged to ten nationalities: 50 per cent were Latvians, 40 per cent were Russians, and 10 per cent belonged to other nationalities." However, as we have seen, Soviet sources reported for Latvia, at least in 1940, very different ratios of nationalities: 76.5 per cent Latvians and only 11.5 per cent Russians.

The composition of Kazakh local soviets is even more revealing: "The membership of deputies to the local Soviets of the Kazakh SSR, elected in March 1955, included 29,393 Kazakhs, 23,040 Russians, 6,546 Ukrainians, 935 Tartars, 797 Tadjiks, 292 Uighurts, 286 Poles, 186 Dungans, and 98 Armenians."[104] The Kazakhs were a minority in their own local soviets. The reason is known, namely the vast resettlements of European populations to this central Asian republic, which thus had her ethnic composition radically changed. The figures for Russian and Ukrainian deputies give an idea of the magnitude of these mass immigrations. Two hundred and eighty-six Polish deputies, a figure reflecting a sizable number of Polish settlers, may cause the reader to wonder what the distant Poles, who have their own state, are doing among the Kazakhs. These settlers are the remnants of over one million Poles who had been forcibly deported by the Soviet Government in 1939–1941 after the annexation of eastern Poland. They were sent either to correctional labor camps or resettled in distant territories, Kazakhstan among others. A few hundred thousand were allowed to quit Soviet territory after the Nazi attack on the USSR; a great many repatriated after the last war, and others are now being repatriated; some still live in distant Soviet lands where they had no desire to settle.

The Kazakh paper *Kazakh Adebiyeti* carried an unusual (under Soviet conditions) complaint by Kazakh intellectuals. They bitterly listed the following: the neglect of the Kazakh language, the inconsiderate attitude towards the interests of Kazakh toilers, the employment of Soviet officials who did not know the Kazakh language, the silencing of protests by accusations of bourgeois nationalism, the relegation to limbo of the Kazakh literary heritage, and the non-admittance to local universities of such Kazakh applicants who could not pass the preliminary examination, given only in Russian, because of their inadequate knowledge of the language of their masters.[105] If one takes into consideration the severity of the Soviet regime, he may take for granted that the Kazakh intellectuals would not have dared to report inaccurate facts; it took unusual courage on their part and that of the editors of the journal to state the true facts. The Russian newspaper *Kazakhstanskaia Pravda* immediately accused them of spreading false propaganda and demanded that sanctions should be taken:

The journal has caused through its articles superfluous and ill-founded disputes among sections of the Kazakh intelligentsia and workers on the cultural front. . . . All this shows that the editorial board of the journal *Kazakh Adebiyeti* has succumbed to the influence of some politically immature people with Philistine views and has been unable to resist national narrow-mindedness and backward and unsound moods. . . . Not only the authors of the articles but also the editorial staff of the journal *Kazakh Adebiyeti*, its editor-in-chief, comrade S. Maulenov, the administrative board of the Union of Soviet Writers of Kazakhstan and its former president, comrade G. Mystafin, are all guilty without doubt of committing these serious errors. . . . The Union of Soviet Writers of Kazakhstan are bound critically to reappraise the mistakes committed by *Kazakh Adebiyeti* and to deduce the unavoidable conclusions concerning improvement in the leadership of its press organ.[106]

Stern admonitions, sanctions (obviously the president of the Union of Kazakh Writers was dismissed, since he is referred to as former president), and the order to keep silent, were the only answer of the anti-colonialist Party to the complaints of an Asian nationality.

12. Resettlements

A nationality may survive foreign oppression if it is able to retain its own nationally conscious educated class, to cultivate its language, the last bulwark of national identity, and if its homeland is not heavily infiltrated by alien settlements. The Soviet policy has, intentionally or not, used all these three weapons in undermining the cohesion of non-Russian nationalities. The educated classes are subject to a Russifying influence; Russian slowly pushes back the use of native languages, while mass resettlements disrupt national cohesion. As a result, the Soviet Government has made the disentanglement of national problems in many of its republics almost impossible.

The policy of Russian and Ukrainian migration to the provinces inhabited by alien nationalities is not new, for it was practiced by the Tsarist Government. It is impossible to make a fair distinction between the results of the economic development of those provinces which required the influx of labor and a conscious nationality policy. In Tsarist and Soviet times both motivations have played their role. The Russian Decree of 1868, which proclaimed the whole land of central Asian nomads state property, allowed for the "establishment by Tsardom of a colonizing fund for the resettlement of the 'superfluous' population from [European] Russia."[107] The total population of Kazakhstan increased from 2,465,000 to 3,835,000 during the short period between 1897 and 1911, but the Russian percentage rose from 20 per cent to 40 per cent. The Russians also settled on the land, but their share in the urban population increased from 15 per cent to 76 per cent during the same period of time. This policy has since been continued by the Soviet Government in central Asia and elsewhere. Between 1926 and 1939, some three million people migrated from European USSR to new industrial centers opened in the Urals, Siberia, and the Soviet Far East; 1,700,000 new settlers came to central Asia during the same period. Russians were resettled during and after the last war on the newly conquered territories of the Karelian Isthmus, Southern Sakhalin, the Kurile Islands, and former northeastern Prussia. Each discovery of natural resources, each industrial or agricultural development, has brought in its wake new waves of Russian and Ukrainian settlers. For instance this was true in 1932 after the finding of oil in the Bashkir Autonomous Republic and the discovery of coal and oil in the Komi Autonomous Republic in 1929. The resettlement brought with it important political benefits for the Russians. For instance implanted Russians in the northeastern part of East Prussia outflanked the Balts, cut them off from the Western nations, and secured the Russian hold on the Baltic coast. The same is true of the Russian colonization of Southern Sakhalin, the Kurile Islands, and strategically and economically important central Asia.

The Kazakhs have been the worst victims of that policy; they have been reduced to the status of a minority in their ancestral homeland. The Russians represented there, as early as 1939, 47 per cent of the total population;

when one adds other non-Kazakh nationalities, it appears the Kazakh numbered less than half of the population. The 1926 Soviet census gave the total number of Kazakhs living in Kazakhstan as 3,627,612 people; the 1939 census, which carefully avoided giving any figures about the national composition of the Republics and produced only total figures of each nationality for the whole Soviet territory, mentioned the figure of 3,099,000 for all Kazakhs living in the USSR within and beyond the borders of Kazakhstan. The same total of all Kazakhs living in 1926 in the USSR was 3,968,000. The Soviet sources never explained what happened to the 900,000 missing Kazakhs. Did they perish during the period of mass collectivization of agriculture, more disastrous for nomads than for settled peasants?

The recent policy of plowing the so-called virgin lands brought new waves of Russian and Ukrainian settlers to territories mostly inhabited by other nationalities. A Soviet source reports on Kazakhstan: "Approximately 600,000 people (mechanics, agricultural specialists, Party and Soviet workers) came to our Republic from the Russian Federation, Ukraine, Byelorussia, and other Republics, for permanent work."[108] This was just one resettlement among many that have taken place here and elsewhere during the Soviet rule. It is small comfort for the Kazakhs, who are losing their own homeland, to know that this vast immigration helped in the cultivation of 20 million hectares of virgin lands.

The hapless condition of the Kazakhs, the principal victim of the policy of Russification and Russian resettlement, may be gathered from these figures:

More than 1,600,000 people . . . study at [9,000 schools]. About 500,000 Kazakh children study at the Kazakh schools in their own instruction language. . . . The Kazakh youth constitutes one-third of all students at special-secondary and higher learning schools.[109]

One-third of the young generation living in Kazakhstan are Kazakhs, or, rather, one-third are those Kazakh children and youngsters who still enjoy the privilege of learning at seventh-grade and tenth-grade schools in their native language and are admitted to professional-secondary schools and universities in their ancestral land, whichever interpretation one prefers. This is the pattern for other numerically small nationalities which are being not only Russified but swamped by large Russian immigrations.

Small wonder that one finds large Russian settlements in all republics, which are wide open to Russian immigration as enforced by the Soviet Gov-

ernment. There is lack of recent Soviet statistics, but Soviet sources sometimes make fairly precise references:

Russians and Ukrainians represent 4.4 per cent in the Armenian Republic.
The Russian population has grown during the Soviet period in the cities.
Skilled workers, technicians, and engineers are being sent to Armenia.[110]

In the Ukraine:

Russians occupy second place according to their numbers. . . . The non-
Ukrainian population lives mostly in the cities and workers' settlements.
Villages are, with small exceptions, entirely Ukrainian.[111]

In Lithuania:

Russians who live principally in the cities number over 10 per cent.[112]

In Latvia Russians represent 12 per cent of the population.[113] Russians
number 10 per cent of the population of the Moldavian Republic.[114]

An important part of the population of Kazakhstan is composed of Russians
living in large numbers in all cities of Kazakhstan and also in the rural
areas.[115]

Russians constitute 11.6 per cent versus 65.1 per cent Uzbeks in Uzbekistan,
the rest being other nationalities such as Tadjiks, Kazakhs, Kara-Kalpaks,
Tartars, Kirghizs, etc.[116] The population of Uzbekistan has quickly increased, one of the reasons being "the influx of population from other
regions, principally from the RSFSR, to the Uzbekistani new industrial
establishments in the cities and to the districts of new irrigation."[117] Russians form 10 per cent of the population of the Tadjik Republic.[118] In
Turkmenistan, "Russians live mainly in the cities, but Russian settlements
exist also in the villages on the frontier of Iran and Afghanistan."[119] These
rural settlements have an obvious strategic objective.

13. Linguistic Russification

The other Soviet attack on the cohesion of various nationalities follows
the linguistic line. Lenin was opposed to any official state language. He
wrote in 1913:

... the Social-Democrats demand an unconditional equality of rights for all nationalities and fight against all and sundry privileges of one or several nationalities. They reject in particular the concept of a "state" language.[120]

He was no less precise in 1914:

We support, of course, the idea that every inhabitant of Russia should have the opportunity of learning the great Russian language. But one thing we surely do not want: the factor of *compulsion*. We do not want to prod people with a stick to enter paradise.[121]

Stalin knew very well the importance of language for every nationality:

The multi-million masses of the people may flourish and develop culturally, politically, and economically only by using their own national language.[122]

Yet it was Stalin who did his utmost to spread the knowledge of Russian by compulsion. A decree issued by the Soviet Government on March 13, 1938, introduced the compulsory teaching of Russian in the whole Soviet territory. Here was the way to implement Stalin's idea of having one regional language for the whole Soviet Union.[123]

There are at present two types of schools in each non-Russian part of the Soviet Union: the one with the Russian language of instruction, and the other with the native language, having also an intensive course in Russian. An official Soviet handbook published in 1956 provided detailed data on the distribution of those schools. Out of the total of 193,963 schools of all descriptions (elementary, secondary, technical, higher, etc.), 114,908 used Russian as the language of instruction, 7,909 both Russian and a native language, and 79,055 only a local language. In the academic year 1955–56, 65 per cent of all students learned in Russian and 35 per cent in other languages. This exceeded by 5 per cent the Russian percentage in the total population. Instruction was carried in 59 languages. The percentage of schools using a non-Russian language of instruction was as follows (for the various republics): the RSFSR—10, Ukraine—86, Byelorussia—95, Uzbekistan—94, Kazakhstan—57, Georgia—93, Azerbaijan—95, Lithuania—97, Moldavia—73, Latvia—79, Kirghizia—81, Tadjikstan—98, Armenia—95, Turkmenia—93, and Estonia—94. More revealing are the percentages of students attending schools with Russian as the language of instruction: in the RSFSR—94 per cent, in Ukraine—26, in Byelorussia—22, in Uzbekistan—20, in Kazakhstan—66, in Georgia—20, in Azerbaijan—23, in Lithu-

ania—11, in Moldavia—33, in Latvia—33, in Kirghizia—49, in Tadjikstan
—16, in Armenia—9, in Turkmenia—21, and in Estonia—22. The apparent discrepancy between the percentages of schools using Russian as the
language of instruction and the much higher percentages of students learning in Russian is easy to explain; the total number of all schools also includes small elementary rural schools with few children enrolled in each.
In every instance the number of students learning in Russian exceeds the
proportion of Russians in the total population of a republic.

These figures reveal not only the advanced process of Russification of
local populations but also the effect of Russian influx into the various republics. The tragic plight of the Kazakhs is clearly expressed in this eloquent figure of 66 per cent of all students studying in Russian. Even the
figure of 94 per cent for the Russian Republic exceeds by far the 80 per
cent of Russians in that republic. The Kirghizian situation, with 49 per
cent of students learning in Russian, is not much better than the Kazakh.
The 33 per cent for Latvia probably reflects a heavy Russian immigration
since the last war. Except for Lithuania, Armenia, and Tadjikstan, the remaining republics have an average of 20 to 26 per cent of all students learning in Russian.

It would be misleading to reverse these percentages and thus deduce the
percentages for students learning in the principal language of their republic because a fraction of those students are taught in other languages spoken
in each republic by the minority groups. For instance five languages of
instruction are used in Ukraine in addition to Ukrainian and Russian—
in Uzbekistan, seven; in Kazakhstan, six; in Tadjikistan, six; except for the
RSFSR, where 45 instruction languages are used, other republics have
from two to seven languages of instruction in addition to the Russian and
the mother tongue of each republic.[124]

These statistics are misleading in one respect, namely, they produce
round figures for all schools, from the elementary to the universities. The
worst situation exists at the universities and similar schools of higher learning from which graduate the intelligentsia, the core of each nationality the
world over. People in former and present colonial possessions have justly
complained of the lack or inadequacy of higher-learning facilities for their
native youth under colonial rule. It is true that the colonial Powers have
not been inclined to promote the growth of a well-trained educated class,
such as would then lead in the promotion of independence or self-government. However, this problem was solved for most of those countries by their

accession to independence or self-government. Great Britain has been modifying the policy in her remaining colonies by opening colleges and by making it easier for native youth to learn at British or foreign universities.

The anti-colonialist Power is not, on the other hand, so eager to produce native intelligentsia at universities using the native language of instruction. Although precise Soviet data are lacking, one may say on the basis of foreign observations that the immense majority of Soviet universities and similar schools use only Russian as the language of instruction. Moreover, non-Russian young people are handicapped in another way. They have intense teaching of Russian at their native schools, but the teaching personnel is not always the best. N. A. Mukhitdinov said in 1956:

The situation regarding teaching of Russian at the general-education [secondary] schools of Uzbekistan harbors serious shortcomings. Many students have not mastered practically and to the required extent oral Russian, cannot freely read Russian literature, express grammatically their thoughts in Russian. The lack of knowledge of Russian on the part of many alumni of [secondary] schools results in the known difficulties which they encounter in furthering their education and in mastering contemporary techniques.[125]

What are these difficulties in furthering education beyond the secondary school? The answer is to be found in Soviet regulations for university entrance examinations. According to the regulations for the academic year 1956–57, each applicant in any republic for admission to any university or similar school must take a written examination in Russian and Russian literature. The required syllabus for Russian literature is very exacting, only an applicant with a thorough familiarity with that literature being able to pass the examination, so that a Russian applicant is obviously favored by these regulations. If an applicant applies for admission to a higher-learning school with non-Russian language of instruction, he must pass the same examination in Russian and Russian literature plus an additional examination on his knowledge of the native language of instruction, but he is not required to take an examination in the native literature. Thus a Lithuanian applying for admission to the Kaunas University, which is one of the few native universities using a non-Russian language of instruction, must know perfectly Russian and Russian literature but is required to know only the Lithuanian language, while he may be ignorant of his national literature.

The 1956 regulations for admission to all secondary-professional schools included a written examination in Russian and an oral examination in

Russian and Russian literature. If the language of instruction at these schools is non-Russian, the applicants must also take an oral examination in the non-Russian language, but only within the program of a non-Russian seventh-grade school. Again the non-Russians are discriminated against, since Russian applicants, of course, know their own language fluently.

In both universities and secondary-professional schools, the examinations in Russian and Russian literature are exacting; those in the native language of instruction are comparatively easy.[126] The admission regulations contain a very revealing rule: "Those applicants who enter the higher schools of the Republics where instruction is given in Russian are not subject to an examination in the language of the Republic."[127] Since most of the universities in non-Russian republics teach in Russian, the students, either Russian or native, are not even required to be familiar with the language of the surrounding population. This is the typical colonial superiority complex.

Of course learning Russian at the secondary school does not present much difficulty for Slavic-speaking Ukrainians and Byelorussians or for the youth of those non-Slavic republics, such as the Baltic or the Transcaucasian, where knowledge of Russian has been widespread for several generations. The real loser is the central Asian, for whom Russian is as foreign as any other European language; moreover, knowledge of Russian having not yet thoroughly permeated central Asia, the native teacher of Russian often has an inadequate mastery of the language he teaches.

Russian has a large share in the curriculum of a Soviet secondary school with non-Russian language of instruction. At present, the seventh-grade school is the universal school, but the Soviet Government proceeds gradually with the extension of eight-grade education for all children. A child attending a seventh-grade school must learn Russian starting with the second grade (at the age of eight). A youngster graduating from a seventh-grade school is expected to speak fairly well and to read Russian. As a Soviet pedagogue puts it:

Children learn [in the non-Russian schools] how to read and write in their native language, the latter language being the medium of instruction and also a subject in itself. Students of elementary schools, besides their own language, compulsorily learn Russian beginning with the second grade.... As the total number of week-hours is almost the same in the Russian and non-Russian schools, teaching of the native language and arithmetic takes in the second, third, and fourth grades [of non-Russian schools] fewer hours than at the Russian schools. By the end of their studies at an elementary school children should master the Russian vocabulary and grammar.[128]

Taking as an example a secondary ten-grade school with the Ukrainian language of instruction, we may observe the following timetable:

Grades:	I	II	III	IV	V	VI	VII	VIII	IX	X
Ukrainian language and literature	13	10	10	6	7-6	6-5	5	3	3	3
Russian language and literature	—	3	4	4	5-6	5-6	6	5-4	4	4[129]

The timetable differs in the case of Russian-instruction schools located on territory of the Ukrainian Republic:

Grades:	I	II	III	IV	V	VI	VII	VIII	IX	X
Russian language and literature	13	10	10	6	7-6	6-5	6	5-4	4	4
Ukrainian language and literature	—	3	4	4	5-6	5-6	5	3	3	3[130]

These timetables disallow the conclusion that Russian language and literature are treated as neglected orphans at non-Russian schools. The time reserved for these subjects during all ten grades amounts to two-thirds of that given to the native language. However, the Party is not yet satisfied, and the drive for the intensification of and improvement in teaching Russian to other nationalities goes on. N. A. Mukhitdinov, as usual, set the pace:

The Russian language is for us Uzbeks a second native language, one of the most important factors in further raising the level of our culture. . . . The carrying out of the recommendations, adopted by the inter-republican scientific conference on the improving of teaching of Russian, a conference that took place last August in Tashkent, will allow for great improvement in the teaching of Russian at the national schools.[131]

The Party approach is best reflected in his characterizing Russian not as a useful official language of the state but as a second *native* language.

The conference to which Mukhitdinov referred was held for the benefit of teachers, teachers colleges, and ministries of education of all Turkic-speaking (Azerbaijan, Uzbekistan, Turkmenia, Kirghizia, and Kazakhstan) and Tadjik republics. But guests from other non-Russian republics attended. Mukhitdinov made the key address, in which he submitted the current Party line:

The Russian language has played a great role in the assimilation by peoples of Central Asia, Azerbaijan, Kazakhstan, and others of the Soviet Union, of the superior world culture, first of all, the Russian culture. Russian is the powerful means of intercourse and of consolidation of friendship among the peoples of our country, and of their internationalist upbringing. The trend among the Uzbek, Tadjik, Kazakh, Azerbaijani, Kirghiz, Turkmenian, and other peoples towards mastering Russian and acquiring knowledge of the culture of the Russian nation was born in the past when those peoples began to have economic and cultural relations with Russia. After the annexation of the Transcaucasus, Kazakhstan, and Central Asia by Russia, which was a deeply progressive phenomenon, this trend among local populations towards both intercourse with leading representatives of the Russian nation and the learning of Russian, incomparably increased. ... The Russian language has become for all of us a second native language and one of the most important means of uplifting our national culture, learning, literature and arts, a means of enriching the vocabulary of our national languages. ... Children of all nationalities have now the opportunity successfully to learn Russian at all schools. Russian has become the national property and the spiritual weapon of each Soviet citizen, independently of his nationality, in the struggle for the construction of a communist society. ... We cannot but feel upset by the fact that students of many Uzbek and other non-Russian schools of general education have not sufficiently and practically mastered oral Russian and are unable correctly to formulate their thoughts in Russian.[132]

The man who thus spoke was not a nationalistic colonial governor but the spokesman of an "internationalist" Party. Yet he himself conceded in another speech: "It is a serious shortcoming that there are only a few textbooks in Uzbek for schools and universities, especially in the technological disciplines."[133] Small wonder that most universities and secondary technical schools in the republics have to use Russian as the language of instruction; of course native languages are used for teaching local philology and literature.

A meeting of Tadjik intelligentsia held in November, 1956, brought out some results of this emphasis on Russian as the language of superior culture:

Writer Djalol Ikrami stressed the fact that one found in our literature and especially in the periodicals a lack of precision, and a slovenliness, often the consequence of the lack of knowledge by our translators and journalists of their native language. ... Comrade Ikrami drew attention to the incompetent teaching of native language and literature at the schools and universities of our Republic. Teachers, who graduate from the teachers' colleges, frequently poorly know their native language and literature.[134]

The Tadjik poet, Dekhoti, is quoted at the same meeting:

Comrade Dekhoti quite sharply presented the problem of learning Tadjik by leading Party and Soviet officials. He remarked that there were among them a certain number who treated their native language with contempt, justifying it by their good knowledge of Russian. Of course, Russian is for us a second native language. We all must learn it. But this does not at all mean that we must forget our own native language.[135]

The hammering on the superiority of Russian culture thus breeds quite naturally a complex of inferiority among other nationalities. It takes only one or two steps from feeling inferior as a Tadjik or an Uzbek to forgetting the native language and eventually becoming a member of the superior Russian nationality.

Ikrami and Dekhoti might have been rewarded, after the conference, for their civic courage by a sharp Party reminder of the danger of falling into "bourgeois" nationalism. Did not Mukhitdinov make a great effort to dispel any illusions that the downgrading of Stalin implied giving a free hand to local patriotism? Did he not say:

In relation to the condemnation of the cult of personality and the liquidation of its harmful consequences, some people begin to say that no nationalism allegedly existed in the past in Uzbekistan and that none exists today. Such attitudes are fundamentally wrong and dangerous. We must fight any form of bourgeois nationalism, nationalist exclusiveness and parochialism.[136]

The Soviet journal for schoolteachers pointed in 1957 to a similar neglect of native language in Kazakhstan: "It is quite justly said that very little time is reserved for teaching native language and native literature at the fifth through tenth grades of the Kazakh secondary schools."[137] Eulogies of Russian never end. A handbook for the principals of schools of the RSFSR, where 20 per cent of people are of non-Russian origin, says:

Our language is that of the great Russian people. . . . The learning of Russian gives to students access to those cultural treasures which have been and continue to be accumulated by the great Russian people. Students who are acquainted with the greatness and might of Russian, are enabled to understand the inexhaustible forces of its creator. Thus the teaching of Russian fulfills the task of educating children in the feeling of Soviet patriotism and national pride.[138]

An author says: "[Russian] . . . is a mighty and invigorating source of spiritual development for all the peoples of the Soviet land."[139] A zealous Uzbek tries not to be outbidden: "Russian is a great, mighty, true, and free language."[140] Another native Asian does his best to justify retrospectively the Tsarist educational policy in the central Asian colonies, which bore a strange analogy to the present Soviet, though much less efficient:

The Reform [of 1868] planned the opening of the so-called Russian-native schools in order to withdraw the native population [of Turkestan] from the influence of mullahs who taught children only how to write in Arabic and how to read the Koran. These schools aimed at training literate officials from among the natives who could then become interpreters and rural mayors. The foundation of these schools was a progressive step, for it opened the door to the knowledge of Russian and world cultures.[141]

This overbearing nationalism naturally befits the new Soviet Russian intelligentsia. Their parents, or at best grandparents, were illiterate peasants or workers who knew nothing about the beauty of the Russian language and the richness and originality of Russian culture. The children and grandchildren discovered the treasures accumulated by their national ancestors. They themselves have built up by their own sacrifice and perseverance a mighty great Power. Their newly acquired status of educated class has produced a pride in the discovered achievements of previous Russian generations and in their own successes and also an inferiority complex shared by all "nouveau-riches." Such an inferiority complex usually breeds its consoling companion, a superiority complex; hence they are inclined to boast about everything—their Russian nationality, the might of the Soviet state, and the progressive nature of a regime which has given them the opportunity of ascending the social ladder. Khrushchev, with his incessant bragging, is a typical representative of this ruling class; the son of an illiterate industrial worker and a self-made man, he reached the crest of Soviet society. No wonder that he and the Soviet Russian intelligentsia feel dizzy at the sight of a Russian culture unknown to their parents and grandparents and of the power of their native land. This spectacle would be both moving and comical but for its tragic side—the existence of other Soviet nationalities, which must crawl before the great Russian nation as though they were ancient barbarians conquered by mighty Rome.

The attack on the national cohesion of these nationalities proceeds on another front that is of special interest to central Asians. They had to accept Russian Cyrillic script instead of their own Arabic, and their vocabulary is constantly changed by the gradual elimination of words of Arabic and Persian origin and their replacement by newly coined words taken over from Russian. This makes the learning of Russian easier, assists the forgetting of the ancient background of their own cultures, and facilitates the gradual adoption of Russian nationality as their own. The Arabic alphabet is looked down on by official Soviet scholars. A well-known historian writes:

Regardless of its complexity, the Arabic alphabet has been used for many centuries by several nations whose languages it hardly fitted. Even now some Eastern nations (Iranians, Afghans, etc.) use it, in addition to the Arabs. According to the claims of Moslem clergy, the Koran was allegedly sent from heaven to Prophet Mahommet written as "the divine word" (*kalomi ollokh*) [in Arabic: Kalimat Allah]; hence the script in which it is written was attributed a divine origin.[142]

The Party did not like this relation between the Arabic alphabet and Islam and liked even less the fact that Moslem central Asians had traditionally looked beyond the frontiers towards other Moslems, among whom were their linguistic brothers, the Turks or the Iranians. Pan-Islamism and Pan-Turkism are the twin nightmares of the Party. The Party is, moreover, committed to a militant atheism; a Soviet pedagogical textbook has this to say about the nature of school upbringing:

Atheistic education constitutes an integral part of moral upbringing. It aims at accustoming students to a truly scientific view of the evolution of nature and society and to the struggle with all sorts of religious superstitions and prejudices, the survivals of an alien ideology and former conditions in the minds of some sections of the population. The scientific-materialistic world outlook and Communist morality are indissolubly linked together; they are inculcated in practical education on one and the same plane; this applies in particular to the atheistic education of youth.[143]

A very effective way of cutting off the central Asian youth from the Koran and Islam, their own ancient Islamic culture, and all thoughts of a spiritual community with other Moslems or Turkic and Iranian linguistic brothers was to eliminate the Arabic alphabet. It did not matter much that they would be thus disabled for reading their own pre-Revolutionary literature, accumulated through centuries; after all, would they not have fewer reasons for harking back to the period of their own independence? The Party inspired a "spontaneous" movement in favor of adopting the Latin alphabet. It was so spontaneous that an All-Union Central Committee for the new alphabet was organized in 1927 to direct the propaganda.[144] The printing presses got busy publishing works in the Latin alphabet. "The reactionary clergy proclaimed the adversaries of the Arabic script 'Kafirs', i.e., infidels."[145] But the Party overcame native resistance, and the Latin alphabet was generally and compulsorily introduced by governmental decrees.[146] Of course the Latin alphabet made the struggle against illiteracy much easier. The objectionable part of the reform was the fact that it was imposed from above by a government composed of people who were alien to central Asian culture and history.

The Party, however, had bad luck. Turkey also introduced the Latin alphabet in the late twenties. Thus the same alphabet could again serve as a link between the Turkic peoples of Soviet central Asia and the RSFSR and the Turks, who were disposed to count them as other Turks speaking different dialects of Turkish. Moreover, the Latin alphabet did not help much in learning Russian; the Party decided to replace the short-lived Latin alphabet by the Russian.

It was not accidental that a broad movement began in the late thirties in several national Republics, including Uzbekistan, in favor of the passage from the Latin to the Russian alphabet. As a matter of fact, the experience of rapidly developing cultural construction, the beneficial influence of the first-class Russian culture on the expansion of cultures of peoples of the USSR, the permanent contact of those peoples with Russian people, and the need for their further cultural development, demonstrated that a new alphabet founded on the Russian script promised a higher level of evolution for Uzbek literature during the historical stage under consideration. The Supreme Soviet of the Uzbek Soviet Socialist Republic adopted on May 8, 1940, a statute which replaced the Latin alphabet by the Russian, and ordered the passage from one to the other alphabet in official administration, in the press and in schools, to take place within the same year.[147]

The other Turkic- and Tadjik-speaking republics, as well as the People's Republic of Mongolia, performed the same quick operation in 1939–40. As two Turkmenian highest officials of education put it quite candidly: "The passage from the Latin to the new national alphabet founded on the Russian script made it easier for the Turkmenian people to learn Russian and to absorb the culture of Russian people."[148] It is noteworthy that one of the two above-mentioned officials is a Turkman and minister of culture in his republic, but the other is a Russian and, at the same time, a Turkmenian vice-minister of culture. This is a typical example of the Soviet policy of having in the non-Russian areas a native as a straw man and a Russian as his controlling assistant.

A Russian linguist found, *a posteriori*, an additional reason for replacing the Latin alphabet by the Russian, a reason which could fully justify a similar reform among the Balts. He discovered that the Russian and other alphabets derived from Greek were definitely superior to the Latin because the Greeks of antiquity were endowed with "the rare gift of precision and a very subtle feeling for phonetics; they expressed the nuances of pronunciation with an unusual perspicacity."[149] The Finns, Estonians, Latvians, and Lithuanians have so far been left in peace; they continue to use the Latin alphabet. The same is true of Armenians and Georgians, who are allowed to write in their own ancient scripts.

The introduction of the Russian alphabet also made easier the carrying out of another linguistic policy, namely, forming new words from Russian roots and simultaneously eliminating words of Arabic and Persian origin and often, as well, of purely local derivation. A historian of Uzbek culture gives as examples such Russian words being introduced in Uzbek after some adjustments to local phonetics: *bonka* (bank), *pochta* (post), *pero* (pen), *tilgirom* (telegram), *dukhtur* (doctor), *zovud* (plant), *anzhirnai* (engineer), *poez* (train), *moshina* (engine), *adris* (address), *iskalod* (warehouse), *istakan* (glass), *kanvert* (envelope), *kantsert* (concert), *kolkhoz* (collective farm), *sovkhoz* (state farm), *brigada* (brigade), *zveno* (link), *traktor* (tractor), *kultivatsia* (cultivation), *dizel* (Diesel), *vint* (screw), *bolt* (bolt), *gaika* (nut), *shatun* (master-rod), *gidrostantsiia* (hydraulic power station), etc.[150] It is not his fault that almost all these words in Russian are of Western derivation; of course he does not mention this.

The reverse side of the coin is the elimination of words of even native origin under the pretext of their feudal or religious meaning:

The Uzbek language has freed itself in the process of its development from such words and idioms which were used only by the upper layers of feudal society but were not understood by the broad masses of people. For instance, such words as *lisson* (language), *mushtarak* (common), *mafkura* (ideology), *mussodira* (confiscation), *azhnabi* (stranger, foreigner), and others of the same type were eliminated from the Uzbek vocabulary and replaced by corresponding words. . . . Likewise, thanks to the successful development of socialist culture of the Uzbek people, words of religious ritual derivation die out and cease to circulate; contemporary Uzbek youth has no notion of their meaning.[151]

These samples of eliminated words have corresponding words in modern Russian and do not denote any feudal past. But they were a part of the ancient literate language, which was, of course, spoken there, as in Russia,

by "the upper layer of society." Why they should not be used by the new
Uzbek intelligentsia, since their Russian social counterparts do so, is a
Party secret.

The Uzbek and other central Asian languages contain many words of
Arabic and Persian derivation for the same reason that European languages use many words of Greek and Latin origin. Language registers the
history of the cultural roots of each people. Even the same Soviet historian
who favors the elimination of Persian and Arabic words from his native
Uzbek inadvertently remarks: "No Uzbek who daily uses these words would
think of them as being of Persian or any other derivation."[152] Yet the
process of de-Arabization and de-Iranization of Uzbek proceeds to make
room for an ever increasing infiltration of Russian words. The statistical
test of the proportions of Arabic-Persian and Russian words used in the
Uzbek newspapers at various times of the Soviet rule produced the following interesting data:

	1923	1934	1940
Persian-Arabic words	37.4%	27%	25%
Russian words	2 %	12%	15%[153]

At the time when central Asians were still relatively free in expressing
their aspirations, there was a distinct trend towards a purification of language, not by replacing Arabic-Persian words by Russian, but by reviving
ancient Uzbek words. The "reactionary," as they are called by Soviet
sources, Uzbek nationalists wanted, after the Russian revolution of 1905,
to free their country from Russian domination but at the same time to
modernize and adjust it to the contemporary world. They had in mind exactly the same objectives as were pursued by Atatürk in Turkey, or are
pursued by national leaders of awakening Asia and Africa in our time.
However, Atatürk, when he was friendly to Soviet Russia (as every Asian
leader hostile to the West), was "progressive" in Soviet terminology, while
Uzbek nationalists are called reactionaries. The only criterion consists in
their being anti-Western or anti-Russian.

A biased Uzbek historian says:

Dzhadids [Uzbek pre-1917 nationalists] proceeded with the reform of old-
fashioned schools by introducing modern lay disciplines and by revising
educational methods. . . . Dzhadid modern schools were permeated with
the spirit of bourgeois nationalism. Dzhadids were spreading through their

press reactionary and counter-revolutionary ideas. . . . The idea of the secession of Turkestan from Russia was popular among the *Dzhadids*.[154]

If one were surprised by the word "counter-revolutionary," used in reference to the events of the Tsarist period of 1905–1917, and did not understand how a central Asian could be counter-revolutionary before the October Revolution, he should realize that the very fact of being anti-Russian at that time is now viewed as a counter-revolutionary phenomenon.

After the Bolshevik Revolution, the Uzbek intelligentsia tried (in 1918–1922) to purify the Uzbek language by reviving the vocabulary of ancient literary language spoken in the great period of Uzbek culture, the so-called Chagatai language:

They fought in particular against borrowing international and Russian words. After the victory of the Soviet authority over the armed counter-revolution [the native *Basmachi* movement] . . . the Communist Party unmasked all counter-revolutionary groups of bourgeois nationalists, including *Chagatai Gurungi*.[155]

Later the "bourgeois" nationalists appeared in the ranks of central Asian Communists:

. . . the bourgeois-nationalists, allegedly defending "purity of language," tried to put sticks in the wheels and to do harm. They wanted in various ways to eliminate from the Uzbek language all words borrowed from other languages, especially international and Russian terms. Some of them propagandized the anti-scientific Pan-Turkic "theory" of a "common language" which had never existed, and others promoted the Pan-Islamic "theory" of "enriching" the language by using words and idioms taken from the jargon of the upper layers of society.[156]

One theory mentioned by the author referred to the concept of unity in the whole of Turkic Turkestan. It was smashed by dividing the administrative division of Turkestan into four republics and by keeping Kazakhstan as a separate unit. Since that time, the Soviet Government has carefully promoted the concept that central Asian Turkic peoples under its rule—Uzbeks, Turkmenians, Kazakhs, Kirghizs, and others—were completely distinct nationalities but that all of them were close to the Slavic Russians.

The other theory consisted in purifying the language by safeguarding the linguistic treasures of the literary Uzbek, which the zealous Communist Uzbek historian calls jargon, without stopping to think that the literate

Russian written by Pushkin and Lermontov, who also belonged to the upper layer of the society, could by the same token be qualified as jargon.

14. Native Literature and Scholars

The net result is a new Uzbek literature. Its spirit may be gauged by this poem written by a contemporary Soviet Uzbek:

> O Russia! Russia, Mighty Fatherland!
> Limitlessly immense like the sky.
> Even the sun, until it wanders around half the globe,
> Cannot embrace Thee at once with its beams.
>
> O Russia! Russia! I am Thy son, not just a guest;
> Thou art my native land, paternal shelter,
> I am Thy son, Thine in my flesh and bone,
> Ready to shed my blood for Thee.[157]

Thus for the poet Hamid Alimdzhan it is Russia, not the socialist Soviet Union, and certainly not Uzbekistan, that is his native land. An Uzbek historian is correct in saying that this poem is "remarkable." It is remarkable as an example of Soviet Russifying colonialist policy.

To be sure, writing in the local languages appears, but the native culture must be socialist in content, and most of these publications are therefore simply translations from Russian classics and current Soviet literature:

The Kazakh people study in their native language works by Marxist-Leninist classics, and the classics of Russian and world *belles-lettres*. One cannot mention without a feeling of pride that 35 volumes of V. I. Lenin's Works and many classic books of *belles-lettres* have been translated into Kazakh and published in mass editions. . . . The translations from Russian into Kazakh of the political, artistic, pedagogical, and scientific-technological literature have played an exceptionally great role in the development of Kazakh language, in the expansion of its vocabulary, and the enrichment of the culture of our people. . . . Translation of outstanding works of Russian literature into Kazakh, and of works by Kazakh writers and learned men into Russian must remain our primary task.[158]

It is much better to read the "socialist" literature, including Russian classics, in the original. The intense teaching of Russian helps in accomplishing this goal:

The peoples of Central Asia, Turkmenians, Uzbeks, Tadjiks, Kirghizs, Kara-Kalpaks, learn Russian and read in Russian the works by the founders of Marxism-Leninism and the works by Russian and universal-literature classics, as well as scientific books.[159]

This passage reads as if not only Lenin but also the two other classics of Marxism-Leninism, Marx and Engels, wrote in Russian.

Russian books and their total circulation (number of copies printed) dominate the Soviet market, as may be seen from the following table:

	1940	1950	1954	1955
Proportion of Russian books	75%	71%	70%	72%
Proportion of printed copies of Russian books	75%	78%	79%	81%[160]

While the percentage of Russian books among all Soviet-published books has remained more or less stationary, the total number of copies in which they have been printed has followed consistently an ascending curve. This denotes the success of Soviet policy in making Soviet citizens of other nationalities bilingual and making them read in Russian rather than in their native languages. The same Soviet statistical handbook from which this table is taken shows in other tables that Ukrainians had an appreciable number of copies printed in 1955 in their own language—63,006,000 by comparison to 776,438,000 copies in Russian printed only in the RSFSR and without counting Russian books printed in the other republics. The other nationalities, less numerous it is true, show from 2,643,000 copies to 16,867,000 copies printed in their languages in the same year.[161]

The handbook produces figures for so-called intellectual workers (scholars, university professors, specialists with higher education). The table is interesting for various reasons and is worth reproducing:

Russians	144,285	Buriats	168
Ukrainians	21,762	Dagestanis	231
Byelorussians	4,077	Kabardinians	70
Uzbeks	1,577	Karelians and Finns	132
Kazakhs	1,172	Komis	188
Georgians	5,271	Maris	78
Azerbaijanis	2,779	Mordovians	212
Lithuanians	1,741	Ossetins	343
Moldavians	305	Tartars	2,142
Latvians	1,764	Udmurts	90
Kirghizs	289	Chuvashes	398
Tadjiks	359	Yakuts	106
Armenians	5,089	Kara-Kalpaks	49
Turkmenians	332	Jews	24,620
Estonians	1,568	Others	2,477
Bashkirs	219	Total	223,893[162]

This table calls for a few comments. First of all, people of Jewish descent are gathered together as Jews, while the Soviet-Leninist doctrine denies the existence of such a nationality, among other reasons that they are dispersed on Soviet territory and cannot point to any region where they constitute a clear majority of the population. They should be included in the total figures of other nationalities, especially the Russian, Ukrainian, and Byelorussian, among whom they usually live. One may be sure that almost all such Jewish intellectuals would feel happier and safer if they were not singled out as a special group. Is this sort of Jewish ghetto in the table a symptom of current anti-Semitism in Soviet leaders, especially Khrushchev?

If one adds the Slavic and Jewish scholars who have in the USSR no other but Slavic culture, one gets the total figure of 194,744, leaving 29,149 for the other nationalities. It comes as a surprise that the Baltic nationalities, which had had before Soviet annexation a highly literate population and a well-developed intelligentsia familiar with modern learning, should now have only 1,741 (Lithuanians), 1,764 (Latvians), and 1,568 (Estonians) intellectual workers while nationalities which had been very recently illiterate and primitive, such as Buriats, Komis, Yakuts, Chuvashes, may boast of the comparatively high figures of 168, 188, 106, or 398 scholars, respectively. Do these low figures for the Balts reflect the Soviet policy of mass deportations of native intelligentsia from the Baltic countries?

There is no doubt that the Soviet Government has made a great effort in spreading literacy and in raising the general cultural level of more primitive nationalities. Every modern colonial Power tries to do the same, since a literate worker or farmer shows a higher productivity of labor and greater ability to learn modern techniques. But Asians and Africans would be the first to say that material progress in colonial possessions must not be equated with political progress towards self-government. This holds true of the Soviet system. Material progress is welcomed by a foreign-controlled nationality if it is accompanied not by denationalization and the perpetuation of alien rule but by a process of emancipation such as has been taking place within the British Commonwealth. There is no trace of such political evolution in the Soviet Empire. Certainly the Soviet sources quoted above do not particularly warrant this optimistic statement by a Syrian Sheik concerning the condition of Soviet Moslems:

The Damascus newspaper *At-Talia* published in January 1956 an interview with a known public figure in Syria, Sheik Muhammed al' Ashmar who had visited the Soviet Union. Al' Ashmar said: "I wish from the bottom of my heart that the condition of Moslems in our [*sic!*] country was such as it is in the Soviet Union." . . . According to Sheik Al' Ashmar, he saw through "the lies and impudence of imperialists . . . who try to mislead religious people and to discredit the Soviet Union in Moslem eyes."[163]

The Sheik was probably blinded by his hatred of the West; he forgot that Frenchmen had long ago quit his native country, that Syrians were free to worship under their own national government; he was blind to the fact that most of the mosques in Central Asia were closed, to the infinitesimal number of Moslem religious schools, and to the Russification of central Asians who had for centuries been culturally close to the Arabs. Did he really wish to "improve" the situation in his independent country to the level of central Asia? Or to have a Russian as controlling assistant to every Syrian in high office? Or to welcome mass Slavic immigration to his homeland?

The depressing uniformity of the Soviet land is perfectly summed up in the following:

The Soviet people is a great co-operative venture of workers, peasants, and the intelligentsia of all nationalities of the Soviet Union who, all of them, are the toilers in one socialist system of economy, and have one Soviet multinational State, one ideology—Marxism-Leninism, one socialist culture uniform in its contents, one Communist Party which is the inspiring and directing force of society, and one goal—building Communism.[164]

A co-operative venture logically implies a compromise between the goals and ideals of those who participate in it. But the Soviet-tailored co-operative venture has only one Party, one culture, one goal.

CHAPTER XIII

SOVIET COLONIAL PROTECTORATES

1. Eastern Europe before the Second World War

THE CONCEPT of a colonial protectorate conveys such basic ideas as the initial preponderant strength of the colonial Power, the imposition of foreign control in the realms of foreign relations and defense, the interference in the domestic life of the protected country, frequently reduced eventually to the status of a colony in everything except name. Asians and Africans were the chief victims of this insidious way of colonization, which left the outward shell of a distinct political unit after destroying its inward content. European nations were conquered outright by their neighbors, but they did not know this form of colonization until 1939. Hitler imposed in March, 1939, a protectorate on the Czechs and a less formal one on the Slovaks. Later, the many European nations occupied by German troops, from France to Greece and from Norway to Italy, were nothing but colonial protectorates for a few years until the crumbling of the Third Reich. Until 1917, Imperial Russia had two protectorates in central Asia: Bukhara and Khiva. But only Soviet Russia applied this concept in eastern Europe. Stalin tried in vain in 1939–40 to reduce Turkey, Bulgaria, and Finland to the status of protected nations but could not secure the necessary German blessing. He succeeded in the postwar period beyond his earlier expectations; the whole of eastern Europe, occupied by advancing Soviet troops, lay at his feet. The process of imposing foreign control, supported by Soviet bayonets, took only a few years and was completed in 1948. A population numbering almost one hundred million people and including several formerly independent nations was reduced to the status of colonial protectorates, deprived of any freedom in the realm of foreign policy and defense, and compelled to adopt foreign ways of life. One hundred million people are more than one-fourth of populous India, more than the whole of Indonesia, and more than the total number of Arab-speaking peoples. At the same time that Western colonialism quickly started to retreat from Asia (a process by now almost completed except for

448

small remnants) and was about to retreat from parts of Africa, Soviet Russia was building her colonial Empire in eastern Europe in addition to the one inherited from the Tsars.

The Soviet colonialism not only deeply affects the political and economic situation of the controlled nationalities who live either within the Soviet Union or in eastern Europe, but, in addition, it eliminates former national fundamental values and ways of life by forcibly replacing them with the Russian-created values and ways. This new type of colonialism, which can be called cultural, infiltrates into the innermost moral life of the subject nationalities. It is just as total as the Communist regime itself. Bearing in mind this forcible imposition of foreign ways of life, one can say that Communists all the world over act as agents of this modern cultural colonialism when they want to transfer the Russian values and ways of life to their native countries. When Khrushchev says that he wants to bury all non-Communist regimes, he proposes, in effect, an extension of the ways of life created by his own nation to the whole world. This attitude implies a rather morbid national superiority complex and seems to relegate the other nations of the world to the inferior position of renouncing their own originality and cultural traditions for the sake of copying the Russian pattern.

This cultural colonialism of Russian Communists calls for the question unwittingly asked by the Political Consultative Committee of the Warsaw bloc countries (*Pravda*, May 27, 1958): ". . . who has granted the right to any State of imposing its doctrine on other countries?"

Let us at once dispel a frequent misconception in the West. It is not true that all eastern European nations had been fascist (some were compelled by Nazi occupation to adopt fascist regimes) before the Soviet conquest while they were later forced to adopt a second totalitarian system, the Communist, thus merely exchanging one evil for another. This unintentional *ex post facto* justification of Soviet extension of Communist regimes to eastern Europe denotes a complete ignorance of the prewar conditions in that part of the world. Many of these nationalities had a long tradition of Leftist parties, peasant or socialist, of free labor unions, and they took part in contemporary western European intellectual trends. They certainly did not invent either form of totalitarianism, the fascist being a western European product, and the Communist, Russian. They began their post–World War I political career by practicing the French type of parliamentary regime; this did not function too well in France and eastern Europe because of the proliferation of political parties unable to produce stable majorities or a sufficiently strong executive. Later, most of them, with the honorable exception of Czechoslovakia, began to shift to authoritarian regimes founded on the army. However, these Latin American type regimes never descended to the debasement of totalitarianism. In several of the countries democratic opposition parties managed legally to survive, though having no influence on the government; opposition newspapers, subject to censorship, usually continued to be published. The whole spectacle before the outbreak of the Second World War was remote from our concepts of political democracy but was also just as remote from either Nazi or Soviet totalitarianism. In the late thirties, the impact of Nazi ideology was felt in sections of the intelligentsia and petty bourgeoisie, but fascists had their nests in western Europe also. Only eastern Europe was hedged in between the two totalitarian systems.

Radical social ideas were far from unknown. The concept of nationalization of industries largely owned by foreign capital was not unpopular; the idea of a directed or planned economy had its followers. Standards of living, except for Czechoslovakia, were low, but they remain low or have fallen even lower under Communist regimes. The reason was obvious; all those countries, again except for the industrialized Czech part of Czechoslovakia, were economically underdeveloped areas. Most of them had been ruled by foreign nations in the 19th century at the time of the great economic expansion of western Europe. Rapid natural increase overpopulated the rural areas, while cities could not shelter the surplus that was accumulating each year for lack of speedy industrialization. Foreign capital was repelled from investing on a large scale in an area hemmed in by two dynamic nations, Germany and Russia, which obviously were not satisfied with the *status quo* in eastern Europe. Low standards of living did not allow for a sufficient accumulation of national capital for large investments in industries. The peasant problem was the most important social question. Of course a land reform that divided up large estates could partly alleviate the situation until further natural increase aggravated it again. The eastern European states proceeded with such reforms during the interwar period. The only exception was Hungary, where 46.4 per cent of arable land was large estates. Bulgaria was a typical country of small farmers, with only 3.6 per cent of arable land owned by estates of more than 30 hectares and only 1 per cent cultivated by tenant peasants. In Rumania, properties of over 50 hectares represented 17.5 per cent of arable area. In Poland, 18 per cent of arable land belonged to landowners having over 50 hectares each. In

Czechoslovakia, 13.8 per cent of arable land was owned by people having over 100 hectares each. Thus there was not much land reserve represented by larger estates to be distributed among peasants either landless or with dwarf holdings. The widely held belief that eastern Europe was, on the eve of the Second World War, an area of large latifundia is ill founded, as is the related view that only Communists distributed large estates among the peasants. Actually Communists did it on a large scale in the only country where large estates still represented a big land reserve, namely in Hungary.

The other belief that these were feudal countries with ruling land magnates is just as false if one considers the whole of eastern Europe. The socially and politically important section of the population was the local intelligentsia of various mixed social derivation (former landed nobility, middle urban classes) and, in the interwar period, increasing by a constant influx of people whose parents were workers or peasants. In some of the countries, the former nobility played no role in the composition of the intelligentsia, for instance, in Yugoslavia, Bulgaria, and Czechoslovakia, where the nobility did not survive the checkered histories of those countries. The real social problem was a gulf created by education and separating the intelligentsia from workers and peasants. The independence of those countries was of fresh or relatively fresh date, and literacy was not always widely spread, though it increased rapidly during the interwar period. In some countries, such as Czechoslovakia and Poland, the system of social insurance for urban populations was, by the Western yardstick, well developed.

These few generalizations, which would require lengthy specification for each country, especially for Czechoslovakia, with its highly industrialized Czech part and its well-built middle class, convey nevertheless a basically correct picture. The Communist land reforms either completed the process already well advanced or brought out no substantial change in, e.g., Bulgaria and Yugoslavia, countries of small landholders. Therefore, the Communist appeal to landless peasants or to those with dwarf holdings, politically so important in economically underdeveloped countries, did not evoke much response in eastern Europe. The slogan of industrialization was more potent, as peasants and other sections of the population saw plainly that the social problem of overpopulation could be met only by a transformation of the economic structure with greater emphasis on non-agricultural production.

Communist parties in eastern Europe were notoriously weak, except for

Czechoslovakia. Eastern Europeans lived too close to the Soviet reality to feel attracted by that regime. Moreover, it was for some of them a Russian regime, and Russians were none too popular, at least in Poland and Rumania. All over eastern Europe the servility of local Communists towards a foreign Power naturally did not endear them to the populations jealous of their independence. Could, for instance, the Poles trust their Communists, whose leaders served the foreign interests of the eastern neighbor? Julian Marchlewski, one of the early leaders, was in turn the Russian unofficial delegate in 1919 to armistice negotiations with his native country and then was appointed, in the summer of 1920, head of the Polish Revolutionary Committee, to be enthroned in Warsaw after the expected Soviet military victory. Later, he served for a short time as a member of the German Party Central Committee and still later was in turn Soviet consul in Berlin and president of the Soviet University for the Western Peoples. Lenin said of Felix Dzierzhinsky, another early leader of Polish Communists and a member of the same Polish Revolutionary Committee in 1920: "It is known that assimilated non-Russians overdo in the matter of hundred per cent Russian attitudes."[1] The Fifth Comintern Congress adopted, with the assent of the Communists of countries concerned, a resolution favoring territorial dismemberment of Poland, Rumania, and Czechoslovakia:

The Congress . . . considers it necessary for the Communist Parties of Poland, Czechoslovakia and Rumania to launch the general slogan of the separation of Ukrainian lands from Poland, Czechoslovakia and Rumania, and their union with the Soviet Ukraine and, through it, with the USSR.[2]

The interwar period, lasting barely twenty years, is too short a time for judgment on the eastern European record of that period. Poverty could hardly be radically obviated for lack of capital, but much more could have been done to include workers and peasants in the stream of national cultural life and to bridge the gulf between the intelligentsia and the manually working classes. Intense nationalism, so characteristic of countries which long lived under foreign control, was present; it bred discriminatory treatment of national minorities, mutual and unending disputes over frontiers, and a lack of understanding for the precariousness of national existence. Eastern Europeans should have looked beyond their rather parochial territorial disputes and remembrances of past quarrels and should have combined in order to have any chance of surviving the strangling by German and Soviet dynamic expansions. Anti-Semitism, bred by poverty, was rampant in many of these countries. There were people who cared for political freedom and who gave their lives for it under the Nazi and Communist regimes; there were others who were indifferent or even hostile to concepts of political democracy. But they never deported wholesale their national minorities, as did the USSR, nor did they invent the summary procedure of gas chambers for liquidating those minorities, as practiced by the Nazis. One must also remember that most of the Danubian and Balkan nations lived for centuries under not particularly enlightened Turkish rule and recovered their independence in the 19th century. Others became independent only after the First World War. Even Imperial Germany and Imperial Austria-Hungary were schools for parliamentary tactics but certainly not schools for a working democracy, for they were ruled by governments appointed by the Emperor independently of parliament. Time was short in which to accumulate experience, the mother of political wisdom. Political democracy cannot be improvised. It takes root through long development and the slow acquisition of habits. It is rather surprising to find (not to speak of Czechoslovakia, which was a working democracy throughout the period under consideration) political parties, such as the peasant and the socialist, together with so many persons attached to its ideals.

Eastern European foreign policies were not an example of wisdom. Even England, with her mature experience, committed some gross errors of calculation in the appeasement period. Few nations have a pure record of wisdom and virtue, so that few could with clear conscience cast a stone at eastern Europeans for all their errors and defects. But the main problem is of a different nature. Asians, Arabs, and Africans would agree that any nationality, whatever its record, has an inalienable right to be master at home, even though a foreign nation claims ability to give it a better system and better administration. The very word "better" is always liable to conflicting interpretations, since basic sets of values vary from country to country. The USSR has, however, deprived eastern European nations of that inalienable right.

2. Prelude to the Sovietization of Eastern Europe. Role of the Soviet Army

Space does not allow for a detailed history of the Soviet policy in eastern Europe between 1944 and the present time. Moreover, such an attempt would be superfluous because of the existence of several books and many articles on the matter. We shall limit ourselves to a condensed survey of events until 1956 and shall devote attention to this memorable year which brought to the surface the consequences of Soviet policy, as pursued in previous years, in the form of a political revolt in Poland and an armed uprising in Hungary. The Polish crisis is interesting for an additional reason, namely it was preceded, accompanied, and followed by a thorough criticism of the Soviet Communist system by Polish Communists whose voice carried a more convincing ring than that of non-Communists.

American rejection, on military grounds, of Churchill's suggestions to combine the main Allied landing in Normandy with Western military operations in the eastern Mediterranean, the Balkans, and in the Danubian region by a break-through from Italy determined the political nature of later events in eastern Europe. In the absence of Western troops, the Soviet army became the only master there. Otherwise, some of the eastern European countries would have been as free as Greece is. Poland and perhaps Rumania could not be saved because of their proximity to Russia, but all or most of the other Danubian and Balkan countries would have escaped being included within the Soviet zone. Churchill acknowledged the political consequences of the military situation as it began to emerge in the fall of 1944. Trying to save what could be saved, he concluded his rather realistic agreement with Stalin that in fact conceded to him Soviet preponderant influence in all the countries which were at that time, or were about to be, occupied by Soviet troops—Rumania, Hungary, and Bulgaria. This agreement mentioned neither Poland (whose fate was prejudged by the Soviet military advance anyhow) nor Czechoslovakia, which Churchill perhaps still hoped to save from becoming a Soviet satellite. Churchill was unusually optimistic in agreeing with Stalin that British and Soviet influences would be equal in Yugoslavia. It is difficult to understand how he expected to enforce this, since he knew that Yugoslavia was firmly in Tito's hands. Albania was not mentioned. But Churchill obtained from Stalin the recognition that Greece would be included within the British zone, thus preventing in advance the USSR's attaining the Mediterranean coast.

Both Western great Powers were prepared to see eastern Europe included within the Soviet zone in the sense that the foreign policies of those countries would follow the Soviet lead. But neither of them expected or gave its diplomatic blessing to Soviet interference in domestic affairs of those nations, nor did they expect that the West would be completely shut off from that part of Europe. Soviet statements were reassuring in this respect, and Soviet obligations had been clearly determined in inter-Allied agreements. For instance, Stalin, uncertain of his own future at the time, assured the world on November 6, 1941, that

We have not and cannot have any such war aims as imposing our will and our regime on the Slavic and other enslaved nations of Europe which expect our help. Our aim is to assist those nations in their liberating struggle against the Hitlerite tyranny and then to leave them full freedom to organize themselves on their territories as they wish. No interference in the domestic affairs of other nations.[3]

The USSR adhered without reservation to the Atlantic Charter of 1941.[4] Its representative at the Allied Conference in London made the following statement on September 24, 1941:

The Soviet Union respects the right of every nation to her State independence and territorial integrity as well as the right to choose such social regime and such form of government as she considers appropriate and necessary to secure her economic and cultural well-being.[5]

Stalin stated on November 6, 1943:

The policy of our government on these questions remains unchanged. We, together with our Allies, must: 1. liberate European nations from the fascist invaders. . . . 2. give to the liberated European nations the full right and freedom to decide for themselves the question of their constitutional regime.[6]

Only on March 13, 1946, was he more frank. Replying to Churchill's Fulton speech on the Iron Curtain separating eastern Europe from the West, he said:

. . . The Soviet Union, wishing to assure for itself a safe future, tries to secure the existence of governments loyal to itself in those countries [Finland, Poland, Rumania, Bulgaria, and Hungary].[7]

This was the first official admission of Soviet interference in the domestic affairs of eastern European countries.

The most important obligation towards Soviet-occupied eastern Europe was assumed by the USSR at Yalta. The three great Powers signed there on February 11, 1945, the Declaration on Liberated Europe, excerpts from which follow:

The establishment of order in Europe and the rebuilding of national economic life must be achieved by processes which will enable the liberated peoples to destroy the last vestiges of Nazism and Fascism and to create democratic institutions of their own choice. This is a principle of the Atlantic Charter—the right of all peoples to choose the form of government under which they will live—the restoration of sovereign rights and self-government to those peoples who have been forcibly deprived of them by the aggressor nations. To foster the conditions in which the liberated peoples may exercise these rights, the three governments will jointly assist the people in any European liberated state or former Axis satellite state in Europe where in their judgment conditions require. . . . c. to form interim governmental authorities broadly representative of all democratic elements in the population and pledged to the earliest possible establishment through free elections of governments responsive to the will of the people; and d. to facilitate where necessary the holding of such elections.[8]

The misunderstanding among the three signatories of the Declaration consisted in their diametrically opposite interpretation of the crucial words "democratic" and "free elections."

If any criticism of the Western governments of the time could be advanced, it would concern their sanguine view of the change of heart they supposed had occurred in Moscow after the Nazi attack. Soviet statements on the perennial obligation of the Soviet bastion to spread the revolution, as well as Soviet expansion in 1939–40, were readily forgotten in the warm atmosphere of the Grand Alliance. Governments concerned assumed that the era of Soviet double talk had ended once and for all. Very few people suspected that when Stalin solemnly talked about free elections in eastern Europe, he actually had in mind the Soviet-type elections, which he had characterized in 1937 as the most free and democratic that had ever taken place in history.

Soviet armies, after entering eastern Europe during the last stage of the war, have not since quit Poland, East Germany, Rumania, and Hungary; they stayed long enough in Bulgaria to determine the course of events. Their role is freely admitted in Soviet sources:

People's democracy was born in the countries of Central and Southeastern Europe as the result of their liberation from the fascist yoke by the heroic Soviet Army. . . . The presence of Soviet troops prevented the reactionary forces in those countries from unleashing a civil war.[9]

Another Soviet author is equally frank regarding Poland:

The entry of Soviet troops and their [later] stay in Polish territory frustrated the plans of foreign imperialists who had enslaved Poland, paralyzed the criminal intrigues of the domestic reaction, and helped the Polish toilers in establishing the people's democratic State and escaping military intervention and civil war.[10]

The admission is made in an esoteric jargon, but it makes sense to anyone even roughly familiar with the situation of the time.

3. Imposing Foreign Ways of Life: Poland

Native Communists were used in Poland, as elsewhere, as obedient tools. The Party was re-created for that purpose in 1942 after its dissolution in 1938 by a decision of the Comintern following the extermination in Moscow of practically all the leaders of the Party. The first obstacle was brushed aside on April 25, 1943, the day the Soviet Government broke off diplomatic relations with the then Polish Government-in-Exile, composed of representatives of all major Polish parties. The quickly changing circumstances had an immediate impact on Soviet policy: the interwar period of peace was accompanied by correct relations with any Polish Government, Leftist or Rightist, democratic or authoritarian. The outbreak of war and co-operation with the Nazis resulted in the denial of the existence of the Polish state, not to speak of the government. The Nazi attack in 1941 had, as a consequence, forced immediate recognition of the Polish Government-in-Exile, while the Stalingrad victory and the Soviet certitude of becoming master of Poland brought the end of diplomatic relations with this government in London and the formation in Moscow of a nucleus of the people's government.

After the rupture with London, the Union of Polish Patriots was established in the Soviet capital. Its members were mainly Polish Communists, with some sprinkling of fellow-travelers. The first official act of the Union was to send, on June 17, 1943, a resolution of fealty to Stalin with the assurance that ". . . we shall not allow people who try to insert a wedge between the Polish people and the Soviet Union to trouble the waters, and we shall make every effort to strengthen the Polish-Soviet friendship."[11] Among the signatory patriots were K. Witaszewski, the present political enemy of Gomulka and a staunch defender of unreserved obedience to Moscow, and Miss W. Wasilewska, who had become a Soviet citizen on the annexation of the eastern territories of Poland in 1939 and was thereafter a member of the Soviet Party and a deputy to the Supreme Soviet; she gained fame as a Soviet literary writer and never cared to go back, even to a Communist Poland. Among other patriots were Ya. I. Berman, who later became the *eminence grise* of the Stalinist regime in Poland and was expelled from the Polish Political Bureau in October, 1956, for his grim role in the period of police terror, and another man dismissed in 1956 from the Polish Government, S. F. Radkiewicz, who was to gain sad fame as the dread Minister of the Interior. Stalin tried to increase their prestige by offering them a dinner at the Kremlin on March 16, 1944, a fact so important in Soviet eyes that it was registered in an official collection of documents.[12]

After the Soviet crossing of the frontier, as established in September, 1939, the "patriots" formed on the Soviet-occupied Polish territory a Polish Committee of National Liberation that was a provisional government in everything but name. The Committee concluded on July 26, 1944, with the Soviet High Command an agreement concerning its administrative duties; the agreement included a passage which meant to reassure the Western Allies: "The Soviet Government declares that it does not pursue the aim . . . of modifying the social regime of Poland."[13] A strange diplomatic situation ensued whereby the London Government was recognized by the United States and Britain and a Communist-controlled Committee actually extended its administration to all areas progressively occupied by Soviet troops. This did not make inter-Allied co-operation easier and was the source of many mutual recriminations. The problem of finding a government for Poland that could be recognized by all three great Powers was to be discussed at the Yalta Conference in February, 1945. Stalin therefore hastened to increase the prestige of his Committee by granting it, on January 4, 1945, recognition as the Provisional National Government of Poland.[14] Only a few days before, on December 31, 1944, the Committee had proclaimed itself such a government. The struggle waged by Great Britain and the United States in 1943–44 to secure an internal autonomy for Poland was nearing its end. Exhausted by Stalin's stubborn refusal to make any true concessions and reconciled to the obvious fact that Soviet but not Western armies were in Poland, the two Western Powers gave in at Yalta; they accepted Stalin's proposal to add a few non-Communist politicians to the existing Communist-run government in Warsaw, and then to grant it recognition as a Government of National Unity called upon to proceed with immediate free elections. During the inter-Allied wrangling over the exact composition of that reorganized government, Stalin further fortified the prestige of his government in Warsaw by concluding with it on April

21, 1945, a treaty of mutual assistance. A reorganized government was set up in June, with Communists retaining the crucial ministerial posts, such as those of the interior and the army, while they and fellow-travelers formed the great majority of the cabinet; a few non-Communists were added, such as the peasant leader S. Mikolajczyk. This government was recognized by the United States and Britain on July 5, 1945. The diplomatic problem of Poland was solved; all that remained to be done was to set up a Communist regime.

The pattern of Sovietization was basically the same in Poland and in other eastern European countries. Small variations in timetable and procedure were allowed. There were three stages in this process. (1) The formation of a coalition government, which was founded either on the genuine co-operation of Communist and non-Communist parties, in Hungary and Bulgaria, e.g., or on a sham coalition that was produced as the façade of a government run from the start by the Communists, as in Poland. But in all cases, Communists, strong because of Soviet troops visible in the backstage, managed to seize control of the crucial posts of command, especially the interior. (2) The second stage was concerned with the systematic disorganization of non-Communist parties through the elimination of their known leaders and by replacing them with people obedient to Communists, such parties being reduced to the status of channels of command for the Communist Party. In addition, national fronts, a common organization of all the parties and their leader, the Communist, were created. The rival party, the Socialist Party, was liquidated through a forcible merger with the Communist Party. (3) The installment of a Communist regime faithfully copied after the Soviet was carried out. By the end of the third stage, nationally minded local Communists were exterminated or imprisoned. The whole process took only a short span of time—from 1944–45 to 1948. By 1948, eastern Europe was already a monolithic Soviet colonial protectorate.

The coalition in Poland was spurious from the beginning because of its derivation from the Union of Polish Patriots formed in Moscow under direct Soviet auspices. After the reorganization of the government in the summer of 1945, the following parties were represented: the Polish Workers' Party (Communist), the Polish Socialist, the Democratic, the Peasant, the Christian Labor, and a new party restored by S. Mikolajczyk, one of the prewar peasant leaders, under the name of the Polish Peasant Party. The four other non-Communist parties were "reorganized" in 1944–45 under the Soviet military occupation, their leadership was purged, and they were manned by people ready to follow Communists through thick and thin. It is characteristic that S. Mikolajczyk had no choice but to form a different Peasant Party, the one existing on his return to Poland being already under firm Communist control.

According to the Yalta inter-Allied declaration, the main and first duty of the reorganized government was to hold

... free and unfettered elections as soon as possible on the basis of universal suffrage and secret ballot. In these elections all democratic and anti-Nazi parties shall have the right to take part and to put forward candidates.[15]

These elections were to give to the country an opportunity to decide what government it wanted to have. The Communists approached Mikolajczyk with the proposal to present one-ticket candidates, his party receiving 20 per cent of parliamentary seats to be distributed in advance of the elections. He declined that offer, being sure that his party, the only one genuinely free of Communist control, could gain the majority of seats in a free competition. The Communists then decided to proceed by two stages. The first was a referendum on questions they drafted and which left no choice for the electors: (1) Should Poland have a bicameral or unicameral parliament? (2) Should the nationalization of industries and the agrarian reform be incorporated into a new constitution as parts of the new social system? (3) Should Poland have permanent frontiers on the Rivers Oder-Neisse?

No Pole cared whether the new parliament would be bicameral or unicameral, as long as it were a genuine parliament. Practically everyone agreed to the nationalization of industries, which before the war were largely controlled by foreign capital or whose owners perished at the hands of the Nazis, and to the completion of the distribution of large estates among the peasants. The country was united on the question of the Western frontier. Mikolajczyk and his party were placed in an awkward position; they decided to challenge the Communist bloc on the relatively indifferent point of the one or two houses of parliament. The Communists, confronted with the prospect that their rule would be questioned by voters casting ballots for a bicameral parliament, had to "organize" the referendum itself. The referendum took place on June 30, 1946. Although the electoral law provided for counting the ballots at the polling stations in the presence of the representatives of various parties, the security police removed ballot boxes immediately after the closure of polling and before the electoral commissions could tabulate the results. Only in one city, Kraków, did the electoral commission appear to have advance notice of the police intentions, and they tabulated the votes before the ballot boxes could be removed. Eighty-four per cent of the votes were cast there against the Communist bloc. For the rest of the country, the Governmental bloc claimed a resounding victory of over 80 per cent majority.

In the first postwar parliamentary elections of January 19, 1947, the Communists sponsored one-ticket lists of candidates selected by their bloc and were again opposed by Mikolajczyk's Peasant Party. The elections were held in an atmosphere of open terror. Local leaders of Mikolajczyk's party were arrested or assassinated; the police was always unable to discover the murderers. His party's electoral lists were disqualified in several constituencies, and his candidates were often beaten and tortured to make them withdraw their candidatures, while his mail communications with various local party centers were disrupted. The Communists organized, at the same time, a public campaign in favor of "open voting." All members of the electoral commissions were Communists, and Mikolajczyk's men were forbidden to observe either the vote or the tabulation of results. Because of disqualification, Mikolajczyk's party was unable to present any candidates in ten districts accounting for about 22 per cent of the registered electorate. On polling day, members of the electoral commissions took the names of voters who dared to place their ballots in envelopes instead of dropping them publicly into the boxes as recommended by the Communist bloc. The results, either determined by open voting or by later tabulation, were truly Soviet: the Communist bloc claimed 9,003,684 votes, conceding to Mikolajczyk's party 1,154,847. Soon after, Mikolajczyk had to flee the country for fear of his life; his party was liquidated.[16]

The only possible rival left on the battlefield was the Socialist Party, which had a long tradition going back to the last decades of the 19th century. It was infiltrated by Communists in 1944–47, a process made easier by the extermination of its popular prewar leaders by the Nazis. This party was "reorganized" in September, 1944, at a hastily improvised Congress which elected all sorts of nonentities as Party leaders. Actually, not one prewar member of the Party Central Executive Committee, its Supreme Council, and its parliamentary group was present at that Congress. K. Puzak, its prewar and wartime secretary-general, was arrested by Soviet military authorities in 1945 and died in prison in 1950. Yet there was potential danger that the prewar traditions of the Party, Polish independence, free labor unions, welfare of the workers, free co-operatives, could still linger among the rank-and-file members. And so this old party had to be erased by a merger with the Communist. As a Soviet author puts it:

The history of the Communist Party of the Soviet Union teaches that the victory of the proletarian revolution is impossible without a complete rout of the petty-bourgeois parties which are active within the ranks of the working class.[17]

There was also the danger that the Polish Socialists could combine with the nationally minded Polish Communists in a joint opposition to Moscow dictates:

The rightist-nationalist elements in the Polish Workers' Party and the reactionary elements in the Polish Socialist Party . . . tried to prove that . . . Poland allegedly should march towards socialism along its own "Polish" road. . . . They also attempted to prove the "inapplicability" to Poland of the experience gathered in the USSR during the process of building up socialism.[18]

The same Soviet author concedes that there was an opposition to the merger, for different reasons, in both the Communist and the Socialist parties:

[The rightist-nationalist elements in the Polish Workers' Party] proposed to include the whole Polish Socialist Party within the United Workers' Party without any purge or re-investigation of its membership. The rightist elements in the Polish Socialist Party also hindered the establishment of one Workers' Party. They claimed that the merger would be artificial, premature, inexpedient, and would annihilate completely their own Party.[19]

The Soviet will was stronger, and both parties were thoroughly purged before the merger:

During the purge preceding the unification Congress 29,000 people were expelled from the Polish Workers' Party. The purge of the Polish Socialist Party before the unification Congress, was carried out with even greater drive; 82,000 people were expelled from the ranks of the Polish Socialist Party.[20]

The total membership of the Socialist Party being at that time about 800,000 people, 10 per cent were thrown out. Twelve members of its Central Executive Committee and twelve members of its Supreme Council were dropped. Thus the two parties were in a proper frame of mind for the merger, which took place in December, 1948.[21] The monopoly of power was safely vested in the united Communist Party, most of its leaders being tested devotees of Moscow. The three small parties included in the Communist-controlled National Front were of no political consequence, their leaders being only too eager to follow Communist instructions.

A monolithic system was created after four years of the presence of Soviet troops on Polish soil. The only thing remaining to be done was to remove the nationally inclined Communist leaders. The Polish Central Committee dismissed W. Gomulka from his post as its secretary-general in 1948. A few months later, he lost his governmental positions of Vice–Prime Minister and Minister of Regained Territories and was also expelled from the Central Committee. He and his political friends were arrested in 1951, to be released as late as 1956. A former colleague of his on the Central Committee called him (in 1952) "an instrument of imperialism, a traitor and a provocateur," following the customary Soviet method of throwing mud at fallen leaders.[22] The appointment of Soviet Marshal Rokossovsky as commander-in-chief of the Polish forces in 1949 came as a symbol of the colonial position of the country.

4. Imposing Foreign Ways of Life: Rumania

The same procedure could be carried out in Rumania, Hungary, and Bulgaria with even greater ease, since these three countries were allies of Germany during the last war. There was less need to observe decorum for the benefit of the West. In none of the three countries were the American and British members of the armistice commissions allowed to have anything to say about the manner in which the Soviet high commands should run the domestic affairs of Rumania, Hungary, and Bulgaria.

King Michael of Rumania arrested on August 23, 1944, the pro-Nazi dictator Marshal Ion Antonescu ordered the cease-fire on the Soviet front and appointed a government under General Constantin Sanatescu, with four parties forming the coalition: the National-Peasant, headed by its veteran leader Iuliu Maniu, the National-Liberal, with Constantin Bratianu as its recognized leader, the small Socialist Party, under Titel Petrescu, and the minuscule (at that time) Communist Party, numbering only about 1,000 members, led by Lucretiu Patrascanu. The Communist Party was included in deference to the USSR, with whom an armistice was to be concluded. The terms of the Armistice included Article 19: "The Allied Governments . . . agree that Transylvania (the whole or a major part of it) should be restored to Rumania." This article provided the USSR with means of pressure. Northern Transylvania had been detached in 1940 by Germany and Italy and given to Hungary. The Rumanians were left guessing as to whether they would get back the whole or part of the lost territory; this depended on their "good behavior." The Soviet troops forbade, for the time being, the extension of Rumanian civilian administration to that territory. After the Soviet military occupation of Rumania, Communist leaders came back from their Moscow exile, and others were released from Rumanian prisons. The Party started to expand under the shadow of the protective Soviet troops.

In October, 1944, the Communists formed a National-Democratic Front composed of their own Party and three other small parties—the Socialist, the Ploughmen's Front (led by a fellow-traveler, Petru Groza), and the equally Communist-infiltrated Union of Patriots. In November, General Sanatescu had to form a second government in which Groza became vice-premier and the Communist leader, Gheorghiu-Dej, minister of communications. But the Ministry of the Interior remained in non-Communist hands. In December, General N. Radescu formed a third government, with a Communist appointed as Under-Secretary of the Interior. All three successive governments were highly unsatisfactory to the Soviet Union, and so the Communist-controlled National Front staged public demonstrations against Radescu in January and February in preparation for what was to come. Vice-Commissar for Foreign Affairs Vyshinsky, who had proved his ability to handle such matters in 1940 in the Baltic States, came to Bucarest on February 7, 1945; he immediately presented the King with an ultimatum: either the King would appoint Groza prime minister (with a government whose list was submitted), or the Soviet Government would decline responsibility for the future of Rumania. The King surrendered and appointed Groza and his Soviet-selected colleagues. None of the acknowledged leaders of the National-Peasant and National-Liberal parties was included. The government was almost entirely composed of Communists and fellow-travelers from the National Front, with a few "dissident" Liberals and Peasants added for decorum. Northern Transylvania was soon after transferred to Rumanian administration.

At the reception of the new Rumanian Government on March 11, Vyshinsky did not beat about the bush:

The circumstances surrounding the question of placing Transylvania under the Rumanian Government's administration have become during the last few months more favorable than they had been in the first period after the expulsion of the occupants. But one most serious and important condition for the carrying out of the Soviet Government's decision was lacking. There was in Rumania no government which would be able to assure order, peace, and discipline in the country. . . . Now this condition has been fulfilled. . . . Such is the reason why the Soviet Government has precisely now concluded that it is possible and opportune . . . to allow the administration by a democràtic Rumanian Government to be established in Transylvania.[23]

In February, 1946, the Groza Government was recognized by the United States and Britain after the addition of two ministers who were prewar members of the National-Liberal and National-Peasant parties. The approaching first postwar elections were preceded by splitting the two most important non-Communist parties, the National-Peasant and the National-Liberal, as well as the small Socialist Party. New parties bearing the same names, the better to confuse the public, were organized in opposition to the old ones. The November 19, 1946, elections produced the expected results: 4,766,630 votes were tabulated for the National Front and 1,204,761 for the three opposition parties. The latter parties were duly dissolved in 1947–48, the National-Peasant leaders, Maniu and Mihalache, having been sentenced to life imprisonment. Although the government was solidly Communist, the King was used to cover up the rapid process of imported revolution. As late as November 8, 1947, the Communist paper *Scanteia* wrote: "The people wish His Majesty the King a long life, good health, and a reign rich in democratic achievements." Two months later, the King was compelled to abdicate and a republic was proclaimed. The second elections, held on March 28, 1948, gave 405 parliamentary seats to the National Front, while the token Communist-controlled "opposition" was allocated nine seats.

5. Imposing Foreign Ways of Life: Hungary

The same process went through slower stages in Hungary but was duly completed in 1948. There is no more convincing record of the history of that process than what Matyas Rakosi, then secretary-general of the Hungarian Communist Party, had to say about it in his notorious "salami speech" made in March, 1952:

We began [in 1945] our work by organizing the Hungarian National Independence Front. . . . The presence in the country of the Soviet Army precluded any attempt at armed rebellion. . . . In the first place the Armed

Forces of the Soviet Union were responsible for the fact that the counter-revolutionaries did not dare resort to bloodshed in order to restore their rule. The Soviet Army also protected us against an imperialist intervention. The Soviet Union shielded us from diplomatic interference by the Western Great Powers, assisted us in concluding the Peace Treaty, and in building up and consolidating our foreign relations. These circumstances naturally helped to strengthen Communist influence. Without these factors our People's Democracy would never have come to life; its development would not have been as quick, powerful, and free from violence. Soviet "interference" in our domestic affairs was quite frequent and of great help in strengthening our Party. . . . We repeat: without the heroic fight of the Soviet Union for liberation and without its well-meant assistance, the Hungarian People's Democracy, and we may add, the others, too, would never have been born. . . .

Our competitor in winning over the industrial workers was the Social-Democratic Party. . . . After the liberation the greater part of the peasants . . . hastened to join the ranks of the Smallholders' Party. . . . The strength of the parties was revealed for the first time at the National Assembly elections, held in November 1945, seven months after the liberation. At these elections the Smallholders' Party won absolute majority, i.e., 56 per cent of ballots. The Communists were running neck-and-neck with the Social-Democrats, getting 17 per cent of votes, but they won one more mandate, thus becoming the second largest party in the country. The Peasant Party did not quite win 8 per cent of votes. . . . Our Party used the results attained in the elections further to consolidate its position. Therefore, it claimed for its members the office of Deputy Premier and the control of the Ministry of Internal Affairs, which was granted after much wrangling.

At the beginning of March, 1946, the Left-Wing Bloc stressed its demands by staging a demonstration of Budapest workers. Under the threatening effect of the imposing and disciplined meeting numbering over 400,000 participants, the Smallholders' Party was obliged to meet the demands. It had to expel 21 of its most incriminated members. . . . Thus, four months after the victory scored by the Smallholders' Party at the elections, our Workers' Party dealt a powerful blow to the reaction. . . . As a sequence to the successful counter-attack launched in March, 1946 . . . the Smallholders' Party was constantly compelled to expel or discard single individuals or groups of its discredited members. This gradual day-by-day "slicing off" of the reaction lurking within the Smallholders' Party was then termed "salami tactics." In the course of our incessant struggle against the enemy, he was gradually frittering away his strength. . . .

[In 1947] the Social-Democratic Party endeavored to unite under its aegis the disintegrating masses of the Smallholders' Party adherents, to assume leadership, in order to carry on the unsuccessful subversive activities of the Smallholders' Party against democracy and the Communist Party. . . . Hinting at the Communist Party they began to announce their readiness to protect the independence of our country against any striving to make of it a "member-State" of the Soviet Union. They took a stand against "any kind of dictatorship." They began to make frequent mention of "Communist terror," promised "life without fear," and assured the peasants that they too were against the "Kolkhoz and chow-line."[24]

In the meantime, the first elections of November 4, 1945, brought the following results: Smallholders' Party—59.9 per cent of votes, Communists—17.11 per cent, Social-Democrats—16.9 per cent, National-Peasant Party—5.6 per cent, other small parties—0.49 per cent. In 1947, the Smallholders' Party, although having a safe majority in parliament but being weakened by Rakosi's "salami tactics," was compelled to replace Ferenc Nagy as prime minister and chairman of the Party, respectively, by docile Lajos Dinnyes and Istvan Dobi. However, the elections of August 31, 1947, showed that the electorate was not yet subdued. Communists got only 22.27 per cent and other parties together 77.73 per cent of all ballots. Let us listen to Rakosi further:

The struggle with the Social-Democratic Party [after the 1947 elections] was longer and tougher. . . . The new Government, in which due to the changed circumstances the role of the Communist Party became even more dominant, was formed at the end of September. . . . On seeing the progress we were making, the "left-wing" Social-Democratic leaders embarked upon a bold venture. In order to save what still could be saved, at a public meeting on February 18, 1948, they excluded their most compromised leaders and expressed their wish to convene a special Party congress at which their merger with the Communist Party would be declared. . . . The merger of the two parties . . . was brought about in June 1948. . . . From then on we made rapid progress. . . . The realization of labor unity and the expulsion from the Party of treacherous Social-Democratic leaders were followed by similar steps in other parties. The Smallholders' and Peasant parties expelled from their ranks most of those elements whose democratic attitude, political loyalty and honesty were doubtful, and intensified their co-operation with our Party. . . . A desperate struggle was waged also for gaining control over the Armed Forces, the Army, the Police, and the State Defense Authority. . . . While the parties of the coalition government demanded commanding posts in the ratio to their parliamentary representation, we, so to speak, postponed the struggle waged for control over the Army. This we attained by preventing the building up of the Army to the maximum strength permitted in the Armistice Agreement and the Peace Treaty. Thus, until 1948 the strength of the Army was only 12,000 instead of the permitted 65,000 to 70,000. . . . When in the fall of 1948 our Party took control of the Ministry of Defense, we could expand our Army. . . . All in all, the struggle fought by us to win a majority in the Army, under the circumstances prevailing in the Hungarian People's Democracy, was of minor significance on account of the presence of the Soviet Army.[25]

The next elections, held on May 15, 1949, were, as Rakosi said in his speech, "a huge people's festival," with the Communist National Front receiving 92.1 per cent of tabulated results. The last step was to purge the Hungarian Party of true or alleged nationalists. The most important among them was the former member of government Laszlo Rajk, who confessed at his trial in 1949 all the sins he had been accused of: having been a stool pigeon for the prewar Hungarian police and having served the French Intelligence Service and the Gestapo and, since 1945, also the American and Yugoslav secret services. Rajk was not saved from death by his previous Party record; he had spent some time in prewar Hungarian prisons, fought in Spain in the International Brigade, was again imprisoned in Hungary on his return in 1941, and in 1944 was placed in a German concentration camp. A member of the Party Political Bureau and, in turn, the interior and foreign minister, he was shot with the same implacability as an ordinary "bourgeois." His self-confessions were posthumously refuted in 1956, his memory was rehabilitated, and his body solemnly exhumed and again interred with great ceremony. His trial companions of Jewish descent confessed to having been linked through the Zionist organization with the American Intelligence Service.

6. Imposing Foreign Ways of Life: Bulgaria

In Bulgaria, a Fatherland Front of opposition parties was formed in mid-1944. This front included the Agrarian Party, the Socialist, the Army political organization *Zveno*, and the Communists. In August, the Bulgarian Government opened secret discussions for an armistice in Cairo with Britain and the United States. In September, a moderate and pro-Western government was formed; it did not include the members of the Fatherland Front. The Russians, fearing that British and American troops would eventually land in Bulgaria, which was not at war with the USSR, suddenly declared war on Bulgaria on September 4, 1944. This enabled them to enter Bulgaria on September 8; the next day, the Fatherland Front staged a coup and formed its own government. One of the four Communist ministers, Anton Yugov, controlled the key Ministry of the Interior. Their party was traditionally much stronger in Bulgaria than in Rumania or Poland. The fact that it looked towards Moscow was not a hindrance, since pro-Russian sympathies had been deeply rooted in the country since the time of its anti-Turkish struggle for independence.

When the time came to think of elections, the Communists proposed to other parties participating in the Fatherland Front that they should proceed with one-ticket elections and distribute seats in advance; they requested at least 50 per cent of seats for their perty. The Agrarians refused and resigned from the government. Their leader at the time was Nikola Petkov, secretary-general of his party since 1945 and vice-premier in the coalition government. The well-known techniques were used against him and his colleagues. A Communist-packed Congress of the Agrarian Party replaced Petkov in May, 1945, with a docile Alexander Obbov. Yugov, minister of the interior, proceeded to arrest Agrarians who remained loyal to their former leader, Petkov. The Socialist Party was also split into two factions, those who were ready to surrender to Communists and who were led by Dimiter Neikov, and those, headed by Kosta Lulchev, who wanted to retain political identity. Thus by the summer of 1945 the Fatherland Front, which had been founded as a genuine coalition of Leftist parties, became a Communist-manipulated front. In November, 1945, Georgi Dimitrov, the famous Comintern leader, came back from Moscow to take over the command of the Communist Party.

With the opposition parties disorganized, the new Fatherland Front managed to tabulate an 86 per cent majority in the general elections of November 18, 1945. Those results looked suspicious; hence the Western great Powers conditioned their recognition of the new Bulgarian government by the addition of two truly representative members of Agrarians and Socialists. This was done, and the Western recognitions followed. On September 8, 1946, a republic was proclaimed, and the child King Simeon went into exile. After new general elections in October, 1946, in which the Fatherland Front got 78 per cent of all votes, Georgi Dimitrov became prime minister.

Then started a short struggle between the Agrarian leader, Petkov, deprived of his party, and Dimitrov, a struggle in which Petkov proved with his courage and his life that political democracy was not a matter of indifference to eastern Europeans. He said of Communists on December 4, 1946: "They threaten, they intimidate, they arrest, they beat people up, they send our supporters to concentration camps, they kill our members, and then they say they are willing to co-operate with us."[26] Answering Dimitrov's charges that the opposition parties were American and British agents, he said: "Let me remind you that I have never been a citizen of a foreign country, nor have I been in foreign service." Dimitrov proudly replied: "I was a citizen of the great Soviet Union, an honor and a privilege!" Petkov then said: "You became a Bulgarian subject two days before the elections. This was officially announced from Moscow." Dimitrov lost patience: "I will teach you a lesson soon!"[27]

Writing several years before the dissatisfied Polish Communists and Djilas had time to revise their previous views, Petkov thus described a Communist society:

If men in power destroy the liberty of speech and press, any excess soon becomes permissible. Such men proclaim themselves infallible, and decide the fate of people arbitrarily, without any control over their actions. The citizens of such a state cease to be a society of thinking men and become a flock of sheep, with no opinions or ideas of their own. Once freedom is destroyed, all other foundations of human society crumble into ruins. A flock of two-legged sheep, even if they look like people, and are well-fed and well-shod, is not a society of human beings.[28]

He was arrested on June 6, 1947, on the floor of parliament and was tried in August of the same year. He refused to indict himself and was hanged on September 23, 1947. Dimitrov, addressing himself to the opposition Socialists, said in January, 1948:

As you remember, from this rostrum I many times warned your political allies from Nikola Petkov's group. They did not listen to me. They took no notice of all my warnings. They broke their heads, and their leader is now under the ground. You should now think it over, lest you share their fate.[29]

Mockingly, and not without reason, he added: "And what happened abroad? . . . The whole incident was soon forgotten."[30] In the summer of 1948, Lulchev and six other Socialists were sentenced to long-term imprisonment; this facilitated the merger of the Socialist with the Communist Party at the end of 1948. The new general elections produced in 1949 a 97.6 per cent majority for the Communist-controlled Democratic Front. The classic pattern had only to be completed by a purge of the Communist Party of its alleged nationalists. The chief Bulgarian victim was Traicho Kostov, secretary of the Central Committee and vice-premier. He had been one of the founders of the Bulgarian Party in 1919, a member of its political bureau since 1935, and had spent ten years in Bulgarian prisons before the war. Removed from his party and state positions in April, 1949, he was executed a few months later as a spy for the prewar Bulgarian police and the British, American, and Yugoslav Intelligence Services. At the trial, Kostov withdrew his written confession and pleaded not guilty.

7. Imposing Foreign Ways of Life: Czechoslovakia

The Czechoslovak story is different but ends in 1948 in the same unhappy way. The Soviet troops were evacuated soon after the war, but the

Communist Party proved in free elections to be the strongest in eastern Europe. Geographically remote from the USSR, the Czechoslovaks had never had any anti-Russian feelings and were eager to co-operate with Russia in order to prevent a resurgence of the German threat to their independence. They all wanted to be allies. One of the leading Czech politicians and a member of the postwar coalition government says with bitter disappointment after the experience of 1948: "The fate of Czechoslovakia demonstrates that the Soviets will not be satisfied with co-operation among allies. What they ask of their partners is not co-operation, but absolute submission."[31] A Czechoslovak government was created on April 4, 1945, in Soviet-occupied eastern Slovakia. It was composed of parties participating in the Czech and Slovak national fronts (the Czech National-Socialists, Social-Democrats, Catholic Populists and Communists, and the Slovak Democrats and Communists); the rightist parties were excluded from political life. Communists received five portfolios, including the key one of the interior. The May, 1946 (first) postwar general elections gave 37 per cent of ballots to the Communist Party, it thereby becoming the largest Party in the country. In July, a new government was formed, the Communist leader, Klement Gottwald, taking the position of prime minister. This coalition government worked smoothly until July, 1947. However, the honeymoon ended when the Czechoslovak Government, Communist ministers assenting, decided to accept the invitation to attend the international conference for the examination of the Marshall Plan. Stalin summoned to Moscow a Czechoslovak delegation and told it to reject the invitation. He probably issued at the same time new instructions to Premier Gottwald, who was on the delegation. Soon Communist Minister of the Interior Nosek started packing the police with his men, while the date for new general elections scheduled for June, 1948, was rapidly approaching. The crucial factor in the situation was the fact that Communist and Socialist deputies had an absolute majority in parliament, 153 out of 300 seats. In the 1948 crisis, the Socialists followed Zdenek Fierlinger, a crypto-Communist. Thus the Communists were able to hide behind a façade of parliamentary majority while liquidating the parliamentary regime.

The non-Communist ministers (National-Socialists, Populists, and Slovak Democrats) decided to put up a fight when the Communist Minister of Interior replaced eight high-ranking police officers with his men. The cabinet instructed him by a majority vote to stop packing the police with Communists. Supported by Premier Gottwald, he refused to obey. Then the twelve non-Communist ministers resigned, hoping that the whole coalition government would fall and the date of general elections be advanced. They expected to have the backing of at least a section of Socialists, of the non-Party Minister of Defense, General Svoboda, and of President Beneš, the veteran statesman whom the Communists could not discard for fear of national reaction. They thought in terms of a legal parliamentary and electoral struggle, but Communists had been packing the police for a different fight. Control of the police safely in their hands, the Communists organized mob demonstrations in Prague and elsewhere that were calculated to terrorize and reduce to silence the opposition parties and their followers. V. A. Zorin, then Soviet vice-minister for foreign affairs, suddenly came to Prague to prove that the USSR was fully behind the Czechoslovak Communists. There were no Soviet troops in the country, but Soviet divisions encircled Czechoslovakia from eastern Germany and eastern Austria through Poland to Hungary. *Pravda* came out openly in support of the Czechoslovak Party on February 23, 1948. The non-Communist parties could use only parliamentary weapons of struggle; the Communists had other means: the police, mob terror and violence, control over radio and press, vested in their own Minister of Information Kopecky, and the support of the neighboring great Power. The struggle was too unequal. Moreover, the Minister of Defense, General Svoboda, sided with the Communists, thus placing the army at their disposal as another eloquent factor. President Beneš, disappointed in his former trust in Soviet good faith but weakened by serious illness, had assured the resigning ministers of his support, but, faced later with mob demonstrations, he surrendered to the pressure of Communist Prime Minister Gottwald. On February 25, he appointed a reconstructed government with Communist and pro-Communist Socialists in full control. The coup was executed with all the appearances of a constitutional transaction. The Czechoslovak Communists eliminated the non-Communist parties as a political force in a one-month crisis, an operation that at least took a few years in the rest of eastern Europe. Parliamentary democracy was ended; a typical Communist regime was quickly introduced.

The well-known Foreign Minister Jan Masaryk committed suicide on March 10, unable to survive the end of a democracy founded by his great father. The elections of May 30, 1948, were for a single list of the National Front, expurgated of all anti-Communists; voters were advised to cast their ballots openly. The result was that 80 per cent of ballots were cast for the

Front. In June, the Socialist Party merged with the Communist. On June 7, Beneš resigned; he died in September, and his place was taken by victorious Gottwald.

The last stage, with sickening conformity, was the show-trial of allegedly or truly insubordinate Communist leaders, Foreign Minister Vlado Clementis, Party Secretary-General Slansky, and others. This, like other "trials," was meant to create an atmosphere of fear and unreserved obedience to Moscow in Communists and non-Communists alike.

The Czechoslovak crisis is more instructive than the events in other eastern European countries in one respect; it demonstrated that an alliance between a non-Communist country and the USSR, as well as a governmental coalition between non-Communist parties and Communists, were short-lived and precarious propositions, as contrary to fundamental Communist concepts. It showed also what the Communists understood by a "peaceful" transition to socialism. One of the ministers who had unsuccessfully challenged Communist preponderance in February, 1948, writes:

No other country has made as many efforts to reach an honest understanding with Soviet Russia, no nation is so deeply Russophile, no other land of Central Europe has carried out so progressive a social policy. . . . If Czechoslovakia failed, who can hope to reach an understanding with the masters of the Kremlin?[32]

8. Communist Great Power *versus* a Communist Small Nation (Yugoslavia)
"A socialist country cannot be uncommitted."

The Yugoslav experience proved that not even independent-minded Communists could reach an understanding with Moscow. There were no Soviet troops in Yugoslavia at the time of the crisis in relations with the Soviet Union. But unlike the setup in Czechoslovakia, the Party was already firmly in the saddle, all other parties having been eliminated and the whole State apparatus being controlled by the Party machine loyal to Marshal Tito. The country had been liberated from German occupation not only by Soviet troops but also by Communist Yugoslav guerrillas armed and supported by the two Western Powers. The USSR had no valid reason to claim that the Communist regime had been installed in Yugoslavia by reason of the presence of Soviet troops. Tito, unlike his colleagues in the rest of eastern Europe, knew that his regime could exist with or without

Soviet support. Yet Stalin treated him with the same contempt he showed other eastern European Communist leaders and studiously applied the same methods used with impunity wherever Soviet armies were on the spot to implement his patterned instructions.

There were several reasons for the ultimate rift between the Communist great Power and this small Communist country:

(1) The not unreasonable fear of Stalin that the example of Yugoslavia, governed by an independent-minded Communist Party basically loyal to Moscow (though unwilling to tolerate direct Soviet interference in their domestic affairs and ready to co-operate but not take orders) would become contagious in eastern Europe. To cite one example, Gomulka and his friends in Poland would have liked to imitate the Yugoslav example of being an ally of the USSR but not its vassal.

(2) Yugoslav resistance to the Soviet plan of keeping Yugoslavia as the cheap source of foodstuffs and raw materials for the USSR and such eastern European countries as, by contrast, were scheduled for further and speedy industrialization. The Yugoslav Communists were eager to industrialize their country.

(3) The unceremonious attempts by the USSR to infiltrate the Yugoslav state and Party apparatus through Soviet "advisers" and native agents. This was a direct challenge to Tito and his friends, rightly fearful that Soviet infiltration, allowed to go unchecked, would eventually confront them with the alternative of either becoming sycophants or of being ousted from power by a pro-Moscow faction within their own Party.

(4) Stalin did not seem too happy about the slow pace of the Yugoslav collectivization of agriculture, though this was a minor reason of conflict, for Stalin tolerated the same slow pace in Poland, which was run, until 1956, by completely subservient Communist leaders.

(5) Accusations hurled from Moscow that the Yugoslav Party had lost its identity by practically merging with the People's Front were not genuine. The Soviet leaders knew very well that the Yugoslav Party was just as much master at home as other eastern European Communist parties and that the front there was, as elsewhere, only a convenient façade for a one-party regime.

(6) Tito challenged the Soviet preponderance in eastern Europe by promoting the concept of a Balkan federation that would include Yugoslavia, Bulgaria, and Albania, and could possibly expand to Rumania. He encouraged other eastern European leaders also to form federations with neigh-

boring Communist states. No great Power, certainly not the Soviet Union, ever liked the idea of a bloc formed by states within her zone of preponderant influence. Tito uselessly challenged Moscow on this score, since he had not the power to back up his ambitious plan. Dimitrov showed an interest in the idea of such federation and even signed with Yugoslavia, on August 2, 1947, a treaty that pledged both countries to work for a customs union and close economic co-operation. He agreed, with the Yugoslavs, to prepare the ground for the gradual formation of a South-Slav Federated Republic that would presumably include Albania. He went so far as to invite, in a speech made on January 17, 1948, Poland, Czechoslovakia, Hungary, Albania, Rumania, and Greece (civil war was going on there, and he expected Greece soon to become another Communist state) to join an eastern European federation. The USSR, whether ruled by Stalin or anyone else, could not allow this dangerous movement to succeed. *Pravda* came out on January 28, 1948, against the scheme, stating that "these countries do not need a problematic and artificial federation or confederation or customs union." Dimitrov immediately submitted to his master's voice and withdrew his support. But Stalin, though he had, through the Bulgarians, killed the whole scheme, unwisely wished to punish Tito, unmindful whether he had the necessary means to enforce his will. Moreover, the scheme would have foundered of itself for other reasons. The Bulgarians wanted a common state with Bulgaria as an equal member with the whole of Yugoslavia, while Tito intended to add Bulgaria as the seventh unit to the existing Yugoslav federal state. There was little chance that they would find a solution mutually agreeable.

(7) There were territorial problems on which the USSR and Yugoslavia could not agree. The Yugoslav wanted to incorporate Trieste and large slices of southern Austria. Soviet diplomacy had supported them up to a point but withdrew its help in consequence of an over-all bargaining with the Western Powers and of the need to retain popularity among the Italian and Austrian Communists. Tito felt that he had been let down.

The USSR had favored in the interwar period, through its Comintern mouthpiece, the idea of independent Thrace and Macedonia conceived as small Soviet satellites providing the USSR access to the Aegean and Mediterranean seas. This scheme was appalling even to Communists of the countries concerned, Yugoslavia, Greece, and no less so to Bulgaria, whose Communists hoped that Macedonia and Thrace would be somehow linked with their own state. Thrace, which belongs to Greece and Turkey, is populated by those two nationalities, no Thracians being there. This scheme was completely artificial; it was invented to serve the great Power interests of the Soviet Union. Macedonia is divided between Greece, Bulgaria, and Yugoslavia. The Yugoslav Vardar Macedonia, with 1,000,000 population, and the Bulgarian Pirin Macedonia, with 200,000 people, are mostly populated by Macedonians, a distinct Slavic nationality. But the Greek Macedonia, densely populated by Greeks after the exchange of populations with Turkey in the twenties, is 90 per cent Greek. Those Greek Communists who protested were expelled from their Party. The scheme was not abandoned after the war; Tito was not prepared to yield on this issue.

All of these reasons brought on an open conflict with the USSR. The Communist Information Bureau expelled on June 28, 1948, the Yugoslav Party from its fold.[33] The same resolution called upon the Yugoslav Communists to fulfill the "honorable task" of overthrowing Tito and other leaders (see Chapter XI). But Tito controlled his Party, and the "honorable task" remained unfulfilled.

This brings up the question of why the Yugoslavs succeeded in asserting their independence of Moscow while the Hungarians failed in 1956? There were two main reasons: the absence of Soviet troops and a different geographical situation. The Hungarians had Soviet troops on their soil which were quickly reinforced by divisions sent from the USSR and Rumania. Their country was surrounded by the USSR and Soviet satellites, a neutral Austria, and a Yugoslavia which did not intend to intervene. Yugoslavia had a broad Adriatic Sea front and common frontiers with Italy and Greece. Stalin did not know whether the punitive military expedition he would send to Yugoslavia would cause Western intervention and a general war which he did not want and which his country, exhausted by the Second World War, was not prepared to fight. His only weapons were excommunication, insults, and an economic blockade, all of them ineffective in breaking Yugoslav resistance.

This conflict between the USSR and a small Communist country threw light on Western policy as well. Yugoslavia had no more chance than Finland or the Baltic States but for the fact that the Western Powers came to her rescue, quite apart from the ideological question, the nature of the Yugoslav Communist regime, and Tito's thorough dislike of capitalism and political democracy. They never asked Tito to become a member of the Western alliance; he was free to pursue his non-commitment policy and to have a domestic policy to his liking. Yet Western assistance, both economic and military, gave him the needed strength to survive Stalin and relentless Soviet hostility. This assistance was not stopped by the normalization of the Soviet-Yugoslav relations and Tito's firm intention of remaining uncommitted to either bloc. This only shows that there is no gulf separating the West from uncommitted nations as long as they stay uncommitted and that the West does not expect other states to copy is own political system.

The angry exchange of letters and notes between Belgrade and Moscow threw a revealing light on the system that the USSR was at that time imposing on eastern Europe. The Soviet Government complained that its advisers in Yugoslavia had been refused, by lower-echelon Yugoslav Party and state officials, full information on domestic, military, economic, and other matters. The Yugoslavs replied that their highest Party and state authorities had been always ready to supply any information desired but could not allow Soviet military and civilian advisers to collect it underhand. This issue boiled down to a simple problem: Who was master in Yugoslavia, the Yugoslavs or Russians?

Tito informed the USSR in 1946 that his poor country could not longer afford to pay exorbitant salaries to Soviet advisers. The USSR refused to demur. One may see from a letter dated April 13, 1948, signed by Tito and Kardelj and addressed to Stalin and Molotov, that this Yugoslav complaint was not far fetched:

The wages of Soviet experts were four times as high as the wages of the commanders of our armies and three times as high as the wages of our Federal Ministers. The commander of one of our armies, a lieutenant-general or a colonel-general, then had 9,000 to 11,000 dinars a month, and a Soviet military expert, lieutenant-colonel, colonel and general, had from 30,000 to 40,000 dinars. At the same time our Federal Ministers had a salary of 12,000 dinars a month.[34]

Faced with Soviet unwillingness to consider the matter, the Yugoslavs decided to ask for a reduction in the Soviet advisory personnel. The USSR replied by withdrawing them altogether. The letter cited still another delicate problem:

. . . we regard it as improper for agents of the Soviet Intelligence Service to recruit in our country, which is going towards socialism, our citizens for their intelligence service. . . . Those being recruited include officers, various leaders, and those who are negatively disposed towards the new Yugoslavia. . . . We cannot allow the Soviet Intelligence Service to spread its net in our country.[35]

The other source of Yugoslav discontent was the open Soviet economic exploitation on the model applied to the whole of eastern Europe. The Russians wanted to penetrate the country's economy through the device of mixed corporations to operate the extraction of raw materials. The Yugoslavs accepted the concept of joint companies, but with an equitable Soviet share, for the development of their industries. The USSR started by proposing to establish a joint corporation for the prospecting, extraction, and distribution of oil. They refused to accept the Yugoslav oil fields as a contribution to the Yugoslav share in the capital. The Yugoslav domestic price of petroleum products had to cover all the cost of production and assure a profit. The company was to be exempt from Yugoslav social insurance laws so that Yugoslav workers might get such insurance benefits as the corporation could "afford." Similar suggestions were advanced for the exploitation of mines. The peak was reached with the Soviet proposal to found a joint Soviet-Yugoslav bank having financial supervision over all other joint companies and Soviet-Yugoslav trade and thus create, through the multiple joint companies, a super-ministry of economic affairs of Yugoslavia. The Yugoslavs finally accepted the establishment of only two such joint companies, for air transport and Danube shipping. The former took over all international traffic and many domestic lines. The joint board met once a year, actual management being vested in a Russian director. The Yugoslavs made the main contribution in the form of airfields and local facilities, the Russians providing planes; financial contribution was equal. The other joint company took over shipping on the Danube, the Yugoslavs supplying the whole fluvial fleet to be used by the company. The Russian manager was master; he fixed freight rates whereby Yugoslavs paid twice as much as the Russians, and half as much as other Danubian states.[36]

When the Russians were eventually told to get out, their irritation knew no bounds. Bulganin said on May 6, 1950: "The Belgrade Tito-Rankovich-Djilas gang, who serve the Anglo-American imperialists as spies and provocateurs, have seized power in Yugoslavia by blackmail and terror."[37] But they could not do much about it. The balance sheet was unfavorable for the USSR, which had lost access to the Adriatic through friendly Yugoslavia and direct land contact with faithful Albania, where, probably, a Soviet naval base was and is located, and had forced Tito to move from membership in the Soviet military bloc to neutrality. Tito, fearing for the security of his country, went even further in concluding a defensive Balkan pact with Greece and Turkey, both members of NATO. He was on the way to becoming indirectly committed to the West. As Khrushchev said in his secret speech:

[Stalin said:] "I will shake my little finger and there will be no more Tito. He will fall." . . . No matter how much or how little Stalin shook, not only his little finger but everything else that he could shake, Tito did not fall.[38]

Stalin's successors decided to accept the situation as it stood and to do their best to repair the damage as much as possible. In 1953, soon after Stalin's death, they restored normal relations between the Soviet bloc and Yugoslavia. This produced a net benefit: Tito gained thereby a greater bargaining power in dealing with the Western Powers and was given a chance to pursue a straight non-commitment policy.

However, Khrushchev was more ambitious and clearly intended to restore the earlier close co-operation between the USSR and Yugoslavia through a full reconciliation between the two parties. He had made a pilgrimage to the Yugoslav Canossa, rather humiliating for a great Power. During his first visit to Yugoslavia, a joint communiqué was signed on June 3, 1955. Tito scored all the points he was interested in: the Soviet promise of respecting Yugoslav sovereignty and of non-interference in her domestic affairs. The communiqué was somewhat self-indicting for the USSR, at least against the background of past Yugoslav experience:

. . . Both Governments accept the following principles: . . . mutual respect, and non-interference in the domestic affairs for any reasons, economic, political or ideological, since questions of domestic regime, differences in social systems and concrete forms of socialist development, are an exclusive matter for peoples of various states; . . . condemnation of any aggression and any attempt at establishing a political or economic mastery over other countries.[39]

Moreover, the USSR had to pay for the reconciliation with large credits to further Yugoslav industrialization. Khrushchev laid the blame for past mistakes first on Beria and then on the equally dead Stalin. If he hoped to assure the gradual return of the prodigal son to the Soviet family, he was greatly mistaken in underestimating Tito's political acumen. Despite the exchange of mutual visits and cordial speeches on each occasion of such visits, the mutual relations have never returned to what they were in the immediate postwar years.

Tito remembers, as an old Communist, that the Muscovite church has

never truly pardoned even a repentant sinner. How could he throw himself on the mercy of the USSR by cutting all links with the West? If he
needed one, he was taught another lesson by Khrushchev himself in 1956–
57 when the USSR suspended for a time the execution of her economic
and financial promises during the sudden new quarrel over Hungary. The
promises were later carried out, but Tito must have wondered at the time
what would happen if he were to isolate himself from the West. Yugoslavia,
as an uncommitted nation, was able, since the reconciliation, to milk both
the Soviet and the Western cows; why, then, should he expel the Western
from his pasture? The whole business of humiliated Soviet repentance did
not produce many results, except for sowing confusion in Hungary and
Poland with the well-known consequences. The Hungarians and the Poles
were quick in deducing from the Soviet statements, made only for the benefit of Yugoslavia, the conclusion that each eastern European country could
practice its own brand of Communism without any further Soviet interference.

National interests prove to be stronger than a common ideology (basically
the same in the USSR and Yugoslavia) where a Communist government is
free, as the Yugoslav is, to assert its interests when they conflict with the
Soviets'. It would be tedious and unprofitable to recount all the scholastic
disputes between the two parties which were going on in 1956–57. They
covered up deep political differences. Tito, somehow forgetting the size of
his state, would like to influence the course of events in eastern Europe and
contribute to an evolution that would result in greater independence of
the Communist states. The USSR could never agree to this, nor is there
valid reason why it should share its influence with small Yugoslavia. Except for Poland, which Yugoslavia could not help in any way, staunch Moscow supporters remain at the helm of governments everywhere in eastern
Europe, including Bulgaria and Albania.

Tito's delicate position was demonstrated during the Hungarian crisis.
He condemned the first Soviet intervention when he hoped that a new
Communist regime, independent of Moscow, would be installed. He approved the second intervention on realizing that Hungary was moving towards a non-Communist regime whose very existence on the Yugoslav
border would afford a bad example to his own countrymen. In the final
account, he did not influence events in any way.

The dispute over co-existence going on in 1956–57 revealed nothing new.
Tito desired peaceful co-existence with both blocs and denied, therefore,

the need for an especially close relationship among the "socialist" states. The Soviet press told him that peaceful co-existence was the formula only for states with different social systems, while socialist states should practice close friendship, i.e., that he should reintegrate the ranks of the Soviet bloc. He wanted neutrality, but the Soviet press replied that neutrality was good only for capitalist states. In 1957, the Soviet Government chose a method, unpleasant for Yugoslavia, of conveying its desire. On March 28, 1957, the USSR and the Yugoslav neighbor, Hungary, told Tito in their joint Party communiqué:

. . . the slogan of so-called "neutrality" is in fact nothing but an aspiration of the reactionary forces to detach Hungary from the socialist camp, to push her onto the road of denial of national independence and of subordination to foreign imperialist states.[40]

But this is actually the road Tito travels. A month later, on April 17, 1957, it was Albania, that Soviet thorn in the Yugoslav flesh, who joined the Soviet Government in admonishing Tito to quit the Balkan Pact:

The two Governments declare that the existence of the Balkan Pact, a closed military grouping of three States, Yugoslavia, Greece, and Turkey, cannot promote peace on the Balkan peninsula and causes a definite distrust among other Balkan peoples regarding the intentions of the countries-members of the said Pact. This is even more true in view of the fact that one of those States is a member of the North-Atlantic Bloc, while the other is simultaneously a member of the North-Atlantic Bloc and the Baghdad Bloc. This circumstance links the Balkan Pact to those [two] aggressive groupings.[41]

Tito thinks that his brand of Communism is better than the Soviet brand and has no qualms in saying it publicly; the USSR cannot accept this view, either for its own or the eastern European benefit, and nothing would compel it to do so. Thus the theological discussions may proceed with courtesy or without, as they did in the period following the Hungarian revolution, but they only disclose two very different approaches to international relations and two disparate sets of national interests.

9. Economic Exploitation and Dependence of Eastern Europe

Yugoslav complaints about Soviet economic exploitation revealed the situation basically prevailing in the rest of eastern Europe until 1956, with improvement after Stalin's death. Stalin was unwise in quickly despoiling eastern Europe immediately after the last war in order to lay hands on as many goods as possible, especially industrial equipment, the more quickly to rehabilitate the war-devastated regions of the USSR. He thus impoverished his own zone of influence, reducing for a time its ability steadily to supply the USSR with annual imports of goods. Soviet troops proceeded with looting but were not so thorough there as they were in Manchuria. The peace treaties of 1947 authorized the USSR, in addition, to remove more goods as reparations from Rumania and Hungary to the total, respectively, of 300 and 200 million dollars. The peace treaties allocated to the USSR all the German and Italian assets in Rumania, Hungary, and Bulgaria without mentioning the fact that a great many German assets had been native property before the war and the forcible Nazi seizure. This gave the USSR an excellent lever for invading the three national economies through the so-called joint companies, to which the USSR had only to contribute the German assets transferred to itself. The total value of these assets was evaluated at some 600 million dollars.

About two hundred enterprises of all sorts in Hungary and one-third in Rumania passed into Soviet hands overnight. Soviet-managed joint companies took over Rumanian oil properties, maritime and fluvial transportation, civil aviation, banking, insurance, lumber, natural gas, coal mining, chemical, building, metallurgical, and other enterprises. Similar companies began to manage Hungarian fluvial navigation, civil aviation, oil, bauxite, and aluminum properties. Much the same joint companies invaded Bulgarian mining, shipping, and civil aviation.[42] All those joint companies, managed by Russian directors, provided large profits for the Soviet partner and, in fact, controlled the economic lives of the three countries. The general pattern of Soviet economic exploitation was not different from the one disclosed by Yugoslavia after the rupture.

All eastern European countries were fleeced through trade with the USSR, trade which arranged prices above the international market level for Soviet commodities, below it for eastern European goods. Neither Soviet nor eastern European sources have ever officially disclosed the true prices charged in mutual trade, but we have some unofficial information, together with general complaints voiced by the Polish press in 1956. For instance, the main Polish export commodity, coal, was largely mortgaged to the Soviet Union by the agreement of August 16, 1945, which obliged Poland to deliver 8 million tons in 1946, 13 million tons each year in 1947–1950, and subsequently from 1951 onwards 12 million tons until the evacuation of Soviet troops from East Germany. S. Mikolajczyk, who was Polish vice-premier at the time of the conclusion of the agreement, says that the price for a ton was only $1.25, while Sweden and Denmark were offering $12.[43]

Poland was thus losing about 100 million dollars annually with which she could have bought machinery in the West. In 1948, the USSR agreed to cut deliveries to 7 million tons annually. It is known from other sources that Czechoslovakia had to supply shoes at 170 crowns a pair while the cost of production was 300 crowns. In 1948, the USSR sold to Italy tobacco acquired from Bulgaria in the same type of trade, at a price 35 per cent lower than the Bulgarian. In 1956, the Polish press could not mention the exact data for fear of provoking Soviet anger, but general complaints were voiced relating to the past. One newspaper referred to

... the criminal shortcomings of our foreign trade personnel which concluded unfavorable foreign agreements and displayed insufficient elasticity in the prices of exported coal that caused certain losses.[44]

It concluded that

... workers and peasants were deeply convinced that products of their labor did not entirely benefit the Polish people and that part of these products was appropriated by other nations. . . . The abnormal nature of our trade relations with the countries of the socialist camp was felt by the Polish public more painfully and bitterly because it remembered the practices of German occupants who had taken away the majority of products of workers' and peasants' labor.[45]

The comparison between the enemy and the Soviet ally was not too flattering for the latter. The principal ideological organ of the Polish Communist Party wrote:

There were commercial agreements, such as the coal agreement of 1946, which were unilaterally beneficial for the Soviet Union and prejudicial to our economic interests.[46]

The ruthless fleecing by the Soviet Union could be contrasted with American assistance given through UNRRA immediately after the war when eastern Europe was still open to the West. The total UNRRA aid to that area amounted to $1,404,000,000. This aid was terminated in 1947, the year of the foundation of the Cominform. Two years later, in January, 1949, the USSR established, together with its satellites, the Council of

Mutual Economic Aid to co-ordinate their mutual economies. Beginning with the Korean War, the USSR compelled all eastern European countries to give high priority to war industries. As Hilary Minc, the former Polish Minister of Economy, said at the October, 1956, session of his party's Central Committee, the supplies originally reserved for other industries had to be diverted to war-material plants. Poland, and probably the rest of the area, installed in 1951–1953 a true war economy. As he admitted, this resulted in "the rise in prices of foodstuffs and consumer goods, and the fall in living standards."[47]

The foreign trade of eastern Europe was largely monopolized by the Soviet Union and in addition was taken up by mutual exchange, this part of Europe having been cut off from its usual trade with the West. Two comparative sets of figures taken from a recent Soviet source give a clear idea of the complete reorientation of eastern European trade:

Trade with all other countries of the Soviet Bloc		Trade with USSR only
In 1937	In 1954	In 1953
(in percentages of total foreign trade)		
Poland	7%	70%	25%
Czechoslovakia	11%	72%	28%
Hungary	13%	70%	29%
Rumania	18%	72%	51%
Bulgaria	10%	87%	58%
Albania	5%	100%	52%
East Germany	—	75%	40%[48]

The same source says:

The share of the Soviet Union in the exchange of goods between the countries of the socialist camp radically changed after the war. Before the Second World War the Soviet Union had commercial relations principally with England, USA, Germany, and France. The share of the USSR in the total foreign trade of Poland, Czechoslovakia, Rumania, and Bulgaria never exceeded before the war one per cent, while Rumania and Hungary had no trade with the Soviet Union.[49]

After Stalin's death, the system of joint companies was gradually abandoned, but the Soviet Union required the repayment of its largely mythical share. Between 1953 and 1955, almost all of these companies were dissolved. Perhaps the Soviet Government considered it unwise to continue this kind of shameless exploitation, which was all too visible to the local population. Perhaps it also found a better way of controlling the economic

life of eastern Europe, not through direct Soviet management of key enterprises, but through Soviet co-ordination of long-term economic plans. The
guiding concepts are two: to assign to each country certain fields of economic specialization, the Soviet Union remaining the only over-all producer of all commodities, and to allocate to each country definite quotas of
goods to be produced for exchange with the USSR, other eastern European
countries, and China. This system creates a complete economic dependence
of eastern Europe, the Soviet Union acting as co-ordinator. As a Soviet
specialist says:

A socialist system of the international division of labor is being created;
each country supplies a share of its goods to the new democratic market in
order to meet the needs of other brotherly countries, and in turn receives
from them goods which are indispensable for its own national economy.[50]

Thus the execution of any Five Year Plan depends on supplies from other
countries, and vice versa. This system would be unobjectionable if the distribution of economic roles and the fixing of prices were freely agreed upon.
However, the same author frankly says:

. . . the law of the cost of production plays a certain [sic!] regulating role
in foreign trade relations, because the socialist states take into consideration
the cost of production for the determination of prices. However the role of
the law of cost of production is limited, as the socialist states themselves
determine . . . the volume of mutual supplies and the price of goods.[51]

A "limited" role of cost of production in fixing prices for commodities
might not be beneficial for weak States facing the powerful Soviet partner:

The long-term agreements determine fixed quotas of exports and imports
of machinery and equipment, of complete supplies of enterprises, of industrial raw materials, and other commodities; . . . each country of the socialist
camp . . . produces such goods which are needed by it domestically and by
the friendly States.[52]

The nature of this division of labor may be seen from the following:

The USSR supplies the countries of people's democracy with the most important types of industrial equipment and machinery for key industries,
raw materials (iron, chrome and manganese ores, cotton), etc. . . . The new
democratic world market receives from Poland coal, coke, zinc, rolled steel
and other metals, machine-tools, a number of important agricultural products, and textiles; from Hungary—transport and electrical equipment,
bauxites, textiles, agricultural products; from Rumania—considerable

quantities of oil and petroleum products, timber, foodstuffs, equipment
for oil industry, locomotives, railroad trucks, and other manufactured
products; from Bulgaria—mainly tobacco, rose oil, fruit, processed agricultural products, lead, zinc, copper, and cement; from Albania—oil,
bitumen, agricultural and livestock products. Industrial equipment and
machinery supplied by Czechoslovakia and the German Democratic Republic play a considerable role in the industrial expansion of some of the
people's democracies.[53]

One may add that Poland supplies ships; Czechoslovakia, railroad rolling
stock, automobiles and trucks, leather and shoes, textiles, glass products
and ceramics; East Germany, electrical equipment, optical and precision
instruments, chemicals and fertilizers, railroad rolling stock, sea and fluvial
vessels; Hungary, locomotives and Diesel engines. Soviet participation in
eastern European trade remains very high in consequence of the close economic integration. The figures for 1955 were as follows:

The USSR share in the foreign trade of (in percentages)[54]

Poland	32	East Germany	40
Hungary	22	Rumania	47
Czechoslovakia	33.7	Bulgaria	46.2

This close economic integration around the USSR reminds one of the
economic exclusiveness of old colonial empires, where foreign trade of the
colonies was monopolized by the colonial Power. It involves certain risks
for eastern Europe rather than for the USSR, with its enormous economic
resources; for instance a breakdown or slowdown in carrying the Five Year
Plan in one country has immediate adverse repercussions on the economy
of some other countries. This was illustrated by the aftermath of the 1956
Polish and Hungarian crises. The virtual stoppage of production in Hungary during the last months of 1956, and the Polish cutting down of exports of coal especially affected East Germany and Czechoslovakia; less
coke from Poland meant less steel produced in East Germany, which, in
turn, could supply less machinery to other eastern European countries and
the USSR; less bauxite from Hungary caused a drop in the Czechoslovak
production of aluminum products. The USSR had to step in by extending
credits and increasing its exports to eastern Europe. Bulgaria received a
570-million-rouble loan; East Germany was helped by a 340-million-rouble
credit, a reduction in the cost of maintenance of Soviet troops, and a raise
in the price of uranium exported to the Soviet Union; Poland got a 500-
million-rouble credit, with the postponement of repayment of her older

810-million-rouble debts; Rumania got a 270-million-rouble credit; Hungary a 1,100-million-rouble loan, etc. Thus Poland, among others, was able to import, on credit, 1,400 million tons of Soviet grain; Hungary, coal, coke, grain, fodder, rubber, cotton, and other products; Bulgaria, machinery, etc.[55]

For the first time, the USSR (probably temporarily because of the unexpected crisis of 1956) had to make an effort in assisting eastern Europe instead of fleecing it in order to prevent its economic decline. However, Soviet credits granted in 1956–57 (a total of a few billion roubles) could not adversely affect the Soviet economy, with its 175 billion roubles of capital investment in 1957. They aimed, among other things, at keeping eastern Europe on the road of industrialization. According to the current Five Year Plans, the average annual accumulation for investment was to be, between 1956 and 1960, the following unusually high percentage of national income: Czechoslovakia, 22; East Germany, 18; Hungary, 18; Poland, 18; Rumania, 25; while the Soviet figure is 24 per cent.[56] This high rate of annual accumulation proved to be untenable, at least in Hungary and Poland, where the 1956 events disclosed widespread dissatisfaction among industrial workers with low wages and hence low labor productivity. Soviet credits might temporarily ease the situation.

There arises the question of why the Soviets displayed intense interest in the quick industrialization of eastern Europe, whereas the other colonial Powers never displayed any such interest. First of all, the Soviet Union is not an exporter of consumer goods, of which they are notoriously short. Secondly, she imports manufactured consumer and even capital goods for her needs from eastern European countries such as East Germany, Czechoslovakia, and Poland. Thirdly, she wants an industrialized eastern Europe to help in the task of assisting China and in the extension of trade with the underdeveloped countries. Fourthly, she is intensely interested in increasing her over-all economic potential as compared to the Western, while the industrialization of eastern Europe means an addition to the Soviet potential. Actually, one colonial Power, Japan, pursued a similar policy of intense industrial development of her Manchurian possession for the quicker growth of the total Japanese potential. The pattern is different from the old colonial one, where the colonial Power wanted to retain the monopoly of industrial products and to keep the colonies in their role of suppliers of foodstuffs and raw materials. However, the common element in both cases is the national interest of the colonial Power as the decisive factor in the economic life of the colonial or protected countries. Poland, once she had recovered autonomy in planning in 1956, immediately began to adjust her Five Year Plan to the requirements of the population and her own ideas of what was best. Other satellite countries would do the same were their Communist leaders less servile to Moscow.

10. Churches. Magic of Fear

It is not surprising that eastern European Communists, all of them committed to a militant atheistic ideology, have pursued a systematically hostile policy regarding all religious denominations. The Catholic church, with its foreign ramifications, has paid the highest price in persecutions. Cardinals, bishops, priests, and clergymen were imprisoned; rival Communist-controlled "patriotic" religious organizations were promoted, and a purely secular education based on Marxism-Leninism was introduced in all schools.[57] That this policy did not correspond to the wishes of the population may be seen from two facts. One of the first acts of Hungarian insurgents was to release Cardinal Mindszenty from prison. One of the first moves of Gomulka after his return to power was to conciliate public opinion by freeing the imprisoned Cardinal Wyszynski and several bishops; he concluded with the Church a sort of armistice agreement which restored freedom of religious activities and the facility to teach religion at schools if parents wished it. The parents soon gave their answer by asking for religious instruction in practically all elementary and secondary schools; the Government complied, much as it disliked this outburst of deep religious feeling.

Looking back at the twelve years of Soviet domination of eastern Europe, we may detect all three features of a colonial protectorate: (1) Depriving the protected nations of freedom in matters of foreign policy. It suffices to consult the records of the United Nations to be impressed by the infallible identity of speeches and votes of all eastern European and Soviet delegations, a fact that could profitably be contrasted with different views expressed by the other Communist state, Yugoslavia. Also, deprivation of national defense; all of the armed forces are closely integrated under the supreme command of Soviet Marshal Konev; all the countries concerned are tied to the USSR by bilateral alliances and the Warsaw Pact; and all, except Poland since the fall of 1956, have their armies infiltrated with Soviet advisers, who often perform commanding functions. (2) Economic exploitation was going on in various forms at least until the crisis of 1956. (3) The protecting Power interfered more than any other in the past in the domestic life of the protected countries, having imposed by stages, in 1944–48, a uniform political-social pattern and rule by its satellite Communist parties. Poland was the only country where its leaders shook off (in 1956) servility to the protecting Power.

The best insight into the nature of the regime imposed from Moscow is to listen to the protests voiced in 1955–56 by the Communist-controlled Polish press (there was and is no other press in Poland), the only one in eastern Europe, except for Hungary, that dared to tell the truth. These protests were very eloquent as an indictment of the Soviet-like pattern of life, although they were moderated by two factors: the fear of a Soviet military intervention, and the fear of eventually convincing the population that Communism in any form was not the kind of regime really suitable for mankind.

The years 1947–48 were those not only of the last stage in the process of Sovietization but also of the full extension of the Stalinist system of mass terror to Party members and the populations of eastern Europe. The weapon of terror was vested in the hands of the political police, which had at its disposal military detachments for quelling riots, torture chambers, and advisers sent by the Soviet police apparatus. The terror struck the guilty and innocent alike. But there was some thought behind this indiscriminate terror, namely, the creation of the mesmerism of boundless and paralyzing fear. People dared not speak out for fear that friend or neighbor might be a police informer. Knowledge that others were tortured or imprisoned made people furtive. Eastern Europe was paralyzed by fear, even as Russia had been by the mass purges of the thirties. A uniform sepulchral atmosphere was created in which everyone distrusted his fellow, the grim fear of terror acting as a more powerful deterrent than terror itself; all opponents within and without the Party were reduced to silence. L. Wudzki, a member of the Polish Central Committee, described this paralysis of will among his own colleagues at the October, 1956, session of this highest Party body, then proceeding for the first time with an honest examination of conscience:

Yet there must have been Communists with strong characters whose moral brakes still worked and who could at least behave like Communists, like men, though they lacked courage to resist. Alas, some obviously could not; others did not want to. In any case those who resisted were broken and imprisoned as enemies and traitors; those who tried to behave like men either were brushed aside or left [the Party]. There were too few of either kind. The majority, resigned to the regime, were building for themselves warm nests close to the generous and full breasts of Beria's system; swilling, they were getting drunk with power and all the accessories and privileges thereof. All moral brakes ceased to work.[58]

Then he described the terror itself:

. . . people were caught in the street and released after seven days of investigation mutilated for life. These people had to be sent to Tworki [a Polish hospital for mental cases]. Others were seeking asylum in Tworki in order to escape the Security Office. They simulated mental illness. Still other honest people were fleeing abroad in panic and alarm. . . . The whole city [of Warsaw] knew that people were murdered, that there were cells where people stood for three weeks in excrement up to their ankles; the whole city knew that Rozanski [a high Political Security official] tore off people's fingernails, and that people were drenched in cold water and left outside in freezing weather.[59]

Another Communist described the effect of this mesmeric fear:

Human fear was like a black thread interwoven into almost all those meetings. People asked questions while remaining seated or hiding behind their neighbor in order that the chairman should not discover who asked the question. This happened although I tried to give the least official character to the meetings and assured them that there would be no topics taboo and that nobody would take down the names of people participating in the discussion or asking questions. In the meeting at the automobile plant, while I noted the questions, someone exclaimed: "You have promised not to take down names but you do it." The discussion immediately died out, questions were asked no longer.[60]

Outwardly, everything was peaceful. Soviet sources could report then, and later, up to the 1956 crisis, the eastern European developments in rosy terms. Everything was for the best in the best Communist world. A Soviet author wrote in 1955:

The results of the fulfillment of the Six-Year Plan . . . disclose for the past years immense successes which the Polish people, led by the Polish United Workers' Party, achieved in the socialist industrialization of the country . . . and in the further rise of the material and cultural standards of people. . . . Big successes were attained in increasing labor productivity. . . . In 1953 the harvest of the four grain cultures from one hectare was 13 centnars for the co-operatives, founded over three years ago, and only 11.3 centnars for individual homesteads. . . . The material condition of the toiling masses of Poland systematically improves. . . . The real income of workers, officials, and peasants increased last year [1954] by an average of 11 to 12 per cent.[61]

A year later, Gomulka, various members of the Polish Central Committee, and the Polish press disclosed that this attractive picture had been interwoven with lies. But general elections in Poland and elsewhere continued to yield the tabulated 97 to 99 quasi-unanimities in support of Communist regimes. Of course voting was by open ballot on one-ticket candidates, and votes were counted by Party members.

11. Revolt in Poland

The fall of Beria and the following reduction in power and prestige of the political police in the Soviet Union and eastern Europe broke the spell of fear. Beginning in 1954, the intellectuals started talking more freely. Except for a short period in Czechoslovakia, Poland and Hungary were the countries most affected by this fresh breeze. But the real shock came with the 20th Soviet Congress and Khrushchev's secret speech, which soon became widely known. The Communists themselves were overwhelmed by this brutal toppling of their idol from the pedestal of a quasi-divine glory. This was done by the same Khrushchev who wrote in 1939, soon after the horrible mass purges, on Stalin's sixtieth anniversary:

Today, on the sixtieth anniversary of Comrade Stalin's birth, all eyes will be turned towards our great leader of nations, our dear friend and father. . . . The working class and all the toilers possess in Comrade Stalin the greatest man of our era. . . . Stalin is the father of the people by virtue of the love he bears them.[62]

Seventeen years later, the same man was to tear the legend to pieces for reasons which are difficult to guess. Perhaps it was an emotional urge shared with army leaders to take revenge for the humiliations and fear Stalin had fed his servants. But the secret speech sowed confusion in the minds of Polish Communists, who were suddenly deprived of their guiding compass. If Stalin, their leader for thirty years, had been a monster and a fallible man, who could be right? Roman Werfel, a member of the Polish Central Committee said:

We believed that Stalin knew better than we did; even where something seemed to be difficult to understand, we were convinced that it should be so. What could Beria's system do in Poland in the years 1938–1939? But we all accepted the liquidation of the Polish Communist Party [by the Comintern]; if we entertained some doubts as to the guilt of people, if we never tired in asking an explanation of the whole affair, if we admitted that many mistakes were committed in 1937 in the USSR, each of us brushed aside the thought that the whole 1937 year [the time of purges] and Stalin's whole policy in this period could have been a horrible mistake. . . . Later came in all countries of people's democracy the anti-Yugoslav resolutions and all that followed [local purges]. Why did we submit? I think that, first of all, because we were convinced that any attempt at a polemic with Stalin or simply having one's own opinion would have meant passing to the camp of counter-revolution.[63]

Gomulka referred to the same cause as late as May, 1957: "The 20th Congress seriously shook the international workers' movement, in particular its Workers' and Communist parties."[64] A young Polish Communist expressed the same thought with the bitterness of a youth whose previous beliefs had been shattered by the Party and whose faith therein was in turn destroyed by Khrushchev's speech:

Our whole faith in the Cause and our loyalty and trust in the Party were transferred to Stalin's person. . . . He was for us the incarnation of the Party ideals and of its struggle. . . . Marxism demolished our faith in all false shrines. . . . While staging sham, false, and varnished images of "our heroic working class," we were in fact turning our backs on it, its opinions and criticisms.[65]

A member of the Polish Central Committee exclaimed: "The 20th Congress helped all of us, and me in particular, to look at yesterday, today and tomorrow with different eyes."[66] A youngster spoke for his indoctrinated generation:

I interpreted to myself and to others every mistake in the policies of the USSR and the Polish People's Republic, every turn in comrade Stalin's policy, as a step forward towards Communism. I tried with the best intentions to believe in what I could not understand. . . . I was 15 years old when I entered the League of Polish Youth. . . . What am I today? A weathercock, after five years of membership. . . . There no longer exist any authorities for me. There are only men. . . . And those men must render their accounts to other men. There will be no men-gods. . . . I am not responsible that Stalin placed himself above the Party. His closest comrades are guilty. . . . Chaos reigns in my mind.[67]

This youngster could see what more sophisticated people abroad sometimes refused to see, namely, that Stalin's guilt was shared by every one of his closest collaborators, who had supported him from fear for their lives or because of their convictions. Like Anderson's child, he told his elders that the king was naked.

Stalin died in 1953, and Beria was executed in the same year. Beginning in 1954, non-conformist views began to be expressed in the Polish press. This trend gathered momentum in 1955–56. Intellectuals, mostly Party members, voiced opinions that would have been unthinkable a few years before. The hypnotism of fear was no longer effective. The same non-conformist sentiment broke out among workers and youth; people instinctively realized that they could now openly express what they had previously only felt. After the 20th Congress, the storm quickly gathered; the whole question of relations with the Soviet Union, and of the nature of domestic regime, came up for re-examination.

Intellectuals aired grievances which the average man had felt for years; they sparked the trouble that culminated in the October days. However, the workers, the alleged rock upon which the Party stood, did not remain passive. As in Berlin in June, 1953, and in Budapest, the workers of Poznań rose against their master, the Party, which claimed to rule the country in the name of the dictatorship of the industrial proletariat. They revolted against low wages and Party indifference to their misery. On June 27, 1956, at seven o'clock in the morning, the workers of the Poznań locomotive plant began an orderly march towards the center of the city. Their ranks swelled with workers from other factories. Placards were raised claiming: "Freedom and bread," "Out with the Russians," "Down with phony Communism." To Lenin's 1917 slogans of peace and bread, these authentic proletarians opposed, almost forty years later, the demand for bread and freedom. An immense crowd of 30,000 people filled the main city square. At 11:30, fighting began between the crowd and the political police; public buildings were attacked. The regular army, with tanks, was called out to quell the revolt, but fighting continued throughout the night, and order was restored only on the following day. According to the official version, 53 persons were killed and more than 300 wounded. The first governmental reaction was to claim, on June 30, that American agents and reactionaries staged the revolt. This was also the explanation given in the Soviet press, which had similarly explained the Berlin riots in June, 1953.[68] But the country was no longer in the mood to accept such explanations. Soon the Polish Government changed its version; it acknowledged that the Poznań events had been due to a genuine dissatisfaction among the workers and that they were a spontaneous outburst of anger.

The later version was approved by the Central Committee in October, 1956. The then First Secretary of the Party, Edward Ochab, said:

We tried in the first period to follow the traditional pattern and to explain superficially the Poznań events by attributing them to the influence of foreign factors. We acted in solidarity with a number of brotherly parties [a clear allusion to the Soviet] which immediately sought in the first place for an imperialist agency.[69]

Joseph Cyrankiewicz, the Polish premier in 1956 and now, who had been the first to attribute the Poznań revolt to foreign agents, retracted himself:

There are also people who see in those moods only an action of the enemy and even construct the thesis about [foreign] agents. This comes from the old barrel-organ, but it has played the tune so many times in former years in our countries that it squeaks, gets hoarse and abounds in false notes.[70]

Another member of the same body said simply: "Poznań shook the conscience of every honest man."[71]

The reaction of the honest man, whether a Party member or not, turned against the hateful Stalinist regime, the great Power that foisted it on Poland, and Soviet agents within the Party itself. The large majority of the Party Central Committee, as if awakened from a bewitched sleep, began to realize that there was something both horrible and contemptible in their taking orders from a foreign Power. A feeling of national pride was taking the upper hand. Matters came to a head at the 8th Plenum of the Central Committee, which lasted from October 10 to October 21, 1956. A man who had dominated the Polish Party's life, B. Bierut, its First Secretary, was no longer alive to restrain the trend towards a greater independence of Moscow; he had died just after the 20th Congress. Another Moscow agent, Berman, was hopelessly compromised by the terror in which he had played a crucial role from behind the scenes. A third, H. Minc, the economic planner, was confronted with the abyssmal failure of his plan and a desperate economic situation. Other members of the Central Committee, who placed loyalty to the USSR above everything else, including their native country, led by General Witaszewski, one of the founders of the Union of Patriots in 1943, were in a definite minority. The First Secretary of the Party, Edward Ochab, picked up by Moscow after Bierut's death, proved to be a complete disappointment; he joined the majority, as did several of top leaders who had never before failed to follow the Moscow line.

The majority finally found a leader in Gomulka, who had been released from prison, together with his political friends, and after several years could again attend the meetings of the Central Committee. He was able not only to provide the majority with a leader but also to inspire confidence in the country which remembered that he had been incarcerated for opposing blind obedience to the foreign Power. Thanks to his record, the Party was able to find with the country a common platform, not in Marxism, but in national resistance to the foreign pressure. It is characteristic that the main issue between Moscow and Warsaw at that time was the question of whether the Soviet Union would be able to maintain on the Polish Political Bureau its viceroy, Marshal Rokossovsky. His membership in the Political Bureau was symbolical for both sides—if he were not reelected, Poland would assert greater domestic independence towards the protecting Power. His person was as significant as that of the Sultan of Morocco in the context of the Moroccan fight for independence.

E. Ochab, opening the session, informed the Central Committee that a Soviet delegation composed of Khrushchev, Mikoyan, Molotov, and Kaganovich had come to Warsaw for urgent conversations with the Polish Political Bureau.[72] His audience was in a good position to understand the meaning of this unexpected visit. One of the members of the Central Committee proposed to elect, first of all, the new Political Bureau, with Gomulka but without Rokossovsky, before consenting to talk to the Russians. The matter was settled by a compromise; Gomulka, already scheduled to succeed Ochab as First Secretary, was to lead the Polish delegation in the talks. There is no official Polish or Soviet record on the nature of those conversations, but informal information about their stormy character is supported by two factors: the simultaneous, ominous movements of Soviet troops towards Warsaw from their base in Lower Silesia, a fact acknowledged by Marshal Rokossovsky himself (see Chapter VII), and the concentration of other Soviet divisions on the western and eastern borders of Poland, and, also, discreet allusions by the Polish delegates to the Soviet representatives' pressure. One of the Poles, Alexander Zawadzki, told his colleagues:

Soviet comrades gave as the reason of their sudden arrival in our country and of the composition of their delegation which is known to you, comrades, the deep apprehension within the Presidium of the Central Committee of the Communist Party of the Soviet Union concerning the evolution of the situation in Poland. . . . The Soviet comrades were also interested in our projects of new composition of leadership which the 8th Plenum of the Party Central Committee was going to elect.[73]

E. Ochab added this information:

I have met completely ill-founded and unheard-of accusations in the conversations with our Soviet friends . . . the sincere, difficult and bitter talks we had two days ago.[74]

Why were those conversations bitter and difficult? The Party and the country at large did not intend to denationalize factories, to restore large estates, or even to overthrow the Communist regime. The only controversial problem was whether Poland would recover her internal autonomy; the new Party leadership did not challenge the existence of the Soviet alliance or the presence of Soviet troops in Poland. Alien control over Polish foreign and military policies was not questioned, as it was in Tunisia and Morocco. The issue was relatively modest by modern standards of revolting colonial populations. It was touch and go whether the USSR would fight a war on that issue. It is difficult to be sure whether the Soviet leaders had in mind merely blackmail in ordering the movement of their troops, in the hope that Polish Communists would be frightened back into their former unquestioning obedience, or whether they changed their former plans during those stormy conversations of the night of October 19–20. They knew that Warsaw workers were mobilized and ready to fight. University students were joining in the movement of national resurgence; the country was awakening. Polish troops could not be relied upon to execute the orders of Marshal Rokossovsky and other Soviet commanders at that time controlling them. Perhaps Khrushchev and his companions were afraid that a regular war in Poland would cause a new revolt in East Germany and thus incite the West Germans to cross the border to help their countrymen. Could they be sure that American troops on the border would fire on West Germans to prevent the flare-up of a general war? Whatever was in the Soviet leaders' minds, they capitulated and accepted the inevitable.

The pro-Russian members of the Central Committee tried to retrieve the situation. One of them threatened and pleaded:

The improvement of the relations with the Soviet Union, already strained, I repeat, strained by the events of the last few days [requires the re-election of Marshal Rokossovsky]. I am afraid that we shall not improve those relations by approving the list [of the Political Bureau] without comrade Rokossovsky. . . . There are certain sacred and permanent principles which it is not permissible to violate. This is, comrades, our great concept of patriotism and internationalism. We must not be unfaithful to this concept.[75]

This rather peculiar concept of patriotism, so frequent among Communists, which placed servility to the protecting Power above one's own country, was repudiated by more than two-thirds of the Central Committee. Marshal Rokossovsky was defeated, the vote being 52 to 23. The new Political Bureau included Gomulka as First Secretary of the Party. The bugaboo of fear was no longer operative. As a member of the C.C. said:

An irreversible thing has happened: today neither the Party nor the public will let their mouths be shut, they will not allow the mouth of the press to be shut. . . . This can be done only despite the nation, against the nation and the Party, by superior force.[76]

The crucial vote was secret, the first secret vote in the Polish Central Committee, as Ochab said.[77]

Soon afterwards, Marshal Rokossovsky and the Soviet commanding officers left Poland. Characteristically, Marshal Rokossovsky, who had been proclaimed a Pole in 1949, had no difficulty in being appointed the Soviet vice-minister of defense and in becoming, in 1957, a member of the Georgian Central Committee. Among the returning Russians was not only the former commander-in-chief of the Polish armed forces but also the commander of the Polish air force, the commander of the Polish artillery, the commander of the Warsaw military garrison, and other such high-ranking former "Polish" officers.[78]

The revolt of a nation kept for twelve years in colonial subjection succeeded. The USSR did not use the ultimate weapon of force, as it did in Hungary. There were two reasons why the Polish drama did not end in the same tragic way; the Poles never challenged either the Soviet alliance or the presence of Soviet troops in Poland. They realized that they would lose an unequal military struggle, since the West could not help in the era of nuclear stalemate. Secondly, the country remained in the hands of a Communist Party that was insubordinate, it is true, but not hostile to Russia. Soon after the Polish events and during the Hungarian crisis, the Soviet Government published, on October 31, 1956, its declaration on the principles governing relations between the USSR and other socialist states (in effect the eastern European, for the declaration scarcely applied to China). The declaration frankly acknowledged the lack of equality in those relations:

There were more than a few difficulties and unsolved problems, and more than a few outright mistakes were committed in the process of building the new regime and carrying out deep revolutionary changes. These difficulties, unsolved problems and mistakes also occured in the relations with the socialist countries. These infractions and errors violated the principle of equality among socialist States.[79]

The declaration promised to establish such mutual economic relations as would be free of anything that would "infringe upon the principles of national sovereignty, mutual benefit, and equality." The same principles were to govern the matter of Soviet military, economic, and scientific advisers. But the eastern European countries were reminded, at the same time, of two conditions *sine qua non* of peaceful co-operation, namely, their participation in the Warsaw Pact and their acceptance of Soviet troops on their territory as the ultimate Russian guarantee. Although the declaration seemed to concede that the matter of Soviet troops could be the object of mutual discussions, it attached a condition that made impossible any request for the withdrawal of these troops:

... The Soviet Government abides by this general principle that the stationing of troops of any State-member of the Warsaw Treaty occurs by agreement among all [*sic!*] its members and with the assent of that State where those troops are or are going to be located at its request.[80]

To the hypothetical Polish request for the evacuation of Soviet troops, the USSR could oppose the lack of assent by other members of the Warsaw Treaty. A few days later, it did not even bother to do this but simply sent reinforcements to its troops in Hungary.

The Polish situation was different from the Hungarian in another respect. Fear of Germany, together with the apprehension that without Soviet support, western Polish boundaries would be revised and German-expelled populations would come back (new Polish settlers being, in turn, expelled from the annexed territories) acted as a brake on any desire to challenge the USSR beyond the scope of internal autonomy. Hungarians acted under no such restraint. Their tragic defeat served as a further warning to the Poles and other eastern European countries. Khrushchev said brutally in 1957: "Such events will not occur in other socialist countries, because the Hungarian events were for all of them an instructive lesson."[81] The sight of Russian troops massacring Hungarians fighting for their national freedom, as the rest of the world watched with horror and also with fear of general complications, must have been an instructive lesson indeed.

The Polish national revolt against the protecting foreign Power is interesting as a proof that attachment to one's own country is stronger in the heart of modern man than any ideology. Those two-thirds of the members of the Polish Central Committee acted as Poles, not as Communists, when they voted for Marshal Rokossovsky's ouster. Their feelings were not basically different from those of Algerian guerrillas or the Indonesians who fought against Holland for their independence. Nationalism is the only factor that may have a disruptive effect on the Soviet Empire; it is the one possible reason for a disintegration of Communist ideological unity.

12. Polish-Communist Criticism of the Regime Imposed by the Protecting Power

Discussions that had preceded and accompanied the Polish crisis, discussions that had begun in 1954, were also deeply interesting from another point of view. For the first time, authentic Communists proceeded with a thorough and critical reappraisal of their system as copied after the Soviet original. It was an incisive criticism by people who lived for ten years under the new regime and who inherited a national tradition hardly adjustable to the Soviet pattern. The influence of a thousand years of close cultural links with the West did not evaporate on the day the first Soviet soldier set foot on Polish soil. The 1948 merger between the Socialist Party and the Communist Party "contaminated" the Communists with the traditions brought with them by former Socialists. These traditions were alien to the Leninist heritage of thought and even more to the Stalinist pattern. Polish intellectuals could outwardly be forced to imitate the Soviet hackneyed phrases and artists and musicians to make genuflexions before the tenets of socialist realism, but, accustomed to free intercourse with Western intellectual and artistic trends, they never changed their innermost convictions. Communist relativist morality, with its justification of the use of all means in the name of revolution, could not take root in a country trained for countless generations in the traditional ethics.

All non-conformist articles published in 1954–56 may be usefully grouped in the following categories: (A) *Protest against the censorship of literature, arts, and learning.* We may understand what that censorship was in Poland, and still is in the USSR and the rest of eastern Europe, by listening to a Polish Communist critic:

. . . Freedom of expression is also that of conscience, because it is the pre-condition of arts and literature. It is a question of restoring to words their true meaning. . . . Only recently freedom meant slavery, sovereignty—dependence, honesty—villainy. Totalitarianism, in whatever form, depraves words. . . . Never before was the public mind cheated so intensely, on such a scale, and with the assistance of so many words denuded by guile of their proper moral meaning, than in our terrible period. . . . Censorship proceeded by impugning not only what could be read in a work, but also what one could not find in it. . . . It was a control over words unknown before in our country and extending to the imposing of silence on certain matters. . . . As in Orwell's fantastic novel, a special Ministry of Learning undertook to change the past. . . . Censorship not only obliterated the past but invaded the most intimate sentiments, eliminating, e.g., pessimism and sadness, because these feelings were considered as having a bourgeois-liberal habiliment. Even death was liable to excision: "A positive hero may not die." . . . We meet even today such writers and men who do not believe in a struggle for truth, for a free word; they are frightened by the sound of tanks and the existence of nuclear weapons. They say: "It is not worth while!" I answer: "It is not true. It is worth while . . . because justice must eventually triumph, and, if its triumph were as brief as human life, it is worth while to live for that moment."[82]

Another writer said:

How false to order people to believe that the socialist system is the only guarantee of human happiness, that some time in the future, after many years, people will be like chronometers showing constantly a brain-cooked "astronomical time" of "eternal happiness." And the worst thing is that writers are supposed to create recipes for such happiness. . . . That would indeed make people unhappy and destroy art.[83]

Another complained about the servility to Russia imposed from above. He recounted the story of an editorial meeting where a proposal was debated to devote 20 per cent of the space in the next issue to Soviet matters. One member of the editorial board wanted to show his zeal and suggested raising it to 30 per cent; his neighbor, not to be accused of disloyalty to the protecting Power, did better and proposed 40 per cent. One outbidding the other, the board finally decided to reserve 90 per cent, but "all members went home fully convinced that 20 per cent would have been enough."[84]

By 1954, the main literary journal admitted: "Let us not suffer from a delusion; the books of Koestler, Orwell, Waugh and Camus are read, circulated and even sought after in Poland."[85] The reading public was not only fed on a meager diet of Party-sponsored "socialist-realistic" literature but was debarred at the libraries from having access to many books placed, as in other "socialist" countries, on an index of prohibited books. A Polish journal gives the retrospective information:

I have before me the "List of books which must be immediately withdrawn from circulation" dated October 1, 1951, and issued by the Ministry of Culture and Arts, Central Library Administration. This list, composed of three parts: pre-war literature, postwar literature classified as obsolete, and books for children, includes 2485 items. . . . It suffices to cite a few items: London's *The Daughter of Snow*, and *Adventure* . . . St. Augustine's *Confessions*, Kautsky's *From Democracy to State Slavery*. . . . The catalogue cards of prohibited books were eliminated from public catalogues to erase even the trace of this literature. No one, except for five trusted librarians at the Jagellon Library for instance, had access to the catalogue of prohibited books. . . . Thus was brought up this generation of "Marxists" who fought against Western-European opportunism, knowing about it only from what Marx, Engels, Lenin and Stalin had written. . . . I am afraid that if Lenin were to visit this Jagellon Library where he worked before the First World War, he would not obtain those books which he had then read. Lenin often refers in his works to Plato's *Republic*. Today he would have received the works of this ancient philosopher only if he could submit a special permit to the main librarian.[86]

He adds that the Ministry asked the librarians to show additional revolutionary vigilance and to withdraw other suspicious books not placed on the official index. The results were rather amazing; an instruction issued in 1956 contained the order to "restore to the shelves books by Dickens, Balzac."[87] The frightened librarians included among the withdrawn books even John Reed's *Ten Days That Shook the World*. Censorship sullied even some of Marx's and Lenin's writings:

The Stalinist inquisition could not tolerate within the Party such an enemy as an authentic Marx or an authentic Lenin would be. They had to play at best the role of the inkpot which Luther threw at the Devil. The question whether there was any ink, or what kind, in the inkpot did not matter. . . . This method bred the catechism-like readings on Marx and Engels. . . . I do not understand why a *complete* history of Marxism seems to be considered a dangerous science.[88]

While Soviet socialist realism frankly became a term of derision in Poland, it has been maintained in the USSR. As the contents of literature and the arts are concerned, it still means the selecting of topics and presenting them in accordance with the current Party line. With respect to form, it promotes 19th-century bourgeois Western standards in literature, the arts, and music. Everything modern, from atonality in music to abstract painting and sculpture, is strictly forbidden. This old Stalinist line, together with his famous Party resolutions of 1946–48, was solemnly reaffirmed in April, 1957, by Shepilov while he was still secretary of the Central Committee in charge of those matters. Shepilov having been proclaimed a double-dealer, Khrushchev upheld, in the summer of 1957, the Party line, warning writers and artists against dangerous Western innovations.[89] This choice of old-fashioned standards, which results in opposing to the 20th-century West its 19th-century image, may be due not only to the pedestrian taste of the Party leaders and to their fear of anything new that smacks of non-conformity but also to the mentality of the new Soviet intelligentsia, which does not yet feel intellectually secure and is afraid of experimentation.

Polish learning was regimented, too. The Polish physicist of world repute, Leopold Infeld, wrote in 1956:

Since the foundation of the Polish Academy of Sciences they held up for us as models to imitate not Copernicus, Curie-Sklodowska or Smoluchowski [Polish physicist], but Lysenko and Lepieshynskaia. . . . We seek in vain for an article on Einstein in the short philosophical dictionary, whose publication will be a monument of shame for the past period. This name is not to be found in the article on space and time where we find however the names of Butlerov and Fiodorov . . . those who claim Russian priority for each important or less important idea, have ridiculed Soviet science by their insistence. . . . How often young men asked me whether Mendeleyev and Pavlov were really great scientists. This is the result of mentioning Butlerov and Fiodorov, but not Einstein in the article on space and time or of attributing the discovery of the famous formula: $E = mc^2$ to Lebiediev and Vavilov instead of to Einstein. . . . I remember a session organized by the Academy to honor Stalin's works. A physicist made the speech. He sharply denounced Einstein, Bohr and Dirac as idealistic physicists. Professor Pienkowski [a well-known Polish physicist] who was seated beside me whispered in my ear: "this idealistic physics must fare not so badly if it produces men of this merit."[90]

University professors were exposed to denunciations by ignorant students. One of them was accused of all sorts of sins, such as refusal to sign Communist appeals and propagating such a subversive view that "the Turgau Gate was blown up with hot air, not with atomic energy."[91] The hapless professor replied:

I have learned about the existence of a Turgau Gate for the first time from the letter [of the investigating commission set up by the Ministry of Higher Education]. I do not know where this gate is located nor how it was blown up. . . . However, I mentioned, while lecturing on gas compression, the use of hot air in piercing the Simplon Tunnel in the Alps. Perhaps the two were confused.[92]

But he was dismissed, whether he had lectured on the Turgau Gate or the Simplon Tunnel. This absurd system failed. As a Communist said: "Thinking is a process which even we could not make people un-learn."[93]

(B) *Moral revolt.* The Polish Communist re-examination of conscience revealed a deep revulsion against Leninist morality. It is impossible to say whether those Communists who protested against the use of immoral means in the name of revolution fully realized that they were challenging Lenin himself and dared not say so or whether the idealized image of the Prophet, a sort of shrine piously worshiped in their minds, made them dissociate Communist morality from its founder. They never mentioned Lenin by name in their debates and attributed all the moral evils to Stalin, as though he had invented the fundamental criterion of Communist behavior, namely, that any act that served the revolution was moral. Whether this omission was due to intellectual timidity or mere political caution, the debate resulted in opposing to Communist morality the traditional one. There lies the deepest meaning of the Polish revolt. A member of the Polish Central Committee said at the October session:

Words, words-symbols with deep meaning, are characteristic for all historical periods. But there is always the danger that the same words have a different meaning for different people. For some they are simply fashionable words devoid of any meaning.[94]

It suffices to remember, in order to understand this criticism, that quasi-unanimous results of elections by open ballot, with one slate of candidates and the tabulation of votes by Communist-composed electoral commissions, were called free and democratic elections, that peace meant the Soviet foreign policy, that police terror was named political freedom. Another member of the same Party body said: "The time when heads served not for thinking but for approvingly nodding at all wisdom flowing from above, has fortunately revolved away forever."[95] Still another bitterly concluded: "I firmly believe that the majority of comrades . . . feel today as I have done since that moment two years ago when I realized that we had fallen victims of the most monstrous ideological and moral fraud."[96]

Communist writers were more explicit:

The system where nobody had the chance of disclosing his doubts and his own opinion, where unconditional obedience to higher instructions and a blind execution of higher directives reigned in our Party and State, is condemned today. . . . This system extended to the whole social and political life.[97]

For the first time, Communists discovered the need for tolerance:

One must say with sadness that tolerance was the Cinderella of people's authority and almost disappeared from our vocabulary. . . . Intolerance . . . is deaf to the new which is always almost "a heresy" in the eyes of the majority. . . . The mechanism of breaking bones of Communists and [Communist] Parties . . . was so precise and consistent that almost no one escaped physically or morally unhurt who had been caught in its iron wheels. . . . The classical and traditional form of intolerance in Party life was the inquisitorial style of the so-called "criticism and self-criticism." It was inquisitorial because people often exhibited self-criticism under the pressure of public opinion at Party meetings, told of mistakes never made, while completely innocent comrades confessed in prisons uncommitted crimes. . . . Freedom becomes in any social environment an empty sound if the rights of those who think differently from the majority are violated. . . . Instead of discussion—invoking authorities; instead of convincing—shouting; instead of proving—insinuations; instead of logic—demagogy; instead of criticism on merits—political denunciation; instead of the human reflex of helping to correct errors—the inhuman tendency to accuse and annihilate the opponent. . . . However, the world is changed not by Philistines with "clean hands" but by rebels and people with restless minds.[98]

A young man ably but bitterly summarized the past:

Lack of trust in men, we called vigilance; absence of independent appraisal —confidence in leaders; lack of collective co-operation—individual responsibility; ossification—abiding by principles; insensitivity to ordinary human injustice—a revolutionary hardness. We talked about awaking enthusiasm with images of achievements, while varnishing was producing false pictures.[99]

The intrinsic value of individual human beings, whom Communists sacrificed so readily for their image of future human happiness, was vindicated, too:

An acquaintance of mine among the personnel officials justified to me discrimination in the past against some categories of people by saying: "It is better to harm a hundred of the innocent than let one enemy escape." This is indeed a weird arithmetic. It was permissible to respect mankind without respecting men. It was rightful to harm individuals in the name of mankind. The sinister paradox of the past consisted in anti-humanitarian practices covered up by humanitarian slogans. . . . It seems that the rules of Communist morality should now include the well-known Kantian principle which counsels us always to treat a human being as a goal in himself, never exclusively as a means. . . . Mankind is composed not of men who can be turned out, but of irreplaceable individuals. Man is a value in himself as truth is. The need to speak truth requires no justification; nor does doing good to others. But one must always justify every pain one inflicts on other men; one must always render account for doing it.[100]

But Communist practice was different:

Political appraisal was theoretically identified with the moral, but practically it had preferential priority. This resulted in such statements, seriously expressed: "X. is morally a universally-known villain but politically is quite, quite decent." The essence of the argument assumed the guise: moral was everything that brought closer the victory of socialism, while socialism was a definite level of production and of production relations, the carrying out of daily [economic] tasks. Hence that man was moral who, independently of his intentions and motivations, scrupulously and conscientiously performed his productive and political tasks. Moral was the man who politically toed the line, and who contributed to increased production. . . . The zealous man, who implemented directives and instructions, and was politically reliable, could become an immoral man by his carrying out those instructions. To avoid the contradiction in evaluations, they created the concept of the "identity of moral and political appraisals" which was in fact substituting political for moral evaluation. . . . Political death was followed by moral death. . . . Thus the trace of people, whose lives could frequently serve as a moral model, was lost in literature, science and propaganda. The theoretical assumption that people mistaken or ideologically hostile were a priori immoral had its not only painful but also comical consequences. We were changing our moral evaluation of people depending on the fluctuations in their political views. Bertrand Russell, "a reactionary English philosopher, one of the leaders of contemporary idealism, a militant ideologist of imperialism" (*The Short Philosophical Dictionary*, 1955, 600), was transformed into a venerable English philosopher after his famous statement on atomic war. J. P. Sartre, about whom a certain philosophical review wrote that he had sold himself to fascism and imperialism, later appeared to be a respectable "eminent French philosopher and a defender of peace." Flabbergasting metamorphoses![101]

An important Party member wrote in the same vein, perhaps unconsciously condemning the Leninist foundation of Communist morality:

The conflict which the Communists experience could be reduced to two words: policy of amorality. . . . The question whether the goal sanctifies the means has again been posed with all sharpness in connection with the

Hungarian tragedy. Speaking more concretely, is Communism to be interpreted as an impersonal and abstract goal or as a closer objective of retaining power at any price; may it justify infringement upon national sovereignty, aggression and terror? . . . The French Communist writer Claude Roy rightly wrote recently: "If we limit ourselves to the thesis that moral and just is everything that serves the working class, we shall adopt the most abject ethics of amorality, a vulgar Machiavellism, a utilitarianism, the old and vile saying that the end sanctifies the means." . . . The Hungarian tragedy places the Communist movement before the problem of humanitarianism. It is known that political and strategic reasons have become ominous abstractions in whose name national sovereignty has been trampled under foot and stinking chauvinist and racialist (the affair of the [Moscow] doctors, for instance) excesses have been justified. . . . All this created an atmosphere where black was called white, crimes—the class ethic; lies were clothed with the dignity of truth; the falsification of history and distortion of facts were called the Party line in learning; varnishing the reality in arts—socialist realism. Man himself was most dangerously forgotten. He became, from a subject of socialism or the struggle for socialism, an object and a blind weapon in this struggle. They swore by the masses, but in practice they had only contempt for the masses and no consideration was paid to their problems and needs. . . . Human dignity was trampled under foot; people who tried to escape from the iron ring of Stalinist dictatorship were defamed. Stalinism destroyed not only the humanitarian ideals of Communism but also the normal principles of human intercourse free of fear and moral terror. . . . It is impossible to have any policy without tactis; but the tactics of Communist parties should not become prostitution. Selling ideals and morality for tactics subverts the Party itself and depraves its members.[102]

Another Communist rehabilitated civic courage, this "enemy of the people" under any totalitarianism:

The crisis, which the international workers' movement is experiencing, is not merely, but perhaps mainly, moral. . . . It is an indisputable truth that democracy inculcates and requires civic courage, while despotism needs intellectual mediocrity and moral debasement. . . . By erasing from the vocabulary the very notion of civic courage they wanted to kill the virtue itself. But universal values may not be indicted, spit upon and shot. Civic courage consists in a resolute defense of one's views and convictions. Only people who have the ability of independent thinking may have their own opinions. Stalinism, intending to kill human capacity critically to think, was murdering the most beautiful human virtue, civic courage. . . . A man without civic courage cannot be a revolutionary. . . . A free man must have civic courage and be guided by the principle: "It is better to die standing than to live kneeling." Civic courage was replaced in recent years by the words: "faithful to principles." . . . A man was faithful to principles if he agreed with the decisions of each Party institution and bravely attacked everyone who fell or who dared not to understand everything or who sought or questioned.[103]

This moral revolt occasioned the printing of a sad, if sardonic, joke apropos of the Hungarian events: "Having to choose between cannibals and those who murder nations, I prefer the former. They kill only as many people as they are capable of eating."[104]

The hopelessness of this situation produced, unexpectedly for Communists, an intensified religious feeling. One of them bitterly wrote:

Look at an official whom all his bosses treat with contempt; where is he to find hope of saving his human dignity if he has lost it on this earth? Look at the worker caught in the web of frequently thoughtless production and unable to prevent the dissipation of his own labor, with a life devoid of rights and no prospect of improvement. Look at the writer, scientist, politician deprived of good name and honor.[105]

The atheists soon discovered to their amazement that almost all Polish parents asked for religious instruction for their school children. As for the Communists, little was left them: "I belong to the generation who went from defeat to disappointment and from disappointment to defeat, who, once the chains that for long years bound their minds and hearts had been broken off, thought that only disgust remained."[106]

This moral revulsion was the most dangerous revolt; it struck at the very heart of modern Communism, its Leninist morality. It was itself a revolution:

The ghost of humane socialism wanders in Eastern Europe and frightens not only capitalists but also Stalinists . . . that what happens in 1956 is not "sterile discussions," but a revolution. He who opposes the revolution is a counter-revolutionary.[107]

This was the worst possible challenge that could be thrown in the face of other Communists (in Poland, eastern Europe, the Soviet Union, and the non-Communist countries), who refused to re-examine their conscience and to look at their cause from a fresh, moral point of view.

The Polish Communist Party now tries hard to stem their moral revulsion. It is compelled to do so for two reasons. First, the Polish Communists realize that one-party rule can hardly be reconciled with traditional morality. Secondly, a Poland free to indulge in such searching re-examination of conscience could become a menace to Communist rule in the rest of eastern Europe and eventually in Russia. Such challenge to the Soviet Union could barely be tolerated for long by the protecting Power.

(C) *The Party machine.* This came in for heavy criticism, though it was

faithfully copied after the Soviet current pattern. A member of the Polish
Central Committee thus summarized the concept of the all-powerful Party
machine, with command centralized in the supreme leaders:

We have built up such a system: the Party, then the Party identity card,
and lastly the Party member. This system led to monstrous results; man did
not count any longer. Every Party member had to accept this system or he
did not count; he had to get rid of all human feelings or at least he could
not disclose them. It was forbidden to protest even when the most horrible
crimes were committed in the name of this system.[108]

He added:

The masses have turned their backs on us, the leadership. Why? Because
we were hypocrites in our actions. We said one thing and did something
else. . . . our meetings were solemn parades, religious services, where we
were giving various truths to people to believe. People recited instead of
thinking. In order to maintain such a system in a nation, which had
glorious traditions of struggle for freedom, we had to create an apparatus
of oppression and have recourse to illegality.[109]

Gomulka's personal friend, Marian Spychalski, who was imprisoned with
him, enumerated the consequences of that system:

Dogmatism in theory which could not be carried out in practice, servility
in politics, lack of principles in ideology, contradiction between words and
deeds, imitation and regimentation in culture . . . the caste-maffia character
of power, with some leaders treating the Party as their private enterprise
and considering that neither the charter nor customary Party rules, neither
laws nor the needs of the masses were binding on them.[110]

His colleague on the Central Committee deplored the fact that there was
no actual worker or peasant on this supreme Party body, which claimed to
rule in the name of the same workers and peasants, and he asked for an end
to "organized" elections: "Let us terminate forever this universal system
of bringing candidates to various posts in attaché cases, people from other
districts and different milieu whom nobody knows."[111] Still another, a
former University of Chicago professor, Oskar Lange, pointed out the consequences of this kind of "dictatorship of the proletariat": "The working
class and the whole toiling people do not want any longer a government
instead of them or in their name; they want to govern themselves and to
become truly masters of their workshops and the country."[112]

The same criticism resounded in the press:

The Party activists and members acknowledged in the best faith the infallibility of Party leadership . . . or reconciled themselves with this state of affairs. Uncritical adoption and carrying out of Party decisions, lack of a free exchange of opinions within the Party and of intra-Party democracy, lack of participation of Party rank-and-file members in the formulation of Party policy and in the control over its realization, absence of publicity in the Party life, all this became the system reigning in the Party. . . . The Party and State policies were determined by the supreme Party leadership . . . while the Party and State apparatus was carrying out these policies without any democratic control by the masses. . . . The time came when not only the masses of workers and peasants but even the mass of Party members had less and less to say about the policy in the State and in every realm of life. . . . The Party lost its compass because . . . it had become indifferent to the reactions, opinions, and what is worse, the true needs of laboring people. . . . The people's government committed very substantial and serious errors in relation to the working people. . . . The principal mistake consisted perhaps in the fact that the representatives of the working class began to rule "in its name."[113]

The result was to be expected: "An unusually ominous and dangerous phenomenon has made its appearance: the weakening of the feeling in the working class that this is its own State, its own factories, and its own society which it should govern."[114] Why should it be otherwise if the principal Party organ conceded:

Hence, not by accident, [administrative] councils, mass organizations, and allied parties became a fiction. They became only a decorative façade for the dictatorship by the Party machine. . . . The Party was transformed from a political leader of the working class into an administrator, a comptroller of the State, a guardian of the alleged "shortest" road to socialism, a road through decrees but not the hearts and conscience of the masses.[115]

Party leaders had a simple device for dealing with opponents:

When a section of Communists, such as had earlier understood the coming danger, stood up against the system and its errors, the Party apparatus . . . struck at them with full strength. Mass repressions began within the Party.[116]

Those were the days of triumph for the professional Party functionary. Political and social work became a well-paid profession. The Party functionaries also ruled the youth organization:

How can people who have no profession, do not belong to the milieu of working people, do not live the normal life of millions of citizens, but only "rule the souls," properly guide a youth organization? The only type of man that this system has created is the dignitary with a desk, a telephone, and frequently an automobile.[117]

A Polish Communist wrote, in the same vein as Djilas, about the emergence of a new ruling class which

concentrated in its hands an economic power unheard of even under capitalism—the administration of the whole industrial and partly other production on the scale of the whole State. One could find during the past years many examples of using this power against the workers; production was a means of enslaving the producers. This was the economic foundation of a new type of dependence not on capitalists but on the political administrators who became . . . the rulers of men. . . . Limited in their freedom, economically and politically dependent, citizens were the object of a systematical and refined oppression. . . . Ideological lies concealed and screened economic dependence and lack of freedom. They had to justify or falsify the tragic image of the material existence of those who were proclaimed the rock of the system. Lodz textile workers lived twelve in one room, including married couples. . . . Terror spread fear; unjust and bestial terror destroyed the ideal which it claimed to serve.[118]

Two Communist writers using the term "Stalinism," which is now taboo in Poland for fear of provoking Soviet anger and which meant the Soviet system, concluded by giving a clear definition:

Stalinism is a system where there exists economic dependence of the popular masses on a group of administrators, and which finds its political expression in the dictatorship of the ruling group over the proletariat.[119]

(D) *Economic and Social System.* The Poznań workers' revolt and the October crisis were due not only to political and moral reasons but also to unbearably low standards of living, inadequate production, and the realization that the economic plan was a failure. The Party could no longer justify its system of oppression by eternally pointing to successes in industrialization. Gomulka, not yet elected First Secretary, was quite outspoken on this topic, seven years after his last speech in the Central Committee. Addressing this Party body in October, 1956, he pointed to the disastrous fall in labor productivity, the lack of co-ordination in industrial production, and the dangerous shortage of foodstuffs because of the deliberate persecution of peasants unwilling to join the collective farms, called in Poland "producer co-operatives." He mentioned that the daily output of the Polish coal miner had fallen by comparison to 1938 by 36 per cent and gave this example of socialist planning:

New industrial establishments have come into being, establishments which produce at disproportionately high production costs only limited numbers of automobiles of an old type which consume plenty of fuel, automobiles which today hardly anyone produces in the world. . . . What kind of benefits can the national economy draw from this?[120]

He also mentioned that many factories were unable to work at full capacity for lack of raw materials.[121]

Speaking of collectivization of agriculture, Gomulka said: "It is a sad picture. Despite great outlays, they [collective farms] had smaller results and greater production cost [than individual homesteads]."[122] Despite large financial assistance to collective farms and the discriminatory treatment of individual homesteads which had resulted, as he said, "in the economic ruin of a great number of peasant farms,"

. . . when estimating the value of over-all production per one hectare of arable land, we arrive at the following picture . . . individual farms, 621.1 zlotys; co-operative farms, 517.3 zlotys; and state farms, 393.7 zlotys.[123]

It was fortunate for the Party that it had succeeded in organizing only 6 per cent of peasant farmsteads into collective farms. Even these had been created by such high pressure that most of them disintegrated in October, 1956, once the peasants were again free to make their choice. The individual peasants, whose farms represented 78.8 per cent of the arable land in 1955, saved the country from starvation and the Party from financial debacle. The measure of living standards was given by Gomulka when he said that 600,000 rooms had fallen into ruin for lack of repair in a country whose cities and villages had been devastated by war and which needed not only to repair its existing housing but to build a great many new dwellings.[124]

The former economic tsar of Poland, H. Minc, conceded that the main error in planning consisted in hasty industrialization at the cost of living standards causing a lower labor productivity. The cup was filled when the Soviet order came to place national economy on a war footing with concentration on war production.[125] It did not help when the Party Central Committee voted a 30 per cent rise in living standards, a promise which could not be kept.[126] Planning and a centralized economic administration brought out a mesh of laws and regulations which paralyzed industrial executives.[127]

The principal organ of the Party published in November, 1956, a thorough criticism of planned and centralized economy; this deserves the attention of those who believe that to make a plan and to nationalize the economy would produce miracles. Polish Communists no longer believe in such thaumaturgy. The author of this frank confession admitted that the principal feature of Communist planning consisted in reducing consumption in order to accelerate accumulation needed for quick industrialization without foreign assistance. The consumer footed the bill. Even so, industrialization was partly artificial because existing plants worked on old machinery which was not renewed while new factories were being built. As he said, "one must distinguish between the net and gross growth of productive establishments; the net growth is obtained by deducting the decapitalization [at existing plants]."[128] Another fallacy of planned economy was the concentration on certain economic branches while paying a heavy penalty for neglect of others:

A one-sided development of heavy or war industries, while neglecting many other industrial branches, results in building a great number of steel mills, cement factories, war factories, etc., but agriculture, processing industries, housing industry, fall in ruin, roads are no longer built, railroads are not kept in good repair, etc. . . . The inadequate development of means of transportation, insufficient housing, defective health service to the population, stagnation in agriculture and in consumer-goods production, make impossible a full use of those factories and plants which have been erected in this one-sided process of industrialization. Usually people do not pay attention to the fact that general economic facilities, such as transportation, roads, housing, etc., play a decisive role in industrialization. . . . Would it not have been better, instead of destroying agriculture for the sake of heavy industries, to develop it and to buy for instance in America machines, industrial equipment, raw materials, radio sets, etc., for exported bacon, butter, eggs? . . . The country becomes richer in steel mills, cement plants, and machine-tool factories, but poorer in consumer goods. . . . Labor productivity has decreased and the masses, dragged from rural districts and packed in the humiliating, degrading and demoralizing environment of workers' hostels, could not be attracted towards cultural processes. . . . Too little was destined for reserves . . . hence lack of continuity in production, long breakdowns during which neither technical facilities nor manpower could be productively mobilized.[129]

It is quite possible that similar complaints could be heard from Russia if complaints were permitted there. Moreover, any small country, Poland, e.g., is not self-sufficient in raw materials. Hence this author, as many others, pointed to breakdowns in production, even at the new plants, for lack of raw materials or delays in their supply.

The workers not only demonstrated in Poznań that they had had enough of being treated as manure for industrialization, they turned the tables on the Party. Parrotwise, the Party repeated that the workers were the masters of the factories which belonged to them. In the fall of 1956, the workers began spontaneously to form councils to participate in running "their own" plants; such workers' councils mushroomed all over the country. This was an instinctive movement which the Party could hardly stop in the upsurging mood of the population. Finally, the councils were officially approved. It would indeed be difficult to prove that those councils corresponded with Lenin's ideas. Did he not say in 1921:

If we should say that it is not the Party which governs and selects candidatures but the labor unions themselves, it would sound very democratic . . . but it would make the dictatorship of the proletariat perish. . . . In order to rule one must have an army of experienced revolutionaries; it does exist, it is called the Party. The whole syndicalist nonsense, these obligatory candidatures of producers, all this can be thrown into the wastebasket.[130]

The Polish workers retrieved those ideas from the Communist wastebasket. The Party temporarily had to accept this unpleasant development; wherefore?

The trend towards the establishment of workers' self-government had principally a political character and was a reaction of the workers to their depressing material condition, to the rupture between the Party and the masses, and to the centralized bureaucratic system of administration of industries.[131]

Some Party members were willing to accept in good faith this new institution and to build up a national system of workers' councils, reaching, eventually, the level of the Diet and being represented there by a second chamber of delegates elected by local councils.[132] Gomulka rejected this and other ambitious concepts in his program speech delivered in May, 1957. He did not agree that the workers' councils should run each enterprise autonomously; he denied that they represented the political power of the proletariat, a role reserved for the Party, and he refused to approve the scheme of having territorial and national bodies elected by the workers' councils. He may have been right that the autonomous administration of each plant by a local workers' council would disorganize planned economy, but it is very strange for the leader of a "proletarian" Party to deny any political role to councils spontaneously created by the proletariat. How-

ever, a Communist Party, even if repentant, never intends to share power
with the proletariat. His own concept of workers' councils is not very ex-
citing; they have to help the management in finding the best ways of increasing production and of using the manpower must appropriately. He
wants the Party to form cells within the councils and to promote its own
candidates. The same method killed (in Poland and the Soviet Union)
labor unions, to which workers opposed their own councils in 1956.[133]

(F) *Resentment against the protecting Power.* Polish Communists laid
the blame for the regime squarely on the Soviet Union. They said and
repeated that the system as introduced between 1947–48 and practiced in
1948–56 had been imported from the protecting Power and consisted in
copying her ways of life. They also complained about the inequality that
reigned in relations with the USSR, although they had to mind their
speech; Soviet troops were stationed on Polish soil. At the October session
of the Central Committee, several speakers alluded to the abnormal condition of these relations and to the Soviet pressure exerted on the session to
assure the election of a Political Bureau pleasing to the USSR. They resented the devious means used by the Soviet leaders in fighting against the
majority of the Polish Committee, namely, the anti-Semitic campaign
waged by the pro-Soviet minority. This campaign, with its slogan of a racial
numerus clausus for the distribution of higher state and party posts, had
two purposes: to strike at such non-conformists among Party members who
were of Jewish descent and to divert the attention of the population from
pressing national problems into channels of racial hatred against their own
countrymen.[134] The Party organ wrote:

For years the thesis was being launched that a Communist must accept,
rather glorify, every move by the leadership of the USSR. . . . It is necessary
to overcome in the whole Communist movement the one-sided orientation
towards studying the Soviet experience as almost the only model. . . . There
can be only one attitude in the Communist movement, namely the recognition of the absolute right of each nation to sovereignty and to equality in
discussing on its merits any debatable question . . . but not from the point
of view of the primacy of this or another State.[135]

The organ depicted the "equality" favored by the anti-colonialist great
Power:

[This process] consisted in rejecting in practice the existing constitutional,
social, economic and cultural heritage of the Polish democratic and revolutionary thought and in replacing it by Soviet models and experience as the

only, sacrosanct and obligatory signposts for action in all realms of life. . . .
Everyone who submitted creative criticism of Soviet shortcomings in one
field or another was exposed to the very serious accusation of "being an
enemy of the Soviet Union." . . . Soviet diplomacy frequently exceeded the
limits of its competence by interfering in the domestic affairs of our country. The system of Soviet advisers, initially helpful, became on the long run
unnecessary and harmful. . . . The Polish October revolt was, first of all,
a revolt of workers against Stalinism, in defense of socialist ideas and of
the independence of the Polish revolutionary movement and true and
full Polish sovereignty in all aspects, ideological, political, social and economic.[136]

Other Communist publicists discovered, at last, that it was erroneous to
identify the policy of the USSR with those of Communist parties. They
pointed to well-known results of such identification:

The scheme of thinking looked as follows: if the Soviet Union concluded
a pact with Germany, then all the Communist parties had to call for the
cessation of war against Germany. Can this type of thinking be called internationalist? It seems that we face here . . . a rather peculiar dominant role
of the USSR which reduces tactics of Communist parties to pure copying
and taking orders while forgetting the interests of a nation represented by
a given Party. . . . The undoubted fact of incomplete equality in our ideological, political, economic and cultural relations with the Soviet Union
caused bitterness in broad public opinion.[137]

They mentioned as examples of Soviet pressure the order not to talk about
the deportation of Polish populations in 1939–41 after the Soviet annexations or the imprisonment of members of the Polish anti-Nazi resistance
movement by the advancing Soviet troops in 1944–45. The glorification of
everything Russian went so far that the Polish press, as they said, had to
pay homage to the Tsarist General Suvorov, who had conquered Poland on
the eve of the last partitions in the 18th century.[138] National reaction to
this arrogance of the protecting Power was thus summed up:

First of all, we did not allow interference in the internal matters of our
Party and our nation in the days of the 8th Plenum. We said clearly, and
have no intention of going back on it, that matters which the Plenum
considered were our internal affair and that nobody except the Polish nation and Polish Communists had the right to decide them. . . . Secondly,
we said that we had our own personnel of trained specialists in many fields,
in particular in the Army, and that the presence of Soviet specialists in
Poland should not continue. . . . Polish commanders replaced Soviet specialists who, such as Generals Turkiel or Andreievsky, had sometimes occupied high positions.[139]

The editorial added rather wistfully: "No country and no nation can be satisfied with the presence of troops of another State on their territory."[140]

For a time, the Soviet press responded by castigating the Polish revisionism in terms of utter opprobrium. The criterion of Polish deviation was as follows:

There is no workers' self-government in the Soviet Union, but the Soviet Union is a socialist country; though there are no workers' councils, there is socialism; workers' councils are contrary to socialism. . . . The collectivization of agriculture took place in the Soviet Union in a way known to all; the question of socialization of agriculture looks different in Poland. The argument runs as follows: as the Soviet road is the model road, while actual modifications in this respect take place in Poland, hence the Polish road cannot lead to socialism.[141]

Polish information centers in other eastern European countries were submitted to a quarantine regime to avoid spreading contagion to other protectorates.[142]

Poland withstood the pressure. The new Party leadership, Gomulka in particular, was compensated for the loss of Soviet trust by a vote of confidence given by the country in the January, 1957, elections. It was not a vote for Communism but for national independence, the platform which Gomulka had presented to the population. It would be risky to forecast the future; suffice it to say that Gomulka has a task almost comparable with that of squaring the circle. It would take a giant to solve such contradictions as the Party's avowed atheism and co-existence with a Church desirous of freedom of religious propaganda and education; industrialization, for which there is an objective reason (namely a 500,000 annual natural increase) and the demand for better living standards; moral integrity and the political monopoly of one party; freedom of discussion within the Party and the monolithic Party ideal (which Gomulka again reaffirmed in his May, 1957, speech)[143] and his simultaneous castigation of those Communists who showed independence of mind; socialization of national economy and individual peasant husbandry, which he himself had conceded; national independence with a Polish road to socialism and the military, political, and economic dependence on the USSR and the presence of Soviet troops in Poland. He will be torn between the will of the country, which was clearly demonstrated in October, 1956, and his own Communist program, in which he believes, between his earnest desire to assure at least domestic independence to his nation and the incessant pressure of a much more powerful Soviet Union. His success would involve finding compromises making no one too unhappy, a herculean task.

13. Hungarian Revolution

Outwardly, Hungary was as peaceful as Poland and the rest of eastern Europe after Rakosi had eliminated the last traces of opposition with his "salami" tactics and terror. Khrushchev, wistfully referring to that period, assured a Japanese journalist in 1957: "Free elections were held there [in Hungary]. The Hungarian parliament was elected in a democratic manner. Truly free elections are strictly held in socialist countries."[144] Tabulated results of elections showed there, as in Poland, a nation most happy at being compelled to adopt Russian ways of life. Matyas Rakosi, for years First Secretary of the Party, in April, 1950, assured the Soviet delegation, headed by Marshal Voroshilov, who had come to Budapest for the celebrations of the fifth anniversary of the liberation by Soviet troops: "You will see in this country . . . with what love and gratitude our people think of the Soviet Union and its leader, the wise Stalin, the greatest friend of the Hungarian people."[145] This happiness and love culminated eventually in the outbreak of a revolution.

Events that took place in Hungary in October and November of 1956 could be reconstructed from various reliable sources, but we shall follow the report of the Special Committee on the Problem of Hungary appointed on January 10, 1957, by the General Assembly of the United Nations. We do this for two reasons: first, because it is the most complete statement of all the facts, carefully checked and screened by the Committee, and, secondly, because of the composition of the Committee. No great Power was represented on this Committee. In addition to representatives from Australia, Denmark, and Uruguay, two countries which had only recently emerged from colonial status, Ceylon and Tunisia, had delegates on the Committee. For the first time, a European colonial problem was investigated by nationals of two non-European former colonial possessions. Their sensitivity to foreign control adds moral weight to the report.[146]

The thrall of fear ceased to be operative in Poland in 1954, and a year later in Hungary; in both countries the lead was taken by intellectuals who started publishing articles asking for greater freedom of expression. The denunciation of Stalin at the 20th Congress had almost immediate repercussions affecting the Hungarian Party leadership. In March, 1956, Rakosi, probably on Soviet orders, announced that Laszlo Rajk and others had been executed on fabricated charges. After this risky step by Moscow, Rakosi, the man responsible for the death of the innocent Rajk, could not remain in office. It is possible that his personal connections with Beria made him *persona non grata* to Soviet leaders. In July, he lost his position as First Secretary of the Party and was succeeded by Ernö Gerö. A. I. Mikoyan attended the meeting of the Central Committee at which this important personnel change was decided. The early October reburial of Rajk, another risky step, symbolized all the injustices and oppression that the Hungarian people suffered under the Soviet-sponsored regime. The same causes which had generated the Poznań revolt and the October crisis in Poland led in the same month to a very tense situation in Hungary, where people wanted and expected a change that should logically have followed Rakosi's dismissal and Rajk's rehabilitation.

There were, however, certain important differences between the situations in the two countries. In both, people revolted against control by a foreign Power and the type of regime that she had imposed on them. In both cases the first reaction, in a country where other political parties had in fact ceased to exist, was to look for a Communist leader who would express national feelings. Gomulka had been stripped of his offices and imprisoned for disobedience to Moscow. But he was not forsaken; the crucial vote in the Central Committee on October 20 showed that he was supported by more than the two-thirds of his colleagues. Thus the Communist Party, despite its pro-Russian faction and Soviet pressure, placed itself at the head of a national movement. This allowed it to keep in its hands the control of events and to limit the outburst of popular anger within bounds acceptable to the USSR. It did not ask for the withdrawal of Soviet troops, nor did it try to quit the Warsaw bloc.

The Hungarians looked towards Imre Nagy, who had been prime minister in 1953–1955 and who had eased the policy notably by slowing the pace of industrialization and trying to improve living standards. His fall, which followed Malenkov's resignation as Soviet prime minister, led to his expulsion from the Party. He was readmitted to the Party on October 13 but was not allowed to play any political role until the uprising. His name became a symbol of opposition to the protecting Power. But he returned to power only after events had gone too far to maintain a Communist regime in any shape and after the Hungarians, who had not expected anything from the USSR in the field of foreign relations, had requested the withdrawal of Soviet troops and also the end of participation in the Warsaw bloc, with a simultaneous proclamation of permanent neutrality of Hungary. Nagy's own party, where he had found too few leaders to support him, practically disintegrated under the impact of events. Differing from that in Poland, the question facing the USSR was not that of internal autonomy for a Communist regime but of the termination of the one-party system and the loss of Hungary, a country strategically important for Soviet control over other Danubian and Balkan countries.

It is difficult to say whether the USSR would have used armed force in any case. On the one hand, floating bridges had been assembled at Zahony on the Soviet-Hungarian border as early as October 20–21, before the first demonstrations in Budapest took place. On October 21–22, Soviet officers on leave in Rumania were recalled to their units. On October 22, Soviet forces in western Hungary were observed moving towards Budapest.[147] This points to the fact that the Soviet Government was sensing that the situation was getting out of hand and was ready for military intervention. On the other hand, Soviet troops were also moving on Warsaw, while others were concentrating on the western and eastern Polish frontiers; this was on October 19, at the time of the visit of the Soviet delegation. The orders were rescinded by Marshal I. Konev, and the troops reintegrated their bases. Was this an intimidating maneuver that failed in both cases? If the Soviet leaders originally intended to use troops in Poland and then changed their minds during their stay in Warsaw, would they have done the same in Hungary, had the Hungarian revolt remained within the same limits as did the Polish?

While the Polish crisis started by workers revolting in Poznań and while workers, intellectuals, and students played the decisive role in October, the crisis in Hungary began with students holding meetings on October 22. By that time the Polish crisis was over, but the limited success of the Poles emboldened the Hungarians. The students, mostly of peasant and working-class origin, had submitted in their resolution sixteen demands which soon after became the program of the revolution. They asked, among other things, for the immediate withdrawal of all Soviet troops, for Imre Nagy to be appointed prime minister, for a public trial of Rakosi and other persons guilty of atrocities committed in the recent past, for general elections by secret ballot with several parties participating, for a revision of the economic plan and of trade relations with the USSR, for the re-examination of the Soviet concession for the exploitation of uranium mines, for improvement in the condition of workers and the restoration of their right to strike, for termination of discrimination against peasants who refused to join collective farms, for freedom of expression, and for the restoration of the old national flag and national holidays. This program amounted to a demand for full external and domestic independence. There was no doubt that free elections, with the participation of various parties, held after the withdrawal of Soviet troops, would result in the establishment of a non-Communist regime. Contrariwise to Czechoslovakia in 1948, the USSR could not be sure that an independent and non-Communist Hungary would have any reason to stay in the Warsaw bloc. Thus this very first program, drafted by the Budapest Building Industry Technological University students and adopted the next day as the spontaneous platform of the Hungarian nation, posed the entire question of both the Communist regime in their country and of the Soviet political and military position there.[148] The Hungarians wanted to recover fully their destined right of national self-determination, as inalienable to them as it is to Americans, Britishers, Indonesians, or the Arabs.

It is no business of a foreign country what kind of a regime a nation wants to have after recovering her independence. But the Soviet statements are unanimous in claiming that the uprising Hungarians planned to establish a fascist regime. Not only all Communists support this thesis but even some gullible Western scholars are inclined to concede them the benefit of the doubt. The United Nations Committee, composed of representatives of five countries, none of which is fascist, refuted emphatically this claim. It said:

... the four parties [taking part in the uprising] were unanimously agreed to retain from the socialist achievements everything which could be used in a free, democratic and socialist country, in accordance with the will of the people. It was made very clear that the condemnation of the old system which the uprising represented would not affect those reforms under which ownership of the land and industrial undertakings had been transferred.[149]

The Committee states elsewhere: "... the insurrection was manned, in its vast majority, by workers who, according to reports, were fully supported by the peasants."[150] In its final conclusion, the Committee says categorically:

The thesis that the uprising was fomented by reactionary circles in Hungary and that it drew its strength from such circles and from Western "Imperialists" failed to survive the Committee's examination. From start to finish, the uprising was led by students, workers, soldiers and intellectuals, many of whom were Communists or former Communists. The majority of political demands put forward during the revolution included a stipulation that democratic socialism should be the basis of the Hungarian political structure and that such social reforms as the land reform should be safeguarded. At no time was any proposal made for the return to power, or to the Government, of any figure associated with pre-war days. "Fascists" and "saboteurs," heavily armed, could not have succeeded in landing on Hungarian airfields, which were under Soviet supervision, and in crossing the Austrian frontier, where a closed zone was shown by the Austrian authorities to the military attachés of France, the United Kingdom, the United States of America and the USSR. The uprising was not planned in advance.[151]

This judgment is corroborated by two Communist sources. Kadar, the present First Secretary of the Hungarian Communist Party, said on November 1, 1956 (before the second Soviet intervention) in an interview with *Igazsag:* "We consider that this insurrection, which became a mighty movement of the people, was caused chiefly by the indignation and embitterment of the masses with a harmful policy and ill-fated methods."[152] A Polish Communist publicist wrote in November, 1956:

It is well-known that Stalinists not only avowed like Rakosi but alleged liberals like Gerö were in the main responsible for the Hungarian tragedy. Gerö stood at the helm of the then Central Committee of the Hungarian Workers' Party which appealed to the Soviet Army. This appeal and equally the assent granted by those people on whom the movements of Soviet troops depended were the most anti-people decisions in the whole complex of Hungarian affairs. This in fact created a situation which only ardent enemies of Communism could have desired—the Army of a State, which thirty-nine years ago had first achieved the victorious revolution, began to fire at people asking for the most democratic postulates. . . . Only protagonists of Stalinism blind to everything, people who "have learned nothing and forgotten nothing" can thus present the reasons and the course of events in Hungary and explain to that extent everything by the activities of "agents," "provocateurs" and "fascist gangs."[153]

By contrast, the official Soviet point of view, generally upheld by non-Russian Communists, is as follows:

The former fascist-Horthyite elements occupied strong positions in Hungary. Precisely they together with the bourgeoisie and landlords were the fundamental force of the counter-revolutionary rebellion. International imperialism played the decisive role in the preparation and the outbreak of bloody events in Hungary. . . . The United States made the plan for the

Hungarian counter-revolution; the Horthyite fascist detachments trained and equipped principally in Western Germany, Horthyites, and armaments were sent to Hungary across Austria.[154]

This hollow defense may be better understood if one remembers that the word "revolution" is reserved for the seizure of power by the Communists and that any anti-Communist movement, as radical socially as it might be, is logically a counter-revolution.

The development of events after the fateful meeting of Budapest students fully supports the interpretation given to those events by the United Nations Committee, the Polish Communists, and Kadar himself before he decided to go over to the foreign side. During the Budapest students' meeting, a representative of the Writers' Union announced that the Union planned to lay a wreath at the statue of Joseph Bem, a Polish general who had fought the Russians in the Polish insurrection of 1830–31 and had later commanded Hungarian troops in 1848–49 in their uprising against Austria and had again crossed swords with the Russians at the time of their military intervention in Hungary in support of the Austrian emperor. This was to be a simple demonstration of sympathy with the Poles, who had just emerged victorious from their own crisis with the common protecting Power. The students then decided to organize their own "silent, peaceful and orderly demonstration."[155] Next day, on Tuesday, October 23, the Minister of the Interior, in turn, forbade and allowed the demonstration. In the afternoon, the huge demonstration of many thousands of students, workers, and other people went to the statue of Bem and to that of Petőfi, the famous Hungarian poet of the 1848–49 uprising. People shouted that they wanted Imre Nagy to be in the government. First Secretary of the Party Gerö and Prime Minister Hegedus had returned the same morning from Belgrade. The demonstration, which had grown, in the meantime, to variously estimated from 100,000 people to 200,000 people, learned at 8 P.M. of Gerö's broadcast, in which he promised nothing and did not even discuss the specific sixteen points. This angered the crowds. A large group of demonstrators went to the radio building, which was guarded by armed members of political police (the AVH). The atmosphere was tense, especially since the radio station had already refused to broadcast the sixteen points. The political police fired. The sight of the dead and wounded transformed a peaceful demonstration into an uprising. Fighting began; workers from the main Budapest plants arrived at the scene; arms came from Hungarian soldiers, ordinary police, the army, and war-factory stores which were thrown open. At no time did the Hungarian army fight against its civilian countrymen; many officers and soldiers joined the uprising. The first battles were fought between the militarized detachments of the political police and armed civilians.

The first Soviet intervention transformed the uprising against the domestic regime into a struggle against a foreign enemy. The nearest Soviet base was seventy kilometers from the capital. The first Soviet tanks appeared in Budapest at 2 A.M. on October 24, the fighting having broken out after 9 P.M. on October 23. It is highly doubtful that Soviet detachments could be alarmed, called up, and arrive in Budapest within this short span of five hours. They were probably pre-alerted to help in dispersing the demonstration, a job too heavy for the Hungarian political police, who could not rely on the Hungarian army. The battle became one between the Hungarians and Soviet soldiers.

Were the Soviet troops empowered to intervene in the domestic affairs of a foreign country? A Soviet international lawyer, writing a year before these events, gives a cautious answer:

"No one has the right forcibly to intervene in the internal life of nations and 'correct' their mistakes by force. Nations have full powers in matters of their domestic life, and have the right to organize themselves as they please." (Stalin, *Works*, III, 209). . . . It must be observed that there are such internal matters which are closely intertwined with the external. In such cases the State concerned cannot remain impassive and not counter-act such domestic measures which infringe upon its interests.[156]

This flexible approach would excuse not only the Soviet intervention in Hungary but any intervention by a great Power to safeguard her external interests. The independence of small nations would be left at the mercy of great Powers.

However, the official statements and international obligations of the Soviet Union did not allow for such an elastic view. The peace treaty with Hungary, concluded on February 10, 1947, obligated the USSR to withdraw its troops from that country, subject to the right to keep such forces as were needed for the maintenance of communications with the Red Army in eastern Austria. Allied occupation of Austria ended in September, 1955, a few months after the signature (on May 15) of the Austrian State Treaty. But the Soviet Union had already taken care of this legal problem. On the eve of the signature of the Austrian State Treaty, the Warsaw Treaty was signed with all eastern European countries, including Hungary. Article 5 of this treaty not only placed all the eastern European armed forces under a joint command exercised by Marshal I. Konev but contained passages highly equivocal; the allied forces "shall be assigned by agreement between the parties," and the Contracting Parties "shall likewise adopt such other concerted measures as may be necessary to reinforce their defensive strength, in order to protect the peaceful labor of their peoples, guarantee the inviolability of their frontiers and territories, and afford protection against possible aggression."[157] This formula allowed for the "assignment" of Soviet troops to the eastern European territories and for their action in defense "of the peaceful labor of their peoples." The decision made by the Warsaw Treaty signatories on the same day clarified the meaning of Article 5 by stating that "the disposition of the Joint Armed Forces in the territories of signatory States will be effected by agreement among the States, in accordance with the requirements of their mutual defense." No such agreements were ever published, the first public agreements concerning stationing of Soviet troops in Poland, East Germany, Hungary, and Rumania having been concluded only after the Hungarian revolution, at the end of 1956 and in 1957. There is little doubt that secret agreements had been concluded before; they might have provided for the Soviet military intervention to uphold Communist regimes in eastern Europe.

The Charter of the United Nations has the priority over other international agreements. Article 2, Paragraph 4 expressly forbids the threat or use of force against the political independence of any state and by implication the armed intervention of one state to uphold or overthrow the regime of another. The General Assembly deduced its conclusion on December 12, 1956, when it qualified the Soviet intervention in Hungary as a violation of the Charter. The treaty of mutual assistance of 1948 between the Soviet Union and Hungary prohibited any interference in the domestic affairs of the other state. Moreover, the Soviet Government insisted many times in the United Nations on reviving its definition of aggression as formulated for the first time in the London Convention of 1933.

Contrary to the popular dictum that all the people cannot be fooled all the time, the Soviet Government apparently believes, not without good reasons, that one may fool most of the people all of the time. Human memory is short, and political memory quickly forgets inconvenient facts. Anyhow, the USSR, which had openly violated the London Convention in 1939–40 in regard to Poland, the Baltic States, and Finland, insisted on this convention being re-enacted as a general international text. As late as

1956 it submitted, again to one of the United Nations committees, the same definition of aggression; this included such clear statements as the declaration of a state as an aggressor if it "promotes an internal upheaval in another State or a change of policy in favor of the aggressor" and the prohibition of aggression perpetrated under such pretexts as: "A. The internal situation of any State as for example: . . . b. alleged shortcomings of its administration; . . . d. any revolutionary or counter-revolutionary [*sic!*] movement, civil war, disorders or strikes; e. establishment or maintenance in any State of any political, economic or social system."[158]

The intervention by a foreign state at the request of the government threatened by internal revolution has not the most pleasant flavor but is legally defensible. Was there such a request by the constitutional authorities of Hungary at the time? Soviet tanks started firing at the Budapest crowds soon after 2 A.M. on October 24. Hegedus was at that time prime minister. Only at 8:13 A.M. did an official broadcast announce that the Party Central Committee had recommended the appointment of Imre Nagy as prime minister and had elected him as a member of the Political Bureau. At 8:45 A.M., another announcement, "signed by Imre Nagy, Chairman of the Council of Ministers," imposed summary jurisdiction. At 9 A.M., a third announcement brought the news that the government had applied for help to the Soviet troops stationed in Hungary. No name was attached to that announcement but the implication was clear that Imre Nagy had himself appealed or at least approved an earlier appeal by remaining in office. The United Nations report established beyond the shadow of a doubt that Imre Nagy was kept under guard and incommunicado at Party headquarters until the afternoon of October 26. He became active prime minister only that afternoon, after the flight of Gerö and Hegedus from Hungary. Yet even after he had moved to his office as prime minister, he remained under the guard of armed agents of the political police for two days. Only on October 28, when these agents had fled, did he truly become master of his decisions and responsible for his acts. The decision to request intervention by Soviet troops was probably made by Gerö and Hegedus as they shifted the blame on Nagy. However, they co-operated in the appointment of Nagy as prime minister, who was the constitutional head of the government, beginning with the announcement of this decision. He thus acquired the right to ask Soviet troops to withdraw, a request he insistently and repeatedly submitted during his short term of office.

The reason for the attaching of Nagy's name to the request for Soviet military help is fairly obvious. He was the symbol for the insurgents in the first period of fighting; they trusted him. Here, then, was the best way of compromising him and depriving the movement of a leader. Actually, many insurgents began to doubt Nagy's patriotism after the broadcast, and he was obliged to make a great effort, after his release from confinement at Party headquarters, to convince them that he had had no part in the Soviet intervention and thus to regain their trust.

"There is evidence also that, even in the first intervention by the armed forces of the USSR, use was made not only of Soviet troops stationed in Hungary, but of Soviet troops from the USSR itself and from Romania."[159] However, the Soviet forces were insufficient to master the situation in Budapest, where fighting lasted without interruption until the cease-fire of October 28. Moreover, the concentration of immediately available Soviet troops in Budapest denuded the provinces, where the revolutionary movements spread like wildfire. Negotiations between Nagy's government and the Soviet Government led to the Soviet agreement to evacuate troops from Budapest. In the last days of October, Soviet troops left the capital and the cities in the provinces; the first intervention ended in a failure.

But the USSR did not intend to give up at any time. What some contemporary commentators, and even Hungarians, took for a graceful withdrawal was, in fact, a temporary evacuation to prepare a full-scale second intervention. As the United Nations Committee says:

In fact, during the last days of October and the beginning of November, the Soviet forces were effecting three types of troop movements in Hungary. The first was the withdrawal from the capital, and from public view in the provinces. The second was the dispatch of new forces from the East to certain strategic centers within Hungary, ostensibly, as announced by Soviet Ambassador Andropov, to assist in the organized withdrawal of Soviet forces. The third was the massing on and within the Hungarian borders of heavy armored units which were to be called upon four days later to crush the Hungarian uprising. . . . By the evening of November 2, Hungary had to all intents and purposes been re-invaded.[160]

The internal developments in Hungary help us to understand this Soviet persistence in quelling the revolution by armed force. On October 25, Gerö was replaced as the First Secretary of the Party by Kadar, who could commend himself to the Hungarian public by his imprisonment under Rakosi and by the known fact that he was horribly tortured in prison. His previous record was checkered. He succeeded to the post of minister of the interior after Rajk and played an active role in inculpating his predecessor. He became a member of the Political Bureau at the beginning of 1951, only to be arrested in April of the same year. He remained in prison until August, 1954, and resumed political activities only in the spring of 1956. In July, after Rakosi's fall, he was readmitted to the Central Committee and its Political Bureau. It seemed that at the helm of the government and the Party stood two men who were among the victims of Rakosi's regime and thus could be trusted.

At the beginning, the spontaneous uprising had no leaders, but the population began to form its own self-government councils. Workers established (as in Poland) workers' councils to run the factories and also to formulate the political and social program of the industrial class; in the provinces, revolutionary councils were formed to take over public administration. Similar councils ran the central ministries and various associations. These workers' and revolutionary councils became the mouthpiece of the Hungarian people; their programs remained within the limits of the students' sixteen points, the quick withdrawal of Soviet troops being the No. 1 demand. The country wanted to be independent. They also asked for the restoration of the various parties as they had existed after the war and before their liquidation by Rakosi, those parties which represented in the elections of 1945 the will of the immense majority of Hungarians. Briefly, the councils wanted to establish a true political democracy, though they never questioned the nationalization of industries or land reform. Externally, they wanted to get rid of the protecting Power. Only in the last days of October did they begin to press, under the adverse impression of the first Soviet intervention, for withdrawal from the Warsaw Pact and the proclamation of the permanent neutrality of Hungary on the Austrian model accepted by the USSR in 1955. Prime Minister Nagy mentioned the termination of Hungarian participation in the Warsaw Treaty for the first time on October 31. After the first news of Soviet troops advancing again on Budapest had been confirmed, the Hungarian Government decided, on November 1, to repudiate the Warsaw Pact and to proclaim neutrality. Kadar was present at that meeting and did not disagree. Thus the two issues of a non-Communist regime and external independence were joined together. The second Soviet intervention solved both of them.

On October 27, Nagy formed a new government in which non-Communists were included and from which Communists who had compromised themselves in Rakosi's era were ejected. The non-Communists formerly belonged to the Smallholders' and the National Peasant Parties. One should recall that the Smallholders' Party had captured a clear parliamentary majority in the 1945 elections. On October 28, the hated political police, AVH, was disbanded. On October 30, Nagy, who was moving along with the deep trend in the country (expressed in the resolutions adopted by the workers' and revolutionary councils) announced that the one-party system had been abolished. Janos Kadar, speaking on the radio after the Prime Minister, expressed the support of the Communist Party for the restoration of a multi-party political life. As a matter of fact, all evidence shows that he co-operated closely with Nagy up to and including November 1. On the same day, Nagy formed within the government an inner cabinet which, in fact, replaced the full government. It was composed of three Communists (Imre Nagy, Janos Kadar, and Geza Losonczy) and three non-Communists, two representing the Smallholders' Party and one the National Peasant. Nagy added in his broadcast that a Social Democrat would be included, thereby acknowledging the cancellation of the forcible merger of the two parties in 1948. This meant a return to the political situation of 1945 when a genuine governmental coalition still existed. On October 30 the three pre-Rakosi era parties were reconstituted: the Smallholders, the National Peasant, and the Social Democratic. One of the first acts of the old Socialist Party (founded in 1880) was to condemn the previous regime: "Not even the most cruel capitalism exploited them [the workers] as have the masters [of our country] during the last eight years. They lied when they said that they were governing in the name of the workers."[161] On November 3, three Socialists were added to the government, which became truly representative and had the right to speak in the name of the whole nation. The reconstructed cabinet included (on November 3) four Communists, three Smallholders, three Social Democrats, and two National Peasants, whose party had shortly before changed its name to the Petöfi Party.

It was that government, supported by the workers' and revolutionary councils, as well as by fighting Hungarian detachments, that was destroyed in the course of the second Soviet intervention. The armed struggle during the first and second Soviet interventions was not a civil war in which a foreign Power intervened but a short war between a whole nation fighting for her independence and the protecting Power, who was determined to maintain her hold on the country. The United Nations Committee says: "It is a significant fact that, throughout the uprising no single unit of the Hungarian Army fought as such at the side of the Soviet troops."[162] The

Committee thus defines the nature of the armed struggle between October 24 and the conquest of Hungary by Soviet troops:

... the fighting which took place in Hungary had nothing of the character of a civil war with one part of the population in armed opposition to another. The military operations were essentially those of a well-equipped foreign army crushing by overwhelming force a national movement and eliminating the Government through which that movement was finding effective expression.[163]

The Communist Party practically disintegrated under the impact of events. Rakosi made a great error in inflating its membership to 900,000 members or about 10 per cent of the total population. This was contrary to Lenin's cautious advice to have a relatively small party of most reliable members. The Soviet Party amounts now to only 3.5 per cent of the population, the Chinese much less than 2 per cent. People enrolled in the Hungarian Party to make careers and for a better livelihood. Their loyalty to the Party could not survive a national crisis. Moreover, it was doubtful whether the Central Committee represented the aspirations of rank-and-file members; this was acknowledged by the Central Committee on October 28, when it decided to transfer all its powers to a Presidium of six members, Nagy and Kadar being included in it "as the best and most honest members of the Central Committee."[164] The assent of the Presidium to the restoration of the multi-party system put an end to the Party as known before or as it is known in other Communist lands; it abdicated its monopoly of power. The bankruptcy of the Party was acknowledged by the change in name to that of the Hungarian Socialist Workers' Party. As last as November 3, the organ of the Party, *Nepszabadsag*, approved the Government's decision regarding the neutrality of Hungary.

Two members of the Soviet Party Presidium, Mikoyan and Suslov (who were not later stigmatized with Molotov, Malenkov and Kaganovich as dogmatists and deviationists and who continue to sit on this supreme Soviet institution of power), twice paid visits to Budapest. They came first during the first intervention to confer with their political friends, Gerö and Hegedus (October 23, 24 and 25), and the second time on November 1, when they discussed the situation with Kadar and Nagy. The first visit resulted in replacing Gerö by Kadar, who was expected to be more popular; the second hastened the mass assault on the country. Yet quite a few people believe that Mikoyan is a kind of "soft" Communist since he had attacked Stalin for his own reasons at the 20th Congress.

The early morning of November 4 saw the second Soviet intervention. In the meantime, Kadar, who had supported Nagy and the new government until November 1, disappeared from Budapest. The United Nations Committee believes that he went to Moscow; no one saw him in Hungary again until November 7. The Soviet Government opened hostilities to the political accompaniment known from its earlier record. The handy device used in Finland, the Baltic States, Poland, and the Transcaucasian Republics in the Leninist period, in Finland in 1939, and in the Baltic countries in 1940 in the Stalinist period was used again in the post-Stalinist era. A broadcast from the Soviet-occupied city of Szolnok announced at 5 A.M. on November 4 that Kadar and a few other Communists had broken with the Nagy Government on November 1 and had formed the Hungarian Revolutionary Workers' and Peasants' Government. Following the footsteps of Kuusinen, this "Government," which did not show its face anywhere in Hungary until after the conquest of Budapest, provided the USSR with the necessary credentials. Of course the same broadcast dutifully stated:

The Hungarian Revolutionary Workers' and Peasants' Government, in the interest of our people, working class and country, requested the Command of the Soviet Army to help our nation in smashing the sinister forces of reaction and restoring order and calm in the country.[165]

Its political program was very moderate, although, naturally, it did not include the question of neutrality and the promise of free elections; but it did mention:

After the restoration of order and calm, the Hungarian Government will begin negotiations with the Soviet Government and with other participants to the Warsaw Treaty about the withdrawal of Soviet troops from Hungary.[166]

The renewal of hostilities came one day after the beginning of negotiations between Nagy's government and the Soviet generals concerning the timetable for the total Soviet evacuation of the country. The mutual atmosphere was so cordial that it was decided to move the place of conversation to Soviet headquarters. The Hungarian military leaders trustfully proceeded there at 10 P.M. on the same day. At midnight, all telephone communications between the Hungarian delegation, composed of General Pal Maleter, minister of defense, General Istvan Kovacs, chief of the general staff, Colonel Miklos Szucs, and others, and the Hungarian Government in Budapest were cut off. The rest of the sad story is told by the United Nations Committee, which affirms that the Soviet-Hungarian military conversations were suddenly interrupted by the arrival of Colonel-General Serov, the chairman of the Soviet Committee of State Security, accompanied by his own officers. He ordered the immediate arrest of the Hungarians.

The reader of this book must have remarked that the Soviet Union has a preference for using tested devices employed to such advantage on many previous occasions. This is true of such snares as people's governments to cover up Soviet military intervention and people's referenda to excuse annexations. It is also true of the mousetrap device of inviting representatives of the opposite side for negotiations and then arresting them. Here is a clever method of getting rid of leaders useful to the opposite party; it was used in 1945 in Poland to decapitate the Polish resistance movement of its principal political and military leaders and to deliver the country to the Communist-controlled government.

The political and military leaders of the Polish resistance movement were invited to meet the Soviet commanding officer, Colonel-General Ivanov, in order to agree on a way in which the movement should co-operate with the Soviet armies. They were offered the most solemn guarantee of their personal security. Three of them went to the appointed place in the Warsaw suburbs on March 27, 1945; thirteen others did the same on the following day. None of them returned home. Pressing inquiries by the British and American governments elucidated no answer from the Soviet Government for several weeks. At length, on May 4, Molotov, who had come to San Francisco to attend the United Nations Conference, casually informed his British and American colleagues that the Polish leaders were held in a Soviet prison. Next day, *Tass* accused them of being guilty of "subversive tactics in the rear of the Red Army" and announced that they were committed for trial in Moscow. Shortly, the Military Division of the Soviet Supreme Court condemned twelve of the sixteen to various terms of imprisonment. Thus the very men who had directed national resistance to Nazi occupation in 1939–1945 at daily risk to their lives were confined to an "Allied" prison soon after the Soviet military occupation of Poland. This method of granting safe-conduct to envoys of the other party and then depriving them of liberty smacks of the Dark Ages, when it was customary, but it scarcely accords with modern international practices.[167]

Premier Nagy announced at 5:20 A.M. (November 4) over the radio that the capital was again being attacked by Soviet troops:

This fight is the fight for freedom by the Hungarian people against the Russian intervention. . . . Today it is Hungary and tomorrow, or the day after tomorrow, it will be the turn of other countries because the imperialism of Moscow does not know borders, and is only trying to play for time.[168]

Thus spoke Nagy during the last hours of his personal freedom, a man who had been a Communist since 1918, who had lived in Moscow for fifteen years and had returned to his native country only in 1944 in the wake of the advancing Soviet troops. When the Soviet troops were about to capture the government building, Nagy, Losonczy, Rajk's widow, and several other Communists took refuge at the Yugoslav Embassy. The Yugoslav Government then undertook negotiations with the Kadar Government for safe-conduct for Nagy and his party. Since the latter group refused Kadar's offer to go to Rumania, it was agreed that they should be free to go to their homes and remain there unmolested. On November 22, a bus sent by the Kadar Government came to fetch the group, who were leaving the Yugoslav Embassy on the strength of this diplomatic pledge. As the group was boarding the bus, Soviet military personnel arrived and insisted on entering it. Thereupon the officials of the Yugoslav Embassy were assigned to accompany the group safely to their homes. However, the bus went straight to the Soviet Military Headquarters, where the Yugoslavs were ordered to leave.

Soviet troops broke down organized resistance in central Budapest throughout November 4, but separate centers of armed opposition to their invasion continued the fight in Budapest and the industrial suburbs until November 11, which was approximately the date of the end of armed struggle in the provinces. During this period of fighting, the Soviet military commanders took over the administration of the reconquered districts. The use of radio stations was reserved for Soviet troops relaying their orders to the Hungarian population. The Revolutionary Government, transported in Soviet army luggage vans, did not function during this crucial period. The United Nations Committee says: "During the early days of the Kadar Government, the administration of the country was, in fact, in the hands of the Soviet Military Command."[169] The Hungarian people offered the one still-possible form of resistance—refusal to go back to work. The Soviet military commanders negotiating with delegates of workers' councils were getting the same answer—that work would be resumed if Soviet troops evacuated Hungary. The USSR replied to this general demand in two ways: by making Kadar and his associates promise the Soviet withdrawal if work were resumed and a policy of arrests, deportations, and other measures of repression. Kadar's newspaper *Nepszabadsag* wrote, for instance, on November 14: "As regards the departure of Soviet troops, this is desired by all, with the exception of a few embittered Rakosi-ites. There is no Hungarian patriot who can be pleased with the fact that Soviet tanks are rumbling through the Hungarian capital."[170] In his cablegram to the Secretary-General of the United Nations, Kadar assured: "After the complete restoration of order, the Hungarian Government will immediately begin negotiations with the Government of the Soviet Union for the withdrawal of these troops from Hungary."[171]

By the middle of December, "order" began to return, and the public position of the Kadar Government concerning Soviet troops started changing too. Work was being resumed, the network of political police was being restored, the native personnel was taking over from the Russians the civilian administration of the country. Kadar was at last able to speak his mind on February 2, 1957: "... They say that there are foreign troops on Hungarian territory, meaning Soviet troops. ... For us they are not foreign troops."[172] On May 27, 1957, the USSR and Hungary concluded a treaty on the legal status of Soviet troops stationed on the Hungarian territory, thus clearly indicating that those troops had no intention of departing.[173] The text of this treaty was copied after the Polish-Soviet agreement on the same matter; however, its Article 1 sounded in Hungary, conquered by Soviet soldiers only seven months before, as a cruel joke at the Hungarian people:

The temporary presence of Soviet forces on the territory of the Hungarian People's Republic in no way affects the sovereignty of the Hungarian State; the Soviet forces do not interfere in the internal affairs of the Hungarian People's Republic.[174]

In the period immediately following the reconquest of Hungary, "order" was re-established by Soviet authorities by various repressive measures, including deportations to the USSR. The United Nations Committee says:

... the Committee has reached the conclusion that, since November 4, 1956, deportations of Hungarian citizens to the USSR have taken place in considerable numbers, which cannot be accurately assessed, but which run into thousands. The Committee has no proof that more than a part of the deportees has been returned to Hungary.[175]

The domestic regime, as before the October uprising, was restored, with the reconstructed Communist Party (now known as the Hungarian Socialist Workers' Party) again in the saddle. The Prime Minister and First Secretary, Kadar, reflected the spirit of his regime when he said on May 11, 1957:

In my opinion, the task of the leaders is not to put into effect the wishes and will of the masses. . . . In my opinion, the leaders' task is to realize the interest of the masses. . . . In the immediate past, we have encountered the phenomenon that certain categories of workers acted against their own interests and, in this case, the duty of the leader is to represent the interest of the masses, not to implement mechanically their incorrect ideas. If the wish of the masses does not coincide with progress, then one must lead the masses in another direction.[176]

Lenin, where he formulated his concept of a revolutionary elite reflecting the permanent interests of the toiling masses (but not following the current wishes of those masses), could not have foreseen that the masses would be led in the name of his doctrine, not by the elite, but by the Russian tanks. Did he not write with sincere indignation in 1914:

No one is guilty of being born a slave. But a slave who not only remains aloof from the striving for his own freedom but justifies and embellishes his slavery (for instance, calls the strangulation of Poland, Ukraine, and other nations, "the defense of the Fatherland" of Great-Russians) calls forth a legitimate feeling of indignation, contempt and horror, and is a churl and a cad.[177]

Did he not express in 1900 this same indignant horror in recalling that Russian troops, on the orders of Nicholas I, had come to the rescue of the Austrian emperor in 1849 and had effectively quelled the Hungarian uprising of the time? "The Tsarist Government not only keeps our people in slavery but sends it to quell other peoples who have risen against their slavery (as happened in 1849 when Russian troops crushed the revolution in Hungary)."[178] This parallels exactly what was done by other Russian troops in Hungary a century later, but this time the orders were given not by the Tsars, but by Lenin's own disciples! Here, as in 1849, the Hungarians fought under the flag of Kossuth, their national leader in the anti-Austrian uprising. In this hour also, as in 1848–49, they recited the poem of Petöfi, the poet of the same uprising:

> Shall we be slaves? Shall we be free?
> That's the question—what's your answer?
> In God's great name we swear, we swear,
> No more shall we be slaves—no more!

The Soviet and Hungarian governments gave an official appraisal of the Soviet intervention on March 29, 1957, which has since become the current Communist version. In the joint declaration adopted by representatives of both governments they said:

. . . the participation of detachments of the Soviet Army in routing the fascist rebels was a supreme act of proletarian solidarity. . . . Both Governments consider that the temporary stationing of Soviet troops in Hungary in accordance with the Warsaw Treaty is imposed by the present international situation.[179]

These people, acting, in turn, as representatives of the two Communist parties, declared on the same day:

. . . The delegation of the Hungarian Socialist Workers' Party has stressed that the conspirators were able to provoke the counter-revolutionary rebellion, first of all, because they had allies in the ranks of the Hungarian Workers' Party in the persons of the treacherous group of Nagy and Losonczy. . . . The Soviet troops fulfill under the present circumstances the function of defending the freedom and independence of the Hungarian people against the aggressive plans of international reaction.[180]

Secretary-General of the Dutch Communist Party Paul de Groot, like almost all foreign Communists, approved this Soviet version of events and explained why Communists had to do it:

He [Lenin] wrote [in 1908]: ". . . the interests of class struggle of the proletariat, or, it would be better to say, of the international movement of the proletariat, represent this one possible point of view from which to examine and solve the problem of the attitude that Social-Democrats must take towards any phenomenon in international relations." . . . One must appraise with the same yardstick the question of the assistance by Soviet troops which Kadar's Government requested. He who does not do so is not a Communist and moreover has no right to call himself a Social-Democrat of the old school.[181]

By applying the same highly malleable yardstick, he came to this disarming conclusion:

Neutrality, guaranteed by both world camps, is a step forward towards national independence for a State which is now subject to American dominion. But it is for a socialist State a step backwards towards subjection to American imperialism and its sphere of influence.[182]

Neither Polish nor Hungarian events in 1956 seemed to confirm this optimistic Soviet appraisal made a year before: "The important superiority of the democratic camp over, and its principal distinction from the imperialist camp consists in the fact that it is not torn apart by internal antagonisms and struggle."[183] Neither the Poles nor the Hungarians seemed to agree with this optimistic statement, also made in 1955: "The relations established between the USSR and the countries of people's democracy are a great example of the true equality, mutual assistance, co-operation and respect for national independence, all of them unheard of in the history of relations between capitalist countries."[184]

CHAPTER XIV

COMMUNIST INTERNATIONAL MOVEMENT

1. Contrasts between the Communist Parties

THE 1956 events in Poland and Hungary shed a revealing light on the mood of the populations in the Soviet eastern European protectorates. It would be insulting for the Czechs, Slovaks, Rumanians, and Bulgarians to assume that they love to be reduced to the status of dependent territories any more than did the Poles or the Hungarians. In both Hungary and Poland, it became evident that the USSR could not rely on the satellite armed forces and that the veneer of Communist indoctrination was very thin, despite the efforts of local Communist parties. The same patriotic spirit which made those eastern European nations resist the rule of other great Powers and fight in the past for their independence and which was at the source of the awakening of Asia and the Near East remains alive in the Soviet protectorates. Even native Communists cannot always be relied upon, as the case of Poland and of a few Hungarian leaders has proved. The clash between the national interests of countries which they rule and the loyalty to the Communist great Power is not always liable to be solved in favor of the latter Power. If there is anything in common between Tito, Gomulka, and Nagy, it is their awakening to the obligations towards the countries where they were born.

We discover here a paradox. Communists who live in the so-called capitalist countries have always shown their supreme loyalty to the USSR as the bastion of the revolution and the center of their political movement. The revolt against the Moscow expectation that national interests of local Communist parties should be subordinated in the last account to the state interests of the USSR materialized from 1948 to 1956 only among the Communist parties which already ruled their own countries. This paradox is easy to explain. A Communist living in a non-Communist country plans to overthrow the existing regime and to install there a different one; he is a professional revolutionary, as Lenin wished him to be. He is at loggerheads with his national environment and is usually suspected of owing allegiance to a foreign Power. He feels like a stranger among his own countrymen. This feeling of isolation and the depressing nature of definitely being unlike the Joneses require a psychological compensation. He finds it in his ties with the Communist great power; her strength becomes, vicariously, his own might. He is in the company of 900 million people ruled by Communist parties, he belongs to the socialist camp, and he is not alone. Were he to revolt against the USSR, he would be reduced to the ungrateful role of a Trotskyite or would have to abandon his revolutionary creed and rejoin his national environment. In either case, he would cease to be a Communist as he understands the term. This explains why Communist parties in the capitalist lands can suffer individual defections as they do but remain as organizations riveted to the mighty chariot of the Soviet Union.

A Communist Party ruling its own native country is in an altogether different situation. It sets the tone and imposes conformity on the population; it splits up and isolates its enemies and is surrounded by large numbers of countrymen who are either resigned to the existence of a Communist regime or acquire vested interests in it by having jobs at the pleasure of the Party. The feeling of isolation disappears. A professional revolutionary is transformed into a ruler. He has to face the responsibility for the fate of his country, even though this responsibility was initially allocated to him by the USSR. He might eventually come to identify himself with his country and then discover a conflict of interests between his nation and Soviet Russia. He is the ruler; his personal ambition might make orders from Moscow rather obnoxious to his personal pride. Eventually, he might try to throw off the foreign yoke, though imposed by a Communist great Power, as Tito and Nagy did, or at least attempt to recover as much national independence as politically possible, as the majority of the Polish Central Committee did in October, 1956.

This might happen, and indeed it did happen in three countries; in Hungary however, the majority of top leaders refused to abandon their allegiance to Moscow. The Communist leaders of Czechoslovakia, Rumania, Bulgaria, East Germany, and Albania figure as colonial puppets. Soon after the Hungarian events, they joined the Soviet leaders in denouncing the Hungarian uprising in Soviet terms. At the beginning of January, 1957, the representatives of the Soviet (Krushchev and Malenkov), Hungar-

ian (Kadar and Munnich), Bulgarian (Zhivkov and Damianov), Czechoslovak (Novotny and Siroky), and Rumanian (Gheorghiu-Dej, Moghiorosh,
and Borila) Communist parties met in Budapest and adopted there a joint
resolution in which they declared:

All the participants in the meeting have come to the unanimous conclusion that the efforts of Hungarian toilers led by the Hungarian Revolutionary Workers' and Peasants' Government, assisted by the Soviet troops,
warded off the attempts at destroying the people's democratic regime and
the socialist achievements of the Hungarian people. The threat of establishing a fascist dictatorship in Hungary was averted, the plans of the domestic
counter-revolution and of the aggressive imperialist circles to transform
Hungary into a dangerous center of a new war in Europe were frustrated.[1]

The satellite Communists did many things by signing this document: they
underwrote the thesis of the protecting Power which they knew to be untrue, condemned in advance any national revolt in their own countries, but
they also excommunicated themselves a priori if any of them were ever
tempted to take the road of a Tito or a Nagy. They acted as other loyalist
natives did in colonial possessions when they pledged their unreserved
fealty to the colonial Power, albeit their motivation was of a more complex
nature. It was very characteristic that the Polish Party was not invited to attend the Budapest meeting. Moscow knew only too well that the Poles, including a great many Communists, sympathized with the Hungarians,
while the Polish Party assumed a very critical position towards the first
Soviet intervention and accepted the second with regret. Gomulka could
not underwrite the Soviet version of Hungarian events, even if he wanted
to (which is improbable), for fear of undermining his precarious popularity
in the country. It was more convenient, both for Moscow and for him, to
avoid being involved in that meeting.

The Chinese Communists, as we said, are in an altogether different situation because their immense country cannot be invaded by Soviet troops.
If they approved the Soviet intervention in Hungary, they did so because
they did not want the empire of their senior ally to crumble, a senior ally
whose economic assistance is of utmost importance to China. By contrast,
they showed sympathy to the Polish Communists, who had not challenged
the existence of the Soviet military bloc but only became a nuisance to the
Russians, thus reducing somewhat their prestige, a fact not unwelcome to a
party that is only a junior ally. On April 12, 1957, the joint Chinese-Polish
declaration was signed; this was not altogether unpleasant to the USSR.

Both governments reaffirmed their intention to build up socialism in accordance with Marxist-Leninist teachings, but with due consideration for national characteristics and conditions, to oppose both dogmatic and revisionist deviations for whatever those terms meant to either signatory, and they pledged their support to the Kadar Government in Hungary. In exchange for the latter provision, the Poles obtained the Chinese reaffirmation of the support for the Polish frontier on the Oder-Neisse and:

The Chinese People's Republic takes note with joy of the successes achieved by the Polish United Workers' Party since the 8th Plenum of its Central Committee. All the people's democratic forces in Poland increasingly rally, each day more closely, around the Central Committee of the Polish United Workers' Party headed by Comrade Gomulka.[2]

The mention of the 8th Plenum of October, 1956, of the rebellious Polish Central Committee, and of Gomulka, whose name had no odor of sanctity in Moscow, was a pique aimed at Moscow but not a challenge, since Moscow had made its own peace, at least for the time being, with the Polish Party and could not object.

2. The 1956 Crisis

The year 1956 brought out a serious crisis within the international Communist movement. This is frankly conceded by the secretary-general of the Dutch Communist Party:

Mankind lived through a serious crisis in the period between the last week of October and the second half of December. We found ourselves in the whirlpool of events. . . . A mixed feeling of fear and doubt veiled the eyes of the masses, including those honest peace partisans and anti-fascists who had no firm ideological ground under their feet and who had not yet completely freed themselves of the ideology of bourgeois society. The proletarian instinct whispered that "it was fine" when the Soviet troops entered the struggle in Budapest. Loyalty towards the Party and discipline kept our Communists on the right path, if one does not count an extremely insignificant number of those who broke off.[3]

"The proletarian instinct" was nevertheless exposed to a great strain by the events of 1956. The sight of Soviet troops murdering people who had risen in the name of their independence was revolting, even to a great many sympathizers of the USSR, those "honest peace-partisans and anti-fascists," who had "no firm ideological ground under their feet" and whose non-proletarian but ordinary moral instinct reacted. Some of them had been pleasantly indulging in great expectations just prior to the Hungarian events. In Stalin's time, they sympathized with the "great social experiment," but they did not relish his regime of terror. They usually found cold comfort in saying that making an omelette required breaking eggs; to be sure, those eggs were human heads, but at least they were not their own. The execution of Beria, the relaxation of the arbitrary Soviet police regime, collective leadership, and smiles and handshakes in foreign relations seemed to usher in a new era; now one could love the USSR without any reservations.

The intervention in Hungary shook, for a time, those confident hopes. Some former sympathizers turned their backs on the Soviet Union. Others were learning in 1956, usually through Polish channels, a great many details about Stalin's persecution of Soviet citizens of Jewish descent and his attack on Jewish culture; they noted the anti-Semitic statements of Krushchev when, for instance, he advised the Polish Central Committee to rid itself of some of its members of Jewish descent and replace them by people of "pure" Slavic origin. They also knew that the pro-Russian faction in the Committee advocated the introduction of a fixed percentage in the state and Party administration for people of Jewish descent and thus hoped to gain national popularity by this anti-Semitic propaganda trick. This persistent information about Stalin's and Krushchev's anti-Semitic bias alienated a number of sympathizers and Communists whose human decency could not approve of racialism.

The publication in America of Kruschev's secret speech was for regular Party members abroad a much greater shock than the Soviet military intervention in Hungary. The Hungarian events could not affect trained Party members permeated with Leninist morality. In their eyes, the threat to the Communist regime fully justified the Soviet intervention. Krushchev's secret speech was an infinitely more serious matter, yet, again, it would be naïve to think that a full-fledged Party member was shocked by the description of terror. He, like any other man, had known very well that the bloody purges included old Bolsheviks, whose ranks had been decimated, and countless other victims. Krushchev did not reveal anything new. The shocking part of his speech was not its contents but his manner and the circumstances which surrounded its delivery. He spoke with indignation and often poked fun at his dead leader. Yet Stalin had been, for the nearly thirty years preceding, the acknowledged symbol of the Soviet

regime and the international Communist movement. To utter an unfavorable word about him was a sacrilege, but Krushchev poured out such
sacrilegious words. No one could tell him that he was a deviationist; the
idol of the movement was toppled down. This placed a thinking Communist in a dilemma.

If Stalin was wrong and yet, as Krushchev said, the dictatorial ruler, then
not only the crimes but the achievements of those thirty years were solely
his. Could, then, the massive collectivization of agriculture, the rapid
industrialization at the expense of consumption, the expansion of Soviet
frontiers and the Sovietization of eastern Europe, also be deemed errors because they were his achievements? If his purges of foreign comrades were
criminal mistakes, was it safe to confide the leadership of the international
movement to Russian leaders? If, on the other hand, as Krushchev said,
there was nothing wrong with industrialization and agricultural collectivization (Soviet achievements allegedly due not to Stalin but to the Party
Central Committee), a different question arose—if the Central Committee
had such influence on those important decisions, were they not to share the
blame for Stalin's crimes? Was Khrushchev himself innocent of human
blood spilled by his former master? Khrushchev did not condemn Stalin
for terror applied to genuine opposition within the Party or to non-Communists, but this did not matter. What hurt was that Stalin, apparently
without any reason and for no practical purpose, decimated loyal Communists.

The Polish Left Wing Communists, who were in a critical mood, deduced
the logical conclusion, namely, that there was something wrong with the
Soviet system which they called Stalinism. Tito took the same view. Others
were not so bold, but they were, for a span of a few months, caught in the
web of logical contradictions involved in Khrushchev's speech. On top of
this, the leaders of foreign parties, most of whom attended the 20th
Congress, were not invited to the secret session. Here was another error, the
leaving of these loyal followers in the dark about such an important matter.
The text of the speech somehow reached Washington and was made public.
Moscow did not deny it. Foreign Communists had to yield to the inevitable
—this was the authentic speech. Palmiro Togliatti could not control his
Italian temper and wrote in June, 1956, an article which reflected his hurt
feelings.[4] He, an old Stalinist, was placed unwarned in a ridiculous position
by his Soviet comrades. His angry reaction was to criticize them for not
mentioning Stalin's merits together with his errors, to accuse them of being

responsible for allowing him to establish a one-man rule, for having exalted him in his lifetime while knowing about his crimes, for shaking the Communists' "limitless faith in the Soviet Communist Party and in its leaders." Togliatti came to the conclusion that the Soviet system was not perfect and that the time had come for a polycentric Communist movement. He probably bitterly regrets this outburst now, but it highlighted the bewilderment caused by Krushchev's speech—a fundamental error made for no apparent rational reasons, but probably an emotional reaction to Stalin's humiliations inflicted on Khrushchev and others, as well as on army leaders. The speech brought no visible benefits to the USSR and sowed confusion in the Communist ranks.

The crisis lasted for several months with steadily declining intensity. The foreign Communists (several parties did not waver for a moment, e.g., the French and the non-European) eventually came to the conclusion that a revolt against Moscow would be the end of the movement as they knew it. They had been exposed to shocks before: the purges in their own ranks, difficult-to-understand expulsions of their own leaders, the trials in the thirties of the old Bolsheviks, whom they had worshiped as heroes of the October Revolution, the Stalin-Hitler Pact, and their own obligation to turn, in 1939-41, the fire of their propaganda from the Nazis to the British and the French "imperialists." All of this they had taken in their stride, as they eventually did the anti-Stalin campaign, especially since, soon after the 20th Congress, the Soviet leaders began to soft-pedal it, mentioning Stalin's merits and concluding that his merits far outweighed his errors. Eventually, "normalcy" in relations with the Soviet Party was restored, and it remained the leader of the movement.

A few small parties in the West were the most affected, especially the American, many of whose members left it in disgust. This was not new; it happened in 1939 when the conclusion of the pact with the Nazis caused a similar revulsion and defections. The parties knew from experience that they could survive the defection of "wavering elements" and that they would be internally stronger by getting rid of them. *Kommunist* expressed this practical philosophy in these words: "It has been known for a long time that the departure of unsteady and wavering members does not weaken but strengthens the proletarian parties."[5] Iron discipline and unquestioning loyalty to instructions from above, even if a later instruction contradicts the earlier, are the mark of a true Communist. The 1956 crisis "purified" the ranks and was not to be greatly regretted. Looking at it retrospectively, one cannot but concede that the movement has not disintegrated and now looks as strong as before, despite several defections which impressed the West more than Moscow. Its ranks still number over thirty-three million members, one-third of them living in the capitalist countries; it continues to control several million "peace-partisans," members of Communist-controlled labor unions, "democratic" women, "democratic" youth, and many unorganized sympathizers. A large fraction of those reserves are on this side of the Iron and Bamboo curtains.

3. The Great Debate: Orthodoxy or Revisionism? One or Several Roads to Socialism?

The really serious problem was of a different kind, namely, the Polish and Yugoslav heresies, which could have had an impact upon other eastern European Communists and populations. Eventually, the epidemic could reach the Soviet intelligentsia, among whom, notably the literary writers, an article in *Kommunist* detected in January, 1957, "people . . . who indulge in deviations from Marxism-Leninism . . . and waste their time on scholastic and abstract speculations on democratic freedoms 'in general.' "[6] The great debate raging in the Soviet press in 1956–57 usually turned on this problem. The "theological" discussions, with their signpost words, concerned a vital political question, namely, who (the USSR or each eastern European Party) should have the right to decide what was a conformist and what was a deviationist view. This involved the important question of who was master in eastern Europe. We may relate this debate by following the signpost words.

(A) *National Communism* was one of them. Soviet leaders knew from the history of their own multi-national state and had learned from the dispute with Yugoslavia, the Polish revolt in 1956, and the Hungarian uprising that a Communist may waver in his loyalty to Moscow as the center of the movement only under the impact of an awakening of his national feelings. Nationalism is the enemy of any imperialist Power, be it the Soviet Union or any other. National reassertion could lead not only to attempts at throwing off the Soviet yoke but to the formulation of local interpretations of Leninism, such heresies undermining the ideological unity of the movement. Lenin said in 1918: "Marx and Engels said many times that our doctrine was not a dogma, but a guide in action. I believe that we must keep this in mind before and above anything else."[7] He took great liberties with Marxism to suit his practical policies. His disciples have done the same, but the monopoly on the interpretation of the doctrine has remained in their own hands and has helped them in devising practical policies. What would happen to the supremacy of the center and the unity of the movement if other parties started invoking the same motto of Lenin in formulating their own interpretations? Moreover, as we have said, there is a core of Leninism which has always been considered sacred. Could foreign Communists revise this also?

Attaching the word "national" to Communism was the worst challenge. However, there is no better word for the revolt of Tito, the Polish Communists, and Nagy and Losonczy. Their views were founded on the assertion of the right of each national Party to decide for itself. The Soviet and Hungarian leaders solemnly condemned national Communism in their joint declaration of March 28, 1957:

The C.P.S.U. and the H.S.W.P. consider the propagation lately by some "theoreticians" of the concept of so-called "national communism" as harmful, having nothing in common with Marxism-Leninism, and pernicious to each socialist country in particular and the whole socialist camp in general.[8]

The Soviet-Albanian joint declaration said the same.[9] M. A. Suslov, a member of the ruling Presidium, warned in April, 1957:

. . . the enemies of socialism try to split up the Communist and Workers' parties and to inflame, under the guise of "national communism," nationalistic views and prejudices. The theory of "national communism," brought to light by the enemies of socialism, unfortunately infiltrated also the vocabulary of some "theoreticians" who call themselves Communists. The idea of "national communism" has nothing in common with Marxism. Its practical fulfillment would result in the disintegration of one single socialist camp.[10]

Nationalism was to remain the unique privilege of Russian Communists. The Soviet press seconded the leaders.[11]

According to Soviet critics, national Communism would result in the following evils: undermining the solidarity of Communist parties, weakening the socialist camp in the face of the enemy capitalist camp, opposing the national road to socialism of one country to that of another, namely, the Soviet, inflaming local national feelings, questioning the position of the USSR as the center of the movement, leading to heretical interpretation of Marxism-Leninism and eventually to its revision, rejecting some of the fundamentals of the residual Communist creed. This makes national Communism nothing but a more refined bourgeois nationalism, the term of supreme opprobrium.[12] To the reprehensible "national Communism" was opposed *proletarian internationalism,* which symbolized the uniformity of the movement without any national deviations and with the USSR remaining its center. The 17th Congress of the Austrian Communist Party held in March, 1957, expressed the heart's desires of the Soviet leadership and reflected the pattern for other parties:

Our indestructible ties with the Soviet Union and the C.P.S.U. as the main force and center of socialism, and the resulting trust in them are founded on objective reality.... Any attempt at alienating the Communist party of any country from the C.P.S.U. and from the Communist and Workers' parties of other socialist countries inevitably leads to the reformist morass.[13]

On the other hand, W. Gomulka reminded his Soviet comrades of the existence of national feelings in eastern Europe, where they were exacerbated by past foreign rule:

Each nation has had her own history that has left its imprint. For instance, the working class of countries subjected by other nations to colonial oppression differs in many respects from the working class of the colonial countries [colonial Powers] or such as were colonial not long since.... The specific feature which history has implanted in the mentality of the Polish nation is, for instance, a particular sensitivity to the sovereignty of the country.[14]

The Soviet leadership was only willing to concede that the forms and modalities of the Soviet pattern might vary from country to country, thus leaving open the big question of who should define the boundary line between a specific form and a deviation.

(B) *Proletarian internationalism* means many things: accepting the USSR as the leading center, never opposing the national interests of an eastern European country to those of the USSR, sacrificing everything on the altar of the movement, maintaining the unity of the socialist camp as the apple of the eye, and admitting that peaceful co-existence stood for cool relations with capitalist states, while international relations between socialist states should be guided by close co-operation, to be defined and determined by the Soviet Union. The Yugoslav and Left Wing Polish Communists served as the whipping boys to teach the lesson of proletarian internationalism.[15] "Only Don Quixotes in the workers' movement can refuse to acknowledge the true fact of the division of the world into two camps: the socialist and the capitalist."[16] "Co-existence is applicable only to countries with different social systems. The principle of proletarian internationalism, not a simple co-existence, is fundamental and determinant in relations between socialist countries, within the socialist system."[17] The same article formulated the basic criterion of proletarian internationalism in words which Stalin would not have repudiated: "Communists throughout the world stress that the attitude one takes towards the socialist camp, with the Soviet Union at its helm [sic!] is the touchstone of proletarian internationalism."[18] To challenge the thesis that the USSR should remain at the helm would be a betrayal of proletarian internationalism. However, the Yugoslavs indulge in the "heresy" that peaceful co-existence should be the mode of living for socialist states, both in mutual relations and in their dealings with capitalist states.[19] This makes it unnecessary for any socialist Power to stand at the helm, and it reduces the concept of the socialist camp to a zero.

Proletarian internationalism entails, for eastern Europe, remaining faithful to the Soviet military bloc: "The strengthening of the Warsaw Treaty organization constitutes the most sacred duty of all the socialist States."[20]

(C) *Stalinism* is taboo. Polish and Yugoslav Communists logically deduced from Khrushchev's speech the conclusion that there was something wrong with the Soviet system because all the errors imputed to Stalin were those of a man who had formed that system. The Soviet system was called Stalinism. However, the equality between socialist states, as Polish Communists observed bitterly, was composed of two facets: freedom of Soviet comrades to criticize shortcomings in the eastern European countries (certainly not in China) and the prohibition for eastern European Communists to utter a critical word about Soviet practices. The motto, as Polish Communists said, was: "Who has given you the right to criticize the Soviet Union?" And so the word *Stalinism* was resented by Russian Communists; the Poles had to drop it from their vocabulary. Yugoslavs, placed in a different geographical situation, could continue to irritate Moscow by talking about Stalinism and Stalinists. It was true, moreover, that a critical analysis of Stalinism entailed a critical analysis of its source, Leninism:

The ideologists of "national Communism" limited themselves for a time to ... attacks on so-called "Stalinism"; ... these attacks ... meant in essence a determined subversion of Marxist-Leninist principles. But if one has said: A. he must sooner or later say: B. And now we may see how the critics of "Stalinism" begin already to pass to a direct attack on Leninism.[21]

Stalin existed and committed certain errors, but there was no Stalinist system under his one-man rule: "Stalinism as a 'system' is the fruit of the imagination of the imperialist bourgeoisie and its spokesmen."[22]

(D) *The Hungarian events* are the touchstone of devotion to the Communist movement. The Austrian Communists loyally said:

The fact that the toilers were dragged, against their own interests, into the black machinations of the Hungarian reaction does not alter at all the objectively counter-revolutionary essence of the Hungarian events. . . . The international working class, including the workers of our country, are grateful to the Soviet Union for its assistance to the Hungarian toilers.[23]

Gomulka sounded unorthodox in May, 1957, when he said:

We may differ with other parties in the evaluation of Hungarian events, but this does not interfere with the general opinion that the assistance by the Soviet Army, in the name of safeguarding the peace and security of all socialist countries, in crushing the counter-revolution, was a sad but unavoidable necessity.[24]

His October, 1956, fear that the same necessity might have materialized in Poland was reflected by his using the word "sad" since no other Communist would have done this.

(E) The problem of national domestic independence involves the question of several *national roads to socialism* or one Soviet highway at best with several lanes along it. What, exactly, ceases to be a particular form of building socialism adapted to local circumstances and becomes a national road? This is a highly controversial matter involving the practical question of the competent authority to answer it, Moscow or the local Party. The Yugoslavs solved this problem in 1948. Gomulka now claims the same right for his Party in defining a Polish national road:

The practice in building socialism has demonstrated that universal forms do not and cannot exist. . . . Stressing the national road to socialism means in a strictly defined sense a different character of this road, i.e., of methods of building socialism in a given country by comparison to the road taken up by socialism in the Soviet Union . . . the concrete road to socialism is determined by the concrete general historic conditions and the concrete class forces existing in a given country. . . . From all I have said one may deduce the general conclusion that the road to socialism which was followed by the Soviet Union . . . is not at all indispensable or convenient for other nations.[25]

After saying that "such [national] a road excludes copying the Russian road," he cautiously moderated his challenge by adding: "However, stressing the historical peculiarities and national features in the construction of socialism does not mean the denial of the existence of general laws and general principles deduced from the experience of building socialism in the Soviet Union."[26] For him, the national road meant several things, such as national domestic autonomy, slower tempo of building heavy industries, improving living standards, abandoning the former pressure on peasants to join collective farms, etc.

Kommunist, seconded by the whole Soviet press, gave him an answer in advance:

The tendency to oppose one's "own road" to the experience of other socialist countries is nothing but an attempt at rejecting the international teachings of Marxism-Leninism. It is not accidental that the imperialists have taken hold of this trend, baptizing it with the name of "national communism" . . . and what is in fact "national communism" but a bourgeois nationalism?[27]

In another article, *Kommunist* said:

The road to socialism is lighted with the Marxist-Leninist ideas but not with so-called "national Communism." . . . All sorts of theories about the "separate roads" to socialism . . . contradict the objective laws of social development which Marxism-Leninism has discovered. This is proved by the experience of the USSR, the Chinese People's Republic and other countries of people's democracy. Communists of all countries attach an enormous importance to the experience of the USSR where socialism was built up for the first time in the whole world. . . . This is the highway not only for the proletariat of the Soviet Union but also a common highway which must be taken by the proletarians of all countries in order to achieve victory.[28]

Kommunist added, however:

The peculiarity in solving the problems of socialist construction results from the creative application of Marxism-Leninism to the particular conditions of various countries which are engaged in socialist co-operation. Thus there is a peculiarity of creative decisions while following the same road.[29]

This again raises the vital question of who shall decide the peculiar national gait for treading the same highway and what constitutes a national
road involving a deviation from Marxism-Leninism.[30] Soviet sources leave
no doubt that, basically, the road to socialism must be the same for all
countries: "The course of history during the last decades bears testimony
to the fact that there is only one scientifically founded road of building
socialism, the Marxist-Leninist road."[31]

(F) Yugoslav and Polish Left Wing Communists have been accused of
open revisionism. The terms *dogmatism* and *revisionism* cover up insub-
ordination, either at home or abroad, to the existing Soviet leadership.
Usually, they mean either the trend to abide by the Stalinist pattern without any change or going too far in modifying the same pattern. Sometimes,
either term is indifferently selected to brand a political opponent. Malenkov, who wanted to change an essential feature of Stalinism, namely, the
neglect of living standards for the sake of speedy heavy industrialization,
was labeled, after his fall, a dogmatist (together with Molotov and Kaganovich, who deserved this label) because this would make him unpopular
with the Soviet public. The Polish press, afraid now to call the pro-Moscow
section of their Party "Stalinists," adorns them with the more innocent
names of dogmatists and conservatives.

Usually, a revisionist is the enemy because he wants to modify the basic
pattern. Polish Left Wingers drew such a fire from the Soviet press that
Gomulka had to come down on them in his May, 1957, speech in order
to appease Soviet comrades, who represented a nuclear great Power. The
revisionists advocated a greater freedom of expression, upheld workers'
councils, which they conceived as autonomous bodies free to have opinions
different from the Party, wanted to leave the peasants completely free to
choose their way, refused to have speedy industrialization at a heavy cost
to the population, vindicated the right to say frankly what they thought
of the USSR, claimed a true equality within the socialist camp, and intended to have freedom of discussion within the Party (see Chapter XIII).
All of this was anathema to the Soviet Communists. The worst offense was
their questioning of Communist morality in the name of traditional standards. How dangerous this was, their sympathy for the Hungarians clearly
demonstrated. The Soviet leaders declared war on all revisionists, for instance, in their joint declaration with the Albanian Communists: "The
participants in the conversations consider it necessary further to rally together the Communist and Workers' parties on the platform of Marxism-

Leninism and to intensify the struggle against any attempts at revising the Marxist-Leninist theory."[32]

Taboo in the guide for action, as Lenin called Marxism, are the following elements. The first is the dictatorship of the Communist Party, which must neither abdicate its monopoly of power nor follow the spontaneous wishes of the workers:

Revisionists make a particular effort to lower the role of the conscious element in the working movement, the role of the revolutionary theory, the role of the political party of the proletariat, and the importance of the organized leadership in the proletarian struggle. . . . The Party works out the policy of the working class. . . . The Party never forgets that there is no homogeneous mass of toilers. . . . There are the leading layers who are deeply conscious of the true interests of the people, and there are backward strata which are imbued with petty-bourgeois illusions and which see only their narrow-private, particularist, purely professional, temporary interests. . . . The Party does not simply reflect the spontaneous views of the masses, but . . . raises the masses to the level of opinions of the vanguard detachment of the working class.[33]

. . . Such fundamental theses, as the dictatorship of the proletariat and the leading role of the Communist Party, are biding for all countries which truly march on the road to socialism.[34]

Of course the Party must, in turn, follow the instructions of its leaders, a phenomenon that is euphemistically named the one-mindedness of its members:

The unity of the Communist and Workers' parties is, first of all, guaranteed by the fact that their ranks unite one-minded people who hold the same views on the goals and tasks of the Party, the forms of its organization and its tactics. . . . The unity of the Party is unthinkable without the liquidation of all factions and groups.[35]

W. Gomulka tried to square the circle by saying: "The unity of the Party does not require at all a sort of one-mindedness of all its members. . . . Such an absolute one-mindedness has never existed, cannot exist and should not exist. . . . The Party must be monolithic."[36] But he claimed the freedom of disagreeing with other parties:

There are in our Party and other parties such comrades who think that the Workers' and Communist parties of the whole world should agree absolutely on every topic and even on the most trifling detail in order to render to the principles of proletarian internationalism what is due to them. We believe that this should not exist and that it is impossible that it exist.[37]

A French Communist rejected workers' councils, unknown to the Soviet Union and the people's democracies but practiced in Yugoslavia and Poland: ". . . in the condition of class warfare any homage to the spontaneity of the workers' movement and every diminution of the role of the proletarian party amount to strengthening the bourgeois influence over the workers."[38] Russian Communists called such "revisionist" institutions "anarchist-syndicalist theories of the protagonists of 'national communism.' "[39]

The worst Polish heresy was the doubt expressed concerning Lenin's dictum that everything was moral that served the revolution. What one Soviet author calls liberalization, Polish Left Wingers called greater freedom of expression:

Some people abroad, who call themselves Communists, act now as apostles of "liberalization" of the social-political life in countries building socialism. . . . The claim of "liberalization" of social-political life under the dictatorship of the proletariat . . . is reactionary and directed against the interests of the people.[40]

Other Soviet publicists took the Polish Left Wingers to task for their whole moral outlook and for their opposition to Stalinism of a "humanitarian socialism" founded on traditional morality. Their rejection of the Soviet idea that power was more important than all other consideration drew back such an answer:

. . . there is not and cannot be any "general concept" of love of your neighbor, justice and humanitarianism, applicable both to the proletariat and the bourgeoisie. . . . As long as capitalism exists, the Leninist approach to the evaluation of all historical events from the point of view: "Who [defeats] whom?" has been and remains fundamental. . . . "For us justice is subordinated to interest in overthrowing capitalism" [a quotation from Lenin]. . . . The rejection of this approach is also the rejection of the substance of Marxism.[41]

It is difficult to deny that the Soviet writer interpreted Lenin more correctly than his Polish opponents.

Contrariwise, the discussion of one or several national roads to socialism could be supported on either side by quotations from Lenin. He said, on the one hand:

The revolution will take . . . its own road in each country. . . . The World Revolution is not built this way as though it would tread the same road everywhere and in all countries. . . . Each country must go through definite political stages.[42]

But on the other hand, he also said:

... all the fundamental and many secondary features of our revolution have an international significance in the sense of their influence on all countries. ... The Russian pattern forecasts for *all* countries something of great importance in their unavoidable and near future. ... Hence the international "importance" ... of the Soviet power as well as of the fundamentals of the Bolshevik theory and practice.[43]

The power of a Party engaged in this debate is the crucial factor in determining which quotation should be cited. *Kommunist*, thinking, no doubt, of its own Soviet Party, said: "We, Communists, call ourselves orthodox."[44] Logically, a deviation by a foreign Party from the Soviet line becomes a revisionist lack of orthodoxy.[45]

4. Co-ordination

Orthodoxy is now assured by frequent bilateral and sometimes multilateral consultations by the Communist parties and their elder, the Soviet Party. The co-operation, the ways of which are not all known to the public, ostensibly has gone through various stages. The first was the Comintern, founded by Lenin in 1919 and composed of the Soviet Party and such foreign parties as had emerged after the Lenin-inspired split within the old socialist parties. It was highly centralized, the various parties being called sections of the Comintern. The Russians, the only ones to have a state and a treasury at their disposal, quite naturally assumed the leadership, which has remained in their hands to the present day. The USSR continues to be, even after the emergence of other Communist states, the only Communist world great Power. It is only too true that "the Russian Communist Party (Bolsheviks) acted as the inspiring spirit and organizer of the Communist International called upon to secure the formation in all countries of parties of a new type, the Marxist-Leninist parties."[46] The Comintern proclaimed in its platform, adopted on March 4, 1919: "Communism is now being born out of the ruins of capitalism; history offers no other way out for mankind."[47]

Stalin dissolved it, at least formally, in 1943 for Soviet tactical reasons. He quite frankly told the Moscow correspondent of the Reuters News Agency that he wanted to prove that Moscow did not interfere in the life of other states and that the foreign Communist parties were not taking orders from abroad.[48] He did this "to facilitate the union of all patriots in the freedom-loving countries," and hence to make it easier for Communists to convince other parties that they were free agents and thus eligible for common action and participation in governments, and, finally, to cement the Grand Alliance and avoid disputes with or suspicions of the Western Powers. In fact, he allayed many fears and helped western European Communists in acquiring a respectable posture and participating in their national governments, a factor not without importance for the USSR, for instance, in France and Italy until 1947. But the policies of the various parties continued to conform to the Soviet strategic objectives; there must have been some sort of co-ordination.

In 1947, Stalin rebuilt a regional organization under the name of the Communist Information Bureau. This included only the Soviet, all eastern European, and the French and Italian parties. It served as a center of guidance for all Communist parties:

The Information Bureau and its press organ: *For the lasting peace, For the people's democracy*, were important factors in strengthening proletarian internationalism within the international Communist movement and in rallying the working class and all the toilers in the struggle for a lasting peace, democracy and socialism.[49]

The new foreign policy, outwardly conciliating, especially regarding the uncommitted nations, dictated in 1956 the decision similar to that which Stalin had taken in 1943. The Cominform was formally disbanded. Neither dissolution meant any interruption in close co-operation among the Communist parties: "The dissolution of the Comintern did not mean that the need for some sort of ties among the brotherly parties had disappeared. A lack of mutual ties among them would be an error and in fact unnatural."[50] The official comment of the parties which had belonged to the Cominform was in 1956 strikingly similar:

The Central Committees of the Communist and Workers' parties, which participated in the Bureau of Information, consider that each party and group of parties . . . will find new useful forms of bonds and contacts between them. The Communist and Workers' parties will no doubt continue, at their discretion and with due consideration for the actual conditions of their respective activities, to exchange views concerning general questions of struggle for peace, democracy and socialism, the defense of interests of the working class and all toilers, and the mobilization of popular masses for the struggle against the danger of war; and will jointly examine, in relation to these questions, the problem of co-operation with [other] parties and movements which are oriented towards socialism as well as with all other organizations which strive to consolidate peace and democracy. All this will strengthen even more the spirit of mutual co-operation among Communist and Workers' parties . . . and will re-enforce their mutual fraternal ties.[51]

For the time being, there is no apparent common organization, and the bilateral talks among various leaders must provide the required channel. As a matter of fact, this form of consultation is less visible and more flexible.

The strengthening of the unity of socialist countries is being realized in their State relations and through the co-operation among the fraternal Communist and Workers' parties. . . . The relations among the Communist parties have an immense impact because these parties stand at the helm of State leadership. . . . The basic interests of the working class stimulate the Communist parties which acknowledge Marxist-Leninist teachings as the foundation of their activities to maintain among themselves much closer ties than the contacts they might have with other organizations. . . . Hence it is fully realistic that the relations among those parties, parties of one-minded people having one common ideological-political background, can and should be closer than the relations between the Communist parties and other progressive and democratic parties. While contacting other parties and co-operating with them on specific matters, the Communists never lose sight of their necessary goal: building a Communist society; they never abandon their principles, and they safeguard their ideological, organizational and political independence. . . . The forms of co-operation have been found—bilateral meetings and also meetings of several parties have been taking place, for instance.[52]

The last three passages refer to all Communist parties either in charge of government in people's democracies or those which are active in the "capitalist" states.[53]

All of these Soviet views have been endorsed by the Chinese Party in the *Zhen'min'zhibao*,[54] with somewhat different nuances and with the reservation against great Power chauvinism, a reservation counterbalanced by the advice given to small nations to overcome their own nationalism. The same basic article conceded, however, to the USSR the role of the center of international proletariat.[55]

Both the unity of the Communist movement and the Soviet Party's central position within this movement were eloquently demonstrated in November, 1957. The 40th anniversary of the October Revolution brought to Moscow for the celebrations innumerable delegates of sixty-five Communist parties representing a total membership of 33 million, with Mao Tse-tung cutting the figure of the senior foreign representative. Gomulka, whom the geopolitical situation of his country left no choice anyhow, was among those pilgrims visiting the Communist Mecca, as was Togliatti, who must have forgotten, in the meantime, his unorthodox statements of the summer of 1956. A Yugoslav delegation composed of Tito's lieutenants attended the celebrations, but Tito himself, although invited, cleverly invoked at the last moment a diplomatic illness as a pretext for declining the Soviet invitation; his two-pronged policy was safeguarded—Moscow was not slighted by the absence of Yugoslav Communists, while the West was consoled by the fact that Tito refused to make the pilgrimage to Moscow personally.

This imposing gathering of top leaders and other prominent Communists represented the parties of the Soviet-Chinese bloc and all the parties from the capitalist countries. In composition, it recalled the Comintern congresses; no such assembly had been held in Moscow for many years past. Its implicit message consisted in telling the outside world that the unity of the movement and the leading role of Russian Communists were not affected by the crisis of 1956. This was a message useful to wishful thinkers who had been sure that this crisis had irremediably wrecked the Communist solidarity with Moscow. Actually, the Soviet preponderance within the movement was, if anything, only strengthened by the display of Soviet technological achievements illustrated by the launching of the two earth satellites. Communists are the last men to despise power. The sputniks and what they stood for proved that the Soviet Party had the right of the stronger to remain the guiding leader of the movement. The central figure at the Moscow gathering was Khrushchev, whose personal prestige had been enhanced by his victory over Malenkov, Molotov, Kaganovich, and Marshal Zhukov. The Leninist morality makes the man who outbids his rivals the best man.

This assembly of Communist parties published two resolutions. The one which was by far less important espoused all the objectives of the Soviet foreign policy couched in the terms familiar to Soviet propaganda. Called "Manifesto of Peace," this resolution, signed by all Communist parties, including the Yugoslav, appealed to "all men of good will" in the name of safeguarding peace.[56] The "capitalist monopolies" (an euphemism for Western countries) were singled out as the enemies of peace; by contrast, the Soviet Union and other Communist states were raised to the rank of foremost apostles and defenders of peace. However, another factor working for peace was named—the uncommitted nations, whose neutrality policy and acceptance of the *Pancha Shila* were duly extolled. Otherwise, this "Peace Manifesto" underwrote the usual Soviet slogans: the termination of nuclear tests, elimination of military blocs and bases on foreign territory, fight against the rearmament of West Germany, opposition to "imperialist designs" in the Near and Middle East, etc.

The Manifesto was signed by the Communist parties from the following countries: Australia, Austria, Albania, Algeria, Argentina, Belgium, Bolivia, Bulgaria, Brazil, Great Britain, Hungary, Venezuela, Vietnam, Guatemala, German Democratic Republic, German Federal Republic, Honduras, Greece, Denmark, Dominican Republic, Israel, India, Indonesia, Jordan, Iraq, Spain, Italy, Canada, China, Colombia, Korea, Costa Rica, Cuba, Luxemburg, Malaya, Morocco, Mexico, Mongolia, Netherlands, New Zealand, Norway, Panama, Paraguay, Peru, Poland, Portugal, Rumania, San Marino, Syria, Lebanon, Soviet Union, Thailand, Tunisia, Turkey, Uruguay, Finland, France, Ceylon, Czechoslovakia, Chile, Switzerland, Sweden, Ecuador, Yugoslavia, and Japan. Yugoslavia placed herself in an awkward position towards the West by espousing the foreign-policy slogans of the Soviet bloc. This act of solidarity with the latter bloc could hardly be reconciled with a true policy of non-commitment. It is possible that one of the Yugoslav reasons for acting in this manner might have been the intimidation by the sudden revelation of Soviet technological progress through the sputniks. Certain other non-Communist states were also shocked by this revelation and reacted at first with an apprehensive reappraisal of the distribution of power on the international scale. The Soviet Government did not hesitate to use this asset of intimidation in its propaganda, making the most of its new position of strength.

The other resolution, much more important, was signed only by those Communist parties which ruled in their respective countries: the USSR, China, Poland, Czechoslovakia, East Germany, Rumania, Hungary, Bulgaria, Albania, Vietnam, Korea, and Mongolia. Only the Yugoslav delegation refused to sign, as though to safeguard the independent policy of its Party and the contacts with the Western "imperialists." Nor did the Communist parties from non-Communist lands sign this resolution, probably in order to prove to their respective countrymen that they remained independent of the Soviet Union and were free agents. However, the implicit assent to the resolution was marked by the words: "While drafting the declaration the participants in the meeting consulted with representatives of the fraternal parties in the capitalist countries."[57]

The declaration itself is an important document for two reasons. It sums up the ideology and objectives of the whole movement, but it does so in terms identical with what Soviet leaders and the press have been saying throughout the last few years. The Soviet imprint is unmistakable in thought and wording. The international stage is seen as the scene "of the competition between the two diametrically opposed social systems."[58] Since only two systems are being referred to, it is clear that not only the Western but also the non-Communist underdeveloped countries, committed or un-committed, belong to the other diametrically opposite camp. After men-tioning the unavoidable ultimate victory of Communism, the declaration repeats what the Soviet 20th Congress said, namely, that the transition to the new order might follow in the capitalist countries either a peaceful or a violent course. But if the Communists were unable to win power by peaceful means, "the ruling classes resorting to violence against the peo-ple" (the non-Communists being, in other words, unwilling to sign their own death warrant and commit political suicide), "the possibility of non-peaceful transition to socialism should be borne in mind."[59] The chances of a non-violent seizure of power should be strengthened by national fronts uniting various parties and organizations but with the leadership of the front being vested in the "vanguard of the working class."[60] Thus the most representative gathering of Communist parties of the whole world dis-played with vigor the Leninist flag of the universal revolution, to be achieved by violence or otherwise. The resolution was adopted in the capi-tal of a great Power which never tires of assuring the capitalist countries of her desire peacefully to co-exist with them.

In foreign policy, the United States was singled out by name as the main enemy, probably because it was the strongest non-Communist state whose defeat would prejudge the fate of the whole non-Communist camp. The declaration again called for a peace zone founded on foreign-policy co-operation between the Soviet-Chinese bloc and the Asian-African coun-tries, co-operation directed against the West, the United States in particu-lar. And the *Pancha Shila* were again offered as the ideological basis for such co-operation. The Soviet plan to petrify the division of Germany was emphasized by the solemn pledge given by the signatories of the declara-tion to support fully the German Democratic Republic. After the usual de-nunciations of the Western blocs (NATO, the Baghdad Pact, and SEATO), the declaration paradoxically called for the "preservation and strengthen-ing" of the Warsaw Pact Organization.

Stalin would have been pleased with his disciples, who reaffirmed his criterion of a true proletarian internationalism:

Today the vital interests of the working people of all countries call for their support of the Soviet Union and all the Socialist countries. . . . The working class, the democratic forces and the working people everywhere are interested in tirelessly strengthening fraternal contacts for the sake of the common cause, in safeguarding from enemy encroachments the historic, political and social gains effected in the Soviet Union—the first and mightiest Socialist power—in the Chinese People's Republic and in all the Socialist countries, in seeing these gains extended and consolidated.[61]

In 1957, as in Stalin's lifetime, the touchstone of a man being progressive, democratic, and peace loving remains his attitude towards the Communist camp and, first of all, the Soviet Union. Otherwise, one is hopelessly confined to the camp of reaction. This means in particular that all Communists and their sympathizers in and out of national fronts must support Soviet foreign policy.

The declaration summed up the Communist residual creed in terms known from the previous Soviet statements: (1) "Effecting a proletarian revolution in one form or another and establishing one form or another of dictatorship of the proletariat" (which means "the leading role of the Marxist-Leninist party" in the post-revolutionary society). (2) Keeping faith with the Marxist-Leninist dialectical materialism as a "world outlook reflecting the universal law of development of nature, society and human thinking. It is valid for the past, the present and the future." Thus any other outlook and philosophy have no place in the Communist-controlled society. (3) Public ownership of means of production. (4) Gradual socialist reconstruction of agriculture (it is interesting to note that Gomulka accepted this tenet by apposing his signature; this carries with it the foreboding that he will try one day to reopen in Poland a campaign for the collectivization of agriculture). (5) Planned economy. (6) "The carrying out of the Socialist revolution in the sphere of ideology and culture" (in plain words, this means a reassertion of the Party claim to set up a single conformist line in all social sciences, literature, and arts). (7) Proletarian internationalism, which spells, at least for the Soviet signatories, an unwavering loyalty to the Soviet Party on the part of all other Communist parties.[62]

The declaration anathematized both dogmatism and revisionism. However, "the Communist parties believe that the main danger at present is revisionism."[63] Small wonder, because the so-called revisionists, notably in Poland, called in effect for some democratization of life both within and without the parties, a lethal medicine for totalitarian parties. Revisionists were dangerous heretics, much more so than Tito, who had challenged only the Russian supremacy, not the main tenets of the faith. The declaration correctly attributed to the revisionists such pernicious ideas as "denying the historical necessity for a proletarian revolution," "denying the leading role of the Marxist-Leninist party," "rejecting the principles of proletarian internationalism" (the Russian supremacy within the movement), and re-pudiating the so-called "democratic centralism" in Party organization (in other words, the strict obedience to the top Party leadership) that would transform the party into "a debating society."[64] Gomulka undertook there an implicit obligation of expelling such revisionists from the Polish Party; he signed this excommunication and the mutual pledge "to ban factions and groups."[65] The Soviet monolithic ideal of the Communist parties was reaffirmed for the benefit of all of them.

The declaration stated that "it is necessary above all to promote the unity of the Communist and Workers' parties, to foster solidarity between the Communist and Workers' parties of all countries."[66] This was, in effect, the reaffirmation of the solidarity between the governments of Communist countries, governments which are controlled by the Communist parties, and the Communist parties in capitalist countries (which were asked in the same declaration to carry out a revolution in a peaceful or other form). This was not very reassuring for the capitalist countries invited to a peaceful co-existence of this kind.

Finally, the declaration announced some unspecified new form of Communist co-operation in addition to bilateral contacts of recent years:

The participants in the meeting have arrived at the conclusion that it is expedient in present conditions to hold as the need arises not only bilateral meetings of leading personnel for mutual exchange of information but to have more representative conferences of Communist and Workers' parties to discuss current problems, share experience, study each other's views and attitudes, and plan concerted action in the joint struggle for the common goals.[67]

This statement carries with it two possible implications: either regional conferences, or world congresses of all Communist parties, such as the one held in November, 1957, or both. The old concept of the Comintern is far from dead, although the new forms of co-operation might by very different. The united Communist movement, with Moscow as its center, remains a living reality.

5. A New Quarrel with Yugoslavia and Other Recent Events

If the Soviet leaders had aimed only at encouraging the Yugoslav Communists to pursue a true policy of non-commitment in 1955 at the time of their solemn reconciliation, no disagreement would have erupted between Moscow and Belgrade in 1958. However, their pronouncements in subsequent years showed that they had in view a more ambitious goal, namely, to make the prodigal sons reintegrate the "socialist" camp. They were bound to reap bitter disappointment. Tito, it is true, followed a strictly neutralist policy and even tried hard to please Moscow by reserving his criticism for Western foreign policies and by sending a delegation to the Moscow international assembly of Communist parties in November, 1957. But, wise after the bitter experience of 1948–1953, he never destroyed the bridges leading to the West and refused readmission to the "socialist family" of states or the acknowledgment of Soviet leadership. Outwardly cordial to his Soviet comrades, he remained discreetly cautious.

The sudden flare-up of Soviet-Yugoslav disagreement over the first Soviet intervention in Hungary had hardly been forgotten when a new and more acrimonious quarrel broke out in April, 1958, over the program submitted to and later approved by the 7th Congress of the Yugoslav Communist League. This time Moscow and the allied parties spoke frankly and brutally. P. N. Pospelov, an alternate member of the Presidium of the Soviet Party and one of the secretaries of its Central Committee, opened fire. On April 22, 1958, on the occasion of the commemoration of the 88th anniversary of Lenin's birth, he addressed a most distinguished audience composed of the social high life of Moscow, including Khrushchev and other Party leaders. He mentioned the draft of the Yugoslav program about to be submitted to the 7th Congress, pointing out the main flaw in this draft:

This draft . . . is characterized by a definite tendency to oppose their [Yugoslav] own position to the single Marxist-Leninist view of all other Communist and Workers' parties. . . . Objectively [*sic!*] the draft of the program of the Communist League of Yugoslavia looks like a document which aims in fact at the weakening of unity of Communist and Workers' parties and of the socialist countries.[68]

The ultimatum was thus clearly spelled out: "If you Yugoslavs want to be treated as Communists, come back to our fold and accept all our views, or we will denounce you as revisionists (heretics)." Yet Pospelov spoke courteously because, as he said, "we hope that the 7th Congress of the C.L.Y. will proceed with necessary improvements before adopting a final version of the program."[69]

He was to be disappointed. Tito and his comrades were prepared to capitulate no more in 1958 than they did ten years earlier. They introduced only minor amendments in the draft of the program, and the 7th Congress adopted it. Moscow then proceeded full blast in the Stalinist style. The delegations from the Soviet and other Communist parties invited to attend the Congress did not come; Marshal Voroshilov canceled his official visit to Belgrade. The Soviet bloc ambassadors left the Congress hall in protest against the vigorous Yugoslav defense of their program. The Communist press all over the world was unleashed against the Yugoslav Communists, accused of serving the interests of American "imperialists." Only the Polish criticism was guarded and mild; the Polish Communists understood that the attempt at imposing full conformity on the Yugoslavs had an ominous ring for them as well. The unanimous verbal offensive extending from Peking to Latin America demonstrated once more the fidelity of all Communist parties to their leader, the Soviet Party. *Kommunist* listed the Yugoslav sins as follows.

(1) They thought that each party had the right to its own autonomous policy. *Kommunist* replied that this was a matter of common concern to all parties.[70] It measured the Yugoslav program by the yardstick of the Moscow declaration of Communist parties adopted in November, 1957, although the Yugoslav delegation had refused at that time to sign this declaration. Every deviation from the declaration was pronounced heretical.[71]

(2) The Yugoslavs did not accept the Soviet thesis of the existence of the two irreconcilably hostile camps, the socialist and the capitalist, with its logical sequence, namely, the obligation for all Communist parties to participate without reservation in the socialist camp. The Yugoslavs could not accept this thesis because of their neutralist foreign policy and their firm desire to remain independent. Instead, they criticized in their program *both* military blocs and accused *all* the great Powers of being responsible for the present international tension and the existence of zones of influence. *Kommunist* indignantly rejected this point of view, which attributed part of the blame to the USSR. It warmly defended Stalin's policies at Teheran, Yalta, Potsdam, and in later years and denied that he ever had thought of

imposing Soviet hegemony on other nations. It objected to any criticism in international affairs being directed to "both addresses."[72] This attitude was of interest to all uncommitted nations because all of them were implicitly notified that it was not permissible to criticize the Soviet "peace-loving" policy or its own military bloc. The USSR made it clear that it expected a "positive" non-commitment friendly to itself and denouncing only the Western "imperialism." A strict political neutrality was not welcome, as the Yugoslavs were told.

(3) The Yugoslav program admitted the possibility of a gradual evolution of capitalist regimes towards socialism through such means as partial nationalizations of means of production, the increasing economic role of the state, and the growing weight of labor unions and other workers' organizations. The Communist press, following *Kommunist*, replied that the only road to socialism led through a revolution controlled by Communists.[73] The Yugoslavs conceded a useful role to non-Communist organizations: "The concept that the Communist parties have a monopoly on all aspects of movement towards socialism and that socialism is expressed only in them and by them, is theoretically incorrect and practically very harmful."[74] *Kommunist* replied: "The struggle of the working class for the revolutionary transformation of the society on socialist foundations can only be successful on the invariable condition of its taking place under the leadership of the Marxist-Leninist party."[75] The reaffirmation of this thesis, as old as Leninism itself, is instructive not only for the non-Communist workers' organizations but also for such politicians in the underdeveloped countries as seem to believe that their sympathy for some sort of socialism creates a platform of understanding with the USSR and China.

(4) The Yugoslavs and, indirectly, the Poles were told that true Communists must proceed with the collectivization of agriculture,[76] the strengthening of state power instead of talking, as the Yugoslavs did, about the forgotten Marxist thesis of the gradual withering of the state,[77] and the assertion of the leading role of the Communist party in every socialist country.[78] They were also reminded of "the general laws of socialist development"[79] (this meaning the acceptance of the Soviet pattern), which were binding on all ruling Communist parties. These uniform "laws" were opposed to the Yugoslav and Polish claims of separate national roads to socialism.

(5) The main bone of contention was the interpretation of proletarian internationalism. The Yugoslavs claimed the right of each Communist party to its own autonomy and again rejected the Soviet "hegemony," as

they called it, within the Communist movement. *Kommunist* replied: "Marxism-Leninism does not deny that one or another Communist Party and one or another socialist country might play the leading role in a given historical period . . . the Soviet Union heads the indestructible camp of socialist states."[80] Small wonder that the same article in *Kommunist* took up the cudgels in the defense of Stalin and his policies against the Yugoslavs' recriminations. His death did not alter the Soviet claim to hegemony.

The article in *Kommunist* was acrimonious but courteous by Soviet standards. It was published before the opening of the 7th Yugoslav Congress in the hopes that Soviet pressure would force the Yugoslavs to capitulate. Their resolute stand at the Congress and their bold answer to the Soviet critics unleashed a violent press campaign in Moscow, Peking, and other capitals. The only difference between this situation and what happened in 1948 consisted in their refraining from calling the Yugoslavs fascists and heaping on them outright insults.

The Chinese Communists were the first to come to the rescue of their Russian allies, to the great disappointment of those wishful thinkers who detected every day a breach in the Moscow-Peking friendship. The article that appeared on May 5, 1958, in the Chinese daily *Zhen'min'zhibao* differed from others only in its frankly impolite tone.[81] It branded the Yugoslav Communists as revisionists and recalled that the November, 1957, declaration of Communist parties had singled out "revisionism, a bourgeois ideological trend," as the main danger facing the Communist movement. The Yugoslav program was stigmatized as anti-Marxist and anti-Leninist and as the product of a reactionary bourgeois nationalism. The Yugoslav Communists were openly accused of serving the interests of foreign reaction and of capitulating before capitalism, as well as of undermining the unity of socialist countries before and after the Hungarian events. It is therefore not surprising that the Chinese newspaper vindicated the basic correctness of the Cominform policy towards Yugoslavia in 1948 and the Cominform contention in the same year that the Yugoslav Party had abandoned Marxism-Leninism in favor of a bourgeois nationalism. The key sentence was as follows: "Yugoslavia has no right to isolate herself."[82]

Pravda proceeded with its own excommunication on May 9, 1958, only after the ground had been thoroughly prepared by *Zhen'min'zhibao*, the French *Humanité*, the Italian *Avanti*, the Belgian *Drapeau Rouge*, the eastern European satellite papers, and scores of others. Repeating the criticism already voiced a few weeks earlier by *Kommunist*, it branded the Yugoslav program as revisionist and as a deviation from the Moscow declaration of November, 1957. The speeches made at the 7th Yugoslav Congress were submitted to sharp criticism. *Pravda* resented greatly the fact that the Yugoslavs had indulged in equal criticism of Soviet and Western policies, thus "treating the Soviet Union in the same manner as the imperialist powers."[83] It indignantly reproached: "To state that the policy of the Soviet Union in the first post-war years consisted in 'achieving domination over other nations,' as was done in the speeches at the 7th Congress of the Communist League of Yugoslavia, is to repeat the concoctions of imperialist propaganda about 'a Soviet Empire' which had surrounded itself with 'satellites.' "[84] Such a statement of actual facts was for *Pravda* nothing but "playing into the hands of imperialists."[85]

While Tito denied at the 7th Congress that the proletarian internationalism was conditioned by participation in the socialist bloc, *Pravda* reiterated that there was no true internationalism without this participation and bitterly reproached Yugoslavia for receiving Western economic aid. It asked the insulting question of why the West was "remunerating" Yugoslavia with this assistance: "For what kind of services? Is it not because the Yugoslav leaders attempt to blacken the Soviet Union and to weaken the unity of the international Communist and Workers' movement?"[86]

The Yugoslavs were accused of all possible sins: bourgeois nationalism, relativist nihilism, and working for the enemies of socialism, the imperialists.[87] At this point, Stalin's ghost could wonder why it had been exorcised in 1955 at the time of Khrushchev's visit in Belgrade and a year later at the 20th Congress of the Soviet Party. His successors were forced by the logic of their fundamental concepts to return to his uncompromising policy towards Yugoslavia. This was no mere coincidence. The unity of the Communist international movement under Soviet leadership requires a strict conformity of views and cannot allow for any polycentrism or any deviation. Heresy must be hunted down to preserve the Soviet hegemony and also to avoid the disintegration of the Soviet empire in eastern Europe. This is, if anything, clearer to the present Soviet leaders after the events in Poland and Hungary.

After these press attacks came the official excommunication. On May 23, the second session of the 7th Congress of the Chinese Communist Party adopted a resolution in which the program of the Communist League of Yugoslavia was stigmatized as anti-Marxist and anti-Leninist. The Yugoslav "revisionists" were accused of betraying Marxist-Leninist doctrine in

order to split up the international Communist movement and thus of serving the interests of imperialism, and the correctness of the Cominform
Resolution of 1948, which had denounced the Yugoslav Communists for
their deviations towards bourgeois nationalism, was upheld. The Chinese
Congress then stated solemnly that "the leaders of Yugoslavia have placed
themselves outside the international Communist ranks."[88]

Soon after this resolution had been adopted, the Soviet Government
officially notified Yugoslavia of its five-year unilateral "suspension" of liberal credits, which had been granted in 1955 as a token of reconciliation.
This meant, in fact, the cancellation of these credits. The Yugoslavs could
on that day recall the economic blockade which Stalin had applied to them
in 1948 and the short suspension of credits during the disagreement between the USSR and Yugoslavia concerning the Soviet intervention in
Hungary. They could wonder whether their former hopes that the Soviet
regime had basically changed after Stalin's death were not a whim of wishful thinking on their part. The other recipients of Soviet credits could ask
themselves whether the Soviet assurances that no political strings were
attached to these credits were true and whether they could safely base their
plans of economic development on pledges so precarious that they could
be unilaterally canceled as a penalty for "misbehavior." The USSR demonstrated that she promoted only the kind of uncommitment she liked.

Khrushchev himself cast anathema in a speech made on June 3, 1958,
in Sofia, where he was the guest at the 7th Congress of the Bulgarian
Communist Party. He chose the capital of a country traditionally at odds
with Yugoslavia as though to make his denunciation even less palatable to
Tito. He lashed at the Yugoslav Communists with a violence which Stalin
would have liked. He accused them of serving imperialist interests: "Why
do the imperialist bosses, who try to wipe out the socialist States from the
surface of the earth and to suppress the Communist movement, finance
at the same time one of the socialist countries and grant it easy credits and
free gifts?"[89] He called them "the scouts of the imperialist camp," "agents
of the class enemy," and "its Trojan horses." He, who, as late as 1956, had
been critical of Stalin's handling of the Yugoslav case, joined the Chinese
Communists in upholding the correctness of the anti-Yugoslav Cominform
Resolution of 1948. He accused the Yugoslav Embassy in Budapest of being
the center for "anti-people" activities in 1956. Tito, whom Stalin had accused of subversive activities in Hungary, was again denounced for the
same crime, this time related to the Hungarian revolution. Khrushchev

finally read the Yugoslav leaders out of the ranks of the Communist movement by saying that they called themselves Communists but followed, in fact, a policy foreign to Communist principles.

The Stalinist procedure was followed in another respect. On June 17, 1958, the Hungarian Government announced the execution of former Prime Minister Imre Nagy, former Minister of National Defense General Pal Maleter, and two other leaders of the Hungarian revolution, while five other defendants were sentenced to various terms of imprisonment.[90] The other well-known Communist who had chosen national liberty in the fall of 1956, Geza Losonczy, was said to have died in prison. It is unknown whether the leaders of the uprising were truly tried by a Hungarian court, as the announcement claimed, or were simply executed in the Soviet Union at that time or much earlier. The announcement did not even say when and where the alleged "trial" had taken place. All of this cannot be checked because the trial, if held, was secret and the defendants were not seen since their arrest in November, 1956, by Soviet troops. The fact remains that the "anti-colonialist" protecting Power took revenge on the people who had stood at the head of the uprising in this Soviet protectorate, an uprising waged in the name of national self-determination.

Rajk and several other dissident Communists of eastern Europe were executed on Stalin's orders under the pretext that they had plotted with Tito. Stalin's successors, on whose orders Rajk had been rehabilitated, voiced this time, through their Hungarian spokesmen, the same charge that Nagy and his collaborators had acted in connivance with Yugoslavia: ". . . the conspirators of the type of Imre Nagy sought refuge where support had previously been granted them."[91] This meant the Yugoslav Embassy in Budapest, where the defeated leaders had obtained asylum. The Hungarian communiqué added that the "conspirators" had issued instructions from the building of the Embassy "to continue armed resistance" and were publishing there an illegal newspaper.[92] While Yugoslavia and Western "imperialism" were jointly accused of instigating and abetting the Hungarian revolution, the uprising was fought, according to the communiqué, under "the black flag of national Communism." This "black" flag is the only one of which the Soviet Communists are afraid. This explains the difficulties in the Yugoslav-Soviet relations because Yugoslavia was the first to deploy this flag in eastern Europe. The Soviet Union is now just as much afraid of the "demoralizing" effect of Yugoslav independence on her satellites as she had been in 1948. Did not Khrushchev accuse Tito, in his speech in

Sofia, of "openly calling on certain forces in other socialist countries to follow the so-called 'Yugoslav policy' "?[93] It was thus no sheer coincidence that the public announcement of the execution of Hungarian leaders came after the new rupture in the Soviet-Yugoslav relations.

The Yugoslav soldier who was out of step, as Khrushchev said in Sofia, was expelled for the second time from the flock of the faithful and the ranks of the orthodox Communists were again closed around their leader, the Soviet Party. The Yugoslav excommunication carried with it an implicit warning to Polish Communists. They had been doing their best since the spring of 1957 to appease their powerful neighbor by trimming down the "liberalism" of the October days. The press was again muzzled. The limited freedom of expression that had existed in 1955–56 was reduced to the freedom of private, but not public, grumbling. The workers' councils were reformed out of existence. The "revisionists" in the Party who had carried Gomulka to power were either expelled or silenced. The Party, again consolidated under his leadership, reaffirmed its control over the country. Poland was toeing the Soviet foreign policy, but the Polish Party continued to deviate in other respects: the agriculture was not yet recollectivized by coercion, the uneasy armistice with the Church was maintained, and greater attention was paid to the living standards. The Party assured the USSR of peace in Poland at the price of the domestic autonomy for itself in deciding the tempo and the ways of imitating the Soviet ways of life. If this arrangement does not suit the Soviet leadership, the Polish Communists will have to yield or face, like the Yugoslavs, the stern Soviet tribunal.

The Yugoslav experience should have ended their own wishful thinking about an "anti-Stalinist" Khrushchev struggling hard with mysterious Soviet "Stalinists" for a more conciliatory policy towards the external world. The uncommitted nations could, if they wished, learn from the Yugoslav story that the Soviet Janus has two faces—one that smiles and the other stern and angry, which is seen only if a particular neutralist policy does not suit the Soviet interests.

President Nasser had the opportunity of seeing both faces within less than a year. During his official visit to Moscow in May, 1958, his host, N. S. Khrushchev, was charming and assured him of his wish to see the Arabs united under Nasser's leadership.[94] They both agreed on a common front against Western "imperialism" and Israel.[95] They met again in July, 1958, immediately after the Iraqi revolt and heartily agreed on their opposition to the American-British landings in Lebanon and Jordan.

President Nasser realized soon after that a change had been taking place in the Soviet and Arab-Communist strategies. The Communists had not opposed his policies in the Near East and had actually co-operated with pro-Nasser nationalists until the domestic developments in Iraq altered the scene. The growing influence of Iraqi Communists, whom General Abdel Kerim Kassem needed to eliminate his pro-Nasser domestic enemies, opened new vistas. Hoping for an ultimate control of the country, the Iraqi Communists deployed the flag of national independence, helped to liquidate pro-Nasser organizations, and firmly opposed an Arab unification under Nasser's leadership. The Iraqi radio, influenced by Communists, passed from attacks on Western "imperialism" to an offensive against Nasser himself. Soon after the failure of pro-Nasser revolt in Mossul in March, 1959, he began to hear the abusive insults broadcast from Baghdad in Arabic, the first such unpleasant experience in his career. He was called a midget Hitler. The Arab Communists also began to capitalize on the discontent in Syria, where the growing Egyptian political and economic control was resented, and thus to undermine the cohesion of the United Arab Republic. The triumphant march of President Nasser was suddenly called to a halt, not by the West, which he had frequently denounced, but by the Arab followers of the very great Power on which he had relied since 1955. President Nasser was given the opportunity of learning a few facts which an experienced politician would have known long time ago, namely, that a small country could not hope to manipulate the policies of a great Power as it wanted, that the Arab Communists co-operated with his followers only as with temporary allies and were ready to discard them as soon as their respective objectives could no longer be reconciled, and, finally, that the Soviet Union, if she only had a reasonable choice, preferred her permanent allies, the Communists, to any temporary "bourgeois" ally.

This sudden challenge from unexpected quarters angered President Nasser, and he replied in the last months of 1958, and even more after the Mossul revolt, with his own denunciation of Communism, which he classed together with the two familiar enemies of Arab nationalism: Western "imperialism" and Zionism. These new developments cast a shadow on friendship with the Soviet Union. It is as yet too early to say whether Khrushchev made a mistake in stepping into the cockpit and openly challenging Nasser. He probably thought that it was a safe course because of the United Arab Republic's dependence on Soviet trade, loans, and military supplies. He might have been reassured by the continuous anti-Western activities of that joint Cairo-Moscow-Peking venture, the Asian-African Solidarity Organization, whose seat in Cairo was not liquidated. Anyhow, Khrushchev decided to show Nasser the stern face of Soviet Janus. The former cordiality and courtesy were forgotten. Addressing the 21st Soviet Party Congress in January, 1959, he found time to answer Nasser's anti-Communist diatribes by tersely stating that "the struggle against the Communist and other progressive parties is reactionary. . . . It is also naïve to compare Communism with Zionism."[96] Nasser was thus called a naïve reactionary. Encouraged by the failure of the Mossul revolt and the growing Communist influence in Baghdad, Khrushchev went a step further at his March press conference. Replying to a question, he assumed the condescending attitude of an elder statesman and advised the "young, hot-headed President" not to interfere in the affairs of other Arab states.[97] He thus called on him not only to leave Iraq alone but to abandon his plan of unifying all the Arabs. Three days earlier, addressing an official Iraqi delegation on the occasion of the signature of agreements for the Soviet economic, military, and technical assistance, he challenged President Nasser on two scores. He again questioned his policy of unification by stating: "However, this does not mean that the countries, liberated from the colonial chains, necessarily must unite in one State and be subject to one government or follow one leader, one chief."[98] He also cast a doubt about the wisdom of uniting Syria with Egypt when he added: "The people of one of the united countries feel, with ever-increasing acuteness, the loss of independence. Its former leaders are either relegated to the second plane or thrown overboard because they do not entirely agree with the leaders of the unified State."[99] These utterances dispelled all doubts concerning the Iraqi and other Arab Communist policies; these policies were evidently co-ordinated with the Soviet Government.

The USSR clearly preferred to deal with a constellation of separate Arab states rather than with a unified one under a non-Communist leadership. Khrushchev justified his interference in the inter-Arab feuds by the newly acquired Soviet position as a Near Eastern great Power: "It is not indifferent to us what is the situation in an area close to our frontiers."[100] President Nasser, who had mocked, in 1957–58, the idea of a vacuum in the Near East created by the Western eclipse, could now see that the Soviet Union did not intend to leave the vacuum long unfilled. The policy of "positive" neutrality, leaning heavily towards the Soviet Union, proved less wise than a strict non-commitment and certainly less safe for a small country like the United Arab Republic.

In the meantime, the USSR added Iraq to the United Arab Republic as another client in foreign affairs. While Cairo provides the propaganda channel, ostensibly non-Communist, through the Asian-African organization, Iraq has withdrawn from the Baghdad Pact and helps the USSR in playing the Kurdish card by her announced intention of granting some kind of autonomy to her large Kurdish population. If Iraqi Kurds are allowed to use Baghdad as their headquarters for a propaganda aimed at the millions of their countrymen in Turkey and Iran, and possibly at the relatively small Kurdish minority in Syria, the Soviet Union will be given the first real chance of playing this potentially important card. The Soviet Government is placed in the enviable position of counterbalancing the local influence of one client by that of another, of supporting General Abdel Kerim Kassem against President Nasser. But she does not want to lose President Nasser. Khrushchev was explicit both in January and March, 1959, on this particular point. He said that the Soviet Union wanted to maintain friendly relations with the United Arab Republic despite the quarrel over Iraq. This meant that Soviet trade, loans, and military supplies would not be stopped, they being the principal Soviet device in keeping the United Arab Republic's foreign policy within the bounds acceptable to the USSR. Of course an outright Communist seizure of power in Iraq would be preferable to the present balancing of the two clients.

Khrushchev's heavy-handed criticism of President Nasser might have been an error only if President Nasser were to respond by seeking to counterbalance the Soviet influence in the Near East by an improvement in the relations with the West and if Krushchev's probable hopes for an ultimate Communist victory in Iraq were to be frustrated.

The events of 1958–59 could also teach a useful lesson to those people in the West who seem to be paralyzed by the nuclear problem. These people feared a nuclear annihilation at the time of each successive crisis: the Near Eastern, the Taiwan Straits, and the Berlin. Each time, such people seemed to forget that nuclear weapons were equally dangerous to both sides and that the Soviet leaders had no interest in inviting a catastrophe. The landing of the American-British troops in Lebanon and Jordan caused the outflow of a torrent of abusive Soviet words, but words should not be confused with action. The Chinese shelling of the offshore islands was as suddenly called off as it had started. The deadline for the evacuation of the Western troops from West Berlin, which Khrushchev haughtily announced in November, 1958, was somehow forgotten by him when the safer prospect of negotiations offered him a way of getting out of an impossible situation in which he had placed himself. The balance of terror limits the freedom of action of both sides. A display of unilateral fear would not only paralyze the West but could embolden the Soviet leaders to assume poorly calculated risks and thus unintentionally to invite disaster.

Addressing the 21st Party Congress, Khrushchev said: "We recall V. I. Lenin's advice that one should never rest on the laurels; we must move forward and strive for new achievements and victories."[101] These new victories he expects to gain, without a nuclear war, in the underdeveloped countries. He reminded the Congress of Lenin's prediction that the final outcome of the struggle against capitalism and socialism depended on the victory in Russia, India, China, and other underdeveloped nations. He boastfully exclaimed: "Vladimir Il'ich Lenin's scientific forecast of genius is being realized."[102]

"The final outcome of the struggle between capitalism and socialism" means much more than successes in foreign policy by making friends with the "capitalist" governments of the underdeveloped countries. It means what Khrushchev said, namely, the ultimate elimination of such "capitalist" governments everywhere. He was as clear about it as possible when he reminded the eighty-three existing Communist parties, seventy of which were represented at the Congress, that the underdeveloped countries did not need to pass through the capitalist stage but could step directly into the socialist stage of development. Put in ordinary language, those countries do not need, according to Khrushchev, to start the process of modernization and economic development under a non-Communist government but can begin and complete the process under a Communist leadership.

Such is the record of Soviet policies towards other states and nationalities. It covers a span of forty-one years and speaks for itself. Its guiding motive cannot be better expressed than in Lenin's terse words: "Who-whom?"

"Who-whom?" is a battle cry, but it is, for Communists, also the watchword for peaceful co-existence, which they prefer to call peaceful competition. "Who-whom?" does not call for a recourse to arms unless odds favor the Soviet Union, as they did in the several cases recounted in this book. But this battle cry certainly calls for struggle against the non-Communist regimes and nations, a struggle which may safely be waged in our nuclear era only by non-military yet possibly more effective means.

NOTES

NOTES

NOTES

INTRODUCTION

1. All of these figures are taken from *Kul'turnoe Stroitel'stvo SSSR, Statisticheskii Sbornik*, 11–39, 214–15, 217, 239. N. S. Khrushchev claimed at the 21st Congress (January, 1959) that the total industrial output of the Soviet bloc amounted, in 1958, to one-third of the world's production. This claim, if true, reflected two things: (1) the quick ratio of the Soviet bloc industrial growth; but also (2) the temporary decline in the Western output because of the recession.

2. *Pravda,* November 26, 1955.

3. *Pravda,* March 27, 1958.

4. *Pravda,* April 9, 1958.

5. *Pravda,* March 27, 1958.

CHAPTER I

1. *Bol'shaia Sovetskaia Entsiklopediia,* XXXVI, 185.

2. *Ibid.,* 186.

3. I. V. Stalin, *Sochineniia,* VI, 108.

4. Editorial, "Nepreoborimaia sila leninizma," *Kommunist,* No. 5 (April, 1957), 6.

5. *Pravda,* October 16, 1949.

6. N. V. Tropkin, *Ob Osnovakh Strategii i Taktiki Leninizma,* 12.

7. I. V. Stalin, *Ob Osnovakh Leninizma,* in *Sochineniia,* VI, 170–71.

8. V. Donskoi, *Razrabotka V. I. Leninym Organizatsionnykh Osnov Kommunisticheskoi Partii,* 35.

9. For an analysis of the social stratification in a Soviet or other Communist society, see Merle Fainsod, *How Russia Is Ruled;* W. W. Kulski, *The Soviet Regime;* David J. Dallin, *The Changing World of Soviet Russia* (New Haven, Yale University Press, 1956); and Milovan Djilas, *The New Class.*

10. Walter Z. Laqueur, *Communism and Nationalism in the Middle East.*

11. V. I. Lenin, *Detskaia Bolezn' 'Levizny' v Kommunizme,* in *Sochineniia,* XXXI, 40.

12. *Ibid.,* 50 n.

13. Donskoi, *op. cit.,* 18.

14. *Ibid.,* 3–4.

15. V. I. Lenin, *Sochineniia,* XXXI, 488.

16. *Ibid.,* 210.

17. *Ibid.*, VI, 457.

18. Donskoi, *op. cit.*, 40.

19. Lenin, *Sochineniia*, XXXIII, 404.

20. Jane Degras, ed., *The Communist International, 1919-1943, Documents*, I (1919-1922), 128-33.

21. Lenin, *Sochineniia*, XIX, 365.

22. Lenin, *Detskaia Bolezn' 'Levizny' v Kommunizme*, in *Sochineniia*, XXXI, 73, 75.

23. Lenin, *Sochineniia*, XXXI, 327.

24. G. Shitarev, "Edinstvo—istochnik nepobedimosti marksistsko-leninskoi partii," *Kommunist*, No. 5 (April, 1957), 30.

25. Lenin, *Sochineniia*, XXI, 85.

26. A. Shishkin, *Osnovy Kommunisticheskoi Morali*, 12.

27. Lenin, *Sochineniia*, V, 430.

28. Lenin, *Detskaia Bolezn' 'Levizny' v Kommunizme*, in *Sochineniia*, XXXI, 24, 27.

29. *Ibid.*, 30.

30. Degras, *The Communist International, 1919-1943, Documents*, I, 133-34.

31. Donskoi, *op. cit.*, 12-13.

32. Editorial, "Leninskoe edinstvo partii—istochnik ee nepobedimoi sily," *Pravda*, July 3, 1957.

33. Lenin, *Sochineniia*, XXI, 188.

34. Tropkin, *Ob Osnovakh Strategii i Taktiki Leninizma*, 17.

35. Al. Romanov, "Nerushimoe ideinoe edinstvo kommunisticheskikh partii," *Mezhdunarodnaia Zhizn'*, No. 11 (November, 1956), 17.

36. *Ibid.*, 19, 22.

37. Shitarev, "Edinstvo—istochnik nepobedimosti marksistsko-leninskoi partii," *Kommunist*, No. 5 (April, 1957), 35.

38. Donskoi, *op. cit.*, 42.

39. *Ibid.*, 42.

40. G. A. Deborin, *Leninskaia Politika Mirnovo Sosushchestvovaniia Dvukh Sistem—General'naia Liniia Vneshnei Politiki SSSR*, 18.

41. Tropkin, *Ob Osnovakh Strategii i Taktiki Leninizma*, 46.

42. Shishkin, *op. cit.*, 167.

43. Lenin, *Sochineniia*, XXXI, 166.

44. Shishkin, *op. cit.*, 75.

45. Editorial, "Nepreoborimaia sila leninizma," *Kommunist*, No. 5 (April, 1957), 16.

46. Lenin, *Sochineniia*, XXVIII, 111.

47. Quoted in I. F. Ivashin and F. G. Zuev, *Mezhdunarodnye Otnosheniia v Period Provedeniia Velikoi Oktiabrskoi Sotsialisticheskoi Revolutsii. Vneshniaia Politika Sovetskovo Gosudarstva v Gody Inostrannoi Voennoi Interventsii i Grazhdanskoi Voiny*, 7.

48. Quoted in *ibid.*, 5.

49. I. F. Ivashin, *Velikaia Oktiabrskaia Sotsialisticheskaia Revolutsia i Raskol Mira na Dve Sistemy*, 4–5.

50. Tropkin, *Ob Osnovakh Strategii i Taktiki Leninizma*, 43.

51. *Ibid.*, 31.

52. V. I. Lenin, *Imperializm, kak noveishii etap kapitalizma*, in *Sochineniia*, XXII, 175–290.

53. Lenin, *Sochineniia*, XXIII, 67.

54. Stalin, *Sochineniia*, VI, 97.

55. Lenin, *Sochineniia*, V, 480 n.

56. *Ibid.*, XXI, 192.

57. Stalin, *Sochineniia*, VII, 94.

58. V. I. Lenin, *Selected Works* (New York, International Publishers, 1943), V, 174.

59. *Ibid.*, X, 127.

60. Lenin, *Sochineniia*, XXVII, 72–73.

61. *Ibid.*, XXIII, 361–62.

62. *Ibid.*, XXIX, 283.

63. Quoted in Jane Degras, ed., *Soviet Documents on Foreign Policy*, I, 79.

64. *Ibid.*, 22.

65. Lenin, *Sochineniia*, XXXI, 371.

66. *Ibid.*, XXVII, 39–40.

67. Lenin, *Selected Works*, VI, 63.

68. *Ibid.*, VII, 282.

69. *Ibid.*, 288.

70. Quoted in *Pravda*, January 30, 1924; see also Stalin, *Sochineniia*, VI, 50–51.

71. Stalin, *Sochineniia*, XI, 54–55.

72. *Pravda*, October 15, 1952.

73. *Ibid.*

74. *Pravda*, February 15, 1956.

75. *Ibid.*

76. *Ibid.*

77. Bela Kun, ed., *Kommunisticheskii Internatsional v Dokumentakh; Resheniia, Tezisy i Vozzvaniia Kongressov Kominterna i Plenumov IKKI, 1919–1932*, 115.

78. *Ibid.*

79. *Pravda*, February 15, 1956.

80. *Pravda*, February 18, 1956.

81. *Ibid.*

82. *Pravda*, February 19, 1956.

83. Stalin, *Sochineniia*, VI, 117–18.

84. W. Gomulka, "Uzlovye problemy politiki partii," *Kommunist*, No. 7 (May, 1957), 73.

85. *Pravda*, February 15, 1956.

86. *Pravda*, February 18, 1956. The new teachings of the 20th Party Congress concerning the violent and peaceful transitions to socialism, the choice of one or the other of these methods (depending on the strength of the resistance of the bourgeoisie), the controlling role of the Communist Party in either case, and the identical meaning of the two phrases "transition to socialism" and "revolution" have been clearly and concisely expounded in "Pod znamenem Marksizma-Leninizma," *Voprosy Ekonomiki*, No. 3 (1956), 3–23.

87. *Pravda*, February 18, 1956.

88. *Pravda*, February 24, 1956.

89. This and other quotations referring to the 8th Congress of the Chinese Communist Party are English translations of monitored Chinese Communist radio broadcasts.

90. A. Berkov, "Edinstvo i splochennost'—zalog novykh uspekhov mezhdunarodnovo kommunisticheskovo dvizheniia," *Kommunist*, No. 6 (April, 1957), 118–19.

91. Lenin, *Sochineniia*, XXXI, 126.

92. Kun, *op. cit.*, 34.

93. *Ibid.*, 680.

94. *KPSS v Resoliutsiiakh i Resheniiakh S'yezdov, Konferentsii i Plenumov TsK*, III (1930–1954), 156.

95. *Ibid.*, I (1898–1924), 405.

96. N. P. Vassil'ev and F. D. Khrustov, eds., *O Sovetskom Patriotizme*, 142.

97. I. F. Ivashin, *Vsemirno-istoricheskoe Znacheniie Velikoi Oktiabrskoi Sotsialisticheskoi Revolutsii*, 45.

98. Tropkin, *Ob Osnovakh Strategii i Taktiki Leninizma*, 15, 16, 26.

99. I. Potelov, "Razvitiie sotsializma i proletarskii internatsionalizm," *Kommunist*, No. 1 (January, 1957), 17–18.

100. Khrushchev's interview with the correspondent of *Asahi-Shimbun*, reprinted in *Pravda*, June 30, 1957.

CHAPTER II

1. Lenin, *Sochineniia*, XXI, 16.

2. *Ibid.*, 141–42.

3. *Ibid.*, XXVII, 342.

4. *Ibid.*, XXIX, 216–17.

5. *Ibid.*, XXI, 85.

6. V. I. Lenin, *Natsional'no-kolonial'nyi Vopros*, 122.

7. Lenin, *Sochineniia*, XXIX, 172.

8. *KPSS v Resoliutsiiakh i Resheniiakh S'yezdov, Konferentsii i Plenumov TsK*, I (1898–1924), 713.

9. I. V. Stalin, *Marksizm i Natsional'no-kolonial'nyi Vopros, Sbornik Statei i Rechei*, 108–109.

10. *Ibid.*, 112, 116.

11. See I. V. Stalin, S. Kirov, and A. Zhdanov, "Zamechaniia o konspekte uchebnika 'Novoi Istorii,'" *Bolshevik*, No. 3 (February, 1936), 65–66.

12. *Vneshniaia Politika Sovetskovo Soiuza v Period Otechestvennoi Voiny*, I, 53.

13. *Ibid.*, III, 45.

14. *Ibid.*, 47.

15. P. N. Shchur, *Sovetskii Patriotizm—Istochnik Sily i Mogushchestva Armii i Flota*, 5–6.

16. Stalin, *Sochineniia*, III, 186–87.

17. Editorial, "Stalin, nasha slava, nasha gordost'," *Sovetskoe Gosudarstvo i Pravo*, No. 1 (January, 1950), 20.

18. *Vneshniaia Politika Sovetskovo Soiuza v Period Otechestvennoi Voiny*, III, 56.

19. *Pravda*, June 30, 1957.

20. N. G. Kuznetsov, "Slavnyi podvig Russkikh moriakov," *Pravda*, February 9, 1954.

21. *Pravda*, April 13, 1954.

22. *Vneshniaia Politika Sovetskovo Soiuza*, Volume for 1947, Part One, 27–28.

23. *Pravda*, June 7, 1954.

24. *Pravda*, October 15, 1955.

25. S. M. Dubrovskii, "Protiv idealizatsii deiatel'nosti Ivana IV," *Voprosy Istorii*, No. 8 (August, 1956), 128.

26. *Ibid.*

27. I. Popov, *Estoniia*, 3–4.

28. I. Baikov, "Voenno-morskaia krepost' na Baltyke, Kronshtadt—250 let od zalozheniia," *Pravda*, May 18, 1954.

29. Vassil'ev and Khrustov, *op. cit.*, 29–30, 41–42.

30. *Ibid.*, 98.

31. *Ibid.*, 15.

32. *Ibid.*, 48.

33. M. A. Zinoviev, *Ocherki Prepodavaniia Istorii*, 74.

34. Shishkin, *op. cit.*, 200.

35. Vassil'ev and Khrustov, *op. cit.*, 6, 278–79, 430, 435.

36. Shishkin, *op. cit.*, 210–11.

37. Zinoviev, *op. cit.*, 71.

38. A. M. Pankratova *et al., Nasha Velikaia Rodina*, 9–10.

39. *Ibid.*, 31–33.

40. *Ibid.*, 85–211.

41. *Ibid.*, 165.

42. *Ibid.*, 90–91, 97, 100, 130, 135–38, 145, 159, 193.

43. *Ibid.*, 88.

44. *Ibid.*, 90, 160, 193.

45. S. Radzhabov, *Rol' Velikovo Russkovo Naroda v Istoricheskikh Sud'bakh Narodov Srednei Azii*, 9–11, 13, 202.

46. Shchur, *op. cit.*, 25.

47. P. N. Shimbiriov and I. T. Ogorodnikov, *Pedagogika*, 248.

48. Baikov, "Voenno-morskaia krepost' na Baltyke, Kronshtadt—250 let od zalozheniia," *Pravda*, May 18, 1954; K. Vershinin, "Moguchiie kryl'ia Sovetskoi Derzhavy," *Pravda*, June 30, 1956.

49. *Pravda Vostoka*, October 13, 1956.

50. Shchur, *op. cit.*, 8.

51. Vassil'ev and Khrustov, *op. cit.*, 436–37.

52. *Ibid.*, 97–98.

CHAPTER III

1. Lenin, *Selected Works*, XI, 205.

2. *Bol'shaia Sovetskaia Entsiklopediia*, V, 337.

3. R. N. Carew Hunt, *The Theory and Practice of Communism*, 6–7.

4. Lenin, *Selected Works*, XI, 666.

5. *Ibid.*, VIII, 239–40; VII, 81.

6. *Ibid.*, VII, 87.

7. A short but complete description of the eventual Communist millenium is to be found in Kun, *op. cit.*, 15–16.

8. Editorial, "Nepreoborimaia sila leninizma," *Kommunist*, No. 5 (April, 1957), 10.

9. *Pravda*, March 29, 1957.

10. Cf. other statements on the decisive role of the Communist Party after the successful revolution: W. Gomulka, "Uzlovye problemy politiki partii," *Kommunist*, No. 7 (May, 1957), 64–66; Editorial, "Eshcho raz ob istoricheskom opyte diktatury proletariata," from the Chinese newspaper *Zhen'min'zhibao*, reprinted in *Mezhdunarodnaia Zhizn'*, No. 1 (January, 1957), 20; I. Potelov, "Razvitiie sotsializma i proletarskii internatsionalizm," *Kommunist*, No. 1 (January, 1957), 21–22; Editorial, "Vyshe znamia marksistsko-leninskoi ideologii," *Kommunist*, No. 1 (January, 1957), 10.

11. Lenin, *Sochineniia*, XXVIII, 309–10.

12. Editorial, "Eshcho raz ob istoricheskom opyte diktatury proletariata," *Zhen'min'zhibao*, reprinted in *Mezhdunarodnaia Zhizn'*, No. 1 (January, 1957), 20.

13. I. Semenov and N. Sokolova, "Stroitel'stvo sotsialisticheskoi ekonomiki v evropeiskikh stranakh narodnoi demokratii," *Voprosy Ekonomiki*, No. 3 (March, 1956), 160.

14. W. Gomulka, "Uzlovye problemy politiki partii," *Kommunist*, No. 7 (May, 1957), 58.

15. English translation of a monitored Chinese radio broadcast.

16. Du Chao-bai, "Razvitiie sotsialisticheskoi ekonomiki i ekonomicheskiie zakony v perekhodnyi period v Kitaiskoi Narodnoi Respublike," *Voprosy Ekonomiki*, No. 1 (January, 1957), 59.

17. S. D. Sergeev, *Ekonomicheskoe Sotrudnichestvo i Vzaimopomoshch' Stran Sotsialisticheskovo Lageria*, 142.

18. Speech at a meeting of the Supreme Soviet of the USSR, *Pravda*, February 13, 1957.

19. Gomulka, "Uzlovye problemy politiki partii," *Kommunist*, No. 7 (May, 1957), 48.

20. Editorial, "Eshcho raz ob istoricheskom opyte diktatury proletariata," *Zhen'min'zhibao*, reprinted in *Mezhdunarodnaia Zhizn'*, No. 1 (January, 1957), 20.

21. Editorial, "Vyshe znamia marksistsko-leninskoi ideologii," *Kommunist*, No. 1 (January, 1957), 10; Potelov, "Razvitiie sotsializma i proletarskii internatsionalizm," *Kommunist*, No. 1 (January, 1957), 22.

22. Sergeev, *op. cit.*, 68.

23. P. V. Galenko, *Stroitel'stvo Sotsialisticheskoi Ekonomiki v Polskoi Narodnoi Respublike*, 187.

24. Lenin, *Sochineniia*, XXXI, 484.

25. Gomulka, "Uzlovye problemy politiki partii," *Kommunist*, No. 7 (May, 1957), 62.

26. Du Chao-bai, "Razvitiie sotsialisticheskoi ekonomiki i ekonomicheskiie zakony v perekhodnyi period v Kitaiskoi Narodnoi Respublike," *Voprosy Ekonomiki*, No. 1 (January, 1957), 72.

27. Potelov, "Razvitiie sotsializma i proletarskii internatsionalizm," *Kommunist*, No. 1 (January, 1957), 29.

28. *Ibid.*, 22.

29. Lenin, *Sochineniia*, IV, 191.

30. *KPSS v Rezoliutsiiakh i Resheniiakh S'yezdov, Konferentsii i Plenumov TsK*, I (1898–1924), 412.

31. V. M. Molotov, *Voprosy Vneshnei Politiki, Rechi i Zaiavleniia, Aprel' 1945–Yun' 1948*, 507.

32. *Pravda*, February 13, 1957.

33. *Pravda*, February 20, 1957.

34. *Literaturnaia Gazeta*, February 9, 1957.

35. Tropkin, *Ob Osnovakh Strategii i Taktiki Leninizma*, 25.

36. Editorial, "Vyshe znamia marksistsko-leninskoi ideologii," *Kommunist*, No. 1 (January, 1957), 8.

37. *Ibid.*, 6.

38. Shishkin, *op. cit.*, 84.

39. *Pravda*, February 13, 1957.

CHAPTER IV

1. *Pravda*, February 17, 1957.

2. Editorial, "Pod znamenem marksizma-leninizma," *Voprosy Ekonomiki*, No. 3 (1956), 8–9.

3. *Vneshniaia Politika Sovetskovo Soiuza* (1948), Part 2, 153.

4. Degras, *Soviet Documents on Foreign Policy*, III, 56.

5. Lenin, *Sochineniia*, XXXIII, 257, 271.

6. Shishkin, *op. cit.*, 8.

7. *Ibid.*, 71, 76.

8. *Ibid.*, 8, 9. Cf. *O Kommunisticheskoi Morali, Sbornik Statei*, 20.

9. Lenin, *Sochineniia*, XXXI, 268, 270.

10. Shishkin, *op. cit.*, 95–96.

11. V. N. Kolbanovskii, *O Kommunisticheskoi Morali*, 10.

12. *O Kommunisticheskoi Morali, Sbornik Statei*, 20.

13. Shishkin, *op. cit.*, 33.

14. *Ibid.*, 77.

15. *Ibid.*, 100.

16. *Ibid.*, 158.

17. *Ibid.*, 118–119.

18. *Ibid.*, 242.

19. Shimbiriov and Ogorodnikov, *op. cit.*, 194.

20. *O Kommunisticheskoi Morali, Sbornik Statei*, 86.

21. Shishkin, *op. cit.*, 93.

22. Tropkin, *Ob Osnovakh Strategii i Taktiki Leninizma*, 3–4.

23. *Ibid.*, 7.

24. Stalin, *Ob Osnovakh Leninizma*, in *Sochineniia*, VI, 146.

25. Tropkin, *Ob Osnovakh Strategii i Taktiki Leninizma*, 21.

26. *Ibid.*, 21, 23.

27. *Ibid.*, 23.

28. *Ibid.*, 24.

29. *Ibid.*, 29.

30. *Ibid.*, 48.

31. Hunt, *The Theory and Practice of Communism*, 8.

32. Stalin, *Ob Osnovakh Leninizma*, in *Sochineniia*, VI, 154; cf. Tropkin, *Ob Osnovakh Strategii i Taktiki Leninima*, 31.

33. Tropkin, *Ob Osnovakh Strategii i Taktiki Leninizma*, 31, 33.

34. *Ibid.*, 42.

35. Degras, *Soviet Documents on Foreign Policy*, I, 57.

36. Degras, *The Communist International, 1919–1943, Documents*, I, 145.

37. Lenin, *Sochineniia*, XXXIII, 271.

38. Tropkin, *Ob Osnovakh Strategii i Taktiki Leninizma*, 14.

39. K. Dubina, "Leninskaia teoriia sotsialisticheskoi revolutsii," *Kommunist*, No. 15 (October, 1955), 73–78.

40. Tropkin, *Ob Osnovakh Strategii i Taktiki Leninizma*, 12.

41. *Ibid.*, 27–28.

42. Louis Carlos Prestes, "Kommunisticheskaia partiia Brazilii v bor'be za mir, svobodu i nezavisimost' rodiny," *Kommunist*, No. 3 (February, 1955), 89–91.

43. *Ibid.*, 91.

44. *Ibid.*, 93.

45. *Ibid.*, 90, 94.

46. M. Danilevich, "Latinskaia Amerika i mezhdunarodnoe sotrudnichestvo," *Kommunist*, No. 2 (February, 1956), 104, 107.

47. *Ibid.*, 110–13.

48. *Ibid.*, 104.

49. Tropkin, *Ob Osnovakh Strategii i Taktiki Leninizma*, 28.

50. *Ibid.*, 37.

51. *Ibid.*, 41.

52. *Ibid.*, 45.

53. Quoted in Shishkin, *op. cit.*, 193.

54. V. M. Molotov, *Soviet Foreign Relations*, 10.

55. V. M. Molotov, *O Vneshnei Politike Sovetskovo Soiuza*, 5.

56. I. P. Pavlov, *Lektsii o Rabote Bol'shikh Polusharii Golovnovo Mozga*, 273.

57. I. P. Pavlov, *Polnoe Sobraniie Sochinenii*, II, Part 2, 345.

58. Yu. M. Pratusevich, "O rechedvigatel'nom analizatore i ievo roli v protsesse poznaniia," *Voprosy Filosofii*, No. 6 (1953), 149.

59. Lenin, *Detskaia Bolezn' 'Levizny' v Kommunizme*, in *Sochineniia*, XXXI, 44.

60. *Ibid.*, 52.

61. *Ibid.*

62. *Ibid.*, 69.

63. *Ibid.*, 75.

64. *Ibid.*, 76–77.

65. N. V. Tropkin, *O Proizvedenii V. I. Lenina: Detskaia Bolezn' 'Levizny' v Kommunizme*, 14.

66. Donskoi, *op. cit.*, 16.

67. Tropkin, *O Proizvedenii V. I. Lenina: Detskaia Bolezn' 'Levizny' v Kommunizme*, 15.

68. *Ibid.*, 24.

69. Tropkin, *Ob Osnovakh Strategii i Taktiki Leninizma*, 40–41.

70. Tropkin, *O Proizvedenii V. I. Lenina: Detskaia Bolezn' 'Levizny' v Kommunizme*, 25.

71. *Ibid.*

72. Tropkin, *Ob Osnovakh Strategii i Taktiki Leninizma*, 33–34.

73. Lenin, *Sochineniia*, XXXI, 167.

74. Tropkin, *Ob Osnovakh Strategii i Taktiki Leninizma*, 35–36.

75. *Ibid.*, 36.

76. *Ibid.*, 47.

77. Hunt, *The Theory and Practice of Communism*, 160–61.

78. Tropkin, *O Proizvedenii V. I. Lenina: Detskaia Bolezn' 'Levizny' v Kommunizme*, 26.

79. *Ibid.*, 27–28.

80. Tropkin, *Ob Osnovakh Strategii i Taktiki Leninizma*, 44–45.

81. Louis Carlos Prestes, "Kommunisticheskaia partiia Brazilii v bor'be za mir, svobodu i nezavisimost' rodiny," *Kommunist*, No. 3 (February, 1955), 97.

82. Lenin, *Sochineniia*, IX, 16.

83. Lenin, *Detskaia Bolezn' 'Levizny' v Kommunizme*, in *Sochineniia*, XXXI, 16–17.

84. Lenin, *Sochineniia*, XXII, 314.

85. *Ibid.*, XXXV, 191.

86. *Kommunist*, No. 5 (April, 1957), 21.

87. Lenin, *Sochineniia*, XXIII, 360–61.

88. Vassil'ev and Khrustov, *op. cit.*, 227.

89. Lenin, *Sochineniia*, XXI, 276.

90. *Ibid.*, XV, 176.

91. *Ibid.*, XXXV, 480.

92. *Ibid.*, XXVII, 299; cf. XXXV, 181, and XXIII, 84; see also Kun, *op. cit.*, 709, 798.

93. Lenin, *Sochineniia*, XXI, 271.

94. *Ibid.*, 272–73, and XXXV, 155.

95. *Ibid.*, XXIII, 67.

96. *Ibid.*, 73.

97. Molotov, *O Vneshnei Politike Sovetskovo Soiuza*, 6.

98. *Vneshniaia Politika Sovetskovo Soiuza* (1946), 29.

99. Lenin, *Sochineniia*, XXI, 271.

100. Kun, *op. cit.*, 799, 810.

101. Lenin, *Sochineniia*, XXI, 271–72.

102. *Ibid.*, 141.

103. *Pravda*, February 15, 1956.

104. *Ibid.*

105. Quoted in Max Beloff, *The Foreign Policy of Soviet Russia, 1929–1941*, II (1936–1941), 153.

106. Lenin, *Sochineniia*, XXVIII, 49.

107. *Vneshniaia Politika Sovetskovo Soiuza* (1948), Part 1, 203.

108. Lenin, *Sochineniia*, XXXI, 414.

109. *Ibid.*, 415.

110. *Ibid.*, 419.

111. *Ibid.*, 404.

112. *Ibid.*, 410–11.

113. Stalin, *Marksizm i Natsional'no-kolonial'nyi Vopros*, 78.
114. *Ibid.*, 96.
115. Tropkin, *Ob Osnovakh Strategii i Taktiki Leninizma*, 40.
116. Ivashin and Zuev, *op. cit.*, 14.
117. Lenin, *Sochineniia*, XXX, 192; cf. *ibid.*, XXX, 153–55.
118. N. L. Rubinstein, *Vneshniaia Politika Sovetskovo Gosudarstva v 1921–1925 godakh*, 14.
119. Quoted in T. A. Taracouzio, *War and Peace in Soviet Diplomacy*, 179.
120. Stalin, *Sochineniia*, XIII, 302–303.
121. Speech delivered on August 31, 1939; quoted in Degras, *Soviet Documents on Foreign Policy*, III (1933–1941), 370–71.
122. A concise description of the events is to be found in Ygael Gluckstein, *Stalin's Satellites in Europe*, 145–50.
123. A. Sobolev, "Vsemirno-istoricheskoe znacheniie sotsialisticheskovo lageria," *Kommunist*, No. 3 (February, 1956), 27.
124. *Pravda*, February 13, 1957.
125. G. A. Deborin, "Leninskii printsip mirnovo sosushchestvovaniia gosudarstv razlichnykh sotsial'nykh sistem," *Voprosy Ekonomiki*, No. 4 (April, 1956), 21–22.
126. *Ibid.*, 18; cf. V. Cheprakov, "Leninskaia teoriia neravnomernosti razvitiia kapitalizma i obostreniie mezhimperialisticheskikh protivorechii v poslevoennyi period," *Voprosy Ekonomiki*, No. 4 (1956).
127. Lenin, *Sochineniia*, XXX, 398.
128. Stalin, *Sochineniia*, XI, 199.
129. Yu. V. Kliuchnikov and A. Sabanin, *Mezhdunarodnaia Politika Noveishevo Vremeni v Dogovorakh, Notakh i Deklaratsiakh*, II, 89.
130. Degras, *Soviet Documents on Foreign Policy*, III (1933–1941), 370.
131. *Pravda*, February 13, 1957.
132. Stalin, *Sochineniia*, II, 277.
133. V. I. Lissovskii, *Mezhdunarodnoe Pravo*, 231.
134. *Ibid.*
135. V. P. Potemkin, ed., *Istoriia Diplomatii*, III, 702.
136. *Ibid.*, 701.
137. *Ibid.*, 703.
138. *Ibid.*
139. *Ibid.*, 707.
140. *Ibid.*, 708.
141. *Ibid.*, 739–40.
142. *Ibid.*, 739.
143. *Ibid.*, 757.
144. *Ibid.*, 709.
145. *Ibid.*, 711.
146. *Ibid.*, 727.
147. Molotov's speech at the meeting of the Supreme Soviet of the USSR

on August 31, 1939; quoted in Beloff, *The Foreign Policy of Soviet Russia,*
1929–1941, II (1936–1941), 275–76.

148. Potemkin, *op. cit.,* 727.

149. *Ibid.,* 701.

150. Lissovskii, *op. cit.,* 70.

CHAPTER V

1. Lenin, *Sochineniia,* XXXIII, 124.

2. Stalin, *Marksizm i Natsional'no-kolonial'nyi Vopros,* 97.

3. Kun, *op. cit.,* 537.

4. Ivashin, *Velikaia Oktiabrskaia Sotsialisticheskaia Revolutsia i Raskol
Mira na Dve Sistemy,* 6.

5. Sergeev, *op. cit.,* 5.

6. Potelov, "Razvitiie sotsializma i proletarskii internatsionalizm," *Kommunist,* No. 1 (January, 1957), 25.

7. *Pravda,* February 15, 1956.

8. "Diskussiia ob ekonomicheskikh i politicheskikh pozitsiiakh natsional'noi burzhuazii v stranakh Vostoka," *Sovetskoe Vostokovedeniie,* No. 1 (1957), 174.

9. *Ibid.,* 179.

10. *Ibid.,* 180.

11. *Ibid.,* 182.

12. *Ibid.,* 183.

CHAPTER VI

1. Quoted in Deborin, "Leninskii printsip mirnovo sosushchestvovaniia gosudarstv razlichnykh sotsial'nykh sistem," *Voprosy Ekonomiki,* No. 4 (April, 1956), 17.

2. Ivashin, *Velikaia Oktiabrskaia Sotsialisticheskaia Revolutsia i Raskol Mira na Dve Sistemy,* 14.

3. Molotov, *Voprosy Vneshnei Politiki, Rechi i Zaiavleniia, Aprel' 1945–Yun' 1948,* 28–29.

4. *Pravda,* August 9, 1953.

5. *Pravda,* February 13, 1957.

6. *Pravda,* February 15, 1956.

7. *Pravda,* June 30, 1957.

8. *Ibid.*

9. V. Kamenev, "Bol'shaia lozh' o 'malykh' atomnykh voinakh," *Mezhdunarodnaia Zhizn',* No. 3 (1957), 97.

10. *Pravda,* March 20, 1957.

11. *Ibid.*

12. *Ibid.*

13. *Pravda,* February 15, 1956.

14. *Pravda,* February 13, 1957.

15. Lenin, *Sochineniia,* XXI, 311.

16. *Ibid.,* XXIX, 133.

17. Editorial, "Kraieugolnyi kamen' vneshnei politiki SSSR," *Mezhdunarodnaia Zhizn',* No. 3 (1957), 3–4.

18. Deborin, "Leninskii printsip mirnovo sosushchestvovaniia gosudarstv razlichnykh sotsial'nykh sistem," *Voprosy Ekonomiki,* No. 4 (April, 1956), 16.

19. *Ibid.,* 27.

20. *Pravda,* April 16, 1957.

21. *Pravda,* June 13, 1957.

22. Deborin, *Leninskaia Politika Mirnovo Sosushchestvovaniia Dvukh Sistem—General'naia Liniia Vneshnei Politiki* SSSR, 22.

23. *Pravda,* February 13, 1957.

24. *Pravda,* June 30, 1957.

25. *Pravda,* April 16, 1957.

26. Potelov, "Razvitiie sotsializma i proletarskii internatsionalizm," *Kommunist,* No. 1 (January, 1957), 15–17, 26.

27. Deborin, "Leninskii printsip mirnovo sosushchestvovaniia gosudarstv razlichnykh sotsial'nykh sistem," *Voprosy Ekonomiki,* No. 4 (April, 1956), 21.

28. *Pravda,* February 13, 1957.

29. Shepilov's speech in *ibid.*

30. Deborin, "Leninskii printsip mirnovo sosushchestvovaniia gosudarstv razlichnykh sotsial'nykh sistem," *Voprosy Ekonomiki,* No. 4 (April, 1956), 25–26.

31. *Ibid.,* 18.

32. *Ibid.,* 20.

33. Deborin, *Leninskaia Politika Mirnovo Sosushchestvovaniia Dvukh Sistem—General'naia Liniia Vneshnei Politiki* SSSR, 27.

34. *Ibid.,* 25–26.

Chapter VII

1. Stalin, *Marksizm i Natsional'no-kolonial'nyi Vopros,* 110.

2. Louis Fischer, *The Soviets in World Affairs: A History of the Relations Between the Soviet Union and the Rest of the World, 1917–1929,* I, xvii.

3. *Ibid.,* xvi.

4. *Ibid.,* 298.

5. *Ibid.*, 383.

6. Quoted in Beloff, *The Foreign Policy of Soviet Russia, 1929–1941*, I, 25.

7. Quoted in *ibid.*, 59.

8. Quoted in *ibid.*, 100.

9. Quoted in *ibid.*, 103.

10. For an analysis of Soviet policies in 1938, see *ibid.*, II, 120–66.

11. The development of the German-Soviet negotiations of 1939 may be seen in captured German documents published by the American Government in 1948: *Nazi-Soviet Relations, 1939–1941, Documents from the Archives of the German Foreign Office*, 1–78.

12. Quoted in Beloff, *The Foreign Policy of Soviet Russia, 1929–1941*, II, 249–50.

13. Quoted in *ibid.*, 256.

14. The texts of the German-Soviet public treaty of non-aggression and neutrality and the attached secret protocol for the division of eastern Europe into the two zones of influence are reproduced in *Nazi-Soviet Relations*, 76–78.

15. See the text of the German-Soviet secret protocol of August 23, 1939, in *Nazi-Soviet Relations*, 78.

16. See the text of the German-Soviet secret protocol of September 28, 1939, in *Nazi-Soviet Relations*, 107.

17. See the terms of the Soviet acceptance of participation in a four-power pact with Nazi Germany, Fascist Italy, and Japan, including the claim to a zone of influence, in *Nazi-Soviet Relations*, 258–59.

18. The maximum Soviet program for a zone of influence in southeastern Europe and the Near and Middle East emerges from the records of conversations held in November, 1940, by Molotov with Hitler and von Ribbentrop; see *Nazi-Soviet Relations*, 217–54.

19. *Nazi-Soviet Relations*, 338.

20. *Ibid.*

21. Tass communiqué quoted in Beloff, *The Foreign Policy of Soviet Russia, 1929–1941*, II, 381–82.

22. For a thorough and well-documented analysis of Soviet-German cooperation in 1939–1941, see Gerhard L. Weinberg, *Germany and the Soviet Union, 1939–1941*.

23. *The Anti-Stalin Campaign and International Communism: A Selection of Documents*, 80.

24. Editorial, "Kraieugolnyi kamen' vneshnei politiki SSSR," *Mezhdunarodnaia Zhizn'*, No. 3 (1957), 3.

25. See for instance, Deborin, "Leninskii printsip mirnovo sosushchestvovaniia gosudarstv razlichnykh sotsial'nykh sistem," *Voprosy Ekonomiki*, No. 4 (April, 1956), 22.

26. *Vneshniaia Politika Sovetskovo Soiuza v Period Otechestvennoi Voiny*, III, 44.

27. Molotov, *Voprosy Vneshnei Politiki, Rechi i Zaiavleniia, Aprel' 1945–Yun' 1948,* 436.

28. *Pravda,* July 11, 1955.

29. *Pravda,* November 18, 1956.

30. *Pravda,* November 19 ,1956.

31. *Pravda,* December 18, 1956.

32. *Pravda,* January 8, 1957.

33. *Pravda,* July 27, 1955.

34. *Pravda,* January 8, 1957.

35. *Pravda,* June 14, 1957.

36. Deborin, *Leninskaia Politika Mirnovo Sosushchestvovaniia Dvukh Sistem—General'naia Liniia Vneshnei Politiki SSSR,* 29.

37. *Pravda,* September 14, 1955.

38. *Pravda,* September 21, 1955.

39. "Zaiavleniie Ministerstva Inostrannykh Del SSSR o planakh sozdaniia Evratoma i obshchevo rynka," *Pravda,* March 17, 1957.

40. *Ibid.*

41. H. L. Boorman, A. Eckstein, Ph. E. Mosely, and B. Schwartz, *Moscow-Peking Axis.*

42. M. I. Skladkovskii, "Razvitiie torgovykh putei mezhdu Sovetskim Soiuzom i Kitaiem," *Sovetskoe Vostokovedeniie,* No. 1 (1957), 122.

43. *Ibid.,* 122.

44. *Ibid.,* 124.

45. *Ibid.,* 126.

46. *Vneshniaia Torgovlia,* No. 2 (1956), 3.

47. *Moscow-Peking Axis,* 84.

48. *Pravda,* June 30, 1957.

49. *Pravda,* October 20, 1956.

50. *Pravda,* June 30, 1957.

51. *Ibid.*

52. *Pravda,* August 9, 1953.

53. T. Belashchenko, "Amerikanskiie voennye bazy—ugroza mira," *Pravda,* February 8, 1956.

54. *Pravda,* January 29, 1956.

55. Molotov, *Voprosy Vneshnei Politiki, Rechi i Zaiavleniia, Aprel' 1945–Yun' 1948,* 293.

56. *Ibid.,* 288, 290.

57. *Vneshniaia Politika Sovetskovo Soiuza* (1946), 73–74.

58. Degras, *Soviet Documents on Foreign Policy,* III, 168–69.

59. Ivashin and Zuev, *op. cit.,* 67–68.

60. Degras, *Soviet Documents on Foreign Policy,* III, 169.

61. *Vneshniaia Politika Sovetskovo Soiuza* (1946), 101.

62. *Ibid.,* 102.

63. *Vneshniaia Politika SSSR, Sbornik Dokumentov,* IV, 450–51.

64. *Ibid.,* 454–55.

65. *Ibid.,* 455.

66. *Ibid.,* 456, 457-58.

67. Hubert Ripka, *Czechoslovakia Enslaved: The Story of the Communist Coup d'Etat,* 23.

68. *Vneshniaia Politika Sovetskovo Soiuza v Period Otechestvennoi Voiny,* I, 431.

69. *Ibid.,* III, 199.

70. *Ibid.,* 175-78.

71. *Vneshniaia Politika Sovetskovo Soiuza* (1948), Part 1, 54.

72. *Ibid.,* 128 and 159 respectively.

73. *Ibid.,* 200.

74. *Ibid.,* 198.

75. *Ibid.* (1949), 89-90.

76. *Ibid.* (1948), Part 1, 52.

77. *Ibid.,* 52-55.

78. For an analysis of the Soviet network of bilateral alliances, see W. W. Kulski, "The Soviet System of Collective Security Compared with the Western System," *American Journal of International Law,* No. 3 (July, 1950), 453-76.

79. *Vneshniaia Politika Sovetskovo Soiuza* (1948), Part 1, 130.

80. *Ibid.* (1950), 59.

81. *Pravda,* May 15, 1955.

82. *Ibid.*

83. *Ibid.*

84. Reported by *Pravda,* May 17, 1955.

85. Kliuchnikov and Sabanin, *op. cit.,* III, 89.

86. *Ibid.,* 90.

87. *Vneshniaia Politika Sovetskovo Soiuza* (1948, Part 1, 181.

88. L. I. Melnikov, "Iz istorii ispol'zovaniia imperialistami territorii Irana kak platzdarma protiv Sovetskoi Rossii (1917–1920)," *Sovetskoe Vostokovedeniie,* No. 1 (1957), 155.

89. *Vneshniaia Politika SSSR, Sbornik Dokumentov,* IV, 451.

90. *Ibid.,* 454-55.

91. *Ibid.,* 457.

92. *Vneshniaia Politika Sovetskovo Soiuza* (1950, 111.

93. *Pravda,* April 18, 1957.

94. *Pravda,* October 31, 1956.

95. *Nowe Drogi,* No. 10 (October, 1956), 18.

96. *Ibid.,* 20.

97. The text of the Soviet-Polish Treaty was reproduced in *Pravda,* December 18, 1956.

98. The text of the Soviet-German Treaty was reproduced in *Pravda,* March 14, 1957.

99. *Ibid.*

100. *Pravda,* March 14, 1957.

101. *Ibid.*

102. *Vedomosti Verkhovnovo Soveta SSSR,* No., 15 ([882], August 6, 1957), 467–72.

103. *Pravda,* May 28, 1957.

104. *Ibid.*

105. Deborin, "Leninskii printsip mirnovo sosushchestvovaniia gosudarstv razlichnykh sotsial'nyhk sistem," *Voprosy Ekonomiki,* No. 4 (April, 1956), 20–21.

CHAPTER VIII

1. *Pravda,* February 20, 1957.

2. I. V. Stalin, *Marksizm i Natsional'nyi Vopros,* in *Sochineniia,* II, 292–97.

3. *Ibid.,* 297 and 301.

4. I. V. Stalin, *Natsional'nyi Vopros i Leninizm,* 13.

5. Vassil'ev and Khrustov, *op. cit.,* 194.

6. R. M. Raimov, *Obrazovaniie Bashkirshoi Avtonomnoi Sovetskoi Sotsialisticheskoi Respubliki,* 8.

7. Lenin, *Natsional'no-kolonial'nyi Vopros,* 60.

8. Lenin, *Imperializm, kak noveishii etap kapitalizma,* in *Sochineniia,* XXII, 181, 264, and 283.

9. Lenin, *Natsional'no-kolonial'nyi Vopros,* 154–55.

10. Lenin, *Sochineniia,* XXXI, 215–16.

11. Lenin, *Natsional'no-kolonial'nyi Vopros,* 63.

12. Stalin, *Sochineniia,* VI, 145.

13. *Bol'shaia Sovetskaia Entsiklopediia,* XXIX, 297.

14. V. I. Lenin, *Natsional'nyi Vopros,* 19, 21, and 26.

15. Lenin, *Sochineniia,* XXI, 377.

16. *Ibid.,* XXII, 135.

17. *Ibid.,* 137.

18. *Ibid.,* XX, 92.

19. Lenin, *Natsional'no-kolonial'nyi Vopros,* 32–33.

20. Quoted in Degras, *Soviet Documents on Foreign Policy,* I, 39.

21. Lenin, *Natsional'no-kolonial'nyi Vopros,* 133.

22. *Ibid.,* 136.

23. *Ibid.,* 135.

24. *Ibid.,* 114.

25. Stalin, *Marksizm i Natsional'no-kolonial'nyi Vopros,* 47–48.

26. *Ibid.,* 51. Cf. Stalin, *Sochineniia,* III, 310–13 and 355–56; VI, 141–42.

27. Stalin, *Marksizm i Natsional'no-kolonial'nyi Vopros,* 87.

28. *Ibid.,* 58.

29. *Ibid.,* 127.

30. *Ibid.,* 50.

31. D. A. Chugaev, *Kommunisticheskaia Partiia—Organizator Sovet-skovo Mnogonatsional'novo Gosudarstva, 1917–1924 gg.,* 18.

32. *Bol'shaia Sovetskaia Entsiklopediia,* XXIX, 291.

33. Sergeev, *op. cit.,* 10.

34. *Pravda,* November 24, 1955, and December 14, 1955.

35. R. P. Dutt, *India Today,* 438, 442–43.

36. *Vneshniaia Politika Sovetskovo Soiuza* (1945), 66.

37. Molotov, *Voprosy Vneshnei Politiki, Rechi i Zaiavleniia, Aprel' 1945–Yun' 1948,* 39.

38. *Vneshniaia Politika Sovetskovo Soiuza* (1948), Part 1, 125–26.

39. *Falsifikatory Istorii,* published in 1948 by the Soviet Information Bureau and reproduced in *Vneshniaia Politika Sovetskovo Soiuza* (1948), Part 1, 110.

40. A. Shvakov and V. Bogoslovskii, *Nezavisimyi Egipet,* 28.

CHAPTER IX

1. Lenin, *Sochineniia,* XXIII, 55.

2. Lenin, *Natsional'no-kolonial'nyi Vopros,* 156–58.

3. Degras, *The Communist International, 1919–1943, Documents,* I, 179.

4. *Ibid.,* 385.

5. Lenin, *Sochineniia,* XXXI, 128.

6. *Pravda,* December 6, 1955.

7. *Pravda Vostoka,* October 13, 1956.

8. E. Zhukov, "Narody Vostoka i sud'by mira," *Mezhdunarodnaia Zhizn',* No. 4 (April, 1956), 45.

9. E. Zhukov, "Raspad kolonial'noi sistemy imperializma," *Partiinaia Zhizn',* No. 16 (August, 1956), 41.

10. *Ibid.,* 46.

11. Degras, *Soviet Documents on Foreign Policy,* I, 17.

12. Stalin, *Marksizm i Natsional'no-kolonial'nyi Vopros,* 84–85.

13. Stalin, *Ob Osnovakh Leninizma,* in *Sochineniia,* VI, 74.

14. *Ibid.,* 94–95, 141–42.

15. Editorial, "Vyshe znamia marksistsko-leninskoi ideologii," *Kommunist,* No. 1 (January, 1957), 8.

16. A. A. Guber, "Gluboko i vsestoronne izuchat' krizis i raspad kolonial'noi sistemy imperializma," *Sovetskoe Vostokovedeniie,* No. 3 (1956), 6–7.

17. *Ibid.,* 7.

18. Lenin, *Natsional'no-kolonial'nyi Vopros,* 84–85, 93, 95.

19. Lenin, *Sochineniia,* XXXI, 124, 127–28.

20. A. Azizian, "Raspad kolonial'noi sistemy imperializma i novye otnosheniia mezhdu stranami," *Voprosy Ekonomiki,* No. 10 (1956), 6.

21. Lenin, *Natsional'no-kolonial'nyi Vopros,* 107.

22. Lenin, *Sochineniia*, XXXI, 124.

23. Degras, *The Communist International, 1919–1943, Documents*, I, 23.

24. *Ibid.*, 386; cf. similar resolutions adopted by the Fifth Congress in 1924 and the Sixth Congress in 1928, in Kun, *op. cit.*, 410–11, 836.

25. Lenin, *Sochineniia*, XXII, 148.

26. *Ibid.*, XXXI, 127.

27. *Ibid.*, 208.

28. *Ibid.*, 219.

29. Stalin, *Sochineniia*, VI, 95.

30. *Ibid.*, 144.

31. Stalin, *Marksizm i Natsional'no-kolonial'nyi Vopros*, 177.

32. *Ibid.*, 161.

33. *Ibid.*, 174.

34. Kun, *op. cit.*, p. 846.

35. *Ibid.*, 40.

36. A. M. Diakov and I. M. Reisner, "Rol' Gandhi v natsional'no-osvoboditel'noi bor'be narodov Indii," *Sovetskoe Vostokovedeniie*, No. 5 (1956), 22.

37. *Bol'shaia Sovetskaia Entsiklopediia*, XXIX, 299.

38. Vassil'ev and Khrustov, *op. cit.*, 10.

39. Zhukov, "Raspad kolonial'noi sistemy imperializma," *Partiinaia Zhizn'*, No. 16 (August, 1956), 45.

40. Editorial, "Velikaia Oktiabrskaia Sotsialisticheskaia Revolutsia i sovremennyi Vostok," *Sovetskoe Vostokovedeniie*, No. 5 (1956), 4.

41. Diakov and Reisner, "Rol' Gandhi v natsional'no-osvoboditelnoi bor'be narodov Indii," *Sovetskoe Vostokovedeniie*, No. 5 (1956), 23.

42. For instance, see Editorial, "XX s'yezd kommunisticheskoi partii Sovetskovo Soiuza i zadachi izucheniia sovremennovo Vostoka," *Sovetskoe Vostokovedeniie*, No. 1 (1956), 3–12; Guber, "Gluboko i vsestoronne izuchat' krizis i raspad kolonial'noi sistemy imperializma," *Sovetskoe Vostokovedeniie*, No. 3 (1956), 3–14; Diakov and Reisner, "Rol' Gandhi v natsional'no-osvoboditel'noi bor'be narodov Indii," *Sovetskoe Vostokovedeniie*, No. 5 (1956), 20–34.

43. Zhukov, "Raspad kolonial'noi sistemy imperializma," *Partiinaia Zhizn'*, No. 16 (August, 1956), 41–42.

44. *Ibid.*, 42–43.

45. *Ibid.*, 45–46.

46. *Ibid.*, 47.

47. *Ibid.*, 44.

48. V. Vassil'eva, "Raspad kolonial'noi sistemy imperializma," *Voprosy Ekonomiki*, No. 4 (April, 1956), 105–106, 117.

49. "Diskussiia ob ekonomicheskikh i politicheskikh pozitsiiakh natsional'noi burzhuazii v stranakh Vostoka," *Sovetskoe Vostokovedeniie*, No. 1 (1957), 174–84.

50. A. N. Kononov, "Stoletiie vostochnovo fakulteta Leningradskovo Universiteta (1855–1955)," *Sovetskoe Vostokovedeniie*, No. 2 (1956), 82–90.

51. *Pravda Vostoka*, October 13, 1956.

52. *Ibid.*

53. N. Mukhitdinov, "K novym uspekham sovetskovo vostokovedeniia," *Pravda*, June 14, 1957.

54. *Uchitelskaia Gazeta*, January 24, 1957.

55. "Pervyi god raboty vostochnoi komissii geograficheskovo obshchestva Soiuza SSR," *Sovetskoe Vostokovedeniie*, No. 1 (1957), 185–87.

56. S. Nazarov, "Sovetskie knigi," *Vneshniaia Torgovlia*, No. 7 (1956), 19, 21.

57. *Ibid.*, 20.

58. Guber, "Gluboko i vsestoronne izuchat' krizis i raspad kolonial'noi sistemy imperializma," *Sovetskoe Vostokovedeniie*, No. 3 (1956), 8.

59. Review of a Soviet book on French West Africa in *Voprosy Ekonomiki*, No. 1 (1957), 135.

60. Review of a Soviet book on African ethnography in *ibid.*, 140.

61. I. Potekhin, "Vozrastaiushchee znacheniie Afriki v mirovoi ekonomike i politike," *Kommunist*, No. 6 (April, 1957), 100, 105, 111.

62. Editorial, "XX s'yezd kommunisticheskoi partii Sovetskovo Soiuza i zadachi izucheniia sovremennovo Vostoka," *Sovetskoe Vostokovedeniie*, No. 1 (1956), 10–11.

63. Guber, "Gluboko i vsestoronne izuchat' krizis i raspad kolonial'noi sistemy imperializma," *Sovetskoe Vostokovedeniie*, No. 3 (1956), 9.

64. "V Institute Vostokovedeniia," *Voprosy Istorii*, No. 3 (1957), 196–201.

65. *Ibid.*

66. Guber, "Gluboko i vsestoronne izuchat' krizis i raspad kolonial'noi sistemy imperializma," *Sovetskoe Vostokovedeniie*, No. 3 (1956), 14.

67. *Ibid.*, 7.

CHAPTER X

1. *Pravda*, November 20–December 18, 1955.

2. Deborin, *Leninskaia Politika Mirnovo Sosushchestvovaniia Dvukh Sistem—General'naia Liniia Vneshnei Politiki SSSR*, 17.

3. *Ibid.*, 22.

4. Vassil'eva, "Raspad kolonial'noi sistemy imperializma," *Voprosy Ekonomiki*, No. 4 (April, 1956), 114.

5. *Pravda*, February 13, 1957.

6. *Ibid.*

7. Lissovskii, *op. cit.*, 83.

8. *Pravda*, April 28, 1955.

9. Vassil'eva, "Raspad kolonial'noi sistemy imperializma," *Voprosy Ekonomiki*, No. 4 (April, 1956), 114.

10. Editorial, "Velikaia Oktiabrskaia Sotsialisticheskaia Revolutsia i sovremennyi Vostok," *Sovetskoe Vostokovedeniie*, No. 5 (1956), 6.

11. *Pravda*, February 15, 1956.

12. Vassil'eva, "Raspad kolonial'noi sistemy imperializma," *Voprosy Ekonomiki*, No. 4 (April, 1956), 114.

13. Romanov, "Nerushimoe ideinoe edinstvo kommunisticheskikh partii," *Mezhdunarodnaia Zhizn'*, No. 11 (November, 1956), 17.

14. Vassilieva, "Raspad kolonial'noi sistemy imperializma," *Voprosy Ekonomiki*, No. 4 (April, 1956), 115.

15. *Pravda*, November 30, December 1, December 11, and December 18, 1955.

16. *Pravda*, May 8, 1957.

17. Kommentator, "Raschety i proschety kolonizatorov," *Mezhdunarodnaia Zhizn'*, No. 1 (January, 1957), 11.

18. V. Poliakov, "Arabskiie strany na puti k ekonomicheskoi nezavisimosti," *Vneshniaia Torgovlia*, No. 9 (1956), 3.

19. Shvakov and Bogoslovskii, *op. cit.*, 4, 5, and 36.

20. *Ibid.*, 55.

21. *Ibid.*, 53.

22. V. B. Lutskii, "Izrail'—orudiie agressivnoi politiki," *Mezhudnarodnaia Zhizn'*, No. 2 (1957), 77.

23. Potekhin, "Vozrastaiushchee znacheniie Afriki v mirovoi ekonomike i politike," *Kommunist*, No. 6 (April, 1957), 110.

24. *Ibid.*, 111.

25. *Ibid.*, 110–11.

26. *Ibid.*, 113.

27. Vassil'eva, "Raspad kolonial'noi sistemy imperializma," *Voprosy Ekonomiki*, No. 4 (April, 1956), 116–17.

28. Danilevich, "Latinskaia Amerika i mezhdunarodnoe sotrudnichestvo," *Kommunist*, No. 2 (February, 1956), 108.

29. Azizian, "Raspad kolonial'noi sistemy imperializma i novye otnosheniia mezhdu stranami," *Voprosy Ekonomiki*, No. 10 (1956), 23.

30. *Pravda*, June 13, 1957.

31. *Ibid.*

32. *Pravda*, December 8, 1955; he developed the same idea in a speech at Banyalor, India; see *Pravda*, November 28, 1955.

33. Pravda, December 6, 1955.

34. Stalin, *Sochineniia*, VII, 293–94.

35. Milovan Djilas, *The New Class*.

36. Stalin, *Sochineniia*, VI, 97–98.

37. Lenin, *Natsional'no-kolonial'nyi Vopros*, 156.

38. Lenin, *Sochineniia*, XXXI, 386.

39. Gomulka, "Uzlovye problemy politiki partii," *Kommunist*, No. 7 (May, 1957), 41.

40. Editorial, "Velikaia Oktiabrskaia Sotsialisticheskaia Revolutsia i sovremennyi Vostok," *Sovetskoe Vostokovedeniie*, No. 5 (1956), 10.

41. *Ibid.*, 9.

42. Ivashin and Zuev, *op. cit.*, 7.

43. Lenin, *Natsional'no-kolonial'nyi Vopros*, 158–60.

44. Guber, "Gluboko i vsestoronne izuchat' krizis i raspad kolonial'noi sistemy imperializma," *Sovetskoe Vostokovedeniie*, No. 3 (1956), 13.

45. T. Timofeev, "O edinstve deistvii partii rabochevo klassa," *Mezhdunarodnaia Zhizn'*, No. 1 (1957), 52.

46. A. S. Kaufman, "Ekonomicheskoe polozheniie Birmy," *Sovetskoe Vostokovedeniie*, No. 1 (1957), 37.

47. He said in Bombay: "The Prime Minister of India, Mr. Nehru, declared that India would also take the socialist road. This is good. Of course we have a different concept of socialism." (*Pravda*, November 26, 1955) Speaking in Rangoon, he made a similar reservation: "The Prime Minister of Burma, addressing me and Nikolai Alexandrovich Bulganin, called us comrades. Yes, we are comrades in the common struggle for peace and friendship." (*Pravda*, December 7, 1955) He wanted to say that Mr. U Nu was not his comrade otherwise, in particular in the battle for Communism.

48. Tropkin, *Ob Osnovakh Strategii i Taktiki Leninizma*, 10–11.

49. *Ibid.*, 13.

50. D. Tumur-Ochir, "O nekapitalisticheskom puti razvitiia otstalykh stran k sotsializmu," *Voprosy Filosofii*, No. 1 (1956), 49–51.

51. *Ibid.*, 56.

52. *Vneshniaia Politika Sovetskovo Soiuza* (1950), 113.

53. A. P. Butenko, "Kitaiskaia revolutsia i eio osobennosti," *Sovetskoe Vostokovedeniie*, No. 3 (1956), 15–17.

54. *Ibid.*, 21.

55. Vassil'eva, "Raspad kolonial'noi sistemy imperializma," *Voprosy Ekonomiki*, No. 4 (April, 1956), 115.

56. Editorial, "Velikaia Oktiabrskaia Sotsialisticheskaia Revolutsia i sovremennyi Vostok," *Sovetskoe Vostokovedeniie*, No. 5 (1956), 8.

57. Tropkin, *Ob Osnovakh Strategii i Taktiki Leninizma*, 18.

58. Lenin, *Sochineniia*, XXXI, 127.

59. Ivashin, *Vsemirno-istoricheskoe Znacheniie Velikoi Oktiabrskoi Sotsialisticheskoi Revolutsii*, 8.

60. Degras, *The Communist International, 1919–1943, Documents*, I, 386–87.

61. V. Mikheev, "Novaia Aziia," *Kommunist*, No. 12 (August, 1955), 88.

62. Tropkin, *Ob Osnovakh Strategii i Taktiki Leninizma*, 10.

63. Fan Zho-yui, "Znacheniie knigi Lenina: *Dve Taktiki Sotsial-Demokratii v Demokraticheskoi Revolutsii*, dlia narodno-demokraticheskoi revolutsii v Kitaie," *Sovetskoe Vostokovedeniie*, No. 2 (1956), 31.

64. *Ibid.*, 33.

65. A. P. Butenko, "Kitaiskaia revolutsia i eio osobennosti," *Sovetskoe Vostokovedeniie*, No. 3 (1956), 22–23.

66. *Ibid.*, 25.

67. *Ibid.*, 25–26.

68. *Ibid.*, 32.

69. For the description of the three stages, see *ibid.*, 30–34.

70. *Ibid.*, 34.

71. A. V. Meliksetov, "Ideologicheskoe perevospitaniie burzhuaznykh elementov v KNR," *Sovetskoe Vostokovedeniie*, No. 1 (1957), 33.

72. *Ibid.*, 33.

73. A. A. Martynov, "Istoricheskii s'yezd kommunisticheskoi partii Kitaia," *Sovetskoe Vostokovedeniie*, No. 6 (1956), 6.

74. Du Chao-bai, "Razvitiie sotsialisticheskoi ekonomiki i ekonomicheskiie zakony v perekhodnyi period v Kitaiskoi Narodnoi Respublike," *Voprosy Ekonomiki*, No. 1 (January, 1957), 61.

75. *Ibid.*, 58.

76. Meliksetov, "Ideologicheskoe perevospitaniie burzhuaznykh elementov v KNR," *Sovetskoe Vostokovedeniie*, No. 1 (1957), 29.

77. *Ibid.*

78. Sobolev, "Vsemirno-istoricheskoe znacheniie sotsialisticheskovo lageria," *Kommunist*, No. 3 (February, 1956), 21.

79. N. V. Tropkin, "O strategii i taktike leninizma," *Kommunist*, No. 1 (January, 1955), 108.

80. Lenin, *Sochineniia*, XXXI, 127.

81. Stalin, *Marksizm i Natsional'no-kolonial'nyi Vopros*, 177–78.

82. Degras, *The Communist International, 1919–1943, Documents*, I, 390.

83. *Pravda*, February 15, 1956.

84. Khaled Baghdash, "Likvidatsiia pozornoi kolonial'noi sistemy postavlena v poriadok dnia," *Pravda*, March 11, 1956.

85. Dolores Ibarruri, "Krepit' edinstvo sil boriushchikhsia za predotvrashcheniie novoi voiny," *Pravda*, March 13, 1956.

86. *Ibid.*

87. *Ibid.*

88. Dolores Ibarruri, "Polozhenie v Ispanii i bor'ba kommunisticheskoi partii za demokratiiu," *Kommunist*, No. 2 (February, 1957), 67–68.

89. F. Miliukov and V. Fuzeev, "Siriiskii narod v bor'be za ukrepleniie natsional'noi nezavisimosti," *Mezhdunarodnaia Zhizn'*, No. 12 (1956), 71.

90. *Ibid.*

91. *Ibid.*, 72.

92. "Iz materialov VII plenuma TsK kommunisticheskoi partii Gretsii," *Kommunist*, No. 5 (April, 1957), 98.

93. Salvador Allende, "Bor'ba naroda Chili za natsional'nuiu nezavisimost'," *Pravda*, August 12, 1954.

94. Egidio Skeff, "Bor'ba brazil'skovo naroda za nezavisimost'," *Pravda*, August 18, 1954.

95. B. Ponomarev, "Sovremennaia mezhdunarodnaia obstanovka i bor'-ba za edinstvo rabochevo dvizheniia," *Voprosy Ekonomiki*, No. 5 (1956), 9.

96. *Ibid.*, 21 and 24.

97. *Ibid.*, 25.

98. *Ibid.*

99. Dr. Sukarno, "Vliianiie Oktiabrskoi revolutsii na probuzhdeniie narodov Azii," *Pravda*, October 11, 1956.

100. *Ibid.*

101. Chandra Shekkhar, "Kolonializm v Azii i Afrike," *Mezhdunarodnaia Zhizn'*, No. 2 (1957), 22–23.

102. *Ibid.*, 18.

103. *Ibid.*, 26.

104. Quoted in Azizian, "Raspad kolonial'noi sistemy imperializma i novye otnosheniia mezhdu stranami," *Voprosy Ekonomiki*, No. 10 (1956), 16.

105. Vassil'eva, "Raspad kolonial'noi sistemy imperializma," *Voprosy Ekonomiki*, No. 4 (April, 1956), 104 and 106.

106. Editorial, "XX s'yezd kommunisticheskoi partii Sovetskovo Soiuza i zadachi izucheniia sovremennovo Vostoka," *Sovetskoe Vostokovedeniie*, No. 1 (1956), 9; cf. Zhukov, "Narody Vostoka i sud'by mira," *Mezhdunarodnaia Zhizn'*, No. 4 (1956), 44–50.

107. E. Zhukov, "Kolonialisticheskaia politika SShA v Azii," *Mezhdunarodnaia Zhizn'*, No. 1 (1957), 71.

108. V. Avarin, "Indiia na puti k ekonomicheskoi nezavisimosti," *Voprosy Ekonomiki*, No. 1 (1957), 81–82.

109. *Pravda*, May 8, 1957.

110. *Pravda*, July 15, 1954.

111. *Pravda*, July 14, 1954.

112. Zhukov, "Raspad kolonial'noi sistemy imperializma," *Partiinaia Zhizn'*, No. 16 (August, 1956), 44.

113. Azizian, "Raspad kolonial'noi sistemy imperializma i novye otnosheniia mezhdu stranami," *Voprosy Ekonomiki*, No. 10 (1956), 23 .

114. Kaufman, "Ekonomicheskoe polozheniie Birmy," *Sovetskoe Vostokovedeniie*, No. 1 (1957), 48.

115. Avarin, "Indiia na puti k ekonomicheskoi nezavisimosti," *Voprosy Ekonomiki*, No. 1 (1957), 83.

116. This section is largely based on the following sources: *Foreign Assistance Activities of the Communist Bloc and Their Implications for the United States, The Sino-Soviet Economic Offensive in the Less Developed Countries*, and the most recent data released in March 1959 by the State Department (*New York Times*, March 22, 1959). Soviet sources supply only fragmentary information on this subject.

117. For the detailed picture of the Soviet bloc's economic relations with Egypt in recent years, see Shvakov and Bogoslovskii, *op. cit.*, 57–63.

118. M. F. Gataullin and M. V. Maliukovskii, "Egipetskaia Respublika na puti k ekonomicheskoi nezavisimosti," *Sovetskoe Vostokovedeniie*, No. 3 (1956), 129.

119. Kaufman, "Ekonomicheskoe polozheniie Birmy," *Sovetskoe Vostokovedeniie*, No. 1 (1957), 47.

120. Avarin, "Indiia na puti k ekonomicheskoi nezavisimosti," *Voprosy Ekonomiki*, No. 1 (1957), 85.

121. *Ibid.*, 85–86.

122. A. Kutsenkov, "Razvitiie ekonomicheskikh sviazei Indii s sotsialisticheskimi stranami," *Vneshniaia Torgovlia*, No. 10 (1956), 7.

123. "Vneshniaia torgovlia Egipeta v 1953–1955 gg.," *Vneshniaia Torgovlia*, No. 10 (1956), 22.

124. *Ibid.*, 23.

125. *Vneshniaia Torgovlia*, No. 3 (1956), 20.

126. *Ibid.*, 4.

127. V. Govinnov and M. Pankin, "Ekonomicheskiie sviazi kitaiskoi narodnoi respubliki so stranami Azii," *Voprosy Ekonomiki*, No. 1 (1956), 63.

128. *Pravda*, February 7, 1956.

129. *Pravda*, January 17, 1956.

130. *Pravda*, December 30, 1957.

131. *Pravda*, January 1, 1958.

132. *Pravda*, December 29, 1957.

133. *Pravda*, December 27, 1957.

134. *Pravda*, December 28, 1957.

135. E. Zhukov, "Postup' vremeni," *Pravda*, December 26, 1957.

136. V. Maevskii, "Dukh Bandunga v deistvii," *Pravda*, January 6, 1958.

137. *Pravda*, December 29 and 31, 1957.

138. *Pravda*, December 29, 1957.

139. The verbatim texts of all the resolutions were published in *Pravda*, January 3 and 4, 1958.

140. *Pravda*, January 3, 1958.

CHAPTER XI

1. Quoted in Kutsenkov, "Razvitie ekonomicheskikh sviazei Indii s sotsialisticheskimi stranami," *Vneshniaia Torgovlia*, No. 10 (1956), 6.

2. *Pravda*, June 29, 1954.

3. *Ibid.*

4. *Vneshniaia Politika Sovetskovo Soiuza* (1945), 77.

5. Degras, *Soviet Documents on Foreign Policy*, I, 349.

6. The text of this treaty is reproduced in Kliuchnikov and Sabanin, *op. cit.*, III, 22–23.

7. *Ibid.*, 92.

8. *Vneshniaia Politika SSSR, Sbornik Dokumentov*, IV, 550.

9. *Ibid.*

10. *Vneshniaia Politika Sovetskovo Soiuza v Period Otechestvennoi Voiny*, III, 364.

11. *Ibid.*, 166.

12. *Vneshniaia Politika SSSR, Sbornik Dokumentov*, IV, 520–21.

13. *Vneshniaia Politika Sovetskovo Soiuza* (1949), 164.

14. Lissovskii, *op. cit.*, 260.

15. *Ibid.*, 250.

16. *Ibid.*, 248.

17. *Vneshniaia Politika Sovetskovo Soiuza v Period Otechestvennoi Voiny*, I, 127.

18. Kliuchnikov and Sabanin, *op. cit.*, II, 91.

19. Degras, *Soviet Documents on Foreign Policy*, I, 1.

20. Kliuchnikov and Sabanin, *op. cit.*, II, 107.

21. *Ibid.*, 120.

22. Degras, *Soviet Documents on Foreign Policy*, I, 61.

23. M. Litvinov, *Vneshniaia Politika SSSR, Rechi i Zaiavleniia, 1927–1937*, 400.

24. Degras, *Soviet Documents on Foreign Policy*, III, 42–43.

25. *Ibid.*, 56.

26. *Ibid.*, 57.

27. *Nazi-Soviet Relations, 1939–1941*, 77. The authenticity of German documents included in this collection was implicitly conceded in an official Soviet pamphlet which complained that the Western Powers had not published other captured German documents relating to the German-British-French diplomatic transactions in the late thirties. This pamphlet said:

The State Department of the United States of America in co-operation with the English and French Ministries of Foreign Affairs, published at the end of January [1948] a collection of reports and various notes taken from the diaries of Hitlerite diplomatic officers. . . . One circumstance attracts attention, namely the published collection includes only materials concerning the years 1939–1941.

(*Falsifikatory Istorii*, reproduced in *Vneshniaia Politika Sovetskovo Soiuza* (1948), Part 1, 59) The description of the collection is incorrect because those documents are German-Soviet agreements and German official reports. But the Soviet pamphlet did not challenge the authenticity of those documents.

28. Kliuchnikov and Sabanin, *op. cit.*, III, 342.

29. *Vneshniaia Politika SSSR, Sbornik Dokumentov*, IV, 550.

30. Quoted in Beloff, *The Foreign Policy of Soviet Russia, 1929–1941*, II, 52.

31. Degras, *Soviet Documents on Foreign Policy*, III, 383–84.

32. *Vneshniaia Politika Sovetskovo Soiuza* (1946), 135.

33. *Vneshniaia Politika SSSR, Sbornik Dokumentov*, IV, 463–64.

34. I. F. Ivashin, *Nachalo Vtoroi Mirovoi Voiny i Vneshniaia Politika SSSR*, 9–10.

35. Lissovskii, *op. cit.*, 336.

36. *Vneshniaia Politika SSSR, Sbornik Dokumentov*, IV, 468.

37. *Ibid.*, 468–69.

38. *Ibid.*, 469–70.

39. *Ibid.*, 467.

40. *Ibid.*, 471.

41. *Ibid.*, 472.

42. *Ibid.*, 472–73.

43. *Ibid.*, 492.

44. Degras, *Soviet Documents on Foreign Policy*, III, 444.

45. Lissovskii, *op. cit.*, 407.

46. *Nazi-Soviet Relations, 1939–1941*, 258–59.

47. Degras, *Soviet Documents on Foreign Policy*, III, 479.

48. *Vneshniaia Politika Sovetskovo Soiuza v Period Otechestvennoi Voiny*, II, 217.

49. *Vneshniaia Politika Sovetskovo Soiuza* (1947), Part 1, 39–54.

50. Eran von Bunsdorf, "Sovetsko-Finliandskiie otnosheniia i ukrepleniie mira v severnoi Evrope," *Mezhdunarodnaia Zhizn'*, No. 6 (June, 1957), 41.

51. Lenin, *Sochineniia*, XXXI, 106.

52. *Ibid.*, 114.

53. Kliuchnikov and Sabanin, *op. cit.*, III, 11.

54. Quoted from Clara Zetkin's book *Lenin*, 268, in Fischer, *op. cit.*, I, 270–71.

55. Lenin, *Natsional'no-kolonial'nyi Vopros*, 22.

56. Lenin, *Sochineniia*, XXXI, 281.

57. Karl Radek, *Vneshniaia Politika Sovetskoi Rossii*, 61.

58. Lenin, *Sochineniia*, XXXI, 179.

59. *Ibid.*, 241.

60. *Ibid.*, 239.

61. *Pravda*, August 3, 1920.

62. *Ibid.*

63. Fischer, *op. cit.*, I, 238.

64. Kliuchnikov and Sabanin, *op. cit.*, III, 47–49.

65. Degras, *Soviet Documents on Foreign Policy*, III, 312.

66. *Pravda*, March 17, 1939.

67. Quoted in Beloff, *The Foreign Policy of Soviet Russia, 1929–1941*, II, 78.

68. Degras, *Soviet Documents on Foreign Policy*, III, 110 and 114.

69. Molotov, *O Vneshnei Politike Sovetskovo Soiuza*, 9.

70. *Ibid.*, 3 and 7.

71. *Ibid.*, 9.

72. *Ibid.*, 5 and 6.

73. Stalin's speech of July 3, 1941, in *Vneshniaia Politika Sovetskovo Soiuza v Period Otechestvennoi Voiny*, I, 30.

74. *Vneshniaia Politika SSSR, Sbornik Dokumentov*, IV, 448.

75. Molotov, *O Vneshnei Politike Sovetskovo Soiuza*, 7.

76. *Vneshniaia Politika SSSR, Sbornik Dokumentov*, IV, 446–47.

77. The treaty is reproduced in *ibid.*, 452.

78. Lenin, *Sochineniia*, XXII, 314.

79. N. N. Petrovskii, *Vossoedineniie Ukrainskovo Naroda v Edinom Ukrainskom Sovetskom Gosudarstve*, 84.

80. T. Gorbunov, *Vossoedineniie Belorusskovo Naroda v Edinom Sovetskom Sotsialisticheskom Gosudarstve*, 179.

81. A. Abramov and K. Venskii, *Zapadnaia Ukraina i Zapadnaia Belorussiia*, 51.

82. Stalin, *Sochineniia*, XIII, 116–17.

83. *Vneshniaia Politika Sovetskovo Soiuza v Period Otechestvennoi Voiny*, II, 65.

84. *Ibid.*, III, 393.

85. Lissovskii, *op. cit.*, 90–91, 123–25, and 127.

86. Kliuchnikov and Sabanin, *op. cit.*, II, 206.

87. *Ibid.*, 207.

88. *Ibid.*, 208.

89. *Ibid.*

90. *Ibid.*, 209.

91. *Ibid.*, 253.

92. *Ibid.*, 345.

93. Lenin, *Sochineniia*, XXVIII, 205.

94. Kliuchnikov and Sabanin, *op. cit.*, III, 6.

95. *Ibid.*, 33 and 45.

96. *Ibid.*, 352.

97. *Ibid.*

98. Quoted in A. Torma and V. Raud, *Estonia, 1918–1952*, 12.

99. Quoted in A. Bilmanis (ed.), *Latvian-Russian Relations, Documents*, 170.

100. Litvinov, *op. cit.*, 362–63.

101. Molotov, *O Vneshnei Politike Sovetskovo Soiuza*, 11.

102. *Vneshniaia Politika SSSR, Sbornik Dokumentov*, IV, 511.

103. *Ibid.*, 512–13.

104. Ivashin, *Nachalo Vtoroi Mirovoi Voiny i Vneshniaia Politika SSSR*, 25.

105. M. Markov, *Sovetskaia Latviia*, 47, 50.

106. Yustas Paletskis, *Sovetskaia Litva*, 65.

107. M. Efimov, *Sovetskaia Estoniia*, 46–48.

108. *Ibid.*, 48–49.

109. Paletskis, *op. cit.*, 67–71.
110. Markov, *op. cit.*, 3.
111. *Ibid.*, 16.
112. *Vneshniaia Politika SSSR, Sbornik Dokumentov*, IV, 411.
113. Molotov, *Soviet Foreign Relations*, 8–10.
114. Lissovskii, *op. cit.*, 408.
115. Gorbunov, *op. cit.*, 166–67.
116. *The Anti-Stalin Campaign and International Communism*, 44–45, 48; similar views on the Soviet unpreparedness at the time of Nazi attack are in E. A. Boltin, "Pobeda Sovetskoi Armii pod Moskvoi v 1941 godu," *Voprosy Istorii*, No. 1 (January, 1957), 20–32.
117. G. N. Cherdantsev, ed., *Ekonomicheskaia Geografiia SSSR*, 137.
118. Quoted in Fischer, *op. cit.*, I, 311.
119. Molotov, *Voprosy Vneshnei Politiki, Rechi i Zaiavleniia, Aprel' 1945–Yun' 1948*, 255.
120. *Ibid.*, 499.
121. Grégoire Gafenco, *Préliminaires de la Guerre à l'Est*, 346–47.
122. *Vneshniaia Politika SSSR, Sbornik Dokumentov*, IV, 516–17; the ultimatum of June 26, 1940, in the same collection, 515–16.
123. *Nazi-Soviet Relations, 1939–1941*, 155–63.
124. Ivashin, and Zuev, *op. cit.*, 14.
125. Molotov, *Soviet Foreign Relations*, 7, 9.
126. *Vneshniaia Politika Sovetskovo Soiuza* (1948), Part 2, 143–44.
127. *Ibid.*, 143.
128. *Vneshniaia Politika Sovetskovo Soiuza v Period Otechestvennoi Voiny*, II, 172.
129. Ripka, *op. cit.*, 7.
130. *Ibid.*, 21–22.
131. *Vneshniaia Politika Sovetskovo Soiuza v Period Otechestvennoi Voiny*, III, 315.
132. Ripka, *op. cit.*, 22.
133. *Vneshniaia Politika Sovetskovo Soiuza v Period Otechestvennoi Voiny*, III, 315.
134. *Vneshniaia Politika Sovetskovo Soiuza* (1949), 175–76.
135. *Ibid.*, 185.
136. I. Korionov, "Oktiabr' i sud'by chelovechestva," *Mezhdunarodnaia Zhizn'*, No. 6 (June, 1957), 15–16.
137. Kliuchnikov and Sabanin, *op. cit.*, II, 95.
138. Degras, *Soviet Documents on Foreign Policy*, I, 239.
139. *Ibid.*, 347.
140. *Ibid.*, III, 33.
141. *Ibid.*, 189.
142. *Ibid.*, 194.
143. *Ibid.*, 200.
144. Molotov, *O Vneshnei Politike Sovetskovo Soiuza*, 17–18.

145. *Nazi-Soviet Relations, 1939–1941*, 258–59.
146. *Vneshniaia Politika Sovetskovo Soiuza v Period Otechestvennoi Voiny*, I, 443.
147. *Ibid.*, 146.
148. *Ibid.*, 165.
149. *Ibid.*, 166.
150. *Ibid.*, 296.
151. *Ibid.*, 272.
152. *Ibid.*, III, 146.
153. *Ibid.*, 163–64.
154. *Vneshniaia Politika Sovetskovo Soiuza* (1946), 169.
155. *Ibid.*, 198.
156. S. Dzhanashia and N. Berdzenishvili, "O nashykh zakonnykh trebovaniiakh v Turtsii," *Pravda*, December 20, 1945.
157. G. V. Khachapuridze, *Sovetskaia Gruziia*, 14.
158. The Royal Institute of International Affairs, *Documents on International Affairs*, 277–78.
159. *Bol'shaia Sovetskaia Entsiklopediia*, XIII, 107–109.
160. *Ibid.*, XLI, 464–65.
161. *Ibid.*, XLIII, 476–78.
162. *Ibid.*, XLIV, 4–6.
163. *Ibid.*, XXIV, 91–92.
164. *Ibid.*
165. Kliuchnikov and Sabanin, *op. cit.*, II, 95.
166. Leonard Shapiro, ed., *Soviet Treaty Series*, I, 150.
167. *Ibid.*, 340.
168. *Ibid.*, 341.
169. *Vneshniaia Politika Sovetskovo Soiuza v Period Otechestvennoi Voiny*, I, 156–57.
170. *Ibid.*, 218.
171. *Ibid.*, 219.
172. *Ibid.*, 220.
173. *Ibid.*, 426.
174. *Ibid.*, II, 275–77.
175. For further information, see *Vneshniaia Politika Sovetskovo Soiuza* (1946), 113–15, 123; *ibid.*, (1947), Part 2, 69–73; and George Lenczowski, *Russia and the West in Iran, 1918–1948: A Study in Big Power Rivalry*.
176. *Vneshniaia Politika Sovetskovo Soiuza* (1950), 187.
177. *Ibid.*, 133.
178. Lissovskii, *op. cit.*, 228.
179. *Vneshniaia Politika Sovetskovo Soiuza* (1947), Part 1, 35–36.
180. *China Year Book* (Shanghai, 1924), 868.
181. *Ibid.*, 870–72.
182. Shapiro, *op. cit.*, I, 138.
183. Degras, *Soviet Documents on Foreign Policy*, I, 370–71.

184. *Ibid.*, 484-87.

185. *Sovetsko-Kitaiskii Konflikt 1929 g., Sbornik Dokumentov,* 8.

186. *Ibid.*, 9.

187. *Ibid.*

188. *Ibid.*, 14-15.

189. Degras, *Soviet Documents on Foreign Policy,* I, 460.

190. *Sovetsko-Kitaiskii Konflikt 1929 g., Sbornik Dokumentov,* 33-34.

191. *Ibid.*, 37-38.

192. *Ibid.*, 76-77.

193. *Ibid.*, 84-86.

194. *Ibid.*, 89.

195. Litvinov, *op. cit.*, 349.

196. *Ibid.*, 348-50.

197. Degras, *Soviet Documents on Foreign Policy,* I, 187-88.

198. *Vneshniaia Politika Sovetskovo Soiuza v Period Otechestvennoi Voiny,* III, 460.

199. *Ibid.*, 474.

200. *Vneshniaia Politika Sovetskovo Soiuza* (1949), 124.

201. *Ibid.*, 171-73.

202. Max Beloff, *Soviet Policy in the Far East, 1944-1951,* 48.

203. *Vneshniaia Politika Sovetskovo Soiuza* (1945), 135.

204. *Vneshniaia Politika Sovetskovo Soiuza v Period Otechestvennoi Voiny,* III, 461-66.

205. *Ibid.*, 467-68.

206. *Ibid.*, 475.

207. *Vneshniaia Politika Sovetskovo Soiuza* (1945), 143-44.

208. *Ibid.* (1950), 59.

209. *Ibid.*, 61-63.

210. *Ibid.*, 122-24.

211. *Pravda,* September 16, 1952.

212. *Pravda,* October 12, 1954.

213. See Dimitrios G. Kousoulas, *The Price of Freedom: Greece in World Affairs, 1939-1953.*

214. See, for instance, Leland M. Goodrich, *Korea: A Study of U.S. Policy in the United Nations.*

215. *Vneshniaia Politika Sovetskovo Soiuza* (1949), 145.

216. *Ibid.*, 146.

217. The Soviet note to Belgrade of August 29, 1949, in *ibid.*, 151-59.

218. *Ibid.*, 105-108.

219. *Ibid.*, 139.

220. *Ibid.*

221. *Ibid.*, 143.

222. *Ibid.* (1948), Part 2, 139.

223. *Ibid.* (1949), 77-79.

224. *The Soviet-Yugoslav Dispute*, 19.
225. *Pravda*, October 12, 1954.

CHAPTER XII

1. See, for instance, Walter Kolarz, *Russia and Her Colonies.*
2. *Spravochnik Propagandista i Agitatora*, 7.
3. *Ibid.*, 170.
4. Cherdantsev, *op. cit.*, 5–6.
5. *Ibid.*, 117.
6. *Ibid.*, 143, 155.
7. *Spravochnik Propagandista i Agitatora*, 191, and Cherdantsev, *op. cit.*, 99.
8. Is. Slonim, *Spravochnik po Georgrafii dla Uchitelei Nachalnoi Shkoly*, 222–23.
9. *Ibid.*, 222.
10. A. F. Yakunin, *Narody Srednei Azii i Kazakhstana vo Vtoroi Polovine 19 Veka: Prisoedineniie Srednei Azii k Rossii*, 15.
11. Radzhabov, *op. cit.*, 170.
12. Lenin, *Sochineniia*, XXIV, 265.
13. Degras, *Soviet Documents on Foreign Policy*, I, 16.
14. Stalin, *Marksizm i Natsional'no-kolonial'nyi Vopros*, 55.
15. Chugaev, *op. cit.*, 31–32, 34.
16. Quoted in *ibid.*, 43–44.
17. *Ibid.*, 44.
18. *Ibid.*, 21 and 25.
19. Kliuchnikov and Sabanin, *op. cit.*, II, 99.
20. Quoted in Richard Pipes, *The Formation of the Soviet Union: Communism and Nationalism, 1917–1923*, 121–22.
21. Chugaev, *op. cit.*, 28–30.
22. *Ibid.*, 38–39.
23. *Ibid.*, 39–40.
24. Kliuchnikov and Sabanin, *op. cit.*, II, 223–24.
25. *Ibid.*, III, 22.
26. *Ibid.*, II, 209–10.
27. Articles 1, 2, and 6 of the Treaty in Kliuchnikov and Sabanin, *op. cit.*, III, 22–23.
28. Kliuchnikov and Sabanin, *op. cit.*, III, 74.
29. *Ibid.*, 76.
30. Quoted in Pipes, *op. cit.*, 230.
31. Kliuchnikov and Sabanin, *op. cit.*, III, 87.
32. Khachapuridze, *op. cit.*, 60–61.
33. Chugaev, *op. cit.*, 46.
34. Klych Kuliyev, *Bor'ba Kommunisticheskoi Partii za Uprocheniie*

Sovetskoi Vlasti i Osushchestvleniie Natsional'noi Politiki v Srednei Azii, 1917-1925 gg., 14-15 and 18.

35. *Ibid.,* 21.
36. *Ibid.,* 25.
37. *Ibid.,* 51.
38. *Ibid.,* 53.
39. Radzhabov, *op. cit.,* 131-32 and 136.
40. Kuliyev, *op. cit.,* 39.
41. Kliuchnikov and Sabanin, *op. cit.,* III, 61.
42. Shapiro, *op. cit.,* I, 98.
43. Kuliyev, *op. cit.,* 53.
44. *Ibid.*
45. Degras, *Soviet Documents on Foreign Policy,* I, 235.
46. Chugaev, *op. cit.,* 47.
47. *Ibid.,* 62.
48. *Ibid.,* 69 and 88.
49. *Ibid.,* 70.
50. *Ibid.,* 72 and 75.
51. *Ibid.,* 87-88.
52. *Ibid.,* 89-90.
53. Pankratova *et al., op. cit.,* 394.
54. *Pravda,* January 12, 1954.
55. Radzhabov, *op. cit.,* 4.
56. "S'yezd intelligentsii Uzbekistana," *Pravda Vostoka,* October 13, 1956.
57. *Pravda,* June 14, 1957.
58. Cherdantsev, *op. cit.,* 322.
59. Kuliyev, *op. cit.,* 9-10.
60. Radzhabov, *op. cit.,* 3-6, 12-13, 22, and 30.
61. *Ibid.,* 33.
62. *Ibid.,* 34.
63. *Ibid.,* 59; the same arguments in defense of the Tsarist annexation of central Asia are submitted in Yakunin, *op. cit.,* 21-22, and T. N. Kary-Niiazov, *Ocherki Istorii Kul'tury Sovetskovo Uzbekistana,* 48-49, 51, and 114-15.
64. I. M. Gassanov and I. V. Strigunov, Review of A. A. Sumbatzade *et al., Prisoedineniie Azerbaijana k Rossii i Evo Progressivnye Posledstviia v Oblasti Ekonomiki i Kul'tury (XIX-nach. XX vv.),* in *Sovetskoe Vostokovedeniie,* No. 5 (1956), 137.
65. *Armianskaia SSR,* 42.
66. Cherdantsev, *op. cit.,* 137 and 198.
67. S. N. Riazantsev, *Kirghiziia,* 48.
68. P. Nikitich, A. Tokombaev and K. Yudakhin, "Zabytoe bogatstvo," *Literaturnaia Gazeta,* June 21, 1956.
69. *Pravda Vostoka,* October 13, 1956.

70. *Ibid.*

71. *Ibid.*

72. Radzhabov, *op. cit.*, 87.

73. "K diskussii o kharaktere dvizheniia gortsev Daghestana pod rukovodstvom Shamiliia," *Voprosy Istorii*, No. 1 (January, 1957), 195.

74. *Ibid.*, 195–96.

75. *Kommunist Tadjikstana*, November 23, 1956.

76. Editorial, "Strogo sobliudat' leninskii printsip partiinosti v istoricheskoi nauke," *Kommunist*, No. 4 (March, 1957), 25–26.

77. Vassil'ev and Khrustov, *op. cit.*, 47.

78. Radzhabov, *op. cit.*, 3–4.

79. A. Kirichenko, "Nasha slava v druzhbe narodov. Ukrainskii narod gotovitsia dostoino vstretit' 40-letie Velikovo Oktiabria," *Pravda*, April 7, 1957.

80. *Pravda Vostoka*, October 13, 1956.

81. *Kommunist Tadjikstana*, November 24, 1956.

82. *Kommunist Tadjikstana*, November 23, 1956.

83. "Za dalneishii rastsvet kul'tury kazakhskovo naroda," *Kazakhstanskaia Pravda*, January 31, 1957.

84. Stalin, *Marksizm i Natsional'no-kolonial'nyi Vopros*, 194.

85. *Bol'shaia Sovetskaia Entsiklopediia*, XXIX, 290.

86. Kary-Niiazov, *op. cit.*, 128–30.

87. *KPSS v Rezoliutsiiakh i Resheniiakh S'yezdov, Konferentsii i Plenumov TsK*, I, 562.

88. *Pravda Vostoka*, October 13, 1956.

89. *Ibid.*

90. *Kommunist Tadjikstana*, November 23, 1956.

91. *Sovetskaia Litva*, December 9, 1956.

92. *Pravda*, December 4, 1956.

93. *Pravda*, April 7, 1957.

94. *Pravda*, June 14, 1957.

95. See Khrushchev's speech of February 25, 1956, in *The Anti-Stalin Campaign and International Communism*, 57.

96. *Ibid.*, 58–59.

97. *Ibid.*, 57.

98. *Pravda*, February 12, 1957.

99. Cherdantsev, *op. cit.*, 35.

100. Quoted in T. Borisov, *Kalmykiia*, 88.

101. Lissovskii, *op. cit.*, 102.

102. Stalin, *Marksizm i National'no-kolonial'nyi Vopros*, 49.

103. Raimov, *op. cit.*, 14.

104. *Kazakhstanskaia Pravda*, February 20, 1957.

105. *Kazakhstanskaia Pravda*, January 31, 1957.

106. *Ibid.*

107. Yakunin, *op. cit.*, 18.

108. *Kazakhstanskaia Pravda,* January 31, 1957.
109. *Ibid.*
110. *Armianskaia SSR,* 51.
111. Cherdantsev, *op. cit.,* 36.
112. *Ibid.,* 143.
113. *Ibid.,* 155.
114. *Ibid.,* 99.
115. *Ibid.,* 279.
116. *Ibid.,* 338.
117. *Ibid.,* 339.
118. *Ibid.,* 391.
119. *Ibid.,* 411.
120. Lenin, *Natsional'no-kolonial'nyi Vopros,* 29.
121. *Ibid.,* 36.
122. Stalin, *Natsional'nyi Vopros i Leninizm,* 19.
123. *Ibid.,* 15.
124. These statistics are to be found in *Kul'turnoe Stroitel'stvo SSSR, Statisticheskii Sbornik,* 186–87.
125. *Pravda Vostoka,* October 13, 1956.
126. The regulations for both types of school are reproduced in *Spravochnik dlia Postupaiushchikh v Vyssheie, Sredniie Spetsial'-nye Uchebnye Zavedeniia (Tekhnikumy, Uchilishcha, Shkoly), i Tekhnicheskiie Uchilishcha Moskvy i Moskovskoi Oblasti v 1956 Godu,* 5–6.
127. *Ibid.,* 6.
128. E. N. Medynskii, *Prosveshcheniie v SSSR,* 70–71.
129. *Ibid.,* 88.
130. *Ibid.,* 89.
131. *Pravda Vostoka,* October 11, 1956.
132. *Pravda Vostoka,* August 22, 1956.
133. *Pravda Vostoka,* October 13, 1956.
134. *Kommunist Tadjikstana,* November 24, 1956.
135. *Ibid.*
136. *Pravda Vostoka,* October 13, 1956.
137. *Uchitelskaia Gazeta,* January 24, 1957.
138. M. M. Deineko, ed., *Spravochnik Direktora Shkoly, Sbornik Postanovlenii, Prikazov, Instruktsii i Drugikh Rukovodiashchikh Materialov o Shkole,* 150.
139. Chugaev, *op cit.,* 102.
140. Radzhabov, *op. cit.,* 191.
141. Yakunin, *op cit.,* 18.
142. Kary-Niiazov, *op. cit.,* 71.
143. Shimbiriov and Ogorodnikov, *op. cit.,* 32.
144. Kary-Niiazov, *op. cit.,* 260–61.
145. *Ibid.,* 261.
146. *Ibid.,* 262–63.

147. *Ibid.*, 272–73.

148. K. M. Kuliyev, minister of culture of the Turkmenian SSR, and I. L. Repin, vice-minister of culture of the Turkmenian SSR, "Razvitiie i pod'-iom sotsialisticheskoi kul'tury i nauki v Turkmenskoi SSR," *Sovetskoe Vostokovedeniie,* No. 2 (1956), 73.

149. A. K. Borovkov, "K voprosu ob unifikatsii tiurkskikh alfavitov v SSSR," *Sovetskoe Vostokovedeniie,* No. 4 (1956), 100.

150. Kary-Niiazov, *op. cit.,* 73–74 and 261–62.

151. *Ibid.,* 266.

152. *Ibid.,* 277.

153. *Ibid.,* 276.

154. *Ibid.,* 106.

155. *Ibid.,* 259.

156. *Ibid.,* 267.

157. *Ibid.,* 322.

158. "Za dal'neishii rastsvet kul'tury kazakhskovo naroda," *Kazakhstanskaia Pravda,* January 31, 1957.

159. Radzhabov, *op. cit.,* 191.

160. *Kul'turnoe Stroitel'stvo SSSR, Statisticheskii Sbornik,* 320.

161. *Ibid.,* 318–19.

162. *Ibid.,* 254.

163. Quoted in Miliukov and Fuzeev, "Siriiskii narod v bor'be za ukrepleniie natsional'noi nezavisimosti," *Mezhdunarodnaia Zhizn,'* No. 12 (1956), 74.

164. Chugaev, *op. cit.,* 100.

CHAPTER XIII

1. Quoted from Lenin's notes on national question, a copy made by Trotsky and held at the Harvard College Library, Trotsky Archive, in Pipes, *op. cit.,* 274.

2. *Communist International,* No. 7 (December, 1924), p. 96.

3. *Vneshniaia Politika Sovetskovo Soiuza v Period Otechestvennoi Voiny,* I, 49.

4. This was done in the Declaration by United Nations, January 1, 1942, which the USSR signed, together with all the other members of a coalition (*A Decade of American Foreign Policy, Basic Documents, 1941–1949,* 2–3).

5. Quoted in Ivashin, *Vsemirno-istoricheskoe Znacheniie Velikoi Oktiabrskoi Sotsialisticheskoi Revolutsii,* 71.

6. *Vneshniaia Politika Sovetskovo Soiuza v Period Otechestvennoi Voiny,* I, 118–19.

7. *Vneshniaia Politika Sovetskovo Soiuza* (1946), 50.

8. *A Decade of American Foreign Policy,* 29.

9. Ivashin, *Vsemirno-istoricheskoe Znacheniie Velikoi Oktiabrskoi Sotsialisticheskoi Revolutsii*, 86.

10. P. V. Galenko, *Stroitel'stvo Sotsialisticheskoi Ekonomiki v Polskoi Narodnoi Respublike*, 34.

11. *Vneshniaia Politika Sovetskovo Soiuza v Period Otechestvennoi Voiny*, I, 399.

12. *Ibid.*, II, 92.

13. *Ibid.*, 155.

14. *Ibid.*, III, 61–62.

15. *A Decade of American Foreign Policy*, 30.

16. See, for the description of events of that period, the books written by two eye-witnesses: S. Mikolajczyk, *The Rape of Poland: Pattern of Soviet Aggression*, and Arthur Bliss Lane, the American Ambassador to Poland at that time, *I saw Poland Betrayed*.

17. Donskoi, *op. cit.*, 73.

18. Galenko, *op. cit.*, 114.

19. *Ibid.*, 182.

20. *Ibid.*, 183.

21. For an excellent description of the merger, see Ygael Gluckstein, *op. cit.*, 173–81.

22. *Głos Pracy*, November 28, 1952.

23. *Vneshniaia Politika Sovetskovo Soiuza v Period Otechestvennoi Voiny*, III, 137–38.

24. The verbatim text was printed in *Tarsadalmi Szemle* in March 1952, and was reproduced in English translation in *News From Behind the Iron Curtain*, No. 5 (May, 1952), 43–47.

25. *Ibid.*

26. Michael Padev, *Dimitrov Wastes No Bullets; Nikola Petkov: The Test Case*, 46–47.

27. *Ibid.*, 49.

28. *Ibid.*, 55.

29. *Ibid.*, 153.

30. *Ibid.*

31. Ripka, *op. cit.*, 2.

32. *Ibid.*, 331.

33. *The Soviet-Yugoslav Dispute*, 70.

34. *Ibid.*, 20.

35. *Ibid.*, 29.

36. See R. L. Wolff, *The Balkans in Our Time*, 336–37.

37. *Vneshniaia Politika Sovetskovo Soiuza* (1950), 163.

38. *The Anti-Stalin Campaign and International Communism*, 62–63.

39. *Pravda*, June 3, 1955.

40. *Pravda*, March 29, 1957.

41. *Pravda*, April 18, 1957.

42. See Kazimierz Grzybowski, "Foreign Investment and Political Con-

trol in Eastern Europe," *Journal of Central European Affairs,* No. 1 (April, 1953); and Wolff, *op. cit.,* 345–46, 517–35.

43. Mikolajczyk, *op. cit.,* 141–42.

44. Editorial, "Patriotyzm a ekonomika," *Po Prostu,* No. 46 (November 11, 1956).

45. *Ibid.*

46. Jerzy Piórkowski, "Suwerenność—rzecz realna i znana," *Nowe Drogi,* No. 11–12 (November-December, 1956), 122.

47. *Nowe Drogi,* No. 10 (October, 1956), 123.

48. Sergeev, *op. cit.,* 38–39.

49. *Ibid.,* 39.

50. *Ibid.,* 29.

51. *Ibid.,* 31.

52. *Ibid.,* 32.

53. *Ibid.,* 37–38.

54. "October's Aftermath," *East Europe,* No. 4 (April, 1957), 3–8.

55. *1956 Economic Survey of Europe* (United Nations, 1957) Chap. 1, 18–19.

56. *Ibid.,* Chap. 2, 2.

57. See V. Gsovski, ed., *Church and State Behind the Iron Curtain.*

58. *Nowe Drogi,* No. 10 (October, 1956) (the verbatim records of the 8th Plenum of the Central Committee of the Polish United Workers' Party) pp. 60–61.

59. *Ibid.,* 61.

60. Mieczysław Górski, "Uwaga, histerja," *Po Prostu,* No. 19 (May 6, 1956).

61. Galenko, *op. cit.,* 190–91, 211, 230, and 244.

62. V. M. Molotov, A. Mikoyan, N. Khrushchev, *et al., Stalin,* 88–94.

63. *Nowe Drogi,* No. 10 (October, 1956), 267–68.

64. Gomulka, "Uzlovye problemy politiki partii," *Kommunist,* No. 7 (May, 1957), 68.

65. Jerzy Kossak, "Do przyjaciela," *Po Prostu,* No. 13 (March 25, 1956).

66. *Nowe Drogi,* No. 10 (October, 1956), 219.

67. Jan Stanisławski, "Czy jestem chorągiewką?" *Po Prostu,* No. 13 (March 25, 1956).

68. *Pravda,* June 23, 1953.

69. *Nowe Drogi,* No. 10 (October, 1956), 116.

70. *Ibid.,* 137–38.

71. *Ibid.,* 162.

72. *Ibid.,* 14.

73. *Ibid.,* 17.

74. *Ibid.,* 113.

75. *Ibid.,* 148.

76. *Ibid.,* 58.

77. *Ibid.,* 146.

78. *Trybuna Ludu,* November 15, 1956.

79. *Pravda,* October 31, 1956.

80. *Ibid.*

81. *Pravda,* June 30, 1957.

82. Mieczysław Jastruń, "O wolność słowa," *Po Prostu,* No. 50 (December 9, 1956).

83. Witold Wirpsza in *Życie Literackie,* May 16, 1954.

84. Henryk Vogler in *Życie Literackie,* May 9, 1954.

85. *Nowa Kultura,* August 22, 1954.

86. Andrzej Borkowicz, "Index Librorum Prohibitorum," *Po Prostu,* No. 24 (June 10, 1956).

87. *Ibid.*

88. Jerzy Szacki, "Uwagi o historji Marksizmu," *Po Prostu,* No. 43 (October 21, 1956).

89. N. Khrushchev, "Za tesnuiu sviaz' literatury i iskusstva z zhizniu naroda," *Kommunist,* No. 12 (August, 1957), 11–29.

90. Leopold Infeld, "O godność nauki," *Przegląd Kulturalny,* No. 25 (June 21, 1956).

91. Janusz Kuczyński, "Administratorstwo i apolityczność," *Po Prostu,* No. 25 (June 17, 1956).

92. *Ibid.*

93. Edda Werfel, "Do towarzyszy z bratnich partii," *Przegląd Kulturalny,* No. 44 (November 1, 1956).

94. *Nowe Drogi,* No. 10 (October, 1956), 171.

95. *Ibid.,* 197.

96. *Ibid.,* 247.

97. J. K. N., "Kto, za co i przed kim odpowiada?" *Nowe Drogi,* No. 1 (January, 1957), 15.

98. Jadwiga Siekierska, "O potrzebie tolerancji," *Nowe Drogi,* No. 2 (February, 1957), 82, 84, 86–89.

99. Kossak, "Do przyjaciela," *Po Prostu,* No. 13 (March 25, 1956).

100. Henry Jankowski, "Jednostka niczym?" *Po Prostu,* No. 38 (September 16, 1956).

101. Henryk Jankowski, "Opinje, moralność, polityka," *Po Prostu,* No. 35 (August 26, 1956).

102. Jadwiga Siekierska, "Czy tragedja optymistyczna?" *Po Prostu,* No. 49 (December 2, 1956).

103. Mieczysław Maneli, "O cywilnej odwadze," *Po Prostu,* No. 47 (November 18, 1956).

104. Mieczysław Wojnar, "Myśli," *Po Prostu,* No. 47 (November 18, 1956).

105. Janusz Kuczyński, "W poszukiwaniu utraconych wartości," *Po Prostu,* No. 49 (December 2, 1956).

106. Edda Werfel, "Do towarzyszy z bratnich partii,"*Przegląd Kulturalny,* No. 44 (November 1, 1956).

107. *Ibid.*

108. *Nowe Drogi*, No. 10 (October, 1956), 60.

109. *Ibid.*, 63.

110. *Nowe Drogi*, No. 10 (October, 1956), 106.

111. *Ibid.*, 174.

112. *Ibid.*, 206.

113. J. K. N., "Kto, za co i przed kim odpowiada?" *Nowe Drogi*, No. 1 (January, 1957), 15–17 and 23.

114. Roman Werfel, "O niektórych sprzecznościach naszego okresu," *Nowe Drogi*, No. 2 (February, 1957), 68.

115. Roman Jurys, "Niektóre problemy naszej partji," *Nowe Drogi*, No. 2 (February, 1957), 75.

116. Kossak, "Do przyjaciela," *Po Prostu*, No. 13 (March 25, 1956).

117. Anna Bukowska, "Przeciw funkcji zawodowego rewolucjonisty," *Po Prostu*, No. 35 (August 26, 1956).

118. Janusz Kuczyński, "W poszukiwaniu utraconych wartości," *Po Prostu*, No. 49 (December 2, 1956).

119. Stanisław Chełstowski and Włodzimierz Godek, "Pierwszy zwiad," *Po Prostu*, No. 44 (October 28, 1956).

120. Paul E. Zinner, ed., *National Communism and Popular Revolt in Eastern Europe*, 200.

121. *Ibid.*, 211.

122. *Ibid.*, 204.

123. *Ibid.*, 202.

124. *Ibid.*, 205.

125. *Nowe Drogi*, No. 10 (October, 1956), 119, 122–23.

126. *Ibid.*, 142.

127. *Ibid.*, 170.

128. Edward Lipiński, "Model gospodarki socjalistycznej," *Nowe Drogi*, No. 11–12 (November–December, 1956).

129. *Ibid.*

130. Lenin, *Sochineniia*, XXXII, 40–41.

131. M. Borowska, J. Balcerek and L. Gilejko, "Miejsce rad robotniczych w naszym modelu gospodarczym," *Nowe Drogi*, No. 2 (February, 1957), 14.

132. *Ibid.*, 27.

133. Gomulka, "Uzlovye problemy politiki partii," *Kommunist*, No. 7 (May, 1957), 47–49.

134. *Nowe Drogi*, No. 10 (October, 1956), 163, 178–79, 197, 198–200, 218, 219, 246–47.

135. Jerzy Wiatr, "Kryzys internacjonalizmu," *Nowe Drogi*, No. 11–12 (November–December, 1956), 110–11 and 117.

136. Piórkowski, "Suwerenność—rzecz realna i znana," *Nowe Drogi*, No. 11–12 (November–December, 1956), 121–23.

137. Jerzy Kossak, Ryszard Turski and Roman Zimand, "Internacjonalizm," *Po Prostu*, No. 44 (October 28, 1956).

138. *Ibid.*

139. Editorial, "Sprawy Polaków," *Po Prostu*, No. 45 (November 4, 1956).

140. *Ibid.*

141. Roman Zimand, "O komuniźmie narodowym," *Po Prostu*, No. 8 (February 24, 1957).

142. Krystyna Zielińska, "Przyjaźń na koturnach," *Po Prostu*, No. 45 (November 4, 1956).

143. Gomulka, "Uzlovye problemy politiki partii," *Kommunist*, No. 7 (May, 1957), 74.

144. *Pravda*, June 30, 1957.

145. *Vneshniaia Politika Sovetskovo Soiuza* (1950), 125.

146. *Report of the Special Committee on the Problem of Hungary* (New York, United Nations, 1957); two other documentary sources on this same problem are: Zinner, *op. cit.*, 317–481, and *The Revolt in Hungary: A Documentary Chronology of Events, October 23, 1956–November 4, 1956* (this publication consists of monitored broadcasts by the Hungarian radio stations).

147. *Report of the Special Committee on the Problem of Hungary*, 5.

148. The text of the sixteen points in *ibid.*, 69.

149. *Ibid.*, 8.

150. *Ibid.*, 43.

151. *Ibid.*, 137.

152. *Ibid.*, 44.

153. Roman Zimand, "Sprawy robotników całego świata," *Po Prostu*, No. 45 (November 4, 1956).

154. B. Ponomarev, "Proval agressivnykh zamyslov mezhdunarodnoi reakstii," *Pravda*, January 4, 1957.

155. *Report of the Special Committee on the Problem of Hungary*, 79.

156. Lissovskii, *op. cit.*, 89.

157. *American Foreign Policy, 1950–1955, Basic Documents*, I, 1241.

158. *United Nations, Report of the Special Committee on the Question of Defining Aggression*, Annex II, Document A/AC 77/L. 4.

159. *Report of the Special Committee on the Problem of Hungary*, 24.

160. *Ibid.*, 26–27.

161. *Ibid.*, 98.

162. *Ibid.*, 28.

163. *Ibid.*, 101.

164. *Ibid.*, 42.

165. *Ibid.*, 46.

166. *Ibid.*

167. See Mikolajczyk, *op. cit.*, 111–12 and 129.

168. *Report of the Special Committee on the Problem of Hungary*, 45–46.

169. *Ibid.*, 107.

170. *Ibid.*, 58.

171. *Ibid.*

172. *Ibid.*, 59.

173. The text of this treaty is reproduced in *ibid.*, 60–62.

174. *Ibid.*, 60.

175. *Ibid.*, 127.

176. Quoted from *Nepszabadsag*, May 12, 1957 in *ibid.*, 112–13.

177. Lenin, *Natsional'no-kolonial'nyi Vopros*, 68.

178. *Ibid.*, 19.

179. *Pravda*, March 29, 1957.

180. *Ibid.*

181. Paul de Groot, "Sovremennye sobytiia v svete leninizma," reprinted from the Dutch newspaper *De Vaarheid in Kommunist*, No. 2 (February, 1957), 65.

182. *Ibid.*, 63.

183. Lissovskii, *op. cit.*, 6.

184. Shishkin, *op. cit.*, 207.

CHAPTER XIV

1. *Pravda,* January 6, 1957.

2. *Pravda*, April 12, 1957.

3. De Groot, "Sovremennye sobytiia v svete leninizma," *Kommunist*, No. 2 (February, 1957), 56.

4. *The Anti-Stalin Campaign and International Communism,* 97–139.

5. Shitarev, "Edinstvo—istochnik nepobedimosti marksistsko-leninskoi partii," *Kommunist*, No. 5 (April, 1957), 32.

6. Editorial, "Vyshe znamia marksistsko-leninskoi ideologii," *Kommunist*, No. 1 (January, 1957), 11.

7. Lenin, *Sochineniia*, XXVIII, 197.

8. *Pravda,* March 29, 1957.

9. *Pravda*, April 18, 1957.

10. *Pravda*, April 17, 1957.

11. For instance, Editorial, "Krepnushchee edinstvo stran sotsialisticheskovo sodruzhestva," *Mezhdunarodnaia Zhizn'*, No. 2 (1957), 3–10; Editorial, "V. I. Lenin i natsional'no-osvoboditel'naia bor'ba narodov Vostoka," *Sovetskoe Vostokovedeniie*, No. 2 (1957), 4–12; T. Timofeev, "O nekotorykh voprosakh proletarskovo internatsionalizma," *Mezhdunarodnaia Zhizn'*, No. 5 (May, 1957), 41–51; Berkov, "Edinstvo i splochennost'— zalog novykh uspekhov mezhdunarodnovo kommunisticheskovo dvizheniia," *Kommunist*, No. 6 (April, 1957), 114–19; Editorial, "Vyshe znamia marksistsko-leninskoi ideologii," *Kommunist*, No. 1 (January, 1957), 3–22; Romanov, "Nerushimoe ideinoe edinstvo kommunisticheskikh partii," *Mezhdunarodnaia Zhizn'*, No. 11 (November, 1956), 16–26; Potelov, "Raz-

vitiie sotsializma i proletarskii internatsionalizm," *Kommunist*, No. 1 (January, 1957), 15–30.

12. Editorial, "Vyshe znamia marksistsko-leninskoi ideologii," *Kommunist*, No. 1(January, 1957), 20.

13. "Iz materialov XVII s'yezda kommunisticheskoi partii Avstrii," *Kommunist*, No. 6 (April, 1957), 97–98.

14. Gomulka, "Uzlovye problemy politiki partii," *Kommunist*, No. 7 (May, 1957), 44–45.

15. "Eshcho raz ob istoricheskom opyte diktatury proletariata," reprinted from *Zhen'min'zhibao*, December 29, 1956, in *Mezhdunarodnaia Zhizn'*, No. 1 (January, 1957), 32–33.

16. Editorial, "Nepreoborimaia sila leninizma," *Kommunist*, No. 5 (April, 1957), 15.

17. Timofeev, "O nekotorykh voprosakh proletarskovo internatsionalizma," *Mezhdunarodnaia Zhizn'*, No. 5 (May, 1957), 45.

18. *Ibid.*, 49.

19. Berkov, "Edinstvo i splochennost'—zalog novykh uspekhov mezhdunarodnovo kommunisticheskovo dvizheniia," *Kommunist*, No. 6 (April, 1957), 116–17.

20. Shepilov's speech on February 12, 1957, in his capacity of foreign minister, *Pravda*, February 13, 1957.

21. Timofeev, "O nekotorykh voprosakh proletarskovo internatsionalizma," *Mezhdunarodnaia Zhizn'*, No. 5 (May, 1957), 50.

22. A. Butenko, "O sotsializme i evo 'gumanisticheskikh' kritikakh," *Kommunist*, No. 5 (April, 1957), 102.

23. "Iz materialov XVII s'yezda kommunisticheskoi partii Avstrii," *Kommunist*, No. 6 (April, 1957), 95.

24. Gomulka, "Uzlovye problemy politiki partii," *Kommunist*, No. 7 (May, 1957), 86.

25. *Ibid.*, 42–44.

26. *Ibid.*, 45.

27. Shitarev, "Edinstvo—istochnik nepobedimosti marksistsko-leninskoi partii," *Kommunist*, No. 5 (April, 1957), 27.

28. Potelov, "Razvitiie sotsialisma i proletarskii internatsionalism," *Kommunist*, No. 1 (January, 1957), 20–22.

29. *Ibid.*, 21.

30. Cf. the joint Soviet-Hungarian Declaration of March 28, 1957, in *Pravda*, March 29, 1957; the joint Soviet-Albanian Declaration of April 18, 1957, in *Pravda*, April 19, 1957 (both declarations stressed that there was only one common road to socialism but allowed for specific forms of adjustments to local conditions); Suslov's speech in *Pravda*, April 17, 1957, in which he insisted on the identity of fundamental features of the process of building socialism but acknowledged the legitimacy of variations in local forms and methods.

31. Editorial, "Nepreoborimaia sila leninizma," *Kommunist*, No. 5 (April, 1957), 14.

32. *Pravda*, April 18, 1957.

33. Editorial, "Nepreoborimaia sila leninizma," *Kommunist*, No. 5 (April, 1957), 6 and 8–9.

34. Shitarev, "Edinstvo—istochnik nepobedimosti marksistsko-leninskoi partii," *Kommunist*, No. 5 (April, 1957), 27.

35. *Ibid.*, 25 and 33.

36. Gomulka, "Uzlovye problemy politiki partii," *Kommunist*, No. 7 (May, 1957), 69 and 74.

37. *Ibid.*, 84.

38. Roger Garaudy, "Problem svobody v svete sovremennoi ideologicheskoi bor'by," *Kommunist*, No. 5 (April, 1957), 49.

39. Editorial, "V. I. Lenin i natsional'no-osvoboditel'naia bor'ba narodov Vostoka," *Sovetskoe Vostokovedeniie*, No. 2 (1957), 11.

40. Shitarev, "Edinstvo—istochnik nepobedimosti marksistsko-leninskoi partii," *Kommunist*, No. 5 (April, 1957), 38.

41. A. Butenko, "O sotsializme i evo 'gumanisticheskikh' kritikakh," *Kommunist*, No. 5 (April, 1957), 105, 107–08.

42. Lenin, *Sochineniia*, XXVIII, 103.

43. *Ibid.*, XXXI, 5–6.

44. Editorial "Nepreoborimaia sila leninizma," *Kommunist*, No. 5 (April, 1957), 17.

45. Cf. editorial, "Vyshe znamia marksistsko-leninskoi ideologii," *Kommunist*, No. 1 (January, 1957), 10–11; the joint Soviet-Albanian Declaration of April 17, 1957, in *Pravda*, April 18, 1957; Editorial, "Krepnushchee edinstvo stran sotsialisticheskovo sodruzhestva," *Mezhdunarodnaia Zhizn'*, No. 2 (1957), 9; the joint Soviet-Hungarian Declaration of March 28, 1957, in *Pravda*, March 29, 1957.

46. *Bol'shaia Sovetskaia Entsiklopediia*, XXII, 259.

47. Degras, *The Communist International, 1919–1943, Documents*, I, 21.

48. *Vneshniaia Politika Sovetskovo Soiuza v Period Otechestvennoi Voiny*, I, 104–105.

49. Potelov, "Razvitiie sotsializma i proletarskii internatsionalizm," *Kommunist*, No. 1 (January, 1957), 28–29.

50. *Ibid.*, 28.

51. "Informatsionnoe soobshcheniie o prekrashchenii deiatel'nosti Informatsionnovo Biuro kommunisticheskikh i rabochikh partii," *Pravda*, April 18, 1956.

52. I. Potelov, *op. cit.*, 19, 27, 29.

53. Cf. Al. Romanov, "Nerushimoe ideinoe edinstvo kommunisticheskikh partii," *Mezhdunarodnaia Zhizn'*, No. 11 (November, 1956), 18–19; Potelov, "Razvitiie sotsializma i proletarskii internatsionalizm," *Kommunist*, No. 1 (January, 1957), 26; the joint Soviet-Albanian Declaration of

April 17, 1957, in *Pravda*, April 18, 1957; Bulganin's speech of April 16, 1957, in *Pravda*, April 17, 1957.

54. Reprinted in *Mezhdunarodnaia Zhizn'*, No. 1 (January, 1957), 16–36.

55. *Ibid.*, 32.

56. "Manifest Mira," *Pravda*, November 23, 1957.

57. "Deklaratsiia Soveshchaniia predstavitelei kommunisticheskikh i rabochikh partii sotsialisticheskikh stran, sostoiavshevosia v Moskve 14–16 noiabria 1957 goda," *Pravda*, November 22, 1957.

58. *Ibid.*

59. *Ibid.*

60. *Ibid.*

61. *Ibid.*

62. *Ibid.*

63. *Ibid.*

64. *Ibid.*

65. *Ibid.*

66. *Ibid.*

67. *Ibid.*

68. *Pravda*, April 23, 1958.

69. *Ibid.*

70. P. Fedoseev, I. Potelov, and V. Cheprakov, "O proekte programmy Soiuza kommunistov Yugoslavii," *Kommunist*, No. 6 (April, 1958), 16.

71. *Ibid.*, 16.

72. *Ibid.*, 23.

73. *Ibid.*, 18–20.

74. *Ibid.*, quoted on p. 20.

75. *Ibid.*, 20.

76. *Ibid.*, 24–25.

77. *Ibid.*, 25–30.

78. *Ibid.*, 31.

79. *Ibid.*, 25.

80. *Ibid.*, 35–36.

81. "Sovremennyi revizionizm dolzhen byt' osuzhden," reprinted in *Pravda*, May 6, 1958.

82. *Ibid.*

83. "V edinstve i splochennosti marksistsko-leninskikh partii—zalog dal'neishikh pobed mirovoi sotsialisticheskoi sistemy," *Pravda*, May 9, 1958.

84. *Ibid.*

85. *Ibid.*

86. *Ibid.*

87. *Ibid.*

88. *Pravda*, May 30, 1958.

89. *Pravda*, June 4, 1958.

90. *Pravda*, June 17, 1958.

91. *Ibid.*

92. *Ibid.*
93. *Pravda,* June 4, 1958.
94. *Pravda,* May 16, 1958.
95. *Ibid.*
96. *Pravda,* January 28, 1959.
97. *Pravda,* March 20, 1959.
98. *Pravda,* March 17, 1959.
99. *Ibid.*
100. *Ibid.*
101. *Pravda,* January 28, 1959.
102. *Ibid.*

BIBLIOGRAPHY

BIBLIOGRAPHY

BOOKS AND COLLECTIONS OF DOCUMENTS

Abramov, A., and Venskii, K. *Zapadnaia Ukraina i Zapadnaia Belorussiia.* Leningrad, Leninizdat, 1940.

A Decade of American Foreign Policy, Basic Documents, 1941–1949. Washington, United States Government Printing Office, 1950.

American Foreign Policy, 1950–55, Basic Documents. Washington, Department of State, 1957. Two volumes.

The Anti-Stalin Campaign and International Communism: A Selection of Documents. New York, Columbia University Press, 1956.

Armianskaia SSR. Moscow, Gosudarstvennoe Izdatelstvo Geograficheskoi Literatury, 1955.

Barghoorn, Frederick C. *Soviet Russian Nationalism.* New York, Oxford University Press, 1956.

Beloff, Max. *The Foreign Policy of Soviet Russia, 1929–1941.* New York, Oxford University Press, 1947–1949. Two volumes.

———. *Soviet Policy in the Far East, 1944–1951.* New York and London, Oxford University Press, 1953.

Berliner, Joseph S. *Soviet Economic Aid: The New Aid and Trade Policy in Underdeveloped Countries.* New York, Frederick A. Praeger, 1958.

Bilmanis, Alfred (ed.). *Latvian-Russian Relations, Documents.* Washington, the Latvian Legation, 1944.

Bol'shaia Sovetskaia Entsiklopediia. Moscow, Gosudarstvennoe Nauchnoe Izdatelstvo, 1949–1958. Second edition.

Boorman, H. L., Eckstein, A., Mosely, Ph.E., and Schwartz, B. *Moscow-Peking Axis.* New York, Harper and Brothers, 1957.

Borisov, T. *Kalmykiia.* Moscow, Gosudarstvennoe Izdatelstvo, 1926.

Caroe, Sir Olaf. *Soviet Empire: The Turks of Central Asia and Stalinism.* London, Macmillan and Co., 1953.

Cherdantsev, G. N. (ed.). *Ekonomicheskaia Geografiia SSSR.* Moscow, Gosudarstvennoe Uchebno-Pedagogicheskoe Izdatelstvo Ministerstva Prosveshcheniia RSFSR, 1954.

Chugaev, D. A. *Kommunisticheskaia Partiia—Organizator Sovetskovo Mnogonatsional'novo Gosudarstva, 1917–1924 gg.* Moscow, Gosudarstvennoe Izdatelstvo Politicheskoi Literatury, 1954.

Dallin, David J. *The New Soviet Empire.* London, Hollis and Carter, 1951.

Deborin, G. A. *Leninskaia Politika Mirnovo Sosushchestvovaniia Dvukh Sistem—General'naia Liniia Vneshnei Politiki SSSR.* Moscow, Izdatelstvo Znanie, 1956.

———. *Sovetskaia Vneshniaia Politika v Pervye Gody Sushchestvovaniia*

Sovetskovo Gosudarstva, 1917–1920 gg. Moscow, Izdatelstvo *Pravda,* 1951.

Degras, Jane (ed.). *The Communist International, 1919–1943, Documents.* New York and London, Oxford University Press, 1956. Vol. I (1919–1922).

———. *Soviet Documents on Foreign Policy.* New York and London, Oxford University Press, 1951–53. Three volumes (1917–1941).

Deineko, M. M. (ed.). *Spravochnik Direktora Shkoly, Sbornik Postanovlenii, Prikazov, Instruktsii i Drugikh Rukovodiashchikh Materialov o Shkole.* Moscow, Gosudarstvennoe Uchebno-Pedagogicheskoe Izdatelstvo Ministerstva Prosveshcheniia RSFSR, 1954.

Djilas, Milovan. *The New Class: An Analysis of the Communist System.* New York, Frederick A. Praeger, 1957.

Dmitriev, N. K. and Chistiakov, V. M. (ed.). *Rodnoi i Russkii Yazyki v Natsional'noi Shkole.* Moscow, Izdatelstvo Akademii Pedagogicheskikh Nauk RSFSR, 1953.

Donskoi, V. *Razrabotka V. I. Leninym Organizatsionnykh Osnov Kommunisticheskoi Partii.* Moscow, Gospolitizdat, 1954.

Dutt, R. P. *India Today.* Bombay, People's Publishing House, 1949.

Efimov, M. *Sovetskaia Estoniia.* Moscow, Gosudarstvennoe Izdatelstvo Politicheskoi Literatury, 1940.

Fainsod, Merle. *How Russia is Ruled.* Cambridge, Harvard University Press, 1953.

Feis, Herbert. *Churchill, Roosevelt, Stalin: The War They Waged and the Peace They Sought.* Princeton, Princeton University Press, 1957.

Fischer, Louis. *The Soviets in World Affairs: A History of the Relations Between the Soviet Union and the Rest of the World, 1917–1929.* Princeton, Princeton University Press, 1951. Two volumes.

Foreign Assistance Activities of the Communist Bloc and Their Implications for the United States. Washington, United States Senate, 1957.

Gafenco, Grégoire. *Préliminaires de la Guerre à l'Est.* Paris, Egloff, 1947.

Galenko, P. V. *Stroitel'stvo Sotsialisticheskoi Ekonomiki v Polskoi Narodnoi Respublike.* Moscow, Gosudarstvennoe Izdatelstvo Politicheskoi Literatury, 1955.

Gluckstein, Igael. *Stalin's Satellites in Europe.* Boston, The Beacon Press, 1952.

Goodrich, Leland M. *Korea: A Study of U.S. Policy in the United Nations.* New York, Council on Foreign Relations, 1956.

Gorbunov, T. *Vossoedineniie Belorusskovo Naroda v Edinom Sovetskom Sotsialisticheskom Gosudarstve.* Moscow, Gosudarstvennoe Izdatelstvo Politicheskoi Literatury, 1948.

Gsovski, V. (ed.). *Church and State Behind the Iron Curtain.* New York, Frederick A. Praeger, 1955.

Gurian, Waldemar. *Bolshevism: An Introduction to Soviet Communism.* Notre Dame, University of Notre Dame Press, 1952.

————. *Permanent Features of Soviet Foreign Policy.* London, Stevens and Sons, 1947.

———— (ed.). *Soviet Imperialism: Its Origins and Tactics.* Notre Dame, University of Notre Dame Press, 1953.

Haines, C. Grove (ed.). *The Threat of Soviet Imperialism.* Baltimore, The Johns Hopkins University Press, 1954.

Hunt, R. N. Carew. *Marxism: Past and Present.* New York, The Macmillan Company, 1955.

————. *The Theory and Practice of Communism.* New York, The Macmillan Company, 1951.

Ivashin, I. F. *Nachalo Vtoroi Mirovoi Voiny i Vneshniaia Politika SSSR.* Moscow, Izdatelstvo *Pravda*, 1951.

————. *Velikaia Oktiabrskaia Sotsialisticheskaia Revolutsia i Raskol Mira na Dve Sistemy.* Moscow, Izdatelstvo *Pravda*, 1951.

————. *Vsemirno-Istoricheskoe Znacheniie Velikoi Oktiabrskoi Sotsialisticheskoi Revolutsii.* Moscow, Gosudarstvennoe Izdatelstvo Politicheskoi Literatury, 1953.

Ivashin, I. F. and Zuev, F. G. *Mezhdunarodnye Otnosheniia v Period Provedeniia Velikoi Oktiabrskoi Sotsialisticheskoi Revolutsii: Vneshniaia Politika Sovetskovo Gosudarstva v Gody Inostrannoi Voennoi Interventsii i Grazhdanskoi Voiny.* Moscow, Vysshaia Partiinaia Shkola pri TsK KPSS, 1955.

Kary-Niiazov, T. N. *Ocherki Istorii Kul'tury Sovetskovo Uzbekistana.* Moscow, Izdatelstvo Akademii Nauk SSSR, 1955.

Kautsky, John H. *Moscow and the Communist Party of India.* New York, John Wiley and Sons, 1956.

Khachapuridze, G. V. *Sovetskaia Gruziia.* Moscow, Gosudarstvennoe Izdatelstvo Politicheskoi Literatury, 1948.

Kissinger, Henry A. *Nuclear Weapons and Foreign Policy.* New York, Harper and Brothers, 1957.

Kliuchnikov, Yu. V. and Sabanin, A. *Mezhdunarodnaia Politika Noveishevo Vremeni v Dogovorakh, Notakh i Deklaratsiakh.* Moscow, Litizdat NKID, 1925–1928. Three volumes (1789–1927).

Kolarz, Walter. *Russia and Her Colonies.* London, George Philip and Son, 1952.

Kolbanovskii, V. N. *O Kommunisticheskoi Morali.* Moscow, Izdatelstvo *Pravda*, 1951.

Kousoulas, Dimitrios G. *The Price of Freedom: Greece in World Affairs, 1939–1953.* Syracuse, Syracuse University Press, 1953.

KPSS v Rezoliutsiiakh i Resheniiakh S'yezdov, Konferentsii i Plenumov TsK. Moscow, Gosudarstvennoe Izdatelstvo Politicheskoi Literatury, 1954. 7th edition. Three volumes.

Kuliyev, Klych. *Bor'ba Kommunisticheskoi Partii za Uprocheniie Sovetskoi Vlasti i Osushchestvleniie Natsional'noi Politiki v Srednei Azii, 1917–1925 gg.* Ashhabad, Turkmenskoe Gosudarstvennoe Izdatelstvo, 1956.

Kulski W. W. *The Soviet Regime: Communism in Practice.* Syracuse, Syracuse University Press, 1959. Third edition.

Kul'turnoe Stroitel'stvo SSSR: Statisticheskii Sbornik. Moscow, Gosudarstvennoe Statisticheskoe Izdatelstvo, 1956.

Kun, Bela (ed.). *Kommunisticheskii Internatsional v Dokumentakh: Resheniia, Tezisy i Vozzvaniia Kongressov Kominterna i Plenumov IKKI, 1919–1932.* Moscow, Partiinoe Izdatelstvo, 1933.

Lane, Arthur Bliss. *I Saw Poland Betrayed.* New York, The Bobbs-Merrill Company, 1948.

Laqueur, Walter Z. *Communism and Nationalism in the Middle East.* New York, Frederick A. Praeger, 1956.

Leites, Nathan. *A Study of Bolshevism.* Glencoe, Illinois, The Free Press, 1953.

Lenin, V. I. *Natsional'no-kolonial'nyi Vopros.* Moscow, Partiinoe Izdatelstvo, 1933.

———. *Natsional'nyi Vopros.* Moscow, Partizdat, 1935.

———. *Sochineniia.* Moscow, Gosudarstvennoe Izdatelstvo Politicheskoi Literatury, 1941–1951. Thirty-five volumes and Index. Fourth edition.

Lenczowski, George. *Russia and the West in Iran, 1918–1948: A Study in Big-Power Rivalry.* Ithaca, Cornell University Press, 1949.

Lissovskii, V. I. *Mezhdunarodnoe Pravo.* Kiev, Izdatelstvo Kievskovo Gosudarstvennovo Universiteta im. T. G. Shevchenko, 1955.

Litvinov, M. *Vneshniaia Politika SSSR: Rechi i Zaiavleniia, 1927–1937.* Moscow, Gosudarstvennoe Sotsial'no-Ekonomischeskoe Izdatelstvo, 1937.

Markov, M. *Sovetskaia Latviia.* Moscow, Gosudarstvennoe Izdatelstvo Politicheskoi Literatury, 1940.

Medynskii, E. N. *Prosveshcheniie v SSSR.* Moscow, Gosudarstvennoe Uchebno-Pedagogicheskoe Izdatelstvo Ministerstva Prosveshcheniia RSFSR, 1955.

Mikolajczyk, Stanislaw. *The Rape of Poland: Pattern of Soviet Aggression.* New York, McGraw-Hill Book Company, 1948.

Molotov, V. M. *O Vneshnei Politike Sovetskovo Soiuza.* Moscow, Gosudarstvennoe Izdatelstvo Politicheskoi Literatury, 1939.

———. *Soviet Foreign Relations.* New York, Workers Library Publishers, 1940.

———. *Voprosy Vneshnei Politiki: Rechi i Zaiavleniia, Aprel' 1945–Yun' 1948.* Moscow, Ogiz, 1948.

Molotov, V. M., Mikoyan, A., Khrushchev, N. *et al. Stalin.* New York, Workers Library Publishers, 1940.

Myrdal, Gunnar. *An International Economy.* New York, Harper and Brothers, 1956.

Nazi-Soviet Relations, 1939–1941: Documents from the Archives of the German Foreign Office. Washington, Department of State, 1948.

1956 Economic Survey of Europe. Geneva, United Nations, 1957.

O Kommunisticheskoi Morali: Sbornik Statei. Moscow, Izdatelstvo TsK VLKSM *Molodaia Gvardiia*, 1951.

Padev, Michael. *Dimitrov Wastes No Bullets; Nikola Petkov: The Test Case.* London, Eyre and Spottiswoode, 1948.

Paletskis, Yustas. *Sovetskaia Litva.* Moscow, Gospolitizdat, 1949.

Pankratova, A. M. *et al. Nasha Velikaia Rodina.* Moscow, Gosudarstvennoe Izdatelstvo Politicheskoi Literatury, 1954. 2nd edition.

Pavlov, I. P. *Lektsii o Rabote Bol'shikh Polusharii Golovnovo Mozga.* Moscow, Akademiia Meditsinskikh Nauk SSSR, 1952.

———. *Polnoe Sobraniie Sochinenii.* Moscow, Izdatelstvo Akademii Nauk SSSR, 1951. Second edition. Six volumes.

Perepiska Predsedatelia Soveta Ministrov SSSR s Prezidentami SShA i Premier-Ministrami Velikobritanii vo Vremia Velikoi Otechestvennoi Voiny 1941–1945 gg. Moscow, Gosudarstvennoe Izdatelstvo Politicheskoi Literatury, 1957–58. Two volumes.

Petrov, F. N. (ed.). *Slovar' Inostrannykh Slov.* Moscow, Gosudarstvennoe Izdatelstvo Inostrannykh i Natsional'nykh Slovarei, 1954. 4th edition.

Petrovskii, N. N. *Vossoedineniie Ukrainskovo Naroda v Edinom Ukrainskom Sovetskom Gosudarstve.* Moscow, Gospolitizdat, 1944.

Pipes, Richard. *The Formation of the Soviet Union: Communism and Nationalism, 1917–1923.* Cambridge, Harvard University Press, 1954.

Pod Znamenem Proletarskovo Internatsionalizma, Sbornik Materialov. Moscow, Gosudarstvennoe Izdatelstvo Politicheskoi Literatury, 1957.

Popov, I. *Estoniia.* Moscow, Gosudarstvennoe Voennoe Izdatelstvo Narkomata Oborony Soiuza SSR, 1940.

Possony, Stefan T. *A Century of Conflict: Communist Techniques of World Revolution.* Chicago, Henry Regnery Co., 1953.

Potemkin, V. P. (ed.). *Istoriia Diplomatii.* Moscow, Gosudarstvennoe Izdatelstvo Politicheskoi Literatury, 1941–45. Three volumes.

Radek, Karl. *Vneshniaia Politika Sovetskoi Rossii.* Moscow, Gosudarstvennoe Izdatelstvo, 1923.

Radzhabov, S. *Rol' Velikovo Russkovo Naroda v Istoricheskikh Sud'bakh Narodov Srednei Azii.* Tashkent, Gosudarstvennoe Izdatelstvo Uzbekskoi SSR, 1955.

Raimov, R. M. *Obrazovaniie Bashkirskoi Avtonomnoi Sovetskoi Sotsialisticheskoi Respubliki.* Moscow, Izdatelstvo Akademii Nauk SSSR, 1952.

Report of the Special Committee on the Problem of Hungary. New York, United Nations, 1957.

Reshetar, John S. *Problems of Analyzing and Predicting Soviet Behavior.* New York, Doubleday and Co., 1955.

The Revolt in Hungary: A Documentary Chronology of Events. October 23, 1956–November 4, 1956. New York, Free Europe Committee, 1956.

Riazantsev, S. N. *Kirghiziia.* Moscow, Gosudarstvennoe Izdatelstvo Geograficheskoi Literatury, 1951.

Ripka, Hubert. *Czechoslovakia Enslaved: The Story of the Communist Coup d'Etat.* London, Victor Gollancz, 1950.

Roberts, Henry L. *Russia and America: Dangers and Prospects.* New York, Harper and Brothers, 1956.

The Royal Institute of International Affairs. *Documents on International Affairs.* London, Oxford University Press, 1956.

Rubinstein, N. L. *Vneshniaia Politika Sovetskovo Gosudarstva v 1921–1925 Godakh.* Moscow, Gosudarstvennoe Izdatelstvo Politicheskoi Literatury, 1953.

Sergeev, S. D. *Ekonomicheskoe Sotrudnichestvo i Vzaimopomoshch' Stran Sotsialisticheskovo Lageria.* Moscow, Vneshtorgizdat, 1956.

Seton-Watson, Hugh. *The East European Revolution.* London, Methuen and Co., 1950.

Shapiro, Leonard (ed.). *Soviet Treaty Series.* Washington, Georgetown University Press, 1950. Vol. I (1917–1928).

Shariia, P. A. *O Nekotorykh Voprosakh Kommunisticheskoi Morali.* Moscow, Gosudarstvennoe Izdatelstvo Politicheskoi Literatury, 1951.

Shchur, P. N. *Sovetskii Patriotizm—Istochnik Sily i Mogushchestva Armii i Flota.* Moscow, Voennoe Izdatelstvo Ministerstva Oborony Soiuza SSR, 1956.

Shimbiriov, P. N. and Ogorodnikov, I. T. *Pedagogika. Moscow,* Gosudarstvennoe Uchebno-Pedagogicheskoe Izdatelstvo, 1954.

Shishkin, A. *Osnovy Kommunisticheskoi Morali.* Moscow, Gosudarstvennoe Izdatelstvo Politicheskoi Literatury, 1955.

Shvakov, A. and Bogoslovskii, V. *Nezavisimyi Egipet.* Moscow, Gosudarstvennoe Izdatelstvo Politicheskoi Literatury, 1956.

The Sino-Soviet Economic Offensive in the Less Developed Countries. Washington, Department of State, 1958.

Slonim, Is. *Spravochnik po Geografii dla Uchitelei Nachalnoi Shkoly.* Leningrad, Gosudarstvennoe Uchebno-Pedagogicheskoe Izdatelstvo Ministerstva Prosveshcheniia RSFSR, 1951. 2nd edition.

The Soviet Prisonhouse of Nationalities: A Study of the Russian Experiment in Solving the National Problem. Calcutta, Society for Defence of Freedom in Asia, 1955.

The Soviet-Yugoslav Dispute. New York and London, Oxford University Press, 1948.

Sovetsko-Kitaiskii Konflikt 1929 g., Sbornik Dokumentov. Moscow, Litizdat NKID, 1930.

Spector, Ivar. *The Soviet Union and the Muslim World, 1917–1956.* (Mimeographed) Washington, University of Washington Press, 1957.

Spravochnik dlia Postupaiushchikh v Vysshie Uchebnye Zavedeniia v 1956 g. Moscow, Sovetskaia Nauka, 1956.

Spravochnik dlia Postupaiushchikh v Vyssheie, Sredniie Spetsial'nye Uchebnye Zavedeniia (Tekhnikumy, Uchilishcha, Shkoly) i Tekhnicheskiie Uchilishcha Moskvy i Moskovskoi Oblasti v 1956 Godu. Moscow, Izdatelstvo *Moskovskaia Pravda*, 1956.

Spravochnik Propagandista i Agitatora. Moscow, Gosudarstvennoe Izdatelstvo Politicheskoi Literatury, 1955.

Stalin, I. V. *Marksizm i Natsional'no-kolonial'nyi Vopros, Sbornik Statei i Rechei.* Moscow, Partizdat TsK VKP (b), 1936.

———. *Natsional'nyi Vopros i Leninizm.* Moscow, Gosudarstvennoe Izdatelstvo Politicheskoi Literatury, 1952.

———. *Sochineniia.* Moscow, Gosudarstvennoe Izdatelstvo Politicheskoi Literatury, 1946–1951. Thirteen volumes.

Taracouzio, T. A. *War and Peace in Soviet Diplomacy.* New York, Macmillan Co., 1940.

Torma, A. and Raud, V. *Estonia, 1918–1952.* London, 1952.

Tropkin, N. V. *Ob Osnovakh Strategii i Taktiki Leninizma.* Moscow, Izdatelstvo *Pravda*, 1955.

———. *O Proizvedenii V. I. Lenina: Detskaia Bolezn' 'Levizny' v Kommunizme.* Moscow, Gosudarstvennoe Izdatelstvo Politicheskoi Literatury, 1951.

Vassil'ev, N. P. and Khrustov, F. D. (eds.). *O Sovetskom Patriotizme.* Moscow, Gosudarstvennoe Izdatelstvo Politicheskoi Literatury, 1952. 2nd edition.

Vneshniaia Politika SSSR, Sbornik Dokumentov. Moscow, Gosudarstvennoe Izdatelstvo Politicheskoi Literatury, 1946. Vol. IV (1935–June 1941).

Vneshniaia Politika Sovetskovo Soiuza v Period Otechestvennoi Voiny. Moscow, Gosudarstvennoe Izdatelstvo Politicheskoi Literatury, 1946–47. Three volumes (June 22, 1941–September 3, 1945).

Vneshniaia Politika Sovetskovo Soiuza. Moscow, Gosudarstvennoe Izdatelstvo Politicheskoi Literatury, 1949–53. Eight volumes (September 4, 1945–December, 1950).

Vneshniaia Torgovlia SSSR so Stranami Azii, Afriki i Latinskoi Ameriki. Moscow, Vneshtorgizdat, 1958.

Weinberg, Gerhard, L. *Germany and the Soviet Union, 1939–1941.* Leiden, E. J. Brill, 1954.

Wolff, Robert Lee. *The Balkans in Our Time.* Cambridge, Harvard University Press, 1956.

Yakunin, A. F. *Narody Srednei Azii i Kazakhstana vo Vtoroi Polovine 19 Veka: Prisoedineniie Srednei Azii k Rossii.* Moscow, Vysshaia Partiinaia Shkola pri TsK KPSS, 1954.

Zinner, Paul E. (ed.). *National Communism and Popular Revolt in Eastern Europe.* New York, Columbia University Press, 1956.

Zinoviev, M. A. *Ocherki Prepodavaniia Istorii.* Moscow, Izdatelstvo Akademii Pedagogicheskikh Nauk, 1955.

ARTICLES

(Only Communist articles, except for those which appeared
in the daily press, are listed)

Alkhimov, V. and Kotkovskii, Ya. "Ekonomicheskoe sorevnovaniie mezhdu sotsializmom i kapitalizmom." *Voprosy Ekonomiki*, No. 3 (March, 1956).

Arutiunian, P. T. Review of the book: *Osvoboditel'naia Bor'ba Armianskovo Naroda Protiv Turetskovo Despotizma, 1850–1870 gg.*, Erivan', 1955. *Sovetskoe Vostokovedeniie,* No. 6 (1956).

Astaf'yar, G. V. "Kitai—velikaia mirovaia derzhava." *Sovetskoe Vostokovedeniie,* No. 5 (1956).

Avakov, R. Review of G. E. Skorov's book: *Frantsuskii Imperializm v Zapadnoi Afrike,* 1956. *Voprosy Ekonomiki,* No. 1 (January, 1957).

Avarin, V. "Indiia na puti k ekonomicheskoi nezavisimosti." *Voprosy Ekonomiki,* No. 1 (January, 1957).

Azizian, A. "Raspad kolonial'noi sistemy imperializma i novye otnosheniia mezhdu stranami." *Voprosy Ekonomiki,* No. 10 (October, 1956).

Berkov, A. "Edinstvo i splochennost'—zalog novykh uspekhov mezhdunarodnovo kommunisticheskovo dvizheniia." *Kommunist,* No. 6 (April, 1957).

Boltin, E. A. "Pobeda Sovetskoi Armii pod Moskvoi v 1941 godu." *Voprosy Istorii,* No. 1 (January, 1957).

Borkowicz, Andrzej. "Index Librorum Prohibitorum." *Po Prostu,* No. 24 (June 10, 1956).

Borovkov, A. K. "K voprosu ob unifikatsii tiurkskikh alfavitov v SSSR." *Sovetskoe Vostokovedeniie,* No. 4 (1956).

Borowska, M., Balcerek, J., and Gilejko, L. "Miejsce rad robotniczych w naszym modelu gospodarczym." *Nowe Drogi,* No. 2 (February, 1957).

Bukowska, Anna. "Przeciw funkcji zawodowego rewolucjonisty." *Po Prostu,* No. 35 (August 26, 1956).

Bulygin, N. F. "K voprosu vossoedineniia Zapadnovo Iriana s Indoneziei." *Sovetskoe Vostokovedeniie,* No. 1, (1957).

Bunsdorf, Eran von. "Sovetsko-Finliandskiie otnosheniia i ukrepleniie mira v severnoi Evrope." *Mezhdunarodnaia Zhizn',* No. 6 (June, 1957).

Butenko, A. P. "Kitaiskaia revolutsia i eio osobennosti." *Sovetskoe Vostokovedeniie,* No. 3 (1956).

———. "O sotsializme i evo 'gumanisticheskikh' kritikakh." *Kommunist,* No. 5 (April, 1957).

Chełstowski, Stanisław and Godek, Włodzimierz. "Pierwszy zwiad." *Po Prostu,* No. 44 (October 28, 1956).

Cheprakov V. "Leninskaia teoriia neravnomernosti razvitiia kapitalizma i obostereniie mezhimperialisticheskikh protivorechii v poslevoennyi period." *Voprosy Ekonomiki,* No. 4 (April, 1956).

Danilevich, M. "Latinskaia Amerika i mezhdunarodnoe sotrudnichestvo." *Kommunist,* No. 2 (February, 1956).

Deborin, G. A. "Leninskii printsip mirnovo sosushchestvovaniia gosudarstv razlichnykh sotsial'nykh sistem." *Voprosy Ekonomiki,* No. 4 (April, 1956).

Diakov, A. M. and Reisner, I. M. "Rol' Gandhi v natsional'noosvoboditel'noi bor'be narodov Indii." *Sovetskoe Vostokovedeniie,* No. 5 (1956).

"Diskussiia ob ekonomicheskikh i politicheskikh pozitsiiakh natsional'noi burzhuazii v stranakh Vostoka." *Sovetskoe Vostokovedeniie,* No. 1 (1957).

Dubina, K. "Leninskaia teoriia sotsialisticheskoi revolutsii." *Kommunist,* No. 15 (October, 1955).

Dubrovskii, S. M. "Protiv idealizatsii deiatel'nosti Ivana IV." *Voprosy Istorii,* No. 8 (August, 1956).

Du Chao-bai. "Razvitiie sotsialisticheskoi ekonomiki i ekonomicheskiie zakony v perekhodnyi period v Kitaiskoi Narodnoi Respublike." *Voprosy Ekonomiki,* No. 1 (January, 1957).

"XX s'yezd kommunisticheskoi partii Sovetskovo Soiuza i zadachi izucheniia sovremennovo Vostoka." *Sovetskoe Vostokovedeniie,* No. 1 (1956).

East Europe. New York, Free Europe Committee. Volumes for 1957–1958.

"Eshcho raz ob istoricheskom opyte diktatury proletariata." Reprinted from *Zhen'min'zhibao,* December 29, 1956, in *Mezhdunarodnaia Zhizn',* No. 1 (January, 1957).

Fan Zho-yui. "Znacheniie knigi Lenina: *Dve Taktiki Sotsial-Demokratii v Demokraticheskoi Revolutsii,* dlia narodno-demokraticheskoi revolutsii v Kitaie." *Sovetskoe Vostokovedeniie,* No. 2 (1956).

Fedoseev, P., Potelov, I. and Cheprakov, V. "O proekte programmy Soiuza kommunistov Yugoslavii." *Kommunist,* No. 6 (April, 1958).

Garaudy, Roger. "Problema svobody v svete sovremennoi ideologicheskoi bor'by." *Kommunist,* No. 5 (April, 1957).

Gassanov, I. M. and Strigunov, I. V. Review of A. S. Sumbatzade *et al., Prisoedineniie Azerbaijana k Rossii i Evo Progressivnye Posledstviia v Oblasti Ekonomiki i Kul'tury (XIX—nach. XX vv.),* Baku, 1955. *Sovetskoe Vostokovedeniie,* No. 5 (1956).

Gataullin, M. F. and Maliukovskii, M. V. "Egipetskaia Respublika na puti k ekonomicheskoi nezavisimosti." *Sovetskoe Vostokovedeniie,* No. 3 (1956).

Gomulka, W. "Uzlovye problemy politiki partii." *Kommunist,* No. 7 (May, 1957).

Górski, Mieczysław. "Uwaga, histerja." *Po Prostu,* No. 19 (May 6, 1956).

Govinnov, V. and Pankin, M. "Ekonomicheskiie sviazi kitaiskoi narodnoi respubliki so stranami Azii." *Voprosy Ekonomiki,* No. 1 (January, 1956).

Groot, Paul de, secretary-general of the Dutch Communist Party. "Sovremennye sobytiia v svete leninizma." Reprinted from the Dutch newspaper *De Vaarheid* in *Kommunist,* No. 2 (February, 1957).

Grzybowski, Kazimierz. "Foreign Investment and Political Control in Eastern Europe." *Journal of Central European Affairs,* No. 1 (April, 1957).

Guber, A. A. "Gluboko i vsestoronne izuchat' krizis i raspad kolonial'noi sistemy imperializma." *Sovetskoe Vostokovedeniie*, No. 3 (1956).

Ibarruri, Dolores, secretary-general of the Spanish Communist Party. "Polozheniie v Ispanii i bor'ba kommunisticheskoi partii za demokratiiu." *Kommunist*, No. 2 (February, 1957).

I. M. "Klasa robotnicza jest i będzie kowalem jutra Polski." *Nowe Drogi*, No. 1 (January, 1957).

Infeld, Leopold. "O godność nauki." *Przegląd Kulturalny*, No. 25 (June 21, 1956).

Ivanov, K. "Bankrotstvo kolonializma i mezhdunarodnye otnosheniia." *Mezhdunarodnaia Zhizn'*, No. 5 (May, 1957).

"Iz materialov VII plenuma TsK kommunisticheskoi partii Gretsii." *Kommunist*, No. 5 (April, 1957).

"Iz materialov XVII s'yezda kommunisticheskoi partii Avstrii." *Kommunist*, No. 6 (April, 1957).

Jankowski, Henryk. "Jednostka niczym?" *Po Prostu*, No. 38 (September 16, 1956).

———. "Opinje, moralność, polityka." *Po Prostu*, No. 35 (August 26, 1956).

Jastruń, Mieczysław. "O wolność słowa." *Po Prostu*, No. 50 (December 9, 1956).

J. K. N. "Kto, za co i przed kim odpowiada?" *Nowe Drogi*, No. 1 (January, 1957).

Jurys, Roman. "Niektóre problemy naszej partji." *Nowe Drogi*, No. 2 (February, 1957).

Kamenev, V. "Bol'shaia lozh' o 'malykh' atomnykh voinakh." *Mezhdunarodnaia Zhizn'*, No. 3 (March, 1957).

———. "Dvustoronnee sotrudnichestvo ili odnostoronnyi grabezh? (k voprosam ob atomnoi politike SShA)." *Mezhdunarodnaia Zhizn'*, No. 5 (May, 1957).

Kaufman, A. S. "Ekonomicheskoe polozheniie Birmy." *Sovetskoe Vostokovedeniie*, No. 1 (1957).

"K diskussii o kharaktere dvizheniia gortsev Daghestana pod rukovodstvom Shamiliia." *Voprosy Istorii*, No. 1 (January,1957).

Khrushchev, N. "Za tesnuiu sviaz' literatury i iskusstva z zhizniu naroda." *Kommunist*, No. 12 (August, 1957).

Kołakowski, Leszek. "Sens ideowy pojęcia lewicy." *Po Prostu*, No. 8 (February 24, 1957).

Kommentator. "Raschety i proschety kolonizatorov." *Mezhdunarodnaia Zhizn'*, No. 1 (January, 1957).

Kononov, A. N. "Stoletiie vostochnovo fakulteta Leningradskovo Universiteta (1855–1955)." *Sovetskoe Vostokovedeniie*, No. 2 (1956).

Korionov, I. "Oktiabr' i sud'by chelovechestva." *Mezhdunarodnaia Zhizn'*, No. 6 (June, 1957).

Kossak Jerzy. "Do przyjaciela." *Po Prostu*, No. 13 (March 25, 1956).

Kossak, Jerzy; Turski, Ryszard and Zimand, Roman. "Internacjonalizm." *Po Prostu,* No. 44 (October 28, 1956).

"Kraieugolnyi kamen' vneshnei politiki SSSR." *Mezhdunarodnaia Zhizn',* No. 3 (March, 1957).

"Krepnushchee edinstvo stran sotsialisticheskovo sodruzhestva." *Mezhdunarodnaia Zhizn',* No. 1 (January, 1957).

Kuczyński, Janusz. "Administratorstwo i apolityczność." *Po Prostu,* No. 25 (June 17, 1956).

———. "W poszukiwaniu utraconych wartości." *Po Prostu,* No. 49 (December 2, 1956).

Kuliyev, K. M. and Repin, I. L. "Razvitiie i pod'iom sotsialisticheskoi kul'tury i nauki v Turkmenskoi SSR." *Sovetskoe Vostokovedeniie,* No. 2 (1956).

Kunaev, D. "Sovetskii Kazakhstan—sotsialisticheskaia industrial'no- kolkhoznaia respublika." *Kommunist,* No. 4 (February, 1957).

Kutsenkov, A. "Razvitiie ekonomicheskikh sviazei Indii s sotsialisticheskimi stranami." *Vneshniaia Torgovlia,* No. 10 (1956).

Lange, Oskar. "Po VIII Zjeździe Komunistycznej Partji Włoch." *Nowe Drogi,* No. 2 (February, 1957).

Lebedinskii, A. "Posledstviia ispytanii iadernovo oruzhiia." *Mezhdunarodnaia Zhizn',* No. 3 (March, 1957).

Lemin, I. M. " 'Doktrina Eisenhowera'—programma kolonial'novo zakabaleniia Blizhnevo Vostoka." *Sovetskoe Vostokovedeniie,* No. 1 (1957).

Lipiński, Edward. "Model gospodarki socjalistycznej." *Nowe Drogi,* No. 11–12 (November–December, 1956).

Lutskii, V. B. "Izrail'—orudiie agressivnoi politiki." *Mezhdunarodnaia Zhizn',* No. 2 (February, 1957).

Maneli, Mieczysław. "O cywilnej odwadze." *Po Prostu,* No. 47 (November 18, 1956).

Martynov, A. A. "Istoricheskii s'yezd kommunisticheskoi partii Kitaia." *Sovetskoe Vostokovedeniie,* No. 6 (1956).

Meliksetov, A. V. "Ideologicheskoe perevospitaniie burzhuaznykh elementov v KNR." *Sovetskoe Vostokovedeniie,* No. 1 (1957).

Melnikov, L. I. "Iz istorii ispol'zovaniia imperialistami territorii Irana kak platzdarma protiv Sovetskoi Rossii (1917–1920)." *Sovetskoe Vostokovedeniie,* No. 1 (1957).

Melnikov, D. "Ugroza bezopastnosti Evropy." *Mezhdunarodnaia Zhizn',* No. 3 (March, 1957).

Mikheev, V. "Novaia Aziia." *Kommunist,* No. 12 (August, 1955).

Miliukov, F. and Fuzeev, V. "Siriiskii narod v bor'be za ukrepleniie natsional'noi nezavisimosti." *Mezhdunarodnaia Zhizn',* No. 12 (December, 1956).

Myshkov, V. "Razvivaiutsia i krepnut sovetsko-iugoslavskiie ekonomicheskiie otnosheniia." *Vneshniaia Torgovlia,* No. 10 (1956).

Nazarov, S. "Sovetskie knigi." *Vneshniaia Torgovlia,* No. 7 (1956).

"Nepreoborimaia sila leninizma." *Kommunist,* No. 5 (April, 1957).

News From Behind the Iron Curtain. New York, Free Europe Committee. Volumes for 1952–1956.

Novikova, V. A. *"Porichoi*—zhurnal progressivnykh pisatelei Bengalii." *Sovetskoe Vostokovedeniie,* No. 2 (1956).

"October Aftermath." *East Europe,* No. 4 (April, 1957).

"VIII Plenum Komitetu Centralnego P.Z.P.R. (10–21.X, 1956)." *Nowe Drogi,* No. 10 (1956).

"Patriotyzm a ekonomika." *Po Prostu,* No. 46 (November 11, 1956).

"Pervyi god raboty vostochnoi komissii geograficheskovo obshchestva Soiuza SSR." *Sovetskoe Vostokovedeniie,* No. 1 (1957).

Piórkowski, Jerzy. "Suwerenność—rzecz realna i znana." *Nowe Drogi,* Nos. 11–12 (November–December, 1956).

"Pod znamenem marksizma-leninizma." *Voprosy Ekonomiki,* No. 3 (March, 1956).

Poliakov, V. "Arabskie strany na puti k ekonomicheskoi nezavisimosti." *Vneshniaia Torgovlia,* No. 9 (1956).

Ponomarev, B. "Sovremennaia mezhdunarodnaia obstanovka i bor'ba za edinstvo rabochevo dvizheniia." *Voprosy Ekonomiki,* No. 5 (May, 1956).

"Postavit' iadernoe oruzhiie vne zakona." *Mezhdunarodnaia Zhizn',* No. 5 (May, 1957).

Potelov, I. "Razvitiie sotsializma i proletarskii internatsionalizm." *Kommunist,* No. 1 (January, 1957).

Potekhin, I. "Vozrastaiushchee znacheniie Afriki v mirovoi ekonomike i politike." *Kommunist,* No. 6 (April, 1957).

Pratusevich, Yu. M. "O rechedvigatel'nom analizatore i ievo roli v prot-sesse poznaniia." *Voprosy Filosofii,* No. 6 (June, 1953).

Prestes, Louis Carlos. "Kommunisticheskaia partiia Brazilii v bor'be za mir, svobodu i nezavisimost' rodiny." *Kommunist,* No. 3, (February, 1955).

"Razvitiie promyshlennovo proizvodstva v Evropeiskikh stranakh narod-noi demokratii. Statisticheskiie materialy." *Voprosy Ekonomiki,* No. 5 (May, 1957).

Romanov, Al. "Nerushimoe ideinoe edinstvo kommunisticheskikh partii." *Mezhdunarodnaia Zhizn',* No. 11 (November, 1956).

Semenov, I. and Sokolova, N. "Stroitel'stvo sotsialisticheskoi ekonomiki v evropeiskikh stranakh narodnoi demokratii." *Voprosy Ekonomiki,* No. 3 (March, 1956).

Shekkhar, Chandra. "Kolonializm v Azii i Afrike." *Mezhdunarodnaia Zhizn',* No. 2 (February, 1957).

Shitarev, G. "Edinstvo—istochnik nepobedimosti marksistsko-leninskoi partii." *Kommunist,* No. 5 (April, 1957).

Siekierska, Jadwiga. "O potrzebie tolerancji." *Nowe Drogi,* No. 2 (February, 1957).

————. "Czy tragedja optymistyczna?" *Po Prostu*, No. 49 (December 2, 1956).

Skladkovskii, M. I. "Razvitiie torgovykh putei mezhdu Sovetskim Soiuzom i Kitaiem." *Sovetskoe Vostokovedeniie*, No. 1 (1957).

Sobolev, A. "Vsemirno-istoricheskoe znacheniie sotsialisticheskovo lageria." *Kommunist*, No. 3 (February, 1956).

"Sovetskii narod—stroitel' kommunizma." *Kommunist*, No. 6 (March, 1957).

"Sprawy Polaków." *Po Prostu*, No. 45 (November 4, 1956).

Stanisławski, Jan. "Czy jestem chorągiewką?" *Po Prostu*, No. 13 (March 25, 1956).

"Strogo sobliudat' leninskii printsip partiinosti v istoricheskoi nauke." *Kommunist*, No. 4 (February, 1957).

Szacki, Jerzy. "Uwagi o historji Marksizmu." *Po Prostu*, No. 43 (October 21, 1956).

Tashenev, Zh. A. "Sotsialisticheskoe stroitel'stvo v Kazakhskoi SSR." *Sovetskoe Vostokovedeniie*, No. 1 (1956).

Timofeev, T. "O edinstve deistvii partii rabochevo klassa." *Mezhdunarodnaia Zhizn'*, No. 1 (January, 1957).

————. "O nekotorykh voprosakh proletarskovo internatsionalizma." *Mezhdunarodnaia Zhizn'*, No. 5 (May, 1957).

Tropkin, N. V. "O strategii i taktike leninizma." *Kommunist*, No. 1 (January, 1955).

Tumur-Ochir, D. "O nekapitalisticheskom puti razvitiia otstalykh stran k sotsializmu." *Voprosy Filosofii*, No. 1 (January, 1956).

Turski, Ryszard and Lasota, Eligjusz. "Polski Październik." *Po Prostu*, No. 44 (October 28, 1956).

Vassil'eva, V. "Raspad kolonial'noi sistemy imperializma." *Voprosy Ekonomiki*, No. 4 (April, 1956).

————. Review of S. P. Tolstoy's book: *Narody Afriki*, 1954. *Voprosy Ekonomiki*, No. 1 (January, 1957).

"Velikaia Oktiabrskaia Sotsialisticheskaia Revolutsia i sovremennyi Vostok." *Sovetskoe Vostokovedeniie*, No. 5 (1956).

"V. I. Lenin i natsional'no-osvoboditel'naia bor'ba narodov Vostoka." *Sovetskoe Vostokovedeniie*, No. 2 (1957).

"V Institute Vostokovedeniia." *Voprosy Istorii*, No. 3 (March, 1957).

"Vneshniaia torgovlia Egipeta v 1953–1955 gg." *Vneshniaia Torgovlia*, No. 10 (1956).

"Vyshe znamia marsistsko-leninskoi ideologii." *Kommunist*, No. 1 (January, 1957).

Werfel, Edda. "Do towarzyszy z bratnich partii." *Przegląd Kulturalny*, No. 44 (November 1, 1956).

Werfel, Roman. "O niektórych sprzecznościach naszego okresu." *Nowe Drogi*, No. 2 (February, 1957).

Wiatr, Jerzy. "Kryzys internacjonalizmu." *Nowe Drogi,* Nos. 11-12 (November–December, 1956).

Wojnar, Mieczysław. "Myśli." *Po Prostu,* No. 47 (November 18, 1956).

Yusupov, D. I. "K piatnadtsatiletiiu arabskovo zhurnala *At-Tarik.*" *Sovetskoe Vostokovedeniie,* No. 1 (1957).

Z. A. "W oczach zagranicy." *Nowe Drogi,* No. 1 (January, 1957).

Zhukov, E. "Kolonialisticheskaia politika SShA v Azii." *Mezhdunarodnaia Zhizn',* No. 1 (January, 1957).

———. "Narody Vostoka i sud'by mira." *Mezhdunarodnaia Zhizn',* No. 4 (April, 1956).

———. "Raspad kolonial'noi sistemy imperializma." *Partiinaia Zhizn',* No. 16 (August, 1956).

Zielińska, Krystyna. "Przyjaźń na koturnach." *Po Prostu,* No. 45 (November 4, 1956).

Zimand, Roman. "O komuniźmie narodowym." *Po Prostu,* No. 8 (February 24, 1957).

———. "Spór o przyszłość socjalizmu." *Po Prostu,* No. 43 (October 21, 1956).

———. "Sprawy robotników całego świata." *Po Prostu,* No. 45 (November 4, 1956).

"Zobowiązania wobec narodu." *Nowe Drogi,* No. 2 (February, 1957).

INDEX

INDEX

H

I

T